Ho's Rants

NOTE: Howard Johnson, the Author, is not responsible for emotional distress caused by these words. Political correctness is not one of his favorite things.

These blogs are all the postings to hojo2rants.blogspot.com from September 18, 2005 to September 17, 2015. They are unedited!

senesis word - st augustine, florida

PHONE: 904-687-1865 **CELL:** 574-265-3386

Website: http://hjwriter.com (May not be active yet)

Email: Senesisword@yahoo.com

Ho's RantsThe Book16830W

604 pages - 300,480 words

CONTENTS

CONTENTS

CONTENTS

CONTENTS

CONTENTS

CONTENTS

CONTENTS

CONTENTS

PART I

Statement of My Current Basic Beliefs and Principles
Howard Johnson - July 17, 2015

The following statements are a collection of my current basic beliefs relating to interactions with other individuals. I provide it so you can better understand the basis and origin of what I say. It explains how I see myself and how to understand my words. I call it my Survival Guide for Senior Years.

I am a believer in myself and those individuals I trust.

I trust no politician, political operative, political activist, government official, celebrity, elitist intellectual, or media reporter or talking head I do not know personally, and few of those I do. I trust no Muslim, ever. Their religious principles make this imperative.

The current actions of their extremists, the hatred and especially their murders of those who do not follow their religion, the silence and even support so called moderate Muslims continue to express in response to the atrocities and evil actions of their extremists are completely unacceptable in my eyes.

I trust and admire the rational opinions and logical judgements of those looked down on by elitists, the so-called *common people*. Their wisdom is far greater than that for which they are given credit. However, I do not trust their opinions or judgements when based on emotions, because they are often influenced and persuaded by those described in the previous paragraph.

Far too often I hear people aping the words they heard over the media, mostly the dictates of the New York Times. They let the media do their thinking and defining for them. I expect that from liberals and all those on the left because that is just who they are, mental lemmings blindly following the crowd and rarely thinking for themselves. Unfortunately, I often hear the same type of things said by many of those who overtly oppose liberalism. They too let the media mislead their thinking and define people and situations for them.

I do not expect anyone to understand any of that which they do not know. I do not even expect them to understand much of what they do know.

I see politics, religion, pseudo science, ethnicity, and culture as powerful belief systems often used by unscrupulous individuals to control others for their own purpose.

Statement of My Current Beliefs and Principles

I am not a follower of or beholden to any ism, ist, group belief system (religious, political, cultural, or other), political party, union, corporation, peer group, boss or officer (political, union, corporate or other organizational at any level), grant committee, dean or head of faculty, or any similar person or organization. This is why I am free to express my own opinions without disrespect, concern for, or apologies to anyone or any group. I will change my own beliefs to fit new realities and knowledge when and if the new information or understanding requires it.

I consider myself a truly independent and quite liberal individual, a realist who knows what it means to conserve, an equal opportunity supporter or detractor. Realism and being a realist are the only *ism* or *ist* I believe in and best describes my political philosophy. Because of this, I know my words and opinions may offend, but it is never my intent to do so. There are exceptions, of course.

I am not ever in any way controlled, intimidated or cowed by any kind of political correctness. I believe it to be a creation of the many narcissist members of the entertainment world and in particular the TV news media. These self-serving hypocrites use PC to coerce people into speaking and thinking the way they determine. It is one more system elitist intellectuals use to try to control others, especially the gullible, unthinking lemmings so many people, including Americans, have become.

I will not accept as a fact, any words, concepts or ideas that do not meet the tests of logic, reason and/or hard science as I understand them. My opinions and beliefs are subject to change when and if new information makes a change necessary. I see the inflexible, closed mind - the mind of the fundamentalist of any flavor: religious, political, social, cultural, or other, right, left, or in the middle - as an evil curse on the individual whose mind is closed for any reason.

I no longer have patience for certain things, mostly personal things, not because I've become arrogant, but simply because I reached a point in my life where I do not want to waste time with what displeases me or hurts me. I lost the will to please those who do not like me, to love those who do not love me, to smile at those who do not want to smile at me, and be around those who cause me pain. I have a strong will to please those who like me, love those who love me, smile at all but those detractors mentioned earlier, and be around those who bring me joy. I no longer spend a single minute on those who lie, fake affection, or want to manipulate. I decided not to coexist anymore with pretense, hypocrisy, dishonesty, political correctness and cheap praise. I have no patience for cynicism, excessive criticism and demands of any nature. However, I do solicit and encourage constructive criticism of my professional actions, especially my writing. I seek that which will improve and add value to my work

It is clear to me that thousands of free and independent individuals and groups working in a favorable competitive environment, under a capitalist system with limited government in a democratic republic, are infinitely superior in every conceivable way to a central decision making collectivist body or government of any kind. The bigger and more powerful the government, the less freedom individuals have to grow and improve their life and the lower will be the standard of living under such government. Examples of this reality abound now and throughout history for at least the last 3,000 years. Freedom works. Collectivism works solely for those running the system and leads to impoverishment, dependency, and ultimately some form of slavery for the masses.

I believe in treating all individuals with respect and honesty. These both deserve, and I will expect, respect and honesty in return. However, I see no reason to be bound to do the same when faced with disrespect or dishonesty.

I try to deal with each person with consideration in all of these things

—Howard Johnson - 2012

"There are many who find a good alibi far more attractive than an achievement. For an achievement does not settle anything permanently. We still have to prove our worth anew each day: we have to prove that we are as good today as we were yesterday. But when we have a valid alibi for not achieving anything we are fixed, so to speak, for life. Moreover, when we have an alibi for not writing a book, painting a picture and so on, we have an alibi for not writing the greatest book and not painting the greatest picture. Small wonder that the effort expended and the punishment endured in obtaining a good alibi often exceed the effort and grief requisite for the attainment of a most marked achievement."

—Eric Hoffer

My expressed opinions may or may not be in accord with the thinking of those who read my words. This includes my views on both of the no-nos of human verbal interaction, religion and politics. Because both areas can be emotionally charged and can be quite devoid of rational thoughts, there is an opportunity to offend, bring to anger, and damage feelings. Those from many emotional persuasions will surely find themselves pricked by barbs from many directions.

I have much respect for the knowledge and wisdom found in the words of many human beings. I even include those deemed foolish and unwise by the multitudes, those whom elitists and intellectuals believe are far beneath them in intellect, or brainpower. This even applies to those who populate flyover country. Genius or mentally challenged, corporate president or ditch digger, priest or sinner, person of any age, sex, culture, race, wealth or education—each of these and others have their own set of knowledge from which can be gleaned words of wisdom and truth if one listens.

I do not judge the worth of a person by any of these criteria. To do so is among the greatest faults of those who shut off all sources of knowledge and understanding that could be gained from those with whom they do not see eye to eye. It extends to even the lowliest among us. This fault is exhibited by political or religious elitists who refuse to be involved in communications of any kind that does not agree with or conform to their personal belief system. As a result, their inbred concepts shut out more and more good, even profound knowledge because it does not fall within the limitations of their beliefs, or confirm them. This is why *political correctness* is the political equivalent of *fundamentalist beliefs* in the broad field of religion including Islam and Atheism. All of these are belief systems driven by emotion, and not necessarily based in reality. One man's belief is another man's anathema.

In 1969, I gave a talk on personal communication at the American Dental Trade Association annual meeting in Chicago. The following comment is from that talk. I used one of my own strong beliefs to illustrate the often hidden but immense value of listening to what even the lowliest among us has to say.

In the areas of human thoughts and ideas, I much prefer to choose my own belief systems based on knowledge, experience, and logical thought processes, rather than adopt those of others. This does not mean I shun the wisdom or counsel of others. It means I accept such only after checking it through my own understanding of how the universe works. That may seem crazy to some. I address the following saying to them:

Those who dance are thought insane by those who can't hear the music.

—*Angela Monet*

Hopefully, you will hear and enjoy some of the music of my heart, soul, and imagination which I poured liberally into these pages.

A few comments from Howard Johnson for before you start reading these words:

Virtually all of the words that follow are taken as originally written, unedited, from the original BLOG. Some spelling, punctuation, grammar, and typos may have been edited, but the thoughts and ideas expressed—the words and their meanings have not.

I have tried to mark all quotes and my own comments for clarity so there is little doubt as to who is saying what. Generally I will mark my own short comments inserted in the words of others with (**parentheses and bold type.**) There may be places where italics and bold italics are used. These will usually be indicated by instructions within the piece. Please excuse those places where this is not clear.

I have tried to be as factual as possible where factual information is included. I try not to mix facts and opinions, a common human failing which can add to emotional confusion. Remember, it is often a reality that one man's facts are another's fantasy and visa versa.

Here is one of my favorite quotes that should be considered by all who read this book.

"Perception, ah yes, perception, it is what drives our decisions, controls our emotions of love, anger, joy, disappointment, friendship, hatred, virtually everything we think or react to. Perception overrules facts, logic, and reality. Whether from love, avarice, or foolishness, and no matter how removed perception is from truth, it still rules us and determines our life decisions. We do not live in a real world, but live totally in a world created by and subject to our perceptions."

—Howard Johnson, 1960

"Blessed are the flexible - for they shall not be bent out of shape."
— Michael McGriffy, MD 1975

PART II

BLOGs are in date order, from latest, September 17, 2015 to earliest, September 18, 2005, a ten year period.

Thursday, September 17, 2015

HJ NOTE: Thomas Sowell is one of my favorite thinkers who is a pleasant, observant **realist** in stark contrast to the ridiculous, unrealistic liberal LaLa Land dwellers of the political left including most of the media. There are a number of his quotes at the end of this seminal piece. The significant thing about most of his quotes is that they have held true throughout history.

Opportunity versus Outcomes - an Op Ed by Thomas Sowell

A hostile review of my new book — "Wealth, Poverty and Politics" — said, "there is apparently no level of inequality of income or opportunity that Thomas Sowell would consider unacceptable." Ordinarily, reviewers who miss the whole point of a book they are reviewing can be ignored. But this particular confusion about what opportunity means is far too widespread, far beyond a particular reviewer of a particular book. That makes it a confusion worth clearing up, because it affects so many other discussions of very serious issues.

The book does not accept inequality of opportunity. Instead, it reports such things as children raised in low-income families usually not being spoken to nearly as often as children raised in high- income families. The conclusion: "It is painful to contemplate what that means cumulatively over the years, as poor children are handicapped from their earliest childhood."

Even if all the doors of opportunity are wide open, children raised with great amounts of parental care and attention are far more likely to be able to walk through those doors than children who have received much less attention. '

Why else do conscientious parents invest so much time and effort in raising their children? This is so obvious that you would have to be an intellectual to able to misconstrue it. Yet many among the intelligentsia equate differences in outcomes with differences in opportunity.

A personal example may help clarify the difference. As a teenager, I tried briefly to play basketball. But I was lucky to hit the backboard, much less the basket. Yet I had just as much opportunity to play basketball as Michael Jordan had. But equal opportunity was not nearly enough to create equal outcomes."

Nevertheless, many studies today conclude that different groups do not have equal opportunity or equal "access" to credit, or admission to selective colleges, or ' to many other things, because some groups are not successful in achieving their goal as often as other groups are.

The very possibility that not all groups have the same skills or other qualifications is seldom even mentioned, much less examined. But when people with low credit scores are not approved for loans as often as people with high credit scores, is that a lack of opportunity or a failure to meet standards?

When twice as many Asian students as white students pass the tough tests to get into New York's three highly selective public high schools — Stuyvesant, Bronx Science and Brooklyn Tech — does that mean that white students are denied equal opportunity? '

As for inequality of incomes, these depend on so many things — including things that no government has control over — that the obsession with statistical "gaps" or "disparities" that some call "inequities" is a major distraction from the more fundamental, and more achievable, goals of promoting a rising standard of living in general and greater opportunity for all.

There was never any serious reason to expect equal economic, educational or other outcomes, either between nations or within nations. My book examines numerous demographic, geographic, cultural and other differences that make equal outcomes for all a very remote possibility.

To take just one example, in the United States the average age of Japanese Americans is more than 20 years older than the average age of Puerto Ricans. Even if these two groups were absolutely identical in every other way, Japanese Americans would still have a higher average income, because older people in general have more work experience and higher incomes.

Enabling all Americans to prosper and have greater opportunities is a far more achievable goal than equal outcomes.

Internationally, the geographic settings in which different nations evolved have been so different that there has been nothing like a level playing field among nations and peoples. . .

Comparing the standard of living of Americans at the beginning of the 20th century with that at the end shows incredible progress. Most of this economic progress took place without the kind of heady rhetoric, social polarization or violent upheavals that have too often accompanied heedless pursuits of unachievable goals like the elimination of "gaps," "disparities" or "inequities."

Such fashionable fetishes are not helping the poor.   —*Thomas Sowell, September 17, 2015*

HJ NOTE: The liberal Democrat **War on America** has been going on for many years. In 1965, Democrats under the leadership of that great moralist, Senator Ted Kennedy, passed an immigration law that has since brought 59 million foreigners into our nation. These mostly poor, ignorant, non English speaking people with virtually no understanding or respect for our Constitution, bloc vote Democrat, and support and use government welfare programs extensively. This act brought in the poorest of the poor, peasants from backward cultures with their high birth rates who will be dependent on government welfare for generations to come. Add to this all of the **illegal immigrants** that have entered our country under a government that does little to enforce existing immigration laws. I wonder how many **illegal immigrants** voted for Obama in the last election? Many of the problems addressed in these BLOGs are directly related to this influx of poor, ignorant, dependent people.

This is Democrat designed system for buying votes with taxpayer money. They win elections. You pay for their votes. The nation suffers. *—HJ 2015*

Following is a collection of Thomas Sowell quotes. Dates are shown where known.

The liberal Democrat party in the US has a record of failure, corruption, lies, hatred, deceit, and greed so blatant that only an intellectual could ignore or evade it. **(There are countless examples of the results of this all over the country. The city of Detroit is but one of countless examples.)**

The most fundamental fact about the ideas of the political left is that they do not work. Therefore we should not be surprised to find the left concentrated in institutions where ideas do not have to work in order to survive.

It is hard to imagine a more stupid or more dangerous way of making decisions than by putting those decisions in the hands of people who pay no price for being wrong. Know-it-alls in the school system do not lose one dime or one hour's sleep if their bright ideas turn out to be all wrong, or even disastrous, for the child. *— 18 August 2000*

People who think that they are being "exploited" should ask themselves whether they would be missed if they left, or whether people would say: "Good riddance"? *— 29 April 2002*

What the welfare system and other kinds of governmental programs are doing is paying people to fail. In so far as they fail, they receive the money; in so far as they succeed, even to a moderate extent, the money is taken away. *— 1980*

Racism has never done this country any good, and it needs to be fought against, not put under new management for different groups. *— June 2009*

It may be expecting too much to expect most intellectuals to have common sense, when their whole life is based on their being uncommon -- that is, saying things that are different from what everyone else is saying. There is only so much genuine originality in anyone. After that, being uncommon means indulging in pointless eccentricities or clever attempts to mock or shock.

Before the Iraq war I was quite disturbed by some of the neoconservatives, who were saying things like, "What is the point of being a superpower if you can't do such-and-such, take on these responsibilities?" The point of being a superpower is that people will leave you alone. *— September 2004*

If the battle for civilization comes down to the wimps versus the barbarians, the barbarians are going to win.

One undeniable accomplishment of Bill Clinton's presidency was that it kept Jimmy Carter from being the worst U.S. president in history.   15 August 2002

Nothing could be more jolting and discordant with the vision of today's intellectuals than the fact that it was businessmen, devout religious leaders and Western imperialists who together destroyed slavery around the world. And if it doesn't fit their vision, it is the same to them as if it never happened.   — *8 February 2005*

When I see the worsening degeneracy in our politicians, our media, our educators, and our intelligentsia, I can't help wondering if the day may yet come when the only thing that can save this country is a military coup.   — *May 1, 2007*

Intellectuals may like to think of themselves as people who "speak truth to power" but too often they are people who speak lies to gain power.   — *February 19. 2008*

If you have always believed that everyone should play by the same rules and be judged by the same standards, that would have gotten you labeled a radical 60 years ago, a liberal 30 years ago and a racist today.

Some of the biggest cases of mistaken identity are among intellectuals who have trouble remembering that they are not God.   — *February 19. 2008*

Too often what are called "educated" people are simply people who have been sheltered from reality for years in ivy-covered buildings. Those whose whole careers have been spent in ivy-covered buildings, insulated by tenure, can remain adolescents on into their golden retirement years.   — *May 5, 2004*

Virtually no idea is too ridiculous to be accepted, even by very intelligent and highly educated people, if it provides a way for them to feel special and important. Some confuse that feeling with idealism.   — *October 15, 2005*

Some of the most vocal critics of the way things are being done are people who have done nothing themselves, and whose only contributions to society are their complaints and moral exhibitionism.   — *October 15, 2005*

Although I am ready to defend what I have said, many people expect me to defend what others have attributed to me   — *September 3, 2007*

As far as party primaries are concerned, both Republican and Democratic Party primaries are dominated by the most zealous voters, whose views may not reflect the views of most members of their own respective parties, much less the views of those who are going to vote in the November general election.

In recent times, each election year has seen each party's nominee selected - or at least subject to veto - by its most extreme wing and then forced to try to move back to the center before the general election.

This can only undermine the public's confidence in the integrity of the candidates of both parties.   — *March 25, 2008*

One of the painful signs of years of dumbed-down education is how many people are unable to make a coherent argument. They can vent their emotions, question other people's motives, make bold assertions, repeat slogans-- anything except reason.   — *September 3, 2007*

Right after liberal Democrats, the most dangerous politicians are country club Republicans.
— *August 26, 2008*

Republicans won big, running as Republicans, in 2004. But once they took control of Congress, they started acting like Democrats and lost big. There is a lesson in that somewhere but whether Republicans will learn it is another story entirely.   — *August 26, 2008*

When we hear about rent control or gun control, we may think about rent or guns but the word that really matters is 'control.' That is what the political left is all about, as you can see by the incessant creation of new restrictions in places where they are strongly entrenched in power, such as San Francisco or New York. (Or Detroit)   — *26 August 2008*

Anyone who has actually had to take responsibility for consequences by running any kind of enterprise — whether economic or academic, or even just managing a sports team — is likely at some point to be chastened by either the setbacks brought on by his own mistakes or by seeing his successes followed by negative consequences that he never anticipated.   — *November 2008*

'Global warming' is just the latest in a long line of hysterical crusades to which we seem to be increasingly susceptible.   — *March 15, 2007*

Both history and contemporary data show that countries prosper more when there are stable and dependable rules, under which people can make investments without having to fear unpredictable new government interventions before these investments can pay off.
— *Sept 11, 2012*

It is amazing that people who think we cannot afford to pay for doctors, hospitals, and medication somehow think that we can afford to pay for doctors, hospitals, medication and a government bureaucracy to administer it.   (chapter: "What society expends?")

Freedom has cost too much blood and agony to be relinquished at the cheap price of rhetoric."
— *1987*

Facts do not "speak for themselves." They speak for or against competing theories. Facts divorced from theory or visions are mere isolated curiosities.   — *1987*

Competition does a much more effective job than government at protecting consumers.

The case for the political left looks more plausible on the surface but is harder to keep believing in as you become more experienced

Understanding the limitations of human beings is the beginning of wisdom.

The key feature of Communist propaganda has been the depiction of people who are more productive as mere exploiters of others.   — *chapter, Is Reality Optional? 1993*

Much of the social history of the Western world over the past three decades has involved replacing what worked with what sounded good. In area after area - crime, education, housing, race relations - the situation has gotten worse after the bright new theories were put into operation. The amazing thing is that this history of failure and disaster has neither discouraged the social engineers nor discredited them.   — *1999*

When you want to help people, you tell them the truth. When you want to help yourself, you tell them what they want to hear.

I have never understood why it is "greed" to want to keep the money you have earned but not greed to want to take somebody else's money.

People who pride themselves on their "complexity" and deride others for being "simplistic" should realize that the truth is often not very complicated. What gets complex is evading the truth.

Those who believe that "basic necessities" should belong to people as a matter of right ignore the implication -- that people are to work only for amenities, frivolities, and ego. Will that mean more work or less work? And if less, where are all those "basic necessities" coming from that the government is supposed to hand out?

Many of the dangerous things that drivers do are not likely to save them even 10 seconds. When you bet your life against 10 seconds, that is giving bigger odds than you are ever likely to get in Las Vegas.

Most problems do not get solved. They get superceded by other concerns.

People who talk incessantly about "change" are often dogmatically set in their ways. They want to change other people.

Maturity is not a matter of age. You have matured when you are no longer concerned with showing how clever you are, and give your full attention to getting the job done right. Many never reach that stage, no matter how old they get.

One of the most ridiculous defenses of foreign aid is that it is a very small part of our national income. If the average American set fire to a five-dollar bill, it would be an even smaller percentage of his annual income. But everyone would consider him foolish for doing it.

Letters from teachers continue to confirm the incompetence which they deny. A teacher in Montana says that my criticisms of teachers are "nieve." No, that wasn't a typographical error. He spelled it that way twice.

If I could offer one piece of advice to young people thinking about their future, it would be this: Don't preconceive. Find out what the opportunities are.

Some of the people on death row today might not be there if the courts had not been so lenient on them when they were first offenders.

If you don't believe in the innate unreasonableness of human beings, just try raising children.

Time was when people used to brag about how old they were -- and I am old enough to remember it.

One of the grand fallacies of our time is that something beneficial should be subsidized.

In the summer of 1959, I worked as a clerk-typist in the headquarters of the U.S. Public Health Service in Washington. The people I worked for were very nice and I grew to like them. One day, a man had a heart attack at around 5 PM, on the sidewalk outside the Public Health Service. He was taken inside to the nurse's room, where he was asked if he was a government employee. If he were, he would have been eligible to be taken to a medical facility there. Unfortunately, he was not, so a phone call was made to a local hospital to send an ambulance. By the time this ambulance made its way through miles of Washington rush-hour traffic, the man was dead. He died waiting for a doctor, in a building full of doctors. Nothing so dramatized for me the nature of a bureaucracy and its emphasis on procedures, rather than results.   — *2011*

Saturday, July 25, 2015

The Brouhaha over Trump and McCain

I never thought much of Donald Trump in the past, nor did I watch any of his TV shows. I guess, like most Americans, I let the media define him for me. Then came the brouhaha over illegal immigrants and John McCain. I too accepted the media's interpretation of his words, at first. Big mistake. Then I dug down and discovered what he actually said and put it in context.

I realized the media, lead by the NY Times, was doing a hatchet job on Trump with lies and innuendo, just like they do with most Republicans and especially conservatives. Politicians should never be candid only politically correct to satisfy the media. Trump's candid remarks, may at times be a bit troubling, but they certainly are refreshing. They certainly are not nearly as bad as the hate filled commentary of our liberal President and his allies. Of course, the media never mentions that or their bald faced lies.

I have gained a lot of respect for Trump as a result. He has gone way up in my opinion. Would I vote for him against Hillary? Of course. But then I would vote against her anyway for almost any other human that breathes. The guy who mows our lawn for example. If Obama and his far left cohorts haven't already destroyed this country, Hillary would most certainly apply the coup de gras.

Here's some of the reasons:

Politics - The New York Times - **HJ Note:** *I have marked all of the lies of the NY Times by marking them bold italics.* **My own comments, corrections and clarifications are in bold.**

Donald Trump Says *John McCain Is No War Hero,* Setting Off Another Storm (**NY Times lie. He never said that or anything similar.**)

By Jonathan Martin and Alan Rappeport July 18, 2015

AMES, Iowa — Donald J. Trump has made his name in politics with provocative statements, but it was not until Saturday, after the flamboyant businessman turned presidential candidate *belittled Senator John McCain's war record,* (**Another NY Times lie. He never belittled his war record.**) that many Republicans concluded that silence or equivocation about Mr. Trump's incendiary rhetoric was inadequate.

Mr. Trump upended a Republican presidential forum here, and the race more broadly, by saying of the Arizona senator and former prisoner of war: "*He's not a war hero*. He's a war hero because he was captured. I like people who weren't captured." (**The NY Times lied big time when they added their own words, "He's not a war hero." Trump did not say it.**)

Mr. McCain, a naval aviator, was shot down during the Vietnam War and held prisoner for more than five years in Hanoi, refusing early release even after being repeatedly beaten.

Mr. Trump and Mr. McCain have been engaged in a war of words over the past week, since the Arizona senator said that Mr. Trump was riling up "crazies" in the party with the inflammatory remarks about illegal immigrants from Mexico.

Yet Mr. Trump's comments on Saturday drew condemnation from his rivals and senior officials in the party at a scale far greater than the response to his portrayal of Mexican immigrants as rapists. (**That last is patently untrue. He did not portray Mexican immigrants as rapists. He said that there were rapists and other criminals among the illegal Mexican immigrants. A statement that is true. The NY Times deliberately left the term illegal out.**) The response was an indication of the reverence many Republicans have for military service and sacrifice. But it was also something more: their best opening yet to marginalize Mr. Trump. (**Another NY Times deceptive trick. Every politician of any persuasion tries to "marginalize" every one of their opponents every chance they get.**)

After weeks when many of them treaded lightly around Mr. Trump, who once again Saturday refused to rule out a third-party run, Republican leaders seized the opportunity to unambiguously speak out against a candidate they see as effectively hijacking their primaries. (**Trying to win is not hijacking.**)

Yet for all the outrage among party elites, some attendees at the Christian conservative conference where Mr. Trump made his comments were not nearly as offended, a reminder of the chasm between the Republican power structure and its grass roots. (**Not so, it's a reminder that some of the attendees actually listened to the remarks and did not accept the NY Times edited version, which the rest of the media immediately picked up and repeated verbatim without checking the facts.**)

With his attack on Mr. McCain, Mr. Trump, whose caustic (**factual**) language about immigration has lifted him in early polls, created a new, revealing litmus test for how the Republican presidential hopefuls are handling the bombastic real estate mogul.

Several of Mr. Trump's Republican opponents immediately denounced his comments, and one said the remarks disqualified him from the presidency. (**They must not have heard the actual** comment but accepted the NY Times revision of his words as gospel, which it certainly was not.)

"Donald Trump owes every American veteran and in particular John McCain an apology," said Rick Perry, the former Texas governor, upon taking the stage. Mr. Perry argued that Mr. Trump's comment made him unfit to be commander in chief. (**He too must not have heard the actual comment but accepted the NY Times revision of his words as gospel. Methinks he could have damaged his chances by speaking out without checking the facts.**)

Senator Lindsey Graham of South Carolina said that anybody serious about being president would not be disrespectful of prisoners of war, and predicted that the early nominating states would render an unmistakable verdict on Mr. Trump's candidacy. (**If that happens, the lies of the NY Times and the rest of the media will be largely responsible, as usual.**)

"Here's what I think they're going to say: 'Donald Trump, you're fired,' " Mr. Graham said to laughs and applause.

For Mr. Perry and Mr. Graham, both retired Air Force officers who have struggled to get traction in the race, Mr. Trump's comments represented an opportunity to highlight their own military service and demonstrate to primary voters that they would not tolerate any impugning of a veteran. (**Trump did not impugn McCain, even though the NY Times lied and said he did.**)

As telling was the difference between how Gov. Scott Walker of Wisconsin and Senator Ted Cruz of Texas reacted to Mr. Trump. Both are running aggressively in Iowa and pursuing the sort of conservative voters who are now considering Mr. Trump.

Mr. Walker, who leads in early Iowa polls, had previously resisted criticizing Mr. Trump. But in a sign of how quickly Mr. Trump's provocation reshaped the expectations of how candidates should treat him, Mr. Walker immediately changed course after Mr. Trump questioned Mr. McCain's military record. (**He did not question McCain's military record. Another NY Times lie, repeated by Walker, a bad mistake, trusting the NY Times.**)

"I unequivocally denounce him," Mr. Walker said at a campaign stop in Sioux City, Iowa. (**He too, must not have heard the actual comment but accepted the NY Times revision of his words as what Trump said, which it certainly was not.**)

Mr. Cruz, who poses a threat here on Mr. Walker's right, was more cautious. He told reporters before his remarks here that Mr. McCain is "an American hero," but added that he would not "say something bad about Donald Trump." (**He may have been one of the few who actually listened to Trump and heard what he really said.**)

Mr. Cruz's reluctance to confront Mr. Trump was perhaps best explained by the reaction to Mr. Perry's denunciation: While many in the crowd applauded, the ovation did not last long and nobody in the audience of nearly 3,000 stood to show their approval. (**They must have heard Trump correctly.**)

"It was not important to me," said Rose Kendall, an attendee from Burlington, Iowa, of Mr. Trump's comment on Mr. McCain. "He said that because John McCain talked him down."

Many Democrats noted that there had been far less opprobrium for Mr. Trump after he began his candidacy in June by saying of Mexican immigrants: "They're bringing drugs, they're bringing crime. They're rapists and some, I assume, are good people." (**All of which is very true of illegals. Note the NY Times did not say illegal immigrants. This makes the quote a lie. The quote has also been edited and not reported correctly.**)

Republicans also treated the businessman more delicately in the 2012 campaign, when Mitt Romney, the party's nominee, sought and publicly accepted Mr. Trump's endorsement even after the businessman had questioned whether President Obama was born in the United States. (**A question that has never been adequately answered and certainly not proven.**)

Speaking to reporters after his turn on stage, Mr. Trump tried to soften (**Trump said clarify, NY Times reported he said soften, the meanings are quite different**) the remarks, saying that any United States veteran who was a prisoner of war was heroic. He also shifted his comments to assuage (appease, mollify, pacify, placate, NY Times word meanings) veterans, saying that Mr. McCain had failed to address their needs. (**Trump has worked to support veterans.**)

"I'm with the veterans all the time," he said. "I consider them heroes."

Asked about his own military draft status, Mr. Trump, 69, said that he received medical deferments from the Vietnam War because of a bone spur in his foot. Mr. Trump could not recall which foot was afflicted.

Yet Mr. Trump's awkward and ill-suited remarks about religion and marriage here may have done more damage to his candidacy, at least with Christian conservatives. (**The man is too candidly honest about his beliefs and person to be a politician. Unlike politicians, he does not cater to the PC crowd. Also, he's one of those hated businessmen, a capitalist.**)

"I'm a religious person," Mr. Trump offered. "I go to church. Do I do things that are wrong? I guess so."

Mr. Trump also struggled to answer if he had ever sought forgiveness from God, before reluctantly acknowledging that he had not. "If I do something wrong, I try to do something right," he said. "I don't bring God into that picture." (**If he were a true politician, especially a liberal one, he would never have been so candid admitting that, or any of the admissions that follow. This is quite refreshing in anyone seeking elective office. If he behaved like virtually all politicians, he would have lied and given the PC answer to appease the media. I really like that in him.**)

And Mr. Trump raised eyebrows with language rarely heard before an evangelical audience — saying "damn" and "hell" when discussing education and the economy — while also describing the taking of communion in glib terms. "When we go in church and I drink the little wine, which is about the only wine I drink, and I eat the little cracker — I guess that's a form of asking forgiveness," Mr. Trump said. (**Candid once more. Candid is the opposite of Politically Correct.**)

If all that was not enough to roil the button-downed crowd, he also described his three marriages in starkly frank terms, conceding that he had difficulty finding a work-life balance.

"It was a work thing, it wasn't a bad thing," Mr. Trump said. "It was very hard for anybody to compete against the work."

Despite his marital problems over the years, Mr. Trump said that he was always available to his children and that he did his best to have dinner with them on most nights even when his work was grueling. He worked hard, he said, to instill good values and steer them away from drugs, alcohol and cigarettes.

"I was actually a great father," Mr. Trump said. "I was a better father than I was a husband."

It was these comments, not his attack on Mr. McCain, that prompted the most muttering and unease in the audience.

"Well, I was turned off at the very start because I didn't like his language," Becky Kruse, of Lovilia, Iowa, said of Mr. Trump, not mentioning his comments about Mr. McCain. Ms. Kruse said she likes Mr. Trump's hard line on immigration and came to the event considering him. "I was not too impressed," she said, noting Mr. Trump's comment about not seeking God's forgiveness. "He sounds like he isn't really a born-again Christian." **(He said he was a Presbyterian. He never ever professed to be a "born again Christian.")**

Find out what you need to know about the 2016 presidential race today, and get politics news updates via Facebook, Twitter and the First Draft newsletter. **(If you can wade through all the BS.)**

A version of this article appears in print on July 19, 2015, on page A1 of the New York edition with the headline: *No Hero, Trump Says of McCain,* Stirring Outrage. **(More lying words by the NY Times.)**

A last HJ comment: It's a sad commentary that Americans get by far the largest portion of their news from the media. For most Americans, the media defines people, events and opinions. Few people bother to check the accuracy of the nightly news or ever hear about the things they deliberately do not mention. I should more accurately say deliberately suppress. I have also noted that apologies and corrections for erroneous front page stories are always buried deep in the bowels of later editions, never given front page status. This is especially true if the correction is beneficial to Republicans, conservatives or any on the right, or detrimental to Democrats, liberals or any on the left.

Letters to the editor, St Augustine Record, July 25, 2015

Threat's not immigrants, It's Ann Coulter's vitriol

Editor: On July 13 Ann Coulter pounded out another inane and vitriolic column against illegal immigrants. Out of the estimated 11 million illegal immigrants (more like 20 million) in our country, she managed to select about a dozen alleged murderers, rapists, drug dealers and burglars as proof of the overwhelming crime wave emanating from immigrant people who are not her idea of deserving. **(She said illegal immigrant, he did not. Big difference.)**

She and Donald Trump may rant and rave about these people. However, I doubt if they have any first-hand knowledge of them and their families: their wishes, anxieties and dreams.

I do!

For the past 12 years, I have worked as a volunteer in a farming community largely populated by Mexican immigrants. **(Legal or illegal?)** I have literally met thousands of these folks and have gotten to know many families quite well. They are no different from the Italian, German, Irish, Oriental and various religious groups that left (their countries) for a better life. Their kids are as American as apple pie, with the added benefit of a second language. The people I have met are hard-working, honest and family-oriented. I am sure somewhere in their community there are some law breakers. Doesn't every community have its share?

But the hate-filled paragraphs of Ann Coulter are meant to inflame, not to inform. This column was particularly misleading and mean, covering millions of innocent people with a broad brush of evil. Comparing immigrants to ISIS is the true evil.   — *Al Moser*

(No, it did not compare immigrants to ISIS. It compared illegal immigrants to ISIS. A completely different meaning.)

HJ Note: If Al Moser had been referring to legal immigrants, he may have been right, but Coulter and Trump were referring strictly to *illegal* immigrants. The actual crime statistics of that group are appalling and well documented. Of course the media hides those facts routinely. But then since *illegals* saw nothing wrong with breaking the immigration laws to get here, why should they then see anything wrong with breaking other laws they wish to abrogate? What's an occasional robbery, drug deal, murder or rape anyway? No big deal. They do that all the time in Mexico. (Or Venezuela, or Honduras, or Columbia, or Iraq, or Pakistan etc. etc.) I responded with my own letter to the editor. It was published a few days later.

Editor: On July 25 you published a letter from Al Moser berating Ann Coulter and Donald Trump for their comments about *illegal* immigrants. About *illegal* immigrants he said, "They are no different from the Italian, German, Irish, Oriental and various religious groups that left (their countries) for a better life. Their kids are as American as apple Pie." That's balderdash. There is one huge, obvious and irreconcilable difference. They are *illegal!* They are **criminals** who disobey our laws to get here and stay here. They are clearly scofflaws. The high school kids in California who took down the American flag, stomped on it, and raised the Mexican flag, cursing in Spanish and shouting "Atzlan (most of the southwest, TX, NM. AZ, and CA) is Mexican." as well as all the members of MECHA, are certainly not, **"as American as apple pie."** Sure, there may be some **illegal** immigrants who might become good American citizens, but they still broke the law to get here. That's a monstrous insult, a slap in the face to all the **legal** immigrants like the Italian, German, Irish, Oriental and others including Mexicans and Latin Americans who did obey the law, entered the country legally and applied for citizenship. Ask them what they think of **illegal** immigrants.

Posted by HoJo at 11:26 PM

Wednesday, December 17, 2014

Seventy-one years ago today - December 17, 1943

My First Love, Dolores

I don't remember when it started, but sometime during the eighth grade, when I was in Roxboro Junior High, I fell for a girl I thought was the most beautiful girl in the world, Dolores Osborn. I pursued her for some time in spite of her lack of interest. Oh, she was pleasant enough with me, and I did manage to take her to a movie or two, but I knew I was not on her list.

I remember walking her home along Fairmont Boulevard after we had a soda at the Dairy Bar, one of the kid's favorite hangouts. She told me about pididdle, a word one says when a car with one headlight appears, an invitation to a kiss, much like standing under mistletoe. If the other one of the couple repeats pididdle, it means they would also like to share a kiss. No sooner had she told me this when a car with one headlight appeared. I bravely said, pididdle, but there was no response. I struck out again.

The ninth grade dance was the social event of the year at Roxboro. To have a date was important, and needed to be arranged early or all the girls would be taken, at least all of the popular girls. At least two months before the dance I took Dolores to a couple of movies and worked up the nerve to ask her, "Would you go to the ninth grade dance with me?"

"Let me think about it for a day or two," she replied. "I'll have to ask my parents. They don't want me to date as yet."

Apparently, her parents did not consider going to the Dairy Bar or movies as dating. I didn't know if this was her way to say no or not, so I would have to wait for her answer on Monday. I thought the day would never come. I sat with Dee at lunch and soon had my answer, yes. I was ecstatic. I now had a date for the biggest event of the year with my dream girl.

Two weeks before the dance my dream was scuttled. Dolores came up to me and said, "I've been going out with Freddie (my buddy Fred Hunziker) for some time now, so I can't go to the dance with you. I'm going with Freddie."

How could any girl be so cruel? Easy, I guess. It was now far too late for me to get a date. All the available girls had long ago been asked. I did get even in a way. Dolores loved to dance and Freddie did not dance. During the evening, I danced every dance, many with close friends of Dolores. She sat at their table with Freddie and never did get to the dance floor.

After the dance, I went with a group of friends, mostly female, to the Dairy Bar for an after party soda. There were one couple and two girls who did not have dates because their parents did not permit them to date. (Shades of a bygone day) I was seated between the two girls who were being quite chummy when who should walk in but Dolores and Freddie. The two girls knew how I had been shafted (as did everyone at school) so they both became, shall we say, amorous—right then and there.

One of the girls, a close friend of Dolores's, put her arms around my neck and called out to Dolores, "We're sure glad you dumped Howie for the dance. We're having a great time with him." It was not long before she and Freddie left.

When I started at Cleveland Heights High, one of my dreams was to sing in the choir. Even though I played an instrument and was in band and orchestra at Roxboro, I joined the chorus, a prerequisite to being in the famous, Heights High School A Capella Choir. When I auditioned, I earned a spot in the second tenor section. I was thrilled, knowing I would be in the next Christmas concert. Another choir member was my old crush, Dolores Osborn. Though I had taken her to the movies a few times, she was not interested in me. I had given up asking her for dates and was reduced to admiring her from afar.

December 17, 1943—everything changed. The choir was to sing downtown at Higbee's department store, an annual event. Given permission to drive the family car, I asked several members of the choir including one girl who lived near Dolores. When she asked if I had room for one more and told me Dolores needed a ride, I, of course, agreed.

After the performance, the choir was treated to a short party with refreshments in a room at Higbee's before we headed home. I sat with Dolores during the party where she did not seem so standoffish as before. As I took everyone home, I happened to end with Dolores as my last passenger. We spent the next two hours in the car in front of her house. I told her how I had felt about her since we met in the eighth grade. Before long we shared our first kiss. After some amorous conversation and quite a few more kisses, I walked her to her door. My feet wouldn't touch the ground, my mind was whirling, uncontrolled, and I was deliriously in love.

At the choir party after the annual Christmas concert, I gave her a card with the words "A penny for your thoughts" and enclosed a bright new penny. Sometime later, she returned the favor and the penny. I still have that penny.

We were to share many Christmases together. We would also walk onto the stage together at Heights as choir alumni many times, sing Emitte Spiritum Tuum, and share memories with choir friends. We managed to sing Emitte one last time in 1996 at our fiftieth class reunion with about forty choir alums.

In September 1949, we were married. I got even with her for standing me up for the ninth grade dance. I never did let her forget that. In the years that followed, we had five children and then were divorced after she betrayed my trust by having an affair with one of my friends. Ironically, our divorce was final on our twenty-fifth anniversary. After our divorce, she married her long time boy friend. I eventually got over it, and we had a friendly relationship for many years, something of great benefit to our children. Fortunately, I am blessed to be one of those who remembers the good parts of life and can forget or minimize the bad. Her husband died of a sudden illness a few years later, after they moved to Detroit.

She passed away some twenty years after our divorce. In a testimony to how positively we had dealt with our children, they asked my wife, Barbara, a Methodist minister, to conduct the memorial service for their mother. Dee and Barb had grown to be such good friends they often went Christmas shopping together for gifts for our children. The service was a celebration of all of the positive things in Dee's life.

In later years I often thought our problems and subsequent parting were a bit of a blessing in disguise for me, once I recovered from the resulting emotional trauma. Had that not happened my life would have been very different. I would probably not have had the several spectacular relationships that I have experienced. There are several stories about these women in my book of memoirs.

Friday, November 14, 2014

Who Can You Trust?

I think you should all read this Outsider Club report. I would have copied it into my BLOG for all to read, but it is copyrighted. It's on the Outsiders Club web site. To view, enter the link below in your browser. I don't know how long it will be available.

http://www.outsiderclub.com/report/who-can-you-trust/1016

Monday, July 28, 2014

Thank You Democrats

It has been nearly a year since I have posted a rant to this blog. I have decided to post a sincere thank you.

I want to thank all of you liberal Democrats for your efforts on behalf of all of us American seniors who have dropped below the poverty line. Using myself as an example, and I am one of those working people who for their entire working life paid the maximum into Social Security and Medicare. I was moved below the poverty line by the huge medical expenses of my late wife's final illness not covered by insurance.

What prompted this email message was a recent headline "U. S. Deficit will cause government to pull back on senior benefits." That's certainly nothing new. It's been going on for at least the last fifty years and especially since 1993. Another thing that prompted this rant was the incident about my Rx costs.

I take several medications since my heart attack and heart surgery. One of those, Effient, an Eli Lilly product, cost me just $6.25 per Rx all of last year. The first time I went to pick it up this year the price was $129 for the same Rx. I didn't have enough money to pay for it. When I contacted the SS office, I was informed that my "Extra help" had expired and I would have to reapply. I went to the SS office and waited four hours to see a lady who helped me fill out a new application. When she told me it would take three or four weeks for my application to be processed I asked her how I was to pay for these critical meds during that period she informed me politely that I would have to pay for them. Then she made a suggestion that I ask my cardiologist for some samples to use until they processed my papers. That was the best thing she did.

What a blessing it was. My cardiologist gave me a month supply of samples. I also found out that unlike most major drug companies, Eli Lilly does not provide even temporary help on the cost of their drugs for poor seniors. When I went to pick up my next Rx of Effient, the price was $6.25. Recently, when I went to pick up a new Rx for Effient, the price was back up to $129. My druggist told me to call my insurance company to find out why. I called them and was told to call Social Security. I called SS and they told me I had to call the Medicare office. Medicare said I would have to call the State Medicaid office. I called them and they said they could find no reason why the price went up, but that I should file another request for Extra Help. Other than the call to my insurance company, each of the calls to government agencies took several days of constant calling at all hours and hearing, "We are experiencing an unusually high volume of calls. Please try your call later." I could not get through to anyone, so I gave up trying and went on the Internet and reapplied once more. Of course by this time I had been without the critical heart medication for nearly two weeks. I finally called my cardiologist and explained the situation. Once more he very kindly supplied me with another month supply of samples.

Now I am waiting for notification that my application for Extra Help is being processed. That will probably take at least a month if all goes well. I hope it comes through before I run out of the samples.

Oh yes, thanks again for the wonderful reductions in Medicare benefits. Visits to my family doctor that cost $17 just four years ago now cost me about $90. One hospital x-ray and tests for my spine, that I have periodically, were free four years ago. Now they cost me about $60. Well of course, we have to find the money to pay for all those hard-working Obamacare bureaucrats somehow. That now falls on those least able to pay, seniors with low or no income. As Obama said about seniors in their eighties (paraphrased), "Take a Tylenol for pain. You're too old for expensive medical treatment like knee replacement or a pacemaker."

That Democrats have gutted SS payments big time while shouting, "Seniors, Republicans want to cut your SS payments. We will protect your Social Security." In 1993 Democrats in control of Congress made some huge cuts in future SS payments and Democrat President Bill Clinton signed these changes into law. What they did was to change the way the Cost of Living Adjustment, the COLA, was calculated. They removed food and fuel from the calculation of the COLA. Apparently they think seniors do not need food or fuel. My current SS monthly payment is $1250.10, an amount lower than what I have been receiving since March 2013. If Democrats had not made those cuts, my current monthly SS payment would be $2,575.81. The same reduction has been proportionally made to all recipients of SS payments. Thank you Democrats.

You would think the public advocates in the media would be screaming about this legislation that so damages seniors, but since they are firmly in the pockets of Democrats, the media never mentions it. In fact, they do their best to hide it from the public while screaming, "Republicans are planning to cut your Social Security." That's what Democrats have already done, gutted Social Security for seniors. Most seniors are either too ill-informed or too ignorant to understand that.

The VA has been in the news recently for the atrocious way they have been handling health care for veterans. This is nothing new, In the late 1960s and early nineteen seventies. There was a very similar scandal in the VA system where several veterans died awaiting treatment that never came. I know because at that time we were supplying goods and services by bid to the VA hospital on Brecksville Road in Cuyahoga County (Cleveland) Ohio. I personally went to the VA Hospital dental clinic to service some of their equipment. The red tape we had to go through to do any work was unbelievably tedious. We had to examine the equipment and then submit a bid for the repairs. That meant two trips for one of our servicemen. As a result, most repairs were bid and then billed at twice our usual rate. Any new problems the dentists pointed out to our men while they were there had to go through the same bid procedure. We tried to work out a system where we bid two hours without knowing what the problem was, but then there was the problem of parts. It also took the VA at least 90 days to process any payments after they were billed.

We doubled our bid prices and included estimates of parts. Even then we were awarded most of our bids for repair service. Another problem was access. Our men often waited an hour or more to gain access to the clinic, even when we had an appointment. Then they had to wait for someone to sign off on the work order, sometimes wasting another hour or more. Actually, I looked at what we were doing and found the delays, paperwork and red tape were costing us more than the actual work. This brought about another increase in our bid prices for repairs. After a few particularly aggravating (and expensive) episodes, I quit biding on repair service. The dentist finally called and begged us to bid on repairs since no one else would. I worked out a system that basically bypassed the red tape and worked well for everyone without all the aggravation. Within a month of putting the system in place I got a call from one of their bureaucrats who accused me of cooking up a "sweetheart" deal for us. I tried to explain why and show that it worked well for both the hospital and us, but he would not listen. I finally told him we would no longer perform any repair service for them at any price. In spite of the begging of the dentist we refused to bid. The VA finally hired a full time dental repair man (from our competitor). We continued bidding and getting contracts on parts and supplies.

I checked our total billings for service labor. It had averaged about $2,000 for the previous three years and probably would have been lower under the last system I worked out. We set the dentist up in private practice as soon as his contract with the VA was over. He told me what a mess their practice was at the hospital and how the dental repair man, who was paid about $17.000 per year, spent most of his time reading books and watching TV in the break room. They still had to issue a work order and get it approved for any repairs their own man did. That was more than fifty years ago and it looks as if nothing has changed since. I can just imagine what a bureaucratic nightmare our healthcare system will become under Obamacare. There will probably be more bureaucrats hired to check on other bureaucrats than there will be workers. Of course, that will mean more bureaucrats paid to do less work and the rolls of government workers will swell accordingly. Since they will be voting to keep their jobs they will overwhelmingly vote Democrat. Isn't that the whole purpose of the government bureaucracy, to provide jobs for Democrat voters who are unable or don't want to work anyway? And all of that featherbedding paid for by workers in the shrinking private sector.

These are all facts I have experienced or have calculated from Federal Government records. Of course, like all good liberals, you will probably adhere to the liberal mantra, "Don't try to confuse me with facts. My mind's made up."

Sunday, September 01, 2013

Subject: THIS IS A TRUE STORY...and a dirty one!

This was sent to me by my cousin below, it is a verified true story on Benaghzi as written by Cynthia Myers whose cousin was one of the ones killed there. The second part was written by Dr. Charles Roots–Senior Pastor, US Navy Chaplin Corps (ret). They are heart breaking stories of the events that have been covered up. Dear God, please be with our brave men and women serving our country over there. Walt

Read carefully and please pass it on. May the truth be told.

Herman "Woody" Hughes, Ph.D.

Captain, USNR, Retired

Professor Emeritus, Pepperdine University

You need to read this true account of what happened to our Ambassador Stevens and the other three who died. If this doesn't make you mad...............Cynthia Lee Myers Wanted to share the truth of what happened over in Libya, you will not find this in the media yet but it airs tonight on FNC.....please read....

"Here is my story. A week out the Embassy in Tripoli began receiving multiple tips about an Al Queda cell in the area planning an attack on 9/11 in response to the killing of Bin Laden. For the next several days, the State Department and Whitehouse were asked for a security force and were denied at least six times. Ambassador Stevens and his team were given the all clear that the Consulate in Benghazi was safe and there was no need for a security force other than his three personal guards(One being my cousin) and a few Libyans who were not armed.

"Then the attack and murders occurred. Immediately the Whitehouse claimed it was a protest gone bad over a you tube video. Obama made a quick speech in the Rose Garden on Sept.12 before catching a plane to Vegas to campaign. He made a generic statement at the end of his speech after placing the blame on an overheated protest over the video. He said "No act of terror will shake the resolve of America. Later that day and over the next two days, the liberal media began saying Ambassador Stevens and the other three men died of smoke inhalation. This was not the case. Out of respect for my cousin, I'm not going to be specific about his murder. However, Ambassador Stevens was brutally murdered. His genitals were cut off. He was sodomized and beaten and cut and stabbed and burned. He was dragged thru the streets and left for dead. This is eyewitness testimony of a local Dr. who found the Ambassador in a ditch and tried to save his life. He had no idea who he was. The other three men, including my cousin, met similar fates. And deaths due to smoke inhalation is a 100% fabricated LIE. The next week I drove my aunt and Uncle and two others to DC to receive his body. We met with Hillary, Panetta, and Susan Rice. ALL of whom apologized and said it was a protest gone bad over a video and exited the area. Next Obama entered with the same story and didn't apologize and wasn't sympathetic. My aunt cried to this man and all he did was hand her flowers and walk away. I tried to get his attention, but didn't. I got upset and yelled "liar" to him, he kept walking. Then a secret service agent grabbed my arm and led me to a room where I was held till the proceedings were over.

"America, I saw firsthand how cold this man is. What kind of liar he is. Most of you haven't a clue about this tyrant and yet you support him. And act like every word he says is Gospel. These murders and the fast and furious cover ups make Watergate look like, a kid who told his buddies secret to the class.

"We must stop this man, and please pass this story along. – God Bless America!"

THIS PART YOU DON'T KNOW, BUT SHOULD.

AMERICAN VALOR, BENGHAZI, LIBYA:

The stunning part of this story is that Tyrone Woods and Glen Doherty killed 60 of the attacking force. Once the compound was overrun, the attackers were incensed to discover that just two men had inflicted so much death and destruction.

The news has been full of the attacks on our embassies throughout the Muslim world, and in particular, the deaths of Ambassador Chris Stevens and three others in Benghazi, Libya. However, there's a little known story of incredible bravery, heroics, and courage that should be the top story.

So what actually happened at the U.S. embassy in Libya? We are learning more about this every day. Ambassador Stevens and Foreign Service officer Sean Smith, along with administrative staff, were working out of temporary quarters due to the fact that in the spring of 2011 during the so-called Arab Spring, the United States cut ties with then president Moamar Gadhafi. Our embassy was looted and ransacked, causing it to be unusable. It is still in a state of disrepair.

Security for embassies and their personnel is to be provided by the host nation. Since Libya has gone through a civil war of sorts in the past 18 months, the current government is very unstable, and therefore, unreliable.

A well-organized attack by radical Muslims was planned specifically targeting the temporary U.S. embassy building. The Libyan security force that was in place to protect our people deserted their post, or joined the attacking force. Either way, our people were in a real fix. And it should be noted that Ambassador Stevens had mentioned on more than one occasion to Secretary of State Hillary Clinton, that he was quite concerned for his personal safety and the welfare of his people. It is thought that Ambassador Stevens was on a "hit list." (Probably on Obamaa's "hit list.")

A short distance from the American compound, two Americans were sleeping. They were in Libya as independent contractors working an assignment totally unrelated to our embassy. They also happened to be former Navy Seals.

When they heard the noise coming from the attack on our embassy, as you would expect from highly trained warriors, they ran to the fight. Apparently, they had no weapons, but seeing the

Libyan guards dropping their guns in their haste in fleeing the scene, Tyrone Woods and Glen Doherty snatched up several of these discarded weapons and prepared to defend the American compound.

Not knowing exactly what was taking place, the two Seals set up a defensive perimeter. Unfortunately Ambassador Stevens was already gravely injured, and Foreign Service officer, Sean Smith, was dead. However, due to their quick action and suppressive fire, twenty administrative personnel in the embassy were able to escape to safety. Eventually, these two courageous men were overwhelmed by the sheer numbers brought against them, an enemy force numbering between 100 and 200 attackers which came in two waves. But the stunning part of the story is that Tyrone Woods and Glen Doherty killed 60 of the attacking force. Once the compound was overrun, the attackers were incensed to discover that just two men had inflicted so much death and destruction.

As it became apparent to these selfless heroes, they were definitely going to lose their lives unless some reinforcements showed up in a hurry. As we know now, that was not to be. I'm fairly certain they knew they were going to die in this gun fight, but not before they took a whole lot of bad guys with them!

Consider these tenets of the Navy SEAL Code:

1) Loyalty to Country, Team and Teammate,
2) Serve with Honor and Integrity On and Off the Battlefield,
3) Ready to Lead, Ready to Follow, Never Quit,
4) Take responsibility for your actions and the actions of your teammates,
5) Excel as Warriors through Discipline and Innovation,
6) Train for War, Fight to Win, Defeat our Nation's Enemies, and . . .
7) Earn your Trident every day

(http://www.navyseals.com/seal-code-warrior-creed).

Thank you, Tyrone and Glen. To the very last breath, you both lived up to the SEAL Code. You served all of us well. You were courageous in the face of certain death.

And Tyrone, even though you never got to hold your newborn son, he will grow up knowing the character and quality of his father, a man among men who sacrificed himself defending others.

Dr. Charles R. Roots - Senior Pastor - Former Staff Sergeant, - USMC Captain, U. S. Navy Chaplain Corps (Ret.)

This should be passed on and on and on.

NO TRUE AMERICAN WOULD OBJECT TO RECEIVING THIS MORE THAN ONCE . . . SO PASS IT ON

And Let us never forget the Hillary Clinton Comment (typical)

"What Difference Does It Make?"

And she wants to be our next president!

"The Beauty of the Second Amendment is that it will not be needed until they try to take it"

—*Thomas Jefferson*

BBC News - 6 February 2013 Last updated at 07:31 ET

French Forces at War in Mali

French forces are embroiled in a "real war" with "terrorists" around the Malian town of Gao, Defence Minister Jean-Yves Le Drian has said.

Islamist militants were swept from Gao last month, but Mr Le Drian said clashes were continuing in the area.

French forces were deployed nearly a month ago to combat al-Qaeda-linked militants who had taken over Mali's desert northern regions.

Al Jazeera TV reported the following additional information about this action:

(Paraphrased) When French forces in Mali overran an Al Queda headquarters near Gao, they captured a computer that had been used to communicate with the Al Queda attackers of the US embassy in Benghazi. In one interesting communique, it said among other things that there would be no US military response to the planned attack, none.

Add that to the fact that several of our military units within an hour of Benghazi were ordered to "stand down" when they initiated a response. There is only one source where those orders could have originated.

I wonder why none of this was reported in the American main stream media? Hmmmm??? I have found Al Jazeera broadcast over British TV to be a much more honest and accurate source of information about events in the Middle East and Africa than American TV. I wonder why this is so? Hmmmm??

Then there was the constant stream of lies about the attack by Susan Rice, Hillary Clinton and Obama. They were most certainly not misinformed. They knew exactly what had happened. **They flat out lied to the world and especially to the American public.** Obedient slaves in the main stream media continued to spread these lies for weeks, even after it became obvious to most thinking individuals that it was a well-planned attack of several hundred Al Queda fighters.

Sunday, July 21, 2013

An angry response to a factual posting and my responses.

The following is a Facebook exchange that brought a lot of flack my way from a number of very upset people. All told, I actually received more positive reactions than negative, but the visceral anger expressed in the negative reactions told a far more significant story. This pointed out to me how poor a communication system, sound bites, or any comments of few words are, particularly in emotionally charged situations. Even well intended comments of limited size are poorly understood or totally misunderstood in these emotional exchanges.

News media and political sound bites are the tools of those who try to incite anger and violence in support of their agenda. These tiny messages are often turned into hate messages by all sides of any controversy. Slogans, placards and signs carried by demonstrators of all kinds are typical, a few words intended to stir emotions. They are simplistic comments that say little or nothing of the realities of extremely complex situations. They are the human equivalent of the barking dog serving only to incite anger or hatred. They are used because they are easy and require little effort. Real communication requires sometimes painful and serious effort. Few people are willing to do so. Much easier to let others define things for us and simply do as they tell us. That is the basis for the power of all politics and religion. Don't think, react like the PC or SC or FC crowd decides for you. Thinking requires work and most people are intellectually lazy. They would rather follow the follower than go out on their own.

NOTE: In this copy of the postings, I used numbers to represent names of three different responders to protect the identity of the author. Several people who knew my email address chose that method rather than use Facebook. Probably that was done to keep from being railed at by angry liberals. I understand perfectly, but since I consider being chastened by angry liberals a complement and testimonial to my integrity, I invite comments.

Here's the comment I posted on Facebook and probably could have worded much better:

"I've seen a lot of static about young black men being killed by police and auxiliary police since the Zimmerman verdict. Here's a reality check. In the first half of 2012, there were 120 black men killed by police. During the same period there were more than 3,000 black men killed by other black men, not police. Where's the hue and cry about that statistic?"

Howard Johnson - July 15 at 8:58pm

~ ~

#1 - "Come to Fort Wayne there is an uproar about the number of black men being killed by black men. At least one shooting a day if not more."

July 15 at 11:28pm via mobile

~ ~

#2 - "so does that make it all right? I guess I shouldn't have expected anything better from bigots like you."

Tuesday at 7:50pm via mobile

~ ~

Howard Johnson, "So the new liberal definition of a bigot is anyone who sites factual data about anything that disagrees with the liberal agenda. Come on. You can do better than that. Name calling is a poor excuse for an argument or attempt to make a point."

Tuesday at 10:42pm

~ ~

#3 - "The media, Hollywood, the Obama administration, and most liberal Democrats are in lockstep in denigrating the police, the military, religion (except Islam), business, white men, and, when things don't go their way, the judicial system. They ramped up their hate rhetoric and sensationalized this one trial while completely ignoring an infinitely more serious problem. In fact, there were a number of killings of black men by other black men in Chicago while the trial was going on. Where is the outrage, the sound bites, the protests, the public outcry about that?"

Via email, Tuesday at 11:20pm

~ ~

#2 - "A piece of isolated data (if in fact true) taken out of context is not a valid argument or justification for any behavior. What is your point anyway? Is it to justify some trigger happy misguided scared white guy shooting an unarmed black kid in a hoody? *After all blacks kill each other anyway!*"

Wednesday at 8:02am via mobile

~ ~

Howard Johnson, "The point of my first posting that #2 did not like and probably couldn't understand is that, at least numerically, the epidemic of black men killing other black men is much larger and more devastating than the problem of police killing black men by a factor of about 27 times. There doesn't seem to be a proportional response from the public, probably because this single incident has been blown to huge proportions with intense emotional reactions by people with an agenda to promote who are screaming for revenge, not justice. This is amplified by the media who use it to sell their product. Apparently there is no profit to calling attention to the realities of life in the black community. Could it be that this hue and cry serves to divert public attention away from a much larger and more serious problem?"

Wednesday at 8:56am · Like · 1

~ ~

#2 "You missed the point. People like myself are not screaming for revenge we are screaming for the end of racial profiling as well as laws like you have in Florida "stand your ground with a gun to kill" I wonder how the public would have reacted if the colors were reversed???"

Sunday at 8:40am via mobile

~ ~

Howard Johnson, "Sure sounds like revenge to me. I too wonder how the liberal public would react if the racial situation were reversed. Added: (When you say "public" I assume you mean those of the public who think the way you do. It is obvious your opinion does not reflect an overwhelming majority of the general public.) Probably just like the liberal public did to the four black teens in Atlanta who beat up a white guy and threw him into traffic where he was killed. Google the Murder of Joshua Chellew. Incidentally, You are way off base about Florida's "Stand you ground law." It is used almost twice as often in the defense of black men than white. Total lack of accurate information never stops a liberal opinion."

Sunday at 12:40pm via mobile

~ ~

#2 "I am ending this conversation and not dignify your comments with a response. Unfortunately ignorance and hypocrisy such as yours is still too pervasive."

Sunday at 1:15pm via mobile · Like · 1

NOTE: more name calling and accusations without shred of substantiation then abdication. Isn't that retreating or running away when they realize they have no valid countering argument.

~ ~

#1 "Never stops the conservative opinion either. I have become more liberal since leaving Leesburg and I am a happier person because of it. There is a public outcry about the blacks shooting blacks in Indiana. Are you not paying attention."

Sunday at 1:19pm via mobile

~ ~

Howard Johnson (for #2) "Typical liberal argument, accuse and name call, but do not offer a single shred of factual evidence, a child's playground activity!"

Sunday at 2:10pm

~ ~

Howard Johnson #1: "Where did you get the notion I was a conservative? Do people have to dichotomize everything? Is it always "them against us?" I am pleased to report that to my right wing friends I am considered a flaming liberal and to my far left family and friends, a fundamentalist right winger. I live in Florida now and have a quite good idea what's going on down here as I am actively engaged in the community. I hear virtually nothing of what is going on in Indiana. Another point: You have absolutely no comprehension of my racial attitudes and beliefs. I have marched in protest with my black friends in the Urban League as far back as 1960. In my business I treated everyone equally as far as pay, promotions and all else was concerned. In our industry, I put the very first full time female salesperson on the road and was given an award for it. My opinions are my own and are based on my understanding of the facts. I am rarely if ever swayed by the emotional diatribes from any position right, left, or a thousand others. Should you want to know more, email me at hobarb@yahoo.com and I'll give you links to a lot of information. I don't feel like posting my BLOG address. Maybe I'll send you one of my books."

Some information I wish I had thought to add to the previous post: I took a young black man who worked for us in delivery and encouraged and trained him to become a service man earning more than twice the pay he had in delivery. Several years later, he asked me how he could become a salesman. I was pleased to train him and give him a territory where eventually he was earning still more. I gave a single, black mom a supervisory position instead of a white man who had been with us longer and felt he had earned the promotion. He had not. He exploded at me in ire, but I did not fire him. Later he begrudgingly admitted he had not been doing his best. As a result and working under the woman as his boss, he became a much more productive employee. He was rewarded with a raise in pay because he was worth it. As a direct result of these efforts, six bright young people were able to go to college. They were the children of the ones I mentioned above.

Here's my response to the above exchanges. It will be in this article only and not posted on Facebook---no barking dog:

I have been cursed, called names, reviled, chastened, lied about, denigrated, ridiculed, and subjected to a lot of other emotional diatribes by people who did not like their understanding of my positions and/or comments on a number of things. These were almost all liberals, many in my family. Honestly, I consider those comments as badges of honor—as compliments considering their sources. I cannot remember a single instance where a rational argument was presented in response to any of my political comments by these people. In a similar vein, I cannot recall a single rational proposal made by any liberal politician in any political campaign. Apparently liberals are totally devoid of constructive ideas and must hide this lack by screaming epithets as arguments. They are masters at accusing those with whom they disagree of all manner of terrible actions, most of which they themselves are far more guilty.

One classic example of this is Howard Dean's screaming, "I hate Republicans! I hate conservatives! I hate Rush Limbaugh!" when he was the chairmen of the Democrat party. As a result of this, and for other obvious reasons, I have renamed our two political parties the **Hate** party and the **Stupid** party. Which is which is obvious to all but the most stupid, biased, or hate driven among the public. The **Hate** party because that is almost all they ever do or say. The **Stupid** party because they recognize the effectiveness of **Hate** party rhetoric, but only use it against members of their own **Stupid** party in primary elections.

I will not spend any time justifying my positions or providing data to back them up. There is a great deal of information available on the Internet, some good, some bad, and some pure non sense. Look it up and find out for yourself. Of course, many of you liberals would not do that as you rely on the liberal media and politicians to do your thinking and research for you. The PC crowd defines most people and situations for you since you seem unable to think for yourselves.

Most of the statistics I use or site, including those in my triggering comment come from the US government. The *isolated data* came from the US Department of Justice. By the way, the comment "Is it to justify some trigger-happy misguided scared white guy shooting an unarmed black kid in a hoody?" is not supported by any of the evidence brought forward by the prosecution in the trial. Didn't the author really mean to say, "That poor little innocent black boy was shot down in cold blood by a wanton white Hispanic racist." Apparently that liberal knew exactly what was going on in the minds of both killer and victim, far better than those involved in the trial or the jury. Too bad they weren't available to the court. That is true of course.

Since my antagonists and most liberals seem to know everything about everything, why is it that since liberals dominate government bureaucracies, control our government schools, predominate among college professors, and have run the government for most of the last fifty years, things are in such a mess? Why has our education system gone to hell, our economy crashed, and our middle classes lost almost all of their wealth? Why is the population of Detroit, that marvelous testimonial to the power of liberalism, now down to about 700,000 and is one of the poorest cities in the nation? Before liberals and the union goons took over, its population was around 2 millions and it had the highest per capita income in the nation. **Those are facts!**

Oh yes, remember the famous and prophetic words of that great liberal, *King* Lyndon Johnson: "Detroit will be our model city, a shining example of the 'fairness' of our policies." Well, he was right on the money. Drive through Detroit on I-75 and you can see some of the burned out homes and factories right from the Interstate. If you are brave and can protect yourself from a car jacking, drive into the city itself and you'll find it looks like a bombed out third world city. **Johnson's liberal buddies and followers under Obama are now doing their best to bring about the same result in the entire country.** Unless there is soon a drastic change in America, they will probably succeed. They have the blessings and support of virtually all of the black community, the Hispanic community, Hollywood, and the main stream media.

As part and parcel of the damage coming is what I think may happen to America in the near future, another civil war. As the left wing fanatics rachet up their hate rhetoric, the white supremacists and other right wing fanatics do the same, MECHA agitates for the take over of Atzlan, the Muslims create general chaos, and our government actually and deliberately incites "their people," sooner or later the lid will blow off. This one will make the last civil war look like a tea party and not the political one. This is merely a conclusion from observations. It is most certainly an event I do not want to happen. It is an event that I believe our current administration and its supporters are working for. I believe they think that during the conflict, the complex food and fuel distribution system will fall apart, the power structure will then break down completely, and they will gain power.

What can we do to prevent this catastrophe that so many seem to be pushing for? **How can we stop this liberal Democrat War on America?**

1. Reduce the size of the federal government by initially reducing federal employment to half of the current level. Reduce the cost of federal employees by cutting all pay and benefits to 95% of the pay of equivalent positions in the private sector.

2. Revise our education system to tell the truth about what made America so successful in providing a high standard of living for most people. Reignite that spirit of American *can do* and *excellence* that our President so despises.

3. Remove a great deal of the power government has usurped from the people in the private sector. I have only a general idea of how to do this, but cutting the government bureaucracy in half and electing constructive people rather than the self-serving frauds that now populate so many of our public offices, would be a start.

4. Remove the power from the labor unions by making a right to work law national so that union membership is no longer compulsory. Outlaw government employee unions. Make unions subject to the sam anti trust laws as companies.

5. Replace Obamacare with a combination of government and private insurance with government providing basic services and private insurance the rest not bounded by state lines.

6. Replace the IRS with a taxing system like the Fair Tax which removes politicians from the power to rake off the system for their own benefit. Make no exceptions and no immunity for anyone or any company. While at it, institute a negative income tax to replace all welfare, unemployment compensation, and social security.

7. Replace existing corporate law with laws that don't favor huge corporations. Provide decreasing controls and reporting requirements as corporations grow smaller. Do everything we can to help and protect small business. The Fair Tax or something like it would take care of the financial part of this.

8. Return to strict rule of the Constitution as it was written, approved, and amended. We have a process for amendment. Use it and not the courts to make necessary changes.

9. Enforce our existing immigration laws. Change the law to prevent gaming of the system. Do not allow the children born of illegal aliens to become citizens.

10. Provide a work permit for aliens so that they can work legally, but must pay taxes to cover the additional costs of their health and educational services for their families.

CHANGE OF SUBJECT: For those who really want to know the realities of firearm violence here are some web sites.

Firearm Violence, 1993-2011 - Statistics on violent crime from the US Department of Justice. Check out the graphs at this site. **http://www.bjs.gov/content/pub/pdf/fv9311.pdf**

About 70% of arrest related deaths were white males including Hispanics. About 30% were black. - **http://www.bjs.gov/content/pub/pdf/ardus05.pdf**

My thoughts and ideas have been affected by many people over many years. My parents, my grandparents, my sisters, the Christian church and my entire broader family were the forces that first taught my mind and helped me to develop my ideas. Since my youth, there have been many influences, mostly ideas and people I learned to at least partially trust and respect. Lately, since I began organizing my thoughts, writing, and becoming active in a number of discussion groups, I have recognized a number of current influences that have had a lot to do with how I think about almost everything. It is interesting that most of the members of these groups are quite liberal in the current, and I think erroneous sense of the word. The following is a sort of credo I am trying to follow in living my life.

In nearly all of my voting, which I do religiously, I am forced to take the lesser evil of the usually two choices on the ballot. In my voting lifetime, a considerable number of years, I have worked and voted *for* a candidate only five, maybe six times. Two of those were Democrats, Harry Truman and more recently, Evan Bayh. Harry worked out. Once he went to Washington,

Even abandoned his laudable Indiana principles and persona and became a career liberal leach. My mistake. The others were Republicans, Dwight Eisenhower, Ronald Reagan, and Francis P. Bolton, Representative of Ohio's 22nd district and a staunch Republican who fought the excesses of King Lyndon Johnson. I voted sort of for George Bush, becoming a staunch supporter after the Daly brothers (the Chicago Democrat machine) came to Florida and tried unsuccessfully to steal the election from him. I noticed they were up to their old tricks in the last election, but were more successful this time.

For more reading that seems to make sense to me, try the links below or Google the names. I placed them in alphabetical order so my actual preferences would not be obvious. Each one was an influence in their own way.

Ray Bradbury - http://www.raybradbury.com

Jared Diamond - http://www.jareddiamond.org/Jared_Diamond/Welcome.html

Stephen J. Gould - http://www.stephenjaygould.org/original.html

Stephen Hawkins - http://www.hawking.org.uk

Eric Hoffer - http://www.hopepubs.com/Hoffer/Hoffer-Books.html
          http://ehoffer.blogspot.com

Thomas Sowell - http://www.tsowell.com

Robert Louis Stevenson

John Stossel - http://townhall.com/columnists/johnstossel

E. O. Wilson - http://www.ted.com/speakers/e_o_wilson.html

Jules Verne

Eric Hoffer probably speaks the closest to my opinions of anyone on the list.

There are many more, particularly those quoted in my book, Memoirs from the Lakeside.

To see an excerpt of my memoirs books, goto http://hjwls.blogspot.com

---

Thursday, July 04, 2013

The Mindset of the Left

On the forth of July, our paper posted an opinion piece by Thomas Sowell, one of the columnists I most admire, and I have posted a copy here.

Sowell is the author of one of my favorite quotes, "Socialism has a record of failure so blatant that only an intellectual could ignore or evade it."

I then wrote my own similar comment, "The liberal Democrat party in the US has a record of hatred, failure, deception, corruption, and greed so blatant that only an intellectual could ignore or evade it."

PERSPECTIVE -   The·Mindset of the Left

THOMAS SOWELL - Inserts in bold italics are comments added by Howard Johnson

When teenage thugs, are called "troubled youth" by people on the political .left, that tells us more about the mindset of the left than about these young hoodlums.

Seldom is there a speck of evidence that the thugs are troubled, and often there is ample evidence that they are in fact enjoying themselves, as they create trouble and dangers for others.

Why then the built-in excuse, when juvenile hoodlums are, called "troubled youth" and mass, murderers are just assumed to be "insane?"

At least as far back as the 18th century, the left has struggled to avoid facing the plain fact of evil — that some people simply choose to do things that they know to be wrong when they do them. Every kind of excuse, from poverty to an unhappy childhood, is used by the left to explain and excuse evil.

All the people who have come out of poverty or unhappy childhoods, or both, and become decent and productive human beings, are ignored. So are the evils committed by people raised in wealth and privilege, including kings, conquerors and slave owners.

Why has evil been such a hard concept for many on the left to accept? The basic agenda of the left is to change external conditions. But what if the *problem* is internal? What if the real problem is the cussedness of human beings?

Rousseau denied this in the 18th century and the left has been denying it ever since. Why? Self preservation.

If the things that the left wants to control—institutions and government policy—are not the most important factors in the world's problems, then what role is there for the left?

What if it is things like the family, the culture and the traditions that make a more positive difference than the bright new government "solutions" that the left is constantly coming up with? What if seeking "the root causes of crime" is not nearly as effective as locking up criminals? The hard facts show that the murder rate was going down for decades under the old traditional practices so disdained by the left intelligentsia, before the bright new ideas of the left went into effect in the 1960s — after which crime and violence skyrocketed.

What happened when old-fashioned ideas about sex were replaced in the 1960s by the bright new ideas of the left that were introduced into the schools as "sex education" that was supposed to reduce teenage pregnancy and sexually transmitted diseases?

Both teenage pregnancy and sexually transmitted diseases had been going down for years. But that trend suddenly reversed in the 1960s and then hit new highs.

One of the oldest and most dogmatic of the crusades of the left has been disarmament, both of individuals and of nations. Again, the focus of the left has been on the externals — the weapons in this case.

If weapons were the problem, then gun control laws at home and international disarmament agreements abroad might be the answer. But if evil people who care no more for laws or treaties than they do for other people's lives are the problem, then disarmament means making decent, law-abiding people more vulnerable to evil people.

Sowell neglects to mention the huge and violent evil that disarming also generates. Laws that control or remove supposedly evil things from law abiding people also make it extremely profitable for criminal organizations to fill the void. Didn't we learn the lesson of prohibition? Wasn't that debacle a clear proof that the left's positions on disarmament are seriously flawed? The Capone syndicate and its deadly offspring were a direct result of this ridiculous idea put into law. Now we have huge and deadly criminal organizations supplying drugs, prostitution, and guns as gun control laws go into effect. They funnel billions of dollars into the campaigns and pockets of lawmakers who write these control laws.

Since belief in disarmament has been a major feature of the left since the 18th century, in countries around the world, one might think that by now there would be lots of evidence to substantiate their beliefs.

But evidence on whether gun control laws actually reduce crime rates in general, or murder rates in particular, is seldom mentioned by gun control advocates. It is just assumed in passing that of course tighter gun control laws will reduce murders.

But the hard facts do not back up that assumption. Gun control laws merely disarm decent, law-abiding people while providing a huge financial bonanza for criminal organizations. That's the hard reality the left totally ignores. That is why it is the critics of gun control who rely heavily on empirical evidence, as in books like "More Guns, Less Crime" by John Lott and "Guns and Violence" by Joyce Lee Malcolm.

National disarmament has an even worse record. Both Britain and America neglected their military forces between the two World Wars, while Germany and Japan armed to the teeth. Countless British and American soldiers paid with their lives for their countries' initially inadequate military equipment in World War II. But what are mere facts compared to the heady vision of the left?

The very vocal leftist critics of our "military, industrial complex" who greatly exaggerate the cost of the defense budget, seem to ignore the realities of history and of the violent enemies free nations have. Or maybe they just are doing what they can to destroy what was the most free and viable nation the world has ever known.

Monday, March 25, 2013

The Wahhabi sect of Islam - the force behind most of the war and killing in the turbulent Middle East.

In a photo, President Obama bows to Saudi King in 2008

Some mental wonderings about the future of our nation under the leadership of a complete and evil, anti-American fraud

Here are a few thoughts from diverse sources about the realities of life in the USA under Obama.. Then there are some details of how Obama's friends, supporters, detractors and enemies have all been conned into helping him in his effort to accomplish his true goals. Didn't someone say, "Those who ignore history are destined to repeat it."

See much more about the Wahhabi sect of Islam starting on Page 42.

THOUGHTS FROM DIVERSE SOURCES:

Socialism has a record of failure so blatant that only an intellectual could ignore or evade it.
—Thomas Sowell.

The liberal Democrat party in the US has a record of hatred, failure, corruption, deception, and greed so blatant that only an intellectual could ignore or evade it.	*—Howard Johnson*

Enlightened people seldom or never possess a sense of responsibility.	*—George Orwell*

The United States will be a socialist dictatorship by 2030. At that time, leftist activists will be happily extolling the joys of socialism while being carted off in cattle cars to the salt mines.
—Howard Johnson

A government policy to rob Peter to pay Paul can be assured of the support of Paul.
—George Bernard Shaw

It seems our present government has deliberately destroyed many Peters and created a huge number of Pauls to ensure compliance with their agenda and support for their enslaving policies.
—Howard Johnson

The problem with socialism is that eventually you run out of other peoples money.
—Margaret Thatcher (England's Iron Lady)

People unfit for freedom—who cannot do much with it—are hungry for power. The desire for freedom is an attribute of a *have* type of self. It says, leave me alone and I shall grow, learn, and realize my capabilities. The desire for power is basically an attribute of a ***have not*** type of self.
—Eric Hoffer

Reality is that which, when you stop believing in it, doesn't go away.	*—Philip K. Dick*

To a liberal Democrat, elitist intellectual, or any collectivist, reality simply does not exist.
—Howard Johnson

Those who are able to see beyond the shadows and lies of their culture will never be understood, let alone believed, by the masses.
—Plato

It is disconcerting that present-day young who did not know Stalin and Hitler are displaying the old naivete. After all that has happened they still do not know that you cannot build utopia without terror, and that before long terror is all that's left.
—Eric Hoffer

Add a few drops of venom to a half truth and you have an absolute truth.
—Eric Hoffer

The new names for our two parties

We now have a two party system for all national elections. The two parties are the **hate** party and the **stupid** party. We have been calling them by other names, but you know which is which. Now whenever you see their old names, substitute **hate** or **stupid**. Of course, a few members of each of the old parties switch when using their new names. Members of the **hate** party have learned that hate of all kinds is the best means of getting elected and they have become masters at using it. Voters are more motivated by hate and hate speech than by any other factor, probably more than all other factors combined. The **stupid** party now loses elections because the only time they use hate and hate speech is in the primaries against members of their own **stupid** party. Brilliant!

Politics is a totally irrational, emotional thing. There are a number of things completely missing from all political campaigning. These include, but are not limited to: truth, honesty, reason, logic, respect, morality, reality, civility, in fact, anything having to do with what we used to call human dignity. Also, the real motives and goals of politicians are carefully hidden beneath layers of deceit. They are kept from public knowledge as much as possible. Most politicians are frauds for this reason alone. None of the current crop of **hate** party members has conducted as effective a hate campaign as has that great unknown, Barack Hussein Obama.

Politicians of the left, the **hate** party, have become single minded in their efforts at inciting lynch mobs (the voters) to hate their opposition. Using class, economic, and race envy, and character assassination, they fan the fires of unreasoning anger and hatred to bludgeon their opponents. Their accusations are almost totally unfounded and devoid of facts. They know that the lynch mob mentality overpowers reason and logic, and will cause ordinary people to do unthinkable evils if guided by the angry rhetoric of the inciters. Obama and his minions are masters of this kind of incitement. Remember the famous rant of then Democrat party chairman, Howard Dean, "I hate Republicans. I hate Conservatives. I hate Rush Limbaugh." That is what motivates liberal Democrats, pure visceral hatred.

Our lying President: Obama for one is a complete fraud, a fabrication. He not only deceives the public, but his friends and supporters as well. It took me a long time to come to this conclusion, but the more I saw the results of his action, the more I examined what he was and is actually doing, the clearer his true purpose came to me. This one conclusion explains all of his actions, his lies and deceptions. There is no other possible conclusion.

I will start with some information published by a black talk show host from Los Angeles.

~ ~

EXAMPLES of Obama's pathological lies:

TERRY ANDERSON, A BLACK LOS ANGELES TALK RADIO HOST, WENT DOWN A LIST OF STATEMENTS, (in bold) SENATOR OBAMA HAS SAID THAT AREN'T EXACTLY CORRECT. (That's being a pathological liar to the uninformed.)

Obama is a fraud, a fabrication. Several of his many blatant lies and their documentation were reported by Terry Anderson, a black talk radio host from LA. One part of his list of Obama's lies are copied in the following paragraphs. They are just a few from his list of several hundred. Obama's lies are in bold. My comments are in bold italics.

1.) Selma March Got Me Born - NOT EXACTLY, your parents felt safe enough to have you in 1961 - Selma had no effect on your birth, as Selma was in 1965. (Google 'Obama Selma ' for his full March 4, 2007 speech and articles about its various untruths.)!! Shades of Hillary being named after Sir Edmond. Those Democrats invent more about themselves than one can keep up with.

2.) Father Was a Goat Herder - NOT EXACTLY, he was a privileged, well educated youth, who went on to work with the Kenyan Government.

3.) Father Was a Proud Freedom Fighter - NOT EXACTLY, he was part of one of the most corrupt and violent governments Kenya has ever had.

4.) My Family Has Strong Ties to African Freedom - NOT EXACTLY; your cousin Raila Odinga has created mass violence in attempting to overturn a legitimate election in 2007, in Kenya. It is the first widespread violence in decades. The current government is pro-American but Odinga wants to overthrow it and establish Muslim Sharia law. Your half-brother, Abongo Obama, is Odinga's follower. You interrupted your New Hampshire campaigning to speak to Odinga on the phone. Check out the following link for verification of that and for more. Obama's cousin Odinga in Kenya ran for president and tried to get Sharia Muslim law in place there. When Odinga lost the elections, his followers have burned Christians' homes and then burned men, women and children alive in a Christian church where they took shelter...Obama SUPPORTED his cousin before the election process here started. Google Obama and Odinga and see what you get. No one wants to know the truth.

5.) My Grandmother Has Always Been a Christian - NOT EXACTLY, she does her daily Salat prayers at 5am according to her own interviews. Not to mention, Christianity wouldn't allow her to have been one of 14 wives to one man.

6.) My Name is African Swahili - NOT EXACTLY, your name is Arabic and 'Baraka' (from which Barack came) means 'blessed' in that language. Hussein is also Arabic and so is Obama. Barack Hussein Obama is not half black. He is the first Arab-American President, not the first black President. Barack Hussein Obama is 50% Caucasian from his mother's side and 43.75% Arabic and 6.25% African Negro from his father's side. While Barack Hussein Obama's father was from Kenya, his father's family was mainly Arabs. Barack Hussein Obama's father was only 12.5% African Negro and 87.5% Arab (his father's birth certificate even states he's Arab, not African Negro). Go to:

_http://www.arcadeathome.com/newsboy.phtml?Barack_Hussein_Obama_-_Arab Americ_

(http://www.arcadeathome.com/newsboy.phtml?Barack_Hussein_Obama_-_Arab-Americ) an,_only_6.25%25_African

7.) I Never Practiced Islam - NOT EXACTLY, you practiced it daily at school, where you were registered as a Muslim and kept that faith for 31 years, until your wife made you change, so you could run for office. 4-3-08 Article 'Obama was 'quite religious in Islam'

#HYPERLINK http://www.wnd.com/index.php?fa=PAGE.view

#HYPERLINK http://www.wnd.com/index.php?fa=PAGE.view&pageId=60559

NOTE: These links probably won't last long.

8.) My School in Indonesia Was Christian - NOT EXACTLY, you were registered as Muslim there and got in trouble in Koranic Studies for making faces (check your own book). February 28, 2008. Kristoff from the New York Times: Mr. Obama recalled the opening lines of the Arabic call to prayer, reciting them with a first-rate accent. In a remark that seemed delightfully uncalculated (it'll give Alabama voters heart attacks), Mr. Obama described the call to prayer as "one of the prettiest sounds on Earth at sunset"' This is just one example of what Pamela is talking about when she says "Obama's narrative is being altered, enhanced & manipulated to whitewash troubling facts."

9.) I Was Fluent in Indonesian - NOT EXACTLY, not one teacher says you could speak the language.

10.) Because I Lived in Indonesia, I Have More Foreign Experience - NOT EXACTLY, you were there from the ages of 6 to 10, and couldn't even speak the language. What did you learn except how to study the Koran and watch cartoons?

11.) I Am Stronger on Foreign Affairs - NOT EXACTLY, except for Africa (surprise) and the Middle East (bigger surprise); you have never been anywhere else on the planet and thus have NO experience with our closest allies.

12.) I Blame My Early Drug Use on Ethnic Confusion - NOT EXACTLY, you were quite content in high school to be Barry Obama, no mention of Kenya and no mention of struggle to identify - your classmates said you were just fine

13.) An Ebony Article Moved Me to Run for Office - NOT EXACTLY, Ebony has yet to find the article you mention in your book. It doesn't, and never did, exist.

14.) A Life Magazine Article Changed My Outlook on Life - NOT EXACTLY, Life has yet to find the article you mention in your book. It doesn't, and never did, exist.

15.) I Won't Run on a National Ticket in '08 - NOT EXACTLY, despite saying, live on TV, which you would not have enough experience by then, and you are all about having experience first.

16.) Voting 'Present' is Common in Illinois Senate - NOT EXACTLY, they are common for YOU, but not many have 130 NO VOTES.

17.) Oops, I Miss-voted - NOT EXACTLY, only when caught by church groups and Democrats, did you beg to change your miss-vote.

18.) I Was a Professor of Law - NOT EXACTLY; you were a senior lecturer ON LEAVE.

19.) I Was a Constitutional Lawyer - NOT EXACTLY, you were a senior lecturer ON LEAVE.

20.) Without Me, There Would Be No Ethics Bill - NOT EXACTLY, you didn't write it, introduce it, change it or create it.

21.) The Ethics Bill Was Hard to Pass - NOT EXACTLY, it took just 14 days from start to finish.

22.) I Wrote a Tough Nuclear Bill - NOT EXACTLY, your bill was rejected by your own party for its pandering and lack of all regulation - mainly because of your Nuclear donor, Exelon, from which David Axelrod came.

23.) I Have Released My State Records - NOT EXACTLY, state bills you sponsored or voted for have yet to be released, exposing all the special interests pork hidden within.

24.) I Took on The Asbestos Altgeld Gardens Mess - NOT EXACTLY, you were part of a large group of people who remedied Altgeld Gardens. You failed to mention anyone else but yourself, in your books.

25.) My Economics Bill Will Help America - NOT EXACTLY, your 111 economic policies were just combined into a proposal which lost 99-0, and even YOU voted against your own bill.

26.) I Have Been a Bold Leader in Illinois - NOT EXACTLY, even your own supporters claim to have not seen any BOLD action on your part.

27.) I Passed 26 Of My Own Bills in One Year - NOT EXACTLY, they were not YOUR bills, but rather handed to you, after their creation by a fellow Senator, to assist you in a future bid for higher office.

28.) No one on my campaign contacted Canada about NAFTA - NOT EXACTLY, the Canadian Government issued the names and a memo of the conversation your campaign had with them.

29.) I Am Tough on Terrorism - NOT EXACTLY, you missed the Iran Resolution vote on terrorism and your good friend Ali Abunimah supports the destruction of Israel.

30.) I Want All Votes to Count - NOT EXACTLY; you said let the delegates decide.

31.) I Want Americans to Decide - NOT EXACTLY, you prefer caucuses that limit the vote, confuse the voters, force a public vote, and only operate during small windows of time.

32.) I passed 900 Bills in the State Senate - NOT EXACTLY, you passed 26, most of which you didn't write yourself.

33.) I Believe in Fairness, Not Tactics - NOT EXACTLY, you used tactics to eliminate Alice Palmer from running against you. He used unethical and probably illegal tactics in every election he has been in.

34.) I Don't Take PAC Money - NOT EXACTLY, you take loads of it.

35.) I don't Have Lobbyists - NOT EXACTLY, you have over 47 lobbyists, and counting.

36.) My Campaign Had Nothing to Do With the 1984 Ad - NOT EXACTLY, your own campaign worker made the ad on his Apple in one afternoon.

37.) I Have Always Been Against our Iraq policy - NOT EXACTLY, you weren't in office to vote against it AND you have voted to fund it every single time thereafter.

38.) I Have Always Supported Universal Health Care - NOT EXACTLY, your plan leaves us all to pay for the 15,000,000 who don't have to buy it.

39.) My uncle liberated Auschwitz concentration camp - NOT EXACTLY, your mother had no brothers and the Russian army did the liberating.

40.) If you like your present health care plan you can keep it. - NOT EXACTLY, one example of the hundreds of lies about the Affordable Care Act.

These are just a few of the hundreds of accurately documented lies pointed out and backed up with recorded facts by Terry Anderson. So, who EXACTLY is this Obama guy and what is he trying to sell us? Please get to work now. Not enough of your loved ones and friends know about this fraud. Now that he is President, his lies about everything have multiplied many fold. Example, his recent blatant lies about the events in Benghazi. The man is a pathological liar. These are proven facts, but their deeper meaning is carefully hidden from the public, Obama's enemies, and even from his friends.

This is easy to understand. By his own words, he is a Muslim. Muslims are instructed by the Koran to "Lie, cheat, steal from, and even murder all who are not true believers in Islam." Modern Muslims believe this is especially true of Christians, Jews, and Hindus. Is it any wonder that Obama lies constantly because of this?

NOTE: About the reliability of snopes.com: Check other sources besides Snopes.com. There have been multiple times they have "debunked" something negative about Obama but the other sites have supported the claims. Do some research and you find they are firmly in Obama's corner and many times will say something is false or will attempt to spin it in a positive light while other sources just as if not more reputable have said the exact opposite. Obama's biggest supporter (with money) is avowed socialist George Soros, who just happens to be the primary "purse strings" and ardent supporter of the infamous SNOPES.COM web site. Draw your own conclusions.

~ ~

Some Barack Obama Quotes - HEJ has added what he actually means in italics.

Change will not come if we wait for some other person or some other time. We are the ones we've been waiting for. We are the change that we seek. *That change is from a free America to a totalitarian dictatorship with me in control. That's more efficient than a republic.*

Focusing your life solely on making a buck shows a certain poverty of ambition. It asks too little of yourself. Because it's only when you hitch your wagon to something larger than yourself that you realize your true potential. *When you become totally dependent on government, it happens. Your government must completely control your life and have and use all your money. We can do a much better job than you can, at least for us. We don't care if you end up in poverty.*

We need to steer clear of this poverty of ambition, where people want to drive fancy cars and wear nice clothes and live in nice apartments but don't want to work hard to accomplish these things. *Michelle and I and our cohorts are the only ones allowed to do this, and we're masters at it. Everyone should try to realize their full potential. Just as long as it doesn't interfere with what I want.*

I will cut taxes - cut taxes - for 95 percent of all working families, because, in an economy like this, the last thing we should do is raise taxes on the middle class. *I actually meant RAISE taxes for working families.*

And I will do everything that I can as long as I am President of the United States to remind the American people that we are one nation under God, and we may call that God different names but we remain one nation. *Of course, I am that God.*

The fact that we are here today to debate raising America's debt limit is a sign of leadership failure. America has a debt problem and a failure of leadership. Americans deserve better. I, therefore, intend to oppose the effort to increase America's debt. *I'm not sorry I said the opposite of what I meant. You understand that of course.*

America and Islam are not exclusive and need not be in competition. Instead, they overlap, and share common principles of justice and progress, tolerance and the dignity of all human beings. *This will be true as soon as I have changed America into an Islamic nation under Sharia law.* It was the labor movement that helped secure so much of what we take for granted today. The 40-hour work week, the minimum wage, family leave, health insurance, Social Security, Medicare, retirement plans. The cornerstones of the middle-class security all bear the union label. *And now I am going to make all of that meaningless and impose poverty on the masses. Unions will be helping me accomplish this.*

It took a lot of blood, sweat and tears to get to where we are today, *and I and my administration have just begun to reverse all those gains.*

Today we begin in earnest the work of making sure that the world we leave our children *is an Islamic world, a whole lot worse than the one we inhabit today for all non Moslems..*

My family, frankly, they weren't folks who went to church every week. My mother was one of the most spiritual people I knew but she didn't raise me in the church, so I came to my Christian faith later in life *when Michelle convinced me to hide my Islamic beliefs and profess Christianity so I could run for political office.* It was because the precepts of Jesus Christ spoke to me in terms of the kind of life that I would want to lead. *That last is, of course, pure Moslem BS because we are urged by our holy Koran to lie, cheat, steal from, and murder Infidels, and especially Christians and Jews.*

It's time to fundamentally change the way that we do business in Washington. To help build a new foundation for the 21st century, we need to reform our government so that it is more efficient, more transparent, and more creative. *That means a totalitarian dictatorship under Sharia law.* That will demand new thinking *(subjugation to our demands)* and a new sense of responsibility for every dollar that is spent. *All money will be spent in support of Islam and my leadership.*

I believe marriage is between a man and a woman. I am not in favor of gay marriage. But when you start playing around with constitutions, just to prohibit somebody who cares about another person, it just seems to me that's not what America's about. Usually, our constitutions expand liberties, they don't contract them. *I don't give a damn what the Constitution says. We are going to act and rule as we see fit.*

I've got two daughters, nine years old and six years old. I am going to teach them first of all about Islamic values and morals. But if they make a mistake, I don't want them punished with a baby. *I'll just have them stoned.*

There is not a liberal America and a conservative America - there is the United States of America. There is not a black America and a white America and Latino America and Asian America - there's the United States of America. *I intend to turn all of those Americas into an Islamic America under Sharia law.*

We can't drive our SUVs and eat as much as we want and keep our homes on 72 degrees at all times . . . and then just expect that other countries are going to say OK. That's not leadership. That's not going to happen, *at least for you. I can do that and send Michelle and our friends on expensive, fuel-consuming jet flights all over the world wherever and whenever we want. I don't give a damn what it costs taxpayers or how much ecological damage it does. We will go and do as we please. Get over it!*

We have an obligation and a responsibility to be investing in our students and our schools. We must make sure that people who have the grades, the desire and the will, but not the money, can still get the best education possible *as long as we can pick and choose who gets that education and what it is they are taught.*

The thing about hip-hop today is it's smart, it's insightful. The way they can communicate a complex message in a very short space is remarkable. *The fact that they promote violence and degrade women is inconsequential. Like Hillary says, who cares?*

I can make a firm pledge, under my plan, no family making less than $250,000 a year will see any form of tax increase. Not your income tax, not your payroll tax, not your capital gains taxes, not any of your taxes. *That is of course pure Obama BS. We are equal opportunity taxers. We will take as much of your money as we can, as soon as we can in never ending cycles, especially if you are a business person or middle or lower middle class American.*

I consider it part of my responsibility as President of the United States to fight against negative stereotypes of Islam wherever they appear. *I will continue to promote negative stereotypes of Christians, Jews, Hindus - in fact, any non Islamic religion.*

If you're walking down the right path and you're willing to keep walking, eventually you'll make progress. *The right path is of course whatever I tell you.*

And we can see the positive impacts right here at Solyndra. Less than a year ago, we were standing on what was an empty lot. But through the Recovery Act, this company received a loan to expand its operations. This new factory is the result of those loans. *Solyndra will be a spectacular financial success and pay back those loans with interest, just like the city of Detroit and the State of California, etc. etc. Is that what actually happened? Of course not, and Obama knew full well it was destined for failure. It sure was a great way to pay off supporters at taxpayers' expense.*

A good compromise, a good piece of legislation, is like a good sentence; or a good piece of music. Everybody can recognize it. They say, 'Huh. It works. It makes sense.' *Good is, of course, defined as that which promotes and furthers my Islamic goals for America.*

If the people cannot trust their government to do the job for which it exists - to protect them and to promote their common welfare - all else is lost. *So trust me.*

But what we can do, as flawed as we are, is still see God in other people, and do our best to help them find their own grace. That's what I strive to do, that's what I pray to do every day. *Of course, Allah is the only God and Islam the only religion and I pray daily for the destruction of America.*

Americans . . . still believe in an America where anything's possible - they just don't think their leaders do. *No, from my own words and from my current leadership they know that I do not believe in America, American exceptionalism, the American Constitution, personal freedom for the masses or any kind of individual liberties. They see me rule by decree, lie to them on a routine basis, ignore the Constitution and bypass Congress when that body does not conform to my orders.*

Let's take a look at Obama's friends and supporters and see how he treats them, identifies with them, panders to them, and then uses them

Democrats: Obama obviously is a Democrat. He accepted the Democrat nomination for President and is the titular head of the Democrat party. He espouses Democrat policies, praises the Democrat's agenda and befriends Democrats everywhere. Is he truly a Democrat or is he using Democrats, fooling them to further a completely different agenda? Hmmmm?

Liberals: Obama obviously is a Liberal. He accepted support of liberals in his nomination for President and during the campaign. He espouses liberal policies, praises the liberal agenda and befriends liberals everywhere. Is he truly a Liberal or is he using Liberals, fooling them to further a completely different agenda? Hmmmm?

Progressives: Obama obviously is a progressive. He accepted progressive support in his nomination for President and during the campaign. He espouses progressive policies, praises the progressive agenda and befriends progressives everywhere. Is he truly a progressive or is he using progressives, fooling them to further a completely different agenda? Hmmmm?

Socialists: Obama obviously is a Socialist. He accepted Socialist support in his nomination for President and during the campaign. He espouses Socialist policies, praises the Socialist agenda and befriends Socialists everywhere. Is he truly a Socialist or is he using Socialists, fooling them to further a completely different agenda? Hmmmm?

Blacks/African Americans: Obama claims to be Black. He accepted Black support in his nomination for President and during the campaign. He espouses Black policies, praises the Black agenda and befriends Blacks everywhere. Is he truly a black or is he an Arab (Caucasian), using Blacks, fooling them to further a completely different agenda? Hmmmm?

Communists: Obama obviously is a Communist. He accepted Communist support in his nomination for President and during the campaign. He espouses Communist policies, praises the Communist agenda and befriends Communists everywhere. He appoints avowed Communists to his cabinet and policy making bodies. Is he truly a Communist or is he using Communists, fooling them to further a completely different agenda? Hmmmm?

Latinos: Obama obviously panders to Latinos. He accepted Latino support in his nomination for President and during the campaign. He espouses Latino policies, praises the Latino agenda and befriends Latinos everywhere. He supports amnesty for illegals. Is he truly a friend of Latinos or is he using Latinos, fooling them to further a completely different agenda? Hmmmm?

Unions: Obama obviously is a Union supporter. He accepted Union support in his nomination for President and during the campaign. He espouses Union policies, praises the Union agenda and befriends Unions everywhere. Is he truly a Union supporter or is he using Unions, fooling them to further a completely different agenda? Hmmmm?

And just what is that different agenda? Hmmmm?

Consider:

1) Who benefitted from the restrictions Obama placed on oil exploration in the US?

2) Who benefitted from the halt in the Canadian oil pipeline.

3) Who benefitted from the money and arms provided to the Moslem Brotherhood in Egypt.

4) Who benefitted from the attack in Benghazi and the orders for our military to "stand down" and not provide the military assistance that was ready and able to respond?

5) What group has renewed rocket attacks on Israel from Gaza?

6) What group would be the most damaged by expanding American oil production?

7) What group would lose the most if the US became energy independent?

8) What group has benefitted the most from the actions of our President?

There is one group and only one that benefitted from each of these eight actions plus many more, not all so obvious.

I'm sure you have your own answers to these eight questions, but here are mine:

1) The oil producing nations and especially Saudi Arabia.

2) The oil producing nations and especially Saudi Arabia.

3) The Moslem Brotherhood

4) Al Queda and in particular the North African organizations.

5) Hamas

6) The oil producing nations and especially Saudi Arabia.

7) The oil producing nations and especially Saudi Arabia.

8) The commonality of the other seven answers is a faction of Sunni fundamentalist Islam.

What is this fundamentalist Sunni faction? The Wahhabi Muslims.

What group did Osama Bin Laden belong to? The Wahhabi Muslims.

What group did the 9-11 terrorists belong to? The Wahhabi Muslims.

What group do most Al Queda members belong to? The Wahhabi Muslims.

What group is Hamas associated with? The Wahhabi Muslims.

What group are members of the Muslim Brotherhood loyal to? The Wahhabi Muslims.

What group comprises the largest portion of Saudi Arabians? The Wahhabi Muslims.

What group are among the most radical Islamic fundamentalists? The Wahhabi Muslims.

To what group does blind Sheikh Omar Abdel-Rahman belong? The Wahhabi Muslims.

What Islamic group plans to control the world? The Wahhabi Muslims

---

Race Whores, Media Whores, and a deliberately factious administration profit greatly from their blatant promotion of racial strife.

There are thousands of examples of racial agitators jumping in at every trial or public gathering of any kind to try to make as much trouble, even violent trouble, as they can. The actions of Al Sharpton, Jesse Jackson, Louis Farrakahn, and Malik Shabazz, the head of the racist and anti-Semitic New Black Panther Party, are clearly aimed at creating racial strife. The reaction to the Trayvon Martin, George Zimmerman case is just the latest in a long line of deliberate efforts to create racial divides in America.

Eric Holder refused to prosecute Shabazz in the voter intimidation case saying, "I'm not going to prosecute my people." Now he has sent the Justice Department Community Relations Service to Sanford, Florida. Holder's CRS didn't travel to Sanford to restrain the mob. They went to Florida to help it. They backed up Al Sharpton and did exactly what Shabazz demanded.

Some reports from the news media:

Outraged NAACP Wants Feds to Prosecute George Zimmerman.

The NAACP was outraged over the not-guilty verdict in the George Zimmerman murder trial and called on the Department of Justice to prosecute Zimmerman for shooting Trayvon Martin.

Senate Leader Harry Reid asks for the Justice Department to prosecute George Zimmerman, "This Isn't Over With."

WASHINGTON (AP) — The Justice Department said Sunday it is looking into the shooting death of Trayvon Martin to determine whether federal prosecutors will file criminal civil rights charges now that George Zimmerman has been acquitted in the state case.

For details on this horrendous evil action go to:

http://swordattheready.wordpress.com/2013/07/14/race-war-commeth/

The main stream media and their yellow journalists tried to out slime the Inquirer with false accusations, headlines, condemnations and even photographs. They and all the members of the race business tried and convicted Zimmerman of murder in spite of the evidence. They have become prosecuting attorney, judge and probably executioner. They don't want justice, they want the opposite of justice, REVENGE. They are a lynch mob with but a single angry, unreasoning and unrelenting purpose. I will be surprised if Zimmerman is not murdered by some slime ball. I wonder how that trial will go and how the media and race whores will treat it?

Special Section on Wahhabi Islam

Most Americans have no concept of Islam, the Wahhabi Muslims and their beliefs and why this is so dangerous?

1) Most Americans are basically honest and respect the integrity of others. Sure, they lie, but not pathologically.

2) Most Americans see others as basically honest and truthful in their day-to-day dealings with others. They expect some degree of honesty from others.

3) Most Americans are therefore easy victims to those who use words and actions with total disregard for truth, honesty, integrity or respect for others. Deception is the universal method of Muslims in their dealings with non Muslims or infidels. It is pathological.

4) As a tenet of their religion, Muslims are instructed it is moral and righteous to be dishonest with infidels in furtherance of the goals of the nation of Islam. They are taught it is perfectly acceptable to lie, chest, steal, and commit murder against infidels and infidel nations. They are only instructed not to do such things against other Muslims. Actually, Muslims are constantly at war with all infidels everywhere in the world. They have practiced this warfare relentlessly since Mohammed came on the scene in the 600s. This is their always ongoing Jihad or Holy War against all non Muslims. It is their basic motivator of interaction with all non Muslims.

5) Wahhabi Muslims, or as they call themselves, the only true Muslims, are a special case.

Wahhabi Muslims see themselves as the only true Muslims. All Muslims who are not true Muslims according to the Wahhabis, are infidels. They are to be treated exactly the same as all infidels or non believers. This gives the Wahhabis full justification to lie, cheat, steal from, maim, and murder those they deem not to be true Muslims or Wahhabis. Incidently, they refer to themselves as true Muslims, not Wahhabis, the name other Muslims use when referring to their members. This makes it difficult to determine if a Muslim is or is not a Wahhabi Muslim. Their actions alone define them, and maybe their location of origin or family. Their words certainly do not as they are completely dishonest in dealings and communication with those they do not consider to be true or Wahhabi Muslims.

Obama practiced Islam daily at school, where he was registered as a Muslim and kept that faith for 31 years, until his wife made him change, so he could run for office.

On April 9, 2009 during the G-20, President Obama clearly bowed to Saudi King Abdullah, stirring a controversy that's been mostly overlooked by the media. (Like so many other of his questionable activities.) Bowing to royalty and dropping your eye contact means subservience! Now you know where Obama's allegiance lies!

See above for examples of Obama's Wahhabi Muslim truthfulness:

One of the basic tenets in the Koran is that Muslims need be honest only with other Muslims. The Koran teaches that it is no sin, and actually a good thing to lie, steal from, cheat, and even murder infidels in the support and furtherance of Islam. Wahhabi Muslims carry this to extremes. The beheading of Americans like Daniel Pearl are one extreme example. The 3,000 deaths in the World Trade Center are another. They gleefully murder innocent civilians at every opportunity.

✳   ✳   ✳

As I predicted and in the way I predicted, Obama the fraud won the election and Democrats won control of the Senate. Fortunately for most Americans, Republicans retained control of the House of Representatives. That may mean little as Obama is not shy about using executive privilege and orders to "Go around Republicans in the House to get what I want done." If he gets away with this, the last four years of economic destruction will seem minor compared with the next four years. This is especially true for the American middle class who will mostly be reduced to poverty. The entire nation will become a Detroit or California. The economic destruction his minions will bring about will make the previous four years seem pale in comparison. We will find out, won't we?

—Howard Johnson · November 2012

Americans have little understanding of Arab cultures, or of Islam.

Americans are quite naive and misinformed about much of Africa and the Middle East, particularly as relates to the make up of nations. This is doubtless because of the way the American media describes all of these so-called nations. Western media has virtually no understanding of Arab culture, Islam, or the Middle East. This is probably why Americans see Middle Eastern nations as though they are all like the nations of Europe after the seventeen hundreds.

Virtually all nations are made up of the remnants of tribal groups diluted by invasions of and joining with other tribal groups. This is the natural human political evolution from family to tribe to state to nation over many centuries.

Consider America before the European invasion. There were thousands of tribal groups, some with alliances, some without. Each tribe had its own government, usually a chief supported or opposed by a religious leader, a shaman or holy man. The succession from one leader to another was hereditary or irregular and often violent. Tribes defended their territory from other tribes and borders flexed frequently during tribal wars and invasions. When the Europeans invaded, the concept of ownership of the land and possession by a nation changed America from tribalism to nationhood. It was a bloody and violent change. Most of Africa experienced the same bloody change when Europeans invaded there with their superior weapons and organized armies. To this day, much of Africa remains tribal resulting in many small bloody wars based on racial or tribal divisions or differences.

The Middle East and the Muslim nations in particular show the same type of tribal identities and conflicts. Afghanistan is certainly not a nation in the European sense, but merely a geographical area. Within that area reside hundreds of tribal groups led by chiefs and shamans very much like the American Indian tribes described earlier. Each tribe is in effect a nation on its own with its own governing body and laws. It has its own chief or warlord and its own religious leader or mullah. Often the warlord and mullah are the same individual. Most of the Muslim nations follow a similar pattern. Even Pakistan which has a governing body and president much like a western nation, has large areas, mostly in the mountainous region bordering Afghanistan, where tribal governments are in control and the central government has little say. One huge mistake Americans and the western media make is describing these areas as nations or parts of nations. In reality, they are not nations in the western sense, but contiguous areas roughly named by westerners for the dominant language or culture in the area. Mostly they are divided into tribal fiefdoms whose only commonality is their submission to the will of Allah, they follow some version of Islam and consider themselves Muslims, part of the nation of Islam.

The Bedouins

In addition to these tribal settlements, there are the bedouins who for centuries lived a nomadic life out in the deserts of Arabia, Sinai, and the Sahara. Bedouins were among the first followers of Mohammed, the first members of the nation of Islam. While nearly all have been forced into settled lifestyles, a few still cling to their nomadic, desert dwelling culture with no land attachment other than the desert. Like the long gone American plains Indians, they are the last remnants of one type of nomadic people, and they are fast disappearing. Even where they have left their nomadic lifestyle and settled in communities, mostly in Egypt, they remain apart from other Arab cultures and peoples. Many Arabs consider them the purest of Arab peoples, admiring them for their toughness and difficult lifestyle.

http://www.bedawi.com/Bedouin_Culture_EN.html - an excerpt follows:

Origins of nomadic peoples are difficult to trace as they leave little evidence behind for archaeologists.

The term 'Bedu'in the Arabic language refers to one who lives out in the open, in the desert. The Arabic word 'Badawiyin'is a generic name for a desert-dweller and the English word 'Bedouin' is the derived from this.

In ancient times, most people settled near rivers but the Bedouin people preferred to live in the open desert. Bedouins mainly live in the Arabian and Syrian deserts, the Sinai Peninsula of Egypt and the Sahara Desert of North Africa.

There are Bedouin communities in many countries, including Egypt, Syria, Israel, Jordan, Saudi Arabia, Yemen and Iraq in the Middle East and Morocco, Sudan, Algeria, Tunisia and Libya in North Africa. Together, the Bedouin population numbers about four million.

The Bedouins are seen as Arab culture's purest representatives and the Bedouins continue to be hailed by other Arabs as "ideal" Arabs, especially because of their rich oral poetic tradition, their herding lifestyle and their traditional code of honor.

The Egyptians refer to the Bedouins as 'Arab', but Bedouins are distinct from other Arabs because of their extensive kinship networks, which provide them with community support and the basic necessities for survival. Such networks have traditionally served to ensure safety of families and to protect their property. The term 'A'raab' has been synonymous with the term 'nomad' since the beginning of Islam.

The Bedouins are recognized by their nomadic lifestyles, special language, social structures and culture. Only few Bedouins live as their forefathers did in camel and goat hair tents, raising livestock, hunting and raiding. Their numbers are decreasing and nowadays there are approximately four million of them. Only 5% of Bedouins still live as pastoral nomads in all of the Middle East. Some Bedouins of Sinai are still half-nomads.

Bedouins have different facial features by which they can be distinguished from other Egyptians and also they generally dress differently.

The Bedouin men wear long 'djellabaya' and a 'smagg' (red white draped head cover) or 'aymemma' (white head cover) or a white small headdress, sometimes held in place by an 'agall' (a black cord).

The Bedouin women usually wear brightly colored long dresses but when they go outside they dress in an 'abaya' (a thin, long black coat sometimes covered with shiny embroidery) and they will always cover their head and hair when they leave their house with a 'tarha' (a black, thin shawl). Traditionally a woman's face was hidden behind a highly decorated 'burqa'ah' but this is now only seen with the older generations. The younger generations cover their face simply with their 'tarha' (shawl).

The Bedouins have a rich culture and their own Arabic 'Bedawi' language, which has different dialects depending on the area where they live.

In former days they emphasized on the strong belief in its tribal superiority, in return to the tribal security – the support to survive in a hostile environment.

'The Bedouin' is aristocratic and they tend to perceive the Arabian nation as the noblest of all nations, purity of blood, way of life and above all noble ancestry. They often trace their lineage back to the times of the Prophet Muhammad and beyond.

The first converts to Islam came from the Bedouin tribes and therefore (Sunni) Islam is embedded and deeply rooted in the Bedouin culture. Prayer is an integral part of Bedouin life. As there are no formal mosques in the desert, they pray where they are, facing the Ka'aba in Mecca and performing the ritual washing, preferably with water but if not available they 'wash' with sand instead.

The Bedouin' is generally open-minded and interested in what is going on in his close and far surroundings since this kind of knowledge has always been a vital tool of survival.

At the same time, the Bedouins are quite suspicious and alert keeping a low profile about their personal background.

Modern Arab states have a strong tendency to regulate their Nomadic lifestyle and modern society has made the traditional Bedouin lifestyle less attractive, since it is demanding and often dangerous, so many Bedouins have settled in urban areas and continue to do so.

The Bedouin people are faced with challenges in their lifestyle, as their traditional Islamic, tribal culture has begun to mix with western practices.

Men are more likely to adjust and interact with the modern cultures, but women are bound by honor and tradition to stay within the family dwelling and therefore lack opportunity for advancement.

Today unemployment amongst Bedouin people is very high. Only few obtain a high school degree and even fewer graduate from college.

However, for most people the word Bedouin still conjures up a much richer and more mysterious and romantic image.

End of excerpt

✳   ✳   ✳

"Wahhabi" Islam: General Overview

Posted on Saturday, July 17, 2004 1:56:56 PM by Steven AU

The terrorist attacks on September 11, 2001 shook the United States to its core. Since those horrific moments, our nation has been thrust into a global war against terror and religious extremism. Now more than ever, it is of the utmost importance that we understand the thought processes of those who seek to destroy the very fabric of Western society. Nothing short of our way of life and our very existence are on the line. We cannot afford to lose.

What could possibly drive people to murder innocent civilians on such a large scale? What would lead a man to sacrifice his own life to take that of another? Why are these terrorists so filled with hate and animosity toward us, that their hate even overshadows their willingness to live? Many questions remain unanswered. Though some politicians would have us believe that the answers to these questions lie in US foreign politics, I believe that there is another force at hand: Wahhabi Islam.

Wahhabi Islam is a term commonly given to a strict Sunni sect of Islam. Followers of Wahhabi Islam do not refer to their religion as "Wahhabi." Many merely call themselves "Muslim," or "True Muslim," for according to their beliefs they are the only true Muslims. Some Wahhabists refer to themselves and their religion as "al-Muwahhidun," "Salafi," "Salafi Da'wa," or "Ahlul Sunna wal Jama'a." Depending on the region and dialect in use, other names also exist. For the sake of simplicity, I will refer to this religion as "Wahhabi Islam" and it's followers as "Wahhabists." By "Wahhabi Islam," I am referring to the forms of Islam that share the strict revivalist vision and beliefs that were preached by Muhammad ibn Abd al-Wahhab in the late 1700's.

Wahhabi Islam counts among its adherents such names as Osama Bin Laden and Saudi Prince Nayef. Various groups such as Al-Qaeda, Pakistan's Jamaat-I Islami, The Islamic Salvation Front, and al-Jihad have also adopted Wahhabism as their official religion (Ahmed; Cline; Haykel; Smith; Hardy). The extremist religion offers many a theological justification and mandate to kill those they deem to be infidels. One should note that according to Wahhabism, the vast majority of Muslims (over 99%) are also to be considered "infidels, heathens, and enemies."

Wahhabists have made their presence known worldwide. From the beheading of Daniel Pearl in Pakistan to the beheading of countless Russian soldiers in Chechnya, from the beheading of Nick Berg in Iraq to the beheading of Paul Johnson in Saudi Arabia 2 days ago, Wahhabists have shown a willingness to use television and the internet to display their gruesome acts of barbarism. To truly understand those that we must fight in this battle against terrorism, one must learn more about Wahhabi Islam and it's extremist teachings.

The Origin and History of Wahhabi Islam

Wahhabism started as a movement within Islam founded by Muhammad ibn Abd al-Wahhab (1703-1792). To fully understand the militancy of Wahhabi Islam, it is important that one learns of the warlike nature of Wahhabi Islam's founder and the brutal times of war in which he lived.

Having been born in a small oasis town in central Arabia, al-Wahhab grew up studying Hanbali Law, one of Sunni Islam's strictest and most conservative schools. He lived and studied with his grandfather until he was in his early teens, at which time he left his home to move to the holy city of Medina, where he continued his Islamic studies.

After completing his studies in Medina several years later and now a young man, al-Wahhab traveled to a city in what is modern day Basra, Iraq. There, he taught Islamic law for approximately four years. Al-Wahhab then traveled to Baghdad where he continued teaching Islamic law. There, he met and later married an affluent woman. She later died and left al-Wahhab a large inheritance, which he used to travel the region.

The early 1730's found al-Wahhab residing in Iran. It was here that he first started to preach his new and radical thoughts on Islam. Al-Wahhab virulently attacked the customs and beliefs of the tribes in the region, many of whom were Sufi Muslim. He also extended his criticisms to the practices of the Twelver Shia, such as paying respect at the tombs of holy men.

With the growing unpopularity of his criticisms against Sufi Islam in Iran, Muhammad ibn Abd al-Wahhab moved back to his native town of Uyaynah in the late 1730's. Upon his return to his birthplace, al-Wahhab began writing the Kitab at-Tawhid, which would later become the main text of Wahhabi Islam's doctrines. It was about this time that al-Wahhab begun to gather a larger number of followers.

Muhammad ibn Abd al-Wahhab's extremist views and doctrines led to controversy in Uyaynah. Many of the town's leaders were not fond of his fundamentalist approach to Islam. After all, merely invoking the name of the Muslim prophet Muhammad was, by al-Wahhab's standards, a grave sin. In 1744, he was expelled from Uyaynah. Al-Wahhab then settled in Ad-Dir'iyah, which was under the control of a powerful tribal leader named Ibn Sa'ud. Ibn Sa'ud became a believer of Wahhab's doctrines and the two formed a strong alliance. Al-Wahhab and Ibn Sa'ud swore a Muslim pledge with each other in which they vowed to establish a new state that would operate under al-Wahhab's strict interpretation of Islamic Law.

And thus began a military campaign that would shake the Arabian Peninsula to its core. The Wahhabi faith provided Ibn Sa'ud with the justification he needed to raid and conquer nearby settlements. Though these settlements were Islamic (and traditional Islamic law prohibits Islamic states from attacking each other), the Wahhabi doctrine viewed all non-Wahhabists as infidels and not true Muslims. It was thus that Ibn Sa'ud found a legitimate purpose to bring the nearby settlements under his control, to spread "true Islam" to the infidels.

The Wahhabists were indiscriminate in their killings of Muslims and non-Muslims alike. They soon garnered a reputation as brutal and fanatical warriors. These Wahhabist warriors were described as being so fanatical that they had little regard for their own lives ... their sole purpose, it seemed, was to kill the enemy. By the time of his death in 1765, Ibn Sa'ud had managed to gain control over most of the region and had spread Wahhabism to those conquered lands.

Muhammad ibn Abd al-Wahhab died in 1792 but the spread of Wahhabism continued under the leadership of Ibn Sa'ud's son, Abd al Aziz. Abd al Aziz continued the Wahhabi campaign and managed to sack the Shia holy city of Karbala and Sunni towns in Hijaz. The Wahhabists were brutal in their treatment of captured lands and brought destruction upon those who had opposed them. In the early 1800's, the Wahhabi army even managed to gain control of Mecca and Medina. Viewing the acts of commemorating dead holy men and praying to saints as unholy acts, the Wahhabists destroyed monuments and gravesites in the holy cities. By doing this, they sought to imitate the Muslim prophet Muhammad's smashing of pagan symbols when he returned to Mecca in 628. Access to the holy sites in Medina and Mecca were severely limited to outsiders.

Shortly after the capture of Mecca, Abd al Aziz died. His son, Sa'ud, assumed leadership of the army but also died shortly after. Sa'ud's son, Abd Allah ibn Sa'ud was then left in charge of the movement.

The majority of Muslims were appalled and horrified at the brutal tactics used by the Wahhabists. Furthermore, the wanton destruction of what was to them holy sites and monuments incensed the overall Muslim community. It was then that the Ottoman Turks, one of the most powerful forces in Islam at the time, united with Muslim forces in Egypt to launch a bloody retaliation against the Wahhabists. Facing such an overwhelming force, the Wahhabists didn't stand a chance. They immediately lost control of Mecca and Media and by 1818 had lost control of the majority of their territories. They were left a mere shamble of their previous power.

The Wahhabists managed to make a slight comeback by 1833, but were once again beaten back. By 1889, the Wahhabi forces were annihilated and the Sa'ud family had fled to Kuwait for refuge. Many hoped that this final victory over the Wahhabi forces would mark the end of the extremist religion once and for all. However, the Sa'ud family would find an unlikely ally in Britain.

By 1920, the Sa'ud family and their Wahhabi forces had built themselves back up. In 1927, the British, who at the time controlled much of the Arabian Peninsula, saw the Sa'ud family as allies from their WWI fight against the Turks, who were allied with Germany. The British signed a treaty with the Sa'ud family in which the Sa'uds assumed control over the Gulf sheikdoms. In 1932, the Sa'uds gave this land the name "Saudi Arabia." And so was born the Wahhabist kingdom that bears the same name to this very day.

Beliefs and Doctrines of Wahhabi Islam

With his strict Hanbali upbringing and militant nature, it comes as no surprise that al-Wahhab's teachings espoused a very extremist interpretation of the Quran. In addition to supporting strict and uncompromising societal obedience to Shariah Law, Wahhabi Islam has additional rules and beliefs that set it apart from other forms of Islam. Some of these doctrines are:

True Muslims – The only true Muslims are those who follow the teachings of al-Wahhab. All other "Muslims" are non-believers and infidels

Tahwid (the essential oneness of God) - Muhammad ibn Abd al-Wahhab championed the notion that people must never, under any circumstances, question the essential oneness of God. He took this notion to its extreme by claiming that prayer or observance to any saints or holy men was a form of raising up human figures to the level of God's power. His belief was that the observance and honoring of the dead, saints, and/or angels detracted from the complete subservience one must feel towards God and only God. Wahhabi Islam thus bans any prayer to saints and dead loved ones, pilgrimages to tombs and special mosques, religious festivals celebrating saints, the honoring of the Muslim prophet Muhammad's birthday, and even prohibits the use of gravestones when burying the dead.

Any Muslim who does not follow these rules is to be considered an infidel. In the mind of the Wahhabist, this automatically places the far majority of Muslims, who indeed do celebrate their prophet Mohammad's birthday and do mention him and various saints in prayer, into the category of non-Muslim infidel. It was thus that al-Wahhab made it a point to destroy all Muslim shrines that he came upon in conquered territories. Upon conquering the Muslim holy cities of Mecca and Medina, al-Wahhab even attack the prophet Mohammad's gravestone and shrine. In his own fanatical mind, al-Wahhab compared this to the prophet Muhammad's destruction of pagan idols when he reentered Mecca in 628.

Bayah (the oath of allegiance) – According to al-Wahhab's teachings, all Muslims must individually pledge their allegiance to a Muslim leader. As long as this leader follows the laws of Islam (as determined by Wahhabi Islam) completely, the individual must give him his unquestionable allegiance. The Wahhabist must make this pledge to ensure his redemption by God after death. The purpose of the bayah is to merge religion and politics into one, ensuring that all Muslims dedicate their lives to following a "pure" leader who upholds all the tenets of Islam while at the same time ensuring that every leader must follow the laws of Islam completely. The Muslim community is thus to become the living embodiment of God's laws and dictates. It is the responsibility of the leader to ensure that all people who live under his control know and follow the laws of God.

Conformity – Wahhabi Islam demands conformity. All people must dress similarly (you may notice in Saudi Arabia, most men wear the same white cloths), behave similarly, pray at the same time, use the same rituals in prayer, and speak in a similar manner. Adherence to the "true faith" is demonstrable in physical and tangible ways. The Wahhabists believe that they can judge a person's faith by observing his actions and level of conformity to the Islamic ways. It is thus the responsibility of each Wahhabist to constantly observe his neighbors and friends in search of unholy actions and behavior.

The Struggle against Jahiliyya – Taken literally, the word Jahiliyya is a reference to a state of barbarism and ignorance. But al-Wahhab used it in a different context. In Wahhabi Islam, all societies that do not follow the true ways of Islam are considered to be in a state of Jahiliyya. All "infidels" are Jahili. Used in this context, Jahiliyya can more accurately be described as a representation of what Wahhabists consider to be the unholy, polytheistic, barbaric, corrupt, and evil state of Arabia before the coming of Islam. Jahiliyya is a representation of the culture that Mohammad fought against and destroyed with the inception of Islam. By so closely comparing their struggle against

Jahiliyya with Mohammad's fight against the polytheists of his time, Wahhabists see the struggle as one of the most holy actions they can take.

According to al-Wahhab, it is the duty of all true Muslims to fight Jahiliyya and the Jahili. Though conversion to "true Islam" is an option, Wahhabists are permitted by their doctrine to "rob, murder, and sexually violate" Jahili. We can find an example of Wahhabi Islam's brutal treatment of what they consider to be Jahili in the gruesome beheadings of such people as Paul Johnson, Daniel Pearl, Nick Berg, etc.

Wahhabists also use many verses from the Quran to support their views on the struggle against Jahiliyya. Two verses commonly used by Wahhabists as justification for their battles are: "Fight those who do not believe in Allah ... until they pay the tax in acknowledgment of superiority and they are in a state of subjection," (Quran 9:29) and "fight with them until there is no more persecution and religion should be only for Allah" (Quran 8:39).

One indication of the strict standards that Wahhabists apply to societies can be found in their current view of the Saudi government. Even though Saudi Arabia's government is by Wahhabi standards Islamic in almost every way, the fact that they allowed "infidels" onto the holy land after the first gulf War, in the eyes of many Wahhabi Clerics, made the Saudi Arabian government Jahiliyya. Some radical Wahhabi proponents such as Osama Bin Laden now even call for the overthrowing of that government.

Original Grandeur of Islam - Muhammad ibn Abd al-Wahhab believed that the Islam of his time was not Islam at all. His contention was that the original purity of Muhammad's teachings and the Quran were watered down and greatly altered from their original form. According to his views, the more time that passed after the writing of the Quran, the more unknowledgeable Muslim scholars got about its true meaning. It is thus that al-Wahhab believed in the original grandeur of Islam. He preached that the Islamic community should return to a strict interpretation of the principles enunciated by the Prophet Muhammad. Al-Wahhab accepted only the authority of the Quran and Sunna along with the issues clearly settled by early jurists. All later reinterpretation of issues and the Quran were to be rejected. Islam would return to the form it had taken shortly after the time of Muhammad. Wahhabists do not believe in reinterpreting issues of Islamic law that were already settled at that time.

With this strong stance against any reinterpretation of Islamic law issues already settled, Wahhabi Islam leaves absolutely no room for any. Wahhabists are thus left with customs and beliefs from ages long ago. Among some of these issues that may not be reinterpreted and reformed are:

1) Women's rights – Women have almost no rights in Wahhabi culture. They are forced to dress in certain ways (usually covered from head to toe in either black or blue), are not allowed to drive, may not speak, not allowed in public without a male chaperone, have no custody of their children, and so on.

2) Dietary laws – Like many other Muslims, Wahhabists may not eat pork or drink wine. They do however follow even stricter guidelines in the form of not being able to drink any alcohol at all or consume any stimulants (i.e.- smoking cigarettes).

3) Exhibition of Wealth - Wahhabists are forbidden to wear any jewelry, including gold, or silk clothing.

4) Culture – Listening to music, dancing, pictures, paintings, loud laughter, and demonstrative crying are strictly prohibited. Men are not permitted to trim their beards shorter than a certain length and are not allowed to grow their hair longer than a certain length.

5) Wahhabi Islam's doctrine of original grandeur thus leaves the Wahhabist in a state of following customs and cultures of ancient times with no possibility of such customs and rules ever being reformed and changed.

The Influence and Effect of Wahhabi Islam

One can easily see the strict and uncompromising nature of Wahhabi Islam. Not only does it entail conformity among people, the observance of ancient customs, a strict and unforgiving interpretation of the Quran, but Wahhabi Islam also glorifies the struggle against Jahiliyya. This leaves the Wahhabist in a position of feeling that the majority of people are infidels and it is his duty to wage war against such Jahili. So it comes as no surprise that Wahhabi Islam has had a significant influence on the world.

Wahhabi Islam has a tremendous effect on all those who live under it's auspices. The individual is first bombarded with the teachings of al-Wahhab as a young child. According to the rules of bayah, it is the responsibility of the leader to ensure that all people who live under his control know and follow the laws of God. And so, the rulers will make religious education a large part of children's lives. In Saudi Arabia, mandatory Wahhabi studies account for over 35% of most schools' curriculums. Parents also have the option of sending their child to a madrassa, in which 100% of the studies are religious in nature.

Wahhabi studies seek to indoctrinate the young children with religious extremism at an early age. One quote from the official school textbook used in many Saudi Arabian schools states:

"The last hour won't come before the Muslims would fight the Jews and the Muslims will kill them so Jews would hide behind rocks and trees. Then the rocks and tree would call: oh Muslim, oh servant of God! There is a Jew behind me, come and kill him. Only "Gharkad" tree, it is of Jews' trees."

Wahhabi Islam views the majority of Muslims as Infidels. It supports violent struggle against all infidels and the young children are indoctrinated with these beliefs from an early age. Ali al-Ahmed, a Muslim who grew up in Saudi Arabia, shares his experiences of the state funded schools:

"The religious curriculum in Saudi Arabia teaches you that people are basically two sides: Salafis [Wahhabis], who are the winners, the chosen ones, who will go to heaven, and the rest. The rest are Muslims and Christians and Jews and others.

"They are either kafirs, who are deniers of God, or mushrak, putting gods next to God, or enervators, that's the lightest one. The enervators of religion who are those they call the Sunni Muslims who ... for instance, celebrate Prophet Mohammed's birthday, and do some stuff that is not accepted by Salafis.

"And all of these people are not accepted by Salafi as Muslims. As I said, "claimant to Islam." And all of these people are supposed to be hated, to be persecuted, even killed.

"Bin Laden learned this in Saudi Arabia. He didn't learn it in the moon. That message that Bin Laden received, it still is taught in Saudi Arabia. And if he dies, and this policy or curriculum stays, we will have other bin Ladens."

In this culture, young children are taught that anyone who is not a Wahhabist is a Jahili and is supposed to be "hated" and "persecuted." It becomes clear why terrorist organizations are able to find so many recruits. Recruits are being raised in Saudi Arabia and indoctrinated by the school system. It is no coincidence that 15 of the 9-11 hijackers were Saudi Arabian.

The environment in which the child grows into a man is also one that leaves no other option open except conformity and religious extremism. The entire student body dresses and behaves in a similar manner. There is no music to entertain the young teenager in his spare time. There are no school dances. There is no mingling with the opposite sex. There are no opportunities to find creative outlets. The young man is left with no other tangible alternative but to turn to Wahhabism as the driving force in his life. Wahhabism teaches the young man hate and intolerance, which become molded into his psyche.

The Wahhabist is also taught to constantly observe his neighbors and friends in search of unholy actions and behavior. He is also aware of the fact that his own actions are being observed. The constant presence of Mutawwiin, "enforcers of public morals" who roam around the towns and cities in search of anyone who violates the cultural rules of Wahhabism (i.e.- someone playing music, not praying at the right time, someone with a beard that is too short, etc), help to sink into the Wahhabist's psyche the notion that he constantly has to be on the lookout. He is in a constant state of having to prove himself and thus acts in an even more devout manner.

We can clearly see that Wahhabi Islam has a huge influence on the individuals who live in such a society. They have little choice but to turn to the extreme and intolerant teachings of Wahhabi Islam as the only viable outlet to their energy. The individual who lives in a truly Wahhabi society is one who is indoctrinated in extremism from an early age.

Wahhabi Islam's influence on culture is also a noticeable one. Al-Wahhab's teachings support a drive towards extreme conformity. And so we find Wahhabi culture to be severely lacking in individuality. Everybody dresses, behaves, and even prays in a similar manner. One could easily recognize the traditional and plain white garment worn by almost every man in Saudi Arabia.

Wahhabi Islam's concept of original grandeur makes its effects known in culture. With the ancient jurists banning music, loud laughter, dancing, alcohol, and even paintings, the Wahhabi artistic and entertainment culture is a bland and boring one. There is little that can truly be called "culture" in Wahhabi society. It is mostly tradition and rules that must be abided by.

Another aspect of culture that Wahhabi Islam has had an influence on is the treatment of women. In this day and age, women in Wahhabi culture are still treated very poorly. They are forced to dress from head to toe in either black or blue garment, are not allowed to drive, may not speak unless spoken too, are not allowed in public without a male chaperone, have no custody of their children, and are even subjected to beatings from the Mutawwiin.

Wahhabi culture dictates the mandatory pledging of an unquestionable allegiance to one's ruler, bayah. It would seem as though after stripping people of any true form of culture, Wahhabism also strips them of any sense of ownership of their own body and mind. By pledging the allegiance, they give up that last bastion of control over their destiny.

Wahhabism has had a significant, yet unfortunate, influence on culture by stifling the creative arts, treating women badly, annihilating any sense of individuality/personal worth, and driving its people to a form of extreme conformity.

One need not look past the terrorist attacks of September 11, 2001 to realize the influence and effect Wahhabi Islam has had on the rest of the world. The extremist religion has indoctrinated hundreds of thousands, if not millions, of Muslims into a system of hate and violence. With its glorification of violent struggle against Jahiliyya and the millions of extremists it has created, it should come as no surprise that Wahhabi extremists have been waging a war of religion since the time of Muhammad ibn Abd al-Wahhab himself.

There has not been a time in its existence that Wahhabi Islam was not in some form or another at war with what it considers infidels. The origins and history of Wahhabi Islam, described earlier in this essay, show the violent and brutal nature it took before the formation of Saudi Arabia. Groups such as the Muslim Brotherhood of the 1940-50's, Al-Jihad and Gamaa Islamiya of the 1970-80's, The Front for National Salvation in Algeria, the Taliban and Mujahideen that fought the Soviet forces in Afghanistan, al Qaeda, etc have kept the violent Wahhabist jihad against what they consider to be Jahiliyya alive to this very day. The violent killing of "infidels" is an influence of Wahhabi Islam that has haunted the rest of the world.

The United States of America has been thrust into a global war against terror. We fought the Taliban in Afghanistan and are now in Iraq. This is no doubt an effect of Osama Bin Laden's Wahhabi theology. But we are not the only ones who have felt the sting of Wahhabi terrorism. Pakistan, Afghanistan, the Philippines, Indonesia, Chechnya, and Bosnia are just a few of the other countries to feel the wrath of Wahhabists. The war against terrorism will be a long and hard war indeed.

The doctrines of Wahhabi Islam are playing another role in this war ... for they are influencing the culture of war itself. Wahhabists are permitted by their doctrine to "rob, murder, and sexually violate" Jahili. Wahhabi extremists are taught from a very young age that all "non-believers" are worthless and subject to persecution and death. This extremist Wahhabist view of "infidels" has led the terrorists to use gruesome and hateful methods. On September 11, mass quantities of innocent civilians were killed. And yet this would mean nothing to them, for the civilians were merely Jahili. The lives of civilians are normally valued and protected in times of war. Wahhabi Islam influenced a major change in those values of war. It is now permissible for our enemies to slaughter and even behead civilians). Violent Jihad against the "infidels" is not only permissible to the Wahhabist; it is mandatory.

Wahhabists and the Saudi government continue to fund Wahhabi madrassas worldwide. A recent figure estimates that the Saudi government alone has spent over 70 billion dollars funding such extremist schools.

The full influence of Wahhabi Islam has yet to be felt by the world. With so many extremists being churned out of Saudi Arabia and its madrassas worldwide, things only appear to be getting worse. The real solution would be to implement some major changes in Saudi Arabia itself. Though some minor changes have been taking place (i.e.-they are cooperating with us more on arresting terrorists), the real changes that need to be made are not ones that Saudi Arabia would be willing to take by itself. For such changes would involve altering the very nature of Wahhabism itself. The Saudi clerics would not stand for such meddling by their own government. So we are unfortunately stuck in this hard place of having to fight terrorists in far away lands with no real end in sight.

References, Works Cited:

1) Alexiev, Alex. WAHHABISM: STATE-SPONSORED EXTREMISM WORLDWIDE. Testimony at the U.S. Senate Subcommittee on Terrorism, Technology and Homeland Security, June 2003.
http://www.globalsecurity.org/security/library/congress/2003_h/030626-alexiev.htm

2) Anonymous. Justifying Wahhabism: The relationship between Muhammad bin Abdul-Wahhab and Ibn Taymiyah. Islamic Web.
http://islamicweb.com/beliefs/creed/wahhab.htm

3) Anonymous. The Rise of Political Islam : Wahhabism and Neo-Salafism. The Media Guide to Islam: A Journalist's Guide to Covering Islam. http://mediaguidetoislam.sfsu.edu/intheworld/04a_therise.htm

4) Anonymous. Wahhabism. Nation Master Online Encyclopedia, June 2004. http://www.nationmaster.com/encyclopedia/Wahhabism

5) Bijlefeld, Willem. Wahhabism: General Information. BELIEVE Religious Information Source. http://mb-soft.com/believe/txo/wahhabis.htm

6) Cline, Austin. Wahhabism and Wahhabi Muslims: Profile and History of Wahhabi Islam. About.com, Religion and Spirituality. http://atheism.about.com/library/FAQs/islam/blfaq_islam_wahhab.htm

7) Idris, Jafar Shaikh. Characteristics of 'Abd Al-Wahhab's Fundamentalism. Islamic Awakening Foundation. http://www.islamicawakening.com/viewarticle.php?articleID=1073&

8) Hardy, Roger. Analysis: Inside Wahhabi Islam. BBC News, September 2001. http://news.bbc.co.uk/2/hi/middle_east/1571144.stm

9) Haykel, Bernard. Radical Salafism: Osama's ideology. Canadian Society of Muslims Online Library, 2001. http://muslim-canada.org/binladendawn.html

10) Hisham, Muhammad. Muhammad ibn 'Abd al-Wahhab. Naqshbandi Sufi Way Website, Febuary 1998. http://www.naqshbandi.org/ottomans/wahhabi/abdulwahhab.htm

11) Lopez, Kathryn Jean. The Good & the Bad: Stephen Schwartz on Islam and Wahhabism. National Review, November 2002. http://www.nationalreview.com/interrogatory/interrogatory111802.asp

12) Metz, Helen Chapin. Kuwait: A Country Study. Washington: GPO for the Library of Congress, 1993. http://www.exploitz.com/Kuwait-Kuwait-cg.php

13) Metz, Helen Chapin. Saudi Arabia: A Country Study. Washington: GPO for the Library of Congress, 1992. http://www.au.af.mil/au/awc/awcgate/loc/sa/saud_wahhabi.htm

14) Mortimer, Louis. Saudi Arabia: Wahhabi Theology. Country Data. http://www.country-data.com/cgi-bin/query/r-11589.html

15) Olasky, Marvin. Islam for terrorists. World on the Web Magazine, October 2001. http://www.worldmag.com/world/issue/10-27-01/cover_5.asp

16) Phares, Walid. Wahhabi vs. Wahhabi. Front Page Magazine, June 2004. http://www.frontpagemag.com/Articles/ReadArticle.asp?ID=13693

17) Smith, Martin. Saudi Time Bomb? PBS Frontline, 2001. http://www.pbs.org/wgbh/pages/frontline/shows/saudi/interviews/

*　　　*　　　*

More about Islam - Keith Elison

I wrote this a couple weeks ago. Hope you find it interesting. I think it's important to know who we're fighting in this war against terrorism and that the Saudi's are really nothing close to an ally.

To say that all Moslem terrorists are Wahhabi is a serious error and is to grossly simplify the situation. The nature of Islam is to elevate many individuals to positions of power, all based on studying and teaching from the Quoran and in submission to those teachings. The history of Islam is one of literally thousands of individuals rising to power through the efforts of devoted followers. These leaders are not elected, they merely talk, fight, and often murder their way into leadership, or are from families who have been hereditary leaders. Osama bin Laden and many other Al Queda leaders are typical examples, as are the Taliban leaders. It is difficult for Westerners to understand the fanatical devotion to such leadership that brings about suicide bombings and other mayhem, often against other Muslims. The history of the expansion of Islam is one of mayhem and murder, often of innocents and always in the name of Allah. The history of Islam is a bloody one indeed. Examples of how Islam encourages Muslims to lie to and cheat Infidels as long as it furthers the cause of the nation of Islam.

Minnesota Democrat Rep. Keith Ellison (aka Keith Hakim or Keith Ellison Muhammad) is the first Muslim elected to Congress. He took the oath of office on January 4 with his hand on the Koran rather than the Bible and sparked much controversy.

Congressmen and other officials are required to take an oath of office as a prerequisite to being seated. Similarly, witnesses in court are required to take an oath before testifying. The purpose of the oath is to encourage people to tell the truth. By swearing under oath, one obligates himself to tell the truth, the whole truth, and nothing but the truth. We, as a nation, take the actions of our elected officials and statements made in court very seriously. Therefore, our oaths are made under penalty of perjury. The legal ramification of knowingly making false statements is the possibility of being criminally prosecuted and jailed. Historically, the oath invoked God based on the idea that those who were religious would be less likely to lie if they feared the wrath of God, in addition to the wrath of the state. It was an additional way through which our legal system emphasized the importance of truth-telling.

While nothing in the Constitution or our state laws mandate a person to swear on the Christian Bible, the legal alternative is to "affirm." This is a promise to tell the truth under pain of perjury, available to those who either do not believe in the Christian God, the Christian Bible, or whose interpretation of the Bible forbids them to swear.

Though some have sworn in on the Old Testament or on different versions of the Christian Bible, all these texts were part of, or variations on the Christian Bible, included the Ten Commandments, and endorsed the same moral value of truth.

The Christian Bible teaches that "The Truth shall make you free," "render unto Ceasar what is Ceasar's and unto God what is God's" (separation of church and state), and preaches freedom and equality for people of all faiths.

The Koran, by contrast, teaches that it's OK to lie to infidels if it furthers the cause of Islam, that nation states have no legitimacy, that the only legitimate nation is the nation of Islam, which has no territorial boundaries; and those who do not submit to the will of Allah should be condemned to a life of dhimmitude (second class citizenry including being lied to cheated and even murdered without consequence to the Muslim doing the lying, cheating or murdering).

NOTE: The Koran also states that it is OK to cheat, steal from, and even murder infidels for the same reason. Because the Koran does not mandate truth telling (honesty, respect, or decent treatment) to infidels and because upholding a man-made constitution conflicts with the literal text of Koranic law, the purpose of the oath is not served by swearing in on the Koran.

An individual cannot subjectively select which text constitutes a "Holy Scripture" appropriate for legal oath-taking. Instead, to determine the intent of the framers who wrote the oath requirement in the Constitution, we must look at the meaning their words held at the time they were written. It is clear that the Founding Fathers intended the oath to be made on the Bible, which espoused the value of truth-telling and in which one of God's Ten Commandments was "Thou shalt not bear false witness." They did not contemplate oath-taking on the Koran.

Swearing in on a text that states the oath does not have to be truthful because it is being made to infidels, or that the individual's allegiance is to a Higher Authority than the Constitution states specifically that the individual does not have to respect our nation's laws to the degree they conflict with Sharia or the Koran, then his oath would not be equivalent to an oath taken on the Bible. To swear on a book that is in direct conflict with the purpose of our oath, renders the oath meaningless. The object of the oath matters.

However, there is no religious test for elected office, and nobody is trying to force anyone to swear on the Christian Bible. An individual can make an affirmation under penalty of perjury, promising to tell the truth and uphold our man-made laws. This would not preclude the individual from practicing the religion of his choice. If that religion is Islam, then his religion encourages him to lie to, steal from, bear false witness against, and even murder infidels in the furtherance of the nation of Islam.

From a legal standpoint, any individual's promise to swear in on the Koran is much ado about nothing, as they are doing no such thing. The official congressional swearing-in ceremony takes place in the House chamber, where the speaker of the House will administer the oath to all House members en masse and no religious texts will be utilized. The subsequent private swearing-in ceremony is nothing more than a photo op and has no legally binding significance. It is at these individual ceremonies that congressmen traditionally pose with the Bible. (In some official positions, the actual Bible is used in the administration of the oath.) Nevertheless, anyone insisting on using the Koran in his is individual ceremony is nonsense—a political/religious statement. It raises questions about the individual's loyalties and values. Do they believe in Sharia law or freedom? Do they respect the authority of nation states or only that of the Nation of Islam? Do they believe in tolerance and equality between Muslims and non-Muslims? Do they believe in freedom of speech even when it slanders Islam? Can they, in good conscience, uphold our man-made constitution even when it conflicts with the Koran?

One example is Minnesota's Democrat Congressman Keith Ellison. (aka Keith Hakim or Keith Ellison Muhammad) In answering these questions, does Congressman Ellison's background allay any concerns. A black convert to Islam, Ellison was active with Farrakhan's Nation of Islam, has a history of supporting anti-Semites, cold-blooded cop-killers (Mumia Abu Jamal) and other questionable characters.

Even more frightening, Ellison's campaign was substantially financed by prominent members of the Council on American-Islamic Relations (CAIR), an organization many experts consider to be a Hamas front group. (See "The Real CAIR" by Joseph Farah on WorldNetDaily; "CAIR's Pro-Hamas Press" by Joe Kaufman on FrontPageMag.com; and "CAIR: Islamists Fooling the Establishment" by Sharon Chada and Daniel Pipes, published by Middle East Quarterly.) He recently spoke at the Muslim American Society and the Islamic Circle of North America, touted by counter-terrorism expert Steve Emerson as terrorist front groups. He also spoke at the North American Imams Federation (NAIF) and his lecture flowed into a session at the American Open University, a radical Wahabbi school that trains many of the NAIF Imams.

Reinforcing his pro-Islamist stance, was Ellison's celebration speech in Dearborn, Mich.—the hotbed of Hezbollah supporters. He promised allegiance to Allah before a crowd cheering, "Allahu Akbar!" (Allah is great!)—the final words of the 9/11 hijackers before crashing into the Twin Towers.

CAIR's charge that any criticism of Ellison stems from "Islamophobia" is bogus. Had Ellison's past demonstrated a condemnation of terrorists, and exhibited moderation, inclusiveness, and tolerance, perhaps we could have entertained this criticism with some degree of credibility. However, Ellison's extremist history makes CAIR's allegation laughable.

At a time when we are engaged in a global war with radical Islam, it is alarming that citizens of the U.S. have elected someone who appears to be in bed with our enemy. **(By both his words and his actions, Obama is another Islamist in bed with our enemies.)** To date, Keith Ellison's alliances have been far from mainstream. But our real war is ideological. We will not achieve victory by appeasing Islamists and ignoring their goals of world domination in the name of political correctness. Freedom, including religious freedom for people of all faiths, is our greatest asset. But when an interpretation of one's private faith crosses the line into a political ideology that conflicts with the freedoms and tolerance of others, we must take heed.

Ellison's insistence on using the Koran at his private ceremony must be seen in the context of the incremental Islamization of America. Some Muslim extremist groups, posing as mainstream, advocate actions to desensitize citizens to their anti-freedom goals and try to silence those who oppose them. Ellison's swearing-in ceremony is just the beginning. Follow his money, his faith, and the company he keeps. I suspect his votes on the House floor will reflect more of the same—an allegiance to values contrary to the Judeo-Christian Bible, contrary to the goals of freedom and tolerance, and sympathetic to political agenda of CAIR.

Ellison is not the only Muslim in American politics who is grossly lying to and cheating Americans in pursuing a political career in furtherance of Islam and Sharia law over freedom. Just who is it that aids and supports radical Islam in speeches throughout the world and with arms and money carefully hidden from public view? Which politician is it that has been a practicing Wahhabi Muslim his entire adult life? Who is this monstrous fraud who's profession of Christianity is purely a device to hide his true belief in Islam and thus help him get elected? Who is this man whose countless documented lies and deceptions are so blatant and monstrous as to be laughable, yet still Americans follow him like the children of Hamlin followed the pied piper?

Surely by now you know of whom I speak. His own words define him yet still Americans follow him like mesmerized sheep or lemmings, even to their own great loss or even death. He is Jim Jones on a monstrous scale asking all to drink his Kool-Aide of political and economic disaster in the name of raw hatred for America and Americans. He also works diligently against everything our founders believed, stood for, and wrote down in our Declaration of Independence and Constitution. That man is the current President of the United States, Barrack Hussein Obama.

As far as I am concerned he is a consummate evil, an enemy of America and of free men everywhere. He is in league with those who attacked us on 9-11 and with all Islamic terrorists throughout the world. He is providing them arms and money, American taxpayer's money and American arms. He is dedicated to the extermination of Israel and probably all Christians and Jews throughout Africa and the Middle East. **Pay no attention to any of his political rhetoric, look only at what he has done.** His record and that of his supporters speaks volumes. You cannot name one thing that has not been or does not promise to be an economic or political disaster for America and all Western nations.

The tragedy in Benghazi and the deaths of four Americans could have been averted. We had the military means to stop the attack and prevent the killing of the four Americans including the ambassador. I would like confirmation of who gave the repeated orders to stand down in the face of the Al Queda attack. Those orders could only have come from the President or with his instructions. And why did Obama, Hillary, and Susan Rice lie through their teeth about the attack being a reaction to that ridiculous video when that was an impossibility?

In my opinion, the Wahhabi influence in our government has been growing for a very long time. I think ACORN is controlled and managed by Wahhabis. I believe it was Wahhabi influence in the mortgage banking system that brought about the collapse of the mortgage market. Jim Johnson and Franklin Raines are not stupid men. I believe they deliberately created the mortgage crisis knowing full well what was going to happen. The achieved their goals and made hundreds of millions personally on the process.

I believe it was early Wahhabi influence that originally helped destroy Detroit. Not only have his Wahhabi minions engineered the greatest loss of real wealth middle class Americans have ever experienced, but they continue decimating the middle class with unemployment and low pay.

One of the countless bald-faced lies he has uttered during the current campaign was said in a Sunday campaign speech. He said, "Unemployment is dropping, jobs are being created, assembly lines are humming again, housing is expanding and a recovery is well underway, all from our policies."

Not one of those statements bore any resemblance to the truth. What is really sad is that the media refused to call him on a single one. So much for our honest, objective, unbiased media.

If that's not enough, If you didn't think your freedom and your life was in danger from Islam before, read this from someone in Holland.

WHAT EXACTLY IS AN INFIDEL?

The author, Rick Mathes, is a well-known leader in prison ministry. The man who walks with God always gets to his destination. If you have a pulse you have a purpose. Rick says:

The Muslim religion is the fastest growing religion per capita in the United States , especially in the minority races.

Last month I attended my annual training session that's required for maintaining my state prison security clearance. During the training session there was a presentation by three speakers representing the Roman Catholic, Protestant and Muslim faiths, who each explained their beliefs.

I was particularly interested in what the Islamic Imam had to say. The Muslim gave a great presentation of the basics of Islam, complete with a video.

After the presentations, time was provided for questions and answers. When it was my turn, I directed my question to the Muslim and asked: 'Please, correct me if I'm wrong, but I understand that most Imams and clerics of Islam have declared a holy jihad [Holy war] against the infidels of the world and, that by killing an infidel, (which is a command to all Muslims) they are assured of a place in heaven. If that's the case, can you give me the definition of an infidel?'

There was no disagreement with my statements and, without hesitation, he replied,

'Non-believers!'

I responded, 'So, let me make sure I have this straight. All followers of Allah have been commanded to kill everyone who is not of your faith so they can have a place in heaven. Is that correct?'

The expression on his face changed from one of authority and command to that of a little boy who had just been caught with his hand in the cookie jar.'

He sheepishly replied, 'Yes.'

I then stated, 'Well, sir, I have a real problem trying to imagine The Pope commanding all Catholics to kill those of your faith or Dr. Stanley ordering all Protestants to do the same in order to guarantee them a place in heaven!'

The Muslim was speechless.

I continued, 'I also have a problem with being your friend when you and your brother clerics are telling your followers to kill me! Let me ask you a question:

Would you rather have your Allah, who tells you to kill me in order for you to go to heaven, or my Jesus who tells me to love you because I am going to heaven and He wants you to be there with me?'

You could have heard a pin drop.

Needless to say, the organizers and/or promoters of the 'Diversification' training seminar were not happy with my way of dealing with the Islamic Imam, and exposing the truth about the Muslims' beliefs.

In twenty years there will be enough Muslim voters in the U.S. to elect the President.

HJ NOTE: Big deal! We already have a Muslim President who is doing his utmost to destroy our nation. What is amazing to me is that people are stupid enough to vote for him.

I think everyone in the U.S. should be required to read this, but with the ACLU, there is no way this will be widely publicized, unless each of us sends it on! This is your chance to make a difference.

FOR FREEDOM'S SAKE...SEND THIS ON

Friday, November 23, 2012

America's Biggest Boom Ever

Is America About to Experience It's Greatest Boom Ever? A Wildly Optimistic Prediction Based on Things Happening Beneath the Public Radar.

All of this is well hidden because the Obama administration and the media want to keep it quiet. They want to act as if it is their policies and effort that have brought on the current slow recovery. The truth is, Obama, the Democrats, and the media are doing everything in their power to stop this boom. Fortunately for many American workers they have not been successful. This is mainly because a Republican House and now Senate have countered most of their efforts. Obama has done what he could by executive order to prevent the boom, stopping the oil pipeline from Canada for instance. Hopefully, a Republican President and Congress will soon correct that and things will really boom. Then workers in the entire country will grow financially like they are in Montana, North Dakota, and Texas.

While everyone including the media has been concentrating on the woes of a depressed economy and a bitter and divisive election campaign, a glimmer of positive hope for things to come has been growing for several years. It's not obvious yet except in places like North Dakota, Texas, and a few other areas. It's growing potential remains unrecognized in most of the nation. Actually, the coming boom is two different but related booms. Both based on the production of fossil fuels, The two resources are enormously plentiful in the US in deposits previously unavailable for economic production.

The first one, natural gas, has already reached glut amounts with production far exceeding demand. The rapidly expanding supply has resulted in record low prices that are now just a bit more than a third of European prices, and just a fifth of prices in Japan. This price difference has brought about a furious effort to produce LNG (Liquified Naturel Gas) tankers to supply American LNG to both Europe and Japan. The opportunity for profits for American gas companies is tremendous. This alone would be a huge positive change in our trade balance of payments and could quickly make us energy independent of imports.

Here is an excerpt from my book, Energy, Convenient Solutions, that describes the beginnings of the natural gas boom economy as far back as 2006.

(1) A Special Case, LNG or Liquid Natural Gas

T. Boone Pickens is promoting a plan for massive conversion of diesel trucks to LNG, Liquid natural gas. His plan would make large amounts of LNG available to power heavy trucks. California set forth a ballot initiative that would free up $5 billion for deployment of a million LNG vehicles on state roads. In 2006, the ports of Long Beach and Los Angeles adopted a plan to reduce drastically pollution from more than 16,800 Class-8 tractor trailers, the only trucks strong enough to transport the heavy containers in and out of the ports. They chose LNG for many reasons including safety and cost. Even with the expense of replacing diesel engines with LNG engines the ports look to save around $350 million each year. The ports have announced the approval of a new $1.6 billion Clean Truck Superfund. Wal-Mart, which operates one of the largest truck fleets in America, is testing four trucks to measure the possible money saved by the switch. I am certain other truck users are carefully watching the results.

Pickens is positioning himself to profit from this with several investments. He has a 40% ownership in Clean Energy Fuels Corp. that provides natural gas for vehicle fleets by designing, financing, building, and operating LNG fueling stations. He also has a 12% interest in a small Canadian company that has designed what could be the most advanced, efficient engine on the planet to replace diesels in new and existing trucks. It is powered by LNG.

Pickens is the type of entrpreneurial investor who will probably solve our energy crisis while generating many good jobs and enriching himself and countless others in the process. His efforts will also result in a great deal of tax revenue for several governments. Many other entrepreneurs and planners are investing in research, development and manufacture of advanced energy systems that will help us solve our energy crisis. Unfortunately the combination of promised new corporate taxes and the economic downturn of 2008 has already caused many valuable projects to be scrapped. Pickens and others have downsized or completely abandoned creative new investments in many things including much needed energy and alternative fuel projects. A more encouraging tax policy could reverse this especially if government would just stay out of the way.

Since the time that was written, the conversion of heavy diesel trucks to LNG has expanded as fast as manufacturers of heavy LNG engines could supply engines. With annual savings in fuel costs between $60,000 and $80,000 per year, conversion to LNG has moved from a luxury with air pollution advantages to an absolute necessity for financial survival. Heavy truck fleets from companies like UPS, Wal-Mart, and trucking companies serving air sensitive areas like LA are no longer testing LNG truck engines, they are converting to them as fast as possible to remain competitive. This quiet, but rapidly growing revolution in the trucking industry is proceeding virtually unnoticed by the public. The new LNG truck engines are not only less fuel costly, but they burn much cleaner, put far less CO_2 into the atmosphere, far less pollutants, and are much cheaper to maintain than the old diesel engines.

Another important factor: Natural gas power plants are much cleaner than either coal or petroleum fired plants and are now a lot cheaper to operate. In 2000 Gas fired power plants made about 20% of our electricity. Gas power plants completed and proposed since then will boost that percentage above 30% within the next ten years, the fastest expansion of any type of power plant including nuclear.

Commercial Gas fired power plants are not the only power generating system to benefit from cheap natural gas. Recently, many gas fired micro turbines were put to use supplying power for emergency services, hospitals, police and others in the aftermath of Hurricane Sandy. Capstone Turbine of California is the largest manufacturer of MicroTurbines in the world. They make various sizes of MicroTurbines: 30kW, 65kW, and 200kW. Products based on the 200kW turbine are also available in 600kW, 800kW, and 1MW configurations. In addition to power systems, Capstone MicroTurbines are used extensively to power busses in China. Capstione's continuing sales to China are one of the few bright spots in our trade with China.

Natural gas is the number one fuel for home heating and is now increasingly supplanting fuel oil in many areas. It is also by far the most popular fuel for cooking. Industrial plants are increasingly relying on natural gas, with many plants drilling their own wells in places like Ohio and Texas.

One of the reason for the rapidly increasing supply of cheap natural gas is the relatively new process of fracking where deep underground shale is shattered releasing the massive amounts of natural gas locked in shale formations. Until this new process was developed, this gas was not economically available. Like any new process, fracking continues to improve in both cost, efficiency, and safety. It has made available vast fields of natural gas previously locked in shale. There is enough gas available in known fields to supply our need economically for many decades to come. Once the LNG tankers are plying the seas, the natural gas boom will be in full swing. That, however, is merely the first boom to hit America.

The same shale that holds vast amounts of natural gas also holds an estimated 1.5–2.6 trillion barrels of petroleum. That's almost half of the world's known deposits. In contrast, the worlds conventional oil reserves are estimated to be 1.317 trillion barrels as of January 1, 2007. The search for new conventional oil deposits has been going on for more than a hundred years and new fields are getting harder to find and more difficult to extract. In contrast, the search for oil shale has been going on for a relatively short period and could be underestimated by a factor of three or more. That means the US could have as much as 4.5–7.8 trillion barrels of petroleum locked in shale.

This graph shows not only the rapidly expanding production in North Dakota, but a similar trend in Texas because of improved methods of extracting oil from old fields. The growth in North Dakota is from a single shale deposit, the Bakken, and there are several other as yet untapped shale deposits that could be just as large. Unless something (like the administration) stops it, the increased production of petroleum will follow the already huge growth in natural gas and a boom in energy will result as the US becomes an energy exporter rather than an importer. How big the boom will be and how long it lasts will be at least partly dependent on the actions of our government. Will the administration support the boom or destroy it? That is the question. To this point their efforts have not been supportive, but the boom continues to grow in spite of their efforts.

Like natural gas, petroleum in shale is yielding to fracking and other new extraction techniques. Experts have estimated that new extraction techniques in shale and even in fields depleted of oil available to conventional extraction, could drop the cost of US produced petroleum at the well head below $5 per barrel. Even with world oil prices at half of their present level, oil from shale is becoming profitable. As of November 1, 2012, world crude prices were $87 per barrel for WTI crude (West Texas Intermediate) and $108 per barrel for Brent crude (North Sea Standard). Rapid expansion of production from the Bakken shale formation in North Dakota has already created an oil boom there. As more investment in infrastructure for extracting crude from shale goes into place, the boom will expand. The Bakken is huge, but it is only one of a number of oil shale deposits in the US, and new fields continue to be discovered. All that is needed is the investment in new drilling and fracking infrastructure, and the transportation system to move the oil to refineries. It is actually possible that the US could move from an oil importing nation to an oil exporting nation within just a few years. This coupled with LNG would generate an unprecedented boom creating many high paying jobs and expanding manufacturing as energy costs go way down. The biggest factor, the billions now going to oil producing nations would be replaced by billions coming in from nations purchasing oil from the US.

There are a few caveats that are quite obvious. The continuing anti energy, anti business policies of the Obama administration could easily stop the booms before they get very far. Increases in taxes could dry up new investment needed in oil production infrastructure and in the transportation of LNG. A plethora of new federal regulations could slow or stop the booms before they develop. Behind all of this is the socialist, anti capitalist agenda of liberal Democrats who, if they were honest would change their name to the Socialist or Communist Party. I see the Republican House of Representatives as the only bulwark against the U.S. becoming a socialist dictatorship. There may still be a concerted effort by the administration, aided by the Senate and the media to have the government take over the entire energy industry, especially the oil and gas industries. They certainly will not let capitalist organizations lead the US into a new boom economy and get the credit for it. Whatever happens, the administration and liberal Democrats will take credit for the boom and their sycophant media will dutifully report this as a fact. If the boom is big enough, Obama will use it to run for a third term in 2016. Count on it.

You can rest assured the anti fossil fuel, global warming crowd will do everything they can to prevent or stop these fossil fuel booms. Unless, of course, their Pied Piper is overwhelmingly given credit for the boom. Such being the case, they will be very quiet about global warming.

They will probably tout the reduction in release of CO_2 as trucking companies and power companies switch to natural gas from coal and petroleum fuels. They will be caught in the dilemma of whether to continue with their anti fossil fuel agenda and go against Obama's claimed economic success, or reverse their agenda and tout the conversion from diesel to LNG as it will cut in half the discharge of CO_2 into the atmosphere by heavy trucks. Then there's a similar reduction in CO_2 emissions as coal and oil fired power plants convert to cheaper natural gas. It will be interesting to see which way their efforts go. It is even possible some will go one way while others go the opposite.

Saturday, July 07, 2012

Who Is it That Really and Truly Pays Taxes - Friday, July 6, 2012

For those of you who don't like my political views, this piece is completely a-political. It is written so people can understand the effects on everyone that taxes have and how many taxes on the "wealthy" are actually paid by average and even poor Americans. As strange as it may seem, corporation, businesses, and professionals **DO NOT PAY TAXES!** They merely act as agents for the IRS, collecting tax dollars from customers and clients and turning your tax dollars lover to the Federal Government. I know that's not what the politicians want you to know, but it is easily demonstrated as a fact.

Who is it that really and truly pays all those taxes, and I mean all, every penny? That includes all payroll taxes, income taxes, FICA, unemployment taxes, sales or value added taxes, real estate taxes, and all those hidden taxes on practically everything. I'm sure you heard all those comments about 51% of Americans paying no income taxes at all, mostly those with low incomes. The Washington ruling elite, their bureaucrats and the wealthiest Americans would like you to believe that, but it is patently untrue. In actual fact, those who pay no income taxes pay a larger portion of their disposable income to the government than those who do pay income taxes. Statistically, the more income above the minimum required for basic necessities one has, the smaller the percentage taxes take out of total income.

Politicians like to use class warfare in their rhetoric about income tax rates for "the wealthy." Unfortunately, those same politicians have built an income taxing system that is extremely complex and that provides endless exemptions and deductions (the infamous tax loopholes) for their friends and supporters. These "loopholes" are finagled by lobbyists for an immense range of beneficiaries. How often do you hear about wealthy individuals or companies who pay virtually no income taxes? Remember GE last year? If you are wealthy enough, you can buy exemptions from almost any tax for a tiny part of that amount in campaign donations or even slipped "under the table" to the right people. Still. that doesn't change anything about who actually pays those income taxes as described in the next paragraph.

Corporations, businesses, professionals, any person or organization that provides goods or services, do not actually pay any of these taxes. They merely pass these costs down to the end users or consumers. The only time they actually pay taxes is when they buy something as an individual consumer. This means that the entire cost of government is borne by those same end users and consumers. At 32% of GDP as it was in 2007, 32¢ of each and every dollar spent by every consumer was tax. This applies to rich and poor alike. Since 2007, liberal Democrat spending aided by Obama's efforts, has upped that to 44% of GDP. That has increased taxes on everyone by 37.5%, more than a third. The estimates the CBO made as to the cost of Obamacare is pathetic. As usual, it will probably cost more than four times the CBO estimate, should it be implemented. This cost will raise the tax portion of everything to at least 50%, another raise in the taxes paid by everyone of 13.64%.. This means that by 2014, the taxes paid by everyone will have increased by 56.25% in just 7 years.

Let's follow some tax dollars and see who actually pays—where the tax debt ends up. The figures reported have been taken from the actual financial statements of real companies. The names have been changed to prevent law suits.

EXAMPLE, STEP 1: XYZ Mining in Arizona digs copper ore out of the ground in several Arizona copper mines. They refine the ore and sell it to copper users. In 2010 their sales were nearly a $billion. Their net earnings before taxes were $211 million, or 21.1% of sales. Federal income taxes on those earnings were $47 million. Taxes other than income taxes were $22 million. These included state and local taxes, franchise taxes, and federal direct mining taxes. Payroll taxes, including both portions of FICA were $67 million. The total tax portion of XYZ's expenses were $136 million or 13.6% of total sales. Out of every $1,000 worth of copper sold, $136 was for taxes that the purchaser of the copper actually paid for. XYZ simply passed that tax burden on to those who bought their copper, a fabricator or manufacturer.

STEP 2: ABC fabricating of Texas bought the raw copper ingots from XYZ and produced copper pipe among many other products. A financial analysis similar to XYZ shows that for every $1,000 worth of pipe sold, $227 was for taxes. Factoring in the portion of the taxes XYZ paid, adds $42 to that amount for a total of $269 out of the $1,000 of sales. This amount is simply passed on down the chain to the purchaser of the pipe, a contractor.

STEP 3: A building contractor in Dallas bought some of this pipe for a major building project. A financial analysis similar to XYZ and ABC shows that for every $1,000 worth of pipe used and priced in the project, $296 was for taxes. Factoring in the portion of the taxes XYZ and ABC paid, adds $84 to that amount for a total of $380 out of the $1,000 of the contract price. This amount is simply passed on down the chain to the purchaser of the pipe, a building owner.

STEP 4: The building owner leases space in the building to a group of dentists. Their financial analysis shows that for every $1,000 of the building lease income attributable to the extensive copper piping in their suite, $198 was for taxes. Factoring in the portion of the previous taxes paid adds $123 to that amount for a total of $321 out of each $1,000 of the rent paid by the dentists. This amount is simply passed on down the chain to the dentists who lease the space.

STEP 5: The group of dentists have many patients that pay for their dental services. Their financial analysis shows that for every $1,000 of the patient fees they receive, $321 was for taxes. Factoring in the portion of the previous taxes paid adds $140 to that amount for a total of $461 out of each $1,000 of the fees paid by the patients. This amount, the entire tax burden applied to each of the 5 steps combined, is actually paid by the end user, the patient who is at the end of the chain, the final or end user.

Conclusion: It is always the end user of any product or service that actually pays every penny of all taxes. This tax burden falls on rich and poor alike and, as in the above example, currently averages about $46 out of every $100 spent by every individual, regardless of income or wealth status. That percentage can be accurately calculated another way. Currently, our federal government consumes about 41% of our GNP. Add to that approximately 5% consumed by state and local governments. It's funny how that adds up to the same $46 out of every $100 spent by every individual, regardless of income or wealth status.

Raising taxes (especially on the wealthy) increases the cost of absolutely everything. From gasoline to bread to apartment rent to health care, increasing taxes will always raise these prices for the consumer. By the same token, lowering taxes will always lower these prices for the consumer. These are demonstrable and proven facts from time immemorial. So, no matter how you slice it, the poor always pay a far higher portion of their needed income from any and all sources, than do those not considered among the poor. The less income one has, the more important that portion is that goes up the chain to pay all those taxes. Said another way, the loss of that $46 out of every $100 spent is much more damaging the less income one has. That $46 is far more important to a low income family trying to get by, than to a slightly wealthy family or even the one down the street making $50k per year.

EXAMPLE 1. A poor family has a total income including welfare payments of $1,600 a month. They pay no income taxes. Assuming they spend all of their income, 46% of what they spend, or $736 is taxes that were passed down the chain. Their total taxes are $736 or 46% of their income

EXAMPLE 2. Another family makes about $5,000 a month. They invest $500 per month in savings and pay $225 for income taxes. They also have a mortgage payment of $1,000 each month. This leaves them with $3,275 of disposable income which they use for all household necessities, food, clothing, transportation, insurance, etc. etc. Assuming they spend it all, 46% or $1,622 is taxes that were passed down the chain. Their total taxes are $1,847 or 34.63% of their income.

EXAMPLE 3. Another family makes about $15,000 a month. They invest $3000 per month in savings and stocks, and pay $2,000 for income taxes. They also have a mortgage payment of $3,000 each month. This leaves them with $7,000 of disposable income which they use for all household necessities, food, clothing, transportation, insurance, etc. etc. Assuming they spend it all, 46% or $3,268 is taxes that were passed down the chain. Their total taxes are $5,164 or 34.43% of their income

EXAMPLE 4: Another "wealthy" family makes about $100,000 a month. They invest $40,000 per month in stocks and savings, and pay $15,000 for income taxes. They also have a mortgage payment of $10,000 each month. They make charitable donations of $5,000 per month. This leaves them with $30,000 of disposable income which they use for all household necessities, food, clothing, transportation, insurance, etc. etc. Assuming they spend it all, 46% or $13,800 is taxes that were passed down the chain. Their total taxes are $28,800 or 28.8% of their income. Lets see, here's the resulting tax table:

Current Income Tax System (monthly figures)

Family	Income	Disposable	Taxes	Tax %	Left to Invest
Poor	$1,600	$1,600	$736	46.0%	$0
Lower middle	$5,000	$3,525	$1,847	34.63%	$500
Upper middle	$15,000	$7,104	$5,220	34.43%	$3,000
Wealthy	$100,000	$30,000	$28,800	28.8%	$40,000

Who thinks this is fair?

The table below gives the same figures with the "Fair Tax" 15-25% base

Family	Income	Disposable	Taxes	Tax %	Left to Invest
Poor	$1,600	$1,600	$0	0.0%	$0
Lower middle	$5,000	$2,295	$750	15.0%	$1,955
Upper middle	$15,000	$6,780	$3,250	21.7%	$4,970
Wealthy	$100,000	$31,200	$25,000	25.0%	$43,800

The table below gives the same figures with the "Fair Tax" 20-30% base

Family	Income	Disposable	Taxes	Tax %	Left to Invest
Poor	$1,600	$1,600	$0	0.0%	$0
Lower middle	$5,000	$2,295	$1,000	20.0%	$1,445
Upper middle	$15,000	$6,780	$4,000	26.7%	$4,220
Wealthy	$100,000	$31,200	$30,000	30.0%	$38,800

It is obvious from this information and from the examination of the P&L statements from any business that **businesses do not pay taxes, they merely collect them from their customers and pass them on to the government.** They represent a substantial part of every end user purchase of goods and services completely paid for by individuals as long as they are not a business expense. In 2006 the percentage that represented tax was 32%. That figure has blossomed to 44% since liberal Democrats took over Congress and the Whitehouse. By 2014 it will swell to at least 50% thanks mostly to the Obamacare tax. While this number is growing, business profits and thus tax revenue, will shrink as the economy sinks farther and farther into the tank.

IT'S A FACT - Corporations do not pay taxes. Businesses do not pay taxes. Professionals in their professions do not pay taxes. Organizations including those who are not-for-profit do not pay taxes. All of these "taxpayers" merely collect those taxes from customers or clients in the price of their products and services and then pass them onto the government just like the much more obvious sales tax. Even the so-called company paid portion of FICA taxes add to the cost of an employee and so are really taken from the employee.

So, I repeat, who really pays the taxes? The truth of the matter is that very few members of the public understand the realities of any taxes. Every business, large or small, every professional, every taxable entity or organization—all workers—appear to pay taxes to many governments. But just who is it that actually pays these taxes?

What happens if lawmakers enact a windfall profits tax on the oil companies at 50% of net profits? It's really quite simple. Every dollar increase in taxes will be met with a slightly larger total increase in fuel prices at the pump to make up for the increased cost of doing business. As with all business, this cost will be passed through to the consumer or end user. That would add as much as another nickel to the price of gas at the pump. So who is paying that excess profits tax? It's the ignorant motorist who voted those self-serving oafs into office just to punish the oil companies.

Thursday, April 05, 2012

A Report on the Coming Financial Disaster

Today, I read the following report on the Internet. It only goes to prove how stupid the human animal is, individually and collectively. Humans are almost exactly like overgrown lemmings, a plague of death and destruction on their own kind. They are reproducing themselves out of existence.

Reports like the following, almost completely ignore the only realistic, rational, effective way we humans can prevent the coming calamity. I seriously doubt humans have the collective intelligence and will to do the only thing that could possibly prevent the mass starvation, food wars, race riots, religious battles, deliberate exterminations, and other violence certain to accompany a worldwide economic collapse. A sad note is that only one nation on the planet has the brains and will to do something about it. That nation is certainly not the United States. Read and weep. My words are in this serif type font.

The report is in this, non serif font.

According to a study released by researchers at Jay W. Forrester's institute at MIT, the world is headed for a "global economic collapse" if humans around the planet do not waver in their consumption of natural resource. Not only is global economic collapse imminent at the current rate of resource consumption and population growth, "precipitous population decline" will also occur.

Recent findings published in the study coincide with those of the Limits to Growth which is an academic report from 1972. Smithsonian Magazine wrote about an Australian physicist named Graham Turner who famously said: "The world is on track for disaster."

According to the report which was produced for The Club of Rome, the researchers conjured a computing model in order to forecast various scenarios based upon the current models of global resource consumption and population growth. A computing model is a mathematical model of a complex process or system which requires conditions for testing.

The majority of the computer scenarios processed indicated imminent economic collapse would occur right around the year 2030. I disagree. I see it as happening much sooner.

Unlimited economic growth potential is still a possibility, however, governments around the world would have to enact policies to limit the expansion of our ecological footprint (human demand on the Earth's ecosystems) in addition to investing in green technologies.

The only possible way humans can limit or reduce our ecological footprint (the current politically correct term) is to stop our ridiculous population growth. Population growth, barely mentioned in one paragraph in the article, is the absolute singular cause of the events that will lead up to total collapse. All the best efforts at slowing resource consumption are feeble, futile efforts. They will make for only a slight slowing of the devastation sure to come, a delaying tactic.

Twelve million copies of the recently published report were distributed in thirty-seven different languages around the world. While there are those, such as former governor of the Federal Research Board and Yale economist Henry Wallich, who strongly disagree with the findings detailed in both the Limits to Growth as well as the more recent MIT study conveying similar findings. Wallich believed that the regulation of economic growth would be equivalent to "consigning billions to permanent poverty."

I would revise Wallich's conclusions and say, economic growth without population control will be equivalent to "consigning billions to permanent poverty, starvation, wars and devastation." Think the Congo wars and desolation expanded to include the entire Earth.

Do you believe that a global economic collapse is truly imminent by 2030 based on the current rate of consumption and population growth as forecast by MIT's computing model?

Read more at http://www.inquisitr.com/215867/global-economic-collapse-imminent-mit-researchers-predict-next-great-depression-2030/#4rHYFWpyoZLboVm4.99

I believe a collapse is not only imminent, but has already begun. The first signs?

1) Food shortages, riots and starvation is growing in the third world. Islamic refugees are streaming out of the Middle East into Europe, some even into America.

2) Total world production of food is declining and has been for a number of years.

3) Several ocean fish stocks have collapsed or are being harvested at unsustainable rates.

4) There are many more signs in evidence, but the overpowering reality is that we are depleting all of our resources at an accelerating rate. Since those resources are limited, it is obvious we will run out. That is true no matter how effectively we deal with economic growth. Even if

we stopped it entirely, that would only delay the end a small amount, a few years at best. Humans are becoming like lemmings, flooding out of overpopulated poor areas into more productive lands.

For a more in depth view of this problem, read: http://decimatenviro.blogspot.com

In my opinion, we could solve this devastating problem, not easily, but effectively. Also, in my opinion, I see us as ignoring it and letting nature take its course to the New Dark Age of Man, whatever that portends.

Monday, March 12, 2012

A Sudden Realization - an Ahah! Moment - Obama's Appeal to Intellectuals

It took several minutes to sink in, but a newly recognized reality found its way into my mind. This startling (to me) epiphany brought a new and deepening understanding of something that had long eluded my mental grasp. This happened during a discussion within a group I belong to of about two dozen members called The Socrates Club. We meet on a weekly basis to discuss subjects and questions submitted by members. They are a bit heavy on the intellectual side with a number of retired professors and PhDs—educators—teachers. I am one of the minority, not an educator, not a PhD.

One of the professors was expounding his disgust at Republicans and their anti education focus—their anti intellectualism. Another professor, also a PhD I believe, was saying how much he liked what Obama was doing as President and that he would certainly vote for him. My instant reaction was to wonder why these intelligent men could possibly approve of what Democrats were doing and what Obama was doing as President. I was a bit upset, thinking, how could they be so blind? I have great respect for the intelligence of each of these men from many discussions we have had.

Then came this sudden burst of brilliance this AHAH! moment—this mental nirvana. I then knew exactly why they expressed these feelings and thoughts. **(In the comics this is portrayed with a lightbulb turning on above an individual's head)** After the light went on it made perfect sense. From their perspective they were absolutely right. I remembered a quotable statement I wrote many years ago and included in my first published collection, Words from the Lakeside.

"Somehow, we always get back to the basics. Right and wrong, good and evil, like beauty, are in the eye of the beholder (or doer). Their rules are not immutable. They are lifestyle—cultural, social, political, or religious creations. They depend entirely on one's own situation and belief system—whose side you are in, what your belief system demands, to what group you belong, or who eats whom. I am sure Genghis Khan, Hitler, and Saddam Hussein had quite different views of right and wrong from their victims."

—*HJ, May 8, 2001*

Why I never connected that thought with the political beliefs of individuals is beyond me. What I expressed in that paragraph more than eleven years ago now seems obvious to me. We each see good or evil, positive or negative, in any situation or activity, in the light of our perceptions of how it affects us, our families and friends. Different people have very different views based on many things including culture, race, sex, sexual orientation, religion, economic conditions—virtually any definable human condition, real or imagined. Right and wrong, good and evil are based on our perceptions, not reality. The next line in the same quotation applies to all creatures in our world including humans.

"Good and evil, right and wrong have very different meanings for a zebra than for a lion."

Group 1, those who favor Obama and liberal Democrats: To many groups of individuals, what Obama and liberal Democrats are doing is commendable. These include almost all members of the following groups: government employees, union leaders, recipients of welfare and other government largess, socialists, communists, African Americans, and all entertainers including sports and TV news. Also in this group are a majority of the following: educators, the intellectual elite, union members, college students, owners and officers of mega corporations and especially of mega banks, trial lawyers, financial professionals, and major investors in the stock market and commodities.

You will note that most of these groups are little impacted by the recession. They believe and agree with those saying economic conditions are steadily improving. For example, investors in the stock market and large corporations are doing quite well, at least better than they were a year or so ago. You will also notice that few if any of these people consider themselves Middle Class Americans. Most of them are toward the top or bottom income segments while few are in the economic middle class. The exceptions are those other members of group1 who happen to fall in the middle income category. To a varying extent, all of these groups are being supported or at least helped financially by government. Consider all of the entitlements these groups receive. Actually there's something from the government, a handout, for almost everyone. And who is it that pays for this growing financial drag on our economy? Hmmmmm?

Group 2, those against Obama and for conservative Republicans: The other groups of individuals see Obama and liberal Democrats as enemies of mostly the middle classes. Those who are the ones not faring so well with what Obama and liberal Democrats are doing, They are losing ground economically and see increasing government control and interference as intolerable. These include almost all Americans of self or independent motivation, such as: the owners and employees of small and medium sized businesses (the ones who create most private sector jobs), family farmers and small to medium corporate farm owners (not the mega corporate farm owners as they're in the other group), entrepreneurs, and inventors. Member of this group were the ones most impacted by the mortgage melt down so skillfully created and manipulated by liberal Democrats.

Not so you say? Media talking heads were so totally committed to the support of group 1 that they hid what was happening at Fannie Mae, Freddie Mac, and Countrywide Financial. They labeled all those who warned of what was going to happen (and did) as racist, or anti poor and worse. If they had done their duty (as they loudly proclaim it), these shenanigans would have been exposed and maybe corrected before the disaster occurred. They deliberately avoided any mention of the real causes of the mortgage crisis and severely castigated those who did. If this had not been done, if the media had investigated and reported honestly, the truth would have been common knowledge and many more of those now in group 1 would be firmly in group 2. I wonder why? Hmmmmm?

One obvious reality is that this debacle moved more real wealth from middle class Americans to the 1% than has ever happened—by far. The number of middle class Americans who lost their entire fortunes, their nest egg for retirement, and were reduced from being somewhat secure financially to being penniless is staggering. Some say as high as fifty percent were devastated by the loss of the entire equity of their homes, the major investment and savings of most. Many went from a 30% to 50% equity to zero or being under water. At the same time, the banks (collectively) went from partial owners of these homes to 100% owners. And who made up these mostly paper losses for the banks, the megabanks who took over most of the small banks? These losses were made up on the backs of the same taxpayers who lost their equity. They received a double whammy.

Another factor is that this group of people usually make political judgements (emotional decisions) on the basis of what politicians say, not what they do. They are also greatly influenced by the media and subject to their obvious bias. I hear even staunch conservatives repeating lies promulgated by the media and directed against conservatives. Why does this happen? Everyone knows that any lie repeated often enough and with enough emphasis will eventually be believed by most people. (A quote from Joseph Goebels, Hitler's propaganda minister) With nearly everyone getting their news from TV news programs, the Politically Correct opinions they present are hammered into the minds of the TV audience. These folks are simply too busy or too lazy to think for themselves. They let TV talking heads do that for them. These news commentators (they are not really reporters) define so many people and ideas for most Americans it is difficult to get the common folks to see the truth, even when they strongly disfavor the lies they are being fed.

These people are more apt to judge a politician by what he does rather than what he says. Still, politics is a totally emotional activity. Reason has very little to do with the selections of any voter.

Group 3, those in the middle, the uncommitted moderates: God only knows who they are and he's not telling. Years ago they were referred to as mugwumps, those who sit firmly on the fence with their mug on one side, and their wump on the other. They are hard to figure, but the TV talking heads have a great deal to say about everything and influence the final decisions of many. Experts who estimate these things say the media move at least half of centrist voters to vote according to their guidance. That is a major factor in any election. As a result, most of the recent Republican nominees for President have been chosen by the media.

A Conservative Black Commentator Predicts an Obama Win in 2012

Here's a prediction from one who is on the conservative side. It bears out what I said about group 1.

By Dr. Walter Williams - October 2011

Can President Obama be defeated in 2012? No. He can't. I am going on record as saying that

President Barak Obama will win a second term.

The media won't tell you this because a good election campaign means hundreds of millions (or in Obama's case billions) of dollars to them in advertising.

And that's why I know Obama will win. The American people are notoriously ignorant of economics. And economics is the key to why Obama should be defeated.

Even when Obama's policies lead the nation to final ruin, the majority of the American people are going to believe the bait-and-switch tactics Obama and his supporters in the media will use to explain why it isn't his fault. After all, things were much worse than understood when he took office.

Obama's reelection is really a very, very simple math problem. Consider the following:

1) Blacks will vote for Obama blindly. Period. Doesn't matter what he does. It's a race thing. He's one of us,

2) College educated women will vote for Obama. Though they will be offended by this, they swoon at his oratory. It's really not more complex than that,

3) Liberals will vote for Obama. He is their great hope,

4) Democrats will vote for Obama. He is the leader of their party and his coat tails will carry them to victory nationwide,

5) Hispanics will vote for Obama. He is the path to citizenship for those who are illegal and Hispanic leaders recognize the political clout they carry in the Democratic Party,

6) Union members will vote overwhelmingly for Obama. He is their key to money and power in business, state and local politics,

7) Big Business will support Obama. They already have. He has almost $1 Billion dollars in his reelection purse gained largely from his connections with Big Business and is gaining more everyday. Big Business loves Obama because he gives them access to taxpayer money so long as they support his social and political agenda,

8) The media love him. They may attack the people who work for him, but they love him. After all, to not love him would be racist,

9) Most other minorities and special interest groups will vote for him. Oddly, the overwhelming majority of Jews and Muslims will support him because they won't vote Republican. American Indians will support him. Obviously homosexuals tend to vote Democratic. And lastly,

10) Approximately half of independents will vote for Obama. And he doesn't need anywhere near that number because he has all of the groups previously mentioned. The President will win an overwhelming victory in 2012.

— Dr. Walter Williams

My own conclusions are fairly simple: People are driven and will vote according to their perceived self interest weighted by their emotions. The self interest of those in group 1 is perceived as being served by the pronouncements of liberals, socialists, the liberal media, and the entertainment world. These left of center groups need only give token attention to group 3. They could care less about group 2 except to immolate their candidates with ridicule, hatred and contempt. (It has become their modus operandi to call any who oppose them racist and other emotionally damaging names at every turn.) They know full well that class and other hatreds trump reason at election time and will use negative campaigning almost exclusively. It always works because it is infinitely easier to destroy than to build.

Sadly, Republicans candidates have adopted the same negative emotional strategy in their presidential primary campaigns. They have abandoned any high ground they had and lowered themselves to the egregious level of their liberal Democrat opponents. How stupid can they get? Their words will be used liberally by Democrats against whoever ends up as the Republican candidate. It's like a comic opera or an old time burlesque routine. But they are politicians so what else could you expect?

I see the point Dr. Williams is making, but I see his predictions as too simplistic. One big and well known factor is that many in parts of the first group simply do not vote, at least not in as high a percentage as those in group 2. Also, I think the mix of ideas and understanding among many members of the first group accurately see socialism and expansion of government for the destructive force it is. In the end, everyone but a very select few will suffer major degradation of their lifestyle. Here's what they know to be true. A government controlled economy has never in history succeeded for very long. A nation with men (and women) free to own property and generate wealth on their own initiative will quickly run circles around any similar nation with an economy controlled by government. This has held true since the Chinese tried it more than three thousand years ago. Look at the very different China of today as compared with the one in Mao's Cultural Revolution between 1966 and 1976. It's amazing what a little bit of economic freedom and the reversal of socialist doctrine can do.

As Margaret Thatcher remarked, "The problem with socialism is that eventually you run out of other people's money."

Or, as George Bernard Shaw said, "A government policy to rob Peter to pay Paul can be assured of the support of Paul." That quote accurately describes the government policy of liberals. That same policy has already generated a great many Pauls and reduced the number of Peters. I think Dr. Williams may be using reverse psychology to frighten the anti Obama forces so they will work harder to defeat him.

My conclusions? People will support and vote for those who they perceive will do the most for them and theirs, even to the detriment of many others. Voting is an emotionally controlled activity. It is completely self serving, the absolute opposite of an altruistic or even rational decision. Many will vote for those they think will punish any who have more than the one voting, even if they lose something in the process themselves. There is a major component of humanity whose most powerful desire is to see those with more, much more, of almost anything, brought down to or below their level. Think the men who flew those airplanes into the Twin Towers. That is an extreme example of this same human trait.

The following quote explains the described political reality in a democracy. It has been attributed to many sources.

"A Democracy cannot exist as a permanent form of government. It can only last until the citizens discover they can vote themselves largesse out of the public treasury. After that, the majority always votes for the candidate promising the most benefits from the public treasury with the result that the Democracy always collapses over a loose fiscal policy, to be followed by a dictatorship."

Monday, February 20, 2012

Lessons from Illinois and Other Liberal, Compulsory Union States

I have several questions for any liberal who reads this.

1) Do you actually believe that spending 2.7 trillion dollars per year on government welfare/entitlements/incentives/grants/social programs, while total revenue is only 2.2 trillion per year and shrinking, is in any way sustainable? That does not include any military expenditures. How long will the Chinese continue to make up the difference?

2) Is there any of this short blog that you can disprove with facts?

3) What is the real reason you continue supporting, promoting, and voting for politicians whose efforts are destroying our nation?

4) What is the real reason you willfully choose those who continue wild spending far beyond our ability to pay?

I would really like to see your answers to my questions.

Here are lessons from Illinois and other liberal, compulsory union states. Is the country as a whole going down the same route?

President Obama's home state is extremely unhappy. This is because Illinois has instituted several severely damaging changes in taxes on both business and individuals. Illinois has demonstrated just how economically devastating bloated government can be.

In January, 2011, the corporate tax rate was increased from 4.8% to 7.0%, a 45% increase. Since that time, the industrial juggernaut Caterpillar has made it clear to Illinois officials that it chose to build its newest manufacturing plant outside of Illinois due to the "business climate and overall fiscal health" of the state. That plant would have added about 1,000 jobs to the state. A number of other large companies are going to do the same thing for the same reasons.

Other smaller businesses have followed suit and actually moved their corporate headquarters from Illinois to neighboring states. Modern Drop Forge Co., which manufactures precision tools and has about 250 employees, along with Internet company, FatWallet.com, an employer of more than 50 workers, are among those businesses that have pulled up stakes and left since the corporate tax increase.

The exodus of companies and reluctance to expand in Illinois provide a great lesson to Obama and his cohorts who plan to increase taxes or limit tax deductions, which are essentially equivalent, on American companies. This will result in fewer American jobs and therefore fewer overall tax dollars as these companies will instead choose to expand overseas.

Obama and others may label this as unpatriotic. What a joke. Is the destruction of our economy, the decimation of the financial health of America's middle classes, the transfer of great wealth to Goldman-Sachs and other Wall Street giants patriotic? The fact is companies must answer to their investors as to the financial decisions they make. If corporate tax rates are substantially higher in America than another potential location, then a decision has to be made that is right for the investors. Investment money always moves to where it will provide the maximum return to investors. This is one immutable law of economics. In spite of this reality, Obama fully expects companies to forego profitability for "the good of the country" even if it bankrupts the company. That is pathetically ridiculous.

At the same time they raised corporate taxes, Illinois raised personal income tax rate from 3% to 5%. That's a 66% increase in the taxes individuals pay to the Illinois Treasury. In the eleven months since the tax increase, the Illinois unemployment rate rose from 9.0% to 9.8%. In 46 states, unemployment rates declined during the same time.

Illinois' own President Barack Obama is calling for increases in the personal income tax rate of American families earning over $250,000 per year by ending the Bush-era tax cuts and by making those earning $1 million or more to have a minimum tax rate of 30%. Do you have any estimates of the net revenue increase these taxes will bring in? Because of the negative effect on our economy, it is far more likely there will be a net decrease in revenue.

When Obama released his budget, he quipped, "At a time when our economy is growing and creating jobs at a faster clip, we've got to do everything in our power to keep this recovery on track." What recovery? According to our government's own employment numbers (not unemployment, a suspect number at best) the number of people employed in the private sector continues to drop. Add to that the rapidly rising cost of food and fuel and his words seem to be more likely evidence of glue sniffing than rational thought. The only indication of the tiniest improvement in the economy is in highly suspect government statistics. They routinely change the method used to calculate these numbers to claim things that are patently untrue.

They claim that massive increases in personal income taxes along with increases in corporate tax bills will help strengthen the economic recovery? Of course that's untrue. Their claims are simply false propaganda. These actions kill jobs and destroy any chance for economic recovery. Illinois is a perfect example of what we can expect overall for the nation.

Illinois politicians said the increases in tax revenues would whittle down the enormous and growing state deficit. Actually, the opposite occurred. Illinois added $2 billion more in debt in 2012 and now has a deficit of some $7 billion. Are these politicians really that stupid or are they dedicated to moving jobs out of Illinois and destroying the state's economy? Historically, when taxes on business are raised, and/or government increases controls and reporting, revenue goes down. The reverse is also true. Why is it that liberals refuse to recognize reality? The only rational conclusion is that they actually want to decimate the American economy—to destroy the wealth of America's middle class and reduce them to dependency on government.

It is informative to note here that by far the largest transfer of wealth from the 99% to the 1% was engineered by liberal bureaucrat thieves who looted Fannie Mae and Freddie Mac with the aid and blessings of liberal Democrats in Congress and Barack Obama. I see this as simply one of many actions designed to destroy America's middle class and turn our country into a Marxist Communist dictatorship.

President Obama says higher taxes are necessary to pay down the debt. He knows higher taxes will produce the opposite results for America, just as in Illinois. It would be advantageous for voters to look at Illinois, and maybe Michigan, California, New York and other liberal, compulsory union states (and at their great financial success) The real fact is, corporate tax hikes will ruin economies and push more companies and jobs out of the state and country.

Another example of the (beneficial?) effects of liberal policies combined with compulsory union membership:

Remember King Lyndon's Great Society programs? Part of that was his Model Cities program which cost billions of taxpayer dollars and was a total failure. I need only repeat one of King Lyndon's pronounced promises: "Detroit will be a shining example of the benefits of our Model Cities program." It is quite telling how accurate Johnson's prediction was. It certainly has become an example of the results of the policies of his "great society" programs now being greatly expanded by Obama and his cronies. Go to the following site for a more in depth description of the results of this example of liberal Democrat efforts and policies.

http://www.thedailycrux.com/content/3247/Government_Stupidity

Or better still, take a drive through the inner city of Detroit and see for yourself the results of fifty years of liberal Democrat policies and labor union efforts. By sure to do so in broad daylight because doing so at night carries a high risk of being car jacked and murdered. Actually, you can see a lot of abandoned homes and buildings just by driving through on I-75. I did that myself a short time ago. Burned out homes and factories were quite evident, even from the Interstate. Much of the city of Detroit looks more like the bombed out center of a third world city than an American one. The media elite boneheads are now beginning to extol a growing renaissance of Detroit in direct denial of realty and in spite of the fact unemployment is nearing

50%. Also, 30% of those working are employed by government. This shining example of liberalism in action has lost 60% of its population in the last 50 years. Those who fled the city were mostly middle class workers and included virtually all of the whites. They have been largely replaced by uneducated and poor Muslims and Hispanics with their huge birthrates.

Now those same morally deficient snake oil salesmen and tyrants are using the same process that has clearly devastated all of the most liberal states, to do the same thing to America with absolute certainty. There may in fact be enough ignoramuses at the public welfare and employment trough, in government unions, and that listen to a totally corrupt and deceptive media, to win the next election. Maybe there are enough of those who have had their fires of hate fanned by emotional blackmail to bring down America. (Thank you reverend Wright!) It is obvious to me that the left's "spread the wealth to equalize economic conditions" means making everyone poor and dependent on government.

When I pointed this out to my Socrates discussion group, one of the many liberal members said I was wrong, that it was not liberal Democrat policies that brought about the demise of the American auto industry that caused Detroit to collapse. I then asked him what he thought was the real cause of the demise of the Detroit's auto industry. "Why, the failure of the auto industry to compete with cheaper and higher quality foreign cars." He replied.

I then asked him what he thought was the reason for that. "Older factories, antiquated equipment and the failure of management to modernize and adapt new manufacturing techniques." He answered.

"I couldn't agree more," was my surprising (to him) reply. "And just who or what was it that prevented the industry from doing those important things?"

He had no concrete answer and mumbled something about greedy executives and poor management, so I continued. "The UAW demanded benefit and labor cost increases that took capital that could have been used for modernization, while union work rules prevented the adoption of new manufacturing methods, especially in the use of automation and robots. These union efforts were backed and supported totally by all liberal Democrats. That's why liberal policies, politics, and support for unions are responsible for the demise of Detroit so I will stand on my original reasoning.

These examples are undeniable realities, and there are many many more. If Detroit is not enough, think New York, California, Illinois, Wisconsin, New Jersey, and all the other blue states that are virtually bankrupt. It certainly wasn't conservatives who ran them into the ground. Now that the voters in several of those states threw out the Democrats and elected Republican governors and state legislatures, Democrats are using every legal and illegal tactic they can to continue the fiscal carnage they have wrought on those states. What do you think they will look like in five or ten more years? And how about Fannie Mae, Freddie Mac, Amtrak and the Postal Service? Competitive private entities clearly beat the pants off these government operations. These private companies make a profit (that word liberals hate) and pay taxes (the word liberals love) to boot. Those four (and every other government operation) are terribly inefficient and require huge infusions of tax payer money to keep operating. Currently they are all drowning in the red ink of substantial losses.

Thursday, May 19, 2011

An Attempt at a Sane Explanation of My Politics

This current blog is an irregular, randomly organized mixture of comments, quotes and observations that are very roughly related to my political and social views. Some are directed at individuals, some to the general public, and some are repeated. I am not a follower of or beholden to any ism, group belief system (religious, political or other), peer group, grant committee, dean or head of faculty, political or other boss, or corporate officer at any level, so I am free to speak my mind, mistakes and all. I consider myself a truly independent and liberal individual and a realist who knows what it means to conserve. No, that is not a contradiction.

This paragraph and the next are about any person's position on anything and how they see where they fit on a representative scale from 1 to 100. The basis is something I learned in a PG class on human motivation I took at Case, Western Reserve University many years ago. Any dichotomous subject will work as an example. I have chosen political opinion, even though that is not really dichotomous and would truly apply only to a single factor—you can imagine one for your own satisfaction. Set the scale at 0 for the most extreme conservative, far right wing opinion and 100 for the most extreme liberal or left wing opinion. All opinions in between can then be represented by a number from 2 to 99. The theory, as explained by our professor, is that regardless of where you are in this spectrum, most individuals will view anyone 10 points or more lower as extremists of the right and those 10 points or more higher as extremists of the left. An individual at 50 would view all of those below 40 as extremists on the right and all of those above 60 as extremists of the left. That would mean that all of those from 40 to 60 would be considered slightly to the left, or right, or middle of the road. It would also mean that those at 80 would see 70 to 90 as the deciding limits while those at 20 would see 10 to 30 as the same limits.

This could generate a conundrum where an individual on the left at say, 90, would view another individual on the left at 70 as a right wing extremist. The individual range of 10 is arbitrarily chosen and might vary from 5 points to 50 points. Still, this basic, very simple explanation of where one can be placed on any such scale would hold true. I hope the reader will keep this in mind. The truth of the matter is that human concepts and behavior are never truly dichotomous even though we tend to treat them as such, a very simplistic action. In truth they range all over the map in three, or possibly even more dimensions. They are not black or white, but many shades of grey, and colors, and intensities, and variations in time—in short, they are extremely complex. Human behavior is individualistic and unimaginably complex Any group, even a harmoniously behaving one, can have individuals that behave and believe differently even when the group is labeled indicating solidarity to a cause or belief.

My political beliefs are based primarily on logical thought processes and the realities of the world in which we live. I realize that human emotions are instinctive and control us more than we care to admit, yours truly included. My effort at not judging emotionally automatically puts me at odds with the almost completely emotional and irrational extremes of both left and right. It seems that feelings determine the political ideology of all extremists, on the left, the right, and in fact, all directions. Their reactions are almost without logical or rational content. But it is not a dichotomy as there are countless variations of almost infinite kinds. I am most definitely not a centrist, but would be called liberal in some ways, conservative in others, in between in still others, and undefinable in most. Part of this was written in response to one very thoughtful person who not only took issue with what I said, but wrote me several paragraphs of her thoughts. In among mostly thoughtful commentaries, she accused me of being a white Caucasian male who thought that made me superior or something like that. She also said she was proud that we had finally elected our first non Caucasian President. My response is several paragraphs down in this blog.

Dictionary Definitions of a few terms often misunderstood, for those who say, "whatever that means."

Leftist - 1: one who espouses the principles and views of the political left; also: the movement embodying these principles 2: an advocate of or adherent to the doctrines of the left— left·ist noun or adjective

Examples of leftist - [the candidate's opponents are working overtime to paint him as an extreme leftist.]

First Known Use of leftist - 1920

Liberal - 1 a: of, relating to, or based on the liberal arts [liberal education] b archaic: of or befitting a man of free birth 2 a: marked by generosity: openhanded [a liberal giver] b: given or provided in a generous and openhanded way [a liberal meal] c: ample, full 3 obsolete: lacking moral restraint: licentious (NOTE: that meaning seems to have reemerged) 4: not literal or strict: loose [a liberal translation] 5: broad-minded; especially: not bound by authoritarianism, orthodoxy, or traditional forms 6 a: of, favoring, or based upon the principles of liberalism b capitalized: of or constituting a political party advocating or associated with the principles of political liberalism; especially: of or constituting a political party in the United Kingdom associated with ideals of individual especially economic freedom, greater individual participation in government, and constitutional, political, and administrative reforms designed to secure these objectives.

In common use today, liberal has become a virtual subset of leftist.

Examples of liberal - [She is a liberal Democrat who married a conservative Republican.]

[She has a liberal attitude toward sex.]

Personal: I consider myself to be a very liberal person, but certainly not in the modern political meaning of the word. which has almost become an oxymoron.

Origin of liberal - Middle English, from Anglo-French, from Latin liberalis suitable for a freeman, generous, from liber free; perhaps akin to Old English leodan to grow, Greek eleutheros free

First Known Use: 14th century

Common usage: in common use there is little difference between leftism, liberalism, communism, socialism, fascism or feudalism. They are all totalitarian systems where a very small number of individuals have power over the masses of common people in a nation or state. Most of such countries are full dictatorships with a single powerful person in complete charge. Some of these countries are dictatorship by a group who are all beholden to a single individual or ideology. Where it is an ideology that rules, there is usually a single charismatic leader, "the meanest son-of-a-bitch in the valley," who rules with an iron fist. Currently, virtually all Islamic nations have this type of rule, the ruling class being either chosen by religious leaders or the leaders themselves. In all of these states, there is very little the masses can say or do about their government. All they can do is endure what happens to them.

Conservative - 1 preservative 2 a: of or relating to a philosophy of conservatism b capitalized: of or constituting a political party professing the principles of conservatism: as (1): of or constituting a party of the United Kingdom advocating support of established institutions (2): progressive conservative 3 a: tending or disposed to maintain existing views, conditions, or institutions: traditional b: marked by moderation or caution [a conservative estimate] c: marked by or relating to traditional norms of taste, elegance, style, or manners 4: of, relating to, or practicing Conservative religion of any kind.

Examples of conservative:

She is a liberal Democrat who married a conservative Republican.

She's more conservative now than she was in college.

First Known Use: 14th century

Racism - 1: a belief that race is the primary determinant of human traits and capacities and that racial differences produce an inherent superiority of a particular race 2: racial prejudice or discrimination.

Examples of racism - the racism that was the basis of apartheid [Hitler's declaration of his belief in a "master race" was an indication of the inherent racism of the Nazi movement.]

First Known Use: 1933

Republic - a (1): a government having a chief of state who is not a monarch and who in modern times is usually a president (2): a political unit (as a nation) having such a form of government b (1): a government in which supreme power resides in a body of citizens entitled to vote and is exercised by elected officers and representatives responsible to them and governing according to law (2): a political unit (as a nation) having such a form of government c: a usually specified republican government of a political unit [the French Fourth Republic]

2: a body of persons freely engaged in a specified activity [the republic of letters] 3: a constituent political and territorial unit of the former nations of Czechoslovakia, the Union of Soviet Socialist Republics, or Yugoslavia

Examples of republic - [when asked by a passerby what sort of government the constitutional convention had formulated for the new nation, Benjamin Franklin memorably replied, "A republic, if you can keep it"]

Origin of republic - French république, from Middle French republique, from Latin respublica, from res thing, wealth + publica, feminine of publicus public — more at real, public

First Known Use: 1604

Idiot - 1 usually offensive: a person affected with extreme mental retardation, mental age of less than 3 years 2: a foolish or stupid person

Examples of Idiot - Don't be such an idiot! [only an idiot would invest in a company just because a casual acquaintance recommended it] [Seeing the universally destructive effects of liberal Democrat policies combined with ruthless union power (example, Detroit, California, etc.) only an idiot, or one completely consumed with hatred for those more successful than they would vote Democrat.]

Origin of idiot - Middle English, from Anglo-French *ydiote*, from Latin *idiota* ignorant person, from Greek *idiotes* one in a private station, layman, ignorant person, from *idios* one's own, private; akin to Latin *suus* one's own — more at suicide

First Known Use: 14th century

NOTE: I am supplying the next three paragraphs to clarify common terms used in my writing and to hopefully remove any and all personal references..

I frequently use the terms liberal and leftist in my blogs. That is not an individual charge aimed at a single person, family or group, but a general classification of those active in movements generally described as liberal, progressive, socialist, communist, unionist, or even Democrat. I know there are a few differences, but these terms are all lumped by me into the group term liberals or leftists. There are many of these groups in the present USA. They include: many of those who hold office, most of the civil servants and bureaucrats who populate our government, and those who directly and indirectly support their efforts such as most of the media and entertainment world. They are generally defined as those who see more government as the answer to virtually every problem, real or imagined. The phrase, "The government should do something about this." is one of their favorite utterances. They seem to overtly despise and speak out disproportionally against anything private including corporations, capitalism, free enterprise, profits, management, conservatives, and the wealthy, often abusing the words fair and fairness in their diatribes. To them, those words apply strictly to laws, ideas, and people that promote liberalism. (Whatever that means) Of course, they clearly exempt from their wrath those wealthy individuals who support their agenda no matter how they accumulated their wealth. They often express contempt for our Constitution and seek to circumvent its limitations on government that our founding fathers designed specifically to protect the people from any intrusive and dictatorial government. Though they claim to be champions of the poor and downtrodden, they actually use the ignorance of these people as tools to obtain power and gain wealth for the select few elitists that make up their ruling class. The leaders of this ruling class can often be identified by their lavish lifestyles, at taxpayer expense, and currently, their constant and liberal use of the labels, racist and racism, cast at their opposition at every opportunity. Their flagrant use of these terms along with other hate speech and negative campaigning with no noticeable rationale, are the hallmarks of virtually every liberal in or outside of any political campaign. Although the left constantly accuses conservative standard bearers of hate speech, it is they who actually do so. By accusing their opposition of evil actions, of which they are primarily guilty, they seek to disarm any pejorative argument against their own actions. They use a constant stream of true hate speech, ridicule, condemnation, and animosity against any who oppose them in any way. Incidentally, there are a number of Republican politicians that fall into the same ruling class category.

I also use the terms entrepreneurial, enterprising, and American in my blogs, words I consider virtually synonymous.. These terms represent those who work to earn a living and in the process, improve our economy and the lives of all our citizens. They are those who care about the realities of life and of bringing those with less up to a higher standard of living by their own efforts and hard work. They are the ones who have driven the American system of capitalism into the greatest engine to remove poverty of the masses that the world has ever known. They do this by being the only ones who create jobs that add to our gross domestic product, the true wealth of our nation. Notice that I did not use the term conservative. That is because I have issues with some so called conservative principals and the issues they favor. They are those who mostly oppose the efforts and agenda of liberals and leftists, who would have you believe that they should do all of your thinking and planning for you, and decide exactly where and for what your hard earned money should be spent. These genuine and independent people—these real Americans with their can do approach to life, believe that thousands of independent, privately owned and competing entrepreneurs, companies, and even corporations can do a far better job of providing for the welfare of all Americans than a government bureaucracy. Consider the success of the private competitors to the Postal Service, Amtrak, and virtually every other government entity. Not only are the private organizations far more efficient, but they make a profit for their owners who pay substantial amounts of taxes. These taxes are then used to subsidize their inefficient government counterparts. That's not an opinion, but a proven fact. Those not on the left do not need to use derogatory terms similar to racism in describing their opposition as liberals do.

These notes are provided so the reader will understand just who the widely diverse groups are that I am speaking about. If I am ever speaking or directing my words to or at a specific individual or organization, I will identify them as such. So attention family and friends. Any remarks you may consider as less than positive or even nasty are generalities. They are not aimed at you individually, except as you identify yourself as a dedicated member of whatever subject groups I am referring to.

I am an active member of a discussion group called the Socrates Club whose members meet every Monday afternoon for about three hours to discuss subjects we select at the start of each meeting. They are almost all seniors from many walks of life from mostly retired professors and other educators to a truck driver, a restauranteur/artist, a couple of local politicians and one lonely engineer/writer/business person, me. We have some often emotional discussions and our moderator tries to restrain anger and contentious exchanges. Among the group, I am the recognized authority on matters of energy, hard science, global warming, and business. They have also learned that I carry with me, the latest printouts from the CBO and other revenue information sources that describe what our government receives as revenue, and what is going out as expenditures. I also carry a complete breakdown of our manufacturing, imports, exports, and consumption of goods and services. As a result, the mostly leftist group has become very careful about quoting financial statistics. One member routinely chides us for having military goods as far and away our largest export. He once claimed military goods and weapons were almost half of our exports. He quit repeating this completely when I provided government statistics showing the average of the last five years was 1.4% of exports

When the group doesn't believe the statistics I provide, I hand them a printed copy and tell them to look it up for themselves. They have become extremely cautious about trotting out their wild data when they know I may drag out a few government statistics to prove them grossly in error.

Email with Maxine - Nasty to the Left

It is extremely interesting to see who responds to my many email thought provokers, and what they have to say. I can almost always predict what those responses I do get will say and the attitudes they will express by whom the response is from. I am proud to say that most of my progeny offer open-minded, thoughtful responses even when they disagree with me. On the other hand, I get typical knee jerk and often nasty, closed minded responses from left leaning friends and family members. I also receive similar responses from extreme right wing individuals as well, surprise, surprise!. My obvious and valid conclusion is that the mind sets of these individuals are locked in a battle with anyone who doesn't accept their emotional, unthinking, fundamentalist belief system. Logic and rationality are completely overwhelmed with unreasoning animosity toward anyone or anything that doesn't agree with their holy belief system. Yes, I sometimes say harsh things about those I see as the enemies of America. Those who take my words as a personal affront always do so when I say something negative, unkind or damaging about the people or belief systems that determine their political views. I see my commentary as a shotgun effect aimed at a system or idea, not at any individual.

For example: I recently forwarded a little humorous bit using the cartoon character Maxine, to which I added my own commentary along with a few harsh comments. Here's what I said along with one or two of the responses I received.

"My daughter sent me this. I think it's priceless. Of course, all you Obama lovers won't like it because the truth hurts. Oh how he and the other far left idiots love to fill the public bird feeders with other people's feed.

"Oh yeah, That French socialist that got his you know what in the wringer in spite of his $3,000 a night hotel suite and his first class seat on the aircraft? (paid for with other people's money) He would fit right in with the Obama/Clinton leftist crowd in every way. Just a poor, humble servant of the people."

One response, not a family member, but from one who doesn't want to be on my mailing list. (He's gone) I think it is typical of what people of any stripe on the left and that react emotionally would say. You'll see my reaction in my response that follows. What is really interesting is that I received three other responses using almost exactly the same words. A mantra? This is the only one that asked to be removed from my email list. Hmmmmm? His email:

Mr. Johnson,

I'm not really sure how I got on your mailing list, but I think you are part of the writer's group from the COA.

Please do me that great honor of removing me from your just to the right of Adolph Hitler mentality platform of hate and racism wrapped up in the robes of Christianity and pillow case halos mailing list.

Sincerely, George (name changed to protect the guilty)

(A typical intellectual response from the left)

My response: George:

Thank you for your kind and thoughtful words and request. Of course I'll remove your address and place it where it belongs.

I have just one question. Do all of you lefties get your orders and words to use in response to anything that doesn't fit your holy all knowing, all seeing opinions from the same high poobah of liberalism/ socialism/ communism/ fascism/ feudalism? It seems you all use the same mantra of name calling of hate, racism, the religious right, and Hitler in every one of your responses to even the slightest deviation from your accepted language. It rather reminds me of play ground tactics where, lacking anything intelligent or creative to say, all that can be done is cursing (which you cleverly avoided doing) and name calling. (Which is all you did) Why don't you try calling me something original or at least creative like Ghengis Kahn or Beelzebub. Heaven forbid you should utter a logical phrase or observation, or exhibit any sense of humor.

May peace and blessings be yours, Ho

Another angry email sparked by the Maxine email:

I saw this and thought oh good, it is not going to be a mean, insulting email. This is the Ho I remember. I was wrong. It is mean, insulting, and disrespectful. Where are your manners? I am very close to marking your emails as junk.

From a good friend who shall remain nameless.

My response:

Sorry you feel that way. That's just the way the world turns. I'll not bother you any more, but I will share another negative response I received from a member of our writers group. (That's three negative and eight positive responses) Incidentally, this guy, George, hates almost everyone and left our group in snit when someone, not me, read something he didn't like.

I included the above exchange with George, and continued:

Please don't get the idea I see you as in any way similar to George. You most certainly are not. Methinks (I'm certainly not sure) maybe a lot of you folks take life far too seriously. As far as my words are concerned, for me it is a fight for survival. At 83 I am long past being useful to the American youth worshiping culture. I am now fighting for my life. Should almost anything happen to me that costs even a small bit like Barb's health problem, I'm dead meat. Already I have been informed that I am too old for having knee replacements (which I am needing more and more) and receiving any help from medicare. Should Obamacare be put in place, I will not be able to get such surgery, or therapy for my bad back, even if I pay for it myself. Maybe I should just blow my brains out if anything serious comes my way. After all, I'm just using up resources that could better be used on some junkie who is twenty-five.

In spite of all that, I am a deliriously happy person with a great life, a spectacular family, a dear lady who loves me and whom I love, and a passion for writing. Only a very small part of my writing is political. That, of course, is what all the fuss is about. I write about people and about real solutions to real problems. I have many dear friends and am active in a number of senior groups, most of whom at least say they like me and my writing. That includes a number of left leaning yet still open minded individuals. The only downers I know are doom and gloom leftists who have little positive or good to say about anything. I'm sure there are those on the right who fit the same bill, but most of my friends are pretty much leftists.

Enjoy life, it's that brief bright light between two black eternities.

Ho

An angry, accusative email response to the Maxine forward from a family member::

You know what, I don't see this as an Obama loving analogy at all. I don't call you an Obama hater, or an idiot, or any of the other names you throw at, well, your sister for one. I do often think you are downright nasty. But you are my relative.

Another:

Please stop assuming what the 'Obama lovers" "far left idiots" 'the leftist crowd" or whatever [pick your own contemptious name] like, don't want to hear, won't accept, etc. etc. etc.

There is a saying: "when you assume, you make an ass of 'u' [you] and me".

Why do you feel compelled to put this type of commentary/snide remark of this in every one of your rants?

I'll make you a deal-stop belittling and assuming what I or any other "leftist" (whatever that means) thinks or will think about a subject, and I won't call every "conservative" (whatever that means) a "lying Limbaugh suck up".

I love you as family; I can't say I love your style of politics-- the opinions I accept and I might even agree with to some degree (surprise!), however, the manner in which they are presented makes me not want to read them. After all, I've already been told I don't want to hear it.

Just some constructive criticism.

BTW, I like Maxine, thought this was funny too, albeit overly simplistic.

I wonder? If I had said, " Obama supporters" "far left proponents" "the liberal Democrat crowd," would those have prompted the comment, ["pick your own contemptuous name"]? Hmmmm?

The following section was my response to the email of my "unnamed friend."

I included the two emails above because their thoughts and opinions do count with me. My political rants and emails go out to more than 200 email addresses—friends, family, and acquaintances—a widely spread group. Some of the responses I receive from family and friends who are liberal are considerate and well thought out. An equal number (my guess, I didn't count) including some family are far nastier than anything I have ever sent to anyone. I just figure it goes with the territory. Some recipients who take my comments as personal and aimed at them individually, which is most certainly not the case, and who respond in a less than hostile fashion, are added to my special l list. I have been sending them more individualized emails once I note their sensitivity. I have just added the two above to that list.

My dear sister once emailed me a speech delivered in the Senate by Senator Robert Byrd of West Virginia, the runner up to Ted Kennedy in pork barrel vote buying. The speech was a purely emotional, "nasty" diatribe against George Bush, Republicans, and conservatives. It was a much longer version of, DNC chairman Howard Dean's famous angry quip, "I hate Republicans, I hate conservatives, and I hate Rush Limbaugh." In the email she said, "We should all get behind this good man." I couldn't believe she would make such a statement.

I emailed back, "Your good man, Byrd, is a typical political opportunist who obviously loves power and prestige, but cares nothing for anyone but himself. I simply cannot imagine my own sister saying anything good about this petty despot. How could you even think of him as good in any way when he was an active member, and even a grand Dragon, of the Ku Klux Klan for many years. It is my understanding (and I am certainly not an expert on the subject) that in order to hold such an office in the Klan one must have participated in at least one lynching. (Doesn't that make him a murderer?) In speeches and interviews over many years, Byrd described Dr. Martin Luther King, Jr. as, 'one of the most dangerous men in America,' even after King was murdered. In my opinion, Byrd is definitely an evil politician with no redeeming qualities. I am in shock that you would even consider using the word good in association with this poor excuse for a man." In retrospect it seems obvious that my sister and I have very different interpretations of the words good and evil. Apparently, to her, the only thing that counts is that Byrd mounted a hate diatribe against George W. Bush. He is forgiven all manner of evil up to and including murder of innocents just because he spoke the liberal party line. I have a very difficult time understanding how this can be, or how anyone, let alone my sister, could call him a good man..

I never did receive a response. Don't get me wrong. I love my sis and her family. Unfortunately, it is extremely difficult to have a rational discussion of anything remotely associated with politics, even social issues, with almost any of them. Their minds seem to be completely closed, at least to me. I would guess that they will rarely listen, read, discuss, or consider anything that disagrees with the mantras of the left. Facts don't count, logic doesn't count, reality doesn't count, it is pure emotion in control. They seem to view me as some sort of right-wing, fundamentalist Christian, highly opinionated nut-job. I know this because several of them have so described me. In truth, they haven't a clue about who I am, what I believe, or how I relate to others. I have learned to just accept that as a reality and not be concerned about it. Their loss, not mine.

When did I ever say that today's problems were new problems? Hell, Socrates and Aristotle (both Caucasian males) spoke of many of the same problems quite a while back. Modern technology and instant access to information makes them flow through a much larger society infinitely faster. That's most of the difference.

You are right about your generation, my kids and grandkids. We tried to have them not endure the seeming hardships we had encountered as children. We were among the fortunate ones who usually had enough to eat. (My father, a Caucasian male, had planned for the depression) My friends and I regularly searched trash throughout the neighborhood for items we could salvage to play with. My very first (and only) bicycle was a wrecked one I salvaged after someone threw it away. I completely disassembled it and saved money earned from my paper route for several months to buy parts to repair it. When I finally got it put together, I was the proud owner of a new bike. Over several years I completely repainted it (purple), put new chrome fenders on it, and was finally able to replace the worn and patched tires. I used that bike on my paper route and as transportation until I graduated from high school in 1945. I sold it for $15 just before I enlisted in the Navy. It would be almost thirty years later, 1975, when I bought my first really new bike.

I knew I had a very good life, even then. I was incredibly happy and optimistic even though I knew I was going to die in the coming invasion of Japan. Then they dropped the bomb and the war was over. Thank you Harry S. and all your helpers! The anti bomb people won't acknowledge that had it not been for that bomb, the invasion of Japan would have taken the lives of probably millions of Japanese and maybe even that many young Americans. No, those are not the facts, but a very reasonable estimate of the probable casualties. Incidentally, the one major firebombing of Tokyo took almost twice as many lives as the bombing of Hiroshima and Nagasaki put together, as did the saturation bombing of several German cities. War is indeed hell.

I don't give a damn what race, ethnicity, or other physical qualities our President has. He or she could be a purple vegetarian homosexual as far as I am concerned. What is important to me is that he or she:

1) respect and obey our laws and constitution.

2) consider that he or she and his or her cabinet are supposed to serve ALL the people.

3) believe in American exceptionalism, brought about by our unusual entrpreneurial spirit.

4) be an honorable and honest individual.

5) understand the basics of math, physics, business, political and religious freedom and true American capitalism.

As far as I am concerned, our current President (who is actually 15/16 Caucasian believe it or not. Arabs are part of the Caucasian race.) misses on all counts as did the previous Democrat President (a Caucasian male) and his (so called) wife. I can't think of any President in my lifetime, Democrat or Republican, who didn't miss on at least two of those. Except for the latest, they were all Caucasian males. In reality, he is just 1/16th Black African. If so, how can he be considered to be a black President?

I think you make a serious mistake in equating the recognition of the stating of a real problem and trying to find a solution with simple prophecies of doom and gloom. Who are all those people shouting doom and gloom anyway??? The first and most important rule of problem solving is to be able to recognize a problem and state it clearly. This I learned in my first year of engineering school. Once a problem is clearly stated, it almost defines a solution. Another rule is, "As long as you keep doing what you have been doing, you will get the results you have been getting." Another is, "Use logic and rational processes to solve problems, and use emotions to make love." Those words make sense to me.

The Prentis/Tyler quotes will be referred to numerous times in this book:

A prediction of where we seem to be headed may have come from far back in history, when the 13 colonies were still part of England. The first quote is often attributed to a Scottish Historian, Alexander Tytler or Tyler. (a Caucasian male) The true origin of the quote is obscure and might actually have originated in the early 20th century from an unknown politician or writer. Nevertheless, this does not detract from its accuracy.

One version of this quote on why democracies always fail and a near exact description of what is happening in our country right now, is:

"A Democracy cannot exist as a permanent form of government. It can only last until the citizens discover they can vote themselves largess out of the public treasury. After that, the majority always votes for the candidate promising the most benefits from the public treasury with the result that the democracy always collapses over a loose fiscal policy, to be followed by a dictatorship, and then a monarchy." He was referring specifically of the Athenian democracy.

The actual author of the second quote, that is frequently included with the first as a part of a single quote, is Henning Webb Prentis, Jr., President of the Armstrong Cork Company. In a speech entitled, *Industrial Management in a Republic*, delivered in the grand ballroom of the Waldorf Astoria at New York during the 250th meeting of the National Conference Board on

March 18, 1943, and recorded on page 22 of Industrial Management in a Republic, Prentis (a Caucasian male) had this to say:

"Paradoxically enough, the release of initiative and enterprise made possible by popular self-government ultimately generates disintegrating forces from within. Again and again after freedom has brought opportunity and some degree of plenty, the competent become selfish, luxury-loving and complacent, the incompetent and the unfortunate grow envious and covetous, and all three groups turn aside from the hard road of freedom to worship the Golden Calf of economic security. The historical cycle seems to be: From bondage to spiritual faith; from spiritual faith to courage; from courage to liberty; from liberty to abundance; from abundance to selfishness; from selfishness to apathy; from apathy to dependency; and from dependency back to bondage once more.

"At the stage between apathy and dependency, men always turn in fear to economic and political panaceas. New conditions, it is claimed, require new remedies. Under such circumstances, the competent citizen is certainly not a fool if he insists upon using the compass of history when forced to sail uncharted seas. Usually so-called new remedies are not new at all. Compulsory planned economy, for example, was tried by the Chinese (not Caucasians, but male) some three millenniums ago, and by the Romans in the early centuries of the Christian era. It was applied in Germany, Italy and Russia long before the present war broke out. Yet it is being seriously advocated today as a solution of our economic problems in the United States. Its proponents confidently assert that government can successfully plan and control all major business activity in the nation, and still not interfere with our political freedom and our hard-won civil and religious liberties. The lessons of history all point in exactly the reverse direction."

These are the real malignancies we must overcome if we are to solve the rapidly growing problems, facing not just the US, but the entire world. The ultimate collapse of America will be death and destruction of unprecedented magnitude unless we reverse course soon. (Please note I did give us a way out.)

You said, "Your doom and gloom emails sound just like an episode of Glen Beck. We will solve our problems. It won't be easy. But we won't be rioting and under total chaos."

That sounds a lot like what many were saying right before the Civil War. Those so saying were dead wrong. We can chalk it all up to "Doom and Gloom," sit and watch TV, or we can try to do something about it. I don't listen to Glenn Beck (a Caucasian male) since he is a problem user, not solver. The media and the entertainment world also are almost exclusively problem users, not solvers. Politicians fall into the same category. I spent ten years writing a book about solutions to our increasing energy problems. I have written extensively about solutions, real and practical solutions, to many of our other problems. That is not doom and gloom, it is an effort to change things for the better. However, I am just one small voice in a sea of far more powerful voices. Still, I keep trying. It is unfortunate that you seem to join the multitude who see realistic observations only as expressions of doom and gloom, rather than efforts to recognize problems and do something positive about them. Do you think being a Caucasian male disqualifies one from being a fair-thinking, responsible member of society?

I concentrated on energy first because absolutely nothing happens without cheap and plentiful energy, and because my education and experience provided much knowledge in the field. As the cost of energy rises so does the cost of everything we call the necessities of life. This includes food, housing, transport, clothing, everything we use and/or consume, even health care. Everything has an energy cost. The standard of living anywhere in the world is almost completely dependent on the cost and availability of one or more forms of energy. There are but two ways to lower the cost of energy to the individual citizen, company, state, or nation. The two are: reduction of use, or reduction of price. Conservation, the reduction of use, is an effort with diminishing results. It can only do so much. No matter how hard you try, there is a limit to how low energy use at any cost can be to keep a house in northern Minnesota warm enough to sustain life. That limit appears to be about half the usual cost. Halving the cost of energy would achieve the same goal. If energy cost were cut to a third, it would exceed that goal. Of course, by using both, the cost to heat that home would be a small fraction, one sixth, of the original cost. That could be expanded to include every use of energy. My book, Energy. Convenient Solutions, has already received some great reviews in newspapers.

Here's one of my descriptions of the book: The author says, "We can replace all fossil fuels with renewable fuels and alternative energy sources within ten years and with only minor disruptions to present manufacturing and distribution systems." He goes on to say, "This book describes most of the existing energy systems and some proposed new ones, all within current technology and present capabilities. Some of these proposed systems are quite unusual and some are very recently announced. It provides many unique and surprisingly workable, long-term answers to the many growing concerns about energy, the economy, and dwindling supplies of petroleum. Adopting these new systems would improve our balance of trade, our economy, our job opportunities, and our technological presence while eliminating the CO2 problem whether it is real or not. The point has been reached where we no longer have the luxury of time. The growing economic menace is here, now, real, and dangerous. If we don't act immediately, the consequences could be catastrophic."

Just because I point out dangers, is not doom and gloom even if the naysayers report that it is. I don't see very many news reports of solvers working on our problems. That's probably because solvers don't make the news, while problem users do. What we really need now are problem solvers and solutions, not problem users.

And why make the point about Caucasian males? I can understand it about British males, German males, and maybe even Scandinavian males, but ALL Caucasian males? Isn't that just a tiny bit of racial bigotry? Notice I didn't include American males because they come in all colors. [grin]

Oh yes, me grumpy? Most people who know me, including those who regularly read my blogs, even the far left contingent, say that I am one of the happiest people they know. Even at 83 with bad knees, a terrible back, lousy balance and hearing, and declining short term memory,

I'm almost disgustingly happy---like a pig up to his middle in mud. Daphne certainly doesn't think I'm grumpy. Barb didn't either. Both were and are really bright lights in my life.

Barb and I certainly enjoyed those last few years together, in spite of all of her health problems. I always wanted her to be the same happy healthy vivacious lady she was during the first ten years of our marriage, but that was not to be. Still, through all of her illness I was very pleased to be able to take care of her. I learned a lot about myself that I liked during those last few years. Either one of us could have become grumpy and made life miserable for the other, but we didn't. We chose to be happy. So I intend to continue to skip joyfully through life, unfazed, or so it may seem, by pain and tragedy around me, yet still affected and offering comfort to those who need it, when they need it.

I like Kipling's poem, If, as well as some of the writings of Elizabeth Barrett Browning, Coleridge and many others of that era. I also like the philosophy of Eric Hoffer - the thoughts of E. O. Wilson - the books of Jared Diamond, Stephen J. Gould, Robert Heinlein, and Leonard Susskind - Nigel Calder's Magic Universe - and many others no one has ever heard of like Sophie Burnham and Anne Lamont. (not all Caucasian males) These are merely examples of a much larger set of similarly different thoughts and ideas by many very different writers. There are many quotes of these and others in my book, Memoirs from the Lakeside.

I devour the magazines, Scientific American, National Geographic, Smithsonian, and Astronomy, reading them from cover to cover. I'm certain that each of you reading this have your own sets of information sources that you value.

Maybe from your standpoint, people who are happy, are actually grumpy and trying to fool people.

My God have I ever wandered about. That's because I love communicating with a person who thinks. As you can tell, I have a tendency to ramble on and on. So keep on challenging me. It will make me. and I hope you, a better member of the human race.

I am so very pleased that so many people take the time from their busy day to respond to my ravings. Just remember, writing is what I do, it is my passion, other than family and friends. I may not always be accurate, I may not always even be lucid, but still I write what is on my mind. My goal is to jolt minds, to get people to think. I'll close with another of my favorite quotes. This one is from George Elliott:

"Oh, the comfort, the inexpressible comfort of feeling safe with a person; having neither to weigh thoughts nor measure words, but to pour them all out, just as they are, chaff and grain together, knowing that a faithful hand will take and sift them, keep what is worth keeping, and then, with the breath of kindness, blow the rest away."

Just a few treasured people fill that bill.

Some facts, opinions, and some wild guesses. You'll have to decide which.

To all of you left leaning souls, even you well meaning ones. I hear in your words echos of the emotionally powerful propaganda of the left that is being promoted by the entire entertainment world including the news media along with leftist politicians. Some of it is very subtle, some quite blatant. I am old enough to have heard many of the same old ideas in the speeches of Eugene V. Debs and Earl Browder, some nearly a century old. You may never have heard of them, but they were the leaders of the communist/socialist party in the twenties, thirties and forties. I believe it was Debs who ran for President several times in the early 20th century as a socialist/communist. Browder was the head of the American communist party and a union organizer for many years. Capitalizing on the depression, he talked about and promoted much the same old disproved socialist promises that the left promotes today. He hated capitalism, business and the wealthy. Those wealthy who espoused socialism/communism were, of course, exempted from his vitriolic speeches. He was a union thug and organizer. During the depression he came a lot closer to leading a Communist takeover of our government than most people will admit. Today he would fit right in with the liberal Democrats and their union cohorts. The last I heard of him was when he was interviewed about the American communist party by Mike Wallace in 1957.

Karl Marx wrote that a prosperous middle class was the biggest deterrent to communism and in effect, that the reduction of the middle class from independence to near poverty was a necessary part of any communist revolution. He also wrote, "Without violence nothing is ever accomplished in history." Marx hated Russia and the Russians. Many people forget that.

A personal experience: Honest curiosity brought me to attend a rally of mostly blacks in the mid sixties outside Western Reserve University. The rally spilled over Euclid Avenue and completely blocked that main Cleveland Street for several hours. There were a number of socialist/communist groups that organized the rally that almost broke out into a race riot. In the midst of the crowd, I found myself very close to one young black speaker who electrified the crowd when he said the following, "There are bottles of cyanide in the school chemistry labs. Just over that hill (pointing south) sits the Baldwin reservoir. (The main water supply for the all white eastern suburbs of Cleveland) It would be unfortunate for a lot of white people if that cyanide found its way into the water in that reservoir." That young man, who I had never heard of before, was the reverend Jessie Jackson. He had come from Chicago to speak at the rally. Now, I ask you, who is a racist? Incidentally, after that comment, I worked my way out of the crowd and headed for home, scared as hell. After I left, a number of white students from Case (now part of Case, Western Reserve University) were beaten badly.

I am a supporter of American capitalism, not the laissez faire or social capitalism of Europe. As such, I consider socialism as a great evil and enemy of the people. From this standpoint, and observing the goings on in our nation for many years, I have made a number of predictions that have been amazingly accurate. I don't know, but I may have sent you a copy of some of my recent predictions. On the non political side (yes, I do a lot of non political thinking and writing. I don't politicize things one tenth as much as liberals and the media do), I quite accurately predicted the dot com bust at least a year before it happened. I also predicted the mortgage melt down several years before it happened. In that prediction I wrote why it would happen and who was responsible. George W. Bush and Dick Cheney were severely criticized and called racists by the left when they tried to stop or prevent this debacle. And just who benefitted the most financially from these destructive efforts? Chris Dodd, Barney Frank and a new Senator from Illinois named Obama. I also predicted Obama's stunning victory and the Democrat sweep of Congress even before he was nominated. I also predicted the insurmountable debt crisis we are now facing including a fairly accurate guess of both the lingering unemployment (which is actually around 14%-15% if figured the way it always was before the Obama era and the changes his administration made in how unemployment is estimated.) and the actual increase in the national debt. My figures for both 2010 and 2011 were about double the CBO estimates. (I was right, they were wrong) All of those predictions are documented. Several from our family, and quite a few of my liberal friends ridiculed every one of my predictions when they were made saying nothing like that would happen. They were, of course, dead wrong, but will never admit it. How were my predictions so accurate? Plain old common sense and a little basic math.

One thing you will never hear from the highly biased news media is what happened to middle America as a result of the mortgage crisis. Middle class Americans lost almost half of the total value of their homes. Many lost them completely to foreclosure. This was the largest transfer of wealth from individuals to banks/government that has ever occurred. In spite of being devastated, America's middle class mostly survived financially. The actions of government officials, liberal governmentalists I call them, could not possibly have been accidental. No one could be that stupid. It is my contention that this was a deliberate effort, orchestrated by leftists in our government, within Fanny Mae and Freddie Mac, to destroy our middle class. In fact, every action taken by liberal Democrats since they took control in 2008 has been aimed at the economic destruction of our country. Obama used trickle down help in the mortgage crisis. Instead of providing mortgage help to middle Americans and small banks, he gave huge banks. Those "too big to fail" billions while middle class Americans and small banks were actually betrayed and defrauded. It would have been far less expensive to provide financial help "from the bottom up" by providing equalizing funds to hundreds of thousands of individuals with guarantees from small banks. Instead, Obama chose to reward his financial supporters in the huge banks on Wall Street, and especially Goldman-Sachs. Did you notice how many Goldman-Sachs executives ended up in his cabinet or among his many Czars?

Several respondents to my predictions said about possible food riots I predicted could happen said clearly, "It can't happen here:" I don't recall if any of those were from our family or not. When the IMF, supported by the five nations of China, Russia, India, Japan, and Brazil, replace the dollar as the world reserve currency, there are many really bad things that could and probably will happen in our country. That time is not far away. I believe the IMF will try to hold off until after the next Presidential election, but they might not be able to do that. This will certainly be the case if we don't reduce government spending drastically and soon. What would the change of the reserve currency away from the dollar mean to Americans? First of all it will mean our government can no longer print money to pay our debts. What will that mean? Probably runaway inflation, rapidly declining paper assets and a government unable to meet its financial obligations. The serious problems will start when the government defaults, not on major debts, but when they can no longer make good on things like food stamps, medical bills, and payments of many types to individuals. How long do you think the millions of folks on food stamps will stay peaceful and quiet when grocers will no longer accept them for payment? What about when your credit card is suddenly unacceptable. How about when no one will cash your Social Security check? Is this a certainty? No. Is it a possibility? Definitely. How probable is it? I certainly don't know, but I'll guarantee it is a much greater probability than the left and their media buddies would even breathe about. They don't want you to know. I know you'll believe whatever suits you about that, but time will indeed tell.

"It can't happen here." is exactly what the folks in Iceland and Greece said. That's what the folks in all of the other at risk nations like France, Portugal, Spain, and even Italy are saying right now, "It can't happen here." Don't bet on it. What can we do to stop it? An immediate reduction by 20% of all federal government payments would be a good place to start. You wouldn't know it, but Social Security payments have already been cut as much as 25%. That was accomplished by Bill Clinton and his Democrat Congress his first year in office. I'll bet you didn't know that. I'll bet you didn't know that Medicare has also been cut almost 30% over the last fifteen years. Welfare payments and health care for illegals has not been cut, but has been expanding during the same period. The details are a bit hard to explain. But they are all there in the federal budget reports if you care to dig for them. That's all part of Democrat vote buying. No, I don't think they are the only ones to blame, but it is almost exclusively their vote buying with taxpayer money that is the cause of our fiscal woes. Three minus four is not one, it's negative one. Democrats don't seem capable of understanding that. They also seem to believe that you can borrow yourself out of debt. That is not remotely rational.

Back to the world according to Obama: As far as I am concerned, we now have the most racist President and administration we have ever had, certainly since just a few years after the civil war. (When millions of Caucasian males died in a war to free their black brothers from slavery) In virtually every political discussion we have, Democrats bring up race as an issue. One example of many clearly racist actions by the Obama administration even reported by the media (since silenced) can be viewed at this site:

http://opntalk.blogspot.com/2011/03/holder-will-not-investigate-his-people.html

There are numerous other examples including one in Ft Wayne in which my friend and neighbor at the lake (a Democrat politician) was involved. Without going into details, it involved six black men, members of ACORN, who used the mortgage system to scam local banks out of several hundred million bucks. They were caught and jailed for a while, but then, all charges were dropped. Can you believe it? As far as I can find out, all the records of this little escapade in Fort Wayne, including newspaper accounts, have mysteriously disappeared. Of course, I'm one of those ignorant people who sees racism as going more ways than one. (Are Latinos or Chinese racists as well?) I'm not accusing anyone, I would just like a little objective clarification.

The debt ceiling is a stupid joke unless we don't raise it. What is the possible purpose of having a debt ceiling if every time you run out of money you simply raise the debt ceiling. If we have the good sense to stick to the ridiculously high debt ceiling as it is, the message to the world and our creditors will be that we are finally doing something about our runaway spending. Another thing we could do to lower the deficit would be to immediately cut all federal government payrolls by

20%. We could use a minimum federal wage (sound familiar) for those low on the pay scale and start a graduated scale of reductions at say $50,000 per year. Then at $200,000 we could up the reduction to 40%. It would do little good to include Congress since they get most of their wealth under the table from lobbyists, the public pork barrel trough, or ear marks. Incidently, did you remember Obama's promise to get rid of earmarks? Yes he did promise that along with thousands of other things he has since reneged on. There have been more earmarks pushed through since the Democrats took power in 2008 than in any similar period in our history. It's kinda like his promises to close Gitmo, end the wars in Iraq and Afghanistan and bring our troops home. But . . . he means well.

Oh yes, the Tea Party. I've been to two of their rallies here in Florida. I have also been to several anti-war rallies organized by the left during the Bush Presidency. There is an obvious and palpable difference between the two groups. Yes there were a few hate based signs at both Tea Party rallies, but not a hundredth as many as at the anti-war rallies. At the so called "peace" rallies, there were many race based signs (read anti white) that had nothing to do with war. I know there are bound to be a few really angry nut cases at any large political rally of any color. Still, there were huge differences in the behavior of those two groups. First of all, there was a great deal of obscenity and even violence at the peace rallies. At one rally, a small group carrying a tasteful banner disagreeing with the premise of the march were attacked by a group of thugs with sticks and beaten quite badly before police arrived to rescue them. Several were bloody and had to be hauled away in ambulances while the crowd around them shouted obscenities as I watched from a relatively safe distance. Some pro peace group that was. After the rally the parks where the rallies were held were cluttered with substantial amounts of trash including all of the signs they had been carrying. Incidentally, the Washington marches produced similar trash records.

In stark contrast, the only violence at either of the tea Party rallies was when a group of Obama supporters rushed one part of the rally crowd and destroyed a banner objecting to Obama's health care plan. Also, the Tea Partiers picked up and carried away all of their trash leaving the site as clean or cleaner than before the rally. I saw no signs that could remotely be considered racist. Of course, Democrats will shout racism at even honest criticism of any non white individual.

I'm sorry, but I just can't stand by silently and watch the system and Constitution that provided the highest standard of living for the most of its citizens be destroyed by a petty, self-serving, would be dictator and his cadre of dedicated and radical progressives who are actually socialist/communist/fascist/feudal elitists who hate America.

By the way, I am still recommending people stash a supply of well preserved food, and maybe invest in some non paper hard assets like gold or silver coins in case paper money goes the way it did for the Weimar republic and many other countries that over spent reality.

I once had in my possession a transcript of a letter written by a Virginian named Jessie Rueben Johnson who wrote about the coming civil war in the 1850s, "I pray it never happens, but I fear it will." The letter was mostly an accounting of his property, famly background, and imprisonment during the Civil War. He was a wealthy owner of several hundred acres of prime farmland, a livery stable, a drugstore, and a tavern. He had added considerably to tracts of land passed down through family from the around 1600 when they were given land grants in the Virginia colony by queen Elizabeth. Unfortunately he was one who on principal, supported the North, Lincoln, and abolition, unlike most of his neighbors. He had all of his considerable property in Virginia stolen—titles transferred to neighbors—while he sat in a Virginia jail as a political prisoner until the end of the war. He stayed behind to protect his property after helping his family move north to escape the war he was certain would come. He was dragged out of his home and put in prison for four or five years. He was lucky he was not murdered as several of his friends were. After the war he and his entire remaining family but for two sons who died fighting for the Union, moved west and settled in Indiana. Virtually all of the family's possessions were lost. They were very poor, but were granted land in Indiana as a reward for the two boys that died while serving in the union army.

This all came to light when I was in my twenties and my father and I met with A Dr. Lorand V. Johnson who sold us a huge book about the Johnsons of Virginia. I have no idea what happened to that book or to the large folder of records, letters, and other papers that went with it. Maybe Lois's family has it or possibly it just got lost or misplaced. According to my dad who found his family listed in the book, and the papers in that folder, that Jessie Johnson was my great grandfather. I have no viable proof, of course, but I would certainly like to get my hands on that book and the papers that were in that folder.

Ho

Tuesday, May 10, 2011 - Posted by HoJo at 10:58 PM

America's Giving Heart

Some time back I blogged about how our friends in the European news media had castigated America for being so stingy with relief for the tsunami that devastated Indonesia. They pointed out that the American government was fourth or fifth largest financial contributor to that relief effort. That is true, but what they neglected mentioning (deliberately, I am sure), was that Americas private giving totaled more than all of the worlds governments combined. Private Americans and American businesses provided more then half of the total relief effort. Also note that Indonesia is a Muslim nation.

Well, we did it again. From the e-news, Real News and Views comes another story you will not read in the New York Times or other government controlled media—or is it the reverse—media controlled government? Who knows?

May 10, 2011 - **Real News and Views**, a direct quote:

The recent earthquake and tsunami in Japan have created a tragic humanitarian crisis. Thousands of homes, businesses and lives have been destroyed. The situation at the Fukushima nuclear power plant remains uncertain. Our thoughts and prayers are certainly with the Japanese people in the midst of this terrible tragedy.

Yet, as with most major natural disasters in our time, the tragedy in Japan has once again showcased the amazing generosity of the American people. As aid pours into Japan from around the world, the United States, in keeping with her magnanimous spirit, has led the way.

So far, USAID and the Department of Defense have spent a combined $32,251,844, which includes sending two professional urban search and rescue teams maintained by the counties of Fairfax, Virginia and Los Angeles, California. The U.S. military immediately dispatched the aircraft carrier Ronald Reagan to Japan, along with other ships, to assist in relief efforts.

However, private donations to relief efforts from Americans already stand at $161 million or FIVE TIMES AS MUCH as public money - including millions of dollars from U.S. corporations such as Goldman Sachs, J.P. Morgan, Walt Disney, and FedEx.

America's generosity arises not only from the faith and altruistic spirit of her people, but also from the fact that Americans have the means and the freedom to be generous. The means is a direct result of America's capitalist economic system that allows for free enterprise, competition, and the creation of wealth, which gives Americans the freedom to give generously to others out of their discretionary funds. While some seek to denigrate wealth creation or tax business into oblivion, it is evident that America - her businesses and citizens - are abundantly generous to people facing crisis and disaster, precisely because they have both the heart and the ability to do so!

In the midst of this disaster we have an opportunity to reflect on America's exceptional spirit, character, and people. Because America was founded on the principle that each person possesses a God-given dignity, her people are always quick to come to the aid of others in their time of need. The American people have always exhibited a great spirit of generosity and concern for the downtrodden, as exemplified now in their outpouring of aid and support to Japan and others at home and around the world. It is in times like these that we should all be particularly proud to be Americans.

End of quote.

I realize governmentalists would prefer to take private money by force and use it as they see fit rather than have the American people contribute directly to the needs and charities of their choice. That's just who you are and what you do; small minded people who are always condemning, but never creating; using problems to build your power, but never solving anything; cursing and calling derogatory names any who oppose your power, but never offering any corrective, constructive ideas. Because you are completely void of any creative, constructive, or realistic ideas, all you can do is label those you oppose with rancid hatred. Your latest idea is to label as racists, anyone and everyone who raises any objections to your lust for power. It's a cheap shot from mindless boobs who, in truth, are the real racists of America.

I'll say one thing for you. You really know how to destroy. You have already virtually destroyed America's education system, America's inner cities (like Detroit), America's middle class (the mortgage melt down), America's once vibrant economy, and much of America's manufacturing. Right now you are doing everything you can to destroy American free enterprise, discredit American exceptionalism, and move wealth from the middle classes to the most wealthy and elite individuals. (The easier to control it my dear.)

I have news for you idiots. True American exceptionalism, free enterprise genius, and fierce work ethic may just be more than you can handle. Just remember, you may bankrupt the government, but America's wealth still lies in the hands of individuals, and I'll wager not even you will be able to change that, not even with your corrupt judges, government bureaucrats, invincible bureaucracy, union thugs, and black militants. There is one single and powerful entity that stands in your way in spite of your efforts to minimize it. That happens to be the US Military. There is another group of real Americans that is growing in numbers and power in spite of all your ridicule and pointed hate speech. That group is the Tea Party. I rest my case. Just once you should try building instead of destroying. I realize just how much harder it is to design and build rather than curse, vilify, and destroy. You're probably just not up to the effort.

Friday, April 01, 2011 - Posted by HoJo at 1:42 PM

Money in politics, The Koch brothers and George Soros

This preamble to the current BLOG points to how political power is for sale.

A review of: The Next Decade: Where We've Been . . . and Where We're Going

by George Friedman

George Friedman is widely respected political scientist and scholar; still one can respect Friedman without necessarily agreeing with him. This review is included to illustrate the rapidly changing economic and related information technologies that are driving what we call globalization.

The review:

In this book, his basic premise that the 21st Century U.S. is an imperial power in the manner of the Roman Empire and British Empire is simply wrong by any rational standards. The Roman Empire, at its height, was a centrally administered political entity in which imperial officials governed subject provinces, provincial subjects paid taxes and served in the Roman army, and the Roman Army (Cohorts and Legions) were stationed throughout the empire to protect imperial frontiers and maintain internal security. The Roman Empire was a discernable political entity with clear lines of authority between rulers and ruled. The British Empire was a centrally administered commercial empire held together by the Royal Navy and the imperial civil service who provided administrators (police and governors) for its colonial possessions.

The United States, by virtue of an extraordinarily high military budget, may be the predominant military power in the world, but its far flung military presence is not any thing like the control exercised by the Roman Legions or the British Royal Navy. Although the U.S. economy is largest in the world, Washington D.C. does not exercise anywhere the same direct influence over world commerce that Rome and London did at the height of their respective empires. In short it is difficult to see how the U.S. can be equated to either empire so the question asked by Friedman, if the U.S. Republic can withstand the strains of empire is a moot one.

Having begun with a false premise, Friedman compounds the error by building a set of prognostic descriptions of U.S. relations with individual countries and regions as the decade of 2010-2020 moves forward. In this effort he apparently fails to understand the effects that the phenomenon of globalization is having on the international stage. Now `globalization' is a widely used term with many interpretations. In this case the term is used to mean the rapidly growing inter-connectivity and inter-dependence of both nation states and geographical regions both economically and culturally. It is a major mistake to treat U.S. relations to specific countries or regions of the world as simply one-on-one relations without recognizing their global implications.

For these reasons, although this book as usual contains a good deal of wisdom, in the end it fails to provide a realistic prediction of U.S. international progress over the next decade.

A major part of globalization is enabled by the tremendous growth and expansion of information/communication technologies including: computers, the Internet, cell phones, and all of the related magic. I use the term magic to describe how these technologies may seem to the vast majority of even those who use them. We are just beginning to see the effects of this revolution. It came about so rapidly that the realization of the profound changes in our lives is just starting to be realized. The political implications have prompted many totalitarian regimes to place controls on access to the Internet with varying degrees of success. The possible results of having free access to all of this information strikes fear into the hearts of all despotic rulers, even more than a free press. These tyrants can rather easily control the press and local media. On the other hand, virtually any access to the Internet will thwart most attempts at control.

Totalitarian regimes of many types are having to deal with the freedom of information exchange provided by the Internet. This freedom is indeed bringing vast changes to the minds and activities of people wherever governments do not shut down or severely limit Internet access. Because freedom of information exchange is the enemy of all who would control the lives of individuals, many political groups, and especially those on the left, will try to control the Internet where they can. Even in the US citizens hear rumblings from some politicians about controlling and/or taxing Internet access. These individuals are the same groups that would destroy individual freedoms and place us all under growing government control. Free men must always be vigilant to protect freedom from those who would take it away. It is obvious to all truly free men and women that the political left will always use government to control people and force them to do their bidding. Just look at what has happened in the United States in the last three years. Our Constitution, originally designed to protect the people from their government, has been abrogated Our indebtedness has tripled while our nation has been economically damaged severely. It is obvious that the agenda of the left is the economic destruction of the middle class in The United States, and the reduction of its citizens to servitude to and dependence on their government. By overburdening entrepreneurs and all businesses other than the very largest with taxes and regulations, these policies have resulted in the largest concentration of wealth in very few hands that we have ever had in our history as a nation.

The recent mortgage debacle resulted in the largest destruction of personal wealth among the middle classes that the US has ever experienced. It also resulted in the greatest transfer of real wealth from most Americans into the hands of a very few, mostly bankers like Goldman Sachs. While those in power decry the evil giant corporations and Wall Street Bankers, they make secret deals with them so they pay little or no taxes, (Like GE last year) have access to political power, can arrange advantageous financial deals and government contracts, and receive advantages denied America's small, medium and even large corporations not in the elite inside group.

EXAMPLE: The Export-Import Bank of the United States' recent deal to provide Petrobras, Brazil's petroleum giant with two billion dollars (that's billions with a "b") to fund offshore drilling, while using federal law to prevent American companies from drilling off our shores. It's strange, isn't it that one of the largest investors in Petrobras happens to be George Soros. The same multi billionaire George Soros who funds and runs moveon.org and other left leaning activist organizations.

This reference to George Soros leads us directly into the meat of this article.

Think Tanks and Political Organizations

In addition to donating directly to political candidates, parties and committees, the Kochs and Soros have funded numerous political think tanks and advocacy groups. These groups are not required to reveal their donors, therefore making it hard to come up with a comprehensive list of organizations that have financial ties to these individuals. The institutions mentioned are those most well-connected with the Koch brothers and George Soros.

Charles Koch co-founded the Cato Institute, a libertarian think tank, along with Edward Crane in 1977. Charles and David Koch, along with Richard Fink and Jay Humphries, co-founded the Citizens for a Sound Economy in 1984. In 2004, CSE broke off into two groups: Koch-linked Americans for Prosperity and FreedomWorks, headed by former congressman Dick Armey. According to its website, Americans for Prosperity "is committed to educating citizens about economic policy and a return of the federal government to its Constitutional limits." In addition to those mentioned above, Charles Koch has helped to build the Institute for Humane Studies, the Bill of Rights Institute and the Market-Based Management Institute.

David Koch is currently on the board of directors at Cato, as well as the Mercatus Center at George Mason University, a research center dedicated to "market-oriented ideas." He is a trustee at the Libertarian Reason Foundation whose goal is to advance "free minds and free markets."

George Soros founded the Open Society Institute which is his primary philanthropy organization. According to the website, "The Open Society Foundations fund a range of programs around the world, from public health to education to business development." While the foundation spends much of its resources on democratic causes around the world, OSI has also contributed to political advocacy groups such as the Tides Foundation. In 2004, Soros pledged $3 million to the progressive think tank, Center for American Progress. Soros is also a major financial backer of the Democracy Alliance, an organization committed to drive progressive activist funding and the recently formed Institute for New Economic Thinking, which was jump started by a $50 million pledge from Soros.

Both the Koch brothers and Soros have given generously to nonpartisan charitable organizations. David Koch, who is still receiving treatment for prostate cancer has donated $120 million to cancer research at the Massachusetts Institute of Technology, $40 million to Memorial Sloan Kettering Cancer Center, $100 million to renovating New York City Ballet and Opera Theater, and $20 million to the American Museum of Natural History, among other donations. Soros recently pledged $100 million to Human Rights Watch, and he has made many other charitable donations such as $50 million for the Millennium Promise initiative to eradicate extreme poverty in Africa. In 2003, PBS estimated Soros had donated more than $4 billion since the 1980s.

VERDICT: Given the difficultly in tracking donations to nonprofits and charitable organizations, it's almost impossible to quantify whether the Koch brothers or Soros dominate this political realm. That said, both the Kochs and Soros have spent incredible riches in this area with no sign of stopping.

Capital Rivals is OpenSecrets Blog's ongoing series that plays political foes against one another on the playing field of money in politics.

Ever since Jane Mayer's recent New Yorker piece earlier this month, much of the media has risen to debate how much influence conservative and libertarian-leaning businessmen David and Charles Koch, the owners of Koch Industries, have in American politics.

Some critics of the article argue that the media cries foul over the Koch brothers, yet largely ignores liberal George Soros, the Hungarian-American currency speculator and stock investor, who has spent millions of dollars on liberal and nonpartisan causes (including the Center for Responsive Politics).

HoJo NOTE: What else would you expect our left leaning media to do?

OpenSecrets Blog is here to investigate the numbers behind these bold-faced names in our new feature, Capital Rivals.

For starters, both Soros and the brothers Koch (pronounced "coke") are incredibly rich. And their political endeavors are numerous.

Koch Industries, started as an oil refiner, and is the nation's second largest private company with about $100 billion in annual revenue. Soros is chairman of Soros Fund Management, a highly successful hedge fund that has provided financial and investment strategies to a variety of funds. As of June 30, 2009, the hedge fund had holdings valued at $4.2 billion.

David and Charles Koch are tied at No. 24 on Forbes top billionaires list with a personal fortunes of $17.5 billion each. Soros is No. 35 on the list with a net worth of $14 billion.

The Koch brothers, Soros and their respective companies have spent millions of dollars on politics, ranging from federal lobbying to candidate support to bankrolling political committees, according to a Center for Responsive Politics review of their political activity.

The Kochs and Soros have also funded think tanks, foundations and political organizations -- money that is sometimes notoriously difficult to track. The Kochs have also funded several scientific research organizations.

These individuals aren't exactly flying under the radar as the Kochs hold leadership positions and are featured on the websites for the Cato Institute, Reason Foundation and the Mercatus Center among others. Soros also runs the Open Society Institute -- website Soros.org -- as well as the recently created Institute for New Economic Thinking.

Still these individuals have provided major funding to groups that aren't particularly transparent, such as Soros-backed Democracy Alliance, which doesn't provide information on the projects it funds.

David Koch's Americans for Prosperity Foundation has a more detailed website, but it is unclear why Koch is seemingly uninvolved in the similar organization, Americans for Prosperity. David Koch contends that no Koch foundations have provided funding to Americans for Prosperity, the citizen advocacy group organizing Tea Party events around the country. A Washington Post article from January of this year connects the Kochs with the Tea Party movement, citing records of their foundation giving $3.1 million to Americans for Prosperity, but according to the Kochs, this is false, as the money only went to the Americans for Prosperity Foundation.

Below is the Center for Responsive Politics' analysis federal political activity by Soros and the Kochs. Note that while direct political donations are relatively easily to track, it's difficult to create a full compilation of the political groups that these individuals are connected with due to secondary and indirect affiliations. Therefore, the groups listed at the end of the are the most well-known organizations linked to these three individuals.

Organization-Driven Political Activity

The Koch brothers' company, Koch Industries, has been a big player in both campaign donations and lobbying. Koch Industries currently leads the oil and gas industry as the top contributor to federal candidates and parties, and is the fifth highest lobbying spender in the industry this year. Soros' hedge fund, Soros Fund Management, has also lobbied at the federal level, but employees have not made campaign donations through a Soros-sponsored political action committee. Because of the notable lobbying involvement of a Soros-funded think tank, the Open Society Policy Center, this group's data is also included for the purpose of this comparison:

Political Action Committee Spending (1989 to 2010)

Koch Industries: $5,938,993 (83 percent going to Republicans)

Soros Fund Management: $0

527 Group Contributions (2001 to 2010)

Koch Industries: $574,998 (100% going to Democrats.)

$186,598 – Democratic Governors Association

$150,000 – Republican State Leadership Committee

$103,400 – Republican Governors Association

Soros Fund Management: $0

Lobbying Expenditures (1998 to 2010)

Koch Industries: $50,972,700

Soros Fund Management: $860,000

Open Society Policy Center: $11,930,000

According to federal lobbying reports, Koch Industries' top issues include energy, environmental, tax and homeland security policies. The Open Society Policy Center has mainly lobbied on issues relating to foreign relations, civil rights, and law enforcement policy. The graph below outlines these organizations lobbying history since 1998:

Koch vs Soros Lobbying Expenditures.bmp

VERDICT: When it comes to the combination of institutional lobbying, 527 group donations and PAC expenditures, Koch Industries far out-spends Soros' hedge fund and think tank, $57.4 million to $12.8 million. Most of this money is attributable to lobbying expenditures.

Individual-Funded Political Activity

Soros and the Koch brothers have all donated to federal political campaigns and committees. While Soros has far out-spent the Koch brothers in donating to 527 groups, especially when considering his incredible $23.7 million in donations to the groups between 2003 and 2004, the Koch brothers have donated more money to federal candidates and committees.

The Koch brothers give almost exclusively to Republicans just as Soros donates predominately to Democrats and Democratic organizations. Overall, Soros has spent $34.24 million and the Kochs have spent $4.06 million. (Note: This study only covers donations to federal candidates - to see donations to state candidates, go to Followthemoney.org and search for Soros and Koch. For example, as Ben Smith of Politico wrote recently, David Koch and his wife have given $74,000 to a Democrat, Andrew Cuomo, New York's State Attorney General.)

Individual donations to federal candidates, parties and PACs (1989 to 2010)

Koch Brothers: $2.58 million
George Soros: $1.74 million
David Koch: $2,224,170
> $667,500 – National Republican Congressional Committee
> $555,000 – Republican National Committee
> $191,400 – National Republican Senatorial Committee

Charles G. Koch: $363,100
> $58,900 – National Republican Senatorial Committee
> $50,000 – Republican National Committee

George Soros: $1,748,627
> $252,670 – Democratic National Committee
> $147,216 – Democratic Senatorial Campaign Committee
> $259,716 – Democratic Congressional Campaign Committee

David Koch's Favorite congressional members:

$17,100 – Todd Tiahrt (R-Kan.)
$7,600 – Elizabeth Dole (R-N.C.)
$7,200 – Mark Foley (R-Fla.)
$6,600 – James Inhofe (R-Okla.)
$5,000 – Sam Brownback (R-Kan.)

George Soros' favorite congressional members:

$6,500 – Hillary Clinton (D-N.Y.)
$6,200 – Jon Cranley (D-Ohio)
$6,000 – Ken Salazar (D-Colo.)
$6,000 – Dan Maffei (D-N.Y.)
$5,500 – Tom Perriello (D-Va.)

Individual donations to 527 organizations (2001 to 2010)

George Soros: $32.5 million   Koch Brothers: $1.5 million

A note from Howard Johnson about NPOs: Non-profit, tax exempt organizations (NPOs) sound great, don't they? These marvelous organizations are without the stigma of that terrible word, PROFITS. However, They do pay their employees, sometimes quite handsomely. They can thus become a practical conduit for all kinds of donations, government grants, and other subsidies, into the pockets of those on their payrolls. These individuals, frequently the organizer of the NPO, may not take out profits, but they can charge travels and stays at fancy hotels and resorts to the NPO in addition to their pay. Although their pay is subject to income taxes, their travel and miscellaneous expenses as well as the costs of often lavish offices and support personnel are not. This certainly applies to 527 groups. They seem to act just like many members of our legislatures, don't they?

So-called 527 groups are non-profit, tax-exempt organizations that are allowed to raise money for political activities including voter mobilization efforts, issue advocacy and other actions. They are allowed to raise unlimited amounts of money from individuals, corporations and unions. Until earlier this year, they could not use these unlimited contributions to expressly advocate for the election or defeat of a federal candidate. Federal court rulings -- including Citizens United v. Federal Election Commission and SpeechNow.org v. Federal Election Commission -- have broken down that restriction.

As mentioned previously, Soros spent $24 million in under two years and did so in his determination to defeat George W. Bush in 2004. He told the Washington Post in November 2003, "America under Bush, is a danger to the world. I'm willing to put my money where my mouth is." Since December 2008, Soros has only donated $4,000 to these types of groups.

NOTE from Howard Johnson: Did you ever wonder why George Soros hated George w. Bush so much that he spent more then $20 million of his own money trying to defeat him in 2004?

Consider the source of his money and then consider the same thing for the Koch brothers. Soros is a hedge fund operator and has made much of his money manipulating currencies using other people's money. This type of speculation generates zero wealth and few jobs. In 1992 he made more than a billion dollars (that's with a "b") by shorting the British pound, one basic method of manipulating a currency if you have enough money and can get enough people with money to go with you. According to many financial experts, "Soros brought down the Bank of England with a $10 billion leveraged position." Many of the records of his financial dealings are hidden from public view so it is difficult to get a full picture. There were few jobs created in the US because of his efforts. I'll only mention the $2 billion that the Export-Import Bank of the United States intends to loan to finance exports to the Brazilian oil company Petróleo Brasileiro S.A., known as Petrobras, over the next several years. This has been heralded by Obama as a plus for the US. Or is it really a payback and a plus for Obama supporter, George Soros, who is heavily invested in Petrobras?

On the other hand, the Kochs, through their parent company, Koch Industries, made their billions in the oil refining, and associated business, right here in the US. Koch Industries is the largest privately owned corporation in the US with petroleum related transport and refining locations on the west coast, mid-west and Calgary, Alberta. Their subsidiary companies include, Koch Minerals, LLC and Koch Carbon, LLC with diverse operations all over the world. Recent acquisitions include, Invista, the world's largest fibers company, and Georgia Pacific, the American pulp and paper products giant. Their companies employ thousands of Americans and make a major contribution to our manufacturing and refining industries. Remember the differences with George Soros organizations as you read the remainder of this blog.

On June 30th of this year, David Koch made a $1 million donation to the Republican Governors Association, his largest one-time donation to date.

David Koch: $1,472,000

        $1,352,000 – Republican Governors Association

        $100,000 – Americans for Better Government

George Soros: $32,506,500

    $12.05 million – Joint Victory Campaign 2004

    $7.5 million – America Coming Together

    $2.5 million – MoveOn.org

    $3.65 million – America Votes

    $3.5 million – The Fund for America

    $150,000 – Win Back Respect

    $120,000 – Majority Action

    $100,000 – Campaign Money Watch

Soros certainly wins the 527 group spending battle, beating the Koch brothers $32.5 million to $1.5 million.

Soros vs Koch 527 donations CORRECT.bmp VERDICT: Soros rules this category, having poured more than $34.2 million into political channels, compared to $4.06 million for the Koch brothers.

Sunday, March 06, 2011

HoJo's Predictions and Some Repercussions

Some very personal reactions and responses 2-15-2011

On Jan 14, 2011, at 8:39 PM, Howard Johnson wrote and sent the following email:

Dear family and friends:

In October of 2004 I emailed the following warning to most of you:

Is a national mortgage collapse imminent? I am certainly no financial wizard and few people pay attention to my predictions, but I very accurately predicted the collapse of the PC market that led to the dot com debacle. I made some very accurate observations that were as plain as the nose on my face to me. Few people paid me any attention.

Well, here I am again with a new prediction that to me is just as obvious. Some time ago, liberals Democrats in our government managed to remove all reasonable controls on mortgages in order to "make home ownership easier for all people." As a result, the government's Fannie Mae and Freddie Mac mortgage banks began providing mortgage money to finance increasingly risky mortgages. In addition, they started bringing pressures to bear on other banks to engage in the same practices. This has resulted in a substantial run up in the price of housing and many new mortgage gimmicks like sub-prime and adjustable rate mortgages. Many of these home buyers hoped to flip these homes in a rising market and make a profit. A rather large percentage of these buyers will not be able to pay their mortgages, especially when the second tier rates kick in in a year or so. It's a risky process with the certainty of dire consequences in the near future.

I believe that because of these practices, housing prices will eventually stop rising and start going down. This will begin accelerating as people begin defaulting on their high risk loans. When this happens, prices of homes will begin dropping precipitously. The mortgage market will very quickly begin to collapse as home owners suddenly find their mortgages are much larger than the new, declining value of their houses, and buyers will be few, even at lower prices..This will then cause the economy to begin shrinking as construction will almost stop. The resulting job losses will then expand, the stock market will crash, and we will be in a major recession. It could even be worse than the great depression that began with the crash of 1929. Consider yourselves forewarned.

END OF 2004 WARNING, my email continued:

I doubt that many people paid attention to my warning because, who am I to have the audacity to predict such things. I have no string of letters after my name to verify my predictions. Despite this, I am now warning you of another financial disaster I see in our future—our very near future. Once more, the media, the pundits, politicians, and especially the government are not talking about it. I think this is a deliberate deception for reasons only known to those who refuse to tell the truth of the situation.

More than 100 cities in the US are now bankrupt. Six states are in even worse condition and 27 others may be bankrupt this year. The federal government cannot bail them out because the federal government is virtually bankrupt as well. The government is printing money as fast as the presses will run. All that does is dilute the value of the existing dollars and scare hell out of our creditors.

I'm certain you all notice the rapidly rising cost of food and fuel, the lifeblood of our economy. With deficits in the trillions, we will soon reach the place where if all of us were taxed at 100% of income it would not be enough to balance our budget. Under liberal Democrat control and guidance, the US has gone from the world's largest creditor to the world's largest debtor in just a few decades.

The Chinese and the Arabs may soon pull the plug. Both have slowed their buying of US treasury notes and are talking of switching to another currency. When, not if, that happens, it will yank the rug out from under our economy as the cost of imports will skyrocket. This collapse has already started as evidenced by the accelerating rises in the prices of precious metals and oil. Today oil passed $91 per barrel and will soon reach $100. The price of gasoline at the pump flew by $3 per gallon several weeks ago and will probably reach $4 by the end of the coming summer. It was about $1.65 here in Florida just a year ago so it almost doubled in just one year. Food prices are following a similar accelerating pace.. Look for cereal to cost $5 a box in six to eight months. Everything else will do much the same.

It is interesting to note that Bill Clinton, aided by his first liberal Democrat Congress, removed food and fuel prices from the federal COLA (cost of living allowance) used to calculate Social Security payments. Had this been left as it was, most Social Security payments would today be almost 25% more than they are now. Democrats deliberately reduced Social Security while at the same time warning the elderly that "Republicans are planning to reduce your Social Security checks." I cannot believe Americans fall for that BS.

Also in recent years, unemployment has been estimated by counting those receiving unemployment checks. Real unemployment, the way it was counted before 1970 is the number who can work, but don't have a job. Today this is about double the number the government reports. 18% would be a far more accurate number than what we get from Washington. To me it verges on criminal that the main stream media does not inform the public of these facts.

I suggest you try to find ways to protect yourself from the mayhem that will follow the economic collapse of our federal government. There could be food riots in many major cities as merchants begin refusing food stamps and credit cards, knowing they will never be paid. As the government runs out of money and the value of the dollar plummets, it will make the great depression look like a cake walk. These things are already happening in Europe. Greece. Ireland, and Iceland have already collapsed and six other European nations will soon follow. All of these things are the direct result of the growth of liberal socialist policies foisted on us by the left.

Be prepared for your government to take over your retirement account. Some members of Congress are already considering this. Then there are your bank accounts, your investments, your home. If they can take your IRA (in exchange for soon to be worthless government notes) they can also take anything else you own. They are even now writing the laws and the regulations that will give them the right to do so. Who says might doesn't make right? They continue to try to abrogate our "right to bear arms" while they have the guns and handcuffs to enforce their laws. As Robert Heinlein said, "When only the police have guns it's called a police state."

I am sure that many of you will say, "That can't happen here." How many of you thought that when I accurately predicted the dot com bust? Or how about the mortgage meltdown? Did my predictions even register with you? I'd really like to hear from you regarding my predictions. Don't say it won't happen simply because it hasn't happened before. If you don't like my prediction and choose a rebuttal, please do not use platitudes and euphemisms, use facts and figures, real figures. While you are at it, look at the lessons of history. You might also tell me how the Greeks are going to solve their economic problems, or the Icelanders, or Californians. Detroit may be beyond help.

I have the answer, but I doubt the short-sighted among our voters will ever let it happen here.

Ho

- - - - - - - -

On Fri, Jan 14, 2011, One of my very dear friends responded:

Ho,

You are so interesting. Below is not the person I have in my mind. Doom and gloom. What's your point? Does this help? Liberals versus conservatives. If there were no liberals, would it be the perfect world? If conservatives ran the world, our economy would be great and our future bright? It is greed that gets us into these sorts of problems. I wish it were so simple as being conservative or liberal. And I can't help but to get the feeling that you enjoy being right about your predictions and would take a certain amount of satisfaction watching our country's demise as you describe below. How does this letter help me? What should I do? My day was not so good. Thanks for making it worse.

- - - - - - - -

Dear friend,

I'm quite sorry I messed up your day.

I want you to know how I treasure your responses to my rants. I read them carefully and try to digest what you have to say. You are one of those few people who question me and work to keep me on track and I really appreciate it. I think you may have missed my point. Possibly because I didn't make it clear enough. Besides, I am actually an optimist.

The dichotomous and emotional positions of liberal vs conservative ignores reality and removes most rational conclusions about what is happening to our nation and what should be done about it. And yes, for a multitude of reasons I believe that application of liberal, socialist ideas, the proven destructive policies of the left, are responsible for the mess we are now in and for the coming, even more damaging debacle. I hear few ideas from liberal Democrats that address the real problems either. It is always my hope that the public, even all humanity, will see what's coming and take the necessary steps to either correct for it, or adapt to it. Sadly, those steps often come too late or are never taken. If I remember, I will attach a little thing I wrote about problems and how they are used. It sort if relates to this whole thing.

No, I certainly do not hope that this will happen. I will certainly take no joy in my predictions being correct. Unfortunately there are many sound reasons I make this prediction. I do not think our politicians on either side have a clue what to do. If they do, they are ignoring their own knowledge. I believe that as a people, Americans have become so luxury loving, self serving, irresponsible, and real work hating that we will not make the hard decisions necessary to stop the train wrecks such as the one we are already in the midst of. I certainly take no joy in my predictions being correct. I hope and pray that I am very mistaken.

Several people profited greatly from my earlier warnings by taking actions based on my predictions. One person sold most of his investments in computer companies when I told him of the coming PC business crash. He told me later I saved him from losing hundreds of thousands. Even though he was just an acquaintance he handed me a check for a thousand dollars in appreciation saying, "That's the cheapest good financial advice I have ever received." I was amazed. I know of no other such dramatic beneficiary.

A fairly close friend who had just sold his house for a handsome price was negotiating the purchase of another home when he read my prediction about the mortgage market. After looking further into what was happening, he decided not to buy right away and moved into a rental house. He called me about six months ago to tell me he just bought a home for around $200,000 that would have cost nearly twice that amount had he bought right after selling. He thanked me for warning him. Of course, he didn't do that on my say so alone. He studied the situation and sought advice of several people in the mortgage business before making his decision to wait. He saw my words not as gloom and doom, but as a positive, a valid warning. Oh, and several of those in the mortgage business laughed at my predictions. They were probably trying to sell him a big expensive house.

My point is to warn people of the menace that is coming their way so they can prepare. It is far better to prepare for a calamity and not have it happen than not to prepare. There are some relatively simple and inexpensive precautions one can take to minimize the damage in any calamity. I assume you have insurance of several types and that your car has seat belts and even airbags. How about considering a little insurance against this probable catastrophe. Oh, I am not selling such insurance so my motive is not to profit.

If I warned you about a train coming loudly down the tracks where you were sitting—if you then noticed the great noise it was making and heard its loud horn, would you consider my words as doom and gloom? If you lived in tornado country and someone warned you of an approaching tornado would you call that doom and gloom? I think not.

Well, the noise from the coming disaster is deafening, if you listen for it. There is a great deal a person can do to prepare. There are even books written about it. A six month supply of staple foods is a good way to start, as long as you tell no one about it. A batch of candles or a stash of flashlight batteries would not be a bad idea should the electric grid fail. There are even flashlights you can crank to charge their batteries. I would even suggest a quantity of bottled water if you don't have a well These inexpensive preparations are minimal and will not go to waste. Necessary medicines are another thing that a six month supply would not be prohibitively expensive and wouldn't take up much room. A cache of silver coins might be another, just in case paper money became useless. Just think about it. These are preparations you would not lose as you could use them from your supply and then replenish as you go along until things go bad. Some of these things we already have as part of our preparations for a possible hurricane here in Florida.

I warn people because I care about them. I want them to be able to prepare, not wring their hands in despair after a disaster happens. Do you think it would be better if I kept silent?

Ho

- - - - - - - -

NOTE: I inserted my comments in (italics.)

Hello,

Sorry for my delay in responding. We are in the midst of a blizzard warning and it made me realize I had not responded. Below makes me feel a little better but I still don't see the person that I met in your writings. Your predictions remind me so much of my own mother who is talking about a revolution (by black folks) etc. Plus all one has to do is listen to Fox radio and hear the same predictions so nothing new in these predictions.

1 **(Actually, my predictions are quite different in detail from those on Fox. Similar in the main, but the devil is in the details.)**

I am surprised that you describe the problems so simply and without nuances. You blame everything on liberals.

2 (No, I merely look at the results, the actual realities. Places where liberals have the most power and where unions are most powerful are always in the most financial difficulty. It was certainly not conservative efforts that drove textiles, then steel, then electronics, then autos, along with most of our manufacturing base overseas, or destroyed Detroit, or bankrupted California, Michigan, New York and other states.)

A remark that changed my outlook forever was a statement made by a German man who gave tours at Dachau (sp?). A young American guy told him that he had heard that the Nazi women were even more vicious than the Nazi men and wanted to know if this was true. This tour guide looked at this young man and told him that the reason he took the 7AM train every morning and did these tours in his retirement was that he wanted people to realize that all of us are capable of the atrocities that were done by the Germans in that era. That in the right circumstances we all have the capability to behave so poorly. In that tour I learned what I never learned in the history lessons in the USA.....that Germany had never recovered after WW1 and there was extreme poverty in the country.

3 (In the public schools I attended, we studied the Weimar republic and what happened to Germany after WWI along with many other parts of history that our dumbed-down schools of later years did not teach. I wonder what group was responsible for that change?)

I find it so interesting that Americans living in their fancy homes and driving their fancy cars can make so many judgments of people that live in conditions that they cannot possibly even imagine. Instead of being grateful we are judgmental.

4 (Hey, lady, you forget. I grew up during the depression when our fancy car was a five year old Nash, we had several dirt streets in our neighborhood and I learned to eat quickly if I hoped to get any of the meager seconds Mom put on the table. Christmas was the only time we had oranges, tangerines, or candy. My buddies and I regularly prowled the trash cans in the neighborhood looking for discarded things we could fix and play with. My first and only bicycle was one I rescued from the trash. It took me at least three months to earn enough from my paper route to buy the parts to fix it up so it was useable. I rode that bike for five years, constantly fixing and repainting it until it looked really good. I sold it for $15 when I graduated from high school. Thanks to my father's hard work and resourcefulness, we were better off than most. That's my reality and we were very grateful for what we had.)

Having digressed a bit I guess my point is this. WE are the reason for the problems. There were so many layers to the mortgage problems that had nothing to do with being liberal or conservative.

5 (It wasn't conservatives that forced banks to write mortgages to folks they knew would never be able to pay for. It wasn't conservatives that ran Fannie Mae and Freddie Mac into bankruptcy. It wasn't conservatives that paid Clinton protégé and Fannie Mae President, Franklin Raines $90 million in bonuses even as this government entity was going bankrupt.)

The common denominator was greed and denial. And we all benefited from the stupidity that was going on. *(No, all of us didn't)* In my case, it was the great returns that

I was getting from the stock market and the low interest rates that allowed us to buy a nicer home than we would have been able to buy in the 80's. Thankfully we were experienced consumers and did not end up like a lot of folks did. But I wonder. Had I been buying my first home at the ripe age of 23 *(as was the case in 1983)* would I have done the right thing? We looked to the bank and the realtor to tell us what sort of home we could afford. Also in 1990 when we bought our second home we were guided by the realtor and bank as to what we could afford. When we bought homes in 2001 and 2007 we were shown homes that were valued at more than 100,000 dollars more than the value of the homes that we eventually bought. And the hint that was given by the realtors......that other people in our salary range were living in much nicer homes. Now, because we humans could not do the right thing, the government will step in with more regulations. And many of those regulations will be just plain stupid. But the people working in the industry nor the consumers were capable of guiding themselves. *(They would have been capable if parents and government schools taught responsibility and self reliance, but no, they taught greed, irresponsibility, and how to be a victim and blame it all on corporations and the wealthy.)*

My predictions for the future are not the same as yours. I predict that health care and education will be the next "crisis". And why? *(Those have both been in growing crisis stages for years, mostly due to efforts of our government.)* Because the so called professionals that work in those fields have let greed and denial guide them. *(As taught by the media and in government schools)* Take my profession. Hospitals have made money from PT's and abused situations where therapy gets involved. Many times I am just pushing an IV pole as someone walks down the hallway. This could easily be done by an aide. So instead of aides walking patients, physical therapy is ordered. This drove up the need for therapists and thus salaries and in the end more expensive for hospitals. Now the government has stepped in with regulations which limits this activity. There has also has been extensive fraud of therapy in various settings which has had to be limited also. *(And just where was it virtually all of that fraud occurred? Answer: taxpayers' money dispensed by government workers under government programs.)* Some of the regs are absolutely ridiculous and actually hurt the patient more than help. However, it was just human nature that created this whole mess and we were unable to guide ourselves. And there are so many other areas of waste in healthcare especially with end of life care. People will lose a dignified death if too many doctors become involved in a case. I have a friend who is a pediatric oncologist. She told me her nickname is Dr. Death. She has the highest number of patients die on her shift. The reason........she explains exactly what is involved with a lot of care and the eventual outcome. She says that many doctors view death as failure and will go to extremes to prevent a patient from dying on their shift. Ironically, she takes her nickname as Dr. Death as a compliment. All of this talk of death panels killed the conversation that needed to be had in this area. I think we are just starting to see the beginning in Arizona where the governor stopped all transplants for it's Medicaid recipients as the state can no longer afford it. And what do most people think? Well those people are on Medicaid/State aid. It won't happen to me. Well guess what? It will happen to everyone. Health care will have to be "rationed". Our technology is too expensive and our ability to keep dying people alive is too good. And now add obesity to the problem. We simply cannot afford it. There will be an adjustment. And we will probably blame each other and it will be very political. In the end I think it may be better. I think it will make people live a healthier lifestyle. That obese patient who is denied dialysis because of her poor prognosis related to her weight will make people take note of their own weight. But there will be lots of outcry first. And people in the USA get so many unnecessary medical treatments that only make the quality of their life worse. This waste will have to stop and the patient will be better off.

6 (A lot of this would take care of itself if it wasn't completely free! A small local hospital near my home in Indiana cut the waste and abuses of their emergency room by charging each patient a $5 cash fee for every patient who used the emergency room. Of course, some people refused to pay and were treated anyway, but the hassle helped cut useless ER visits down to almost none and the hospital made much better use of its ER. I have often wondered why our helpful government hasn't forced the hospital to stop this practice because of the efforts of some do gooder.)

As far as education goes, I can't explain it like my husband can who was in the field from the mid 80's to 2007.

7 (You can very easily see the effect the teachers union has had on education by what's happening in Wisconsin and elsewhere. The unions would rather have half their members laid off than give up a tiny part of their income to keep them all working.)

But back to your emails. I can appreciate the entertainment in provoking people. But there are some difficult issues ahead of us. And when people of your intellect only add to the problem, well, I lose my patience. Your emails mostly promote blame. And yes, I can hear you say that you offer solutions but they start off with a lot of blame and putting people on the defense. Problems will not be solved with this strategy. Your emails also many times just address one side to an issue. Again, someone of your intellect should be able to see both sides and the nuances. Makes me think of an article that I read that promoted staying involved in Afghanistan. Then I read another article that discussed all the reasons to leave Afghanistan. Both had very good points. Big problems are complex. My concern now is that there is so much negative communication out there. Yours and my generation did not grow up with all the negativity and inflamed news stories that run 24/7 now. Someone with you age, experience, intellect, and most importantly, the ability to articulate should be offering encouragement to the next generation. Assuring them they have the ability to solve these problems. That we have faced many problems in the past and overcame them. It doesn't matter if there is a black, yellow. or purple president, or that Congress is liberal or conservative. What matters is us. And talking about people taking up their guns and taking your money just does not help us. Those worries are better kept from the written word and forwarded to lots of people.

8. (The first step in finding a solution to any problem is to define the problem. Doing so frequently requires calling attention to those responsible for the problem. If you call that

blame, that is your choice. I call that defining the problem. Once the problem is defined, the next step is to use that definition to find a solution. I do not buy that there are two sides to every problem. There is only one side to a person who is being drowned by another. Stopping that person and getting the victim out of the water and give them air to breathe. There is only one side to any organization, group or whatever when they are drowning in debt, stop spending more than you take in. Most problems have a nearly infinite number of solutions, an infinite number of "sides," not just two. There is much more in my full response after the end of your message.)

I will end this email as I started it. The blizzard warning. After 9-11 and the anthrax scares my husband assured me that these were not major concerns for him..... that we had an immediate danger right next to our house that he worried about. I must back up and tell you that Larry taught a Risk Assessment course at Cornell so his outlook has always been interesting. I asked him what that danger was. His reply......the railroad tracks a mile away from our house. He then noted all the containers of chemicals that passed through on a daily basis on those tracks. One derailment could cause a lot of problems. So it never hurts to be prepared. His other comment. People mostly die in bed. Given that statistic, is bed a dangerous place? Should we avoid laying in our beds? Complexity and simplicity.......Oh, and one other of my husband's comments when, as a toxicologist, is asked about dangers......Wear your seatbelt.

Your friend

Hi there:

This is a very long response to parts of your last email message. You took the time to say what you thought and wanted me to hear. I appreciate that and listened carefully to what you said. I thought I would return the favor, so here it is. Incidently I don't care much for sound bytes. They are emotional chirps that miss virtually all of the nuances, subtleties, and rational parts of any idea, proposal, or position. Sadly, the sound byte has come to constitute the majority of communications of news and many personal communications. Maybe that is because so many people now text message or use facebook or twitter. Sound bytes, text messages and postings on social networks are more like dogs barking than communications between thinking humans.

Oh, and about seat belts? I first installed seat belts in my car in 1952 when the only ones you could find to buy were surplus military or aircraft seat belts. I have used them ever since then, even when I had to install them myself. Like the boy scouts, I like to be prepared.

Perhaps I have not provided you with an adequate understanding of where I get the basis for my opinions or what my political reasoning is. First of all, I am not a follower of or beholden to any ism, group belief system (religious, political or other), peer group, grant committee, dean or head of faculty, political or other boss, or corporate officer at any level, so I am free to speak my mind, mistakes and all. I consider myself a truly independent and liberal individual and a realist who knows what it means to conserve. No, that is not a contradiction.

I have written extensively about things like:

1) the decimation of our environment, and impending menace that is more likely to end humanity than anything else. See http://decimatenviro.blogspot.com.

2) legalizing drugs to remove the money from illegal drugs and stop all associated criminal activity, http://hjdrugprb.blogspot.com.

3) a completely new taxing system that will remove tax revenue from the control of politicians, http://jtax.blogspot.com. My tax plan would include a negative income tax to replace welfare. It would also make it difficult for a few people to control a large number of industries, corporations, or political patronage.

Does that sound like I am a right wing conservative?

My personal social, environmental, and political beliefs are based closer to the world of science and humanity described in books like those by Eric Hoffer - The True Believer and The Temper of our Times, E. O. Wilson - several books, Jared Diamond - Collapse, The Last Chimpanzee, and Guns, Germs, and Steel, Stephen J. Gould - Bully for Brontosaurus, Nigel Calder - The Magic Universe, consumer advocate, John Stossel - Give Me a Break and Myths, Lies, and downright Stupidity, and even parts of the Bible. Lately I have become an admirer and reader of the writing of Thomas Sowell. Included in my regular reading are several magazines: Scientific American, Astronomy, National Geographic, and Smithsonian, each of which I read cover to cover. No, I don't agree with everything they have to say, but I don't always agree with everything I have to say, either.

In truth, I do not blame everything bad on liberals. The blame actually falls on the idiots who vote for politicians: that use class hatred and promise voters things impossible to deliver: or that use taxpayers money to buy their seats in legislatures, be they professed Democrat, Republican, libertarian, liberal, socialist, conservative, or whatever. I am not specifically anti liberal, but I am definitely anti government, and in particular, the huge, self serving Jaba the Hut monster our government has become. It has doubled in size in the last thirty years and more than doubled in cost. Since liberal Democrats took control of Congress in 2007, our government has expanded from about 32% of GDP to as much as 44%. This after holding steady at around 30% for many years. Our current government has been growing in power and wealth at the expense of primarily the American middle class, and the benefit of mega corporations, politicians, the super wealthy, and Wall Street bankers and others mad for power. (Check how many on Obamas cabinet or among his czars are ex Goldman-Sachs executives, for instance.)

The latest crop of self serving egomaniacs (there are a majority of these in all political parties) have conspired to move great wealth and power out of the hands of the American people and into those of the elite royals in government. The unbelievably expensive vacations of the Obamas, Nancy Pelosi's private jet (now taken away and sold), Hillary's extravagant senate offices she used for such a short time, are but recent examples of the personal excesses of those elitists who have been running our government for most of the last fifty years. They have been running it as if it were their own private property and with our money. They do these things because they have learned that the power to control great wealth is at least the equal of actual ownership.

Obama's just proposed budget represents $30,500 spent for each American household or $11,290 spent for each man, woman, and child in the nation. That's your money he and Congress propose to confiscate, control and spend. Much and possibly most of it goes for purely political pay offs to keep incumbent politicians in office. For those not aware of such things, that's buying votes.

In all the years I have voted in national elections, I have only voted FOR a candidate five, maybe six times. Two of those were Democrats, Harry Truman and Evan Bayh of Indiana. The others were Republicans Dwight Eisenhower, Ronald Reagan, and Frances P. Bolton in Ohio's 22nd congressional district. I came to regret voting for Bayh who once he arrived in Washington, quickly changed, joined the Washington elite ruling class, and became a dedicated, fiscally idiotic, liberal Democrat, beholden to lobbyists. Who knows why?.

I'll give you my reasons for being so anti government in a few examples of the thousands available for anyone who looks. They are in concert with my idealism tempered by a logical acceptance of reality. The best example is quite simple and it consists of just one question and an answer:

Do you think our country—any country—and the populace are better off with economic freedom or a government controlled economy?

Same question stated differently:

Are thousands of independent entrepreneurs and corporations with the freedom to make their own choices and stand or fall in a competitive, capitalist environment where profit is necessary for survival better able to control an economy for the benefit of the most individuals, or is a single government bureaucracy with employees that cannot be fired , managed by individuals appointed and/or chosen by politicians and unions, and not beholden to any profit motive or performance standard controls?

Here's another example taken from my HoJo2Rants blog at: http://hojo2rants.blogspot.com.

Remember King Lyndon's Great Society programs? Part of that was his Model Cities program which cost billions of taxpayer dollars and was a total failure. I need only repeat one of King Lyndon's pronounced promises: "Detroit will be a shining example of the benefits of our Model Cities program." It is quite telling how accurate Johnson's prediction was. It certainly has become an example of the results of the policies of his great society programs now being greatly expanded by Obama and his cronies. Go to the following site for a more in depth description of the results of this example the efforts and policies of liberal Democrats and their union bosses.

http://www.thedailycrux.com/content/3247/Government_Stupidity

Or better still, take a drive through the inner city of Detroit and see for yourself the results of fifty years of liberal Democrat policies and labor union efforts. Be sure to do so in broad daylight with several friends in your car because doing so at night or alone carries a high risk of being car jacked and murdered. Actually, you can see a lot of abandoned homes and buildings just by driving through on I-75. I did that just a few days ago and burned out homes and factories were quite evident, even from the Interstate. Inner city Detroit looks more like the bombed out center of a third world city than an American one. The media elite boneheads are now beginning to extol a growing renaissance of Detroit in direct denial of realty and in spite of the fact unemployment is nearing 50%. Also, 30% of those working are employed by government. This shining example of liberalism in action has lost 60% of its population in the last 50 years. Those who fled the city were mostly middle class workers and included virtually all of the whites. They have been largely replaced by uneducated and poor Muslims and Hispanics with their huge birthrates and dependence on welfare.

Now those same morally deficient snake oil salesmen and tyrants are using the same process that has clearly devastated all of the most liberal states, to do the same thing to America with absolute certainty. There may in fact be enough ignoramuses at the public welfare and employment trough, in government unions, and that listen to a totally corrupt and deceptive media, to win the next election. Maybe there are enough of those who have had their fires of hate fanned by emotional blackmail to bring down America. (Thank you reverend Wright!) It is obvious to me that the left's "spread the wealth to equalize economic conditions" means making everyone poor and dependent on government. Well, that's one way to level the field of economic opportunity in America, take it away.

When I pointed this out to my Socrates discussion group, one of the many liberal members said I was wrong, that it was not liberal Democrat policies that brought about the demise of the American auto industry that caused Detroit to collapse. I then asked him what he thought was the real cause of the demise of the Detroit's auto industry. "Why, the failure of the auto industry to compete with cheaper and higher quality foreign cars." He replied.

I then asked him what he thought was the reason for that. "Older factories, antiquated equipment and the failure of management to modernize and adapt new manufacturing techniques." He answered.

"I couldn't agree more," was my surprising (to him) reply. "And just who or what was it that prevented the industry from doing those important things?"

He had no concrete answer and mumbled something about greedy executives and poor management, so I continued. "The UAW demanded benefit and labor cost increases that took capital that could have been used for modernization, while union work rules prevented the adoption of new manufacturing methods, especially in the use of automation and robots. These union efforts were backed and supported totally by all liberal Democrats. That's why liberal policies and politics are directly responsible for the demise of much of America's auto industry and the city of Detroit. I will stand on my original reasoning. He had no response.

These examples are undeniable realities, and there are many many more. If Detroit is not enough, think the entire states of Michigan, New York, California, Wisconsin, New Jersey, and all the other blue states that are bankrupt or nearly so. It certainly wasn't conservatives who ran them into the ground. Now that the voters in several of those states threw out the Democrats and elected Republican governors and state legislatures, Democrats are using every legal and illegal tactic they can to continue the fiscal carnage they have wrought. What do you think they will look like in five or ten more years?

And how about Fannie Mae, Freddie Mac, Amtrack and the Postal Service? Competitive private entities clearly beat the pants off these government operations. These private companies make a profit (that word liberals hate) and pay taxes (the word liberals love) to boot. Those four (and every other government operation) require huge infusions of tax payer money to keep operating.

Then there were my predictions on the mortgage melt down. These were based on some unique realities in my experience. Barb's younger son is a mortgage banker, has been since the 1990s. More than ten years ago he told me about some of what he was seeing in the mortgage markets that made him nervous. The relatively small bank he worked at then was told by agents of our federal government to make loans to disadvantaged (read mostly black or Hispanic) home buyers that were far riskier than the bank's rules allowed. When his bank refused, the government stepped in and actually seized the bank with some technical nonsense, turning it over to a much larger area bank. The bank owners received about twenty cents on the dollar, a major rip-off. Adam did not stay with the new bank, but went to work for another regional bank that had been trying to hire him for some time.

This bank also was ordered to make risky loans and also refused. Fortunately, they were big enough to weather the resulting storm even though they could no longer sell their mortgages to Fannnie Mae and Freddie Mac. (the federal government mortgage banks). We talked about the situation for some time and that's when I made my prediction about the coming collapse of the mortgage market. What would eventually happen was as plain as day to anyone who looked at it rationally. Yes there were a number of greedy people who bought houses to flip and make a fast buck, but the billions in loans to people who would never be able to fulfill their obligations was infinitely larger. This was a financial house of cards that had to crumble. When the Bush administration and conservative Republicans in Congress tried to check this fiscal lunacy, they were ridiculed and called racists by many in the media and shouted down in Congress by the likes of Maxine Waters, Barney Frank, Chris Dodd and most of the other liberal self servers.

Along with all the other solvent homeowners, my six children each lost a major portion of the equity in their homes. Fortunately, none of them became upside down. Each retained some equity.

In actual fact, that debacle was by far the largest financial loss the American middle class had ever suffered both from a dollar and a percentage standpoint. It resulted in the transfer of more than half of the percentage ownership of all American homes from individuals to banks. (I'm sure you can understand that math.) Then the government forced hundreds of small and medium sized banks to close their doors or be taken over by larger banks. The total value of the nearly 400 banks that were closed between 2008 and the present was in excess of $633 trillion. Who ended up with those assets? Remember those few huge "too big to fail" banks? So much for liberal Democrats taking care of the small business owner. "Let's give those megabanks a few hundred billion in taxpayer money and let all those small banks go under." No wonder Goldman Sachs is now in bed with the Obama administration. Talk about interlocking directorates. How about interlocking ownership between the megabanks and federal government. Wall street bankers and the Whitehouse are definitely sharing the same bed. The media screams about corporate executive bonuses, but never mentions the huge bonuses paid to Fannie Mae and Freddie Mac executives—$90 million to Clinton buddy Franklin Raines of Fannie Mae alone—even as those two were going bankrupt. That's reality, an undeniable fact. It sure as hell does not have "another side."

Why the dichotomous "two sides to everything" stance anyway? If the truth be known, there are usually more sides to any question of opinion than there are people interested in it. Sometimes, there is only one side. For example: statements of truth (not opinions) have but one side, the factual. One plus two equals three does not have another side. That the sun rises every day does not have another side. The reality of the mortgage debacle does not have another side. The deliberately engineered mortgage collapse does not have another side. These are undeniable realities, they happened.

On the other hand, opinions almost never have two opposite sides, but usually many different sides.. Some are very close to the same while others can be quite different. Different does not mean opposite and visa versa. The enemy of my enemy is not necessarily my friend. He or she could be an even worse enemy.

A Nearby Example of the Results of Liberal Democrat efforts

While all this mortgage business was going on, my neighbor in Indiana (he ran for Congress a couple of years ago and lost) told me about a little problem the Fort Wayne banks were having. It seems there was a group of six men who cooked up an interesting real estate scheme. All were south side politicians, three were lawyers, two were real estate agents, and one was a professional appraiser. They would buy a run down south side (the slum neighborhood) house for between $5,000 and $15,000 and fix it up cosmetically for as little as they had to spend, usually between $5,000 and $10,000. Then they would find a buyer or someone to pose as a buyer. They would sell them the house for say, $100,000 and, using the appraiser and with government aid and guarantees, obtain a loan for still more than the appraisal. They would cut a check for the home buyer for $20,000 or a bit more, and pocket the difference, usually between $50,000 and $90,000. (Talk about greed) Neither this nor even the whole mortgage collapse would have happened if it were not for housing and mortgage policies put in place by liberal politicians under Carter and then Clinton. These policies were opposed by Republicans and by the Bush administration as I mentioned earlier. Their rational efforts brought them scalding condemnation from liberals and their friends in the media. The fact that they were so right will never be mentioned by the liberal propagandists we call the main stream media.

What happened next was quite predictable. The owners would finally default on their mortgage, walk away from the place and leave it empty. Within a week or so, strippers would remove everything useable from the house including pulling the wiring. (copper sold as scrap) sometimes they even removed doors and windows. When they foreclosed, the bank got a property with a house that would cost far more to fix than it would ever be worth. Many of them were set afire before they could be bulldozed down. Others became crack houses or shelters for transients and drug dealers. The city received no taxes and the resulting blighted neighborhood rapidly went down hill. I don't know it for a fact, but I'll bet the same thing happened on a much larger scale in Detroit. Drive through parts of the south side of Fort Wayne and you'll see what I mean. It's Detroit on a much smaller scale.

The six men were sued by the banks. The city was working up a criminal suit as well. My neighbor knew all the details about this while it was happening. (and told me plenty) He knew because he was a member of the law firm involved in the suit for the city. The six men were—guess what—black liberal Democrats. They were also higher ups in the local ACORN group. Surprise, surprise! After making news in all the local media for about a week, things suddenly became very quiet. Remember, this was the spring of 2009 and ACORN's buddy was in the Whitehouse. To make a long story short, the whole thing quickly and quietly was swept under the rug. No more mention in any of the media—ever. The criminal suit was gone and so was the bank suit. I could find no records of either in a search of Fort Wayne public legal records on the Internet. Those records disappeared or at least public Internet access to them disappeared. They were there one day and gone a few weeks later. My friend now claims he knows nothing more about it and no longer will talk about it, even in private. Hmmmmmm? You can make your own assumptions about what happened there. Incidentally, I often wonder if the newspaper accounts of this are still in the archves? I'll bet they too have mysteriously gone missing.

The things described in these paragraphs are all hard realities, not opinions. You can see them, photograph them, even buy them. Both Detroit and Ft Wayne would love some new owners who would pay taxes. Wherever government controls anything, you will find huge waste, crippling graft, crime, corruption, gross inefficiency and almost total financial irresponsibility.

You mentioned health care, your field, and the unconscionable waste and poor use of resources. Isn't most of this paid for by medicare, medicaid and health insurance? Do you think a government single payer system would do better? And about rationing of healthcare I have had two experiences with government agencies that reflect the realities of government running anything. When Barb became ill with PPS in 2000 and had to step down from the pulpit, her healthcare was covered for one entire year by the Methodist church. During that year we tried obtaining a new healthcare policy with little success. We then applied for SSI which would have helped us quite a bit. She was denied coverage many times (at least ten times) over the next few years with no explanation or recourse. In 2003, after her surgeries and heart attack cost us half a million dollars (really), a friend of ours put us in touch with Mike Pence, a Republican Congressman, not from our district, but whose wife I believe also had PPS. He was wonderful. Within a month we started receiving Barb's SSI checks. Incidently, our own Republican Congressman did nothing for us.

About two years ago I applied for a federal grant from the Department of Energy to help with the publication and promotion of my book on energy, Energy, Convenient Solutions. I jumped through all of the hoops, filled out all of the forms, and made certain that I was income qualified. After dozens of phone calls I was given an appointment for an interview with a grant officer in Jacksonville. It was fifteen months after my application was sent in. When I walked into the office and saw the grant officer I was certain I was in trouble. The officer who had just called me in was a black woman about fifty weighing at least 350 pounds. I walked over to her desk and handed her my papers. She took them, compared them with some papers she had on her desk, picked up a large rubber stamp, stamped and signed my papers and hers. Then without a word she handed them back to me and called out the name of her next victim. The big *Denied* in red told me everything I would ever learn about why the grant request was denied. (And there was no appeal) If I wanted to try again for a grant I would have to go through the entire process again. She must have felt a great sense of satisfaction in turning down my application without a word of explanation or help. I wondered what would have happened if I had been black or had slipped a few $100 bills inside those papers. Those are my two latest experiences with the federal bureaucracy. I can only imagine what a chaotic mess our government will make of our health care system if Obamacare becomes law.

Obamacare, VA style healthcare for the entire nation.

Oh yes, now even the Obamacare proponents are admitting the bill will not save any money. My estimate of the cost of Obamacare is at least double the cost of our present system. It will be run like any government operation, a monstrous, overburdening bureaucracy with all the waste, inefficiency, corruption, and political favoritism that guarantees. My cost estimates of government expenditures have routinely been far more accurate than those of the CBO. The history of their estimates of expenses is one of missing the final costs by factors of from two to four. I wonder why? Is there another side to those facts, or are they merely conjured up out of thin air in Lalaland?

Incidentally, have you ever spent any time in or visited a VA hospital? When I was in the dental business we did a lot of maintenance work on dental equipment in the VA hospital near Cleveland. We actually had to jump our bid prices about a third higher than what we charged private dentists because of all the costs associated with dealing with their red tape and special requirements, few of which made any sense at all. It finally became so expensive to deal with them we quit bidding. The first time we didn't bid, their purchasing agent called and begged me to bid, admitting no one else had either. Then he said the following, "I don't care if you double the regular price, we need that service." I bid on two more small jobs and then quit for good. I have no idea how or from whom they purchased their service and supplies after that.

I was going to list the similarities between the Carter and Obama effects on our country and compare them to those of the Reagan years, but everyone knows the difference in the budgets, the deficit, the unemployment rates, and inflation. Remember Carter's 20% interest rates, 12% inflation, and double digit unemployment? They say inflation is under control, but is it? Have you noticed the price of gasoline, diesel, and heating oil has doubled in the last year? (It just went from $3.14 a gallon to $3.55 a gallon in two weeks here.)

And how about food prices? Have you seen that they have increased by 50% or more during the same period? Ever wonder why those increases don't seem to affect the government's inflation index, or bring about an increase in COLA, the cost of living allowance used for Social Security and military pay? That's because liberal Democrats under Bill Clinton, removed food and fuel from those calculations. This has seriously affected the poor who can least afford it because food and fuel consume a major portion of their income. And the unemployment rate that was 4.2 % when Reagan left office is only 9.4% under the way it is calculated using Obama's new method. The current way to figure the unemployment rate does not include those who have stopped actively seeking work or are no longer receiving unemployment checks. If figured the same way it was during previous administrations including Reagan's, the current rate would actually be close to 18%. And these deliberate deceptive manipulations of statistics by our government go on and on. I wonder, where is the media outrage about those two hidden, but hugely deleterious changes?

Is it any wonder that our federal government is mired in debt along with virtually every blue state in the nation? I ask you again, who is more responsible, liberals or conservatives? Few people will pay any attention, and certainly few politicians are willing to address these serious problems. Could we correct these problems and once again become the dynamic leader of the free world? Yes, with the right leadership. Will we? I seriously doubt it. I am going to use two very telling quotes and related information that will explain why we will probably end up on the trash heap of history.

Why Democracies Always Fail

See quotes on Page 91

Those words of Prentis clearly echo your comments about the health industry, indeed, it probably holds true for any industry or functioning body deeply dependent on insurance, government, or any other source of money poorly controlled by the rules of economics. It is so very clear that laziness, fraud, and being wasteful, ignorant, and destructive are easily accomplished by a growing section of our populace while hard work, honesty, thrift, and being creative and constructive are now limited to a shrinking number.

In stark contrast, look at China. After decades of oppressive economic conditions, the government permitted an expanding number of economic freedoms including private ownership of farms, businesses, and even industries. The results of this complete reversal of policy has been the amazing growth of their economy and the creation of a rapidly expanding middle class of consumers, and a number of newly created, quite wealthy entrepreneurs. I believe that this economic growth and freedom will lead to more personal freedoms for the Chinese. They have let the capitalist free enterprise genie out of the bottle. It is hard to predict just where it will take them, but it is obvious that their direction is the opposite from where we in America along with most of the Western world are heading. The road up is a lot happier then the road down. Quite obviously, they are between courage to liberty; and liberty to abundance, while we are between apathy to dependency; and dependency back to bondage.

Yes, these last two paragraphs are personal opinions, but just look at the present realities of America compared to China. The factual realities are so obvious I think you would find it impossible to come to any very different conclusions. The lessons of history are pretty damned hard to deny. They have repeated over and over again.

Oh yes, wasn't it Pogo who said, "I have met the enemy, and he is us?"

Wisconsin and the Power of Government Unions, the SEIU

It is easy to see that two opposing groups have squared off for battle in Wisconsin and elsewhere over mostly government unions who are married to the liberal Democrats. This battle is over whether the SEIU, the teachers union, and their like run things or the voters of Wisconsin do. Voters who have finally awakened to see the ruthless self-service of government unions.

Incidentally, one of our esteemed US Presidents said, "Government workers, however, don't generate profits. They merely negotiate for more tax money. When government unions strike, they strike against taxpayers. Such an action is unthinkable and intolerable." Which one was it? Here's a hint, it wasn't a Republican.

Here's another quote, "It is impossible to bargain collectively with the government."

That wasn't Newt Gingrich, or Ron Paul, or Ronald Reagan talking. That was George Meany -- the former president of the A.F.L.-C.I.O -- in 1955. Government unions are unremarkable today, but the labor movement once thought the idea absurd. My how times and politics have changed. Unions now routinely extort money and gain power by threatening to shut down critical government services. And who do the unions, Democrats, and the government media slaves blame for the shut downs they brought about? One guess.

Here's another link you might want to check out.

http://www.youtube.com/watch?v=tsH8xvjTAlo. It tells how Obama and Eric Holder are joining in supporting a foreign nation and a criminal drug cartel against the state of Arizona. This is an evil unprecedented in our entire history.

Incidentally, I have the perfect answer to the illegal drug problem. It would remove all of the incentives for criminal activity and put the drug cartels out of business permanently. Check out http://hjdrugprb.blogspot.com. The only problem is all the drug cartel's money that is paid to American politicians to keep drugs illegal and keep the Mexican border porous for the drug cartels. Why do you think Obama and Eric Holder are suing Arizona for enforcing federal law when they won't? Hell, it's pretty plain to see they want the drug cartels to keep on making money and killing Americans. I wonder how much of that Mexican drug cartel money flows into their coffers? Hmmmmm?

Remember prohibition? Of course you don't. You are too young. Prohibition created many huge and powerful criminal gangs, the remnants of which still operate in many America cities. Just think Al Capone, Big Bill Thompson, (Republican and one of the most corrupt politicians in American history), Jake Arvey, the Daleys, and the current Democrat political machine in Chicago as one example. These criminal gangs pour billions into keeping drugs, prostitution, guns, and who knows what else illegal. They love those laws because they know it secures their illegal businesses. Just as prohibition created thousands of criminal organizations to supply alcohol, drug laws create thousands of criminal organizations to supply illegal drugs. The same thing applies to prostitution and guns wherever they are illegal.

Good old Rom Emanuel, remember him as Obama's right hand man? Anyway, as a member of the current version of the Capone gang structure, was there any doubt he would be able to run for mayor even when his candidacy was illegal according to Chicago law? We all knew a way would be created to circumvent that law. As with any law they want to break, they simply get one of their judges to rule in favor of what they want, regardless of any law. On the larger scale, it looks as though that same criminal organization is now running the country, and running it into the ground.

Tell me where I've been wrong and have sweet dreams!

Cordially, Ho

INSERT, 9-18-2015 - It's truly amazing what has happened in Wisconsin and to Scott Walker, the Republican Governor who fought for the people of Wisconsin and won against union goons and money sent in from all over the nation to Wisconsin to defeat him. At this point his campaign is faltering a bit because of a lack-luster performance in the latest debate. Of course, the CNN moderators asked Walker only three questions, less than anyone else.

How the European Leftist News Media Misrepresents America, and how Americans are fighting back via the Internet.

Some time back I blogged about how our friends in the European news media had castigated America for being so stingy with relief for the tsunami that devastated Indonesia. They pointed out that the American government was fourth or fifth largest financial contributor to that relief effort. That is true, but what they neglected mentioning (deliberately, I am sure), was that Americas private giving totaled more than all of the worlds governments combined. Private Americans and American businesses provided more then half of the total relief effort. Also note that Indonesia is a Muslim nation.

Well, we did it again. From the e-news, Real News and Views comes another story you will not read in the New York Times or other government controlled media—or is it the reverse—media controlled government? Who knows? However, they are now joined at the hip, the media gushingly in attendance. They will, of course, be widely separated and antagonistic the instant Republicans regain control in 2012. (I hope!)

May 10, 2011 - Real News and Views:

The recent earthquake and tsunami in Japan have created a tragic humanitarian crisis. Thousands of homes, businesses and lives have been destroyed. The situation at the Fukushima nuclear power plant remains uncertain. Our thoughts and prayers are certainly with the Japanese people in the midst of this terrible tragedy.

Yet, as with most major natural disasters in our time, the tragedy in Japan has once again showcased the amazing generosity of the American people. As aid pours into Japan from around the world, the United States, in keeping with her magnanimous spirit, has led the way.

So far, USAID and the Department of Defense have spent a combined $32,251,844, which includes sending two professional urban search and rescue teams maintained by the counties of Fairfax, Virginia and Los Angeles, California. The U.S. military immediately dispatched the aircraft carrier Ronald Reagan to Japan, along with other ships, to assist in relief efforts.

However, private donations to relief efforts from Americans already stand at $161 million or FIVE TIMES AS MUCH as public money - including millions of dollars from U.S. corporations such as Goldman Sachs, J.P. Morgan, Walt Disney, and FedEx.

America's generosity arises not only from the faith and altruistic spirit of her people, but also from the fact that Americans have the means and the freedom to be generous. The means is a direct result of America's capitalist economic system that allows for free enterprise, competition, and the creation of wealth, which gives Americans the freedom to give generously to others out of their discretionary funds. While some seek to denigrate wealth creation or tax business into oblivion, it is evident that America - her businesses and citizens - are abundantly generous to people facing crisis and disaster, precisely because they have both the heart and the ability to do so!

In the midst of this disaster we have an opportunity to reflect on America's exceptional spirit, character, and people. Because America was founded on the principle that each person possesses a God-given dignity, her people are always quick to come to the aid of others in their time of need. The American people have always exhibited a great spirit of generosity and concern for the downtrodden, as exemplified now in their outpouring of aid and support to Japan and others at home and around the world. It is in times like these that we should all be particularly proud to be Americans.   **End of quote.**

I realize you liberals would prefer to take private money by force and use it as you see fit rather than have the American people contribute directly to the needs of their choice. That's just who you are and what you do. You are small minded people who are always condemning, but never creating; using problems to build your power, but rarely solving anything; cursing and calling derogatory names any who oppose your power, but offering very few corrective, constructive ideas if any. Because you are relatively void of creative, constructive, or realistic ideas, all you can do is label those you oppose with rancid hatred. Your latest idea is to label as racists, anyone and everyone who raises any objections to your lust for power. It's a cheap shot from mindless boobs who, in truth, are the real racists of America.

I'll say one thing for the left. They really know how to destroy. They have already virtually destroyed America's education system, America's inner cities (like Detroit), America's middle class (the mortgage melt down), America's once vibrant economy, and much of America's manufacturing. Right now you are doing everything you can to destroy American free enterprise, discredit American exceptionalism, and move wealth from the middle classes to the ruling class of relatively few, wealthy and elite individuals and corporations. (The easier to control it my dear.)

I have news for you anti patriots. True American exceptionalism, free enterprise genius, and fierce work ethic may just be more than you can handle. Just remember, you may bankrupt the government, but America's wealth still lies in the hands of individuals, and I'll wager not even you will be able to change that, not even with your corrupt judges, government bureaucrats, invincible bureaucracy, union thugs, and black militants. There is one single and powerful entity that stands in your way in spite of your efforts to minimize it. That happens to be the US Military. There is another group of real Americans that is growing in numbers and power in spite of all your ridicule and pointed hate speech. That group is the Tea Party. I rest my case. Just once you should try building instead of destroying. I realize just how much harder it is to design and build rather than curse and destroy. You're probably just not up to the effort.

Tuesday, January 25, 2011

The "experts" who cry wolf

The constant warnings of persistent attention-seeking doomsayers among, college professors, environmental extremists, PBS, the New York Times, Washington Post and other Newspapers, are becoming like the story of the boy who cried wolf. In their efforts to bring attention to themselves, gain celebrity, and sell themselves and their products to the public, these so called pundits have exaggerated possible dangers out of all proportion to reality. These scare tactics sway a lot of people who are ignorant of the facts. They are so seldom correct in either action or scale that most reasonable people pay them scant attention anymore. The worrisome thing about this is that should a real dangerous menace come along (a real wolf) the predictions will be viewed as just another exaggeration and ignored by the public and those who could counter the menace.

EXAMPLE: When the very first primitive steam powered locomotives appeared at least one newspaper predicted people would die riding in theses conveyances that could go as fast as forty miles per hour because they would be unable to breath moving that fast. You may laugh, but how many erroneous and equally dire predictions have been foisted off on a gullible public in the same way since then?

As PBS releases a special about the oil delivery system, the Business & Media Institute goes back in time to recall environmentalists pipe dream: stopping it.

* By R. Warren Anderson

Wednesday, April 19, 2006 10:00 AM EDT

Alaska Pipeline Doomsayings Revisited

After the discovery of oil in Prudhoe Bay, Alaska, it didn't take long for environmentalists to cry gloom and doom and for the media to hype those claims. From caribou dying to earthquakes to all hell breaking loose, there was no shortage of catastrophic predictions though the Alaska pipeline now boasts great success roughly 30 years later.

Construction on the pipeline began in 1975, and oil first moved through it on June 20, 1977. Former Secretary of the Interior Gale Norton summed up its success in 2003 that Today the pipeline produces 17 percent of our domestic petroleum. It has pumped nearly 14 billion barrels of oil and $400 billion into our economy. We need the pipeline even more now than when it was built.

Just in time for the PBS special, The Alaska Pipeline, set to air April 24 on PBS, the Business & Media Institute compared predictions from the pipelines inception to the realities of the past three decades.

Propaganda, Not Policy: Approval of the pipeline was not based on facts but on oil industry propaganda, according to some of the Department of Interiors top ecologists, reported The Washington Post on Feb. 11, 1971. The New York Times ran an editorial that began, passage of the Alaska pipeline bill is the triumph of scare propaganda and economic pressure over reasoned public policy on Nov. 14, 1973.

Reality: Despite those claims, the pipeline has had tremendous policy implications. It created tens of thousands of jobs, from the construction of the pipeline in Alaska to the manufacturing of the pipe in Pennsylvania, to the building of the tankers to transport the oil in Louisiana.

And as gas prices rise going into another summer driving season, the pipelines effect on the oil market bears mentioning. Alaska produces about 800,000 barrels a day or about 1 percent of the world market of 73.5 million barrels a day, said Peter Van Doren of the Cato Institute.

A loss of that production would increase prices by at least 10 to 16 percent. In the 1980s, when production was 1.8 million barrels a day and the world market was smaller (54 mbd), the loss of Alaskan oil would have increased world oil prices by 30 to 50 percent.

Bye-bye Caribou?: Many people suddenly developed a passionate concern for the mating habits of Alaska caribou and campaign noisily against intrusion of Arctic pipelines into this essential activity, reported The Christian Science Monitor on Oct. 10, 1972. The New York Times on Oct. 14, 1973, said the question is whether the caribou will go the way of the buffalo.

Reality: Thirty years later we can see the effects of the pipeline on the caribou. Walter Hickel, a former U.S. Secretary of the Interior and governor of Alaska, said that the caribou herd has not only survived, but flourished. In 1977, as the Prudhoe region started delivering oil to America's southern 48 states, the Central Arctic caribou herd numbered 6,000; it has since grown to 27,128. Alaska's Department of Fish and Game Web site reports that in general, caribou have not been adversely affected by human activities in Alaska. Pipelines and other manmade objects have been built to accommodate caribou movements, and the animals have adapted to people and machines.

INSERTED NOTE: There have been many reports of caribou huddling near and even against the pipeline to stay warm in extremely cold weather and storms. It is quite possible that this could explain at least part of the herd's growth. So much for the doomsayer's predictions.

Earthquake Risk: Larry Moss of the Sierra Club stated in the Los Angeles Times on June 14, 1973, that the oil industry has continued, single-mindedly, its attempt to turn a sows ear into a silk purse. Support for this claim was that the pipeline had basic design flaws which cannot really be overcome by engineering ingenuity. This was supposedly because the pipe would cross one of the most active earthquake zones in the world, would scar and despoil vast tracts of magnificent, undisturbed country and would threaten extensive oil spills in the numerous rivers which the pipeline would cross.

A report from top ecologists at the Department of the Interior claimed that dangers of severance in earthquake prone areas were inadequately dealt with, read The Washington Post on Feb. 11, 1971. The Alaskan area involved is renowned for its extreme seismic activity, the Post reiterated on May 7, 1972. In the 70 years before 1972, 23 major earthquakes had clobbered the terrain where the Alaskan pipeline would be built, any one of which could have caused a catastrophic break in the pipe, the Post article continued.

Reality: The time passed since the construction of the pipeline allows for testing of this claim. On Nov. 3, 2002, a 7.9-magnitude earthquake struck Alaska. It was the worst earthquake recorded on Alaska's Denali fault, and considered a once-in-600-years event. The New York Times on Nov. 5, 2002, called it one of the largest earthquakes in American history, which, had it struck a major city, would have destroyed hundreds of buildings and killed many people. Tremors caused movements around Yellowstone National Park and even rocked boats in Louisiana. In comparison, the great San Francisco earthquake of 1906 was weaker at 7.8.

Yet the pipeline withstood the powerful quake just as designed damaged but not ruptured, according to the Nov. 10, 2002, Los Angeles Times. If anything, last week's powerful earthquake shows that the pipeline could have withstood more, the pipelines seismic design coordinator said. The New York Times article said that After an aerial survey today, pipeline officials said they found no leaks in the structure.

Gale Norton summarized the effects: The Alaska pipeline was just 60 miles from the quake's epicenter. It shook back and forth, some supporting struts broke. But the pipeline held. It did not crack. Not a drop of oil was spilled. No one was injured. The safety systems put in place worked to perfection. The predicted design flaws that supposedly couldn't be overcome by engineering ingenuity werent mentioned after the earthquake occurred.

Misplaced Effort: Less than five months after the announcement of the oil discovery and proposed pipeline, members of the Sierra Club complained that they were invited to only two superficial meetings where they were told nothing significant, according to The New York Times on July 5, 1969. The Sierra Club and their fellow environmentalists from the Wilderness Society, Friends of the Earth, and Environmental Defense Fund Inc. delayed pipeline progress with lawsuits. The Feb. 13, 1973, New York Times said the delay in construction is the best the oil companies can expect, while the possibility grows ever livelier that after years of misplaced effort the Alaska pipeline will join such forgotten and costly fantasies as the South Sea Bubble.

Reality: That misplaced effort has pumped 15 billion barrels of oil into the U.S. economy. Adrian Herrera of Arctic Power, an Alaska-based group that advocates oil drilling in the Alaska National Wildlife Refuge, said the effects of the pipeline have been huge. The benefit is both economic and social. Infrastructure that was built in conjunction with the pipeline has a trickle-down effect that has helped all businesses. Nationwide the effect has been quite profound, he continued. Not just a direct benefit there's indirect benefits too. Jobs supporting the pipeline have been spread across the nation, as have the advantages from having more oil available.

Pipeline Breaking: On May 6, 1970, The New York Times said that the head of the Naval Arctic Research Laboratory warned that the proposed trans-Alaska oil pipeline might break and wreak great damage to the environment.

Reality: Despite leaks in the past, the pipeline has improved and is leaking less. The United States has the most stringent environmental controls on oil. Any spill of more than a teaspoon is reported. The whole pipeline is scanned every day from the ground or helicopters for leaks. Despite being three decades old, the pipeline is more modern than many others around the world.

All Hell to Break Loose: The New York Times on Nov 10, 1974, quoted an internationally known professor on Arctic soils from Rutgers University. He predicted all hell will break loose on Alaska's north slope within five years after hot oil starts flowing through the trans-Alaska pipeline. He then compared the spread of damage to the permafrost to a cancer that takes five years.

Reality: Of the 800-mile pipeline, 420 miles are above ground to avoid the permafrost. When above ground, it has a 2-inch heat pipe containing pure ammonia. When the air is cooler than the ground, the ammonia vaporizes and draws the heat from the earth. The ammonia then condenses on the pipe, starting the process again.

Major Oil Incidents Not Caused by Pipeline

The pipeline has not been without accidents but the biggest ones did not involve pipeline malfunctions. On Feb. 15, 1978, there was a leak of 16,000 barrels. There are some indications that it is sabotage. You have to suspect foul play, said Morris Turner of the Alaska Pipeline Office, according to The Washington Post on Feb. 16, 1978. No one was ever charged in that incident. On Oct. 4, 2001, Daniel Carson Lewis, who had been drinking, shot the pipeline and caused a leak of more than 6,000 barrels of oil. The Los Angeles Times on Oct. 21, 2001, quoted a state policeman as saying, Alcohol and a guy with a gun nothing deeper than that.

The largest oil-related incident in Alaska since the pipeline was built was the Exxon Valdez incident not a pipeline failure, but a ship crashing because of human error. On March 24, 1989, a ship hit a reef and spilled more than more than 11 million gallons of crude oil into Prince William Sound. The ships captain, Joe Hazelwood, had been drinking before the ship left, which was illegal. But the time of the ships departure changed, and had it not, then he wouldn't have broken the law. Hazelwood also left the deck to do other work, leaving the ship with an under-qualified sailor a breech of company policy.

While many animals were killed and the environment was damaged, it has since bounced back. The 2005 salmon run was so large that millions of fish were left to die and rot in hatchery areas. Exxon has paid out $3.5 billion in relation to the oil spill. Alyeska, a consortium of oil companies of which Exxon is a part, spends around $60 million a year on oil spill prevention in Prince William Sound.

Tuesday, November 23, 2010

America's new Fat Cat Royalty, the Washington Elite Ruling Class

Showdown in November: Political Elites, Ruling Class vs We, The People

July 20, 2010 - By Mondoreb

BRAVE TALES of the politically-elite RULING CLASS

A few brave Tales of the Political Elite. After reading them, voters may decide it's time for the Ruling Class to relearn who the boss is in America.

WASHINGTON, D.C.:

Where the "public servants" are the masters over everyone paying the bills.

The ruling elite are different than us: Mostly, they are more arrogantly incompetent.

Time's almost up for many in the Ruling Class that is made up of the Political Elite and their porker hangers-on. November 2 will be here before they know it. It's truly time for the "public servants" who populate the DC petty nobility to find out who the real bosses in American politics are. With all of the country's challenges, it's hard to figure just exactly how the elites stay in power when their performance has been absolutely horrible.

Examples abound almost daily.

Maybe the partying-while-the-USA-burns mentality of the President is merely a disguise for his angst at diminished power come November?

Even though Washington Elites are pampered and spoiled–with pay and perks almost double those in the private, money-making sector––they justify it to themselves in the time-honored way of Ruling Classes throughout history: they feel they deserve it, of course.

Just how do the few continue to rule the many?

One way is to fan the flames of class envy, usually a British affliction. It's all detailed in Janet Dailey's fine piece, American Politics has caught the British disease. See it later in this blog

There was a warning of what was to come during the election campaign with Joe the Plumber, to whom Mr Obama unwisely confided his intention to "spread the wealth around". Americans who have risen from poverty to become qualified tradesmen or entrepreneurs generally believe that they have a right to put what wealth they produce back into their own businesses, rather than trusting governments to spread it around among those judged to be deserving.

But Joe's warning was not heeded. Most of the constituency whose instincts were the same as his voted for Obama, and have now lived to regret it. This in itself is not especially surprising: it could simply be seen as the self-interested politics of personal survival. What is more startling is the growth in America of precisely the sort of political alignment which we have known for many years in Britain: an electoral alliance of the educated, self-consciously (or self-deceivingly, depending on your point of view) "enlightened" class with the poor, ignorant, and deprived.

America, in other words, has discovered bourgeois guilt. A country without a hereditary nobility [but with an unreasoning emotional attachment to celebrities of all kinds, even criminals.] has embraced noblesse oblige. Now, there is nothing inherently strange or perverse about people who lead successful, secure lives feeling a sense of responsibility toward those who are disadvantaged. What is peculiar in American terms is that this sentiment is taking on precisely the pseudo-aristocratic tone of disdain for the aspiring, struggling middle class that is such a familiar part of the British scene.

The American Spectator's July/August print edition offers the following cover story, now featured at AmSpec's website, America's Ruling Class — And the Perils of Revolution. The author, Angelo M. Codevilla, relates exactly when it was that the misadventures of the piggish political elites first became apparent to most common folk.

As over-leveraged investment houses began to fail in September 2008, the leaders of the Republican and Democratic parties, of major corporations, and opinion leaders stretching from the National Review magazine (and the Wall Street Journal) on the right to the Nation magazine on the left, agreed that spending some $700 billion to buy the investors' "toxic assets" was the only alternative to the U.S. economy's "systemic collapse." In this, President George W. Bush and his would-be Republican successor John McCain agreed with the Democratic candidate, Barack Obama. Many, if not most, people around them also agreed upon the eventual commitment of some 10 trillion nonexistent dollars in ways unprecedented in America. They explained neither the difference between the assets' nominal and real values, nor precisely why letting the market find the latter would collapse America. The public objected immediately, by margins of three or four to one. [The unwashed proved far wiser than the elites, as usual.]

When this majority discovered that virtually no one in a position of power in either party or with a national voice would take their objections seriously, that decisions about their money were being made in bipartisan backroom deals with interested parties, and that the laws on these matters were being voted by people who had not read them, the term "political class" came into use. Then, after those in power changed their plans from buying toxic assets to buying up equity in banks and major industries but refused to explain why, when they reasserted their right to decide ad hoc on these and so many other matters, supposing them to be beyond the general public's understanding, the American people started referring to those in and around government as the "ruling class." And in fact Republican and Democratic office holders and their retinues show a similar presumption to dominate and fewer differences in tastes, habits, opinions, and sources of income among one another than between both and the rest of the country. They think, look, and act as a class.

Make no mistake: they feel they are better than the people they supposedly serve—as do their advisers and staff, elite-educated that most are. One of the few times the One-Party Media* casts a favorable light on Republicans is when one graduates into the Ruling Class. John McCain is one of the Ruling Press' favorites—outside of a presidential election season, that is.

* – "One-Party Media" from University of San Diego School of Law Professor Maimon Schwarzschild writing at The Right Coast (via PowerLine, The One Party Media).

The folks in Arizona have been laboring to remind McCain that he represents them—not his chroniclers at the Washington Post or New York Times.

There are Ruling Class wannabees. Former Senator Trent Lott comes to mind [Lott confirms he's a paid tool of the Washington Establishment]. Though out of power, apparently Lott hasn't forgotten how to employ the royal sneer. (Like all ruling class elitists, his words ring of the famous verbal sneer of another ruling class elitist, "Let them eat cake," Marie Antoinette.)

Any possible shred of doubt remaining in anybody's mind about former Senate GOP leader Trent Lott's true allegiance have now been definitively removed: Lott is a paid tool of the Washington Establishment who hates the Tea Party and all other insurgents who have had it with politics-as-usual.

"We don't need a lot of Jim DeMint disciples. As soon as they get here, we need to co-opt them," Lott told The Washington Post in an incredibly revealing story.

Sen. Jim DeMint, of course, is the South Carolina conservative Republican who last year formed the Senate Conservatives Fund to back precisely the kind of insurgent conservative Senate candidates most feared by the Lotts of the world.

One can almost hear Lott's disdain for the "little people" coming through the pixilated page.

So it's not like the Ruling Class excludes Republicans. It doesn't. But as anyone who has had many associations with the snobby can attest, they prefer "their kind of people."

And their kind of people are most often Progressive Democrats. But there are no shortage of Establishment Republicans hungering for power on the taxpayers' dime. The Establishment GOP joins the Democrats in thinking that they know best how to mandate for other lesser-blessed lives; that's why some in the GOP are dumping on the Tea Party and Right-Blogs.

Erick Erickson blogged this Washington Post item last night. His post contains an anecdote about a Tea Party favorite GOP politician mocking Tea Partiers after attending a TP rally. That happened later, while sitting in the Capitol Club. I've had off the record conversations on the topic with Hill Republicans. It's not surprising to hear one say something akin to, well, you know those bloggers, they're not very bright people, a bit crazy, with too much time on their hands. Then they'll catch themselves and say, present company excluded, of course.

This is but one reason why the clock is ticking on the GOP. The party has the 2010 and 2012 election cycle to "get it."

What to do if they don't?

After all, The Ancient Regime Isn't Going Out Without a Fight. Already, there are elites trying to bypass the Electoral College. The Dems in Massachusetts are the latest to run this trick up the flag pole.

Some have speculated that the elite won't wait until 2012–they'll uncork an "October Surprise" in order to keep their hands on the levers of power.

Again, what to do?

For one, voters can demand of the GOP–and the Democrats, though the remaining Dems will be those mostly representing "safe" districts (a rough American equivalent to the English "rotten boroughs")–that there is no more time to kick the can down the road for the next generation.

The next generation is now.

* No compromises while the country is burning in debt.

* Repeal the mad monster that is ObamaCare. Those who make their peace with the abomination in the interests of "governing" can and will be shown the door like the representatives they replaced.

* Campaign relentlessly against all those of the Politically-elite Ruling Class. Defeat them wherever they are found–though VDH says that the Postmodern Cultural Elite (not exactly the same thing; the Ruling Class is more of a subset) are to be pitied. Pity them better when they no longer hold power over the ones they profess to serve.

* If Republicans don't stop the Federal Leviathan–while it still can be stopped–dead in its tracks over the next four years, their cries of "But the Democrats will win and they are worse than us" will have no meaning or truth.

Better to create a political party that truly represents the millions not represented now by the Ruling Class outside of both Republican and Democrat's reach.

Because when you get down to it: the Ruling Class is neither Republican or Democrat. It's about scratching the backs of their fellow Classmates–while the rest of the country continues to pay for them for doing it.

These have been a few of the TALES OF THE POLITICAL ELITES. We provide them for informational and agitprop purposes.

The Ruling Class has revealed itself for the country to see.

The only antidote is an active, engaged citizenry intent on stamping it out wherever it raises its greedy, arrogant hooves.

Come November 2, it will be well past time for voters to employ the same language that the Ruling Class has been using.

Voters don't have much time to learn the lingo.

By Janet Daley in the UK Telegraph - Published: 9:00PM BST 17 Jul 2010

American Politics Has Caught the British Disease

Under Barack Obama, the phenomenon of class resentment is a live political issue, says Janet Daley in the UK Telegraph.

When David Cameron visits the United States this week, he will find a country whose national political argument has become more like our own in Britain than probably he – and certainly I – would ever have imagined. For America has learned, thanks to Barack Obama's crash course in European-style government, about the titanic force of class differences. The president's determination to transform the US into a social democracy, complete with a centrally run healthcare programme and a redistributive tax system, has collided rather magnificently with America's history as a nation of displaced people who were prepared to risk their futures on a bid to be free from the power of the state.

They are talking a lot about this in the US now. Suddenly the phenomenon of class resentment is a live political issue. Some commentators describe it as the Democrats' "middle-class problem", which means that there has been a spectacular collapse of support for the administration among the core blue-collar voters who should constitute its base. (This terminology may be confusing: the "middle class" in the US means the skilled working, or lower middle, class. University-educated professionals are described as the "upper middle class" which, in this country, tends to mean a notch or two below titled aristocracy.)

Related Articles * Barack Obama needs to find his voice

There was a warning of what was to come during the election campaign with Joe the Plumber, to whom Mr Obama unwisely confided his intention to "spread the wealth around". Americans who have risen from poverty to become qualified tradesmen or entrepreneurs generally believe that they have a right to put what wealth they produce back into their own businesses, rather than trusting governments to spread it around among those judged to be deserving.

But Joe's warning was not heeded. Most of the constituency whose instincts were the same as his voted for Obama, and have now lived to regret it. This in itself is not especially surprising: it could simply be seen as the self-interested politics of personal survival. What is more startling is the growth in America of precisely the sort of political alignment which we have known for many years in Britain: an electoral alliance of the educated, self-consciously (or self-deceivingly, depending on your point of view) "enlightened" class with the poor and deprived.

America, in other words, has discovered bourgeois guilt. A country without a hereditary nobility has embraced noblesse oblige. Now, there is nothing inherently strange or perverse about people who lead successful, secure lives feeling a sense of responsibility toward those who are disadvantaged. What is peculiar in American terms is that this sentiment is taking on precisely the pseudo-aristocratic tone of disdain for the aspiring, struggling middle class that is such a familiar part of the British scene.

Liberal politics is now – over there as much as here – a form of social snobbery. To express concern about mass immigration, or reservations about the Obama healthcare plan, is unacceptable in bien-pensant circles because this is simply not the way educated people are supposed to think. It follows that those who do think (and talk) this way are small-minded bigots, rednecks, oiks, or whatever your local code word is for "not the right sort".

The petit bourgeois virtues of thrift, ambition and self-reliance – which are essential for anyone attempting to escape from poverty under his own steam – have long been derided in Britain as tokens of a downmarket upbringing. But not long ago in America they were considered, even among the highly educated, to be the quintessential national virtues, because even well-off professionals had probably had parents or grandparents who were once penniless immigrants. Nobody dismissed "ambition" as a form of gaucherie: the opposite of having ambition was being a bum, a good-for-nothing who would waste the opportunities that the new country offered for self-improvement.

But now the British Lefties who – like so many Jane Austen heroines looking down on those "in trade" – used to dismiss Margaret Thatcher as "a grocer's daughter", have their counterparts in the US, where virtually everybody's family started poor. Our "white van man" is their Tea Party activist, and the insult war is getting very vicious. It is becoming commonplace now for liberals in the US to label the Tea Party movement as racist, the most damaging insult of all in respectable American life.

[**NOTE:** Liberals use "racist" and other demeaning labels wily-nily against all opposition in usually personal attacks. Their actions prove that they are the true racists and never hesitate to play the race card against any and all opposition. That is their only argument because they are devoid of rational, constructive ideas or proposals and must resort to tactics more commonly used in childish schoolyard verbal "Nyah! Nyah!" battles. It is a sad testimonial to the efficacy of American voters that this, class and ethnic hatred, and other destructive tactics used by the left actually motivates them.]

So the Democrats, who once represented the interests of ferociously self-respecting blue-collar America, are now seen – under their highly educated president, who wholeheartedly embraces the orthodoxy of the liberal salon – as having abandoned their traditional following. Which is precisely what Labour did here when it turned its back on what used to be called "the respectable working class" because of its embarrassing resentments and "prejudices" against welfare claimants, immigrants, and anti-social youths. Bizarrely, among people who see themselves as profoundly empathetic, there was an utter failure to understand why the spirit of benevolent understanding and tolerance did not flourish among those whose daily lives were directly affected by a mass influx of foreign workers, or local delinquency, or a welfare system that rewarded inertia.

So who will speak – both here and over there – for the aspiring, the enterprising, the law-abiding, and, perhaps most important of all in these economic times, the productive classes? Mr Cameron seems unsure whether he wishes to recapture the Thatcher constituency of C1s and C2s, or to cultivate the liberal drawing rooms with a green/overseas aid/gay marriage portfolio. He speaks warmly of the virtuous and hard-working, but his tax policies will make them pay off most of the national deficit out of their own pockets.

In the US, there is probably no going back for the Obama administration. It has definitively lost faith with the "little guy" voters who once thought of a Democratic presidency as a form of divine protection, and this president does not seem to have the ingenious flexibility of a Bill Clinton, who swung Right after his first disastrous years in office, partly under pressure from a Republican Congress.

What is most depressing about this – apart from the injustice of it – is that the people who have been disenfranchised and disowned are the very ones on whom both countries' economic recovery depends.

The One-Party Media

July 19, 2010 Posted by Scott at 9:22 PM in Powerline

University of San Diego School of Law Professor Maimon Schwarzschild was my classmate in Mrs. Mullenbein's Temple Beth El pre-k class in Fargo back in 1955 or so. Even then his smarts made him stand out. Over at The Right Coast, Maimon draws the big picture that emerges out of the fabricated tale of the congressmen and the phantom n-word:

The usual disillusioned phrase is "mainstream media" or MSM. The problem, of course, is not mainstream-hood. Angrily talking about the "state-run media" is even more misguided: the media were anything but state-run, or state-sympathetic, when Bush was president; and Republican or conservative officials or judges can expect relentless hostility now as much as ever.

What we have is One-Party Media: newspapers, broadcast networks, news magazines which represent the views and preoccupations of the Democratic Party and the political left, and consistently denigrate or ignore the views and preoccupations of the political right or centre-right; and which very often systematically ignore any news or information which might reflect badly on the one party, or reflect well on the policies, proposals, or values of the other. (Fox is the exception - and how it is reviled for it! - although in its actual news stories, Fox often, although not always, follows the "narrative" of the other media.) (The Wall Street Journal is the other partial exception, but with the same proviso for many of its actual news stories, and at any rate the Journal is still largely a specialized business paper with a specialized readership. There are essentially no other major exceptions in either print or broadcast news.)

This really cuts deep: It is extraordinary, and I think unprecedented, that a free press has voluntarily transformed itself into something not very different from the controlled press in an undemocratic country. But that is what has happened. There are, to be sure, alternative sources of information and commentary in the US for anyone who seeks them out. (There are often such sources in undemocratic countries as well: foreign broadcasts, "underground" or samizdat circulation, and so on.) But the mainline, and still collectively very powerful, media are overwhelmingly a One-Party media. It needs to be said plainly.

The story of the congressmen and the phantom n-word presents a case study in the phenomenon of the one-party media. But, as Maimon says: "There are innumerable examples, every day."

The left just does not tolerate any view or person who does not ape their mantra as spelled out dutifully by the New York Times and moveon.org. It's as if no liberal has a mind of his or her own. It's not enough that they ridicule and vilify in the nastiest way possible, any one who opposes or disagrees with their "holy" pronouncements. Now, NPR, one of their propaganda organs, has shut down one of the very few really fair voices to be heard on NPR, Juan Williams.

To read their side of the controversy, goto: **http://www.npr.org/templates/story/story.php?storyId=130713285** for an article supporting their position. It's a pretty weak argument when you look at those, like Nina Tottenberg, who made far more egregious personal comments, but are still welcome at NPR. Apparently, even more flagrantly negative comments made by Tottenberg and others about Republicans, conservatives, capitalists, and Christians are perfectly acceptable to NPR. That is because Tottenberg and those others support the liberal party mantras. Juan makes the mistake of being honest and expressing his feelings. Free speech has long been a casualty of the ruling class at NPR. Stray from saying purely positive things about liberalism, socialism, communism and now Islam and you're apt to be fired. Say all the negative or nasty things you want against capitalism, business, Republicans, conservatives, Christianity, or even America, and you'll get no negative comments and maybe even a pat on the back.

To read an unbiased view of the firing read, http://www.washingtonpost.com/wp-dyn/content/article/2010/10/21/AR2010102101474.html

A quote from that piece, "NPR officials say they have repeatedly told Williams that some of his statements on Fox violate NPR's ground rules for its news analysts. The rules ban NPR analysts from making speculative statements or rendering opinions on TV that would be deemed unacceptable if uttered on an NPR program. The policy has some gray areas, they acknowledged, but it generally prohibits personal attacks or statements that negatively characterize broad groups of people, such as Muslims."

Liberalism is an almost religious belief system with little basis in reason or reality. Those blind sheep who follow the "holy" rules, mantras, and ideology of the left will do so religiously even to their own obvious detriment. I recently sent an email message and request for comments to a broad spectrum of family and friends, a number of whom are far left politically from yours truly. I received a few very interesting responses, mostly predictable.

Here is that email about taxes:

Here's something that puzzles me and I would like to hear from anyone, especially liberals, who would explain it to me.

U. S. Government figures show conclusively that an increase in marginal income tax rates always results in a decrease in income tax revenue, and conversely a decrease in income tax rates always results in an increase in income tax revenue. Since this is true, at least for the last sixty years, what are the real motives of those currently in power who constantly promote an increase in income tax rates? Do they actually want a decrease in federal tax revenue? Why are they so avidly pursuing a policy that will result in lowered tax revenue for the federal government?

HoJo II
– – – – – – – –

Hi Daddy-doo,

I suppose most people, like me, think that naturally more money in taxes = more money in the coffers. Most folks would not consider that building in other factors that occur when taxes increase offsets or reduces the increase. It is a matter of people, myself included, not doing their homework because I don't know where to look for that information. Where is it that one could locate the statistics? It is probably not simple math or even simple economics but a complex interplay of factors that provides the end results.

Love, Deb
– – – – – – – –

October 18, 2010

Deb: There are many sources for information on the subject available on the Internet. Just search tax rates and tax revenue, and you will find more information than you really want to know. I just researched some new information on the Cato Institute web site and found the axiom I described actually applies clear back to when the income tax was first levied in 1913. Here's a quote based on what happened in the early 1920s.

"Changes in marginal income tax rates cause individuals and businesses to change their behavior. As tax rates rise, taxpayers reduce taxable income by working less, retiring earlier, scaling back plans to start or expand businesses, moving activities to the underground economy, restructuring companies, and spending more time and money on accountants in order to minimize taxes. Tax rate cuts reduce such distortions and cause the tax base to expand as tax avoidance falls and the economy grows. A review of tax data for high income earners in the 1920s shows that as top tax rates were cut, tax revenues and the share of taxes paid by high-income taxpayers soared"

That held true in more recent years with the Kennedy tax cuts, the Carter tax increases, the Reagan tax cuts, the first Bush "no new taxes" increase, the G.W. Bush tax cuts, and the Obama tax increases and threat of tax increases. In fact, business and individuals react to the threat or promise of tax rate changes even before they happen. The record of this consistent human behavior is about as consistent as anything political has ever been.

Love, Dad

Democrats Decimate Social Security Payments for Seniors

Hi All:

Just a little commentary on continuing Democrat false accusations and lies. This one is about Social Security, you know, that program Democrats are constantly accusing Republicans of planning to reduce or change to the detriment of seniors. Seniors please note this fact. The only major reduction of SS benefits for seniors was put in place by Democrats under Bill Clinton, not Republicans. Bill Clinton and the Democrats changed how the COLA, cost of living adjustment, is calculated so that today, SS checks are about 20% less than they would have been had the Democrats not reduced SS benefits.

What did they do? They removed food and fuel from the mix used to determine the COLA. I guess Democrats figured senior didn't need food or fuel. This was a direct blow to seniors dependent on SS, as food and fuel are a larger portion of senior's expenses than any other age group. This change made for an extremely false indication of the real cost of living. It resulted in most SS checks today being from $200 to $250 less than they would have been. So to use a typical Democrat strategy on them, Democrats took between $200 and $250 per month away from most seniors. And they have the gall to say Republicans will reduce SS? Get real!

Ho

Response 1 - What else would you expect from a liberal?

Response 2 - FACT! 85% of all debt our country has incurred in 230+ years of our existence has come not from "tax and spend liberals," but from the three presidencies of Ronald Reagan, Bush the elder, and Bush the idiot. Letting the Bush tax cuts expire (2.5Trillion to debt) would put us back to the tax rates of the Clinton era, which was the most prosperous decade in American history

regards ????

Reply to Response 2 comment. Typical for a liberal who knows little of our Constitution.

Question: What constitution are you living under? Our President is the executive branch of government and does not control our nation's purse strings.

FACT #1: The US Constitution places all responsibility for legislating federal expenditures in the house of representatives. All any President can do is propose, Congress legislates what we spend.

FACT #2: Except for 1947-1948, Democrats controlled the house and the federal purse strings from 1945 to 1994 when the Republicans took control. Reagan's proposed tax cuts were approved by the House, but none of his proposed reductions in expenditures were. Federal revenue soared, but the Democrat "tax and spend" Congress spent even more of it. That's why the national; debt soared. Reagan couldn't do a thing about it but complains and everyone knows how the one-party press spun his reactions to that.

FACT #3: Through six of the 8 years our infamous philanderer-in-chief was in power, Republicans controlled the House and the purse strings. If indeed it was the most prosperous era for Americans, they can thank the Republican House and Senate for that. Clinton had virtually nothing to do with it.

FACT #4: Democrats took control of the house in 2007 and look at what has happened since then. Have you been smokin' some of that Democrat weed. The records would tend to indicate that when Republicans control the House, the economy booms, and when Democrats do, well, look at us now. Obama and liberal Democrats own this financial debacle and the high unemployment. They could cause a boost to the economy, lower unemployment and probably increase federal revenue by lowering taxes, but they are far too intent on punishing those who create wealth for everyone to do anything as positive and helpful for America as that. **There are two factors alone that are responsible for the recovery** we are experiencing and liberal Democrats did everything in their plower to scuttle those. Thank God their efforts failed. The first was the rapid expansion of our own oil and gas production which has caused an unprecedented boom by greatly reducing our energy imports and lowering the cost of transportation considerably. The second is the Republican control of the house that has at least stopped the Democrat effort to destroy our economy and make the middle class dependent on government. Unfortunately, very little of their unprecedented wasteful spending has been reversed as yet.

Oh, and about that typically liberal hate comment, "Bush the idiot." It merely demonstrates the total inability of liberals to mount a rational argument about anything. Instead, they call names, curse, and personally denigrate others like school children on a playground. You'd think that they would be able to mount a rational defense of their positions, but apparently not.

Regards, Ho

There was no response from #2 responder of course.

Sent: Oct 18, 2010 9:31 PM

More on taxes and revenue

Hi All:

I have received a number of responses to my email about taxes and revenue. Most asked where I found the information. No one answered my why question. So here's a little additional information.

There are many sources for information on the subject available on the Internet. Just search tax rates and tax revenue, and you will find more information than you really want to know. I just researched some new information on the Cato Institute web site and found the axiom I described actually applies clear back to when the income tax was first levied in 1913. Here's a quote based on what happened in the early 1920s.

"Changes in marginal income tax rates cause individuals and businesses to change their behavior. As tax rates rise, taxpayers reduce taxable income by working less, retiring earlier, scaling back plans to start or expand businesses, moving activities to the underground economy, restructuring companies, and spending more time and money on accountants in order to minimize taxes. Tax rate cuts reduce such distortions and cause the tax base to expand as tax avoidance falls and the economy grows. A review of tax data for high income earners in the 1920s shows that as top tax rates were cut, tax revenues and the share of taxes paid by high-income taxpayers soared"

That held true in more recent years with the Kennedy tax cuts, the Carter tax increases, the Reagan tax cuts, the first Bush "no new taxes" increase, the G.W. Bush tax cuts, and the Obama tax increases and threat of tax increases. In fact, business and individuals react to the threat or promise of tax rate changes even before they happen. The record of this human behavior is about as consistent as anything political has ever been.

I still wonder what the real motives of those who increase taxes are. Those politicians certainly cannot be so stupid as to not know this reality, so what is their real goal? Use of class envy and resentment of those who have more than less successful individuals is an emotional reward that the stupid and ignorant see as gain even if, as is actually true, they suffer more than those they seek to punish. Once more it is the old, "cut off nose to spite face" attitude of so many people.

In an example of this close to home, I was involved in two law suits over computers I sold that one of my bitter associates, Dennis Schaaf, convinced customers to file against me and Hoosier 500 computers. Both were absolutely false accusations pretty much proven by my attorney with the information I gave him. Both suits were settled by arbitration where no one admitted or proved any guilt on my part. Because I had product liability insurance with a $500.00 deductible, all of my legal fees and settlement amounts were paid by my insurance. In the end, the sum total it cost me for each suit was that $500.00.

One guy, a trucker, paid his attorneys $4,400.00 to "get" me. The other, A local business owner, paid the same attorneys at least $3,000.00. Incidently, these particular attorneys from Syracuse make a pretty good living filing cases like these against all kinds of merchants. That's about all they do, file lots of small cases, use the same boilerplate for each one and rake in the cash whether their clients win. lose or draw. In both cases against me, all of the computer equipment I sold them was returned to me as part of the settlement. I cleaned both systems up and sold them as used for a total of almost $1600.00. So I ended up about $600.00 ahead.

Of course, I had to go through all the hassle of depositions and the other legal crap, but it sure cost me a whole lot less than it did those two jerks who were talked into suing me. About a year after this happened I had the great joy of telling this to the local business owner and suggesting that he thank Dennis for getting him to waste all that money. Sometimes, what goes around, comes around.

HoJo II

Monday, November 22, 2010
It's Becoming a Feudal World

This section contains the words of a number of intelligent and concerned individuals that all FEUDALS should read, but probably won't.

FEUDAL: one who espouses, promotes and/or blindly believes in the left, liberalism, socialism, communism, marxism, fascism or any form of government where an elite few control and do all the thinking and deciding for the rest of the people—the peons, serfs, or peasants. In other words, elitist totalitarianism masquerading under such titles.

Do Feudals ever read or listen to anything that doesn't support their ancient ideology?

Just a few thoughts that bear on the current federal government's efforts to destroy free enterprise, private property, and of course, personal freedom. I wonder who or which important private organization or company they will choose to demonize next? Incidently, all socialists, communists, marxists, fascists, and even the present liberal democrats, can be lumped together as a single, united ism—that is totalitarianism. I called them The Feudals in my book of the same name. Regardless of their intent, their idealism, their noble (???) purpose, their superior intellectual elitist attitude, or any other purpose they claim, the result is always the same. It has been so for many millenia. Ultimately hate becomes their banner and total control of the many by a few their goal. As Lord Acton's famous words:

Socialism in general has a record of failure so blatant that only an intellectual could ignore or evade it. The most fundamental fact about the ideas of the political left is that they do not work. Therefore we should not be surprised to find the left concentrated in institutions where ideas do not have to work in order to survive.

—Thomas Sowell

The judgments of men are formed not from facts as they are, but as they wish them to be. They root through tons of good wheat to find three pieces of chaff if the chaff lends weight to their beliefs and argument. It is not that they want others to know the truth, but to have those others believe as they do. Beyond this they do not care. The conceit of man ordinarily forms his criterion of truth.

—Anonymous

The Santa Barbara Newspress runs "What the World is Saying"; seems they forgot to print this.

Ever wonder why we have to depend on the foreign press to find out what's "really" going on in our own country. It's a good thing that Obama and the democrats don't own the Canadian press.. Here is what Howard Galganov predicts for Barack Hussein Obama - PLEASE READ:

Barack Hussein Obama: I Told You So - Yes I Did

By Howard Galganov

Montreal, Quebec , Canada

http://www.bing.com/images/search?q=Galganov#focal8d200795e6b26f56aaf4108af3 fc3&furl=http://www.bilan.usherb.ca/voutes/voute3/postbilan/yvesduhaime_1976.jpg

When Obama won the Presidency with the help of the LEFTIST Media, Hollywood, And Entertainment Liberals, Ethnic Socialists (ACORN), Stupid Non-Business Professionals, and Bush Haters, I wrote:

It won't take six months until the People figure this guy out and realize how horrible a mistake they've made. And when they come to that realization, the damage to the United States of America will be so great it will take a generation or more to repair - IF EVER.

The IDIOTS who not only voted for the Messiah, but also worked [hard] to promote his Lordship, are now left holding the bag.

Here are two things they will NEVER do: They will NEVER admit to making a blunder out of all proportion by electing a snake-oil salesman with no positive social history or management experience of any kind. They will NEVER take responsibility for the curse they've imposed upon the immediate and long-term future of their country.

In essence, the people responsible for putting this horror show in power are themselves responsible for every cataclysmic decision he makes and the Consequences thereof.

In just six months, the Messiah's polls are showing the following:

1. On Healthcare Reform - He's going under for the third time with polling well Under 50 percent, even within his own Party. Even though he might be able to Muscle a Healthcare Reform Bill by using Chicago BULLY tactics against his Fellow Democrats, it will just make things worse.

2. On Cap and Trade (Cap and Tax) - The Fat-Lady is already singing.

3. On the Stimulus Package (Tax and Spend) - His popularity is in FREE-FALL.

4. On the TARP package he took and ran with from President Bush - It's all but Good-Night Irene.

5. On the closing of GITMO and "HIS" war on what he no longer wants called the War On Terrorism - He's standing in quicksand with his head just about to go under.

6. On a Comparison between himself and George W. Bush at the same six months into Their respective first term Presidencies - Bush is ahead of him in the Polls.

7. On a comparison between He Who Walks On Water and the 12 preceding Presidents between WW II and now - Obama ranks 10th.

8. On a Poll just Conducted, that asks who would you vote for today between Obama and Mitt Romney - It's a dead heat. Between Obama and Palin - Obama's ONLY ahead by 8 Points and she hasn't even begun to campaign. (That in spite of a media backed ridicule and hate campaign of unprecedented proportions they have mounted against her. This campaign never considers her considerable accomplishments, only distortions of her personal life and activities.)

It seems to me that Obama Wants to be everywhere where he shouldn't be.

He's personally invested in 'totally insulting' America 's ONLY REAL Middle Eastern ally (Israel) in favor of Palestinian Despots and Murderers. He's traveling the world apologizing for the USA while lecturing others on how to do it right, when in fact and truth he has no experience at doing anything other than getting elected.

He went to the Muslim world in Egypt to declare that America IS NOT A CHRISTIAN NATION while he heaped praises on Islam, where he compared the "plight" of the Palestinians to the Holocaust.

The Russians think he's a putz, The French think he's rude. The Germans want him to stop spending. The Indians want him to mix his nose out of their environmental business. The North Koreans think he's a joke, The Iranians won't acknowledge his calls. And the British can't even come up with a comprehensive opinion of him.

As for the Chinese, he's too frightened to even glance their way. [After All, China now owns a large portion of the United States .]

Maybe if America's first Emperor would stay home more, travel less, and work a little bit instead of being on television just about everyday or stop running to "papered" Town Hall Meetings, perhaps he would have a little bit of time to do the work of the nation.

In all fairness, it wasn't HARD to be RIGHT in my prediction concerning Obama's presidency, even in its first six months, so I'm going to make yet another prediction:

OBAMA WILL PROBABLY NOT FINISH HIS 4-YEAR TERM, at least not in a Conventional way. He is such a political HORROR SHOW, and so detrimental to the USA and his Own Democratic Party, that the Democrats themselves will either FORCE him to Resign or figure out a way to have him thrown out.

Who knows, maybe he really isn't a BORN US Citizen and that's a way the Democrats will be able to get rid of him. [If he is a natural born citizen, why has he actively and at great expense, to taxpayers of course, sealed all records of his birth from public view?]

Or - MORE LIKELY THAN NOT, the Democrats will make Obama THEIR OWN LAME DUCK PRESIDENT.

I don't believe the Democrats have nearly as much love for their country as they do for their own political fortunes. And with Obama, their fortunes are rapidly becoming toast.

Subject: History Unfolding

This is enlightening. Lest you think it was written by some right-wing kook, David Kaiser is a respected historian whose published works have covered a broad range of topics, from European Warfare to American League Baseball.. Born in 1947, the son of a diplomat, Kaiser spent his childhood in three capital cities: Washington D.C., Albany, New York, and Dakar, Senegal. He attended Harvard University, graduating there in 1969 with a B.A. in history. He then spent several years more at Harvard, gaining a PhD in history, which he obtained in 1976. He served in the Army Reserve from 1970 to 1976.

He is a professor in the Strategy and Policy Department of the United States Naval War College and has previously taught at Carnegie Mellon, Williams College and Harvard University. Kaiser's latest book, The Road to Dallas, about the Kennedy assassination, was just published by Harvard University Press. Dr. David Kaiser

"My friends, we live in the greatest nation in the history of the world. I hope you'll join with me as we try to change it."

—*Barack Obama*

History Unfolding

I am a student of history. Professionally, I have written 15 books on history that have been published in six languages, and I have studied history all my life. I have come to think there is something monumentally large afoot, and I do not believe it is simply a banking crisis, or a mortgage crisis, or a credit crisis. Yes these exist, but they are merely single facets on a very large gemstone that is only now coming into a sharper focus.

Something of historic proportions is happening. I can sense it because I know how it feels, smells, what it looks like, and how people react to it. Yes, a perfect storm may be brewing, but there is something happening within our country that has been evolving for about ten to fifteen years. The pace has dramatically quickened in the past two.

We demand and then codify into law the requirement that our banks make massive loans to people we know they can never pay back? Why? [This resulted in the largest financial loss to the largest number of people (mostly the American middle class) that the world has ever seen. In one deliberate action, the left destroyed most of the hard earned wealth of most Americans. In the process, Chris Dodd, Barney Frank, and Barack Obama led the list of Democrats who profited greatly from middle America's loss. Clinton appointee, Franklin Raines walked away with bonuses totaling $90 million while heading Fannie Mae and engineering the mortgage meltdown.]

We learned just days ago that the Federal Reserve, which has little or no real oversight by anyone, has "loaned" two trillion dollars (that is $2,000,000,000,000) over the past few months, but will not tell us to whom or why or disclose the terms. That is our money. Yours and mine. And that is three times the $700 billion we all argued about so strenuously just this past September. Who has this money? Why do they have it? Why are the terms unavailable to us? Who asked for it? Who authorized it? I thought this was a government of "we the people," who loaned our powers to our elected leaders. Apparently not.

We have spent two or more decades intentionally de-industrializing our economy. Why?

We have intentionally dumbed down our schools, ignored our history, and no longer teach our founding documents, why we are exceptional, and why we are worth preserving. Students by and large cannot write, think critically, read, or articulate. Parents are not revolting, teachers are not picketing, school boards continue to back mediocrity. Why?

NOTE: Our wonderful President has announced often and loudly, "Americans are NOT exceptional." and/or "America is not an exceptional nation." Now that he has made those statements, he is doing everything in his power to make it so.

We have now established the precedent of protesting every close election (violently in California over a proposition that is so controversial that it simply wants marriage to remain defined as between one man and one woman. Did you ever think such a thing possible just a decade ago?) We have corrupted our sacred political process by allowing unelected judges to write laws that radically change our way of life, and then allow mainstream Marxist groups like ACORN and others to turn our voting system into a banana republic. To what purpose?

Now our mortgage industry is collapsing, housing prices are in free fall, major industries are failing, our banking system is on the verge of collapse, social security is nearly bankrupt, as is medicare and our entire government. Our education system is worse than a joke (I teach college and I know precisely what I am talking about) - the list is staggering in its length, breadth, and depth. It is potentially 1929 x ten... And we are at war with an enemy we cannot even name for fear of offending people of the same religion, who, in turn, cannot wait to slit the throats of your children if they have the opportunity to do so.

And finally, we have elected a man that no one really knows anything about, who has never run so much as a Dairy Queen, let alone a town as big as Wasilla, Alaska . All of his associations and alliances are with real radicals in their chosen fields of employment, and everything we learn about him, drip by drip, is unsettling if not downright scary (Surely you have heard him speak about his idea to create and fund a mandatory civilian defense force stronger than our military for use inside our borders? No? Oh, of course. The media would never play that for you over and over and then demand he answer it. Sarah Palin's pregnant daughter and $150,000 wardrobe are more important.)

Mr. Obama's winning platform can be boiled down to one word: Change. Why?

I have never been so afraid for my country and for my children as I am now.

This man campaigned on bringing people together, something he has never, ever done in his professional life. In my assessment, Obama will divide us along philosophical lines, push us apart, and then try to realign the pieces into a new and different power structure. Change is indeed coming. And when it comes, you will never see the same nation again. And that is only the beginning.

As a serious student of history, I thought I would never come to experience what the ordinary, moral German must have felt in the mid-1930s. In those times, the "savior" was a former smooth-talking rabble-rouser from the streets, about whom the average German knew next to nothing. What they should have known was that he was associated with groups that shouted, shoved, and pushed around people with whom they disagreed; he edged his way onto the political stage through great oratory. Conservative "losers" read it right now.

And there were the promises. Economic times were tough, people were losing jobs, and he was a great speaker. And he smiled and frowned and waved a lot. And people, even newspapers, were afraid to speak out for fear that his "brown shirts" would bully and beat them into submission. Which they did - regularly. And then, he was duly elected to office, while a full-throttled economic crisis bloomed at hand - the Great Depression. Slowly, but surely he seized the controls of government power, person by person, department by department, bureaucracy by bureaucracy. The children of German citizens were at first, encouraged to join a Youth Movement in his name where they were taught exactly what to think. Later, they were required to do so. No Jews of course.

How did he get people on his side? He did it by promising jobs to the jobless, money to the money-less, and rewards for the military-industrial complex. He did it by indoctrinating the children, advocating gun control, health care for all, better wages, better jobs, and promising to re-instill pride once again in the country, across Europe, and across the world. He did it with a compliant media - did you know that? And he did this all in the name of justice and .... change. And the people surely got what they voted for.

If you think I am exaggerating, look it up. It's all there in the history books.

So read your history books. Many people of conscience objected in 1933 and were shouted down, called names, laughed at, and ridiculed. When Winston Churchill pointed out the obvious in the late 1930s while seated in the House of Lords in England (he was not yet Prime Minister), he was booed into his seat and called a crazy troublemaker. He was right, though. And the world came to regret that he was not listened to.

Do not forget that Germany was the most educated, the most cultured country in Europe . It was full of music, art, museums, hospitals, laboratories, and universities. And yet, in less than six years (a shorter time span than just two terms of the U. S. presidency) it was rounding up its own citizens, killing others, abrogating its laws, turning children against parents, and neighbors against neighbors. All with the best of intentions, of course. The road to Hell is paved with them.

As a practical thinker, one not overly prone to emotional decisions, I have a choice: I can either believe what the objective pieces of evidence tell me (even if they make me cringe with disgust); I can believe what history is shouting to me from across the chasm of seven decades; or I can hope I am wrong by closing my eyes, having another latte, and ignoring what is transpiring around me.

I choose to believe the evidence. No doubt some people will scoff at me, others laugh, or think I am foolish, naive, or both. To some degree, perhaps I am. But I have never been afraid to look people in the eye and tell them exactly what I believe-and why I believe it.

I pray I am wrong. I do not think I am. Perhaps the only hope is our vote in the next elections.

David Kaiser

Jamestown , Rhode Island

United States

"Socialism is great until you run out of everyone else's money."

—*Margaret Thatcher*

Obama is Setting the Foxes to Guard the Henhouse

Can you even believe this??

Well, boys and girls, today we are letting the fox guard the henhouse.

Tomorrow, the wolves will be herding the sheep!

Obama Appoints two devout Muslims to homeland security posts. Doesn't this make you feel safer already?

Obama and Janet Napolitano Appoint Arif Alikhan, a devout Muslim as Assistant Secretary for Policy Development Source for announcement: Homeland Security Press Room.

http://atlasshrugs2000.typepad.com/atlas_shrugs/2009/06/obama-appointment-arif-ali-khan-asst-secretary-dhs.html

The American-Arab Anti-Discrimination Committee (ADC) is proud to announce that the DHS Secretary Janet Napolitano swore-in Kareem Shora, a devout Muslim, who was born in Damascus, Syria as ADC National Executive Director as a member of the Homeland Security Advisory Council (HSAC). **http://www.adc.org**

NOTE: Has anyone ever heard a new government official being identified as a devout Catholic, Jew or Protestant...? Just wondering. Doesn't this make you feel safer already??

Devout Muslims being appointed to critical Homeland Security positions? That should make our homeland much safer, huh!! Was it not men of the "Devout Muslim Faith" that flew planes into U.S. buildings not too long ago in the name of Islam. What the heck is this president thinking?

This announcement was made on Aug 20. Why are we just now hearing about it???

Ho's comment: Don't be naive. He knows exactly what he's doing. Most of his actions are achieving exactly what his backers intended. You don't think using the government to precipitate the mortgage crisis that cost average Americans most of their hard earned investment in their homes was an accident, do you? C'mon! You can't be that blind. How about that billion dollar (taxpayer's money) payoff to George Soros? Who do you think is really calling the shots and running our ship of state? And how about the recent move to have the TSA exempt Muslim women from airport security measures put in place because of threat of attack by, who else, Muslims? The implications of that bit of idiocy are horrifying.

Significant (and revealing) Differences Between Conservatives and Liberals

If a conservative doesn't like guns, he doesn't buy one.

If a liberal doesn't like guns, he wants all guns outlawed.

If a conservative is a vegetarian, he doesn`t eat meat.

If a liberal is a vegetarian, he wants all meat products banned for everyone.

If a conservative sees a foreign threat, he thinks about how to defeat his enemy.

A liberal wonders how to surrender gracefully and still look good.

If a conservative is homosexual, he quietly leads his life.

If a liberal is homosexual, he demands legislated respect.

If a black man or Hispanic are conservative, they see themselves as independently successful.

Their liberal counterparts see themselves as victims in need of government protection.

If a conservative is down-and-out, he thinks about how to better his situation.

A liberal wonders who is going to take care of him.

If a conservative needs a job he looks for one in the private sector where he will compete and risk being fired or laid off.

If a liberal needs a job he looks for one in government where ability doesn't matter, and he can't be fired or laid off. (And all he really needs to do is vote for Democrats.)

If a conservative doesn't like a talk show host, he switches channels.

Liberals demand that those they don't like, be shut down (the "fairness doctrine")

(Fox News - Rush, Glen, Bill, Sean, & Greta RULE!!!) .

If a conservative is a non-believer, he doesn't go to church.

A liberal non-believer wants any mention of God and religion silenced. (Unless it's a foreign religion, of course!)

If a conservative decides he needs health care, he goes about shopping for it, or may choose a job that provides it.

A liberal demands that the rest of us pay for his.

When a conservative considers tax policy he realizes higher taxes cost jobs and result in lower tax revenues and acts accordingly.

When a liberal considers tax policy he knows what conservatives know, but he raises taxes in spite of this because it punishes those rascally wealthy people. His definition of "wealthy" is any one with a job or business in the private sector.

If a conservative slips and falls in a store, he gets up, laughs and is embarrassed.

If a liberal slips and falls, he grabs his neck, moans like he's in labor and then sues.

If a conservative reads this, he'll forward it so his friends can have a good laugh.

A liberal will delete it because he's "offended".

Conservative on "global warming." "I seriously doubt it is much of a problem."

Liberal on Global Warming. "Who cares if it isn't so. Look at all the new taxes we can add because of it and all the liberal organizations that can use it to raise money."

Conservative businessman on taxes and investment: "I can't invest much in expanding my business because new taxes will take most of the part of my profits I usually set aside for growth capital. For the same reason I can't hire new people so there will be no new jobs."

Liberal on business taxes and investment: "You wealthy business people and your obscene profits will just have to do without like the rest of us. Those taxes are absolutely necessary so the people you would have hired can get jobs in the government."

More Politically Significant Quotes:

We have no government armed with power capable of contending with human passions unbridled by morality and religion. Avarice, ambition, revenge or gallantry would break the strongest cords of our Constitution as a whale goes through a net. Our Constitution is designed only for a moral and religious people. It is wholly inadequate for any other. 　　　　　*—John Adams*

I always wondered why liberals so disregard our Constitution. Now I know. Thanks John 　　　　　　　　　　　　　　　　　　　　　　　　　　　　　　　　　*—HJ, 2007*

The function of socialism is to raise suffering to a higher level. 　　　　*—Norman Mailer*

The sick in soul insist that it is humanity that is sick, and they are the surgeons to operate on it. They want to turn the world into a sickroom. And once they get humanity strapped to the operating table, they operate on it with an ax.   *—Eric Hoffer*

Foreign aid might be defined as a transfer from poor people in rich countries to rich people in poor countries.   *—Douglas Casey*

A government policy to rob Peter to pay Paul can be assured of the support of Paul.

—George Bernard Shaw

Without violence nothing is ever accomplished in history.   *—Karl Marx*

[Karl] Marx never did a day of work in his life, and never took the trouble to find out how a worker really feels when on the job. He naturally assumed that workers were a lesser breed of intellectuals.   *—Eric Hoffer*

There's no such thing as life without bloodshed. I think the notion that the species can be improved in some way, that everyone could live in harmony, is a really dangerous idea. Those who are afflicted with this notion are the first ones to give up their souls, their freedom.

—Cormac McCarthy

People unfit for freedom—who cannot do much with it—are hungry for power. The desire for freedom is an attribute of a have type of self. It says: leave me alone and I shall grow, learn, and realize my capacities. The desire for power is basically an attribute of a have not type of self.

—Eric Hoffer

The golden rule is of no use to you whatever unless you realize that it is your move!

—Dr. Frank Crane

The Democrat Golden Rule, "Do onto others things you would never do to yourself and let the taxpayers pay for it.   *—Howard Johnson*

Thought for the day: In today's topsy-turvy world, it is **not** okay to call a person a slut or whoremonger, but it is okay to be one!   *—HJ, 1999*

Every former protester I know passionately defends the actions of the 1960s and early '70s as exercising our First-Amendment right to criticize government policies. None seems to have read the First Amendment to the end where it speaks about peaceably to assemble, and to petition the government. More importantly, even in their advanced years, many seem incapable to confront the reality of having served the interest of America's enemies.   *—Balint Vazsonyi*

The desire to transcend the human condition is an invitation to tyranny.

—Gertrude Himmelfarb

Reality is that which, when you stop believing in it, doesn't go away.   *—Philip K. Dick*

When only cops have guns, it's called a "police state."   *—Robert Heinlein*

With our progress we have destroyed our only weapon against tedium: that rare weakness we call imagination.   —*Oriana Fallaci*

The United States will be a socialist dictatorship by 2030. At this time those leftist activists will happily extol the joys of socialism as they are being carted off to the salt mines.
                                                                                    —*HJ, 2008*

A trained flea can be taught to do most the things a congressman does.   —*Mark Twain*

Add a few drops of venom to a half truth and you have an absolute truth.   —*Eric Hoffer*

Enlightened people seldom or never possess a sense of responsibility   —*George Orwell*

To know a person's religion we need not listen to his profession of faith but must find his brand of intolerance.   —Eric Hoffer

Choose, and take the consequences. Choose to command, and learn the pain of the barbed treachery of envy. Choose to obey, and learn how soon obedience begets contempt. Choose the philosopher's life, and learn the famished waste of thought that, like a barren woman, lusts unpregnant. Choose . . . or become the victim of others' choosing.
                                                           —*Talbot Mundy in Tros of Samothrace*

There only two possible results when the lion shall lie down with the lamb. The lamb will be eaten, or the lion will starve.   —*HJ, 2004*

Friday, November 19, 2010

How the left twists quotes into falsehoods to serve their agenda of hate.

In his 1953 confirmation hearing for Secretary of Defense in the incoming Eisenhower administration, former General Motors CEO Charles "Engine Charlie" Wilson was asked how he would handle conflicts of interests in the Defense Department's dealings with his old firm. Wilson replied that "for years I thought that what was good for our country was good for General Motors, and vice versa."

For decades, Wilson's comment -- misquoted as "What's good for General Motors is good for the country" -- has been paraded by liberals as an example of conservatives putting the concerns of a giant corporation ahead of those of the rest of America. This is typical of how liberals expound bald faced lies through the biased media. It's but one example of how they "redesign" their quotes of what so many people say into even the exact opposite of what they actually said. NEVER will the main stream media correct these misquotes or even consider apologizing for their grievous lies.

But since GM's multi-billion dollar bailout and government takeover, the misquote from Wilson has become the philosophy of the Obama administration. They are treating the success of the initial public offering of the new GM, which will likely happen this Thursday, as proof positive that the auto industry rescue and much of the rest of Obama's economic policies must be good for the country. While they loudly (and falsely) proclaim GM has paid back the taxpayer's loan, they brag about the "new" GM and its profitability.

Consider this quote from John Berlau in The American Spectator,"But what exactly is so remarkable about a company coming back to life after a $65 billion taxpayer bailout, additional billions in tax breaks not available to other companies, (no corporate income taxes for the next few years), and even an amazing "sovereign immunity" exemption for this IPO from anti-fraud securities laws and lawsuits? With this massive infusion of government aid and favors, even a company selling ketchup Popsicles to women wearing white gloves would likely show a profitable quarter! (Hat tip for the Popsicle analogy to David Spade in Tommy Boy."

The sorry reality is that the bulk of the bailout money went to the UAW pension fund at the expense of less well connected pension funds of police and teachers. While GM would certainly have weathered a chapter 11 bankruptcy using a tried and proven system, our government arbitrarily went around the procedures that would have fairly treated all debtors from pension funds to bondholders to stockholders and trade suppliers. They instead simply pushed all private debtors out of the picture, took over the company and gave everything to the UAW which was probably the largest single factor in GM's financial; plight in the first place. This was a purely political payoff made with $59 billion of taxpayer's money. It was also a massive transfer of wealth from the private to the public sector. Had GM and Chrysler been able to follow Ford's lead they would still be in private hands today. Your government does not care how much of your money they spend as long as they gain power and control. Look for this procedure to become a standard in their arsenal of weapons against private business in the future.

Just because there has been a temporary setback in the recent elections does not mean the left will slacken its assault on private business, capitalism, and free enterprise. Remember those millions of anti-business leftist activists still employed by our huge government bureaucracy? Not only are they a huge controlled voting block, (they're voting to keep their cushy jobs and pensions), but they control much of the day to day operation of our far left government. All of these individuals, groups and departments will work hand-in-hand with leftist politicians to turn our once free nation in a totalitarian state. If you look closely, we're almost there already. My guess is the left is working on another plan to destroy our free economy. If you think the mortgage debacle they orchestrated was bad, wait 'til the next shoe drops.

Remember these actual, unedited words of DNC chairman Howard Dean, "I hate Republicans. I hate Conservatives. I hate Rush Limbaugh." I consider that a mantra of the left, an expression of what every liberal really feels and the hatred they express. If I were to use the left's standard policy about quotes I would have added, "I hate the stupid common people. I hate everyone who wants to be free. I hate anyone who won't follow my agenda." and claimed it was what he intended to say. Incidently, those added words are probably not far off the mark of what he and the rest on the left think. Of course, actions speak far louder than words and it is the actions of the left, and not their words that are driving this once free nation toward totalitarian socialism.

Unless this new Congress does everything it can to fulfill the promises that got them elected, I will stand by my prediction made in 1992 that the United States will be a totalitarian socialist dictatorship by the year 2030. We will then all be equally poor and starving. Except for those in power of course. That's the left's way of making everyone "equal." I am reminded of a sentence from Animal Farm, "We are all equal, but some are more equal than others."

October 12, 2010.

An email from MoveOn.org

NOTE: I joined MoveOn.org to keep abreast of what the enemies of America, capitalism, and free men are doing in their effort to destroy America. I have edited out the lies and fakery from the original email and substituted the truth, *in italics,*

Dear MoveOn member,

Forget the *great joy* from the *real* media about this year's elections.

We're quietly building a mighty volunteer army to *try to* continue our *destruction of Capitalism and America*. In the last month, MoveOn members around the country have organized nearly 1,000 events. Made over 200,000 phone calls recruiting get-out-the-vote volunteers for those *crooked* Democrat candidates. And turned out thousands of volunteers to talk to their neighbors *and curse at Republicans* about the election, with more coming every day.

We're doing *as much damage to the country as we can*. And we have got to keep it going.

This week our goal is to make 20,000 phone calls to *potential hoodlums and union thugs* to volunteer through our online calling program. With our handy calling tool, it's super-easy. Can you spend 15 minutes making phone calls? Click to sign up:

http://pol.moveon.org/2010?id=241312-9724911-nwGZA6x&t=3

We're facing a *rapidly failing* uphill battle. Just Friday, The New York Times' top election analyst gave a *glorious* report that Republicans now have a 72% change of taking over the House this fall.[1] And polls continue to show *socialist leftist thieves and criminals* like Alan Grayson and Russ Feingold are *losing big time*.

But in cities and towns across the country, *a hate filled elitist campaign* to stop the *loss of our power* and *return* our *socialist* leaders to their *destroy America program* is evident. Last weekend, MoveOn members held 350 "Yes We Can *Destroy America*!" house parties from Cave Creek, AZ to South Hadley, MA. At 48 events coast to coast this week, MoveOn members are releasing *made up* hard-hitting reports *cursing decent American organizations* that are helping Republicans try to *wrest* Congress *from the control of the leftists, communists, marxists, and other haters of America.* And in California, we've seen *one of our biased polls show socialist leader*, Barbara Boxer, pull ahead in her race against Carly Fiorina[2] *by the most vile hate-based campaigning.*

If you haven't yet gotten involved in this election, now's the time. And if you have, it's critical to keep going—and to get your friends, neighbors, co-workers, and anyone you can get your hands on involved.

Can you help out by calling MoveOn members in key areas to recruit them to volunteer with the most important campaigns for destroy America candidates? Click here now to sign up to get started calling:

http://pol.moveon.org/2010?id=24112-9724911-nwGZA6x&t=7

Thanks for all you do.

–Steven, Adam, Lenore, Duncan, and the rest of the *destroy America* team

Sources:

1. "Projected Republican Gains Approach 50 House Seats," The New York Times, October 8, 2010
http://www.moveon.org/r?r=91943&id=24112-9724911-nwGZA6x&t=5

2. "Boxer pulls ahead in polls as Calif. senate race closes in," San Diego News Room, October 7, 2010
http://www.moveon.org/r?r=91946&id=24112-9724911-nwGZA6x&t=6

Want to support our work? We're entirely funded by our 5 *remaining* members—no corporate contributions, no big checks from CEOs. *All we get is tons of money from US hating Hungarian billionaire, George Soros, ACORN, SEIU, the communist party, and many other worker repressing unions.* Chip in here.

This email was sent to Howard E. Johnson on October 12, 2010.

October 7, 2010

This Is How You Fix Congress!!!

Let us all promote a "Congressional Reform Act of 2010". It would contain ten provisions, all of which would probably be strongly endorsed by those who drafted the Constitution and the Bill of Rights. For those of you who say, "this is impossible," let me remind you, Congress has the lowest approval of any entity in Government, now is the time when Americans will join together to reform Congress - the entity that is supposed to represents us, but actually only represents itself and those who provide them all that money. In case you didn't notice, members of Congress buy their membership with taxpayer dollars. The more they can steal from taxpayers, the more they can spend to get elected. They have careers as tax thieves. Every time they write an earmark or pork bill, they are stealing tax dollars to buy their next election

We need to get a Senator to introduce this bill in the US Senate and a Representative to introduce a similar bill in the US House. These people will become American hero's. On second thought, that's undoubtedly an impossibility, so lets have a referendum and pass the law ourselves.

Thanks,

A Fellow American

Congressional Reform Act of 2010 based on the following:

Serving in Congress is an honor, not a career. The Founding Fathers envisioned citizen legislators, serve your term(s), then go home and back to work like the rest of us.

1. Term Limits: 12 years only, one of the possible options below.

> A. Two Six year Senate terms
>
> B. Six Two year House terms
>
> C. One Six year Senate term and three Two Year House terms

2. No Tenure / No Pension:

A congressman collects a salary while in office and receives no pay when they are out of office.

3. Congress (past, present & future) participates in Social Security: All funds in the Congressional retirement fund moves to the Social Security system immediately. All future funds flow into the Social Security system, Congress participates with the American people.

4. Congress can purchase their own retirement plan just as all Americans.

5. Congress will no longer vote themselves a pay raise. Congressional pay will rise by the lower of CPI or 3%. In no instance will Congressional pay ever be more than the average of the pay of a randomly selected group of middle managers from 100 medium sized American companies.

6. Congress loses their current health care system and participates in the same health care system as the American people.

7. Congress must equally abide in **all laws** they impose on the American people.

8. All contracts with past and present congressmen are void effective 1/1/11. The American people did not make this contract with congressmen, congressmen made all these contracts for themselves.

9. Expenses and travel: Members of Congress will be granted an expense allowance in exact accord with IRS rules for business expenses and must keep substantiating records. They will be limited to twelve round trips for themselves and four for their families by commercial air from Washington to their home states and districts. Additional travel or if you want to travel in a private jet, Nancy, you'll pay for yourself with your own money. Accepting anything worth more than a total of $100 per year from anyone for any reason is cause for expulsion from Congress and forfeiture of all rights and privileges as a member.

10. No more than 100 attorneys will be permitted to be nominated to run for Congress in any single election. The first 100 who file are in. After that no more filings of attorneys will be permitted. As an alternative, let as many file as want to, then select up to a hundred from those by random lottery along with fifty alternates (one from each state). The alternates will be available in case one of the original group cannot run for any reason.

These 10 would have to be fleshed out for use, but the essentials are there. Incidentally, did you know that until Lyndon Johnson became president the government represented just 4% of our economy. Right now our government represents slightly more than 40% of a much larger economy? At that accelerating growth rate, the government will represent 100% of our economy in just forty-two years.

Tuesday, September 21, 2010

An open letter to LaLa Land dwellers

This includes most Democrats from the center to the far left

Dear moderates, Democrats and other leftist supporters of the present administration:

You are all victims of a colossal fraud. Because of your prejudices and fears, you will probably—no—certainly misunderstand the intent of these words. It is my observation that facts and realities have little to do with your opinions and expressions. Emotions driven by LaLa Land hopes, class envy, and illogical hatred of profits and capitalism, will always override any rational thoughts that might come into your heads.

You must be happy as clams with what the anointed one and his followers have accomplished to date in their war against free enterprise. Let's see:

1) They brought about the biggest destruction of personal wealth for the most middle class people in history. And, yes it was started during the Bush administration, but it was liberals in the government bureaucracy like Raines and Johnson supported by Senators Dodd, Frank, and Obama who deliberately forced it through over the strenuous objections of George Bush and Dick Cheney. Both were called all manner of racists and anti-home owners by the left including the media for trying to prevent the debacle they saw coming. Barney Frank in particular is on record saying Fannie Mae and Freddie Mac were in excellent shape and that Bush and Cheney were trying to stop a policy that was providing homes for low income families. Ha! Typical of the left it was all condemnation and contrived hate speech with no substance or rational information of any kind. All of this is in the records even if the biased media refused to report it. I think it was a deliberate action designed to do just what it did. It's all part of Obama's announced plan to spread the wealth which is really a plan to spread poverty and make everyone dependent on government. Right now I think they are gearing up to do it again—to finish the job of destroying all private wealth of middle Americans and make them dependent on government.

2) They succeeded in severely damaging the greatest machine for spreading the wealth among the most people the world has ever known. Because of the new taxes and controls Obama threatened, along with his soak those nasty wealthy people promises, unemployment exploded and continues to rise. Despite their efforts to hide it, real unemployment has risen steadily to about 17%, far above the nearly 10% that is being reported. While private sector employment plummets, government employment is rising rapidly. Meanwhile our government of change prints money as fast as the presses will run. Question: what do we do when China, Middle Eastern bankers, and the rest of our creditors, decide not to loan us any more money? Or when tax revenue dries up as private businesses and corporations disappear?

3) Their so-called stimulus or porkulous package, a thinly disguised political payoff system, has created few, if any private sector jobs. I do believe it did precisely what it was intended to do, appear as an effort to help the economy while actually providing money to support political activities of a number of leftist support organizations. Doubt me? Just follow the money trail to who ended up with that money. While much of that trail is well hidden, those individuals identified as direct or indirect recipients are all Democrats. You won't find a single conservative or conservative organization among them.

4) They turned a struggling auto industry over to the UAW for political expediency and as a payoff for support. While the momentum of GM and maybe even Chrysler will keep then going for a while, sooner or later the management style that makes Amtrak and the Postal Service such expensive, poorly run and unprofitable operations will prevail and no amount of public tax dollars will keep them afloat. I certainly wouldn't buy a car from either of those companies whose raison d'etre is no longer profit, but support for the UAW pensions. Because of their efforts of the last five years, their current models may be excellent, but I sure wouldn't trust things to stay that way. GM now stands for Government Motors. Remember the East German "peoples car," the Trabant? The 1975 model was dubbed tops of the list of the 50 worst cars ever built by Time magazine. Is that what we can look forward to from Government Motors when the UAW decides current models are too extravagant? To read the entire article, go to:

http://www.time.com/time/specials/2007/article/0,28804,1658545_1658533_1658030,00.html

5) Internationally, they have given political recognition, aid, and support to many of our enemies while kicking a few of our loyal friends in the butt. Their UN people sat uncomplaining when that pig-headed idiot, Iranian president Mahmoud Ahmadinejad, called for the destruction of capitalism and a "war without borders" against the West and especially America. This pocket Hitler is about to have possession of atomic bombs and will certainly use them against us as soon as he can. Appeasement never worked against Hitler and I can guarantee it will not work against this petty tyrant.

There are many more, but who cares. If the first five don't convince you, the next 100 won't either. I realize many of you could use ignorance or stupidity as an excuse, but that still leaves hope for some of you. Do you know the difference between ignorance and stupidity? - - -Ignorance can be corrected.

For years I have dealt with the reality that many of you who I know personally haven't a clue who I really am, what I fervently believe, how I conduct my life, the people I respect and honor, why they have earned my respect, or what seems to me to be important and for the greater good of all humanity. Sadly, many from all kinds of political beliefs—individuals that I would call extremists to some degree—refuse to discuss or consider any ideas or even words that do not fit into their ideology. It's easy to have a friendly, rational discussion with people who agree with you, but it is far more stimulating and instructive to have these types of discussions with people who have different opinions. For this reason I often seek discussion with those of widely differing opinions. My active membership in the Socrates discussion group here in St Augustine is but one example.

I can remember having very few rational, open political conversations with any members of the left, and those only on rare occasions. What I do remember are emotional diatribes verging on hate speech against virtually anything having to do with capitalism, industry, business, corporations, indeed, the whole string of things that are the heart of American success and the major provider of jobs for the vast majority of Americans. I learned long ago to keep my mouth shut and my opinions to myself when conversing with those on the left most of the time. I try to act thus, even when the most egregious condemnations are made about things those doing the condemning know little or nothing about. The closed mind is far more the devil's workplace than is the idle mind.

In every single discussion I can remember about virtually any subject with the slightest political content, I have always received the same kind of "You poor thing. You just don't want to see how right we are." attitude from virtually every one on the left. I have heard lots of hatred—class hatred, race hatred, religious hatred, hatred of the wealthy, (see definitions of wealthy later in this piece) and lots of condemnation of those not on the left. I also see lots of problems used to blame on those on the right, (mostly conservatives and those hated capitalists), and lots of name calling—racist and other demeaning epithets. Never, let me repeat, NEVER, have I heard any leftist propose any rational solution to any problem. All I hear from the left is condemnation of those they seek to blame for virtually any problem. Their universal solutions are always more government bureaucracy as in "give us money," or "put us in charge," or "lets tax it," or "take money from the wealthy to pay for it," or "give us control." That's virtually all I've heard out of Washington since long before the far left Democrats took control of Congress in 2006. It actually dates back to the depression of the 1930s. Even you biased ones on the left should be able to see what has happened since the anointed one took control and began his campaign to economically destroy the middle class and private enterprise, and replace it with government bureaucracy. At the rate things are going, this once free nation will be a socialist dictatorship in a very short time. We may be there already. Events related to the coming election will answer that question. When that happens, the entire nation will soon look like inner Detroit, a bombed-out, third-world country where most are equally dirt poor and the super wealthy, including many elite politicians, have all the wealth. Such will be the triumph of the left. Apparently, that is what you people on the left want. I'll say one thing, it is one way to make us all equal—equal in poverty that is.

A word about the often abused adjective wealthy in our country. A recent opinion study showed that most Americans generally view the wealthy as anyone who has more than twice as much stuff or income as they do. This means a family making $50,000 a year views all families making more than $100,000 a year as wealthy, and those making $200,000 view as wealthy only those making more than $400,000 a year etc. The same study described how people view the source of wealth as good or bad. Most Americans view those who achieved their wealth, even modest wealth, through business investment or the employment of others as bad or even evil, no matter how hard they worked. Strangely, they expressed little negative and mostly positive feelings about those individuals achieving wealth through celebrity, politics, the arts, entertainment, or sports. Those whose wealth was inherited also received mostly positive responses. Even attorneys' wealth was seen as more positive than negative, better than business people, but less than celebrities.

Successful business people get a bad rap from others for many reasons, but by far the most obvious reason is jealousy and class envy. That's because it's far easier to ridicule and use hate speech to demean a person or group than it is to learn and/or earn ones way up to a comparable position. Do those curses and angry condemnations make those on the left feel any better about themselves? I doubt it. But it certainly diverts attention from and provides an excuse for their failures.

It is difficult for me to understand why those who provide the vast majority of jobs and employment in America should be so despised by so many people. Actually, I think it is because of the I hate my boss attitude of so many employees. This is nurtured and fomented by the deliberate hate speech of union activists, Democrat politicians and the main stream media. It probably originated in the sixteenth or seventeenth century with the great disdain the elitist, privileged, upper class held for merchants and trades people. Isn't that precisely how the elitist leftists treat business people in the present America? This attitude is aggravated by legions of anti boss stories in books, movies, TV, radio, and even professional sports. From Simon Lagree to the Dabny Coleman character in the movie, From Nine to Five, business people or bosses, almost always Caucasian men, are portrayed as evil, stupid, nerdy, or hopelessly ridiculous. Universally they are depicted as the main antagonist to the good, clever, hard working, often oppressed worker, woman, subordinate, or even slave as protagonist. They are right up there, high on the hate scale with all those evil right wingers. They are of course in great contrast to those loving, wonderful left wingers who are incapable of doing anything but good. Dr. Paul Joseph Goebbels conducted just such a propaganda campaign against Jews in the early thirties and everyone knows where that led. It could be said the current propaganda campaign in America is against Caucasian men of business and industry, and that would be fairly accurate.

Then there are those wonderful Hollywood geniuses. Those brilliant celebrities who are pampered, worshiped, adored, and emulated by legions of idiot fans because they are either physically beautiful, very sexy, or can play act. (That's faking being someone other than who they are, or, in effect, lying.) Amazingly, fans actually expect these narcissistic, emotional junkies to have something intelligent to say about anything. They hang on their words as if they were meaningful or of value. The trouble is, these caricatures of human beings are so used to following scripts, and doing or saying what promotes their careers or what their publicity agents tell them to say in public, that I doubt they have an opinion or intelligent thought of their own. They merely repeat the mantras provided them by the likes of George Soros and his moveon.org propagandists.

I belong to an active group of seniors who hold a few holds barred discussion for three hours every Monday afternoon under the auspices of our Council on Aging. There are from twenty to thirty active members at each meeting. They are mostly retired people from many different walks of life equally divided between the sexes.. The group includes several college professors, other members of academia, two politicians, a few corporate employees, truck drivers, housewives and quite a few whose professions and backgrounds are obscure. This diverse group are mostly on the left politically. The only rabid right winger (not me) in the group couldn't take the heat and left more than a year ago. Even those I see as fundamentalist leftists enter into our open discussions. They have learned that they must back up their many accusations against "big business" and capitalists with referenced facts because they know I will research those with which I disagree and call them to task with cold hard facts that are often far different than their claims.

Among the members who are of the far left are several who constantly demean and condemn business, corporations, Republicans and conservatives. In discussions, we frequently clash, mostly over emotionally held positions where I try to point out practically any known factual data. Example: it is a proven fact that every time federal tax rates have been lowered (the Kennedy, Reagan, and Bush tax cuts), tax revenue increased. Also, every time federal tax rates have been raised, tax revenue went down. That has been true for at least the last fifty years. Then I ask, "Why do Democrats constantly refer to increasing tax rates on the wealthy, but never mention increasing tax revenue for the government? In my opinion, it's because Democrats are far more interested in punishing the wealthy and successful than in increasing tax revenue. That's total fiscal nonsense." When I point this out, they will grumble and say something like, "It's not that simple." or "There were other factors at work." The reason for this is quite obvious to all but the dimmest light bulb or most prejudiced ideologue of the left. None of them will ever acknowledge these proven facts. That to me is ultimate stupidity. A childish, cut off nose to spite face, activity.

One of these leftist members made this comment to me after a particularly spirited discussion, "Howard, I have a hard time figuring out just where you stand on this. One minute you sound like a right wing corporate slave, the next, I hear ideas with which I completely agree."

I replied, "First of all, there are no corporate slaves, and secondly, I am no slave of any kind, so get real. No corporation, member of any corporation, or individual can force or control an individual or group to do or not to do any activity, legal or illegal. Only government can legally do so, and they can enforce their impositions with guns, handcuffs, and threat of prison. Your "corporate slave" remark is simply meaningless. Furthermore, I am no ideologue of any ism. I owe no allegiance to any political party, faction, union, employer—no group of any kind. I have no peer revue group, membership committee, or board of directors to satisfy. I do not have to pander to any grant committee or government agency for funds. I'm sure this confuses you. To me, you appear to be an ideologue of the far left. This because I hear the mantras of the left repeated virtually verbatim in all of your arguments. Let me read to you from an Op Ed piece I wrote for this group a few months ago." Here is that piece:

"The populist, anti business attitude and activists who fought the robber barons of a hundred and more years ago are still fighting a long vanquished enemy. Some of these so called titans of industry conspired to control everything. As powerful and hated as many of them were, not all of them were evil, but they were all human. I speak against today's power hungry robber barons all of whom also are not evil, but are human and would control everything far more than those earlier ones ever dreamt of doing. Today those robber barons sit in the halls of Congress and populate our government bureaucracy. Incredible amounts of legislation has been enacted to blunt the potency of these power-mad individuals in the private sector. So much that most of that power has been taken over by government, the new lair of the robber barons. The big difference is that government has men who can enforce their rules with guns and handcuffs and prisons. That kind of power is extremely easy to abuse. The private sector has no power even close to that. Any person working for any other always has the option to quit and find another job.

Beware the military/industrial complex - is now - beware the government/banking complex

Several of our Socrates members have reminded us of President Eisenhower's warning, "Beware the military/industrial complex." This statement was made at a time when the government represented less than 3% of our nation's economy while the private sector was a huge 97%. Now the government has exploded to more than 40% of the economy while the private sector has shrunk to a mere 60% or less. It shows an amazing feat of strength and adaptability in the private sector that the entire 40% of the economy that is government, is paid for by taxes levied on that 60% that is the private sector.

"Also, who owns and controls the military? The government of course. Who controls the procurement of military hardware, including weapons and supplies, and military services including software and electronic processes? Congress. Who decides what weapons are to be used? Congress. Who finances the industries who manufacture those items and services? The major banks. Who now controls the major banks? The government. As a result I think it imperative that we reword Eisenhower's statement to, "Beware the government/banking complex."

That evil private sector that generates profits and pays all taxes, is now under direct and devastating attack by a far left government that doesn't seem to give a damn that it is destroying America's economy, impoverishing her people, and building an elitist governing class that are becoming the new Lords and Ladies of a Feudal dictatorship. The Sheriff of Nottingham would fit right in with this oppressive class. One of the saddest realities of this situation is that the vast majority of those sworn to expose this evil chicanery are acting as if they are card carrying members of these elitists. That's most of the media to you slow ones out there.

I have formed many friendships with members of the group in spite of our political differences. I daresay my expressed views have earned me a great deal of respect, even from those with whom I disagree. One member of the group is a retired professor of psychology, Jewish, an atheist, and fairly far to the left. We have become good friends. He is always reminding the group about Eisenhower's warning, "Beware the military/industrial complex." In one of our discussions I explained that the military is an arm of the federal government and that industrialists realize far less profit from military procurement than do the big banks which are so obviously in bed with our current administration and Congress. With the government now at more than 40% of the American economy, what we should truly fear is the "Government/banking complex." Abe begrudgingly agreed I could be right. He then paid me what I consider to be a great compliment. He said, "Howard, you are the only conservative with whom I have ever been able to hold a rational political discussion."

Incidently, before King Lyndon and his great society came along, the government was less than 4% of our economy, and even then that was too much. At the 40% it is now, we have passed the point where the private sector can pay for government. Good old math tells us it now takes two jobs in the private sector to pay for each government employee. This is why we are going in debt at three times the rate of just a few years ago. As soon as we reach 51%, America will be a committed feudal (socialist, communist, marxist, liberal) dictatorship. I believe only a bloody revolution will stop this dictatorship and that will happen only after the nation has been deeply impoverished. It looks to me as though many European nations are even closer to collapse than we are. The total collapse of cultures, nations, and most organizations happens very quickly. History provides countless examples. If you would like to read about how and why societies and nations collapse, and maybe even some helpful ideas to prevent such a happening, I suggest you read Jared Diamond's book, Collapse. He's the author of the Pulitzer Prize winning book, Guns, Germs, and Steel, and also, The Third Chimpanzee. I've read all three by this learned professor of geography, physiology, evolutionary biology, and biogeography who cuts across many fields of thought. I respect him and others like him who are realistic idealists, much as I try to be.

Here are some things I would like you to know about me that I'm sure you would not imagine. In my entire political life I have voted for no more than a dozen major candidates. Of those dozen or so, two were Democrats. One of those, Evan Bayh, betrayed his avowed principles and became a liberal Washington insider. I'm certain political ambitions were the driving force that moved this otherwise well intentioned man to adopt the posture of the left. The other Democrat is now a Libertarian and despises what the Democrat party has become.

In the vast majority of elections I find myself choosing the lesser of two or more disasters. Along those lines, I haven't voted **for** a president since Ronald Reagan, and before that, Goldwater, and Eisenhower. Had I been old enough I would have voted for Harry Truman, (in spite of my father's opinions) I missed that election as my 21st birthday was just a few weeks after the election.

I think the vast majority of our elected officials (of all parties) are self-serving egotists, much more interested in money and power for themselves than in serving their constituents. I have read and admired the well turned phrases of Eric Hoffer for many years. Ageless, they are far too numerous to mention here but for a few I must repeat because they fit most politicians so well.

"People unfit for freedom—who cannot do much with it—are hungry for power. The desire for freedom is an attribute of a have type of self. It says: leave me alone and I shall grow, learn, and realize my capacities. The desire for power is basically an attribute of a have not type of self."

"Passionate hatred can give meaning and purpose to an empty life. Thus people haunted by the purposelessness of their lives try to find a new content not only by dedicating themselves to a holy cause but also by nursing a fanatical grievance. A mass movement offers them unlimited opportunities for both."

There arc so many liberal Democrats now in power who fit those descriptions precisely. That last one reminds me of the words of the then chairman of the Democrat party, Howard Dean, "I hate Republicans, I hate conservatives, and I hate Rush Limbaugh." Though your party hacks try to label those same three as purveyors of hate, it is almost exclusively Democrats who use volumes of hate speech almost every time they open their mouths. Apparently, any words that disagree with, are negative about, or even poke fun at liberal Democrats and their agendas are labeled hate speech no matter how true they are. Of course, that is merely my opinion.

I would like to call your attention to the major achievements of liberal Democrats in league with labor unions. These are undeniable facts you can see and touch.

1. Take a trip through central Detroit to see what unionism and liberal politics has accomplished there. You'll see a city literally destroyed. It looks like the bombed out capital of some third world nation. Block after block of destroyed homes, homes that have been looted and many burned, those still standing that is. Many if not most of the neighborhoods in the center of this once vibrant city are totally destroyed. The city has been run by a whole series of corrupt politicians, all liberal Democrats beholden to union power. There are even small sections on the south side of Ft Wayne that look nearly the same for similar reasons.

2. The most liberal states are all reeling in the throes of financial disaster, because liberal politicians spend money (mostly to buy votes) far beyond the states' ability to generate tax revenue. Michigan, New Jersey, New York, California, and several other liberal states are virtually bankrupt. Businesses and industry that hasn't already fled, or can't flee overseas from those states are moving to states and even countries with more business friendly attitudes and tax rates. As they flee, they take revenue and jobs with them. Each of those states is controlled by spendthrift liberal Democrats, has monstrous tax rates, is losing population (at least working population), has a high unemployment rate, and is deeply in debt (and rapidly going deeper). Maybe New Jersey can come out of it now that they have a fiscally responsible Republican at the helm. The state of Indiana is a good example of what can happen under a hard working conservative Republican governor even with a Democrat dominated legislature. The state is one of the very few that are in the black, where private sector employment numbers are growing, and where state revenue is climbing. Businesses and workers are moving to Indiana in droves, many from those liberal states including California. And those on welfare? Many are leaving Indiana for more liberal states with welfare programs easier to scam.

3. The mortgage and then the stock market collapse, certainly engineered by liberals, their policies, and government pressure on banks, resulted in by far the largest destruction and transfer of wealth from middle class Americans. The really wealthy didn't lose much and the super wealthy, mostly supporters of the left, actually profited from the economic disaster. No one mentions it , but the mortgage melt down wiped out about two thirds of the wealth of the American middle class. Apparently liberals think the way to level the economic playing field is to make everyone (except people in government and unions) as poor as the poorest Americans. It is quite obvious, that the entire financial fiasco was deliberately engineered by liberals (who profited substantially) including Barney Frank, Chris Dodd, and the anointed one, our wonderful president. Then there were those bureaucrat leftists like Franklin Raines who used their appointed positions to wield the wrecking ball that demolished the mortgage industry and brought about the economic disaster that followed. In my opinion it was designed to do just exactly what it accomplished, the destruction of much of the personal wealth of the majority of Americans. In the process, the four mentioned, along with quite a few other liberal Democrats, profited greatly, all paid from taxpayer funds while deliberately striking a major blow to America's financial health, its private sector.

I could list dozens of similar facts, but why bother. Fifty years of liberal action to dumb down the populace by devastating our once top-notch education system, coupled with punitive taxing systems and election processes designed 200 years ago has created a monstrous, bloated government whose sole purpose is to perpetuate itself. Back then it took many days to get from one place to another, even on horseback, and the best and fastest communication was in days or weeks compared with the millisecond transfer of today. Another sign of politically directed education. Few of the younger generation have any idea who their congressman is or why he was elected. Many don't know who their senators are. Recently (2006) I heard one of those man-on-the-street interviewers asking college seniors who the vice president of the US was and who were their representative and senators. Less than a third of them got any right, and none knew all of them. That's appalling. That's also why so few Americans vote.

These are realities, not the pie in the sky or the rosy pronouncements of politicians.

And how about our glorious main stream media? The New York Times, the LA Times, ABC, CBS, NBC and their spin-off cable news services have become the propaganda arm of liberal Democrat government. On a daily basis, they hide all negative news about the government and Democrats while front paging any positive news or spin, even if they have to lie. They have become so blatant in their lopsided, leftist promoting propaganda, they have become a pathetic joke to many, and suspected of chicanery by most Americans. There was even some information leaked about how they were scheming to have Fox news taken off the air along with all right wing radio talk show hosts like Rush Limbaugh, Glenn Beck, and Sean Hannity. Unable to compete or even discredit these far more truthful and accurate news and opinion sources, they are trying to get their far left cohorts in Congress to force them off the air. That I call dictatorship in action!

In comparison to the success of conservative talk radio and the hosts just mentioned, look at what happened to the most popular left wing talk-radio mouthpiece, Al Franken. All of his programs were disastrous failures. So he decides to run for the Senate in a liberal Democrat state with a political machine that rivals in corruption, that of Cook County, Illinois. In spite of all the tricks Democrats could pull, his Republican opponent bested this clown by between 200 and 700 votes in a close election. During the recount, previously uncounted ballots started appearing from unusual places. Some were even found in the trunk of a poll worker's car. I predicted (correctly) that while the recount of known ballots would not change things significantly, there would be many new, uncounted ballots found, the vast majority of which would be for Franken. Well, you know the outcome.

Over the years I have received occasional bits of correspondence from leftist friends that were quite critical of what they believe my political beliefs to be, the causes and people they assume I support, and/or almost any person who does not believe as they do. I have received some responses, but those have mostly said they don't like my writing about controversial subjects, but only those soft warm fuzzies I write about in my short stories during the time when I was growing up. Well, you leftists won't like what I've written in my book, *Energy, Convenient Solutions,* or my latest version of *Words from the Lakeside*, either. No, they are not filled with hate speech. I leave that up to you folks on the left. They are liberally sprinkled with the words of wise and famous men and women who often point out the folly, greed, anger, and deception, of those on the left. I even include myself in that group as a rational, thinking individual, who does not have a closed mind. The energy book is also filled with information that could lead to solutions to many of our energy related problems. Solutions, that's a word absent from the vocabulary of the left. Apparently leftists believe that solutions are the last thing they want because a solution usually removes a problem and so removes a destroy and control weapon from the liberal arsenal.

I have come to believe that liberalism, socialism, communism, nazism, and feudalism are all just different names for political totalitarian systems of government. In each of these, the people serve the government rather than the government serving the people as our Constitution outlined. I believe each of these isms to be consummate evils that subjugate free men and, like the kingdoms and sheikdoms of old, place all the power and wealth under the control of a few elitists including, royals, commissars, lords, sheiks, emperors, senators, presidents, (and their appointed czars) etc.

I could fill a book with examples of how stupid our politicians believe the public to be. I will provide just two examples. The first is the Congressional Budget Office, the CBO. During the recent ramming of Obamacare down our throats against major public resistance, Democrats announced gleefully that the CBO numbers on the costs of Obamacare showed it would not add to the nations financial obligations, it was a tax-neutral law. In the past, cost estimates by the CBO averaged about a quarter of what any proposed bill eventually cost. That's averaged! So you can count on Obamacare to cost at least four times what the CBO says it will cost. Oh yes, did you know that one part of the bill no main-stream media person would mention is a heavy tax placed on home sales. That's right, if you now sell your home you must pay a substantial portion of the sale to the government as a health care tax. That's one more of the many taxes the federal government levees on everyone, regardless of their financial condition. It will fall disproportionately on middle class and poorer Americans. Did you know that between 20% and 26% of every dollar spent for goods and services goes to the federal government in the form of hidden taxes. Those taxes are paid by everyone, the poorest and the wealthiest, regardless of their income or financial status.

Another example is taxes and federal revenue explained earlier in this article. Apparently those idiots in Congress don't even believe their own reports on taxes and revenue. In truth, they must think that revenge against the hated wealthy is worth any price the people must pay, usually in higher tax rates and unemployment. Please note, The super wealthy are not included since they are allied with the left. It's a strange alliance until you look closely.

The current stagnant economy and unemployment is the direct result of the tax policies and pronouncements of controls made by Democrats and the administration. Of course, since they are the government, they have voted themselves immunity to these problems. In fact, employment in Washington is booming (4.14% unemployment) as government employment grows and private employment continues to sink.

Interesting note: ten years ago there were about 9,500 publicly traded corporations in America. By 2008 that number had shriveled to about 7,000. In January, 2010 we learned it had plummeted to 4,100. The same relative numbers apply to individual enterprises and privately owned corporations. Thanks to the war against business now being waged by our leftist government, small businesses are disappearing at an alarming rate along with the jobs they have provided. For many years, small business has been the creator of most new jobs. It is obvious that our government has become the enemy of business and small business in particular in spite of all the hoopla (BS) about help for small business from the administration. (That so called help comes with many oppressive regulations and hundreds of bureaucrats telling you how to conduct your business.) What I would like to know is who is going to pay for the burgeoning bureaucracy when those 4,100 publicly traded corporations and the remaining millions of small businesses are gone? China anyone?

Oh yes, just the other day, right after our glorious president made remarks about the improving economy, the Bureau of Labor Statistics released a report that more than half a million private sector jobs were lost during the previous week. That's the largest number of job losses in more than a year. That's why I believe nothing our government, or any liberal or leftist says. I merely watch what they do, how they act, and register the results of their efforts. I also take most of what the government controlled media says with a pound or two of salt. It's not just that they lie, they hide negative news about Democrats and positive news about Republicans while loudly trumpeting the reverse. Unfounded accusations that are splashed all over the front page of the New York Times are routinely recounted or corrected way back in the paper where no one looks.

Thursday, July 15, 2010

A Friend from Dearborn Michigan relocates his manufacturing company

Speaking of the results of their efforts reminds me of what a friend of mine from racing days told me earlier in the year. We've kept in touch off and on since the 1960s when we were competitors in sports car racing. Several years ago I mentioned in an email that I was coming to visit my daughters in the Detroit area. He asked me out to lunch while I was there. During our meeting he asked me questions about Ft Wayne and northern Indiana as he was considering moving his business from Dearborn to a more business friendly location. He manufactures highly specialized construction equipment he sells to distributors and contractors. "I've about had it with Michigan taxes and union pressures here." he told me. "I've heard things are much more business friendly in Indiana so fill me in on what you can."

Among other information I gave him was the name and address of a Republican politician who is currently in charge of new business development in the Ft Wayne area. I told him what I knew about the business climate in Indiana and how there were numerous small manufacturers who had already moved here from Michigan. He thanked me and that's the last I heard from him until this summer. I was floored when I read his email. He had moved everything possible from his entire business in Dearborn, including more than half of his labor force, about 35 people into a new facility called, I-Park Lemminkäinen, in Kaluga, some 180 km south of Moscow. He moved his entire family along with those 35 employees and their families into an American community near Kaluga. The children will attend English speaking schools that cater to Americans.

He wrote, "I ran across the I-Park developers while searching for a new location in the states. They flew me there and gave me a VIP tour. I was impressed. Then they took me to the American community and I talked with several Americans who had been there for some time. I was amazed. Many familiar names in the automotive and construction fields were already operating there. Business taxes including capital gains are a straight 15% of profits under a plan they call STS. That includes pensions and insurance, less than half comparable costs in the US and the record keeping and reporting is a small fraction of what we did in Dearborn. Since we are now here, it is obvious we took the deal. They way things looked to be going with the mortgage debacle and the looming 2008 election made up our minds. We were not the only ones. There is a big shortage of housing in the developing American section. Homes and apartments (mostly apartments) are being built at an astounding rate. Still, there is a long wait to get a place to live, much longer than when we moved here. More Americans seem to be moving here every day."

I wonder if those are some of the twice as many talented Americans who moved out of the country in 2009 as did in 2008? (A little known fact the media would never report.)

"The business part is better than we expected. Our business has taken off and we still ship to a number of our old customers in the States and Canada. Those American customers still account for more than half our business. The unskilled pay scale is much lower than in the States, but highly technical or skilled personnel are roughly equal to the States, and in short supply. (That's why they are tapping the American market for skilled and technical people.) With the cost of living mostly much less including housing, and business and personal taxes so much lower, our real business and living costs are little more than half that of Dearborn. There are a few negatives. The quality of goods and services is much lower than we are used to, and some things are just poorly made. There is a concerted effort to change that, but it will take time and some new attitudes among the Russians. Also, personal travel is a red tape nightmare. I think that's a leftover from the old Soviet Union. Except for travel, personal freedom seems about the same, but not so for criminals. The ACLU would scream. Of course, they would probably soon be in jail. Health care is OK, but wait times are long, and exotic tests and services readily available in the US are simply non existent. I'm sure Obama will soon change that in the US."

He went on to invite us to visit him if we ever get to Moscow. Oh yes, because of their increase in retained profits they send every employee that wants to go, back to the states for two weeks every year, all at no cost to the employee. The employee doesn't even have to pay income taxes on the value of the trip. Can you see liberals allowing such a tax evading thing here?

So what does it all add up to? No rational group of people would do what this administration is doing unless their intention was the deliberate and destruction of America. It is impossible for them to do what they are doing out of ignorance. No one is that stupid or ignorant. Therefore it is a deliberate action ensuring destruction of the current Constitutional system of government so they can impose a new and totally different system. Sharia law, anyone? That is the only rational conclusion an intelligent person could come to. Ahmadinejad for president of America, Obama for president of the world under sharia law. Is that what you leftists really want to wake up to some day? Don't think it's impossible.

For several good reasons I now believe our president is a devout and committed Muslim who is not even a legal citizen of this country. That is not because of what others say, but the result of my own intensive research. Even though he won't produce it I believe he has a Hawaiian birth certificate that he purchased just like hundreds of other foreign nationals including a number of Far Eastern leaders, politicians, and wealthy citizens. The reason he won't produce his Hawaiian birth certificate is that it will list the actual location of his live birth. I checked this out from several sources including the Hawaiian statutes that provide for this.

Additionally, there are no hospital records available that show Obama was born there. The group that published this information and the state of Hawaii both testify this to be the truth. Check the following web site which explains how a foreign national can get US citizenship by obtaining a Hawaiian birth certificate..

http://logisticsmonster.com/2008/12/04/foreigners-become-a-us-citizen-get-your-haw aii-birth-certificate-here/

Obama could easily counter all these claims by 1) producing his Hawaiian birth certificate or 2) unsealing the records of Mombasa Coastal Hospital in Kenya. Neither of these is likely to happen since each would establish his true birthplace as Mombasa Coastal Hospital in Kenya. Even Snopes does not dispute these facts.

The media will not investigate this out of fear of retaliation. I believe the carefully hidden threat of violent retaliation is behind all of this. The New Black Panther Party has been getting a lot of publicity lately. Its Philadelphia leader, King Samir Shabazz was recorded professing his hate for all white people. He specifically called for the murder of "cracker babies", a racist term referring to white infants. For several weeks, pundits have been hammering the Obama administration for its handling of the New Black Panther Party voter intimidation case. The main part of the argument is that the Obama administration cancelled a certain conviction because it won't go after minorities for even the most egregious civil rights violations.

During the presidential election, New Black Pather Party members Jerry Jackson and King Samir Shabazz were accused of making intimidating remarks to both white and black voters as they stood outside a Philadelphia polling place. They were dressed in black military-style uniforms and Shabazz brandished a nightstick, a clear violation of the law. Incredibly, the men asked a camera man why he was taping them. This was caught on video.

The Department of Justice filed a civil action in federal court before Obama took office. The suit accused the two men, as well as the New Black Panther Party and its leader Malik Zulu Shabazz, of engaging in voter intimidation. In typical fashion, none of the defendants responded to the complaint. Then, the Department, under the instructions of Eric Holder, decided to drop its case against all but King Samir Shabazz, the one with the nightstick. The department received an injunction prohibiting Shabazz from displaying a weapon within 100 feet of a Philadelphia polling location until 2012. That was an inconsequential slap on the hand for the New Black Panther Party which will certainly encourage them to ratchet up their plans for intimidation in the next election. Many pundits decried the government's position as outrageously lenient, and evidence of an Obama administration double standard on race issues.

It doesn't take much of a stretch to think that threats of violence by similar activists could be behind the current rash of Republicans, defeated in their primaries, who are planning to run as independents, mainly to divide the Republican vote and help liberal Democrats. There are already four that have announced such plans and several more that may consider doing so if they lose to Tea Party candidates in upcoming primaries. Poles show there is little chance of any of them garnering enough votes to be serious contenders. Democrats love it since each of these campaigns give them a leg up in areas where otherwise they would have no chance. I smell liberal efforts, hidden promises, and possibly even threats of violence behind these divisive actions.

Remember the movie, The Manchurian Candidate? I firmly believe we are experiencing just such a carefully orchestrated fraud being perpetrated by Islam in their efforts at world domination.

They desperately want control of our industry and military and this is one way to get that control while our people sleep at the switch. It is the only way they can counter the growing threat from the Chinese who at present, could easily march through Iran and conquer all of the Middle East including Saudi Arabia. With their growing military and economic power, I doubt either Russia or America would try to stop them as both are terrified of the nuclear war that could ensue. Should Islam succeed in taking over America before the Chinese could act it would be a whole different ball game. They would use nuclear weaponry even if the result was the destruction of all life on Earth. Believe me, the idiot that pressed those final launch buttons would only be thinking about all those virgins.

Islam has one big advantage. They do not care if their actions destroy life on the planet, we, at least most of us in the West, do. Even the Communist Chinese are free of the religious fanaticism that drives Islam with their disdain for all life on the planet. They know the only way to stop Islam is to cripple them economically. That is, of course, what Islam is currently trying desperately to do to us. Why we do not recognize this and even help them by trading huge amounts of cash for oil. Could their agents be behind the mortgage debacle? It's not an impossible scenario. It certainly fits into the overall picture.

Unless main stream America wakes up very soon and takes effective action, we are looking at a future of extremely violent destruction, far worse than any man has yet experienced. Islam has fomented bloody battles and revolutions against any and all who didn't submit to their brutality since they came on the scene in the seventh century. They don't seem to care how many people they murder, even slaughtering their own to impose their Sharia law. There is no freedom, only submission to a male chauvinist culture that murders women at the slightest provocation and whose males are immune from criminal prosecution for such murders. Nice people.

Personally, my hope is that the Chinese will wake up and wage a major war against Islam, and soon. They did it before and with their awakening power they may be the only force now willing to go against Islam. I can see them going through Iran and Saudi Arabia with a scorched earth invasion and taking control of their oil. They have none of the resistance to taking aggressive action in the face of a major threat that we seem to have. They did it in Tibet when they had far less power, wealth, and military equipment.

Maybe I will write a novel with this reality as the background. I could title it, *"The Destruction of America."*

Thursday, July 01, 2010

The Realities of the Gulf oil disaster

As this is written it has been more than seventy days since the explosion that resulted in the sinking of the deep water oil platform that loosed a torrent of raw oil and gas from the mile deep floor of the Gulf off the shore of Louisiana. The resulting string of stupid blunders by BP and the companies running the oil rig combined with the bureaucratic ineptitude of our competing government agencies has created a nightmare of accusations and claims by all parties. In addition, long delays face most actions for a variety of ridiculous reasons, including jurisdictional disputes between government agencies, domestic and foreign companies and unions. Example, the sand berms to keep the oil from gaining access to extensive Louisiana marshes: After a rather long delay, the federal government finally granted permission and Louisiana started pumping sand to build the berms to keep the oil from reaching the marshes. Shortly after the pumping started, environmentalists convinced the government the pumping might endanger the Chandeleurs, the sand islands that offer some protection to the Louisiana coast over time. The government stopped the berm building until a study could be conducted to determine the environmental affect of moving the sand. Who knows how many months that study would take. Actually, it would be mostly an ongoing argument between conflicting views. In the meantime, the oil damage to the vast wetlands will probably cause a thousand times more environmental damage than the worst the sand pumping would do.

This is but a single example of the many skirmishes occurring over what to do and how to do it. It's a classic case of too many chiefs and too few indians typical of the ridiculously complex, conflicting agencies of our obese government. Each agency and often each head of this or that trying to make themselves more important. All this with complete and total disregard for the costs paid by taxpayers. To add to the confusion, many if not most members of both private and public organizations have little understanding of their own rules. Another example, also from the oil spill, is the various interpretations of the Jones Act of the 1920s by various individuals.

Witness words from one private source: "The Jones Act only applies within three miles of shore. Therefore, foreign skimmers, along with American skimmers, are already at work beyond three miles. The Deepwater Horizon spill is occurring 50 miles from shore, and the vast majority of oil is beyond 3 miles"

Response from another source: "I believe you will find the Jones act applies to the territorial waters of the United States. In the 1920s, when the Jones act was written into law, those territorial waters extended 3 miles from shore. Since 1982 the United Nations law of the sea defines territorial waters as 'a belt of coastal waters extending twelve nautical miles from mean shore line.' These waters are considered sovereign territory of the state owning the land. In addition and in response to several nations (including the US) arbitrarily declaring the extension of their territorial waters 100 to 200 nautical miles from shore, the UN defined an Exclusive Economic Zone extending 200 nautical miles from the defined shoreline. In this zone, 'a coastal nation has control of all economic resources including, fishing, mining, oil exploration, and responsibility for any pollution of or by these resources.' The Jones act has been considered by many as covering this economic zone."

This plethora of confusing authorities, both written and personal, that are negatively affecting the efforts to fix the oil spill is typical of both government and corporate bureaucracies. It's everyone trying for a share of the credit when things go well, and everyone pointing fingers of blame at others when things go wrong. All of this is fueled by greedy lawyers eager to sue anyone with deep pockets on any side of any controversy, and a media more interested in sensationalism than facts. Frequently, viable solutions to the real problems are ignored or lost in the melee and uproar of conflicting accusations.

Add to this confusing mix a president who is a political hack with virtually no experience at running or managing anything other than a political campaign. He is a master of platitudes and euphemisms, an orator who is quite obviously without a clue as to how to manage or direct any real situation. His handling of the McChrystal situation was that of a schoolboy ego that couldn't bear the tiniest slight. "McChrystal's error was to blow off steam and allow his subordinates to grumble about their civilian overlords—which one assumes is pretty standard fare in military circles—in the presence of a journalist." says Rabbi Shmuley Boteach in his blog.

It's about time members of groups, that constantly denigrate and condemn others out of class or economic envy, or those with whom they have a jurisdictional dispute, began to honor and respect the achievements and rewards of those others. I see it as important that we recognize the realities of our situation and the real reasons we are where we are. There has been enough of this destructive and debilitating blame game and all of its political distortions and emotional hate-filled activities. We have been engaged in terrible inner political warfare, while our enemies stand on the sidelines urging on the various sides, and gleefully watching our self destruction.

Many web sites and news reports disappear soon after being posted for many reasons including obvious inaccuracies, editorial revisions, and/or real changes that make them invalid. A single powerful caveat exists about Internet information. Many charlatans lurk well hidden behind attractive facades on the Internet. Even a cursory examination will reveal there are magic, energy out of nothing, and secret smoke and mirror articles readily available. Many of these are driven by hidden agendas. Every searcher must be certain that information comes from a reliable source, and truly is from that source. All information must be checked and confirmed from other reliable sources. Even those sources can be in error for many reasons.

The following section deals with political, jurisdictional, corporate, and communications problem in greater detail. This is the background of where we are, why we are there, and what we must do to go forward. It has little to do directly with energy and fuels, but everything to do with what we must overcome in order to counter this growing menace before it destroys us.

It is my personal conclusion that government and corporate bureaucracies along with political and media activists are among the most powerful forces against solutions to the serious problems facing humanity. Rather than use those problems as a focus for knowledgeable people to find creative solutions, these negative groups use these problems as bludgeons with which to punish and if possible, destroy those who do not support their agendas. The vast majority of ordinary citizens of the world are swayed this way and that by intense and usually hate-filled rhetoric of persuasive individuals in politics and the media. It is no wonder they get angry because of frustration at leaders who quite obviously are feathering their own nests at the expense of the common folk while blaming all the economic woes they have created on those, like the wealthy who have achieved more. Of course, they exempt themselves from the wealthy no matter how much power or wealth they possess.

Thursday, March 25, 2010

Who Really Pays All Those Taxes?

The truth of the matter is that few members of the public understand the realities of any taxes. Every business, large or small—every professional—every taxable entity or organization—every worker, all appear to pay taxes to many governments.

> **IT'S A FACT** - Corporations do not pay taxes. Businesses do not pay taxes. Professionals in their professions do not pay taxes. Organizations including those who are not-for-profit do not pay taxes. All of these "taxpayers" merely collect those taxes from customers or clients in the price of their products and services and then pass them onto the government just like the much more obvious sales tax. Even the so-called company paid portion of FICA taxes add to the cost of an employee and so are really taken from the employee.

If that is so, who is it that actually pays these taxes?

The truth is, all of these "taxpayers" merely collect those taxes from customers or clients in the final price to the consumer of their products and services and then pass them onto the government. They collect taxes exactly like the much more obvious sales tax. Even the so-called company-paid portion of FICA taxes add to the cost of an employee and so are actually taken from the employee. Those who actually pay every one of those federal and state taxes are, guess who—you! All those soak-the-rich taxes are finally paid for by the end user of all goods and services. Guess what portion of the bicycle you bought, or that movie you took your girlfriend to see, or the dinner you and your family had for your birthday, was actually taxes passed down to you through the distribution chain. Is is 5% or 20%? How about from 35% to 60%? Add to that the sales or VAT taxes collected by your state or city. You could be paying as much as 75% tax on every purchase if you live in New York City.

What happens if lawmakers enact windfall profits tax at 50% of net profits? It's quite simple. Every dollar increase in taxes will be met with a slightly larger total increase in fuel prices at the pump to make up for the increased cost of doing business. As with all business, this cost will be passed through to the consumer or end user. That would add as much as another nickel to the price of gas at the pump. So who is paying that excess profits tax? It is the ignorant motorist who voted those incompetent oafs into office just to punish the oil companies. Cut off nose to spite face, is the reality they ignore.

No matter when or how they are levied, taxes are ultimately paid by the final consumer. This is true of buyers of products or users of service. At the present time, hidden taxes amount to between 20% and 26% of every dollar the public pays for everything. Every dollar paid for every nail, hammer, car, vacation, legal service, doctor visit, and so on, now contains between twenty and twenty-six cents in hidden federal taxes. Add to that federal and state income taxes on all the pay for the workers, or profits for the business involved in providing that item or service. Don't forget FICA taxes or others that add to the cost of those goods or services. Actually, the hidden taxes on fuel are a bit lower than that because of the rapid rise of the cost of imported oil now around 70% of the price at the pump. A large part of that is appropriated by the governments of the oil-rich nations where we have no control. It goes directly into the coffers or certainly the complete control of their leaders. The socialist/communist welfare state will ultimately collapse economically when its natural resources run out, or it no longer has enough private capitalist enterprises generating profits to tax.

Currently and almost unbelievably, it is the capitalist machines of the Chinese state that are supporting the American socialist state systems by loaning that government vast amounts of money. What does the reader think will happen when the US owes China more than its net worth? With the trillions of dollars of debt we are now assuming, that time is rapidly approaching, thanks to the deliberate efforts of our current administration. Just who will be the ones to pay this enormous, outlandishly foolish debt?

When the American military suddenly finds itself paid, supplied, and owned by the Chinese and China takes over America in a bloodless coup, a group of Chinese bureaucrats will be running Washington for their own benefit.

Will Americans wake up then? Not likely

Thursday, March 18, 2010

That Wonderful Health Care Bill

In 2001 I finished writing a book titled "The Feudals" in which I compared the America that the liberal agenda was working to create to Europe under the feudal system of the middle ages. In that book I made the following prediction:

The United States will be a socialist/marxist/communist/fascist/feudal dictatorship by 2030. At this time those leftist activists will happily extol the joys of socialism as they are being carted off to the salt mines by the brown shirted storm troopers of the new America.

—HJ, 2001

I am afraid I was wrong. It has already happened. The reality is we are now an oligarchy ruled by an elite who have circumvented our Constitution, lied to us about virtually everything they are doing, and made law by a dictatorial process against the overwhelming demands of the American public. Here's what they have already done to gain and consolidate their complete control of our nation and its people by flaunting total disregard for our laws and Constitution:

1) They have deliberately destroyed more than half of the wealth of our middle class by manipulating the mortgage system. The next step will be to destroy the remaining wealth of the middle class and make them totally dependent on government..

2) They have nationalized two of our major auto manufacturers. Which of our major corporations will suffer the same fate during the next round of economic collapse? The coming collapse is of course being engineered by the despots who are working to control our country.

3) They have nationalized several banks, insurance companies, and who knows what else. Isn't it interesting that so many officers and executives of Goldman Sachs are now in powerful

positions within the Obama administration? Isn't it also interesting that all of them received a special presidential exemption to the federal law that states such individuals had to divest themselves of all stock in the banks they formerly worked for. Hmmmm?

4) Somehow, they have taken complete control of much of the media, principally TV networks and newspapers making them virtual propaganda machines of the administration.)

5) They are now in the process of illegally passing a so called "health care" bill that is aimed directly at destroying the best health care system in the world. Most of this was done in defiance of the law in secret meetings held by the administration and liberal Democrat leaders. Health care is to be placed under the complete control and operation of the same bureaucratic idiots who have done such a marvelous job of running the Postal Service, Amtrak, and all the other failing government systems.

6) Their same destructive economic policies that have virtually bankrupted our nation, have also bankrupted a number states under the same liberal Democrat control. New York, Michigan, and California are the worst with several others close behind.

The amazing thing to me is how completely blind most Americans are to what is happening. Our nation in its history has indeed taken those fateful steps and moved from bondage to spiritual faith to courage to liberty to abundance to selfishness to apathy to dependency, and is now on the verge of taking the last step into bondage once more. Our freedoms are being eliminated at a steadily accelerating rate in the name of security. The ultimate security is of course slavery and that is where we are rapidly headed.

So here is my opinion of you liberal Democrats who voted for and are supporting this madness. You will fall into one or more of these sorry groups of people:

1) You are a completely emotional ideologue with out a rational thought in your head who thinks using a phrase like, "We should all just love each other" will solve everything. You do little or nothing productive.

2) You are an idealist, also under emotional control, who actually believes there are no evil, power hungry liberal Democrat politicians, or people for that matter. You also do little or nothing productive.

3) You are a government employee who can't be fired and who's main job is to make more work for other government employees in order to expand your department and create more government jobs. That's the government's main job creation program. You vote Democrat to ensure your job. You do nothing productive.

4) You work for a giant corporation and your job depends on your company getting more of those lucrative government financed programs. You also do nothing productive

5) You work for GM, Chrysler, AIG, or Goldman Sachs. You also do nothing productive.

6) You are a member of moveon.org, ACORN, SEIU, UAW, or some other labor union. You also do nothing productive.

7) You are on welfare and probably wouldn't work if given the opportunity. You also do nothing productive.

8) You work for federally funded schools. You also do nothing productive.

9) You work in academia at the university level. You also do nothing productive.

10) You are a trial lawyer. You also do nothing productive.

11) You are an entertainer, a media or sports personality, or some other celebrity. You also do nothing productive.

12) You are a dyed-in-the-wool Democrat who would vote that way even if the likes of Hitler, Stalin, Che Guevera, or Osama bin Laden were on the ticket. There is a very slight chance you could do something productive.

13) You are a typical politician with your hand in everyone's pocket spending tons of other people's money on your election campaign while syphoning much of it off into your own family's pockets. You also do nothing productive.

12) You are a multi million or billion dollar executive of one of the companies in bed with government officials and bureaucrats. You also do nothing productive.

13) You are a college or university professor accepting government grant money to do research providing results designed to satisfy the government's needs. You also do nothing productive.

20) You are employed by one of the thousands of organizations aboard the global warming tax bandwagon. You only extol things that support AGW and all this carbon footprint crap. You also do nothing productive.

21) You have never been gainfully employed because the world owes you a living. You live on other people's money. You also do nothing productive.

22) You are a criminal, an illegal alien, or a foreign terrorist, but I repeat myself. You also do nothing productive.

23) You are one of the stupid, ignorant, lazy, criminals, gang members, or just plain ne'er-do-wells that wander about in our nation looking for something to steal or someone to mug. You also do nothing productive.

For those very few decent human beings in any of these categories, my apologies. You are just inherently out of it or totally ignorant. I suggest you take a remedial math course where you will learn that 6 is not the same as 10 and 1 minus 3 does not equal 2.

I suggest the math course because of today's revelation by the CBO about the health care destruction bill. The CBO reort said, "The $940 billion health bill would help cut deficit over 10 years." Of course, the CBO (Congressional Budget Office) is staffed and run by liberal Democrats. If that alone or combined with all the previous errors in CBO and other government reports about costs (they average out to be less than half of the actual costs) doesn't convince you this is a fairy tale, you are dumber than I thought. Here's an example of typical liberal Democrat math.

The CBO used estimated tax revenue from the bill over the next ten years compared with estimated costs over the next ten years. Sounds rational doesn't it? What they are very careful to keep from you is that while the tax revenue is for ten years, the cost estimate is for only six of those years. This is a typical Democrat ploy about costs and taxes.

Don't believe me? Well read this and weep. The tax increases start right away while the benefits (costs) do not start until 2014. That makes the cost period for the next ten years only for the last six years while the income (taxes) are being used for the entire ten years. If we take the CBO at their word a quick calculation would reveal costs from 2014 to 2020 would be $940 billion while tax revenue would be $564 billion, a deficit for the program of $376 million. And that's using the CBO's own gloriously optimistic figures. If past experience is any indication the real deficit should be somewhere around a trillion dollars. That's trillion with a T.

I can absolutely guarantee that no media person will explain that to the American public. They lie through their teeth. I often wonder why. What payoff are they getting from our new dictatorship? Maybe their lives have been threatened or those of their families. It is a complete mystery to me.

There is one more bit of information that it is important to know. If you average out the errors the CBO has made in all of its cost projections for the last twenty years you come up with a factor of 3.7 times. That means that on average, actual costs of programs turn out to be 3.7 times the CBO estimates. In other words, CBO estimates have averaged to be only about 27% of the actual costs. That demonstrates the sorry state and unreliability of the CBO. Actually, they have been fairly consistent in their errors so to get a real estimate just multiply whatever they provide by 3.7. For example, take the $940 billion CBO estimate for the Obama care bill, multiply it by 3.7 and you get a far more accurate estimate of $3478 billion or $3.478 trillion. That's trillion with a "T." Do you suppose the Chinese will actually be stupid enough to underwrite such an increase in our debt?

Another prediction made in my book, "The Feudals" was about the specific process and the exact moment when our republic dies and is replaced by a "feudal" dictatorship. Here is that quote:

"At some point in time the powers commanding the feudal horde will realize or believe they have pushed America too far and fear a major backlash in a coming election and the loss of their power. At this point in time a major civil disturbance, possibly a reaction to a rapidly sinking economy or some other artificial catastrophe will bring out a secret army who, like Hitler's brown shirts, will enforce the new America laws. As part of the effort to quell these disturbances this "secret army" will suddenly become known and will enforce martial law on the entire nation. It is only one small step from there to the suspensions of elections, shutting down the legislature and the Supreme Court, and ruling by decree."

—HJ, 2001

For info on Obama's own "brown shirts,"

goto: **http://www.hyscience.com/archives/2009/03/obama_brownshir.php**

This is precisely what Obama was referring to when he stated in a speech last year, "We need a National Civilian Security Force, an organization as big and well-funded as the U.S. military." What other purpose would such an organization serve other than to enforce the laws after just such a coup. I believe we already have such a force in ACORN, the SEIU, and several other militant groups that have been organizing since Saul Alinsky started in motion his plan to destroy free America. At this moment we are perched on the brink of a revolutionary change from a representative republic to a dictatorship. Make no mistake, the fine print in Obama's undefined health care bill will deal the final death blow to the republic and to freedom in America. It will be over before most of the public know what is happening. They will know the reality when Social Security checks begin to bounce, food riots erupt and Obama's "Brown Shirts" come marching down Main Street USA. This last sentence is not a prediction yet, just a gnawing fear in my heart and mind.

It looks like the road to serfdom has finally led America there. The Road to Serfdom is a book written by Friedrich von Hayek (recipient of the Nobel Memorial Prize in Economic Sciences in 1974) Welcome all to the serfdom of Feudal America, right out of the European middle ages.

If it doesn't happen, there are some growing benefits and new industries coming because of the health care bill. Should it pass, I am predicting a huge increase in such operations. Private hospitals are growing in Costa Rica as are associated services. Because trial lawyers don't have a strangle hold on doctors or insurance companies in Costa Rica, fees are much lower, a fraction of fees for the same services in the US. Plastic surgery and orthopedic replacements are at the top of the list as a growing number of Americans opt to go there for expensive surgery. With rapidly expanding and state of the art health care facilities staffed with experienced, well trained staff, even picky Americans are already flocking there for surgery and other treatments. A few insurance companies are testing the water about offering catastrophic care insurance for treatment there.

One could ask, "Doesn't Costa Rica have socialized health care?" but they also have a private system catering to those able to pay from not only the US but from elsewhere in the world as well. It has been estimated that the Obama health care bill will bring about a huge boom in Costa Rica as both patients and medical professionals from the US are disrupted by the realities of Obama care. Coming from the US and elsewhere, immigrants will fill the rapidly growing need for medical professionals in their rapidly expanding system. A side effect has been a small real estate boom supplying housing for those that have already moved there. A huge boom is predicted to start should Obama care become a reality.

This brings me to another thought. The administration controlled media have been ridiculing and talking down talk radio for years. They have recently stepped up their attacks to an unprecedented level with constant lies and distortions about what this host or that has said. They and their lackeys, even Democrat politicians, use only vituperative language and name calling against any of the major talk radio hosts. Time and time again these hosts have challenged those individuals to debate or to prove what they say was not true. Not a single word of denial of facts has ever been uttered by any of the left leaning media. They will simply not engage in a factual, substantive, honest debate because they know they will lose. In stead they use partial quotes, misleading innuendos, outright lies, and common ridicule in order to besmirch anyone who speaks out against the left. While the power of talk radio, the Internet, and other alternative information sources is growing and the influence of the main stream TV and leftist propaganda papers like the New York Times is waning, most Americans still get most of their "news" from the highly biased "Main stream" media. What amazes and encourages me is the growing realization by the public of this reality. I am fully expecting our totalitarian leftist government to find a political way to silence talk radio.

Another encouraging movement from grass roots America is the tea parties. These protest meetings are drawing more attendees than any type of protest meetings ever yet the media plays them down and refuses to show video of them because they are so huge. I've been to several and they are peaceful and very well attended. They are also ridiculed and have their attendance grossly under reported by the media. In fact, media reporters and cameramen will not attend and I am sure they are ordered not to do so by their news organizations. Recently there was a gay protest meeting in I believe Denver, where about 75 protesters marched about some obscure complaint. The pictures shown on national TV of the marchers concentrated their shots so the screen was filled with protesters. I don't remember exactly what was said but it was claimed to have been a crowd of hundreds. The number 75 came from a news photo of the entire group that was printed in the paper. At the same time this was going on there was a tea party in he same city where about a thousand showed up. This was of course deemed "not newsworthy" by the press and no reporters or cameramen covered it. That certainly demonstrates the extreme bias and agenda of the news media. They are obviously propagandists for the left and not news people at all.

I have just one more little commentary. We have a wonderful, adorable, loving little dog named Charlie. He really has a great life for a dog. He is loved, petted and treated with kindness all day every day. All his needs are cared for. He has all the food he wants and gets occasional treats. He has numerous toys he loves to play with. He has a warm comfortable bed in which to sleep. If he gets sick we take him to the vet. When we travel in our motor home he sits in the window and watched everything. We cleanup after him and bathe him when he gets dirty, one activity he doesn't particularly care for. We let him out, on his rope when he wants and let him in when he wants. His greatest joy is when we go out and take him with us on our four wheeled pedal car. When he knows we are going, and he frequently asks us to take him, he bounces around with great excitement. But as happy as he is, he is not free. On those rare occasions when he does get loose he is often gone for hours who knows where, but so far he has always come back because he is completely dependent on us. When we travel, Charlie goes to "camp" at his vet's kennel. He has no say in the matter. As a matter of fact he has little say about anything he does. We control where he goes, what, when and where he eats and sleeps, what toys he has, in fact, everything he does is very much under our control and direction. Then, when he gets up in years and we determine it's time, we will have him euthanized, one more thing we decide with out any input from him. Charlie lives in the ideal socialist state. But what happens if this ideal state goes bankrupt? Then Charlie would be on his own. He would either struggle aga inst all the world throws at him until he starves to death or he gets adopted into the same kind of slavery by another person (state).

Isn't that precisely how a socialist state works in the real world? It's cradle to grave security, but of course everything you do or have is determined by the state. The Obama health care destruction bill is one more giant step into the dull gray abyss of socialism, marxism, communism, fascism, feudalism. I use all five, as they are each merely a slight variation of totalitarianism. We are all being forced to be like Charlie, totally dependent on our masters for everything. If you think state determined euthanasia isn't in the package you don't know what is happening in all states with socialized medicine. That includes Canada and Norway. You are now much closer to being pups like Charlie with the Washington elite as your masters.

Enjoy your leashes and just say woof!

Monday, February 22, 2010

Hojo's Predictions, an Unbelievably Sad Revelation since 1994

Since about 1994 I have been writing political and economic predictions. In 1998 I started writing a book I titled, The Feudals about those political ideologues of the left I saw as taking us down that fatal road to a socialist, communist, marxist, fascist, feudal dictatorship. In that book I included many predictions based on information from my experience and that I had gathered first from the news media and then from other sources that I use to confirm news media stories. It was not a very big surprise to discover how many news media "objective reports" were misleading because they simply left out significant facts or they just pain lied. As a result I have adopted the following rules for collecting data.

1. Believe nothing you hear or read uttered by any politician, media personality, or proponent of any political philosophy. Always use the source person or persons' proven track record to pass judgement on what ever they say. Believe only what they do, never what they say. In fact, question everything using the tests that follow.

2. Confirm anything you hear or read with sources you trust to be accurate and honest. Just remember that anyone who professes any political or religious philosophy will only provide information favoring their philosophy.

3. Accept as fact only those things that meet the following tests:

a. All laws of physics, chemistry and/or mathematics must testify to its veracity.

b. If a physical test is not possible it must still meet your personal belief system and/or be agreed with by several reliable sources, not necessarily sources with which you agree philosophically.

c. If neither of these is sufficient and it is important, research it from as many confirming sources as necessary before deciding what it means and whether it is true or not

4. Accept no one's opinion on anything, even those who agree with you. If it doesn't make sense or seems strange to you keep digging until you are satisfied you have the answer.

5. Refrain totally from believing any political or religious power pronouncements. They are all designed to remove your independent thought from you and replace it with their dogma.

In 1996 I made the following prediction: "The United States will have become a socialist/communist/marxist/fascist/feudal dictatorship---an oligarchy by the year 2030." I wrote that in an introduction to a political book I was writing titled later, The Feudals. I believe that far more now than I did then. I wonder if those believers in far left ideologues will be happy when that comes to pass? As of March of 2010 I believe the destruction of our existing democracy will happen much sooner, possibly within a few months. All the signs are there. The ramming of the left's health care destruction bill through in defiance of the law in our Constitution, will push us over the cliff. Make no mistake, this so called health care bill is actually a huge power grab by leftist despots. Once enacted it will be very difficult to repeal.

In 1998 I predicted the current mortgage system collapse. I wrote that the two government mortgage companies, Fannie May and Freddie Mac were deliberately destroying the mortgage banking system. Earlier that year, a mortgage banker I know very well told me about our government ordering banks to make not just risky, but also noncollectable mortgage loans. With that information it became obvious to me what was happening. I also wrote it was being deliberately orchestrated by leftists in the bureaucracy of our government to do precisely what it did. That was to destroy much of the wealth of the middle class which it certainly accomplished. Not only did it accomplish its unspoken aim, but the architects of the collapse made tons of money personally at taxpayer expense.

Who were those who brought the mortgage collapse about? Franklin Raines and Jim Johnson both walked away from Fannie May with millions in their pockets. Both were far left, unelected government bureaucrats who cooked the books to gain millions in bonuses. Franklin Raines was paid bonuses of $90 million over five years. When that was exposed, he promised to return all of it. So far not one red cent has been returned and no political or media person has once mentioned that fact. Ken Lay of Enron gained far less for his chicanery and was awarded a prison sentence. His crime was penny ante compared with Raines and Johnson who are now both working in the Obama administration. That demonstrates the fairness and policies of the left. They were not the only ones to gain huge sums of money from Fannie May and Freddie Mac. And just who received millions in campaign contributions from those self same government banks? Chris Dodd, Barney Frank, and a brand new Senator from Illinois named Obama were the three largest recipients. The only ones to complain about what was going on and try to do something to stop it were those two evil Republicans, George Bush and Dick Cheney. And where were the Democrats in this? They were screaming at Bush and Cheney and calling them names for opposing such a noble effort to provide housing for the poor. Their complaints were echoed loudly by the left's captive media.

There was another little local Indiana action that I found out about by digging into some sketchy reports in the local media. It seems there was a group of at least six community organizers in Fort Wayne who had a neat little scam going. The group were buying up low value homes in the poor sections of Ft Wayne and turning them into gold mines. Here's how it worked. They would find a poor family with nothing to lose to work with them. The group would put a few thousand dollars in dolling up one of these old houses and then have one of the bank appraisers they owned value it for say $120,000. They would then apply and get a loan for those people of say $135,000 backed by one of the two government mortgage companies. Once they got the money they would hand $25,000 to the family who would then walk away while they pocketed the balance of $85,000 less their expenses. Not a bad deal, eh? Sometimes the family lived in the home for awhile and a very few even stayed and tried to pay the mortgage—didn't take the pay off money. Mostly they just walked away without even having seen the place. It didn't take long for the house strippers to realize the house was empty so by the time the bank foreclosed, the place had been completely stripped of all appliances, fixtures, and even the copper wiring in the walls was pulled and sold for scrap.

I'm sure Ft Wayne was not the only place where this little deal was going on. In Indianapolis the city was paying the same kind of community organizers $500 to $1,000 for every mortgage they wrote. I wonder who set up that marvelous system? Need I tell the name of the parent organization of these community organizers? It seems to me there was another public figure who claimed that title on his resume. Hmmmm!

I wrote down quite a other few predictions about the political and economic future of our nation that have come true including both that Obama would be the candidate and that he would be elected carrying a majority for Democrats into both houses of Congress. Both predictions were written down long before they became actualities. I also wrote predictions about what the Obama administration would be doing and why. Nobody listened or believed me then and I certainly don't expect anyone to listen to me now. After all, what could I know?

I'll say one thing. My Socrates discussion group here in St Augustine have gained and expressed amazement at the accuracy of the predictions I have shared with them in writing during my three year membership. Even those who ridiculed my predictions when I made them now listen when I make them. I personally am terribly disheartened that I was right. I'll make another really far out prediction about the very near future. I don't believe the power systems are yet in place to make it happen, but they could be and very well hidden. Here goes.

What would happen nationally if suddenly major riots broke out. Racial or food riots in places like Detroit, Philadelphia, Atlanta, New Orleans, and even Cleveland? Why the Obama administration would have to do something to stop it. Out would come the President's Civilian National Security Force to deal with the problems under martial law. As he said, "We cannot continue to rely on our military in order to achieve the national security objectives that we've set. We've got to have a civilian national security force that's just as powerful, just as strong, just as well-funded." It would be just one more step "necessary for the personal safety of the people" for civil liberties to be suspended "until we get things under control." Of course then elections would have to be suspended until all the rabble rousers were dealt with. Sound familiar? Read you history books as it has all happened before.

That's actually not a very good prediction for the immediate future because I don't believe his civilian national security force, CNSF, is quite ready. Of course, I could be wrong about that Maybe he can be stopped before his CNSF has gathered enough power. I certainly hope so. My guess is that under another name like ACORN they already have the personnel, the organization, and the weaponry. I just think they need a lot more training, but I could be wrong about that as well. Could you tell me just what possible need could he have for a separate and independent military force "just as strong, just as well-funded" as our military if he didn't intend to use them in this way? Give me a break!

Friday, January 29, 2010

America is in rapid decline - can we stop it?

Doing things exactly the wrong way

Growing rancor of political campaigning is one example of the power of inciting hatred to sway voters. The preponderance of personal attacks over substantive proposals shows how much easier it is to tear down a political opponent than to build one's own stature and make serious proposals. Negative campaigning is easy and especially effective in the age of the "sound bite." Like war, it is easy. All you have to do in war is break things and kill people. Any idiot can do that with little training. In political campaigns it is pure emotion that drives voters. Serious proposals, even solutions for all-important problems, rarely get the media play and public attention that hate-filled rhetoric prompts.

For similar reasons, it takes far less skill or organization to demolish a home or even the World Trade Center than it does to conceive, design, and build the same thing. Conflict is easy. Cooperation and creative building are far more demanding, require careful consideration, dedication, creative effort and hard work. They are infinitely more rewarding. This is what we sorely need right now.

Often attributed to Lincoln in error are these words penned by William J. H. Boetcker, in 1916.

You cannot strengthen the weak by weakening the strong.

You cannot help small men by tearing down big men.

You cannot help the poor by destroying the rich.

You cannot lift the wage earner by pulling down the wage payer.

You cannot keep out of trouble by spending more than your income.

You cannot further the brotherhood of man by inciting class hatreds.

You cannot establish security on borrowed money.

You cannot build character and courage by taking away a man's initiative and independence.

You cannot help men permanently by doing for them what they could and should do for themselves.

Yet are those not precisely the short lived, instant gratifications politicians and media personalities regularly wield against those they oppose for any reason?

See quotes on Page 91

These are the real malignancies we must overcome if we are to solve the rapidly growing problems facing not just the US, but the entire world.

It's about time members of groups that constantly denigrate and condemn others out of class or economic envy began to honor and respect the achievements and rewards of those others. I see it as important that we recognize the realities of our situation and the real reasons we are where we are. There has been enough of this huge and debilitating blame game and all of its political distortions and emotional hate-filled activities. We have been engaged in terrible inner political warfare while our enemies stand on the sidelines urging on the various sides and gleefully watching our self destruction.

Socialism has a terrible record of providing a decent living for its subjects. An examination of all socialist nations shows that in order to be successful they must have a huge source of income outside the government to survive. Those that do not, universally house a population in poverty like Haiti and many African nations. Most are actually dictatorships where one or a very few individuals wield all the power and control all the wealth. That source of income is usually a valuable natural resource which capitalists throughout the world require to feed their economy. Petroleum is probably the biggest source of income for socialist nations. Those that have it usually have wealthy despots running the country and wasting that income. Other natural raw materials include iron, wood, diamonds, agricultural produce and others. Even tourism is a source of supportive income for some socialist nations.

Venezuela is a good example of how quickly the income from raw materials can destroy the economy. With their fat little dictator squandering this valuable resource in many ways in a controlled economy, Venezuela is suddenly on the verge of economic collapse. The people of Venezuela, used to low prices on all kinds of goods subsidized by the government including 25 cents per gallon gasoline, have suddenly been awakened by run away inflation as government excesses quickly outran income when oil prices dropped. Many things now cost five or ten times what they did a year or two ago. This includes food and—you guessed it—gasoline. Shades of the old Soviet Union, Cuba, North Korea—every socialist utopia whose outside income suddenly dropped or disappeared.

Socialists are quick to point out socialist nations that are doing quite well—whose citizens enjoy a high standard of living—free education, health care, and all manner of benefits. Take a look at those nations, where their income is coming from. Each has either a major source of income from natural resources (oil, minerals, etc.) or a capitalist manufacturing base of privately owned organizations. There are no exceptions! The growth of foreign trade income from all manner of private enterprises has fueled the explosive economic growth in China, Korea, Taiwan, and every other awakening Asian economy. Even India is getting into the act. Look at what happened to them when our economy took a nose dive. Now they are striving to grow their own domestic economies by—can you guess? Advertising and consumerism at home!

While these nations move toward the wealth distribution of a capitalist economy, we are sinking into dull gray socialist poverty. Our manufacturing base has long fled to other shores, our technology industries are now doing the same and what do we have left? Agriculture! We are about to become a nation of poor farmers and wealthy politicians running things for their own benefit. Don't think our investors and entrepreneurs who haven't already done so won't soon head for more attractive shores with lower taxes and less government interference. We are being strangled by an out-of-control tax and spend monster whose only incentive is class hatred and money envy.

I have but a single question for you capitalist hating liberal idiots. Once capitalism is dead and its profits no longer can be taxed, where are you going to get the money to pay for all your social programs? Or do you plan to hand the entire nation over to the Chinese capitalists who will soon own everything in America anyway.

Saturday, January 16, 2010

Some Comments on That Utopian Marvel, Socialism

The most fundamental fact about the ideas of the political left is that they do not work. Therefore we should not be surprised to find the left concentrated in institutions where ideas do not have to work in order to survive.   *—Thomas Sowell*

The function of socialism is to raise suffering to a higher level.   *—Norman Mailer*

A government policy to rob Peter to pay Paul can be assured of the support of Paul.
—George Bernard Shaw

Socialism in general has a record of failure so blatant that only an intellectual could ignore or evade it.   *—Thomas Sowell*

A Painful Prediction Followed by Some Observations

The United States will be a socialist dictatorship by 2030. At this time those leftist activists will happily extol the joys of socialism as they are being carted off to the salt mines.   *—HJ, 2008*

Why is it people seem to want to replace a very successful capitalist system with a socialist system that has proven to be a failure and should actually be called feudalism? The American capitalist system where a few are extremely wealthy, a great many more are wealthy, the vast majority live quite comfortably, a small minority are just getting by and a very small number are in poverty, is in the process of being deliberately destroyed so socialism can take over. Socialism which has been proven time and time again to provide power and extreme wealth for the very few in government while the vast majority are in or close to abject poverty. Just look at the nations of the world. There are hundreds of examples—obvious examples—of the failure of socialism. Socialism has inevitably lead to dictatorship where "the meanest SOB in the valley" takes over complete power, just like the "monkey king" of troops of our simian relatives. Just like our current crop of socialists in Congress (who still call themselves Democrats) all these would be totalitariqn tyrants promise anything to get in power, forget those promises when in power, and use that power doing anything to ensure they will always remain in power

Why is it people can't see the multitudes of failures? I have one opinion that goes to basic human nature. It is easier for have nots to destroy the haves than to work to join them. Class envy whipped into a frenzy is the tool used by those seeking power and control to destroy any who oppose them. It's the child on the beach who has not the skill or the patience to build a sand castle, but can gleefully destroy it. It's the men who have neither the skill nor patience to design and build the WTC who destroyed it killing 3,000 human individuals. It's the thousands of government bureaucrats who daily shuffle papers delaying and preventing benefits promised by the government to individuals who have become desperately dependent on them.

I'll excuse all you leftists who hate America and think Americans should be punished for working hard and being successful. You are just too stupid, self pitying, and even pathetic to consider seriously. Bluntly put, you prefer destruction and personal injury to construction and cooperative behavior. Unfortunately it is far easier for a few of your depraved idiots to destroy what hard working Americans have built than for those Americans to defend what they have built from a few determined thugs. What's worse, you are too ignorant and hate filled to realize how wrong it is for all but a very few individuals.

The Saul Alinsky school for the destruction of Americanism, capitalism, individual freedom and the promotion and ascension of Utopianism/socialist dictatorship/slavery.

"Obama learned his lesson well. I am proud to see that my father's model for organizing is being applied successfully beyond local community organizing to affect the Democratic campaign in 2008. It is a fine tribute to Saul Alinsky as we approach his 100th birthday." --Letter from L. DAVID ALINSKY, son of Neo-Marxist Saul Alinsky

Hillary, Obama and the Cult of Alinsky: "True revolutionaries do not flaunt their radicalism, Alinsky taught. They cut their hair, put on suits and infiltrate the system from within. Alinsky viewed revolution as a slow, patient process. The trick was to penetrate existing institutions such as churches, unions and political parties.... Many leftists view Hillary as a sell-out because she claims to hold moderate views on some issues. However, Hillary is simply following Alinsky's counsel to do and say whatever it takes to gain power.

"Barack Obama is also an Alinskyite.... Obama spent years teaching workshops on the Alinsky method. In 1985 he began a four-year stint as a community organizer in Chicago, working for an Alinskyite group called the Developing Communities Project.... Camouflage is key to Alinsky-style organizing. While trying to build coalitions of black churches in Chicago, Obama caught flak for not attending church himself. He became an instant churchgoer." (By Richard Poe, 11-27-07)

These are the criminal conspirators that are now running our nation. Realizing that most Americans will catch on to what they are doing within a very short time they are moving as quickly as possible to consolidate their power and never face another election. With massive new taxes announced and unannounced, the powers in Washington are forcing major corporations, banks they do not control, and other economic entities toward economic disaster and destruction. Using this as an excuse "They're just too big to fail" they took over two of our three major auto companies and gave them to the UAW to run. That figures! The UAW is their constituency and who they take care of, not the American public.

Their end purpose became obvious when they refused even to negotiate the sale of Pontiac, Saab, and/or Saturn divisions to private investors eager to purchase and run them. One famous automotive entrepreneur after making a generous offer for Saturn, withdrew his offer after the government refused to bargain in good faith. His comment, "They obviously prefer to trash the company and get nothing for it than let it become a private company and increase private enterprise and investment". The pending multi million dollar deals for three of the GM divisions have all been scrapped because of government intransigence. As a result, all three potential buyers are making deals with foreign auto manufacturers to pick up the market being deserted by GM.

With Goldman-Sachs in bed with the administration—they have supplied how many members to the Obama administration? Here's a report from Global Research:

"For a speech to Goldman Sachs executives, Summers walked away with $135,000. This is substantially more than double the earnings for an entire year of high-seniority auto workers, who have been pilloried by the Obama administration and the media for their supposedly exorbitant and "unsustainable" wages."

A series of articles published over the weekend, based on financial disclosure reports released by the Obama administration last Friday concerning top White House officials, documents the extent to which the administration, in both its personnel and policies, is a political instrument of Wall Street.

Policies that are extraordinarily favorable to the financial elite that were put in place over the past month by the Obama administration have fed a surge in share values on Wall Street. These include the scheme to use hundreds of billions of dollars in public funds to pay hedge funds to buy up the banks' toxic assets at inflated prices, the Auto Task Force's rejection of the recovery plans of Chrysler and General Motors and its demand for even more brutal layoffs, wage cuts and attacks on workers' health benefits and pensions, and the decision by the Financial Accounting Standards Board (FASB) to weaken "mark-to-market" accounting rules and permit banks to inflate the value of their toxic assets.

Read the entire report at:

http://www.globalresearch.ca/index.php?context=va&aid=13208

JUST KNOW THIS! These people are enemies of free men everywhere. They are on an orchestrated path to the total destruction of free America and the eradication of the economic/political system that created the most wealth for the most people more equally spread among the common folks than any other system in history. It was an excellent demonstration of the wealth that free people working in an open competitive environment with little interference from the dictates of politicians seeking self agrandizement. Their ultimate goal is an America under Soviet style socialist dictatorship where a very few control everything and the common man is a mere slave serving their leaders. They would replace a capitalist system where virtually thousands of organizations under diverse and creative management with a socialist system where there are a very few extremely wealthy and powerful members of the government who can virtually do as they please.

Look at the example already set by the members of the Socialist party in power. Michelle Obama spends huge sums on lavish luncheons on taxpayer's money. If you don't think a $400/00+ lobster "snack" is extravagant you belong on another planet. In the Socialist monopoly, one doesn't have to be personally "wealthy" to be truly wealthy. All that is necessary is access and control of "public" money. "Princess" Hillary spent millions of taxpayers dollars for lavish Senate offices she only used for a few years. She says it was so she could better "serve" her constituents. It was actually an ego trip so she could live "better than those business executives" and have "the most expensive and luxurious office of any Senator." That huge government expense had little to do with serving constituents.

Another "princess" in the new socialist royalty, Nancy Pelosi, insists on expensive luxury jet aircraft to whisk her wherever she wants at great and unnecessary expense to the taxpayers. Witness the recent jaunt be she and a number of her faithful to Copenhagen for no conceivable reason. Using a number of expensive military jets, they went on what could accurately be described as a pleasure excursion for themselves and some family members. They had no possible legitimate purpose in taking that trip which cost American taxpayers hundreds of thousands, if not millions of dollars we could ill afford to spend. Are we going to stand for those greedy, self serving ego maniacal politicians to live like kings and queens on our money (they want all kinds of new and punitive taxes) while we face economic disaster—a very personal disaster—that they have brought upon us?

Just in passing, did you realize that the mortgage meltdown, deliberately engineered by liberals in government, resulted in the largest transfer of wealth out of the hands of individuals in the history of the world? People with moderate homes with normal mortgages consistently lost between 60% to 100% of their home equity. The liberal executives in the government's Fannie May and Freddie Mac walked away with hundreds of millions of dollars for engineering this debacle which ultimately resulted in the recession. Nothing will ever convince me this wasn't a deliberate effort to destroy middle America and our capitalist system. Government ownership of virtually all of America's businesses is the ultimate goal.

As early as 2003 my son-in-law who worked as a mortgage salesman for a bank in Dayton was telling me of extreme government pressure exerted on his bank to make shaky loans. When the bank refused they were cut off from all access to government loan guarantees or referrals. His words, "Howard, I can hardly believe it but our federal government is deliberately inflating the housing bubble which I think will burst with dire consequences in a few years."

Tuesday, January 12, 2010

Liberals on education

Liberal mecca, Berkeley, California is a perfect example of how liberals tackle problems and demonstrates how they will always make things worse, sometimes catastrophically worse (the mortgage meltdown) when they try to do anything. It's a small example of why they are doing such a fantastic job of running Amtrak, the Postal Service, Fannie May, Freddie Mac, Medicare, etc. etc. etc. Now they want to take charge of health care? That's all we need, 60 bureaucrats (all of whom vote Democrat because they know who gave them their jobs) sitting around drinking coffee, playing cards and occasionally approving, or more likely disapproving our requests for critical medical services. But I digress.

The liberal masterminds that run Berkeley found there was a problem with their high school science program, in particular a science lab. It seems that Black (notice the capitalization) and Hispanic students were not doing nearly as well as their white counterparts in this science lab. Well, something had to be done about that. After all, everyone is equal, right? The liberal wizards running things had several options. 1) They could study the problem and take steps to bring the failing students up to the standards of the "white" students. That could take some extra effort, but it has been done successfully elsewhere and certainly could be done in Berkeley with the liberal intelligentsia (an oxymoron) in residence there. 2) They could have researched how other schools were dealing with the problem, learn from their experience and adopt the best of their methods. I'll not list the several other options, but surely you get my drift!

So what did these geniuses do? Why of course, they aborted the science lab, condemned it to non existence, killed the whole project. Just think of the wonders that kind of progressive thinking could bring to our entire education system. Wait a minute, isn't that what's been happening all over the US? Isn't that the very reason our education system has progressed to it's present glorious, exemplary state? The logic? If a course, or class, or school has a problem with one or more ethnic/racial groups performing in a far superior manner to other ethnic/racial groups there is a universal solution. CLOSE DOWN THE COURSE, OR CLASS, OR SCHOOL. Problem solved!

Same logic—if there are 500 students of varying abilities, set the curricula to fit the slowest student. It's the best way to level things out and make everybody equal. Besides, those loyal members of the teachers union who couldn't teach a starving dog how to eat won't have to work so hard and strain their gray matter. Of course, should anything fail, those at fault, pardon me, those dedicated educators with a problem not of their making, could fall back on that universal excuse all liberals rely on for everything, GEORGE BUSH. Yeah! Blame it on George. Or maybe Halliburton, or big corporations, or conservatives, or Republicans or . . .

Remember the first law of liberalism — **Liberals or their policies are never to blame for anything!** OH, for the good old days!

Tuesday, December 15, 2009

Who's predictions? Prophecy?

Just today one of my blogger friends reminded me of a blog I wrote in February 2006 in response to an email sent to me by Arianna Huffington. Read it and see what you think.

My, how things really don't change. Check out the following post. It is on page 242

http://hjarianna6210.blogspot.com

Friday, October 09, 2009

Some musings and quotes

The financial crisis explained in simple terms.

NOTE: This is a version of a story heard on talk radio and embellished by the author of this blog, who adds, "The crisis was created deliberately by Liberals aided by greedy bankers and politicians buying votes."

~ ~

Heidi is the proprietor of a bar in Berlin . In order to increase sales, she decides to allow her loyal customers - most of whom are unemployed alcoholics - to drink now but pay later. She keeps track of the drinks consumed on a ledger (thereby granting the customers loans).

Word gets around, promoted by liberal politicians and their adoring media and as a result increasing numbers of customers flood into Heidi's bar.

Taking advantage of her customers' freedom from immediate payment constraints, Heidi gradually but steadily increases her prices for wine and beer, the most-consumed beverages gradually. Her sales volume increases massively as do her profits (and tax payments)

A young and dynamic customer service consultant at the local bank recognizes these customer debts as valuable future assets and increases Heidi's borrowing limit. Deciding to expand she opens several new bars on her greatly expanded credit.

He sees no reason for undue concern since he has the debts of the alcoholics as collateral.

At the bank's corporate headquarters, expert bankers transform these customer assets into DRINKBONDS, ALKBONDS and PUKEBONDS. These securities are then traded on markets worldwide. No one really understands what these abbreviations mean and how the securities are guaranteed. Nevertheless, as their prices continuously climb, the securities become top-selling items.

One day, although the prices are still climbing, a risk manager (subsequently of course fired due his negativity) of the bank decides that the time has come to demand payment of the debts incurred by the drinkers at Heidi's bar and by Heidi for her greatly expanded business.

However they cannot pay back the debts.

Heidi cannot fulfill her loan obligations and claims bankruptcy.

DRINKBOND and ALKBOND drop in price by 95 %. PUKEBOND performs better, stabilizing in price after dropping by 80 %.

The suppliers of Heidi's bar, having granted her generous payment due dates and having invested in the securities are faced with a new situation. Her wine supplier claims bankruptcy, her beer supplier is taken over by a competitor.

The bank is saved by "the Government" following dramatic round-the-clock consultations by leaders from the governing political parties.

The funds required for this purpose are obtained by a tax levied on the non-drinkers.

Finally an explanation I understand...

~ ~

In addition, the non-drinkers are mostly business people, some very wealthy, who hire 90% of the people employed and generate most of the new jobs. Seeing their profits deeply cut by the expanded taxes, they reduce their one-year and five-year financial budgets, cut their plans for expansion, reduce their payroll (that's lay off many of their employees), and cancel orders for new equipment.

The stock market drops by 50% as investors move their holdings to safer places (like gold and Ireland). The media morosely reports the layoffs and order cancellations announcing, "We are now in a terrible recession brought about by greedy businessmen." Consumer confidence (a very nebulous quality) drops precipitously, profits (and taxes) take a huge drop, and more and more businesses fail.

The government (who can't manage anything and would seriously "screw up a one car parade") takes over those failing "business that are too big to fail." Between feuding and self-serving politicians and anal retentive government bureaucrats the economy collapses in line with a quote often attributed to a Scottish Historian, Alexander Tytler or Tyler.

See quotes on Page 91

For more information about these quotes and their sources go to http://www.lorencollins.net/tytler.html

A very interesting interview about Obama's "share the wealth" plan.

INTERVIEWER: Hello.

SUBJECT: Hey! How are you doing?

INTERVIEWER: Very well, sir, thank you.

SUBJECT: All right. My wife had a hard time trying to understand why Obama's plan to "spread the wealth" was unfair. She couldn't see (sigh), you know, what was wrong with taking from those who have and giving to those who don't have so what I did was I simplified it for her. She's a woman that prides herself on education. She's working on a PhD at Vanderbilt and she makes excellent grades.

INTERVIEWER: Oh, no.

SUBJECT: Now, I told her, I said --

INTERVIEWER: Wait a minute, wait a minute, wait a minute. You are depressing me. Your wife's a PhD, working on a PhD, she makes excellent grades.

SUBJECT: Yes, and we have four kids.

INTERVIEWER: No, it makes total sense that she would think what she thinks because the culture she's immersed herself in, academia, is teaching her this stuff.

SUBJECT: (laughing) Well, let me finish. Let me show you what I did.

INTERVIEWER: Yes. Sorry for the interruption.

SUBJECT: That's okay. Let me just show you what I did to bring her around. I said, "You know, what if you made a hundred on a test and another guy in your class made a 60? This guy has a failing mark and you have a high passing mark. Would it be fair to give say 20 of your points, bring you down to an 80, give the 20 to the guy that made the 60 and bring him up to 80 and everything is equal?" She said, "No." I said, "Why?" She said, "Because I earned that grade." I said, "Don't you think rich people earned the money that they get?" And so she was speechless. She couldn't say anything. She'd said, "No, I earned it." I said, "Think about it, Baby. "You're bringing a guy up from a failing grade to a passing grade, and we gonna bring you down to his level." I said, "Now you apply that type of example with everybody in the classroom, everybody being dumber. Nobody would ever get out of your class because everybody would have a failing grade." So she then understood the point I was trying to make. Sometimes you have to use other examples to get other people to think, you know, to try to get the point across of what you're trying to say. That's all I wanted to say.

INTERVIEWER: Well, you did a great job out there. I don't know how much you made her "think" as you made her "realize."

SUBJECT: Yeah.

INTERVIEWER: But I need to ask you something, Tim.

SUBJECT: Go ahead.

INTERVIEWER: Has this conversion held? Does she still get it now that you've explained it to her.

SUBJECT: She gets it but she hates it.

INTERVIEWER: Well, I tell you, if she goes back to class where she's studying for her PhD and she runs this story either by a fellow student -- or even worse, a professor -- the professor will say, "Well, here's what you shoulda said when your husband posed this question: 'The people who have a lot of money didn't earn it. They have stolen it.'" This is Obama's belief. This is why they've stolen it. They have unfairly taken what's not theirs. They haven't earned it. That's the whole point, they cheated and steal and had lied to get it and that's why he's going to take it from them and give the money to like these poor people lining up at Cobo Hall in Detroit for it. (See Page 197) That's what he believes. You gotta stay on this, my man, because a professor's going to tell her that if she dares tell this story, and the professor is going to say, "Well, you can't compare wealth to grades because there isn't anybody else... You can't take somebody else's grade but you could take somebody else's money from them while they weren't looking. You could cheat 'em, you could steal." They'll work on them like this. This is going to be an ongoing thing. You did a great thing here, a great thing. You've taken a big, giant step here.

SUBJECT: Oh, yeah. Well, I just appreciate that. She doesn't like to listen to anything that disagrees with her beliefs. I'm like, "Whatever." I think sometimes she just don't want to listen because people are realists.

INTERVIEWER: Well, look, she's like a lot of people. Her world view is safely wrapped inside a cocoon in which she lives, and if anything penetrates it that upsets this security blanket she's living in, you're right, she doesn't want it.

SUBJECT: Yep.

INTERVIEWER: She does not want to be challenged with anything that would question her beliefs.

SUBJECT: Yeah.

INTERVIEWER: You have a huge challenge out there.

SUBJECT: Well, I'm teaching the four kids, bringing them up in the right way, teaching them.

INTERVIEWER: God bless you. This is a great interview. I appreciate the fact that you're doing this, and I appreciate the fact that you are telling us.

SUBJECT: All right, have a good one.

INTERVIEWER: Thank you, Thank you very much. Well, sometimes it's just a simple little explanation like that is all it takes when you make it personal.

Another difference between public and private enterprise.

Cheats and thieves in private business pay heavy fines and are sentenced to prison when caught. Liberal Democrats in government who do even worse are rewarded with bonuses and plush jobs. Ah, the blessings of liberalism/socialism/communism/feudalism.

One example of the results of the tireless efforts of Barney Frank, Chris Dodd, (then Senator) Barack Obama, Franklin Raines, Jim Johnson, was the melt down of the mortgage market.

Fannie Mae and Freddie Mac problems were started by democrat administration personnel. Two Senators receive more campaign contributions from Fannie Mae and Freddie Mac than all others from 1989-2008. Number 1 – Senator Chris Dodd, (D) CONN Chairman Senate Banking Committee and former 2008 Democrat candidate for President. Number 2 - Senator and now President Barack Obama. How did Barack Obama do this after only 3 years as a Senator? You fill in the blanks.

Remember when Barack Obama stood up for his Vice Presidential Search Committee member Jim Johnson? It was June 2008 and Jim Johnson had to resign because of a "controversy" about his time at embattled Countrywide Mortgage. It was not important that Jim Johnson received loans at a below market rate.

It was also largely ignored that Jim Johnson was former CEO of Fannie Mae. It seems that the CEO's of Freddie Mac and Fannie Mae were cooking the books. The CEO's had been inflating yearly earnings to receive their annual bonuses! They would then amend the earnings statements later in the year. Typical government chicanery, like base line budgeting.

Those CEOs cost several orders more Americans to lose several orders more of their hard earned equity than Enron's executives. Ken Lay who was demonized in the media, sent to prison by the government, and was held up as an example of "evil capitalists." Not a single CEO of Fannie Mae and Freddie Mac missed their annual bonuses. For example, Franklin Raines made $90 Million in bonuses from Fannie Mae in 6 years! It seems capitalists go to prison and pay heavy fines while liberal Democrats in government are paid bonuses and are even awarded jobs in government when they do the same thing. Ah, the blessings of liberalism/socialism/communism.

One other note: I find it hard to believe that these people, who directly brought about the mortgage collapse, are that stupid. Ergo, this was a deliberate action intended to do just what it did. For instance, in California, homeowner's equity in the housing market dropped from around 60% to about 30% while the banks' equity (mortgages) increased from about 40% to 70% of the housing market. Sure, some foreclosures cost banks a bit, but overall they almost doubled their share of the mortgage market. I wonder how much of that is controlled by Goldman Sachs? Hmmmmm!

Obama money at Cobo Hall in Detroit

A huge crowd assembled at Cobo Hall in Detroit when it was announced that the federal government would disperse several millions in recovery funds to individuals in hard hit Detroit. A reporter from radio station WJR went there and interviewed several who were there waiting to apply for some of the money.

WJR interviewer finds a Model Obama Citizen - October 7, 2009

ROGULSKI: Did you get an application to fill out yet?

WOMAN: I sure did. And I filled it out, and I am waiting to see what the results are going to be.

ROGULSKI: Will you know today how much money you're getting?

WOMAN: No, I won't, but I'm waiting for a phone call.

ROGULSKI: Where's the money coming from?

WOMAN: I believe it's coming from the City of Detroit or the state.

ROGULSKI: Where did they get it from?

WOMAN: Some funds that was forgiven (sic) by Obama.

ROGULSKI: And where did Obama get the funds?

WOMAN: Obama getting the funds from... Ummm, I have no idea, to tell you the truth. He's the president.

ROGULSKI: In downtown Detroit, Ken Rogulski, WJR News.

Another woman is questioned:

ROGULSKI: What are you doing here?

WOMAN: We're all here to get some Obama money.

ROGULSKI: How much money will you be getting?

WOMAN: I don't know, but it will be worth the wait.

ROGULSKI: Where's the money coming from?

WOMAN: I don't know. It's government money Obama's giving us.

ROGULSKI: Where did he get it from?

WOMAN: It's Obama money. He's got lots of money.

ROGULSKI: And where did Obama get the funds?

WOMAN: He's the President. He promised us money. God bless Obama.

ROGULSKI: In downtown Detroit, Ken Rogulski, WJR News.

NOTE: There were 65,000 who went to Cobo in hopes of getting a cash handout. Only 3,500 will actually receive any money. What do you think is going to happen in Detroit when those 61,500 find out they will not get any money?

Some interesting facts about American car sales:

The latest sales figures from the auto industry tell a great deal about the people's faith in their government when it comes to running auto companies. (Or anything else for that matter.)

GM reported a drop of about 44% in sales from a year ago. Chrysler reported a 48% drop. Ford, the only major American auto company still in private hands, reported a drop of just 4%. That's a pretty good indicator of the faith the American people have in their government, at least the car buying public. Roughly the same trend was shown in the results of the "cash for clunkers" program. The public has eloquently expressed their opinion!

I had to add this exchange with one of my SFN friends

Al:

Don't worry about idealists on the left coming down on you. Mostly they are decent, caring people who see everything remotely political in their own definition of black and white, no shades of gray anywhere. White is anything that follows the emotional mantras handed down by their high priests. Black is anything that does not. They are firmly indoctrinated in the fundamentalist religion of the left and live in a la la land with hardly a clue as to what is actually happening. No matter how factually wrong they are or how factually right you are, their belief system overrides facts, and logic never comes into play. I have a whole bunch of them in my family that I love dearly.

Remember that great liberal Democrat Howard Dean's rant of a few years back, "I hate Republicans! I hate Conservatives! I hate Middle America! YEEEARGH!!!" This is the brand of unreasoning passion that controls the minds of so many liberals.

Add to that this thought. I hear echos of the old Al Capone/Big Bill Thompson/Jake Arvey/Richard Daly I and II machine now ringing through Washington. I lived enough in Cook County to have personal experiences with that gang. In fact, the son of Capone's accountant was a long time drinking buddy of mine. I could tell hundreds of horror stories. Of course, most libs wouldn't listen to any of them, let alone believe anything counter to their liberal belief system. Most idealists on the left haven't a clue what that gang is really up to. Doesn't bode well for our country unless the people wake up soon. I'm encouraged because I see that beginning to happen. I just hope it is not too late.

Ho

Ho:

I agree. I expected more intelligence out of Don, but Liberalism seems to carry its own set of blinders. My elder brother is a retired Physics professor. Very intelligent. UNTIL politics is mentioned. Then he reverts to his Pavlovian conditioning and his brain flies south. You'd think a "scientist" would apply scientific rigor to politics as well (if it doesn't work, the theory is wrong), but that doesn't seem to be the case. But then, he was never a researcher, just a teacher in California where the teachers are all super libs. You'd think an ex-Navy career officer would be able to withstand the peer-group propaganda better.

Al

Friday, September 18, 2009

Not so fast on the H1N1 vaccines

What is the real reason for all the emotional promotion by government and media of the fear driven panic over H1N1 flu and the supposed dire need for vaccines? All for a disease that has already proven extremely mild? Do you actually believe all that propaganda foisted off on a gullible public by a patently dishonest government? Somebody must be making lots of moolah. I wonder who?

By doubting we are led to inquire; by inquiring we perceive the truth. —*Peter Abelard*

Here are excerpts from a couple of articles that pose serious questions that should certainly be answered. The web addresses of the articles are included so the full articles can be easily read.

http://truth11.wordpress.com/2009/09/18/why-millions-of-americans-don't-need-the-swine-flu-vaccine-all-of-the-risk-none-of-the-benefit/

Wednesday, September 16, 2009

Mike Adams,

Natural News

(NaturalNews) The FDA has now suddenly granted approval to four different H1N1 vaccines, all on the same day! With virtually no testing, these fast-tracked vaccines are now approved for use on everyone: Infants, children, adults, senior citizens and even expectant mothers. But does everyone really need these vaccines? And all for a disease that is little more deadly than the common cold?

Even for those who got sick, virtually everyone survived the sickness. After a few days of extra rest in bed (and hopefully some nutritional supplementation), they were able to kick the virus and return to normal life. This is all a normal part of beating any flu.

All these millions of people who were infected by H1N1 and didn't die have naturally made their own swine flu antibodies. They are now immune to the swine flu, and they now have zero risk of being infected or killed by this H1N1 swine flu in the future. The actual risk of serious illness or death from the H1N1 flu may be statistically less than the risk of taking the vaccine.

Wednesday, September 28, 2005

The Johnson Tax Code

- HJ - Nov 27, 2000 - Rev Jan 25, 2006 -

I have long thought about new ways to simplify our tax codes and provide a comprehensive welfare program at the same time. I believe the greatest difficulty facing any new or revised tax system proponents would be simply getting it passed onto law. Our current tax codes are so complex and full of corporate and individual welfare programs in the various specific deductions, abatements, rebates, exemptions and other complicated falderal that an army of attorneys, accountants and other tax consultants has grown just to interpret these laws for the public. I would really like to know just how much it costs the people to support this monster and the corresponding counter organization in our governments. I will wager it is in the billions!

The IRS code is an effective welfare program for attorneys, accountants and other tax professionals. For that single reason it will be difficult to simplify. Like so many of our increasingly complicated laws, it is written specifically so attorneys are required to interpret it. I see a great reluctance in our overwhelmingly attorney-based congress to pull this financial rug out from under so many of their professional colleagues. How many ex-IRS people are among those tax professionals? I know of several so there must be tens if not hundreds of thousands of them making their living on the backs of working people because of the IRS code. That army against simplification would be galvanized against any revision and especially against the plan outlined in these pages which could completely do away with the need for their services.

In looking for a workable plan, I set down the following criteria:

A) It should not be used for benefit of certain organizations, groups, industries, individuals or pet causes of members of Congress. NO EXEMPTIONS! Let Government grants do that job so recipients of handouts would all be identified with those who did the handing out.

B) It would not be "fair" as that is such a relative term, so abused by politicians as to be totally meaningless. It should be designed to treat all people equally, not "fairly" as that still has some objective value and meaning.

C) It must have simplicity in all facets so most people can understand it and know where they stand, how to figure out their taxes and know the other guy hasn't gained an advantage by hiring a tax professional.

D) It should make cheating extremely difficult and quite obvious, even for the most expert cheat. Policing should then become easy and enforcement costs relative to collections should drop dramatically.

E) No loopholes of any kind should be left open and provisions should be made to immediately close any kind of loophole which may appear at any time in the future.

F) The "Negative Tax" concept should be used to provide welfare in such a way that it encourages people to work to make a better living while providing a base income for those who can't work either temporarily or permanently.

G) As optional components, provisions could be made for healthcare and Social Security that would provide superior results for less money.

H) The individual states should administer and collect the tax and be charged with reporting all tax receipts and passing the Federal portions on to the Federal Government.

I) Extreme income and wealth of individuals should have special status and be subject to higher tax rates than the average American. These rates should not be so high as to inhibit individual enterprise or creativity. These should also consider those who receive high incomes over short periods in their lives by averaging out that income over the individual's lifetime.

J) It should address trade with other nations for a possible application of special taxation applied to benefit those nations where we have special interests or needs.

K) Properly designed, it could replace all the myriad taxing systems: federal, state, county and city. As outlined here it would replace only the federal and state systems.

I came up with a three pronged system of taxation as follows:

I - A Transfer Tax on all things of value

A) The individual states responsibility: The individual states would administer the tax and set the amount of the tax which must be at least 8%. The states would then be responsible for collecting the tax and paying the Federal Government their share of the tax revenue. This tax would be applied equally to all transfers of property between individuals and/or organizations.

B) The Added Value Tax: For the benefit of commerce, the tax would apply at the time of the transfer and exempt the item or items from any additional tax on the original value for a period of one year from the originating transfer. If the item is transferred again during that year, a tax at the same rate would be applied to any increase of value over the amount original taxed. Reporting and payment of the tax would be handled by the party who originally owned the item. This is precisely the system used to collect sales taxes in our current state systems except there would be no tax-free sales.

C) All property transfers would be included: This would cover exchanges of all kinds of property, including even trades without any money being involved. Included would be real property of any kind including all personal items, real estate, stocks, bonds, cash, and any other item that has value. Also included would be things like patents, copyrights, legal judgements, fees for any kind of service, and all intangibles exchanged for money, goods, or services. The same rules and relatively low tax rate would apply to gifts, inheritances, money transfers of any kind where ownership passed from one person and/or organization and another. The only transactions exempt from this tax are wages and amounts paid directly to an individual for labor. Fees for services paid to corporations, businesses and recognized professionals would not be exempt.

D) Not-for-profit entities: The only possible exception would be the transfer to any legitimate not-for-profit enterprise. The structure for determining and identifying those enterprises are already in place. Any transfer from those not-for-profit enterprises to another person or entity would be taxed at the normal rates except for true charity donations. Should that charitable gift be turned into cash for any reason, the tax would then be applied.

E) The very few exceptions: Since most personal gifts would be given during the year following purchase they would not be taxed as gifts. Large gifts of considerable value like real estate, stocks and businesses with values more than thirty thousand dollars, may not have been transferred or taxed during the preceding year and are special cases. Gifts of property to members of the immediate family would be exempt from the tax on the established basis currently in use.

F) Possible abuses by low transfer value: There must be provision to prevent abuses such as a sale of property for an amount far less than the current value for the purpose of establishing a low tax basis. In such instances where sales or transfer values are deemed to be lowered for the sole purpose of lowering the tax, the tax paying entity who originated the transfer becomes responsible for justifying the value. Means to determine actual market value of property are well established and should be used in these cases. Should the appraised value be more than that used as the tax basis, the standard tax rules and rates will apply to the appraised value. A penalty equal to the total amount of the additional tax will also be applied. Should the difference be small, the additional tax and penalty will be small, thus protecting honest errors. If the appraised value is less than the tax basis used there will be no tax or penalty.

There is another effective way to block these kinds of abuses, bidding. All sales or transfers over a certain amount ($5,000 for instance) could be made subject to a bidding procedure similar to that used by Ebay. Example: An individual sells a piece of property of any kind for $10,000. This is then listed on a bidding entity (like Ebay) with the minimum bid placed at $11,000 or 10% above the stated value or sale price. Anyone, including the original seller could then bid on the property. The highest bidder would then pay the transfer tax on the amount of the bid. Once the bidding was over and closed, the original seller could either accept the high bidder and sell the property to them or place a larger bid and pay the transfer tax on that amount. This procedure would make the system completely self policing and leave little room for mischief.

G) Transfers in and out of the country: All transfers in and out of the country would be recorded and taxed in the exact same manner with a few exceptions. Since it may not be easy to collect taxes from foreign entities, taxes on all incoming as well as outgoing transfers are to be reported and paid by the American entity receiving or sending the transfer. The amount is exactly the same. Only the payment method is different. In addition, there is no one year exemption period for these incoming transfers. The second transfer, or the very first one after the incoming transfer, will be reported and taxed as an original transfer. The only difference is those taxes on the second transfer will be paid to the state receiving the second transfer. All following transfers will be treated in the normal fashion.

II - Federal/State Income tax - low income protection

A) A grossly simplified Federal Income Tax system is in addition to the transfer tax. It is a four-step, graduated plan which funds and replaces all welfare programs, State and Federal. It is a negative income tax for low income people and its simplicity is its value. Equal application to all citizens and an incentive to work for those who can work. It would replace the minimum wage laws which have sent so many jobs out of the country.

Click on http://hjminwage.blogspot.com/ to learn why the minimum wage is a miserable failure.

B) A base level of individual income: The first step is to establish a base level of individual income, an amount sufficient to support a single individual at a subsistence level. This level would be established by the individual states to reflect that state's living costs. We will use $15,000 as an example. An individual citizen of the US would start receiving that amount in monthly payments from their state once they reached their eighteenth birthday, registered to vote and began living on their own. Non-citizens would not be eligible to receive any of this income. We will call this Negative Tax or NT income.

C) How this program encourages people to work: Whatever amount in income an individual receives in any fashion or from any source will reduce his NT income by half of that amount. Employers will deduct half of any NT employee's pay as a withholding tax to be paid directly to the state. Once this withholding amount reaches $1,250 in any single month or a total of $15,000 in a year, additional amounts are not withheld for that period. NT users are required to file monthly reports of income from all sources, cash or items of value including gifts of more than $100 in value. The 50% reduction rule will be applied to all this income. Any amount paid for by others, including such things as insurance, rent, debt repayments, fines and tuition, is to be included in this reported income. The following month's check will reflect the effect of all income. Once the aggregate value of all sources of income as listed above reaches $30,000, the individual will no longer be an NT recipient. This means a married couple who have together income of $60,000 will receive no money from the state and will pay no income taxes. I t will also mean that a welfare recipient will receive a net gain equal to half of every dollar he earns, a real incentive to work.

D) Penalties for breaking the rules: These can be applied easily by imposing a fine and reducing subsequent payments by the amount of error or deception plus the fine. The fine for any error is half the amount of the error if it is deemed an actual error and is not contested. It is double the amount of the error if it is contested or if it is due to deception of any kind. Monthly errors of $100 or less or annual errors of $1,000 or less will bear no fine if the error is corrected and repaid.

E) Households and deductions: A household has been defined quite well by existing law. Basically it is a group of related people, sharing a dwelling of some type. There may be several wage earners in a household, all contributing to the members as a group. For tax purposes, a household will be counted as having one to five members according to how many dependent members live there. If there are more than five members, the count will remain as five for tax purposes no matter how many are there. This sets the maximum deduction for the household at five. As a member of a household, an individual may apply for the NT income, but the maximum is reduced by $6,000 annually, an amount representing housing costs. This amount is also set by the individual states. Individuals receiving NT income may not be considered as dependents for tax purposes even if they live in the household. Individuals living in households with aggregate income in excess of $150,000 will be ineligible for NT income unless they are dependent and over 65, or so physically or mentally handicapped as to be unable to work. The usual rules for disabilities will apply.

F) Tax rates and exemptions: Once an annual income of $30,000 is reached by an individual, the basic tax rate of 10% begins. In a household that plateau is raised $18.000 for each dependent up to the maximum of five including the head of the household. This puts the maximum untaxed income at $102,000 for households with five or more members. There are no deductions of any kind so the tax is applied to gross income. Once gross income for any individual or household reaches $1,000,000, all further income is taxed at 50%.

G) Taxable income: This includes all income of any kind from all sources including, but not limited to wages, fees, rent, interest, dividends and capital gains. Deferred income, IRA's, pensions and the like would be taxed in the same manner as they are under present law, but at the new rates. All current tax free municipal bonds and other tax exempt income vehicles would remain tax free. True gifts of any kind would not be included as taxable income as they are covered by the transfer tax. To keep a possible gift loophole from being abused, true gifts are defined as gifts that can in no way be considered as taxable income as listed above. This will prevent avoiding tax payments by simply calling or renaming any kind of taxable income as a "gift" or "gifts."

H) The plan would replace the current Social Security payment program with more income for those who really need it. Medicare as it is now operated would be replaced by a multi-tiered system for seniors providing for private insurance and prescription drugs. While the details would have to be addressed by addition to the system or by a completely separate system, a basic program could be funded by raising the NT or negative tax on an age related basis. The NT income basis could be raised to $20,000 at age sixty, $22,000 at age sixty-five, $24,000 at age seventy, $26,000 at age seventy-five, and $30,000 at age eighty. The amounts could easily be adjusted to satisfy actual needs. Health care premiums for all who use the NT income would be automatically deducted from the recipient's monthly checks. This would, in effect, provide health care benefits to all Americans and solve the current healthcare problems. See the section on health care.

III - How the States and the Federal Government decide on tax rates and divide the money between them.

A) Of the base 8% transfer tax, states would pay half to the Federal Treasury. The remaining 4%, or more if the state raised the rate above 8%, would be used for state income. It should roughly equal the combined state income and sales taxes currently in effect in most of the country. Together with the property tax, this currently averages 10% of GNP going to taxes at the state and local level. States could make weekly or monthly payments into the Federal Treasury. In order to maintain the current level of taxation, effort would have to be made to determine the actual income from such a rate and adjust it if required.

B) The negative Income Tax or NT: This could be set by state legislatures to fit the needs of their state. The Federal Government could set minimums, but the states will decide on the actual amount in the same way they decide the amount of the Transfer Tax. The numbers used in this essay may not be realistic and a serious effort to find a realistic base amount would have to be done. The statistics should all be there. All we need to do is to find and use them.

C) Corporation taxes could be eliminated, but the resulting screams and emotional diatribe from the left and their hate campaign against the source of nearly all of America's wealth, corporations and profits, would drown out all reason. Either the current system or a more reasonable, flat tax on gross profits of say, 8% would work. The transfer tax like any sales tax, falls equally on business expenses as well as non-business and that seems to work OK. By removing all expenses from exempt status, the tax rate could be lowered substantially and tax considerations would be removed from business decisions. Business could then concentrate on good business practices to make a profit and not be so involved in the complicated tax codes for so many business decisions. The screams of agony from Wall Street would be heard coast to coast, but in the end they would benefit from lowered overall taxes. Many abusive practices would disappear and the tax connivers would literally be put out of business.

IV - Why Congress doesn't want a simple Tax System.

A) I repeat from the beginning of this essay: "The IRS code is an effective welfare program for attorneys, accountants and other tax professionals. Huge amounts of money are syphoned out of business' and individuals' pockets and into those of people and organizations in this artificial profession. For that single reason it will be difficult to simplify. Like so many of our increasingly complex laws, it is written in such a manner as to require attorneys to interpret it. I see a great reluctance in our attorney-based congress to pull this financial rug from under so many of their professional colleagues." Any simplification of the IRS Code faces this high hurdle.

B) Once a system is put in place that so benefits a powerful group with an insider connection to legislators, it is extremely difficult to dislodge. This difficulty is completely out of proportion to the relatively small number who will oppose any changes that don't improve their position. It is so unfortunate that small groups of "insiders" can wield such power, but they do. Washington is full of these small groups seeking to feather their own nests at the expense of the average working American. Such is the price one pays for constantly growing and intrusive government. Systems like the IRS code grow constantly in size and complexity, sometimes maliciously and always in the direction of serving the few at the expense of the many. It takes a catastrophe or a miracle to stop this juggernaut and replace it with a simple, reasonable, less costly and more effective alternative.

D) The wealthy would object strenuously since the transfer tax would hit them proportionally. Unlike the sales tax which disproportionally taxes lower income people, the transfer tax would hit the wealthy when they transferred property of any kind. Since sales of real estate, stocks, bonds, businesses and the like are now exempt from almost any kind of taxation, this would increase taxes on wealthy investors and speculators. Taxes on sales by speculators would only be on the financial gain when the property was resold in less than a year. It would certainly replace the capital gains tax and would level the tax field between rich and poor. Since it would not be a punitive tax like inheritance taxes, it would be a much fairer distribution of the tax burden. Everyone would be in nearly the same boat and with zero loopholes (that could be done), there would be very few wealthy people who could avoid taxes altogether.

Wednesday, September 28, 2005

A Solution to the Identity/Security Problem

- ONE WE CAN LIVE WITH

Current technology enables us to accurately and positively identify individuals by facial pattern or iris scan of the eye. The equipment to do this is expensive, but not prohibitively so. The only real problem seems to be the privacy issue. A unique method will overcome that without stepping on toes.

First, regardless of the system used, a personal identifying card or token combined with a database of the confirming identity information would be necessary. Let's go with a card like a credit card or driver's license now in wide use. Let's also suppose we chose the facial recognition scan method.

Data on the card: Minimum data on the card could be used for identifying the individual only. Name, address, phone number, citizenship and such optional information as the person desired like driver's license number, social security number blood type, allergies etc. By making these optional, the person would not be forced to provide information that might endanger or challenge privacy. For the sake of avoiding the usual "ID" problem, let's call the card a "travel card" and make it optional and not compulsory. Read later on how making it optional is the key to its success.

The Facial scan database: We now have the technical capability to develop a database of facial scans which could be used to positively identify anyone, anywhere and under many different conditions. This could be an invaluable aid to all who would need their identity positively proven. Using the same type of communication and equipment similar to the credit card approval system, a person's identity could be confirmed almost instantly. Let's run through a scenario at an airport gate.

1. A person steps up to the check in counter and presents their travel card. They face a small camera which enters a facial scan into the system. The system uses the information on the travel card to locate the facial scan in the database and compare it with the new scan. With a match, the person proceeds.

2. Their checked baggage is tagged with an ID that ties it to the individual. After the individual is on the plane the bag is matched to its owner. Carry-on bags are screened as they are now.

3. When the person enters the aircraft another facial scan is taken to confirm their identity and record them as "on the plane." This makes certain that the person who appeared at check in is the same as the one who is on the plane. If the scans of those on the plane do not match those from check in, the plane doesn't leave.

This same procedure could be used in every instance where positive identity is required. For example: check cashing, money transfers, license applications, hospital check-in, any form of transport, even bars to prevent underage drinking. No borrowed or forged Ids could ever be used.

The OPTIONAL issue: Earlier it was mentioned that there was a value to making the use of the travel card optional - that is not absolutely required by law. Those sticklers for privacy who would insist that such a system, if compulsory, infringed on their individual rights would be technically satisfied. They could simply exercise that right and refuse to participate. The fact that there would be many activities in which they could not participate would not change that fact. They would be unable to fly commercial, obtain a driver's license, cash a check (except where the establishment chose not to require identity) or obtain a credit card. In short, they would not be able to access anything where positive identity was required of a stranger.

The airline industry would not be required to use the system, but who would fly on any airline that would not? Can you imagine a state that would not require it for licenses of all kinds? Life would be very difficult for those who chose not to participate; difficult, but not impossible. Private transportation would be available, driven by someone else. Cash transactions would still be available without problem. Can you imagine a credit card company that would issue a credit card with out a positive ID? Maybe there would be some, but you can imagine their rates would be astronomical.

How about immigrants or foreign travelers? Passports and positive IDs are required of all who enter the US legally. Cameras at all points of entry could be used to enter a record into the database of every single person who entered the country. These records could be checked instantly against international databases of criminals and terrorists.

Tuesday, September 08, 2009, 2:07 PM

Is The United States Becoming an Atheocracy?

Atheism is a religion and has become the defacto state religion of the U.S.

In direct defiance of the Constitution and with total disregard for the supreme law of the land, Atheists are seeking to use the courts to impose their belief system on all Americans. These self-serving, arrogant activists are actually fundamentalist atheists who want to abolish Christianity in particular and impose their own belief system on all of us.

The removal and abolishment of anything remotely resembling religion or religious beliefs from all public places has for a long time been the focus of the atheist fundamentalists. Their constant efforts to remove "In God We Trust" from our coinage and remove the pledge of alligience from everywhere. Eventually, they like the Taliban, will try to remove all the brass and stone statuary and symbols and especially the ten commandments from all buildings in the Capitol.

They have already succeeded with removals of the ten commandment from numerous places including from a state judicial building in Alabama by an order of the Fifth Federal District Court. This order was based on a faulty interpretation by the Supreme Court of the words of the First Amendment of the United States Constitution. Their ruling is precisely the opposite of what the First Amendment meant and clearly says. That amendment states, "Congress shall make no law respecting an establishment of religion, or prohibiting the free exercise thereof...." The ruling definitely establishes Atheism as the state religion and specifically prohibits the "free exercise thereof." That is in direct opposition not only to the wording, but specifically to the obvious intent.

American Atheist activists, the ACLU, and the Taliban are precisely the same animals, but cloaked with differing coverings. They use the law to force their belief system on everyone. No other organizations in America seek to impose their own belief system on others and destroy all who don't agree by using the courts. That means employing men with guns and handcuffs to control and punish any persons who do not submit to their control. If that's not unconstitutional then nothing is. Our Constitution was written specifically to defend the people against just such intolerance. Now these fanatics are twisting the courts to say those words mean the opposite of what they so clearly state.

"Congress shall make no law respecting an establishment of religion, or prohibiting the free exercise thereof...."

Read the article that follows for a more in-depth explanation.

Tuesday, September 13, 2005

Is the United States Becoming an Atheocracy?

Excerpt from the start of the lecture

A•the•oc•ra•cy (a'thi·ok'rà·si), n., pl. -ceis 1. government in which there is no God as the supreme being and ruler and where no law or moral value is immutable. 2. government by atheists or where atheism is the state religion. 3. country or nation ruled by an atheocracy.

The removal and abolishing of anything remotely resembling religion or religious beliefs from all public places has become the current focus of the atheist left. Recently, a monument engraved with the Ten Commandments was removed from a state judicial building in Alabama by an order of the Fifth Federal District Court. This order was based on a faulty interpretation by the Supreme Court of the words of the First Amendment of the United States Constitution. Their ruling is precisely the opposite of what the First Amendment meant and clearly says. That amendment states, "Congress shall make no law respecting an establishment of religion, or prohibiting the free exercise thereof...."

The first part clearly states the Federal Congress shall make no law which establishes a religion. That includes only the United States Senate and House of Representatives. In other words, any federal law which establishes a religion as the official, federal religion is constitutionally illegal. In Thomas Jefferson's own words this was included in response to the fear that congress might choose one denomination as the official, sanctioned, federal religion to the exclusion of all others. This fear was based upon English religious law and the religious persecution of principally Roman Catholics by the Episcopal church, the Church of England. The statement about a wall of separation between church and state is not a part of the Constitution, but was made in a letter on January 1, 1802, by Thomas Jefferson to the Danbury Baptist Association of Connecticut. The congregation heard a widespread rumor that the Congregationalists, another denomination, were to become the national religion. This was very alarming to people who knew about religious persecution by the state established church in England. Jefferson made it clear in his letter to the Danbury congregation that the separation was to be that government would not establish a national religion or dictate to men how to worship God. Jefferson's letter from which the phrase "separation of church and state" was taken, affirmed First Amendment rights. Jefferson wrote:

"I contemplate with solemn reverence that act of the whole American people which declared that their legislature should 'make no law respecting an establishment of religion, or prohibiting the free exercise thereof,' thus building a wall of separation between church and state."

The reason Jefferson choose the expression "separation of church and state" was because he was addressing a Baptist congregation; a denomination of which he was not a member. Jefferson wanted to remove all fears that the state would dictate policy to the church.

It is quite evident that the removal of the monument with the Ten Commandments is precisely the kind of action the amendment was written to prevent. Alabama Chief Justice Roy Moore, most certainly acted within his rights in placing the monument with the Ten Commandments in the Judicial Building. Those commandments and many other "laws" from the Bible were the basis for the law of the land. Clearly, the order to remove the monument was an action by the Federal Court to promote and "establish" Atheism as the state religion of the United States. In addition, this action is clearly guilty of "prohibiting the free exercise" of religion for a great many people. It is truly akin to the Taliban blowing up the huge, centuries old, stone statues of Buddha in Afghanistan.

Our federal judiciary has not only reversed the meaning of those very clear words of the Constitution, but extended it to include all non-federal governments, government agencies and even public schools, none of which was included in the amendment. The Constitution says "Congress" and does not mention state, county or other municipality or agency thereof which are all included in the recent rulings. Are corporations, social and business organizations next on this ever expanding list? After all, they are "public" entities in that they are open to the public and are authorized or licensed by government. If you think that a ridiculous prospect, consider that all male schools have recently been forced by judicial ruling to accept female applicants, in direct violation of their charters, even when the female applicants don't meet entrance requirements.

FEUDALs - **Fundamentalist European United Demagogic Atheist League**

There are many in the Islamic world who, if they could, would impose their own fundamentalist laws on the entire world. Their fondest wish is that the United States fall to their onslaught as the twin towers did on September,11. As one of the most Christian nations in the world and one of very few with complete religious freedom, we are their sworn enemy. Lurking amongst us there is another, even more dangerous enemy of Christians in America. Members of this insidious, loosely connected group are working feverishly to destroy us from within our own nation. I call them FEUDALS. They originated in Europe when they sainted Marx, Lenin and Engels. Other saints include Frenchman, Jean Paul Sartre, and American, Madeline Murray O'Hare. Their goal is to stamp out all recognized religions and replace them with their own belief system. In direct defiance of the First Amendment to the United States Constitution, Feudals are working to make Atheism the official state religion of our country. Make no mistake, fundamentalist Atheism is a religion and Atheist activists are currently succeeding in making their belief system the official federal religion.

Their legal arm and the spear point of their attack on Christianity, is the ACLU with the mainstream media, the Hollywood left and the American Trial Lawyers Association helping at every opportunity. ACLU should actually stand for, Atheist Control by Liberals Union. These enemies of true religious freedom have convoluted the United States Constitution and promoted the myth about the separation of church and state with a constant stream of lies and deceitful lawsuits. The true goal of this group is to make Atheism the state religion of our country by destroying all other religions, especially Christianity. They would have us part of a Godless, socialist world state with them running things much as the Lords ran Europe's feudal empires during the middle ages. So far they seem to be winning. With all religious messages and symbols except those which promote Atheism already removed by force from public institutions including schools, they have succeeded in having their message of atheism alone promoted to all American school children and to adults who contact or deal with government. Our national motto, "In God we trust," is certainly their next target and could even be replaced with "In Atheists we trust" by these religious zealots. Already they have forced the removal of "Christmas" from many printed calenders, and stopped numerous school choirs from performing Handel's "Messiah" or other Christian music, even during the Christmas season. Doesn't this sound like what the Taliban did? Will they next strike from the Declaration of Independence, or at least change Jefferson's words, "We hold these truths to be self-evident, that all men are created equal, that they are endowed by their Creator with certain inalienable Rights, that among these are Life, Liberty, and the pursuit of Happiness?" . . . .

Vaccine makers are given immunity from US lawsuits.

http://truth11.wordpress.com/2009/07/21/now-legal-immunity-for-swine-flu-vaccine
-makers

Global Research

July 20, 2009

The US Secretary of Health and Human Services, Kathleen Sebelius, has just signed a decree granting vaccine makers total legal immunity from any lawsuits that result from any new "Swine Flu" vaccine. Moreover, the $7 billion US Government fast-track program to rush vaccines onto the market in time for the Autumn flu season is being done without even normal safety testing. Is there another agenda at work in the official WHO hysteria campaign to declare so-called H1N1 virus—which has yet to be rigorously scientifically isolated, characterized and photographed with an electron microscope—the scientifically accepted procedure—a global "pandemic" threat?

Now just why would she do that?

With no legal liability, could it be that Baxter (a pharmaceutical company) is preparing to sell hundreds of millions of doses containing highly toxic aluminum hydroxide as adjuvant?

The current official panic campaign over alleged Swine Flu danger is rapidly taking on the dimensions of a George Orwell science fiction novel. The document signed by Sebelius grants immunity to those making a swine flu vaccine, under the provisions of a 2006 law for public health emergencies. Now just why would she do that?

This could easily mean that Sebelius knows that the expensive (and profitable) vaccines will pose more of a health risk than the disease itself.

With this immunity, vaccine makers can completely ignore safety testing costs. I wonder who benefits from the millions of dollars thus saved? Just where does all that money go? Who gets the payoff? I wonder how much will flow into Sebelius' coffers?

Thursday, September 03, 2009

GM - Government Motors

Have you seen the GM ads for the Equinox?

"The all new Equinox - 32 mpg highway - better than CR-V, Rav4, and even Escape Hybrid"

You'd better take that number with a substantial grain of salt. Now that the "government" owns and operates GM (Government Motors) we should expect projected favorable numbers to be skewed as far afield as possible just like their estimates of the finances of any favored program. These cost numbers are usually understated by a factor of two while income or revenue is overstated by the same factor.

Such being the case the Equinox should get about 16 mpg. But just maybe the Government Motors new owners are afraid the motoring public wouldn't accept their usual highly suspect estimates and didn't stretch them as far from reality as usual. Such being the case let's say they only exaggerated a little and the reality is about 24 mpg, still not up to the three vehicles they claim to beat. I'll wager that's a bit closer to the truth.

Like the honesty of their statement, "We don't intend to run GM." After making this public statement they fired the President and who knows who else, ordered corporate headquarters moved from Warren into the inner city of Detroit, and closed nearly 2,000 dealers (many highly profitable ones and nearly all supporters of Republican candidates). The new Obama auto "CZAR" (or is it Kommisar), basically put the UAW in charge. That sure sounds like running the company to me. They'll probably do the same excellent job of managing their auto company as they have Social Security, Medicare, Medicaid, Fannie May, Freddie Mac, the Postal Service, Amtrak, and the list goes on and on. Lots of taxpayer money going down federal rat holes, lots of political payoffs, graft, corruption, and why not? It costs those politicians and bureaucrats not one penny. Mr. Taxpayer Sucker pays for it all as two previously major tax paying companies become major tax consuming companies.

The response of Mr. Average American car buyer to the "Cash for Clunkers" program demonstrates clearly how the public thinks. Overwhelmingly they rejected GM and Chrysler products whose sales dropped far below last year while Ford, the only remaining privately owned American car company, posted substantial gains. Of course, by far the largest sales gain was posted by Toyota. The public knows how poorly any government operated entity is run. I surely wouldn't buy a new car from such an operation. I seriously doubt either Chrysler or GM will be around for long and I certainly wouldn't buy any of their stock.

Oh yes, the management and stockholders of Ford want to thank the Obama administration for making them the only remaining privately owned American car company and for giving them such a huge boost in sales.

Wednesday, August 12, 2009

The truth about health care, several views

From moveon.org, an Internet mouthpiece for the far left, with a little corrective information, the real truth.

Top Five Health Care Reform Lies—and How to Fight Back

Lie #1: President Obama wants to euthanize your grandma!!!

The truth: These accusations—of "death panels" and forced euthanasia—are, of course, flatly untrue. As an article from the Associated Press puts it: "No 'death panel' in health care bill." What's the real deal? Reform legislation includes a provision, supported by the AARP, to offer senior citizens access to a professional medical counselor who will provide them with information on preparing a living will and other issues facing older Americans.

The real truth: "Death panels" and forced euthanasia are only the worst possible result of medical decisions being made by bureaucrats when they run out of money which they certainly will. Look at what's already happening in some European nations under similar circumstances. Let the camel's nose in the tent and before long it fills your tent and you are forced out.

Lie #2: Democrats are going to outlaw private insurance and force you into a government plan!!!

The truth: With reform, choices will increase, not decrease. Obama's reform plans will create a health insurance exchange, a one-stop shopping marketplace for affordable, high-quality insurance options. Included in the exchange is the public health insurance option—a nationwide plan with a broad network of providers—that will operate alongside private insurance companies, injecting competition into the market to drive quality up and costs down.7

If you're happy with your coverage and doctors, you can keep them.8 But the new public plan will expand choices to millions of businesses or individuals who choose to opt into it, including many who simply can't afford health care now.

The real truth: Apparently the writer of the above has not read the only health care plan in the Democrats' arsenal. (If Obama has a plan, where is it?) The only existing Democrat plan specifically states that changes in plans or in the supplier of the plan will not be permitted. The only point of that section of their plan is to drive private health care insurance out of the business.

Lie #3: President Obama wants to implement Soviet-style rationing!!!

The truth: Health care reform will expand access to high-quality health insurance, and give individuals, families, and businesses more choices for coverage. Right now, big corporations decide whether to give you coverage, what doctors you get to see, and whether a particular procedure or medicine is covered—that is rationed care. And a big part of reform is to stop that.

Health care reform will do away with some of the most nefarious aspects of this rationing: discrimination for pre-existing conditions, insurers that cancel coverage when you get sick, gender discrimination, and lifetime and yearly limits on coverage. And outside of that, as noted above, reform will increase insurance options, not force anyone into a rationed situation.

The real truth: Obama's non existing plan, if it follows the house Democrats' plan, will result in weeks, months, or even years of waiting as demands for care will far outpace the medical profession's ability to supply it. Just look at Canada, Scandinavia, or England, and the realities there.

Lie #4: Obama is secretly plotting to cut senior citizens' Medicare benefits!!!

The truth: Health care reform plans will not reduce Medicare benefits. Reform includes savings from Medicare that are unrelated to patient care—in fact, the savings comes from cutting billions of dollars in overpayments to insurance companies and eliminating waste, fraud, and abuse.

The real truth: There is no government run system ever created that has come close to competing with private operations. The truth is waste, fraud, and abuse are the hallmarks of government bureaucracies because employees call most of the shots and are notoriously inefficient. Compared to private organizations they have never been able to effectively compete on anything close to a level playing field without massive subsidies. UPS, FedEx, USPS, the perfect example. I rest my case. Oh yes, have you ever heard of any government cost estimates that have been even close to the final cost. Usually the final costs are five to ten times the original estimates, and that's conservative.

Lie #5: Obama's health care plan will bankrupt America!!!

The truth: We need health care reform now in order to prevent bankruptcy—to control spiraling costs that affect individuals, families, small businesses, and the American economy.

Right now, we spend more than $2 trillion dollars a year on health care. The average family premium is projected to rise to over $22,000 in the next decade—and each year, nearly a million people face bankruptcy because of medical expenses. Reform, with an affordable, high-quality public option that can spur competition, is necessary to bring down skyrocketing costs. Also, President Obama's reform plans would be fully paid for over 10 years and not add a penny to the deficit.

We're closer to real health care reform than we've ever been—and the next few weeks will decide whether it happens. We need to make sure the truth about health care reform is spread far and wide to combat right wing lies.

The real truth: If you speak only of health care insurance, most people without it are without it by choice (they don't want to spend the money) or are illegal aliens. If you are speaking of health care, since 1968 it has been illegal by federal law to deny medical care to anyone in need This includes those without insurance, or the money to pay for services, including illegals. So, anyone needing health care in America will get it. There is no health care crises other than the excess of demand over supply. We don't have enough health care professionals available to serve the demand. Any federal health care insurance system will not even address this problem, and will certainly make it much worse. What we really need is a massive program of growth in education of health care workers at all levels. We need acceptance of new medical intermediates to do many of the simple services that now must be done by doctors. These could include many examination, diagnostic and treatment procedures that could be handled by professionals with much less time and money consuming education. There is a growing shortage of physicians and trained nurses. What is needed are training systems for professionals at several levels between nurses aides and nurses and between technicians and physicians.

We're closer to the major desolation of the best health care system in the world than we've ever been. This so called reform proposal is a recipe for the destruction of that incomparable health care service.

Currently, all levels of health care professionals are entering the US in substantial numbers from all manner of education systems from all over the world. They are staffing our hospitals, clinics, and all manner of health care facilities in steadily increasing numbers. Why is it our schools and colleges are not turning out enough graduates? That is indeed the biggest problem and it is not even mentioned in the Democrats' only proposal.

Another thing that would reduce costs considerably would be limits on the fees trial lawyers could collect from suits against members of the health professions and health organizations.

These statements are the real truth about our situation with health care. They may not be as emotionally stimulating from either political standpoint as they are not fightin' words, just realty that must be dealt with.

Remember one thing, Obama's promise on the government's plan, **"If you like your present healthcare plan, you can keep it."**

NOT EXACTLY!

Monday, August 03, 2009

A collage of tasty bits of information

All you leftists should be ecstatic with the Obama administration and Democrat Congress. They are systematically destroying or nationalizing private business. Banks and Auto companies fell first, the insurance industry is next and the oil business will soon follow. I wonder where it will stop? Probably not before the government owns and runs all industry and business. They're well on their way as it is. I wonder what you have to say about the following short bits of info?

The deliberate action of the federal government brought on the mortgage collapse. They succeeded in cutting 35% to 60% of the value of personally held real estate, most of which was mortgaged an average of around 55%. In a single action, government destroyed more than 90% of personal equity in real estate. Banks (like Goldman Sachs, loved and rewarded by Obama) now own more than 90% of privately owned real estate. Isn't that great that we have soaked those evil wealthy people that own their homes.

The "governmentalists" in Washington are doing everything they can to destroy private enterprise and replace it with inept government workers.

Reporting from Orange County and Washington — Regulators took on the mortgage industry's best-known figure Thursday, accusing former Countrywide Financial Corp. Chief

Executive Angelo Mozilo of hiding his alarm about risky loans the company was making at the height of the housing boom while he was reaping nearly $140 million in profits on stock sales.

In a fraud and insider-trading lawsuit against Mozilo, the Securities and Exchange Commission

quotes e-mails in which the executive derided certain Countrywide loan products as "toxic" and "poison" more than three years ago -- well before "toxic debt" entered the popular lexicon as the cause of the housing crash and the resulting global financial crisis and deep recession.

I wonder why so many Goldman Sachs executives are in the government? Read:

http://thinkprogress.org/2008/09/22/paulson-goldman-bailout

Re: Fannie Mae & Freddie Mac:

Fannie Mae executive Franklin Raines reaped 90 million in bonuses while Fannie Mae collapsed due to bad loans. Barney Frank was reporting, "Fannie Mae and Freddie Mac are sound financially." even after they were already bankrupt. He then denied he said it in spite of TV recordings of his speech.

As I understand it, the common and preferred shareholders are basically being wiped out, but the government is backing Fannie and Freddie's existing debt, the value of which therefore rose. So here's my question: if Fannie and Freddie were heading for bankruptcy but for the government's intervention, why didn't the Treasury Department bargain hard with major holders of their existing debt (such as the Chinese government), and threaten to let Fannie and Freddie go bankrupt unless the debt holders agreed to write down the value of the debt? After all, there was no explicit guarantee of such debt, and Treasury still could have agreed to explicitly guarantee FUTURE Fannie and Freddie debt.

The way the bailout is structured, it seems that Fannie and Freddie shareholders, and the American taxpayer, are paying the price, but holders of the GSE's debt get made whole at the latter's expense. Why?

The Country Wide debacle went right along with Fannie Mae and Freddie Mac.

Acorn real estate deals in Ft Wayne:

Some time ago I heard on local radio in Ft Wayne about a real estate loan scam that was conducted in that city. Three local banks charged a number of people (5 or 6 were members of Acorn by the way) with conspiracy to defraud the banks with loans made based on fraudulent appraisals. I checked the website they sighted and copied the following information about how they did it:

They bought up low value inner city homes in Ft Wayne for between $20,000 and $40,000. Then they did some cosmetic improvements that cost between $3,000 and $6,000. Next they had appraisals made for 3 or four times their cost by their appraisers. (I wonder how much of a kick back those appraisers received.) Then they found local people to buy these houses securing loans from these banks backed by Fannie Mae for 100% of the purchase price. They paid these people

$15,000 to $30,000 from the loan proceeds and pocketed the remainder. When the buyers realized they could not keep up the payments they walked away. When the banks finally foreclosed they were left holding mortgages three or four times the value of the homes. In many cases strippers moved in soon after the house was vacated and stripped everything of value including copper piping and wiring that was sold as scrap. These stripped houses lost their entire value as repair costs were prohibitive. The losses to the mortgage holders were substantial. Recently I went back on the Internet to get links for this paper and, lo and behold, they were gone without a trace. I searched under every name and title I could think of and nothing turned up. I wonder how that happened?

For more info on Acorn goto:
http://www.fortwaynenews.com/index.php/2008/09/28/democrats-seeking-to-line-the-pockets-of-acorn/

The Obama Government paid healthcare bill is not about healthcare. It is principally an effort to destroy private insurance companies and replace them with government bureaucracies. It includes the eventual replacement of all private insurance with single payer government run healthcare. It also includes euthanasia and withholding services from the elderly, and rationing. It has never worked in any nation that tried it. Ask the French, Britons and Canadiens.

The entire Democrat campaign is based on class warfare with hate for the wealthy. Apparently Obama's method of leveling the playing field for income is based on reducing the income of all productive, middle class and wealthy individuals to that of the poor. They have sure got a good start on doing just that. It doesn't help the poor one little bit but it sure does punish those evil wealthy people. Wouldn't it be better to help bring those on low incomes up rather than tearing the rich down? I guess Democrats are so filled with hate they would rather hurt successful people and punish them for being successful than try to raise the incomes of the poor and enable them to be more productive .

Obama's promise of no tax increases for those earning less than $250,000.00 per year were absolutely useless. Now he says that even the poor will be taxed. I wonder, did he forget that everyone including the poor already pay 20% to 25% of every dollar they spend in hidden taxes on virtually everything.

The promise of a max of 8% unemployment after the stimulus was pure fiction. It is already above 9.5% and heading higher.

This unemployment is a direct result of the expected reduction of business profits as increases in taxes prompt business executives to cut employment and plans for growth which must be paid for out of profits.

The Obama administration's predictions of the results of their actions have all been terrible failures.

Government bureaucracies cost at least twice as much as private businesses doing the same things. They are also much less efficient.

Tax cheat Timothy Geitner promises massive tax increases. Michael Rozbruch, a Certified Tax Resolution Specialist says, "Unfortunately, the Obama Administration may be sending the wrong message to the American taxpaying public by apparently condoning the behavior of Tim Geitner and Tom Daschle. Although Daschle withdrew his name as a nominee for the Health and Human Services Secretary is still leaves a bad taste in people's mouths. And I am positive that if he weren't named as a nominee he would still owe the IRS $120,000 + today."

Raising taxes above 15% on business profits will always result in lower revenue receipts. Lowering taxes on business profits down to 15% has always resulted in higher tax revenues.

The Chinese who hold most of our debt are about to cut off our credit line.

Income tax receipts down 22 %, business tax receipts are down 28% from a year ago. That's the biggest drop since the great depression. Nice going, Obama!

~ ~

A few Obamaisms:

"If you are a family with income of less than $250,000 my plan will not raise your taxes one iota." Obama. - Ha!

"If you are a family with income of less than $200,000 my plan will give you a reduction in your taxes." Obama. - Ha!

"My health care plan will let you keep your present insurance." Obama. The truth is just the opposite.

"We will not be running the Auto companies." Obama.

Hey Pres! Firing the president and ordering the main offices moved from Warren to downtown Detroit is running the company. Try doing anything the government doesn't approve and you'll see who's running the company.

~ ~

The Post Office is hemorrhaging money at such a rate they are considering closing as many as 1,500 post offices (and releasing 10,000 employees). I thought government employees couldn't be fired or cut.

Democrats plan on repealing the 22nd amendment. I wonder why?

Thursday, July 09, 2009

Michael Jackson - The Power of Celebrity

First of all it is sad whenever anyone dies, sad for family, sad for friends, especially when they pass at a relatively young age. But the exercise in celebrity worship over Michael Jackson was a circus. It would have been comedic had it not been about a death. The aim of this article is not to condemn Jackson, but to point out how celebrities, the wealthy, and the powerful can get away with actions that would bring disgrace and even jail time on ordinary people. The bigger the celebrity, the greater their wealth, the more powerful the individual, the more they can get away with. Think of Henry the Eighth, the ultimate combination of celebrity, wealth and power.

The TV funeral showed clearly how some people, and especially celebrities and other "fans" can get caught up in an almost religious fervor over a celebrity who was never directly connected to their lives. Oh, maybe a few of the "big" celebrities (I won't comment about their eulogies) met him or knew him professionally, but most of those only knew him from his performances. They came seeking the spotlight and in hope some of his celebrity might "rub off" on them.

Of course, there were those "look at me" self promoters like Jessie Jackson and Al Sharpton, who appear at most newsworthy events seeking the media spotlight. Then there were some of the Hollywood crowd, darlings of the media and overflowing with tears—acting? I saw a few cuts of their actions and words on the news as I chose not to watch the media circus. Granted, Jackson displayed great talent and for that gained super celebrity status, but just look at some of the realities of his life.

He must have hated being black, something none of his "fans" ever mentioned or considered. Just look at him. He had all semblance of his racial origins changed to Caucasian. Just compare early pictures of him, before the surgeons and dermatologists reworked him into a pasty faced, non-black. Then, did he choose a black woman to mother his children? This alone should have angered or at least upset the black community. Of course, his wealth and celebrity overwhelmed any of that and the many celebrants at his funeral oozed adulation.

Then there was his notorious actions with young boys that resulted in several charges, later dropped after multi million dollar payments. In a taped interview with Martin Bashir he said about young boys, "Why can't you share your bed? The most loving thing to do, is to share your bed with someone."

The entire interview can be read at:

http://www.wnd.com/news/article.asp?ARTICLE_ID=30853.

But for his celebrity and wealth he would be a registered sex offender who spent time in prison. True, there are some of these famous folks that take a fall, but these are usually minor celebrities with little wealth or power. Look at the known but well hidden parade of females Lyndon Johnson and John Kennedy had, even in the White House. Then there is Bill Clinton who did the same thing but with far less panache compared with the other two. Clinton was so crude he got caught, but even then he got away with it in spite of lying publicly to the entire nation. The dalliances of powerful public figures have been known for a very long time and will probably continue. As someone once said, "Hell, if you have enough money and power you can get away with murder."

Such is the power of celebrity. Michael Jackson is just one example of the very different playing field the rich and famous have compared to ordinary people. There are many other obvious and a few less obvious examples. It is apparent that to the American media, celebrity, wealth and power count far more in positive news than honor, honesty, integrity or even decency. And a large number of Americans follow and believe the main stream media whose celebrities are right there amidst the Hollywood crowd. It's no wonder instincts and emotion override logic and rationality in the judgement of so many people. "Like diarrhea, it runs in the genes." Thinking and logic have become quite unpopular in recent years. Today with the majority of Americans it's all about "looking good," "following the crowd," "being cool," and "me first." Oh yes, one final remark: if you happen to be a successful business person or politically a non-liberal no matter how decent, you will be reviled, cursed and condemned while your equally wealthy celebrity or leftist is admired, emulated, praised, and excused for all manner of evils. You can thank the media part of the entertainment world for that.

Friday, June 05, 2009

America descends into dark, gray Marxist totalitarianism

Note from HJ: When I read this it confirmed what I have been saying in many different ways for many years and is at the heart of my book, The Feudals, that I have been working on for at least twelve years. That's why it is repeated here.

Note from Don Wildmon: For years I have refused to use words such as Marxism, socialism or similar words when describing our current situation. However, it is time to call a spade a spade, regardless of how those who oppose us label us. Rome is burning. The article below was written by Stanislav Mishin, a blogger and columnist for the Russian newspaper Pravda.

American capitalism gone with a whimper . . . . .

It must be said, that like the breaking of a great dam, the American decent into Marxism is happening with breath taking speed, against the back drop of a passive, hapless sheeple, excuse me dear reader, I meant people.

True, the situation has been well prepared on and off for the past century, especially the past twenty years. The initial testing grounds was conducted upon our Holy Russia and a bloody test it was. But we Russians would not just roll over and give up our freedoms and our souls, no matter how much money Wall Street poured into the fists of the Marxists.

Those lessons were taken and used to properly prepare the American populace for the surrender of their freedoms and souls, to the whims of their elites and betters.

First, the population was dumbed down through a politicized and substandard education system based on pop culture, rather than the classics. Americans know more about their favorite TV dramas than the drama in DC that directly affects their lives. They care more for their "right" to choke down a McDonalds burger or a BurgerKing burger than for their constitutional rights. Then they turn around and lecture us (Russia) about our rights and about our "democracy". Pride blinds the foolish.

Then their faith in God was destroyed, until their churches, all tens of thousands of different "branches and denominations" were for the most part little more then Sunday circuses and their televangelists and top protestant mega preachers were more then happy to sell out their souls and flocks to be on the "winning" side of one pseudo Marxist politician or another. Their flocks may complain, but when explained that they would be on the "winning" side, their flocks were ever so quick to reject Christ in hopes for earthly power. Even our Holy Orthodox (Russian Orthodox) churches are scandalously liberalized in America.

The final collapse has come with the election of Barack Obama. His speed in the past three months has been truly impressive. His spending and money printing has been a record setting, not just in America's short history but in the world. If this keeps up for more than another year, and there is no sign that it will not, America at best will resemble the Wiemar Republic and at worst Zimbabwe.

These past two weeks have been the most breath taking of all. First came the announcement of a planned redesign of the American Byzantine tax system, by the very thieves who used it to bankroll their thefts, loses and swindles of hundreds of billions of dollars. These make our Russian oligarchs look little more than ordinary street thugs, in comparison. Yes, the Americans have beat our own thieves in the shear volumes. Should we congratulate them?

These men, of course, are not an elected panel but made up of appointees picked from the very financial oligarchs and their henchmen who are now gorging themselves on trillions of American dollars, in one bailout after another. They are also usurping the rights, duties and powers of the American congress (parliament). Again, congress has put up little more then a whimper to their masters.

Then came Barack Obama's command that GM's (General Motor) president step down from leadership of his company. That is correct, dear reader, in the land of "pure" free markets, the American president now has the power, the self given power, to fire CEOs and we can assume other employees of private companies, at will. Come hither, go dither, the centurion commands his minions.

So it should be no surprise that the American president has followed this up with a "bold" move of declaring that he and another group of unelected, chosen stooges will now redesign the entire automotive industry and will even be the guarantee of automobile policies. I am sure that if given the chance, they would happily try and redesign it for the whole of the world, too. Prime Minister Putin, less then two months ago, warned Obama and UK's Blair, not to follow the path to Marxism, it only leads to disaster. Apparently, even though we suffered 70 years of this Western sponsored horror show, we know nothing, as foolish, drunken Russians, so let our "wise" Anglo-Saxon fools find out the folly of their own pride.

Again, the American public has taken this with barely a whimper...but a "freeman" whimper.

So, should it be any surprise to discover that the Democratically controlled Congress of America is working on passing a new regulation that would give the American Treasury department the power to set "fair" maximum salaries, evaluate performance and control how private companies give out pay raises and bonuses? Senator Barney Franks, a social pervert basking in his homosexuality (of course, amongst the modern, enlightened American societal norm, as well as that of the general West, homosexuality is not only not a looked down upon life choice, but is often praised as a virtue) and his Marxist enlightenment, has led this effort. He stresses that this only affects companies that receive government monies, but it is retroactive and taken to a logical extreme, this would include any company or industry that has ever received a tax break or incentive.

The Russian owners of American companies and industries should look thoughtfully at this and the option of closing their facilities down and fleeing the land of the Red as fast as possible. In other words, divest while there is still value left.

The proud American will go down into his slavery with out a fight, beating his chest and proclaiming to the world, how free he really is. The world will only snicker.

Stanislav Mishin

Thursday, March 26, 2009

Feudalism Rears its Ugly Head

by Howard Johnson

Straight out of the medieval period, feudalism is about to turn all American common people into serfs—virtually the property of their wealthy and powerful masters, the politicians. We are now facing the comprehensive controlling power of governmental officials—the kings, queens, lords and ladies now in control of our growing feudal political system.

Socialism, Communism, Fascism, Liberalism—no matter what it is named, it is the current version of the cruel, totalitarian feudal system of the middle ages. The Sheriff of Nottingham would be right at home in our new government of "change." For those educated in our failing government schools, I suggest you read "The Legend of Robinhood" to learn about the Sheriff of Nottingham. If you can't read, go to your video store and ask for the movie, "Robinhood of Sherwood Forrest."

Names and dates of movies about Robinhood

The Robin Hood legend has long been popular with movie makers, inspiring the silent version starring Douglas Fairbanks, the Errol Flynn classic of 1938, Sean Connery and Audrey Hepburn's "Robin and Marian" in 1976, Disney's own live-action version "The Story of Robin Hood and His Merrie Men" in 1952, and Kevin Costner's latest version in 1991.

"We cannot continue to rely on our military in order to achieve the national security objectives that we've set. We've got to have a civilian national security force that's just as powerful, just as strong, just as well-funded."

President Barack Obama, July 2, 2009

He may already have this force in place. It's now called ACORN.

Sounds like Hitler's Brown Shirts in 1929 to me. See later at the end of this blog

I have had it! I have listened to hatred spewed from the mouths of idiots, fools, and buffoons for years. Hatred and animosity is constantly aimed at anyone who disagrees with the "HOLY" positions, actions, pronouncements, and agendas of the left. This vilification comes with curses and damnation from so-called "objective" and "compassionate" liberals. I myself have been cursed, called all manner of names like stupid, ignorant, and received many other abusive and demeaning labels and actions. All from the colossal frauds, the minions of the liberal left, that pass themselves off as humanitarians saviors of "the people." Over many years you leeches on the left have succeeded in using ignorant mobs of blind followers to put in public office all manner of self-serving low lives: liars, thieves, cheats, and worse—men and women without honor or human decency.

All your politicians of the left seem to want is more power, more money, and more control. Just listen to what your President said today, March 27, 2009. He actually said, "The government will tell you when to turn the lights in your homes on and off." He obviously intends to do just that. This is pathetic!

Powered by a voting public of celebrity worshiping, historically ignorant people, the power hungry tyrants that have driven the corrupt Cook county Democrat machine for decades have invaded and taken over our national government. There is an old phrase reserved for people of high and mighty reputation—those that rise to the top. That phrase is "la creme de la creme," literally, the cream of the cream. Well let me tell you, there is another material that "rises to the top." If you have ever seen the disgusting slurry that fills a cesspool or septic tank you will remember the foamy scum that floats on the top. That could be described as "la scum de la scum." This is a deceptively accurate description of those who have "risen to the top" in the federal government, both elected, appointed, and hired into the bureaucracy. These are la scum de la scum of America. The few exceptions in the federal government merely make the evil majority all the more visible. They have been caught in so many lies and other deceptions in recent years as to have lost credibility with all but the blindest of their slavish followers. As this is being written many protesters are at "TEA" parties shouting, "No more bailouts!" Is it possible the public are finally catching on to what is going on?

Actually, I don't blame you on the left for your emotional diatribes. To borrow one of your mantras, "It's not my fault. I can't help myself." Maybe it just like one comedian of years ago often said, "The Devil made me do it." You are merely exhibiting those very human animal instincts, those emotionally driven processes, the instincts that provided homo sapiens the reproductive success that is now overrunning the planet. Humanitarian concerns and reason are completely overwhelmed by angry emotions incited into hatred by the mob leaders you have selected. The bus of state is being driven by a committee of permanent adolescents with little real experience, and questionable backgrounds. These include tax cheats controlling the financial powers of our government. They are so disorganized they frequently counter each other's arguments. Democrat legislators are passing major legislation virtually none of them have read. I wonder who it was that actually wrote the $800 billion "porkulous" bill? And how about that huge Democrat boondogle, "The Federal Budget?" Who wrote that? Those who would destroy our nation could hardly have dreamed in their wildest imagination that such an instrument of our devastation could been proposed by our own government.

This condition has been brought about by a selection process designed two and a quarter centuries ago for people who mostly walked from place to place, sent mail by horse or boat, traveled on the water by canoe or sail, and couldn't read. There were exceptions, mostly among the "wealthy," people who could read and had horses for transport. To use this ponderous, antiquated, and unwieldy process in the age of instant access to the Internet, world wide transport in hours rather than months, and the vast technology available to rapidly expanding numbers of people in most of the world. Because of this, I propose we make a huge change in the selection of all elected officials, federal and state. We will need a major revision of our Constitutionally defined process of selecting all political offices and positions. This proposal is described as a simplified method and easily instituted system for selection of legislators and executives as well as other offices.

Friday, March 19, 2009

A New Process for Selecting Public Officials that are Currently Elected

I propose we do away with elections which have enabled self-serving, power hungry individuals and groups to bully and buy their way into control of the election process for the legislature. This new process would remove completely the power money and influence have over our current election process. A lottery system for selection of legislators would accomplish the replacement of all financial influence with chance, removing virtually any undue influence by anyone. Any legislature chosen at random from the public would be relatively free of the influence now so powerful a force in government. It couldn't possibly be any worse than what we have now.

Here's a first effort at how it would work: Using the social security system, all those with social security numbers would be able to enter the "pool" of citizens for the lottery. Entry into the pool would be optional. Those who did not want to participate could merely not register. Registration would be conducted by the current systems being used to register voters. Current Congressional districts could be used to determine the numbers of representatives and the constituency from whom they would be chosen. All those registered in any district would be in that district's pool. Each district would draw numbers of nine individuals from the pool. This would provide the members of the second level pool.

The second level pool: The entire group for each state would meet and elect one member as their Senator along with an alternate for each Senate seat. Once the Senators and alternates are chosen, the groups of nine would meet and select two of each group to be their representatives in Congress. Two alternates would also be chosen in each group. Representatives would be selected every two years while Senators would serve four years. By using nine members in each group, the possibility of a tie would be avoided. The purpose of the two alternates would be to replace the one originally chosen should that person be unable to perform their duties for any reason. Any felony conviction would be cause for immediate expulsion.

Reselection: Once their terms in office are over, sitting members of both houses would automatically be included in the next selection group from their district or state. This would make selection groups of eleven and add one more Senate candidate in each state group. These "Incumbents" would face the same election process as other members of each group. Terms would be limited to three for any one office. That is six years for Representatives and twelve years for Senators.

States could set up similar systems for selection of their legislatures. This new lottery system would apply only to legislators. Other offices could still be elected by the existing system.

"Seek not the favor of the multitude; it is seldom got by honest and lawful means. But seek the testimony of few; and number not voices, but weigh them."

—Emmanuel Kant

"All our knowledge begins with the senses, proceeds then to the understanding, and ends with reason. There is nothing higher than reason."

—Emmanuel Kant

"All our passions begin with emotions—instinctive reactions driven by millennia of evolution. There is no reason, rationality, or knowledge in passion, only the animal actions of flight, consummation, procreation, self-preservation, or combat."

—*Howard Johnson*

Friday, March 13, 2009, 3:10 PM

Something of Historic Proportion is Happening

by Pamela Geller

Pamela "Atlas" Geller began her publishing career at The New York Daily News and subsequently took over operation of The New York Observer as Associate Publisher.

She left The Observer after the birth of her fourth child but remained involved in various projects including American Associates, Ben Gurion University and being Senior Vice-President Strategic Planning and Performance Evaluation at The Brandeis School.

After 9/11, Atlas had the veil of oblivion violently lifted from her consciousness and immersed herself in the education and understanding of geopolitics, Islam, terror, foreign affairs and imminent threats the mainstream media and the government wouldn't cover or discuss.

Her website, www.AtlasShrugged.com, winner of the "Best New Blog" 2005 Jewish and Israeli Blog Award and finalist in the 2005 Weblog Awards, is a counter terrorism site fighting the great fight, changing the world one word at a time. Leading authorities are regularly interviewed. She routinely confers with leading scholars on the Middle East, Islam, Eurabia , China and Russia ..

The objective of her website is to cover related but little reported events of great import. She provides an unblinking, glaring examination of global affairs and is a member of Pajamas Media.

href = "http://atlasshrugs2000.typepad.com/a...ing-of-hi.html

Subject: "Something of Historic Proportion is Happening" by Pam Geller

I am a student of history. Professionally. I have written 15 books in six languages, and have studied it all my life.. I think there is something monumentally large afoot, and I do not believe it is just a banking crisis, or a mortgage crisis, or a credit crisis. Yes, these exist but they are merely single facets on a very large gemstone that is only now coming into a sharper focus.

Something of historic proportions is happening. I can sense it because I know how it feels, smells, what it looks like, and how people react to it.

Yes, a perfect storm may be brewing, but there is something happening within our country that has been evolving for about 10 - 15 years. The pace has dramatically quickened in the past two.

We demand and then codify into law the requirement that our banks make massive loans to people whom we know can never pay back. Why? We learn just days ago that the Federal Reserve, which has little or no real oversight by anyone, has "loaned" two trillion dollars (that is $2,000,000,000,000) over the past few months, but will not tell us to whom or why or disclose the terms. That is our money. Yours and mine. And that is three times the $700B we all argued about so strenuously just this past September.

Who has this money? Why do they have it? Why are the terms unavailable to us? Who asked for it? Who authorized it? I thought this was a government of "We the People," who lent our powers to our elected leaders..Apparently not.

We have spent two or more decades intentionally de-industrializing our economy. Why? We have intentionally dumbed down our schools, ignored our history, and no longer teach our founding documents, why we are exceptional, and why we are worth preserving. Students by and large cannot write, think critically, read, or articulate. Parents are not revolting, teachers are not picketing, and school boards continue to back mediocrity. Why?

We have now established the precedent of protesting every close election (now violently in California over a proposition that is so controversial that it wants marriage to remain between one man and one woman. Did you ever think such a thing possible just a decade ago?). We have corrupted our sacred political process by allowing unelected judges to write laws that radically change our way of life, and then mainstream Marxist groups like ACORN and others to turn our voting system into a banana republic. To what purpose?

Now our mortgage industry is collapsing, housing prices are in free fall, major industries are failing, our banking system is on the verge of collapse, Social Security is nearly bankrupt, as is Medicare and our entire government. Our education system is worse than a joke (I teach college and know precisely what I am talking about.) The list is staggering in its length, breadth, and depth. It is potentially 1929 x 10. And we are at war with an enemy we cannot name for fear of offending people of the same religion who cannot wait to slit the throats of your children if they have the opportunity to do so.

And now we have elected a man no one knows anything about, who has never run so much as a Dairy Queen, let alone a town as big as Wasilla , Alaska . All of his associations and alliances are with real radicals in their chosen fields of employment, and everything we learn about him, drip by drip, is unsettling if not downright scary (Surely you have heard him speak about his idea to create and fund a mandatory civilian defense force stronger than our military for use inside our borders? No? Oh, of course. The media would never play that for you over and over and then demand he answer it. Sarah Palin's pregnant daughter and $150,000 wardrobe is more important.)

Mr. Obama's winning platform can be boiled down to one word: Change. Why?

I have never been so afraid for my country and for my children as I am now. This man campaigned on bringing people together, something he has never, ever done in his professional life. In my assessment, Obama will divide us along philosophical lines, push us apart, and then try to realign the pieces into a new and different power structure. Change is indeed coming. And when it comes, you will never see the same nation again.

And that is only the beginning.

I thought I would never be able to experience what the ordinary, moral German felt in the mid-1930's. In those times, the savior was a former smooth-talking rabble-rouser from the streets, about whom the average German knew next to nothing. What they did know was that he was associated with groups that shouted, shoved, and pushed around people with whom they disagreed; he edged his way onto the political stage through great oratory and promises. Economic times were tough, people were losing jobs, and he was a great speaker. And he smiled and waved a lot. And people, even newspapers, were afraid to speak out for fear that his "brown shirts" would bully them into submission.

And then he was duly elected to office, with a full-throttled economic crisis at hand [the Great Depression]. Slowly but surely he seized the controls of government power, department by department, person by person, bureaucracy by bureaucracy. The kids joined a Youth Movement in his name, where they were taught what to think.

How did he get the people on his side? He did it promising jobs to the jobless, money to the moneyless, and goodies for the military-industrial complex. He did it by indoctrinating the children, advocating gun control, health care for all, better wages, better jobs, and promising to re-instill pride once again in the country, across Europe , and across the world.

He did it with a compliant media - Did you know that? And he did this all in the name of justice and .. . . change. And the people surely got what they voted for. (Look it up if you think I am exaggerating.) Read your history books. Many people objected in 1933 and were shouted down, called names, laughed at, and made fun of. When Winston Churchill pointed out the obvious in the late 1930's while seated in the House of Lords in England (he was not yet Prime Minister), he was booed into his seat and called a crazy troublemaker. He was right, though ..

Don't forget that Germany was the most educated, cultured country in Europe . It was full of music, art, museums, hospitals, laboratories, and universities. And in less than six years - a shorter time span than just two terms of the U. S. presidency - it was rounding up its own citizens, killing others, abrogating its laws, turning children against parents, and neighbors against neighbors. All with the best of intentions, of course. The road to Hell is paved with them.

As a practical thinker, one not overly prone to emotional decisions, I have a choice: I can either believe what the objective pieces of evidence tell me (even if they make me cringe with disgust); I can believe what history is shouting to me from across the chasm of seven decades; or I can hope I am wrong, close my eyes, have another latte and ignore what is transpiring around me.

Some people scoff at me; others laugh or think I am foolish, naive, or both. Perhaps I am.. But I have never been afraid to look people in the eye and tell them exactly what I believe—and why I believe it. I pray I am wrong. I do not think I am.

"Democracy is two wolves and a lamb deciding what to have for dinner. Liberty is a well-armed lamb."

—Benjamin Franklin

See if you see any similarity to the present U.S. - NAZIs in the 1920s

The National Socialist German Workers' Party, (German: Nationalsozialistische Deutsche Arbeiterpartei, abbreviated NSDAP), commonly known in English as the NAZI Party (Nationalsozialistische Deutsche Arbeiterpartei), was a political party in Germany between 1919 and 1945. It was known as the German Workers' Party (DAP) before the name was changed in 1920.

The party's last leader, Adolf Hitler, was appointed Chancellor of Germany by president Paul von Hindenburg in 1933. Hitler rapidly established a totalitarian regime known as the Third Reich.

Nazi ideology stressed the failure of the economy, the failure of democracy, and the failure of laissez-faire capitalism.

During the 1920s Hitler organized the De-Sturmabteilung.ogg Sturmabteilung, abbreviated SA, (German for "Assault detachment" or "Assault section", usually translated as "stormtroop(er)s"). Originally a "civilian security force" (sound familiar?) that functioned as a paramilitary organization of the NSDAP – the German Nazi party. It played a key role in Adolf Hitler's rise to power in the 1920s and 1930s.

SA men were often called "brownshirts", for the color of their uniforms; this distinguished them from the Schutzstaffel (SS), who wore black and brown uniforms. I wonder what color shirts members of ACORN wear?

"History is the witness of the times, the light of truth."   --Cicero

"Unfortunately, historians are not. Frequently their writing is guided or controlled by those who put their actions in the best light while denigrating those of their opponents and enemies."
—Howard Johnson

"Those who ignore history are doomed to repeat it."   --*George Santayana*

"Half of human history was made by drunkards in their cups and written down by slaves of one imposter or another in the hope of table leavings."   *—Talbot Mundy*

Saturday, March 21, 2009

NASA's Global CO2 Surveyor

My son recently sent me an article about NASA's global CO2 surveyor satellite that unfortunately didn't achieve orbit and was destroyed. I could not find any links to the article, so I attached it to this email. In it I found some interesting statements that prompted the following response:

Dear Mike:

I often become suspicious of the veracity and the political motives of articles published by some "scientists" when those articles contain statements that are patently false or at least misleading. I also view as suspect the common assumption made that CO2 generated by human activity is a major factor in and causes catastrophic global warming. This one assumption runs counter to conclusions from many long studied and well known factors that affect climate. The following paragraph is from that article. It caught my eye because one little sentence in italics, the basis for the accuracy of the entire project, is untrue.

"Carbon dioxide molecules aren't measured directly; the instrument tabulates the absorption of sunlight by CO2 and molecular oxygen molecules before and after sunlight is reflected off the Earth's surface. Since each molecule has a unique infrared signature, they can be singled out and counted. There are two detectors for CO2 because it is easier to spot near the Earth's surface at 1/61 microns and in the atmosphere at 2.06 microns. The molecular oxygen A-band channel acts as a survey control because its presence in the atmosphere is constant."

In rebuttal I offer a substantiated quote from my book, A Convenient Solution, and an article I published in 2007. The full article on global warming can be found at: **http://hjgulfstream.blogspot.com**. Should you want to read the section in my book it is available on the web at **http://acsexcerpts.blogspot.com**.

From page 47 of the book: With the exception of hydrogen, all gaseous, liquid, and solid fuels produce carbon dioxide when burned in any energy process. In addition, the production of hydrogen by any means other than by electrolysis, using energy from nuclear, wind, water or tidal power plants will add carbon dioxide to the atmosphere from both the energy and the raw materials used to create the hydrogen (coal-fired power plants for instance). It is interesting to note that for each pound of carbon oxidized to carbon dioxide, four pounds of oxygen are removed from the atmosphere. For every thousand tons of CO2 added to the atmosphere, eight hundred tons of oxygen are removed. In all the concern about CO2 there has never been a single mention of that fact.

The obvious conclusion is that the amount of oxygen in the atmosphere is not a constant as stated in the article in Aviation Week.

It should be interesting to note that I do not agree with those who say atmospheric CO2 has a catastrophic effect on climate or with those who argue it has absolutely no effect. It is just that the amount of that effect, though real, is so small as to be insignificant compared to other, well known factors. In just the same way, pouring a bucket of water into Lake Erie raises the lake level. I do not think shore dwellers need to fear that will flood their homes. This puts me solidly against global warming proponents in government who use it to gain power and as a huge cash cow of tax revenue. In addition there are literally thousands of groups using proven tactics to frighten the public into compliance donations, and mindless support.

From my article on global warming: Any global warming from the effects of CO2, if indeed it exists or poses any danger at all, is grossly distorted relative to the facts at hand. Most of the data used to show global warming are at best statistical and at worst, anecdotal. Both of which provide great opportunities for opinions (and agendas) to mitigate the data we can obtain. We know for certain that addition to the atmosphere of any gas will contribute that gas's infrared absorption properties with all its complexities. Actually, all gases in the atmosphere have some "greenhouse" effect. This includes, nitrogen (75.0% - 78.08%), oxygen (20.11% - 20.95%), argon (0.89$ - 0.93%), and carbon dioxide (0.035% - 0.038%). The percentages in parentheses are of air at sea level. Ranges are shown because air also contains a variable amount of water vapor (from 1- 4% ±0.25%) and trace amounts of other gases. Each gas has a complex rate of infrared absorption and emission at various infrared frequencies. Water vapor has from 30 to 90 times the temperature effect of CO_2 depending on various conditions.

The warmer air becomes, the more water vapor it can hold. Remember the weatherman's favorite "dew point" predictions? When the temperature lowers to that point, the air can hold no more water vapor so it condenses out as "dew" or rain in the big picture. Using the same rationale as the global warming folks use for CO_2, increasing amounts of water vapor would cause a much larger increase in atmospheric temperatures than CO_2 resulting in still warmer air and still more water vapor. Shouldn't this lead to a runaway greenhouse effect? Wouldn't this drive atmospheric temperatures higher and higher until the oceans boil and all life is extinguished? Obviously this has not happened so something about these assumptions must be wrong for water vapor and CO_2 as well.

Water vapor adds still another factor to the mix. That is the heat of vaporization or condensation of water. Tremendous amounts of the sun's radiant energy evaporates water all over the earth. All of that energy enters the atmosphere in water vapor. The warmer the ocean or wet land, the more energy goes into the air. When all this water vapor condenses out as rain, that energy is released and the air warms. This is the driving energy that causes the air to move and creates windstorms, tornados and hurricanes. For all practical purposes, the CO_2 content of the air has zero effect on the amount of energy that goes into the atmosphere or heats the air when water condenses.

One huge factor that man has affected greatly is the water vapor that green plants give off and particularly dense rain forests. Our continuing decimation of all types of rain forests is removing a huge source of water vapor that formerly entered the air. One example of this effect was used incorrectly as an example of global warming, which it was not. The disappearing snows of Mount Kilimanjaro are not an effect of global warming. Studies have shown that the cutting of the forest around the base of the mountain so reduced the amount of water vapor in the air flowing up the mountain that both the rainfall and snowfall on the higher slopes has been reduced dramatically. This is one correct example of where human activity has interfered with nature. Deforestation worldwide has done far more damage to our environment and effected climate far more than even tripling the amount of CO_2 in the atmosphere could do. It alone could arguably be responsible for any temperature increase over the last hundred years as a reduction in the amount of water vapor would reduce cloud cover resulting in less of the sun's energy reflected away. Why don't we do something about that?

Whatever the effect of carbon dioxide, it is so small in comparison as to raise questions about the real amount of the danger it poses. Certainly it is not the degree of danger claimed by the high priests of global warming. I seriously question the validity of the often quoted phrase, "Overwhelming numbers of scientists support the theory that man's use of fossil fuels is bringing about catastrophic global warming." In the first place, the worldwide destructive clearing and burning of rain forest results in putting far more net carbon dioxide into the air than all the vehicles in the entire world. Second, shrinking rain forests mean less water vapor is released into the air. This could in turn mean less rain and snow where the air over land is drier. The questions remain, does the evaporation from the oceans increase and make up for this loss, and what effect does the drier air have on cloud cover and the resulting reflection of the sun's energy away from the earth? All of these interacting variables have much larger net effects on global temperatures than $CO2$.. Because of this, "Overwhelming numbers of scientists" may have no real clue about the degree of effect that $CO2$ might have on atmospheric temperatures leading to global warming. Obviously it is much smaller than that of water vapor.

Thursday, March 12, 2009

The Card Check bill in Congress

I know a lot of you are extreme liberals, but even you should be up in arms about what labor bosses are trying to ram through Congress.

Wake up Americans! Democrat politicians are about to reward labor unions for their help in the last election by doing away with a basic right of all Americans, the right to a secret ballot for elections. First they said they were bailing out the American auto industry with your billions of dollars. That is pure BS. All they were doing was padding the pay checks of lazy and conniving UAW workers with money from the public treasury. No wonder Toyota, Honda and the other off-shore auto companies are beating the pants off of UAW auto companies with their autos, even those built by American workers in American factories. Their labor costs are about half of what the UAW members get paid for the same work. They have crippled our once great auto industry that will certainly go down the tubes anyway, just like our electronics industry and many others that were highly unionized.

Now the Democrat controlled government is about to demolish the foundation of our Democratic Republic, the secret ballot. The American public should be screaming against this destruction of a basic right. Where is the massive outcry from the third estate? Are the masses just so stupid they can't see what's happening? Maybe they just don't give a damn. It's beyond my comprehension.

And how about those so called protectors of human rights in the media? They should be haranguing everyone to urge their representatives to throw this evil proposal out. Where are all their calls of "foul?" Perhaps they are over enamored with the "Royals," now controlling our government. Maybe they're getting a payoff of some sort to ignore what's happening. Something is very rotten there and it ain't in Denmark.

Next the Democrats will be rewriting our election laws and doing away with the secret ballot in public elections. How will you like it when politicians know exactly how you vote? There wouldn't be any goons using coercion and beatings on those who didn't vote their way, would there. Of course not! This is America. Americans don't do those kinds of things. Ha!

The Cook County Democrat machine is, in fact, already doing that in a round about way. They know quite well who votes how in the local precincts and their goons are not shy about punishing those who don't toe the line. Now we have a product of that corrupt machine as our President. Democrat machine politics with all its intimidation, corruption, payoffs, ballot box stuffing, votes by dead and non existent voters, and associated criminal activities—those machine politics have completed their take over of Washington. I wonder how long it will be before we see Democrats elected by 100% of the vote just like Kim Il Sung was in North Korea.

Newt Gingerich explains what is happening in a much less pointed manner than I do. Here's what he has to say:

March 11, 2009 | Vol. 4, No. 10

Dancing to Big Labor's Tune

by Newt Gingrich

After spending an astounding $61 million to elect Democrats in the 2008 elections, union bosses are getting their payback this week.

Yesterday, so-called "Card Check" legislation was introduced in both the House and the Senate.

Card Check strips American workers of the right to a secret ballot and gives the federal government the right to impose labor contracts on workers.

The timing of this assault on the freedom of the American workplace could not be worse. A new study shows that for every three workers coerced into joining a union under Card Check, one job will be eliminated by besieged American businesses.

Card Check Could Eliminate 600,000 Jobs In Its First Year

Card Check is a job killer. Even Obama supporter Warren Buffet opposes it, saying "I think the secret ballot is pretty important in the country. I'm against card check." Watch him here.

But as far as Big Labor is concerned, a deal's a deal. Their goal is to get their allies in Washington to ram Card Check through Congress this week, before anyone notices that American workers and businesses are losing fundamental rights.

What's happening in Washington this week is old style, quid-pro-quo politics - the kind President Obama pledged as a candidate to end. Supporters of the so-called Employee Free Choice Act (that's their Orwellian name for Card Check - it would more correctly be called the

Union-goon authorization-to-bash-your-head-in-if-you-don't-vote-us-in act.) claim to be all about protecting American workers.

But leave it to Vice President Joe Biden to inadvertently tell the truth.

In a meeting with the AFL-CIO last week, Biden made it clear who's calling the shots when it comes to American workers, businesses and jobs. He told the gathering of union big-wigs:

"You all brought me to the dance a long time ago, and it's time we start dancing."

82% of Democrats Oppose Eliminating the Secret Ballot

For big labor and their allies in Washington, it's time to start dancing - and dancing fast.

Vice President Biden and the union bosses hope to duplicate with Card Check the Obama Administration's success in rushing the mammoth $787 billion stimulus bill through Congress so quickly most members never had time to read it.

The reason they have to act quickly is simply this: The vast majority of Americans - 77 percent of Republicans, 82 percent of Democrats and 79 percent of independents - oppose what they're trying to do.

Not only that, but the latest surveys show that a full 82 percent of Americans say they don't want to belong to a union.

The Stakes Are High This Week

But it's precisely this kind of pro-secret ballot, pro-freedom sentiment among the American people that makes union bosses so eager to pass Card Check.

Under Card Check, union organizers and their enforcers will be able to go into any small business, hospital or construction site and coerce workers into signing cards. If they get 50 percent plus one, the deal's done, and the workers are forced into a union. And if management and the new union fail to reach a negotiated contract, the federal government will just impose one. Coerced unionization allows for what is effectively a new, unaccountable form of forced taxation. Workers will have a portion of their paycheck going to the union to be spent as the bosses (many are convicted extortionists) see fit, including political donations to parties and candidates that the workers may not even support.

Talk about an "offer you can't refuse." There's no vote. No secret ballot. No right to freely negotiate the contract. The workers, the workplace, and a portion of the worker's paychecks are controlled by the union bosses.

For Americans like you and me, the stakes are high this week. Hanging in the balance are literally hundreds of thousands of jobs, not to mention fundamental freedoms like the ability of small businesses to create and sustain jobs, the freedom of American workers to have a say in how their workplace is organized, and the freedom of American workers to freely choose whether they want to give money to politicians and political parties.

Congress Is Holding Hearings This Week

Make Your Voice Heard at www.AmericanSolutions.com/FreedomNotFear.

The time to act is now - this week, while Congress holds hearings on Card Check.

You can make your voice heard by the people who matter most by joining in American Solutions' "Freedom Not Fear" campaign.

Freedom Not Fear is grassroots petition drive to preserve American jobs and preserve the right of the secret ballot for American workers. Over 80,000 Americans have already gone to AmericanSolutions.com/FreedomNotFear and signed the petition, but we need more help.

Remember the "Drill Here, Drill Now, Pay Less" campaign from last summer? With your help we were able to change hearts and minds on Capitol Hill about the necessity of using more safe, clean American energy.

We can do the same with Freedom Not Fear. Congress needs to hear from the sweeping majorities of Americans of all political parties who oppose this massive power grab by Big Labor.

The union bosses want to silence the voices of American workers and businesses. Go to Americansolutions.com/FreedomNotFear today and let them know that we won't go down without a fight.

Responses from the Pro and Anti Labor Forces

This is a balled faced lie! Get your facts straight! Card check does not do away with the secret ballot, it simply offers an alternative. As your Quoted hero Newt proclaims,"the secret of Politics is to Lie, Lie, Lie, and then Lie some more." Have a good misinformed day. (Typical liberal misinformed misinformation.)

Another response:

You and Newt sure got it right. I was working in a small automotive supplier in Ft. Wayne for many years, right from the git go. Once the company got big enough to be noticed, the UAW moved in. It didn't take most employees long to realize that if you didn't support the union, you were in for a bad time. I only lasted about a year until I found a job with Volkswagen in Ohio. It was for a little less money, but the atmosphere was very much better. Everyone worked. We were all part of "the team." The goon squads and intimidators will love the power the new law will give them. Once the unions come around, extreme coercion will be the norm. Look what they've done to the big three as it is.

By way of correcting any misunderstanding, here are some facts and some opinions. Of course, the emotionally intense hatred most liberals express for anyone with whom they disagree causes great confusion on their part as to just which are facts and which are opinions. (See pro-labor comment back two paragraphs.) This makes sensible communication damn near impossible, but I try anyway. Incidentally the first responder did what so many liberals do constantly, misquoted Newt out of context. I have searched high and low, but can't come up with the exact line quoted. The closest is a line given in a speech to a Republican organization in Atlanta, date unknown. In that speech he said, "The secret of liberal politics is to lie and lie, cheat and cheat, and tell the victims of your efforts you are working for them." But Newt was correctly dubbed as one of my political heroes along with so many who have stood up for independence, freedom and personal responsibility. Men like Washington, Jefferson, Madison, and most of our founding fathers as well as Reagan and a few other so often vilified by the left. At least Newt is not trying to destroy what they so masterfully built.

Reality trumps intentions every time. This new law would remove the right of the company to request a secret election, a right they now enjoy. This offers protection to workers who really don't want a union, but are intimidated to sign the cards. In its place the new law gives that option over to the employees. The law states clearly that only the employees can request a secret ballot election. This gives union goons an open invitation to intimidate employees to sign cards requesting a union and not ask for a secret ballot. They use the same kind of intimidation organized criminals use to intimidate witnesses. I wonder where they learned that? Once more than 50% signed, the union is in, even without an election. I'm sure those disgruntled union members would request a secret ballot election, wouldn't they. Ha!

One Example of the Effects of Unionization

I've seen the UAW in action unionizing one company started in 1920 in a small town in Indiana. The company and town shall remain nameless to protect the author. It was a small family owned business with about 100 employees that built bodies on Ford and GM truck chassis. Their wage and benefit scale was actually above union standards at the time. The UAW wanted to collect dues and impose their own work rules. During 1948 we were in the plant as part of our engineering studies at Purdue during the time we were here, the union began trying to "organize" its employees. None of the employees I spoke with were favorable to the union. Most said the "The old man (the owner) and his boys take good care of us. We don't need a union."

We were at the plant several times a week for three weeks. By the time we left things changed and there were some nasty incidents. Employees who spoke out against the union often had an "accident." Several ended up in the hospital and one died. No one was ever charged. There were three elections several months apart. The union lost in the first two, but won on the third. Within the year the owners decided it was no longer in their best interest to continue operating the plant. Pickets marched in front of the plant as it was shut down and dismantled. The owners shut down their assembly line after finishing the bus contract already underway. They sold their remaining contracts, inventory and machinery to a manufacturer in Tennessee, and all moved to Florida.

(There was a rumor that the company in Tennessee belonged to a member of the family, but I have no confirmation of that rumor.)

The small town was devastated as this was one of their largest employers and a sizable portion of the town's economy. During the year, we studied the effects on the town and determined that there were more than a dozen dependent businesses that soon closed their doors and about 300 additional people lost there jobs. The fallout undoubtedly left the city's economy in ruin for a long time. The plant stood empty for many years. I happened by the plant many years later and found a paved parking lot full of weeds, a battered fence and a few empty buildings. I have no idea what became of the owners or their family, but I'm sure they had a good and successful life wherever they went. Maybe they took over that plant in Tennessee. I do know that they remained substantial financial supporters of Purdue University for many years after they closed their Indiana plant. Great job, UAW.

Some of my liberal family and friends constantly vilify me as a Rush Limbaugh worshiping, George Bush loving, far right Republican member of the extreme right, a Christian fundamentalist homophobe, racial bigot and all that other crap on their long hate list. The truth is they all hate anyone who doesn't go along with their "holy" far left agenda handed down to them from the George Soros crowd and the New York Times. (I wonder why he doesn't just buy the Times? It's going broke, you know.) Talking to them is like negotiating with Al Queda or the Taliban. It's their "holy" way or off with your head. Well, it's hasn't come to that quite yet, but one never knows when. I notice they **never** propose a rational argument. All they do is call names and ridicule.

No amount of reason or logic will ever sway their emotional attachment to what they are "supposed" to believe or to "political correctness." Talk about mind-numbed robots, I realized long ago how fruitless it is to have a rational conversation with any of them about virtually anything with the remotest hint of political content. To me, liberalism is one of the most fundamentalist religions on the planet. It is totally devoid of any rational content, often exuding pure hatred.

One of my very liberal friends was visiting a few years ago and ran across a pamphlet titled, A Real Answer to the Drug Problem laying on our coffee table. He read through it while I was doing something else and asked if I had read it.

When I allowed I had, he immediately said, "I think it's a great idea. I suppose you are very much against it, aren't you?"

I replied, "Take a look at the back of the pamphlet." The back of the pamphlet listed seven "solutions" I had developed and written down. It offered pamphlets like the one he held on all of the ideas—my ideas.

"You . . . wrote this?" he asked with great incredulity.

"And all of the others as well."

"That's amazing!" he exclaimed. "That sounds more like a liberal idea, than one you would come up with."

I smiled. "It only goes to show how little you really know about me, doesn't it? And how little you know about anyone you consider a conservative, or for that matter, anyone who isn't inside that tight little exclusive box of ideas you virtually worship."

"Now, don't get nasty." he warned.

"By getting nasty I suppose you mean saying anything that doesn't fit inside your tight little box of 'liberal' ideas. It has been my observation that most liberals consider anything proposed or even uttered by a non-liberal that doesn't fit in that box is considered hate speech."

"Not really."

"No? Tell me please, what political proposal that violates any of the holy tenets of liberalism by what Republican politician has not been labeled as hate speech."

He couldn't think of any. Incidentally, I wrote the original in 1999 and posted it to my blog in September 2005/ It was updated once in 2008, but still remains essentially as first written down. It's at **http://hjdrugprb.blogspot.com**. Check it out if you'd like to see it.

In light of what is happening near our border with Mexico as I write this, my solution could put an immediate stop to all those murders. I am working on revising my proposal in this light very soon.

Sunday, February 15, 2009

Observations about trust and major disappointments

Observations about trust - a short one

I have a very simple rule regarding trust for friends and family. I trust them recognizing that they, like myself, can be mistaken or fooled. It's a whole lot easier to trust those I know than to bother with doubts. I have been stung a very few times, but as I have always said, "Fool me once, shame on you. Fool me twice, shame on me." It simply makes sense and I don't believe I've ever been fooled twice.

As far as those who are not family or friends:

I believe nothing I hear on TV, radio, movies or the Internet that does not make logical sense to me or I cannot personally prove, especially if it doesn't pass a scientific test. That's the basics, math, physics, and chemistry.

I believe nothing I hear from the so called, "unbiased" main stream media that I don't personally know to be true from other sources. Their biggest lie is not reporting or minimizing news that does not promote their leftist agenda.

I believe nothing any politician says, ever. Even things that make sense to my logical mind. I always think there must be something I'm missing, usually about who is the real beneficiary and where the money is going.

Major Disappointments:

I am particularly distressed when I hear these man-on-the-street questions that stump so many Americans, particularly about our government. These interviews usually conducted by late night TV or talk radio make me wonder if those people being interviewed ever attended any school or read anything but advertising copy in their entire life.

Then there are the political fiascos like the senate race in Minnesota. How anyone could vote for that idiotic failed comedian and caricature of a human, Al Franken, for the US Senate is beyond my comprehension. Of course, that's just Minnesota. Then watching the blatant vote fraud conducted by Democrats who used the recount process to "find" more than a thousand "misplaced" ballots, all for Franken, even finding more ballots for two precincts than there were voters in those precincts. Of course, as soon as they produced enough votes to push Franken over Stevens, the Democrat secretary of state certified the election and pronounced Franken the winner.

For my money the Democrat party is totally corrupt, buying and manufacturing votes with total impunity, right out of the Cook County Illinois Democrat machine play book. (A machine left over from the Al Capone days.) Meanwhile their coconspirators in the "unbiased" main stream media completely ignore these blatant unethical if not illegal activities and fawn over Obama and his wife. Our new President obviously was and probably still is involved up to his eyeballs in Cook County Democrat machine crooked politics. Of course the MSM (Main Stream Media) will never even breathe any of this so it has to be found from other more reliable sources.

I hate to admit it, but many Republicans are as crooked and self serving as their Democrat counterparts. Unfortunately they are amateurs at vote stealing and don't have the adoration of the MSM so they are quite unpopular.

I am amazed at how the American people seem to accept all this criminal activity as normal and acceptable. I guess the new Americans believe that the way to get what you want is to lie, cheat and steal. It's all right as long as you don't get caught or are a Democrat politician and get a pass. Perhaps that is the new American ethic replacing the old hard work ethic of previous generations of Americans and new immigrants. Never in our history have so many politicians become so wealthy so fast as Democrats like the Clintons, Reid, Pelosi, Raines, Obama, and others. I wonder where all that sudden new wealth came from—I mean really came from, not the conveniently opportune immediate source. The real sources are doubtless hidden by several untraceable steps. No wonder there are so many felons and criminally indicted in the halls of our nation's federal buildings. It seems like criminal accusations and indictments are almost a testimonial for so many Democrats. There are so many it would be foolish fo me to list them here. They run continuously from Bobby Baker (remember, he took a fall for Lyndon Johnson) to Jessie Jackson's protégée, Mel Reynolds (sent to prison for bank fraud and having sex with a minor) to William Jefferson from Louisiana (unexplained $100,000 found in his freezer - is he still in Congress?). How about Barney Frank having a male prostitution ring run from his home? (He says he knew nothing about it, snicker, snicker.) Any Republican or Conservative in these circumstances would have been hung, drawn, quartered, and boiled in oil by the main stream media.

To refresh you memories check out these websites:

Bobby Baker - . . . http://educationforum.ipbhost.com/index.php?showtopic=4332

Mel Reynolds - . . . http://baic.house.gov/member-profiles/profile.html?intID=57

William Jefferson - . . .
http://theoryequalsdogma.blogspot.com/2008/12/congressman-money-in-freezer-william.htm
l

Barney Frank - . . . http://www.time.com/time/magazine/article/0,9171,958598,00.html

Some interesting quotes:

"Natural science does not consist in ratifying what others have said, but in seeking the causes of phenomena."   —*Saint Albertus Magnus*

"More tears are shed over answered prayers than unanswered ones."

—*St. Teresa of Avila*

"Tradition means giving votes to the most obscure of all classes, our ancestors. It is the democracy of the dead."   —*G. K. Chesterton*

"You shall not go about spreading slander among your kinsmen; nor shall you stand by idly when your neighbor's life is at stake. I am the LORD."   —Leviticus Chapter 19:16 NAB.

"Where is all the knowledge we lost with information?"   —*T. S. Eliot*

"There's no such thing as life without bloodshed. I think the notion that the species can be improved in some way, that everyone could live in harmony, is a really dangerous idea. Those who are afflicted with this notion are the first ones to give up their souls, their freedom."

—*Cormac McCarthy*

"If there were no God, there would be no atheists."   —*G. K. Chesterton*

"In children we have an innocent audience not yet hardened and brutalized and made cynical. They look to us trustingly for information and enchantment. How very few of us are worthy of such trust."   —*Sterling North*

"Hollywood has unfortunately become a memory. It's nothing but a sign on the side of a hill."

—*Mickey Rooney*

"The quickest way of ending a war is to lose it."   —*George Orwell*

Tuesday, January 20, 2009

Reflections on Inauguration day

I am not very hopeful our new President will acknowledge and follow the many excellent policies and programs of the last administration in spite of the attitudes he has shown on this up to today. Once he is President with a majority in both houses of Congress and an adoring press corps he will probably take a very different course. No matter what he does, the media will proclaim his greatness to the skies even as they cursed and damned our last President. The orgasmic reaction of the media will prove a real problem once Obama faces the realities of the office. Only then will we find out what he is made of. My guess is he will be a disappointment to many of his adoring subjects who almost all have their hands out. The political money machine is currently in deep doo doo and will probably continue to decline simply because those who make it work see Obama's "change" as a black hole of new and oppressive taxes and are planning accordingly.

The financial realities of nations like Ireland who radically lowered taxes on business and realized huge increases in economic growth even in tax revenue, are lost on those American liberal socialists who's mantra is "soak the rich." There is no question but that Obama's announced policies caused many businesses to quickly cut back on investment and employment in their plans for the years ahead. All because business must plan at least a year ahead and many plan for five or even ten years. Looking at and planning for huge new taxes and their effects on profits, investors, owners, and business managers had no choice but to cut employment and expansion to the bone in order to survive. Add that to the government created and promoted mortgage crisis and the media's constant harping, "the worst economy since the great depression" and you have a recipe for econoomic disaster. Incidently, the Carter years were much worse than the current crisis by any measure you can use and that is something the left including their media completely ignore. Together these factors make a serious and long depression like that of the thirties an almost certain result. Incidently, government jobs will definitely exacerbate the depression. Only private sector expansion and job creation has a positive effect on the economy. I firmly believe that the policies Obama and his liberal Congress will put into effect will prevent any recovery and will lengthen and strengthen the current economic woes in our nation. At this point in time I see Nancy Pelosi and her control freak Marxist efforts as even more dangerous for America than Obama's, but the reality of that opinion remains to be seen.

I think we can get some idea of where Obama will take us from several salient facts. First of all, this inauguration is costing tax payers more than the last four inaugurations put together. And this at a time of dire financial conditions. Second, maybe small, but indicative of things to come. Michelle Obama has spent more money on food, entertainment and clothing since her husband's campaign began that Laura Bush spent since GW took office. Her penchant for $400 lobster "snacks" at expensive hotels is well documented. Incidently, all of those tabs were picked up by "others." The media panned Sarah Palin for spending so much Republican money on clothes during the campaign, but they never mentioned the bills the Democrat party picked up for Michelle, and she wasn't even a candidate. I wonder why?

On the brighter side, we had a former President who, like Obama, was the product of a corrupt political machine yet who history now sees as one of our best Presidents. Harry Truman was disdained by many of his democrat colleagues, a number of whom tried to keep him out of the Presidential race. On spite of this he won the Presidency even with pundits predicting a Republican landslide. He surprised everyone with his performance, friends and foes alike, and is now called one of the best Presidents ever. Then there was the peanut farmer who's policies brought on interest rates in the twenties, double digit inflation and unemployment, and a recession that was far worse than the current one, at least to this point. Perhaps Obama can rise above his corrupt beginnings and become a good President for all the people. I certainly hope so.

One other prediction—the media will change their tune soon after Obama takes office and will begin commenting on how the situation is now beginning to improve. Anecdotal success stories of "ordinary Americans" will begin replacing the doom and gloom stories so common for the last few years. The media will try improving the public's confidence rather than destroying it as they did while the Bush administration was in power. It will be a miraculous "change" brought about by "the messiah." Don't kid yourself, this will happen.

As a result of the sickeningly fawning media, I absolutely refuse to watch any TV on inauguration day. I will listen to his speech over the radio, but most of the media are so orgasmic over our new President and his wife that it sickens me greatly. For obvious reasons, he is receiving the exact opposite treatment from that Bush and his wife received eight years ago. The media are providing Michelle the same adoration heaped on Jackie and then Princes Di. Elitism, royalty, and pop culture rule in the current main stream media.

That a product of one of the most corrupt political machines in the country who was ushered into the political process by known mobsters and radical, hate-filled so-called "holy" men should receive such adulation is pathetic. The extremely biased reporting of the media far out shadows the really important and historic fact that America has elected a "black" man President. They are treating him and his wife much more like rock stars or Hollywood celebrities than President and first lady. He was elected our "pop culture" President by hordes of celebrity worshipers who couldn't care a rat's annie about any of his policies except maybe his promise to "soak the rich." But wait a moment, his promise to "soak the rich" applies only to businessmen and then only to those who don't contribute to the liberal cause. That is apparent from the number of private jets that flew into Washington for his inauguration. There were so many at Dulles they had to close a runway to park them. At more than 600, twice as many as had ever been there before, this was an unprecedented turnout of the wealthy privileged few who scoffed at the environmental impact of burning all that fuel and flaunted their wealth while thousands of ordinary citizens were losing their jobs and homes. Remember the brouhaha when three auto execs flew to Washington for a handout in their corporate jets? Hmmmmm! I wonder how many who came in those 600+ jets are looking for bail-out money for themselves?

Yes, "Hollywood" has taken over and that includes the media. They have triumphed over capitalism, business, Republicans, the religious right, and common sense with hatred and bluster. These promoters of celebrity worship more and more control the thoughts and actions of those who react emotionally without thinking and refuse even to listen to any who do not toe their "politically correct" lines on anything. When an asinine and inept comedian like Al Franken can become a U. S. Senator by stuffing ballot boxes and a totally inexperienced, stammering debutante looks to be appointed the next Senator from New York simply because she has the name Kennedy in her repertoire, our government has sunk to unprecedented new lows. Both along with numerous others should be an embarrassment and an insult to the American public. But wait, we've already proven that integrity, honor, intelligence, respect, experience, and most other attributes of personal excellence do not matter to the pop culture adherents in the entertainment world. There are only two things that count, celebrity and complete submission to the emotional and hate driven agenda of the far left. I wonder but one thing. When capitalism and business are destroyed in this country, who's going to pay the taxes to support the rapidly expanding and money consuming monster our government has become?

Two years ago I responded to a scathing message from Arianna Huffington condemning George Bush and the Republicans for virtually everything including natural disasters while praising the actions of Democrats. That response never made it to the Huffington Post, but did trigger a vitriolic email response from Arriana to your's truly. I include my response verbatim.

Saturday, February 11, 2006

Response to Ariana Huffington's email to me, February, 2006

My dear Ariana:

As usual, you are close to being right, but are looking in precisely the wrong direction. I see your Orwellian predictions as at least equal to and probably truly more applicable to those on the liberal left than the conservative right. Of course, I am quite disappointed in Republicans who seem more intent on aping the worst behavior of the liberal Democrats than applying a steady conservative hand to the nation. Democrats are on a rampage of hate and destruction simply because they are out of complete power. Like spoiled brats who can't have their way, they scream destruction for the very nation that serves them. Republicans, so long out of power, seem unable to handle the power they do have, falling into the trap of mostly reacting to the constant stream of charges and accusations from Democrats who have behaved even worse for decades. The whole thing would be just another comedic struggle between groups of fairly equal idiots hungry for power were it not for the vast number of Americans who really care about their country and want their leaders to do the right thing democratically. These people in the middle, and I don't mean moderates, but the poor individuals caught in this titanic and completely indefensible warfare between politicians and their media cohorts from the two sides are the ones who will ultimately suffer as they are forced to choose between the lesser of two evils in so many elections.

Myopic, and totally adversarial gadflies like your self from both political extremes help polarize the nation into warring factions who are becoming increasingly radical in what they say and encourage. Can major violence be far behind? I don't think so. It appears to me even our general populace has sunk to new lows in recent years.

America has apparently become a nation of hate filled, boob grabbing, irrational, bed hopping, lying and cheating men with no understanding of culture, honor, responsibility, reverence, or respect, and who adore politicians who act, talk and posture as they do. Could it be the American male has sunk so far from civilization as to be almost completely controlled by his basic instincts? Has the macho, baby making culture of the Latin American males and the killing culture of the inner city males (and of many Muslims, I might add.) taken control of our young people? How about the women? American women have become vulgar, violent, vain, vindictive, venereal, vicious and vacant in a sorry imitation of the latest version of the male of the species, indeed trying to out do most males in cursing, fighting and sexual activity. Has the self-serving, self-centered, self-righteous, sex-obsessed, cursing "anti-lady" become the new feminist icon? Have Madonna and Hillary become the idols and heros of Americas "new" women?

The most primal primate instincts seem to have risen to the fore as the controlling force for so many. Freed from the moral constraints of religion, the emotional constraints of family and the cultural constraints of community while being constantly bombarded with the unbridled promotion of sex and violence, American young people are growing in anger, animosity and activism against everyone and everything they see as opposing their absolute freedom from any moral constraints. In addition, they are increasing in hatred for those who are benefitting from the existing system. This seems true no matter how hard those they hate have worked, how positive the results, or how many people benefitted or were carried to success by their efforts. Listen to and watch the music videos that our young buy in the millions and to the adulation they express towards their chosen icons who star in them. Exempted from the outpouring of hate and venom despite promoting it are the carriers of the message: the politicians, media icons, educators, sports heros, and activists who are whipping up this violent class warfare. In their diatribes they have been very careful to grant themselves immunity from all this hate and venom.

Is this the future of America? How far are fundamentalist liberals from the killings and mob violence of fundamentalist Muslims? I don't think that kind of violence is very far away. It is infinitely easier and quicker to get attention by violent, destructive action than by peaceful, constructive efforts. 9-11 provides us with a prime example. Eric Hoffer gave a powerful description of these sick and sorry individuals many years ago when he wrote,

"Passionate hatred can give meaning and purpose to an empty life. Thus people haunted by the purposelessness of their lives try to find a new content not only by dedicating themselves to a holy cause but also by nursing a fanatical grievance. A mass movement offers them unlimited opportunities for both."

It truly amazes me that Hoffer so accurately describes the political climate, actors and actions of today in words written during the forties, and fifties. That he so deftly describes the activist left of today, so very long ago is amazing. I shall use his quotes freely in this essay.

It is well known that intense hatred can unite people in a way nothing else can. People who dislike each other intensely will work together, even pause their own battles, to fight a common enemy, real or imagined. It is the power behind the lynch mob, the underlying force within riots, the basic motivator for war and the real enemy of peace. As is often the case, the so called, "peace movement" in our country is a movement that will lead us unerringly to hatred, violence and warfare. It is the last resort to those who have lost the legal, political, intellectual or practical battle against the other side for whatever reason. "When you can't convince them or counter them democratically, bury them with protests and screaming hatred to silence them completely, or finally, blow them up." could well be the mantra of most protest groups. Freedom and individual independent and democratic action is the enemy of these groups that exist only because their programs or ideas do not convince the majority to adopt them. These are the sour grapes losers in democratic elections or determinations that would use any means to impose their will on the majority who did not agree with them in the first place. Once more, the prophetic words of Eric Hoffer,

"The basic test of freedom is perhaps less in what we are free to do than in what we are free not to do. People unfit for freedom - who cannot do much with it - are hungry for power. The desire for freedom is an attribute of a "have" type of self. It says: leave me alone and I shall grow, learn, and realize my capacities. The desire for power is basically an attribute of a "have not" type of self."

Believe me, there are far more "have not" types than "have" types and the percentage seems to be growing. Maybe it's because the "have not" types breed more frequently and so expand their genes in the human pool much faster and wider than the "have" types. In spite of strong economic growth and the widening breadth of middle income types, the numbers of individuals in the lowest economic and educational groups continues to expand. The trap of birth into the lowest economic and educational level is a trap these groups have great trouble overcoming despite countless government programs designed to provide just such a lift. This trap is certainly aided and abetted by self-styled "leaders" of these groups who desperately want to keep their minions in poverty and ignorance so they can control them. Why is this and how did it come to be?

In my own perception the biggest cause is cultural bias aided and abetted by a system of education geared to the poorest students. Excellence is almost deemed an evil in so much of our present culture. That there is a concerted effort to label those who excel intellectually and in earning power in a negative light is obvious. Poor students are told that the reason they are not successful is outside of their control and is being imposed on them by others for their own benefit. People told they are not to blame for their own problems will rarely if ever make any effort to solve their problems. They have a valid and highly touted "reason" not to succeed constantly being rammed down their throats. People who assume the responsibility to solve their own problems will usually solve these problems themselves, even those few problems for which they lack complicity or responsibility. Again, the prophetic words of Eric Hoffer:

"The untalented are more at ease in a society that gives them valid alibis for not achieving than in one where opportunities are abundant. In an affluent society, the alienated who clamor for power are largely untalented people who cannot make use of the unprecedented opportunities for self-realization, and cannot escape the confrontation with an ineffectual self."

Here is a classic example from my own experience: My church as part of their outreach program sponsored a Cambodian refugee family each year. These families, often with three generations, were provided a house to live in, a program to learn to speak English, and help in obtaining employment. Few of their members had any job skills and the language barrier was another major obstacle to normal employment. Fast forward three years for the very first family. The parents and three children are now fluent in English. The grand parents speak some English, but because they stayed home to care for the children they did not have the pressing needs of the parents. All three children rank very highly in a school system known for its high achieving students. Both parents have good jobs and have advanced steadily because of hard work and good skills development. By the time of my last contact with this church, the family has paid back almost ninety percent of the down payment made by the church for their house. They would soon have the title and mortgage in their own names. They were not required to repay the church, but insisted, saying the church could use the money to sponsor another family. They had become successful, contributing, tax paying Americans with no drag on the local economy or welfare programs. Every Cambodian family our church sponsored followed this same pattern.

Why is it that many inner city families, and in particular, African American families are unable to do this? In my opinion it is the vast difference between cultures and an indictment of our own culture that so demeans the unfamilied, the poor and the uneducated. For all their pious pronouncements, so many so-called leaders of inner city communities not only blame everything under the sun except the poor themselves, but insist the poor will remain poor unless they (these leaders) are given the power and the money to dole out to them. Apparently they have never heard the old Chinese saying, "Give a man a fish and he has food for a day. Teach a man to fish and he has food from then on." In actuality, programs to educate and help the poor to pull themselves up by their bootstraps along with a great deal of individual initiative by some of these same people has brought a massive movement of the poor into the ranks of middle and even higher income folks. This in spite of being told constantly they cannot do so on their own.

Do these same "leaders" talk encouragingly about this progress and how individuals have worked hard within the system to succeed and advance themselves up the educational and economic ladder? No! They not only hammer away at absolving the poor from any culpability in their sorry state, but even condemn someone like Bill Cosby when he dared to suggest that the poor have some responsibility for helping themselves. In effect they loudly proclaim, "The enemy is the system that is deliberately denying you any opportunity to climb out of your lowly state. They owe you (lots of money) just for being poor and you should demand it now." It seems to me they are doing everything in their power to keep the poor poor and subservient to their leadership. Why do they do this? I believe it is because they know that hate unites and they use hate skillfully to get their serfs to do their bidding.

Once more I turn to Eric Hoffer for appropriate thoughts:

"All mass movements avail themselves of action as a means of unification. The conflicts a mass movement seeks and incites serve not only to down its enemies but also to strip its followers of their distinct individuality and render them more soluble in the collective medium."

"There is apparently some connection between dissatisfaction with oneself and proneness to credulity. The urge to escape our real self is also an urge to escape the rational and the obvious. The refusal to see ourselves as we are develops a distaste for facts and cold logic. There is no hope for the frustrated in the actual and the possible. Salvation can come to them only from the miraculous, which seeps through a crack in the iron wall of inexorable reality. They asked to be deceived."

Could anyone better describe those who support the liberal left? And then:

"There are many who find a good alibi far more attractive than an achievement. For an achievement does not settle anything permanently. We still have to prove our worth anew each day: we have to prove that we are as good today as we were yesterday. But when we have a valid alibi for not achieving anything we are fixed, so to speak, for life. Moreover, when we have an alibi for not writing a book, painting a picture, and so on, we have an alibi for not writing the greatest book and not painting the greatest picture. Small wonder that the effort expended and the punishment endured in obtaining a good alibi often exceed the effort and grief requisite for the attainment of a most marked achievement."

The liberal left and their subservient gadflies have honed victimism, individual irresponsibility, hate for the productive, and envy for the successful into a high art form. They look at their own failings and evils and loudly accuse their opposition of doing the same things. Their message to their eager hate-filled mob is, "Our opposition is just as evil and conniving as we are, but we'll take a whole lot more from the rich and successful and bring them down to your level— really make them suffer. Who cares if we destroy the country, you'll at least get your revenge." That is indeed a powerful, motivating message and it is working.

I agree with Osama bin Laden in one of his statements. "America will soon collapse into oblivion. All we have to provide is a tiny bit of terror every year or two. It will fan their internal flames of hatred and disturb their already precarious internal power balance. They will soon destroy each other. Islam will then march triumphant over the rotting corpses of these satanic monsters. Their passion for things of the flesh and not of the spirit will surely destroy them." I pray this is not prophetic, but fear that it is.

June 15, 1858 Abraham Lincoln said, "A house divided against itself cannot stand! I believe this government cannot endure permanently..." (paraphrased from this point on) half left and half right. I expect the Union to be dissolved in a massive, violent...

Leaders of the liberal left are indeed doing everything in their power to divide our nation with hate and vitriol while at the same time claiming it is their opposition that is causing the division. Somehow they seem to think that by destroying the nation they will come to power, permanently as a socialist, atheist dictatorship arises from the debris and ashes of the capitalist nation that once was America. The prophetic words of the Scottish historian, Tyler will have come to pass. (See quotes on Page 91) The "shot heard round the world" will have at last been silenced. The serfdom of the middle ages will once more prevail with all new masters–lords and ladies. Virtually all people except those in power will have been reduced to the lowest common economic, social and educational common denominator. We will then have true liberal equality?

I'm sure you get lots of emails and lots of links to blogs, but do you ever read or listen to any who disagree with your opinions? Most liberals I know of listen to or read only the words of those who agree with them. You might browse through a list of my blogs. It has links to lots of stuff you may never hear about. Click on **http://hjbloglist.blogspot.com** and see some different views about a lot of things.

Howard Johnson

Sunday, November 23, 2008

Where now? The economy, down or far down?

Most of our politicians do not seem to be about solving problems. They seem to have become more about creating them with increasing frequency and severity, and using them as clubs with which to bludgeon opponents. Now it looks as if they are going to kill off all America's spirit and incentive to work and create by punitive taxation and wealth redistribution. Read that as take from the haves and give to the have nots. Or, as Karl Marx put it, "From each according to his abilities, to each according to his needs." (taken by threat of prison and enforced by men with guns and handcuffs.)

It looks like the government (who can't manage anything and would seriously "screw up a one car parade") will take over those failing "business that are too big to fail." Between feuding and self-serving politicians and anal retentive government bureaucrats our economy will surely collapse in line with a quote often attributed to a Scottish Historian, Alexander Tytler or Tyler. The true origin of the quote is obscure and might have originated in the early 20th century from an unknown politician or writer. Nevertheless, this does not detract from its accuracy.

See quotes on Page 91

For more information about these quotes and their sources go to **http://www.lorencollins.net/tytler.html**

The recent election was all about money from the public treasury—money for this group or that group—lowering taxes for those who currently pay the least and raising taxes on those who now pay the most. We are among the highest taxed nations in the world and the incoming congress and administration promise more and bigger taxes. Within a year the US will have the highest overall rate of taxation of any nation. This is an indicator of economic doom. Here are the facts.

After the Fannie Mae and Freddie Mac debacles came the gifts of $700 billion in our tax dollars to financial institutions who, because of their own greed amplified by government interference, seriously damaged our economy costing billions of dollars in losses for a great many people. And just how many hundreds of millions did those individuals responsible for the mortgage debacle stick into their own pockets and walk away with? They should be stripped of their property and dumped in jail, but what's really going to happen to them? Well, glory be! They are now in charge of fixing the very fiasco they orchestrated. Something is very wrong here.

Since then we have seen several other leaches with their hands out come to Washington to ask for billions to save their own sorry butts, some even flew there in their private jets. I see no reason why the big three can't do what the airlines did by using chapter 11 to reorganize and become competitive again. I know most pilots had their pay cut in half and many lost most if not all of their pensions. With big three auto workers at about $74 per hour while foreign auto makers in America (who are not asking for a bail-out) pay their employees about $43 per hour. Gimme a break! This is more a bail out of the UAW than the auto companies. Unless they dump those ridiculous pay and benefit scales and become truly competitive, all that money will just disappear down the usual political payoff rat hole. How many more companies are waiting in the wings to dip their hands into the till? Why can't we afford to let them fail? All that money is just sending good money after bad and will only postpone the inevitable. It's bite the bullet now or bite a bigger bullet harder later.

At present, government creates problems because our elected officials ignore or deliberately refuse to see the realities going on all around them. Without exception in virtually all nations, the higher their taxes, the slower their economic growth. It has even been shown that virtually every time taxes are increased, total tax revenue decreases. The opposite is also true. When taxes are lowered, business thrives and grows, the economy becomes more vital, more new jobs are created, and tax revenue increases. Certainly there is a point of no return, but the result of Ireland's drastic cut in business taxes to 12.5% including capital gains clearly demonstrates the efficacy of business taxes far lower than what we have currently. To increase business taxes is one certain way to lower tax revenue and damage an economy. It may make some people feel good to see politicians punish the "wealthy" by taking their hard earned money, but when it costs them their job things may look a bit different. It's low tax rates and a business friendly atmosphere that makes for a successful, growing economy. There have been countless examples throughout history and all over the world. Government taxes and controls stifle creativity, productivity, satisfaction, incentive, and the creation of wealth. The less government controls and taxes the more incentive the people have to be creative and work diligently. This always results in greater creativity, productivity, satisfaction, and the creation of wealth. Even the Chinese have realized that and acted on it. I have asked numerous liberal leftists about this fact but they have no answer. They seem more interested in punishing the "wealthy" (a relative term) and bringing them down than in rewarding diligence, thrift, and inventiveness and so bringing up those on the lower income levels. At the same time they seem to want to reward those who for any reason are unable or unwilling to work to earn their keep.

A look at America's tax systems.

US personal CGT (Capital Gains Tax) is now 15% (5% for lowest income brackets) (Obama has proposed to at least double this rate)

US corporation CGT is 35% (Obama proposed to immediately raise this to 39%)

US Corporate income tax rate is now 35% (Obama has hinted at rates as high as 55%.)

SS tax rates are 15.4% of gross income (that's a flat tax on the first dollar earned up to $103,000,00 per year, no deductions) (Obama has proposed we tax all income at this rate.)

VAT(Value Added Tax) varies from 0% to 9% by state and municipality.

State income tax rates vary from 0% in seven states (2 states tax only dividend and interest income) to 8.14% in NY and 10.2% in CA. New York City adds a 4% city income tax.

Total state tax burden varies from a low of 6.4% in Alaska to a high of 11.9% in New Jersey. Most of the high rate states are in the north east with New York second at 11.7%. California is 4th at 10.8%

Hidden federal taxes on purchases (excise, transport, license fees, etc.) amount to between 15% and 24% of every dollar spent by every individual for everything purchased. This tax falls heaviest on those with the lowest incomes.

Federal gas and oil excise taxes are 18.4¢ per gallon for gasoline and 24.4¢ per gallon for diesel. Since fuel is taxed by the gallon, when gasoline prices fall the percent taken by taxes rises and visa versa.

There are many other hidden and specific taxes and tax exemptions that transfer money from private citizens to the federal, state and municipal treasuries.

All of these taxes—all of them—are actually paid by the public, the consumer, the end user.

IT'S A FACT - Corporations do not pay taxes. Businesses do not pay taxes. Professionals in their professions do not pay taxes. Organizations including those who are not-for-profit do not pay taxes. All of these "taxpayers" merely collect those taxes from customers or clients in the price of their products and services and then pass them onto the government just like the much more obvious sales tax. Even the so-called company paid portion of FICA taxes add to the cost of an employee and so are really taken from the employee.

THEY ARE A COST OF DOING BUSINESS! Just like rent, utilities, advertising, and all other business expenses they end up on the "expense" side of any business ledger and must be balanced by income. All expenses are added into the price of goods and services supplied by the company or individual who is in any business or profession. I really don't know why this is so difficult to understand. The result is that when taxes are raised, the total amount of that increase is passed on to the consumer.

Example: Take a hardware store that sells paint. Say that at present the paint sells for $20.00 per gallon and that the store makes a gross profit of $5.00 on each gallon of paint that yields a net profit after expenses and taxes of $2.00. That's 10% of sales. Now comes the government and raises the tax on net profit to the tune of 50¢ on each can of paint. The store owner realizes this and in order to maintain his level of profitability and be able to support his family, he raises the price of the paint to $20.50 per gallon. He also raises the price of every other item in his store by the same percentage, 2.5%. His competitors, faced with the same tax increase, will raise their prices as well.

You can apply this rule to every business, profession, individual, and corporation in the world. All taxes are ultimately paid by the end user. You can rest assured the guy who is the head of the hardware conglomerate that supplies the paint had his taxes raised as well so his price to the hardware store has gone up another 25¢ which he passed on to the hardware store owner as a wholesale price increase. This 25¢ added to the cost of the paint means the store owner must add that in as well so the paint now sells for $20.75 per gallon. Now think about all the components that go into that one product: the pigment, the oils, even the can and label, all have added to the cost of the can of paint. Let's say all these little increases from the raise in tax add up to another 20¢ in the wholesale cost of that paint. The store owner must now raise his selling price another 20¢ to $20.95.

But wait just a moment. This leaves the store owner with the exact same income he had last year and because of the tax increase everything is now about 5% more expensive. He does some quick calculations and decides that in order to maintain his living standard he must raise the price of the paint (and everything else in his store)at least 5% just to stay even. Then his clerks come to him complaining their take-home-pay has dropped and in the face of rising prices for everything, they need at least a 10% raise. His landlord raises his rent and on and on until that can of paint is now selling for $21.29. So, who really pays for tax increases?

Now let's look at one of those wealthy taxpayers who are going to get soaked by all those raises in corporate and capital gains taxes. Joe is a multi millionaire with a large stock portfolio, some real estate and a good chunk in the bank. His investment counselor called him early last year and suggested that the future didn't look good for several reasons including specifically a drastic drop in the real estate market and a huge increase in income and capital gains taxes. It took Joe more than two months to liquidate most of his real estate and sell many of the American stocks he held. He flew to Ireland and looked into some real estate and business investments there. He lost nearly 25% of his holdings because of the declining markets, but is certain he will gain in the long run because of the vigor of the Irish economy and the Irish capital gains tax of 12.5% instead of the 39% CGT America is facing. He had started a small energy research company in California several years ago that had grown to thirty employees. In August he moved the entire operation and all but five employees to Dublin. He also moved most of his cash to the Bahamas. He will wait to see how the new administration and congress act before deciding what else he must do to maximize his asset growth. His home in Palo Alto has been put up for sale. When asked about his losses from liquidation he replied, "I will be receiving a larger after tax income from a smaller but growing investment so I should make up my losses rather quickly. Right now I am considering moving to Ireland permanently."

The Tax Policy Center, a joint venture of the Brookings Institution and the Urban Institute, two center-left think tanks, said that, "a lower corporate tax rate and a lower capital gains tax would encourage multinational corporations to invest more in the United States and, for a given amount of investment, to report a larger share of their worldwide taxable income to the United States instead of foreign treasuries." With investment capital deserting our economy in huge quantities because of punitive business taxes is it any wonder the American stock market is crumbling? It is interesting to note that as Obama's poll numbers dropped the market gained ground and visa versa. Since the election the stock market has been in a virtual free fall. This drop is the direct result of the anticipated tax increases that are already a major factor in our failing economy.

Let's look at some tax consequences at today's rates:

First, take Ahmed, a resident of New York City at the lowest income level. Assuming no federal income tax look at what happens to $100.00 he earns. FICA tax takes 15.4%, State Income tax takes 8.14% and New York City takes 4%. That takes from Ahmed $27.54 reducing his after tax earnings to $72.46. Then when he spends that amount to purchase life necessities lets say these have the minimum hidden taxes of 18% or $13.04 giving him a total tax burden of $40.58 out of the original $100.00 he earned. That's a rate of taxation of the poorest NYC wage earner of more than 40%. Who said the poor don't pay taxes?

Second, the same earnings in December of Louise, a person in the highest tax bracket. Under the present law, state and city income taxes take the same amount, $12.14. (She pays no FICA tax because she has passed the maximum income) The highest Income tax bracket of 35% takes another $35.00 reducing her after tax earnings to $52.86. When she spends that amount, minimum hidden taxes of 18% take $9.51 for total tax burden of $56.65 out of the original $100.00 she earned. That's a rate of taxation of the wealthiest NYC wage earner of 56.65%, just 41.65% higher than the poorest. This means that the wealthiest New Yorkers pay less than 50% higher taxes than the poorest New Yorkers. Sounds more like soak the poor than soak the rich. Like Joe in the earlier example, Louise has options Ahmed does not.

Let's look at the third example. Louise is not a wage earner. Instead, she makes her living with investments, holding, buying and trading stocks. By holding them for more than a year and then reporting her income as capital gains she would only be liable for 15% tax on her capital gains and dividends. She would have 6.85% NY state CGT and 2.3% city CGT (capital gains tax). So, how does this shake out. Federal CGT would be $15.00, State CGT $6.85 and city would be $2.30 or a total of $24.15, a rate of taxation of 24.15%, lower than the tax rate of the poorest taxpayer. But look at it another way. Of that $100.00 earned, she would retain $75.85. If her ordinary expenses were $5.85 out of that, it would leave her with $75.00 to reinvest to grow business and create jobs for other people. The more investment capital she had, the more jobs she could create and the more the total economy would grow.

Small business owners employ the largest number of workers in the private sector. Recent interviews with many of these businessmen show their planning for the next few years has been scaled back considerably. Most have put off or cancelled expansion plans and new jobs. Some are planning facility closings and layoffs. Some that can are moving off shore while others are closing their doors and going out of business. This does not bode well for our economy and is all a direct result of promised tax increases. I know why rank and file workers are so blind to these realities, but why is it that politicians and the media refuse to recognize them?

Would any of you liberals out there tell me where my math is wrong or what should actually be done that will not destroy the American economy? Facts and logic please!

Thursday, October 23, 2008

Predictions of dangerous factors promising possible economic disaster

For the last year I have been a member of a discussion group here in St Augustine. Called the Socrates Discussion Group, we have between fifteen and twenty-five members, mostly seniors of both sexes, who discuss many subjects, often controversial, for two hours every Monday afternoon. After one heated (but quite civil) discussion late last year I decided to make some predictions for the next year. Here's what I wrote and submitted to them at our meeting on January 7.

Observations and predictions for the future, for the Socrates Discussion Group, Jan 5, 2008.

Howard Johnson

There are several dangerous factors promising possible economic disaster for our nation in the immediate future. That those already in play have not already precipitated an economic collapse is amazing to this writer. I will list them in chronological order.

1. **The trade deficit:** We continue buying more than we sell on world markets. Even as our economy grew in recent years, billions have left our shores for other nations, enriching foreign businessmen and despotic rulers in the process. This money is increasingly used to buy American businesses, stocks, and real estate. More and more foreign investors are also buying up our debt.

2. **Oil, a special case:** As domestic supplies of oil dwindle and limits are imposed on drilling for new oil in our lands, more and more oil must be imported at higher and higher prices to supply our hunger for fuel for our vehicles. This has become the largest exodus of dollars from our economy in our entire history. Many of those dollars go to nations whose rulers hate us and plot our demise.

3. **Mounting debt:** The three tiers of American debt are also growing. Our Federal debt fed by excesses of an irresponsible Congress bent on buying their way into power at any cost to the future taxpayer has doubled in the last ten years. With Social Security and Medicare costs rapidly expanding, entitlements will soon overpower federal revenue. Mortgage debt also has grown, driven by steadily increasing prices for homes and business property, often far beyond real value. People are driving the prices of property steadily upward and often assuming mortgages far beyond their ability to pay. They plan to "flip" their purchase, pay off their mortgage and pocket

the difference for a tidy profit. One blip in the real estate market, actually long overdue, and these mortgages will go into default. Consumer debt for cars, appliances and credit cards is another mounting pressure on a banking system already strained to the limits and fed by the very money we send abroad. With oil sheiks, despots like Hugo Chavez, and Chinese banks supplying the capital, what happens if and when they withdraw their financial support? The likelihood of just one of these collapsing will surely precipitate the rest to do the same. Once America's ability to pay its debts comes into question, everything will collapse and quite suddenly.

4. **The political situation and the next election:** It is this writer's opinion that not only will Barack Obama be the Democrat nominee for president in the coming election, but that he will win in a landslide and will carry a large Democrat majority in Congress with him. Aided by an adoring and highly biased media, Democrats will have complete control of the Federal government.

The result: As soon as the polls show this trend and possibly before the actual election, several things will happen driven by the promise of doubled capital gains taxes along with other tax increases. The housing bubble will collapse, the stock market will crash, and consumers will default wholesale. As debt defaults multiply and investment capital flees our shores, the entire debt support system will collapse. Because we are in a world economy, investment capital will move to places like Ireland, China, India, and even Russia. The loss of the American market will bring with it the collapse of much of the world economy. The result will make the "Great Depression" look like a mild recession. It is my opinion that this is the goal of those on the far left. The chaos that will follow such a total economic collapse is precisely the opportunity they want to take control. Eugene Debs and Earl Browder almost put the Marxists in power during the great depression and I'm afraid their successors will succeed this time. I'm afraid their successors, the far left liberal Democrats led by Obama, will succeed this time and America will sink into a dull gray version of the old Soviet Union, a Socialist/communist dictatorship.

Prediction update, October 16, 2008: Unfortunately, while many of the predictions in the previous paragraphs have come true, revelations of many of the actual reasons are never even mentioned by the highly biased media as they seek to be the determining factor in making the election a liberal Democrat landslide in November. Democrats and the media have been touting a depression for most of the last eight years, repeating the left's mantra, "The worst economy since the great depression," an absolute untruth. In fact, until the Democrat orchestrated mortgage collapse, the economy was among the best ever with low unemployment and high wages. Another of their mantra's, "Bush tax cuts for the wealthy" is also an absolute lie. In actuality, the Bush tax cuts increased income taxes paid by the wealthiest Americans by 2% and decreased those paid by the bottom half of wage earners by 2%. This information comes directly from government statistics. You'll never hear those statistics mentioned by the media for obvious reasons. Incidently, whenever "the left" is used in this article it includes liberal Democrats, entertainers (actors, media personalities, sports figures, etc.) and anti-capitalists of all kinds.

As has been the case numerous times, tax cuts by the Bush administration greatly increased federal tax revenue even as the Democrats predicted a huge loss of revenue. As expected, their grossly erroneous predictions are never mentioned by the media who's extreme bias has become obvious to all but the dimmest lightbulb. By whipping up and encouraging a very successful class hate campaign against business people—the wealthy, big business, and big oil in particular—liberal Democrat politicians and their cronies in the media have created an emotional anti-business, anti-success attitude within much of the public, particularly those ignorant of the facts. Profit has long been an evil thing in the lexicon of the left including the media. This in spite of the fact that in America, profits are the sole source of investment capital, by far the largest force in job creation, and the largest source of federal revenue. There is no question—class envy and hatred for business works, politically. Ultimately it will destroy our economy, and that is quite obviously the goal of the left.

Here are some remarks by Newt Gingerich:

"Today marks the end of one of the most dishonest, relentlessly one-sided campaigns of bias and distortion by the mainstream media in American history.

"The latest tactic in this elite media campaign has been to declare the presidential race over in an effort to discourage some voters from going to the polls. After all, if Barack Obama has already won, why should supporters of John McCain even bother to vote?

"But this election won't be decided by Keith Olbermann, or CNN, or the New York Times. It will be decided by you.

"So annoy the mainstream media. Remember 2000. Remember how close it was. Remember how every single vote counted."

Do any of you readers ever consider the fact that only wealthy business people are included in this organized hate campaign? Many entertainers including sports figures and media talking heads earn far more than most business owners, yet the media dotes on them while ridiculing and condemning virtually everyone in business. Likewise wealthy attorneys like Edwards make millions bilking corporations by misleading courtroom actions inflaming class hatred in juries. Anyone who does not comply with their results are forced to do so by the power of men with guns. Attorneys will only go after those with "deep pockets" for purely economic reasons. Yet these types are held in high esteem by the media. Sleazebags like Edwards are virtually immune to media criticism as long as they are Democrats. Incidently, have you ever heard of a Republican trial Attorney?

While most attorneys in movies and TV shows are portrayed with adoration no matter how wealthy, business people are almost always portrayed as evil, sinister cheaters or stumble bums. There have been and now are many lawyer shows from LA Law to Boston Legal glorifying the legal profession, but have you ever heard of similar shows glorifying business people? Of course not. Those who become wealthy in movies or TV, on the professional game fields, or in the courtroom are praised and held up as role models no matter how crass, immoral, evil, or self indulgent they are. On the other hand, business people who become wealthy are universally reviled, insulted, ridiculed and portrayed as evil monsters. For decades, the evil cattle baron as the villain and the lone poor farmer or cowboy as the hero has been a staple plot for thousands of films and TV shows. This pattern has morphed into the staple of poor employee against evil business man employer in many of today's entertainment offerings.

That many people get their economic and political information from these shows is obvious no matter how in error they are. Emotions almost always triumph over logic. Case in point, the movie The China Syndrome almost by itself convinced the American public that nuclear power was a very bad and dangerous thing and so shut down our entire nuclear power program. This in spite of the fact that nuclear power has the safest record with the least health dangers of any form of power generation. The movie, based on an actual incident at the Three Mile Island nuclear facility, was a fictional story—a fabrication. The facts of the actual incident were the direct opposite of the story. The emergency safety features and precautions built into the plant worked perfectly. The accident was confined to the facility and the safety systems worked perfectly. No dangerous radiation was released and no one was injured. Nevertheless, this Hollywood fabrication falsely convinced the American public that nuclear energy would kill or sicken us all. As a result, no nuclear power plants have been built since, a great loss to our economy.

While the left continues their hate campaign against them, Republicans seem reluctant to speak out with the truth about the root causes of our economic problems. Newt Gingerich is one who does speak out as in a recent article, "A candidate with the courage to tell the truth about Franklin Raines, Chris Dodd, Barney Frank, the Carter and Clinton-era pressures for bad loans, the ACORN pressure for bad loans (trained in Chicago by Barack Obama in his community organizer days) would have an enormous response from a country which is sick of predatory politicians, arrogant bureaucrats, and elitist reporters." Unfortunately, the left (and especially their propagandists in the media) is very capable of personal attacks on anyone who points out these truths with ridicule, hate speech, and false accusations of racism. Together with completely ignoring any negative information about Democrats or positive information about Republicans and conservatives, this produces an extremely false impression of reality in the minds of impressionable (and usually ill informed) voters and the young in particular. Does Tom Brokaw actually expect us to believe that in all the questions submitted for the debate he managed there was not a single one about Jeremiah Wright, Bill Ayers, Father Pfloeger, or Acorn? Give me a break.

Here's a modified quote from my unpublished non-fiction book, The Feudals:

See quotes on Page 91

That is precisely what has happened to our country thanks to the efforts of liberal Democrats. Their "tax the rich and spend taxpayer money to buy votes" philosophy is based in this reality. By pledging more and more money to more and more people, and promising to take it away from the "rich," the Feudals are buying votes motivated by class envy and hatred. It is easy to see that Obama's constant mantra, "Tax reductions and government checks for most Americans while the wealthiest 5% get taxed to pay for it. I'll punish those rich bastards for you." No, those are not his exact words, but that's the appeal of his message, loud and clear. At least the words of Jeremiah Wright, his spiritual mentor, **"God Damn America"** were an honest expression of his feelings. The liberal Democrat campaign follows the same hate driven pattern of racism, class and wealth envy, ridicule, and denigration because they have no ideas or plausible proposals and because hate campaigns work. Their main effort is to accuse Republicans of precisely what Democrats have been doing all along.

Here's what really scares me. I believe liberal Democrats mean to do precisely what they say they intend to do. This includes: 1) Checks for the lowest half of the citizens. That's definitely blatant vote buying right out of Tyler's prediction. 2) Just the promise of the doubling of the capital gains tax is already causing a monstrous flight of investment capital from America. That's what is depressing the stock market and causing job loss. 3) The so-called "fairness doctrine" will probably be passed to silence talk radio. This is actually an attack on our freedom of speech and numerous Democrats are already talking about it. 4) Several McCain-Palin campaign workers have been attacked. I see this violence against Republicans as growing in intensity and number. Incited by the class envy and hate speech from the left, these attacks could quickly escalate. The left doesn't hesitate to use violence to serve their ends. Just ask Obama cohort, Bill Ayers.

A prediction: In addition to what I predicted in January, it is my opinion that given a large Democrat majority in Congress, Obama will continue the destruction of our capitalist economy that the left has worked so hard to achieve. The left will then move us down the road to socialism. Incited by all the hate speech, violence against Republicans, conservatives and those perceived as "rich" will grow in frequency and intensity. From the chaos that follows, a socialist dictatorship similar to the old Soviet Union will eventually emerge just as predicted by Professor Tyler. It will be a bloody and devastating change. As the Bolsheviks did in Russia, or the French did with the guillotine, the wealthy, then the intellectuals, educators, and idealists that started the revolution will be murdered or otherwise disposed of, and the media will be controlled. I wonder how those political satirists from the entertainment world will fare? In the Soviet world dissent was silenced with a bullet or knife. (Trotsky in Mexico for example) My specific prediction is that within the next twenty years the United States will become a socialist dictatorship much like the old Soviet Union.

Right now, during the 2008 national election, here are numerous incidents of voter intimidation like what was recorded by a CNN reporter in Philadelphia. He recorded two Black Panthers in their uniforms blocking the entry to the polling place. One was even wielding a night stick. When he spoke to them he was threatened and recorded the remark, "We are going to elect a black President and nothing is going to stop it." Numerous citizens were so intimidated they left without voting. The left does not hesitate to use intimidation and violence to gain their political ends. Once in power, the left will even use murder as a political incentive to enforce their edicts. It is my firm belief such violence is soon coming to our nation.

Now Obama announces he wants a civilian military force with equal power to the regular military. What for? Maybe he is continuing to follow another leader who brought "change."

The Sturmabteilung (help·info), abbreviated SA, (German for "Assault detachment" or "Assault section", usually translated as "stormtroop(er)s"), functioned as a paramilitary organization of the NSDAP – the German Nazi party. They played a key role in Adolf Hitler's rise to power in the 1930s.

SA men were often called "brownshirts", for the colour of their uniforms, and to distinguish them from the Schutzstaffel (SS), who wore black and brown uniforms (compare the Italian blackshirts).

The SA was also the first Nazi paramilitary group to develop pseudo-military titles for bestowal upon its members. The SA ranks would be adopted by several other Nazi Party groups, chief among them the SS. They were very important to Hitler's rise to power until they were superseded by the SS after the Night of the Long Knives.

I wonder what color shirts Obama's civilian military will wear. Maybe the same uniform now worn by the Black Panthers as they intimidated voters in Philadelphia.

Don't say it can't happen here—it can.

Oh yes, who will Obama pick for his cabinet? How about Franklin Raines for Treasury Secretary, Bill Ayers as the Secretary of Education, and Tony Rezko as head of the Justice department.

Realty check: No, this didn't happen, but it still could eventually. Instead, several of his picks declined, withdrew or otherwise were chastened by gross misconduct, usually tax fraud and deliberate non payment of federal taxes, or in the case of one Republican, withdrawal because of "irreconcilable differences."

Subject: Bar Stool Economics - - Our tax system explained for average Americans

Suppose that every day, ten men go out for beer and the bill for all ten comes to $100.

If they paid their bill the way we pay our taxes, it would go something like this:

The first four men (the poorest) would pay nothing.

The fifth would pay $1.

The sixth would pay $3.

The seventh would pay $7.

The eighth would pay $12.

The ninth would pay $18.

The tenth man (the richest) would pay $59.

The ten men drank in the bar every day and seemed quite happy with the arrangement, until one day, the owner threw them a curve. 'Since you are all such good customers, he said, 'I'm going to reduce the cost of your daily beer by $20. Drinks for the ten now cost just $80. The group still wanted to pay their bill the way we pay our taxes so the first four men were unaffected. They would still drink for free. But what about the other six men - the paying customers? How could they divide the $20 windfall so that everyone would get his 'fair share?' They realized that $20 divided by six is $3.33. But, if they subtracted that from everybody's share, then the fifth man and the sixth man would each end up being paid to drink his beer. So, the bar owner suggested that it would be fair to reduce each man's bill by roughly the same amount, and he proceeded to work out the amounts each should pay.

And so:

The fifth man, like the first four, now paid nothing (100% savings).
The sixth now paid $2 instead of $3 (33%savings).
The seventh now paid $5 instead of $7 (28%savings).
The eighth now paid $9 instead of $12 (25% savings).
The ninth now paid $14 instead of $18 (22% savings).
The tenth now paid $49 instead of $59 (16% savings).

Each of the six was better off than before And the first four continued to drink for free. But, once outside the restaurant, the men began to compare their savings.

"I only got a dollar out of the $20," declared the sixth man. He pointed to the tenth man, "but he got $10!"

"Yeah, that's right," exclaimed the fifth man. "I only saved a dollar, too. It's unfair that he got ten times more than I!"

"That's true!!" shouted the seventh man. "Why should he get $10 back when I got only two? The wealthy get all the breaks!"

"Wait a minute," yelled the first four men in unison. "We didn't get anything at all. The system exploits the poor!"

The nine men surrounded the tenth and beat him up.

The next night the tenth man didn't show up for drinks, so the nine sat down and had beers without him. But when it came time to pay the bill, they discovered something important. They didn't have enough money between all of them for even half of the bill!

And that, boys and girls , journalists and college professors, is how our tax system works. The people who pay the highest taxes get the most benefit from a tax reduction. Tax them too much, attack them for being wealthy, and they just may not show up anymore. In fact, they might start drinking overseas where the atmosphere is somewhat friendlier.

David R. Kamerschen, Ph.D.

Professor of Economics, University of Georgia

For those who understand, no explanation is needed.
For those who do not understand, no explanation is possible.

~ ~

St Peter and the Senator

While walking down the street one day a US senator is tragically hit by a truck and dies. His soul arrives in heaven and is met by St. Peter at the entrance.

"Welcome to heaven," says St. Peter. "Before you settle in, it seems there is a problem. We seldom see a high official around these parts, you see, so we're not sure what to do with you."

"No problem, just let me in," says the senator.

"Well, I'd like to, but I have orders from higher up. What we'll do is have you spend one day in hell and one in heaven. Then you can choose where to spend eternity.'

"Really, I've made up my mind. I want to be in heaven," says the senator.

"I'm sorry, but we have our rules."

And with that, St. Peter escorts him to the elevator and he goes down, down, down to hell. The doors open and he finds himself in the middle of a green golf course. In the distance is a clubhouse and standing in front of it are all his friends and other politicians who had worked with him.

Everyone is very happy and in evening dress. They run to greet him, shake his hand, and reminisce about the good times they had while getting rich at the expense of the people.

They play a friendly game of golf and then dine on lobster, caviar and champagne. Also present is the devil, who really is a very friendly guy who has a good time dancing and telling jokes. They are having such a good time that before he realizes it, it is time to go.

Everyone gives him a hearty farewell and waves while the elevator rises ... The elevator goes up, up, up and the door reopens on heaven where St. Peter is waiting for him.

"Now it's time to visit heaven."

So, 24 hours pass with the senator joining a group of contented souls moving from cloud to cloud, playing the harp and singing. They have a good time and, before he realizes it, the 24 hours have gone by and St. Peter returns.

"Well, then, you've spent a day in hell and another in heaven. Now choose your eternity."

The senator reflects for a minute, then answers: "Well, I would never have said it before, I mean heaven has been delightful, but I think I would be better off in hell."

So St. Peter escorts him to the elevator and he goes down, down, down to hell. Now the doors of the elevator open and he's in the middle of a barren land covered with waste and garbage. He sees all his friends, dressed in rags, picking up the trash and putting it in black bags as more trash falls from above...

The devil comes over to him and puts his arm around his shoulder. "I don't understand," stammers the senator. "Yesterday I was here and there was a golf course and clubhouse, and we ate lobster and caviar, drank champagne, and danced and had a great time. Now there's just a wasteland full of garbage and my friends look miserable. What happened?"

The devil looks at him, smiles and says.......ized."Yesterday we were campaigning. Today you voted."

~ ~

A president's pension currently is $191,300 per year, until he is 80 years old.

Assuming the next president lives to age 80. Sen. McCain would receive ZERO pension as he would reach 80 at the end of two terms as president. Sen. Obama would be retired for 26 years after two terms and would receive $4,973,800 in pension.

Therefore it would certainly make economic sense to elect McCain in November. The results certainly indicate the economic acumen of America's voters.

~ ~

It's not looking good for that bailout plan..... true story.

Back in 1990, the Government seized the Mustang Ranch brothel in Nevada for tax evasion and, as required by law, tried to run it.

They failed and it closed.

Now we are trusting the entire economy of our country to a pack of nit-wits who couldn't make money running a whore house and selling booze?

~ ~

New Rules for the Workplace to Achieve Change and Fairness

You small business owners out there are preparing for life under a Barack Obama presidency. Here are some new rules for small businesses based on Obama's ideals of change and fairness:

As of November 5, 2008, when President Obama officially becomes president-elect, our company will instill a few new policies which are in keeping with his new, inspiring issues of change and fairness:

1. All salespeople will be pooling their sales and bonuses into a common pool that will be divided equally between all of you. This will serve to give those of you who are under-achieving a "fair shake."

2. All workers below management lavel will be pooling their wages, including overtime, into a common pool, dividing it equally amongst you. This will help those who are "too busy for overtime" to reap the rewards from those who have more spare time and can work extra hours.

3. All top management will now be referred to as "the government." We will not participate in this "pooling" experience because the law doesn't apply to us.

4. The "government" will give eloquent speeches to all employees every week, encouraging its workers to continue to work hard "for the good of all."

5. The employees will be thrilled with these new policies because it's "good to spread the wealth around." Those of you who have underachieved will finally get an opportunity; those of you who have worked hard and had success will feel more "patriotic."

6. The last few people who were hired should clean out their desks. Don't feel bad, though, because President Obama will give you free healthcare, free handouts, free oil for heating your home, free food stamps, and he'll let you stay in your home for as long as you want even if you can't pay your mortgage. If you appeal directly to our democratic congress, you might even get a free flat screen TV and a coupon for free haircuts (shouldn't all Americans be entitled to nice looking hair?)!!!

New rules for professionals in keeping with Obama's change and fairness:

Since most professionals are licensed by their states, pooling of income, fees, awards, prizes, etc. will be done on a state by state basis. For example, all New York attorneys will give all of their income, fees, awards, prizes, etc to the NY attorney pool. This pooled money will first be used to pay the federal income tax and the remainder will be divided equally between all NY attorneys. This will serve to give those attorneys who are under-achieving a "fair shake".

The same state income pooling process will also be used for physicians, dentists, football players, actors, accountants, race car drivers—anyone in any recognized profession that is not working as an hourly employee of a company. Those professionals who have underachieved will finally get an opportunity and reward; those who have worked hard and had success will feel more "patriotic."

If for any reason you are not happy with the new policies, you may want to—WELL, YOU KNOW.

A Bit About our Probable Next President

Website about Obama - (No longer available)
http://ahwatukeemusings.blogspot.com/2008/10/barack-obama-william-ayers-acorn.html

Now for the serious stuff, as hard as it is to take politicians seriously.

I am amazed at the responses many of my "Rants" have evoked from the far left members of my family. I have been cursed, ridiculed, called numerous unsavory names including liar and moron, denigrated by members of my family, and ordered never to send emails (that disagree with their political views). It is plain to me that their logic is so weak and their arguments so poor That all they can do is hit me with emotional clubs. It seems to me that is the sum total of arguments from the left. Like DNC chairman Howard Dean's famous rant, "I hate Republicans. I hate

Conservatives. I hate Rush Limbaugh." all they can offer is ridicule, hate, class envy, and name calling. I challenge you liberals to list any positive proposals your politicians have made. I'll wager that those few proposals are laced with bigger government bureaucracy, playing to class envy in most Americans, increased taxes on the "wealthy," or vote buying.

It's an amazing time to be alive in America . We're in a year of firsts in this presidential election: the first viable woman candidate; the first viable African-American candidate; and, a candidate who is the first front running freedom fighter over 70. The next president of America will be a first.

We won't truly be in an election of firsts, however, until we judge every candidate by where they stand. We won't arrive where we should be until we no longer talk about skin color or gender. Now that Barack Obama is the Democrat candidate, we need to stop talking about his race, and start talking about his policies and his politics.

Sadly, the Hollywood left including the main stream media had a major part in selecting the candidates of both parties. This may even have been the single most important factor in terms of the results. In an age when celebrity has become by far the most important factor for any selection, the celebrity treatment afforded any candidate by the Hollywood/New York media looks to far outweigh issues and even reality. Never mind inexperience, animosity toward middle American values, or mentors shouting, "God Damn America," Obama has the celebrity so many Americans worship, especially the young.

The reality is this: Mr. Obama is the current odds on choice to be our next President. Its time America takes a closer and deeper look at him. Some pundits are calling him the next John F. Kennedy. He's not. He's the next George Mc Govern. And it's time people learned the facts.

Because the truth is that Mr Obama is the single most liberal senator in the entire U.S. Senate. He is more liberal than Ted Kennedy, Bernie Sanders, or Mrs. Clinton. He is the presidential frontrunner whose rhetoric is so farther removed from his record than any previous candidate. Walter Mondale promised to raise our taxes, and he lost. George Mc Govern promised military weakness, and he lost. Michael Dukakis promised a liberal domestic agenda, and he lost.

Yet Mr. Obama is promising all those things, and he's not behind in the polls. Why? Because the press has dealt with him as if he were in a beauty pageant. Mr. Obama talks about getting past party, getting past red and blue, to lead the United States of America . But let's look at the more defined strokes of who he is underneath this superficial 'beauty.'

Start with national security, since the president's most important duties are as commander-in-chief. Over the summer, Mr. Obama talked about invading Pakistan, a nation armed with nuclear weapons; meeting without preconditions with Mahmoud Ahmadinejad, who vows to destroy Israel and create another Holocaust; and Kim Jong II, who is murdering and starving his people, but emphasized that the nuclear option was off the table against terrorists - something no president has ever taken off the table since we created nuclear weapons in the 1940s. Even Democrats who have worked in national security condemned all of those remarks. Mr. Obama is a foreign-policy novice who would put our national security at risk.

Next, consider economic policy. For all its faults, our health care system is the strongest in the world. And free trade agreements, created by Bill Clinton as well as President Bush, have made more goods more affordable so that even people of modest means can live a life that no one imagined a generation ago. Yet Mr Obama promises to raise taxes on "the rich." How to fix Social Security? Raise taxes. How to fix Medicare? Raise taxes. Prescription drugs? Raise taxes. Free college? Raise taxes. Socialize medicine? Raise taxes. His solution to everything is to have government take it over. Big Brother on steroids, funded by your paycheck.

Incidently Obama is running many ads saying he will only increase taxes on the top 5% of Americans and leave the bottom 95% alone. This "soak the rich" strategy may please many poor and middle income families with its class envy retribution, but let's look at it realistically. What happens to the vast majority of the income of the 5% wealthiest Americans? A portion is used to buy things and build things that provide jobs and income for many other Americans. By far the largest amount is invested and most of that investment capital is used to build companies that hire employees and create jobs. This builds the economy and creates wealth. Let's use the favorite target of liberal "Big Oil" class envy abuse. Exxon paid $28 million in taxes on about $42 million in profits for 2007. That's as much as the entire lower half of all individual American taxpayers combined. The remaining after tax profits of

Finally, look at the social issues. Mr. Obama had the audacity to open a stadium rally by saying, "All praise and glory to God!" but says that Christian leaders speaking for life and marriage have "hijacked" - hijacked - Christianity. He is pro-partial birth abortion, and promises to appoint Supreme Court justices who will rule any restriction on it unconstitutional. He espouses the abortion views of Margaret Sanger, one of the early advocates of racial cleansing. His spiritual leaders endorse homosexual marriage, and he is moving in that direction. In Illinois , he refused to vote against a statewide ban - ban - on all handguns in the state. These are radical left, Hollywood, media , and San Francisco values, not Middle America values.

The real Mr. Obama is far from what the American public want from every poll taken on the subject of socialist programs. But Mr. Obama will win if people don't start looking behind his veneer and flowery speeches. His vision of 'bringing America together' means saying that those who disagree with his agenda for America are hijackers, racists, or warmongers. Uniting the country means adopting his liberal agenda and abandoning any conflicting beliefs. Should you express any opposition to any of his words or actions the media will brand you as racist.

Other than raising taxes, what has he proposed? Change? What kind of change? Repudiation of the Bush policies? All of them? Rescind the bush tax cut "for the wealthy?" The Bush Tax "cuts" not only resulted in a huge increase in federal tax revenue but the actually resulted in an increase in taxes paid by the top 50% of taxpayers and reduced taxes on the bottom 50%. It would be generous to not say Obama is lying, just that he is grossly misinformed, but I doubt that is the case. It is quite clear to me that he knows precisely what he is doing and where it will take us.

Thursday, September 04, 2008

The T. Boone Pickens Plan for Wind Power and Natural Gas

You've probably seen those T. Boone Pickens natural gas TV ads. Like you, I wondered why. I spent several hours of research to find out just what T. Boone was up to. As one of those evil capitalists he was obviously after increasing his wealth. Here's what I discovered from one source, The Alternative Energy Speculator. Please read my commentary at the end of this article excerpt. It's about a piece describing Pickens and his efforts I read in one liberal newspaper. It reveals just how wrong the entire liberal establishment is about wealth, taxes, investment, profits, and how these harm or benefit Americans.

Dear Reader,

If you follow the energy industry at all, you've undoubtedly heard of the Pickens Plan the massive effort by Texas billionaire T. Boone Pickens that calls for an estimated $1 trillion investment to displace electricity currently produced from natural gas with clean wind power. The Pickens Plan would allow the excess natural gas capacity to be used to power trucks and even cars. What's more, California has already set forth a ballot initiative that would allow the state to invest in the burgeoning market for natural gas-fueled vehicles. The measure, which currently faces no opposition, would free up $5 billion to fast-track the deployment of a million natural gas vehicles on California's roads.

That's all very interesting, yes, but why am I telling you about it today? Well, you see, T. Boone Pickens is no dummy. He may very well believe in the environmental benefits of his plan but he also stands to take enormous profits from it. And you can follow his lead.

To Your Best Days,

Paul Amos

Associate Director, HIS

"One undeniable beneficiary of the Pickens Plan would be Pickens himself. He has bet $12 billion on a massive new wind farm in rural Texas and his BP Capital hedge fund is heavily invested in the natural gas industry."

-The Guardian, UK

How T. Boone Pickens and The "Pickens Plan" Can Make You Rich

Dear Reader,

T. Boone Pickens recently revealed a plan that he believes could be the only real solution to reducing our dependence on foreign oil. I know, that's a pretty bold statement to make. But this is T. Boone Pickens we're talking about--the former Texas oilman who's worth about $3billion...and just so happens to be the 117th richest person in the United States!

I can assure you, Pickens didn't become a self-made billionaire by being on the wrong side of the energy markets. So when he says he's found the only real solution to reducing our dependence on foreign oil, you might want to see exactly what he's talking about.

The Pickens Plan:

A $1 Trillion Transition

You may have only recently seen the ads for the Pickens Plan. But the fact is, this thing's been building momentum for a few years now. You see, Pickens Plan calls for an estimated $1 trillion investment to displace electricity currently produced from natural gas with clean wind power. This allows the excess natural gas capacity to power cars and trucks.

It's an excellent "transitional" plan that can help alleviate hundreds of billions of dollars currently spent on oil, while creating thousands of U.S. jobs.

But the truth is, this "transitional" plan didn't begin with Pickens. It actually began in California, with a little-known "Clean Air Action Plan" that Pickens capitalized on the moment it launched. Back in November of 2006--in an effort to drastically reduce pollution--the ports of Long Beach and Los Angeles adopted a clean air action plan. Within three years, this action plan requires the ports to:

Achieve a 47% decrease in diesel particulate matter (PM) emissions from port-related activity (shipping AND trucking).

Cut smog-forming nitrogen oxide (NOx) by 45%

Achieve a 52% reduction of sulfur oxides (Sox).

Now understand, this is an area where more than 16,800 Class-8 tractor trailers are the only machines strong enough to transport the heavy containers to their destinations. And they transport a lot of them. In fact, combined, these two ports move more than $260 billion worth of traded goods per year. And that number is expected to reach $1.3 trillion by 2025. With that kind of money in play, you know there's a major opportunity for investors. And T. Boone Pickens was the first to the party.

You see, in order to meet the new emission-reduction requirements, the South Coast Air Quality Management District, the state Air Resources Board and the EPA called for the replacement of more than 5,300 trucks with clean-burning Liquid Natural Gas (LNG) trucks.

LNG Fast Facts:

As a liquid, LNG is not explosive. LNG vapor will only explode in and enclosed space within the flammable range of 5-15%. [It must be kept in insulated or vacuum bottle containers as it is very cold. It is kept cold bythe constant vaporization of the liquid in the containers. The less highly insulated the container—the faster the LNG evaporates.]

Benefits of LNG in transportation applications:

LNG is produced both worldwide and domestically at a relatively low cost and is cleaner burning than diesel fuel. Since LNG has a higher storage density, it is a more viable alternative to diesel fuel than compressed natural gas for heavy duty applications.

In addition, LNG in heavy-duty natural gas engines achieves significantly lower NOx and particulate emission levels than diesel.

Essentially, they decided to go with LNG because it could help the ports meet their reduction requirements--but without having to add a hefty price tag to the transition. And guess who got an early piece of that action?

You got it! The one and only, T. Boone Pickens. Pickens owns 40% of a company called Clean Energy Fuels Corp. (NASDAQ:CLNE). This is a company that provides natural gas for vehicle fleets in the U.S. and Canada. It actually designs, builds, finances, and operates the fueling stations too.

Bck in July, 2007, the stock was trading around $13.24 a share. By October of 2007, the stock hit $19.60 a share--giving a gain of more than 48% in less than 4 months.

You see, although Clean Energy Fuels Corp. supplies the LNG, someone still has to supply the engines that run on the stuff. After all, it's not as if GM and Ford are cranking these things out. They can barely stay in business as it is. But there is a small Canadian company (of which 12 percent is actually owned by Pickens) that has designed what could be the most advanced, efficient engine on the planet. And it's powered by LNG. In fact, it's so revolutionary it was awarded the 2007 Industry Innovation Award for alternative fuel trucks.

Bottom line: This engine and this fuel source, which is cheaper and cleaner than diesel, has proved to be the best stop-gap available that can handle the heavy workload, wear and mileage required by the ports and the drivers.

It doesn't hurt that Clean Energy Fuels Corp. is already supplying the infrastructure in the way of LNG fuel and fueling stations too. But the best part is, this engine can actually be swapped with existing diesel truck engines that are already in service. So no need to purchase brand new trucks!

In fact... This Revolutionary Engine Could Actually Save Truck Drivers and Companies Over $353.8 Million per Year! Let's face it...everything comes down to the bottom line. And that's why this particular engine manufacturer is going to make investors an absolute fortune. You see, as I write this, diesel fuel in the port areas in California is already well over $4.96 a gallon...and steadily on the rise. And with the skyrocketing costs of fuel set to go even higher in the near future, truckers are desperately looking for ways to save on energy costs. For them, even a drop of $0.05 gallon would save each truck, traveling 80,000 miles per year and getting an average of six miles per gallon - over $650.

But this engine has proved even better. Once retro-fitted to a current semi, the new engine could save over $21,000 a year in fuel costs! And with more than 16,800 of them servicing the port area, companies and drivers (depending on how the fuel arrangement is met) are looking at a total savings of more than $352.8 million per year. With that kind of money staying in their pockets, it came as no surprise when, just this past January, the ports of Los Angeles and Long Beach approved a $1.6 billion Clean Truck Superfund.

Since the announcement of the $1.6 billion "superfund," this little engine manufacturer has watched its share price skyrocket more than 96.2% And this is in the wake of one of the most volatile markets in recent memory! Now that the Pickens Plan is in full swing, we're expecting share prices to rise least another 143%

Check it out... Ports of Los Angeles and Long beach announcement to approve a new $1.6 billion Clean Truck Superfund. The fund will assist replacing many of the 16,800 Class 8 trucks serving the ports with LNG-powered vehicles. The ports have also introduced a new progressive ban that will remove all pre-2007 trucks by 2012. This company's LNG fuel system is the only alternative fuel technology currently qualified for financial support under the ports' Clean Truck program, within the next 8 to 10months.

In fact, even retail giant Wal-Mart, which operates one of the nation's largest fleets, has joined this company in their natural gas revolution... having picked up four test vehicles to measure the money saved by the switch.

While Wal-Mart, the leader in low cost providers, is claiming the move is for "Clean-Energy Purposes,"the reality is... they're looking at saving several million dollars a year in transportation costs. And as more LNG fueling stations appear across the country (thanks to the Pickens Plan), and with the proven environmental AND cost savings of the switch--investors are now lining up for their share of what this little-known company is about deliver.

How Wrong the Entire Liberal Establishment is

Here's a revelation of just how wrong the entire liberal establishment is about wealth, taxes, investment, profits, and how these harm or benefit Americans.

I just read a full page article about T. Boone Pickens in a typical liberal newspaper. From the article's attitude and description one would think Pickens was the worst kind of scoundrel. They wrote disparagingly of his wealth, the profits he made in oil, and how now he's "cornering the market" on new sources of energy. These include wind and LNG. The article is just another example of the left using class envy to inflame hatred against successful entrpreneurial capitalists and make "profits" a dirty word especially when they tie it in with "excessive." **Liberals just don't get it.** They have no concept of how profits and wealth turn into jobs and economic prosperity and how taxes result in lost jobs and economic depression—"but they mean well."

The Pacific tigers get it. The Irish get it. Even the Georgians get it. The Indians get it and the Chinese get it in spades. All have realized the fact: that "profits" and "profitability" provide job opportunities and build economic abundance, that low taxes encourage savings and investment to fund those projects that create jobs and generate more wealth, and that in the current worldwide economy, the capital to fund these projects goes where it gets the best return. This is why lowering taxes always results in economic success and higher tax revenue and raising taxes always results in a recessive economy and lower tax revenue. This is so pervasive and exceptions are so rare it is virtually axiomatic.

Why then don't the liberals get it? Why are the current liberal Democrats planning to double the capital gains tax and rescind the Bush tax cuts? I find it hard to believe they are so ignorant of reality. There are but three possibilities. 1) They know these facts, but believe voters are so stupid they would sacrifice thousands of jobs just to hurt those rascally wealthy people by electing liberals. 2) They are so ignorant or stupid that they don't know these facts. 3) They know the truth and want to use taxes to "get even with America" and bring us to our economic knees.

The T. Boone Pickens example - While the newspaper article denigrated Pickens for his wealth in comparison with so many poor Americans (those dirty profits from oil), it never mentioned how many good jobs his companies provided, how many families his investments have fed, clothed, and housed, how many young people his enterprises have sent to college, how many seniors are enjoying retirement after working for him, or how much he paid in taxes. How about his wind farm? This was a financial risk that provided jobs for many people and environmentally favorable energy for Americans. Why didn't the paper give him accolades for his efforts for the environment? Was it because he dares to make profits from his efforts? I wonder how long that paper would be in business if it didn't make a profit? Newspapers are dying all over America and the reasons given include low circulation, high labor costs, loss of advertising, and the Internet. The real reason is lack of profit. None of these businesses (newspapers are a business) would go out of business if they were profitable. The reasons given for newspapers dying are actually what caused them to become unprofitable.

Profits - what do they do?

1. They enable companies (that's organized groups of workers) to expand, grow, and create jobs.

2. They enable companies to provide their employees with better pay and benefits.

3. They enable companies to access investment and loans to expand.

4. They enable companies to pay taxes - (Exxon paid 28 million for 2007. That's as much as the entire lower half of all individual American taxpayers combined.)

5. They provide stockholders (owners) a financial return on their investment.

This begs the question, would all you who are castigating profits work without pay? Profits are to business what a pay check is to a worker. Why isn't a paycheck subject to the same disdain as profits.

So kudos to T. Boone and all the other successful capitalists who among other things, provide nearly all the jobs, make almost all the investments, create and develop the technologies, and build the American economy, while paying for most of our bloated, inefficient, and self-serving government. They are the ones who really build our country, not those self-serving, egotistical politicians with their strutting, posturing, and under-the-table grabbing for cash. There was much ado about the famous "bridge to nowhere" in Ketchikan, Alaska. Why didn't Ted Kennedy's "Big dig" in Boston bring out some of the same objections? It was certainly in the same category as it merely moved four miles of a surface freeway underground while not improving anything but the view above ground. It also cost more than 16 billion dollars, many times the cost of the "bridge to nowhere." In spite of the comments of its detractors, the "bridge to nowhere" did have a positive result. It would have gained sorely needed access to nearby land for expansion of Ketchikan. I've been there and seen the possibilities first hand. T. Boone should look into funding that bridge. Under the right circumstances it could be a money maker. Maybe Sarah could convince T. Boone to get the job done.

If the Obama crowd has their way and implements their announced tax changes, the resulting flight of capital from America to elsewhere in the world will make the flight of manufacturing jobs of the past forty years look like a trickle. The resulting depression will make the Jimmy Carter years and even the great depression look like a day in the park.

Saturday, August 02, 2008

Facts, Opinions and Brainwashing - The Liberal Propaganda Machine

I recently had a response to one of my political emails from one of the more liberal members of my extended family. Their words are brief—a typical liberal sound byte—aimed at just a few words, "America's enemies" and "brainwashed," among the several paragraphs of thoughtful commentary. I will list the resulting exchange in oldest first order.

~ ~

Hi all:

I'll bet you don't know I'm a member of moveon.org. Well, why not? That way I can know what America's enemies are saying and planning. It also tells me what line the news media and liberal Democrat politicians are going to use before they use it. Recently I received an email right up my alley since it talks about oil, drilling and alternative energy. I can't believe people actually believe this stuff. Here's the email along with my commentary in italics.

~ ~

Dear MoveOn member,

Last month, conservatives led by Newt Gingrich and Rush Limbaugh sent over a million messages to Congress calling for offshore oil drilling. Then John McCain joined the push for drilling. Now he's running ads saying Obama's responsible for high gas prices, because Obama's energy plan focuses on alternative energy not drilling.

That's mostly true except for the twist at the end. Obama's energy plan focuses on preventing as much drilling, pumping, refining and delivery of domestic petroleum and petroleum products as possible in order to force us into alternative energy regardless of the cost to Americans and to our economy. His plan just incidently includes unspecified alternative energy, but mostly calls for cut backs in energy use—conservation he calls it. McCain's plan provides for price relief at the pump while encouraging the private sector to develop practical and cost effective alternative energy. This is a positive, creative approach compared with Obama's regressive one.

It's a scam. Offshore drilling won't save any money at the pumps for years (although it will boost oil company profits). But some senior Democrats are showing signs of caving under all this pressure and polls show McCain's attacks may be hurting Obama.

The scam is Obama's and moveon.org's foolish statements like that one. The mere threat of offshore drilling after Bush signed the executive order resulted in a rapid drop in world petroleum prices to around $120 a barrel and a corresponding drop in gas prices at the pump of more than thirty cents a gallon in just a few weeks. That reality sure puts the lie to their words. Americans are still able to read the prices at their local filling stations and actually know this is happening.

Here's the truth: Right now, progressives are losing this argument. (Naturally! Because it's false!) We all need to fight back. If we don't, we could end up losing the election AND the fight for clean energy. Substitute the word "expensive" for their "clean" and their statement is true.

We've got a simple, powerful new ad that tells the truth about the Republicans' drilling scam. Will you check it out, and chip in $25 to help get it on the air right away?

Go ahead and watch the ad. Then take a look at the gas prices at your local gas station and see if they're telling the truth. No amount of lies can change an every-day reality we can all see.

---

http://www.moveon.org/r?r=3996&id=13372-9724911-hmXEUhx&t=4

Mostly this web site is a plea for money. Not much real information.

McCain is so focused on drilling because he knows people are anxious enough about energy costs to make this the issue of the 2008 elections. When you're worried about how you're going to afford the drive to work, or how you're going to get your kids to school, and you have no other short-term options you'll be open to anything that might help. McCain is preying on that anxiety by offering offshore drilling as a quick fix. That last sentence should read, "McCain is answering that anxiety by offering offshore drilling as a shot in the arm to ease our pain at the pump while encouraging alternative energy research and development for the long range. It's certainly no quick fix."

Offshore drilling won't fix gas prices or our dependence on foreign oil. There simply isn't enough oil offshore or in the Arctic, and it will take up to a decade to get what little is there. Even then, we would only save 3 or 4 cents a gallon! That's a pathetically untrue statement when we can all see that just the threat of renewed off shore drilling by American oil companies has already resulted in a 30 cents per gallon savings. Who are they trying to fool? I know that few Americans understand commodity futures markets, but those moveon.org geniuses certainly should. That price drop was fully predictable in the futures world where oil prices and thus gasoline are determined. They just can't be so stupid they don't understand that.

Offshore drilling is a gimmick but it will be the gimmick that works for John McCain if we don't push back now. Our new ad has a regular-looking guy telling the truth straight into the camera. Isn't that the best thing for people to hear right now? That "regular looking" guy has to be kidding! Maybe he just has been cooped up so long with his moveon buddies he hasn't seen what's already happening to gas prices at the pump.

If you can, contribute to help get the ad up in more cities so more people see McCain's drilling gimmick for what it is:

http://www.moveon.org/r?r=3996&id=13372-9724911-hmXEUhx&t=5

The only gimmick I see is that foolish little charade on Youtube. I suppose there are some who are so brainwashed with the left's propaganda they believe it lock, stock, and barrel in spite of all the actual realities to the contrary.

Thank you for all you do.

Noah, Ilyse, Laura, Andrea and the rest of the team

Sources: "Will More Drilling Mean Cheaper Gas?", Time Magazine, June 18, 2008

http://www.moveon.org/r?r=3834&id=13372-9724911-hmXEUhx&t=6

No wonder their information is so far from the facts, look at their sources. Liberal leftist propaganda magazines like Time are not about to publish anything but pro Obama and anti oil articles. And their other source, themselves, how arrogant can you get? You can't use your own words to prove your own words. But of course, how else could moveon.org confirm anything they say?

Ho

~ ~

One liberal reply:

How can you claim to be a fair, objective commentator when you use such phrases as "America's enemies?" I'm pretty convinced by your tirades - convinced that you are the one who is brainwashed (your label for anyone who doesn't agree with you).

~ ~

My response:

Not so. It's my label for almost anyone who DOES agree with you.

Did I ever say I was a fair, objective commentator? In all honesty I don't believe there is a single "fair, objective" commentator in the world in spite of those who claim to be. We all have our opinions and prejudices and particularly so as relates to the political arena. Politics is a completely emotional purview with less rationality than anything except possibly religion. Nothing makes the blood boil more than an opposing political or religious opinion. The driving force in both is almost pure peer pressure, a very powerful influence. Birds of a feather. . . .

America's enemies: I should have elaborated on that phrase you objected to. I see America as an entrpreneurial, capitalist, free market nation. I believe that is what made us the large nation with the broadest spread of wealth for the widest range of common people. Poor in America generally have far more than in most other nations of the world. There probably are a few small nations with a more equal distribution of wealth, but I don't know for certain which ones, maybe Switzerland? I believe having the power, control, and driving force of our economy in the hands of literally thousands of corporations, cooperatives and individuals as being infinitely superior to a single corporate entity, government. As I understand the politics of the left, liberals etc, they consider just the opposite to be the superior system and despise capitalism, free enterprise, and even the word, profits. Therefore, I consider those individuals and organizations who propose European style atheistic socialism as the style of government for America as America's enemies. Certainly they are in opposition to the America I love and enjoy.

I believe American capitalism with all its obvious faults is far superior to socialism (see the latest two articles starting on page 187 for more of my opinions on this. The current economic blossoming of Ireland, China, India, and other similar nations is a direct result of free enterprise capitalism exploding when the chains of socialistic governments are removed. If that doesn't make socialism the enemy of capitalism it certainly places them in opposition to each other. I realize that it is not a completely black and white issue and there are many variations in the application of laws and rules in the nations mentioned, but there is no question about free enterprise capitalism beating the pants off of socialism in virtually every respect. Maybe what we really have is a battle between big, expensive, bureaucratic, all intrusive, and all powerful government with liberal socialists in control of everything (your side) versus a much smaller monitoring and law making and enforcing government that guides and helps entrpreneurial entities of all sizes achieve success, wealth, and yes, profits, (my side).

Oh yes, read the comments starting on page 267 for an example of a more typical, earthy liberal response. There is not a single rational comment in that entire response.

I also believe strongly in our Constitution and Republic. I believe our Constitution and its Bill of Rights to be a fabulous protection of individuals from an intrusive and controlling government as the founders intended it to be. I certainly would not want any kind of theocratic government and that includes atheocratic. See my blogs, **http://hjchurchandstate.blogspot.com** and **http://hjatheocracy.blogspot.com** for more on this. I know you and many on the left disagree with my opinions expressed in these blogs, but reading it might just do you good—at least cause you to think outside your normal box.

Ah, brainwashed, a much abused catchall phrase for lumping all who disagree with one's belief systems. Later on in this BLOG I'll give you some examples of how I have been "brainwashed" into my "tirades." Still, I should know better than to use such an overused and misunderstood phrase. Just one question: what do you call it when one is brainwashed with actual facts?

I belong to an active discussion group who meets in St Augustine every Monday at one in the afternoon to discuss virtually anything from global warming to city government to the price of fuel. The "Socrates discussion group" includes a wide variety of seniors with diverse backgrounds and opinions. From far-left atheists to far-right Christian fundamentalists, this group is an amazing collection of great minds that somehow manage to have civil discussions on the most sensitive of subjects. Two members in particular have become really good friends in spite of our opinion differences. Bob is a far right wing Roman Catholic and Abe is a far left atheist. I find myself in opposition to some of the statements of each in about equal measure. I tend to have friendlier arguments with Abe than with Bob. Believe it or not I have become the defacto arbiter of the group, often refereeing passionate arguments and getting us back to the point of the discussion. I sorely miss those wonderful gatherings of such diverse minds when I'm not in St Augustine.

The fact is, I love diverse opinions and the deep thinking they bring about. I listen, make my own points and learn many new viewpoints. Maybe I am being "brainwashed" by all these diverse opinions. Abe paid me what I consider a fine compliment at our last meeting when he expressed how he enjoyed our discussions. He said, "Howard, you are the only person I consider a conservative with whom I can have rational discussions. I'll miss your comments while you're away." That from one who is at least as far left politically as most of the Grimm clan.

I have never let differences of opinion get in the way of the love and respect I have for family and friends and especially the entire Grimm clan. I have had several meaningful (mostly friendly) exchanges with you and a few other Grimms over the years. Incidently, I find it far easier to make a point with my brother-in-law than with my sister. I think she still reverts back to those heated dinner table discussions from the late 30s and early 40s where we were always at each other's throats and neither would give an inch. We argued constantly, but our deep love for each other was never in question.

I'm always pleased to word joust with you. Unlike some who take issue and simply curse at me and my opinions without saying anything of consequence, your replies are usually intelligent opinions. I really appreciate that. Of course, there's not much rebuttal in your latest terse response, but you didn't use pointless vulgarities and that's a plus. About the "brainwashing." Au contrair, mon cheri! To me being brainwashed is believing in and espousing things in direct contradiction of the facts even when the facts, not opinions, are simple, obvious and provable.

Current example: Obama promises that if elected he plans to more than double the capital gains tax. Sounds great, doesn't it. Soak the rich. Get more tax income. The historic facts show just the opposite. Without exception, every time the capital gains tax has been raised, revenue from this tax has gone down. Every time the capital gains tax has been lowered, revenue from this tax has gone up. There are lots of valid reasons for this phenomenon but basically investment money goes where it earns the best return. Capital gains taxes directly affect income on investment money (capital). You wouldn't pay fifty bucks for an item if you could get the same thing elsewhere for twenty bucks, would you? In a world economy, the really big money (like the bankrolls of the oil sheiks) goes where it earns the best return. Doubling the capital gains tax in effect doubles the cost of investment in America and will drive billions in capital out of the US and into places like Ireland, China, India and other nations without such punitive taxes. Those billions will no longer be available for American business expansion—read that as good jobs and economic success, prosperity. So, go ahead, soak the rich with increases in capital gains and other taxes, and watch our economy take a real nosedive while unemployment skyrockets. It will be the American worker who will get punished. The wealthy individuals and businesses will merely move their capital to places other than America where they receive a better net return.

Just like the threat of American oil companies being permitted to drill on the continental shelf offshore has had a major affect on the price of petroleum fuel, the mere threat of massive tax increases is already driving capital out of the US. You idiots! WE NO LONGER DRIVE THE WORLD'S ECONOMY! WE'RE NOW JUST ANOTHER COG IN THE GEARS!

Some years back when Boeing was laying off thousands and Seattle was taking a serious economic nosedive there was a sign erected on one of the main roads out of town. The sign read, "Would the last person to leave Seattle please turn off the lights?" Well, let me assure you that if Obama is elected with a liberal majority in both houses of Congress, and if he implements the programs he is promising, all you hard-working Americans can kiss prosperity and the good life goodbye as investment capital and expansion will flee our shores far faster than manufacturing jobs did forty years ago. The resulting crash will make the early thirties look like the good years. The new sign on the New Jersey Turnpike will read, "Will the last person to leave the US please turn off the lights?" I ask all you class hatred types, what are you going to do when there are no companies left to hate—or to work for? How will you get health care then? (See Detroit.)

Sure, lots of what I said in the preceding three paragraphs represents my opinions, particularly the projections of disaster. Unfortunately there are substantial historic facts to back those opinions. I'd like to hear some really rational rebuttal. How about explaining to me how and why Obama's planned tax increases will not result in what I said it would. How it won't deprive the poorest Americans of their jobs while the wealthy move their money making investments overseas. And don't tell me it's illegal. Just consider the oil sheiks, George Soros and Marc Rich. Also, explain why petroleum prices dropped so precipitously after the Bush announcement. I wonder, do liberals ever offer factual, rational arguments to anything?

Five Brainwashes

Brainwashing: I did mention earlier I would say more about that, so here it is, at least an example of how I have been "brainwashed."

Moveon.org wrote: "It's a scam. Offshore drilling won't save any money at the pumps for years (although it will boost oil company profits)."

BRAINWASH #1: Those profits will benefit American workers with jobs, American stockholders with income, American investment with a good return and yes, even pay more taxes to the American government. Not to mention that it would mean less money for oil sheiks to ship their Lambhorginis by air all the way to England for a proper oil change. Wouldn't that be a shame. Apparently moveon.org is against new jobs, new investment opportunities, and new prosperity for Americans. (The last sentence was an opinion that could be a fact.)

BRAINWASH #2: Monday, July 14, 2008 - George Bush signed an executive order lifting the ban on offshore drilling.

See: **http://www.foxnews.com/story/0,2933,381761,00.html** for details of the order.

BRAINWASH #3: The mere threat of offshore drilling after Bush signed the executive order resulted in a rapid drop in world petroleum prices to around $120 a barrel and a corresponding drop in gas prices at the pump of more than thirty cents a gallon in just two weeks. That reality certainly puts the lie to their words.

BRAINWASH #4: Americans are still able to read the prices at their local filling stations and actually know this is happening.

Moveon.org wrote: "**Offshore drilling won't fix gas prices or our dependence on foreign oil. There simply isn't enough oil offshore or in the Arctic, and it will take up to a decade to get what little is there. Even then, we would only save 3 or 4 cents a gallon!**"

BRAINWASH #5: That is a pathetically untrue statement. The amount of recoverable petroleum in offshore deposits and the time required to drill for it is merely an educated guess of known fields. Many times actual drilling finds much more (and sometimes less) than predicted. There is also the probability of finding new, undiscovered fields. We can all see that just the threat of renewed offshore drilling by American oil companies has already resulted in a 30 cents per gallon savings. (see BW #3) Who are they trying to fool? I know that few Americans understand commodity futures markets, but those moveon.org geniuses certainly should. That price drop was fully predictable in the futures world where oil prices and thus gasoline prices are determined. Liberal Democrats just can't be so stupid they don't understand that. Maybe it's just, "Don't bother me with the facts, my mind's made up."

Saturday, June 28, 2008

It Is Impossible for Liberal Media and Politicians to Tell the Truth

Liberals probably won't want to read this because these indisputable facts indicate some basic truths that don't agree with their la la land agenda of non ideas. But, hey! Mr. and Ms. Liberal, you can't counter the truth by ignoring it.

Liberal politicians and the liberal media are flat-out lying to the public about the effects of taxes and how their tax policy differs from the conservatives. Here are some facts right out of the US Government. After Bill Clinton increased income taxes in 2002, the wealthiest half of taxpayers, the top fifty percent, paid 84% of the income taxes. That meant the bottom half, those with lower incomes paid 16%, right? Liberals and the media kept saying Bush's tax cuts were "Tax cuts for the wealthy." Since the Bush tax cuts took effect, guess what! The wealthiest 50% have paid 86% of the income taxes meaning the lower earners, the bottom 50% paid only 14%. And those percentages were of a much larger federal revenue because lowering taxes gave business the incentive to invest in expansion and create jobs. That sure puts the lie to the liberal's mantra, "Tax cuts for the wealthy." According to my math that meant the wealthiest taxpayers had an increase in taxes of 2% while the poorer tax payers paid 2% less. That sure doesn't sound like "Tax cuts for the wealthy" to me.

The truth is—and you will never hear this from Democrats or the main stream media—lowering taxes and especially capital gains taxes, always generates more jobs, lowers taxes more on the poor than on the wealthy, and increases tax revenue totals. Raising taxes always does the opposite. It makes me wonder, did any liberal ever take basic math in grade school? Does any liberal understand that10 % of $100,000 is a lot more than 20% of $20,000? Does any liberal understand that doubling the capital gains tax will stop a lot of business expansion, cost many jobs, and send more business offshore resulting in major damage to our economy? If the idiot you are trying to put in the Whitehouse gets what he promises, the Jimmy Carter years will look like a bonanza. Of course, who ever accused a liberal of rational thinking or action.

There's another proposal being pushed in Washington that scares me. It's called, "The Fairness Doctrine." Sounds really nice, doesn't it? Good old fairness. It's actually a free speech suppression doctrine right out of NAZI Germany in the 1930s. It is designed to silence talk radio, the single strongest voice of dissent against an oppressive and dictatorial American government. Hey you idiot voters! If you don't like talk radio, TURN IT OFF! No one is forcing you to listen. Of course the left would like to muzzle talk radio. They want to turn it off for everyone permanently since it tells the truth about them. The next thing these NAZI liberals will be doing is burning all the books that disagree with their agenda.

There was an interesting broad spectrum survey of more than a thousand Americans taken about a year ago and one of the questions was something like, "What percentage of Americans do you think are having a hard time financially, are worse off than they were six years previously?" This cross spectrum of Americans answered on average 47%. Remember that number. Another question asked in the survey was are you personally better off, about the same, or worse off than you were six years ago? 55% said they were better off, 30% said they were about the same, and

15% said they were worse off. Think about that! Their perception was that 47% of others were worse off while the reality was only 15% considered themselves worse off. The other interesting question was about job security. The survey showed a whopping 67% thought the average worker was afraid they were going to lose their jobs while only 8% of those questioned thought they were in danger of losing theirs. That is amazing. I think it really demonstrates how the doom and gloom media distorts reality in the minds of the average American. Of course, that's how they make their money.

People want to hear and see about murders, accidents, disasters, famine, pestilence and all other kinds of human and creature misery. Did you ever see one of those ads soliciting donations to charity showing happy, healthy, well clothed children? Of course not. There might be millions of those, but photographers seek out the sick, starving, disease ridden, dying, little ones to try to get your sympathies and open your wallets. Misery like sex, sells. It's the stock-in-trade of Hollywood and the entire entertainment world including the news media and the ad writers. That's in spite of the fact that it portrays a grossly distorted view of virtually everything. Throw in a whole lot class envy and hatred for business and those who provide the vast majority of jobs and you have a real case of making the worst out of a good situation.

I see many of these distortions every day. One murder in a city of millions. What about the 999,999 who made it through the day without getting murdered? Five and a half percent unemployment. That means that 94.5 out of every 100 people that could work actually have a job. Sounds like 94.5% employment to me. With all the media hype about recession and supposed bad economic times it's a wonder the economy continues to grow. We've yet to have a quarter of negative economic growth in spite of all the doom, gloom, and constant recession talk in the media. Looks to me like those imbeciles actually want a recession. At least they are doing a powerful job of selling the idea to the unsuspecting public. I wonder why they didn't do this when things really were worse during the Clinton years and certainly during the Carter fiasco. Hmmmmm!

And oh yea! Attention all you anti-war people. Did you know there is a war going on right here in America that is rapidly overtaking Iraq and Afghanistan in violence and death? Why aren't you up in arms and protesting this war? Do you even know the war I'm speaking of? Add up the killings and mayhem along our southern border with that in most American cities and you'll find a death toll that is higher than that in both Middle Eatsern wars together, and that toll is rising. Yes, it's a drug war, not a war on drugs. The drug cartels virtually own our neighbor to the south. At least they are able to operate in relative impunity and have complete control of many areas along our border. I'm sure they are waiting impatiently for the opening of the border for Mexican truckers so they can move their operations north into the US. Take a look at one of their drug banks in Mexico. It's shown in my earlier rant of January 14 2008. Scroll down to the rant on that date and see the photos.

I wonder what will happen if the liberals and their champion of unidentified change do end up controlling our government. Well, I can tell you one thing. It will no longer be our government. It will quickly become their government. Government of the people, by the elite, and for the elite. That will give us a real recession or depression which they will promptly blame on the Republicans and George Bush just like every other calamity they have engineered. I have found there was one president who, during his administration, drew more blatant hatred and animosity even than George Bush. So George, don't sweat the idiots that spew hate at you. You are definitely in pretty great company. The president I mentioned who was hated even more than GW? Abraham Lincoln.

Thursday, June 05, 2008

Some Disturbing Observations Seldom Reported by the Media

Here are a few facts and opinions I have collected from many sources. Quite a few were gleaned during my research for my book, A Convenient Solution, on the future of fuels and energy in the US. Please note that my comments about the negative press given business, profits, capitalism and especially "Big" oil by no means indicate these are all pure, honest and blameless. It's just that their negative aspects are grossly distorted while their positive are completely ignored. It's one hell of a lot easier and popular for those with limited knowledge of business and industry to condemn and vilify than to take the time to learn and understand the truth. Those who would destroy us know and use this to incite hatred among the masses for those institutions that have been instrumental in creating the greatness that has been America, including the highest standard of living and the broadest distribution of wealth among its people of any nation.

Consider these facts:

1. One of the biggest problems among America's "poor" is obesity.

2. Millions of people from all over the world are trying to come here.

3. With the exception of the oil-rich dictatorships, the cost of motor fuels to the consumer in the US is lower than in any other country, even if you remove the taxes on fuel in the rest of the world.

4. We still have the best health-care in the world and the most productive pharmaceutical industries. (That will change with Obamacare.)

5. Home ownership is much higher here than anywhere else in the world.

~ ~

These are just a few of the many positive observations. But now read about a few troubling observations and realities. Keep in mind my comments in the opening paragraph.

The success of Al Gore's ridiculous book, movie and his receiving the Nobel prize.

The complete, unquestioning stance of the media about global warming, its cause, and the extreme danger it poses for humanity. The unwavering political correctness of human caused global warming and the suppression of any doubts, negative information (facts), or commentary regarding global warming.

21,000 scientists have signed a petition saying human caused global warming is bunk. One of these, the President of the Czech Republic, offered to debate global warming with Al Gore. The Pied Piper of the global warming crowd refused as he has refused to debate any other of these scientists.

Virtual any dissent from the holy tenet of global warming is greeted with ridicule and disdain by the politically correct media. Rarely is supporting evidence provided.

Global warming even accepting it as true and under its worst possible reality, is not nearly as dangerous or threatening a menace as several other problems we are virtually ignoring. The rising cost of energy, the associated transfer of trillions of dollars from our economy to those of nations, mostly Islamic and socialist dictatorships that urge our destruction, and the active prevention of our use of all but a tiny portion of possible new and available energy and fuel sources are all far more immediate and dangerous facts than global warming at its worst.

The introduction of the cap and trade bill in Congress, a bill that promises huge, unprecedented increases in fuel costs, taxes, and debt in our country. The only beneficiaries being politicians.

The idiocy that is our handling of our borders and the invasion of millions of illegal aliens from all over the world. This includes the invasion of criminals and the many murders and other crimes now committed by illegals especially along the border. The facts, deliberately hidden by the media and government officials, about the war going on near our border with Mexico and even inside our country that has now become far deadlier than the war in Iraq.

The prohibition of our drilling for oil in Anwar, along our coasts and virtually every domestic source of crude.

The complete silence of the media about the huge oil field in North Dakota, a field that has as much as 400 billion gallons of recoverable sweet crude. That's enough to supply all of our domestic need for at least the next fifty years. Drilling is now underway, but it will be several years before the field can produce significant amounts of crude. I would not at all be surprised to see efforts mounted to block drilling in this area as well. (See Boom on page 62.)

The completely unfounded and distorted accusations and threats made by liberal politicians against our oil companies and the constant reporting of this in the media.

The continuing harangue against American oil companies by liberals and the media is the main cause fuel prices are so high. This in spite of the fact that government takes a minimum tax (profit) of twelve times as much money from fuel prices as do the oil companies.

The blocking of construction of any new refineries for 32 years.

The blocking of construction of any Nuclear power plants for the last thirty years.

The ongoing prohibitions against needed coal-fired power plants.

The efforts being made to shut down some major hydroelectric plants and remove their dams and water impoundments.

The constant hate filled harangues against "Big" business, capitalism, entrepreneurship, and free enterprise by liberals and the media. This includes the successful convolution of the word, "profit" as an evil thing. This is sophisticated use of class or economic envy to incite anger against those very institutions that built the nation and economy that has provided the highest standard of living for the most people the world has ever known. Hell! The biggest problem our poorest people face is obesity.

Taxes - Is it conceivable that the ordinary citizens of this country hold so much class hatred for the wealthy that they will sacrifice their own well-being in order to inflict a little financial punishment on the "wealthy?" Do those same citizens realize the dirty little fact that they are paying about 25% in hidden federal taxes for every dollar they spend from the very first dollar they earn? Do they realize those hidden taxes amount to more than the total of all income taxes? Do they realize the wealthy do not have to pay that much on a large portion of their income. Do they realize that corporations including individuals who incorporate as professionals, businesses, professionals — any one who sells any product or service — **do not actually pay any taxes** but merely pass them on to the consumer? Do they realize that every dollar paid by corporations is one less dollar those corporations have available to invest in expansion and new jobs? Do they realize how wantonly their elected represented spend their tax dollars on getting themselves reelected using earmarks and pork barrel projects? Do they wonder how much of that money finds its way into the politician's pockets by devious, untraceable routes? Do they remember how a thousand dollars magically grew into a hundred thousand dollars in cattle futures? Do they ever wonder who the lobbyists and contractors are that benefit from those give aways? Do they ever wonder how many of them are related to the one who instigated the project? Just ask Harry Reid.

The people of Ireland finally realized the folly of massive taxes and controls on business and reversed their tax policy, controls on and attitude toward business. In less than thirty years they have gone from virtually a third world country where no foreign capital and little of their own was available to the single most dynamic national economy in Europe with thousands of major investors pouring money into the fastest growing business-driven economy, maybe in the entire world. The Irish finally got it!. Their low taxes and business friendly environment has moved them from dirt streets, outside plumbing and horse drawn carriages in just thirty years to manicured concrete city streets and neighborhoods, modern bathrooms, more jobs than the populace can fill, and a shortage of BMWs and Porsches. I've been there and I've seen it. (**2015 added note:** Unfortunately, between efforts of left leaning politicians in the European Union and in Ireland, along with some home-grown excesses, their prosperity has waned since.)

The rise to Presidential candidate of a virtually unknown man with few significant accomplishments other than compelling oratory.

The most significant call of Obama's oratory is change with absolutely no words about what that change might be. The hints he's made about what he will do if elected do not bode well for our economic survival as a nation.

The only significant proposals hinted at by Obama are deliberate defeat and withdrawal from Iraq, the cancellation of the Bush tax cuts and the imposition of massive new additional taxes.

The newly revealed hate filled racist rants of The Reverend Right and Father Michael Pflager. Add to these, the long standing hate rhetoric from their close friend Louis Farakahn.

The ridiculous false positive comments of Nancy Pelosi regarding Iran's President, Mahmoud Ahmadinejad's actions in Iraq.

The constant efforts of the left to bring about our defeat in Iraq.

The efforts of our media to describe our troops in Iraq in the worst possible light while describing the Islamic terrorists as insurrectionists or even freedom fighters.

The constant implication that our forces in Iraq are torturing Iraqis in the face of overwhelming evidence to the contrary.

The complete absence of any media reports about the overwhelming support and appreciation our forces are receiving from ordinary citizens in Iraq. Contrast this with the frequent portrayals of the terrorists hate for Americans as being that of the majority of Iraqis. (**2015 Added note: We sure screwed that up, didn't we?**)

~ ~

There are many more observations from all over the world, but those listed are enough to make one wonder. It would be impossible for anyone to devise a better, more effective, or more complete plan for the destruction of America than the efforts covered in this list. I cannot believe this is not being done by plan. There is just too much that does not make sense for it not to be deliberate and directed. I believe there are many individuals in politics, in the media, in the entertainment world and in other venues that are actively promoting the complete destruction of our economy and nation. I cannot conceive of at least some of the liberal Democrats in Congress, in the states, and in the judiciary not being fully aware that their actions as noted in the above observations are going to destroy us. I also cannot conceive of the main stream media being duped by these people. They can't be that stupid. They have to be involved. I am sure there are a large number of well meaning Americans that are aiding and abetting this cabal unwittingly.

I wish to cite one simple political example. Every member of our Congress has to know the following facts: A reduction in taxes has almost always resulted in increased federal revenue. Movement in the capital gains tax rate has always resulted in associated counter movement in total tax revenue. When the rate is raised, tax revenue goes down. When the rate is reduced, tax revenue goes up. In spite of this fact having been proven time and time again, Liberals are now promising huge tax increases. Those people just can't possibly be that stupid so the only rational conclusion is that they are making every deliberate effort to destroy our economy. The only rational explanation for that is that they either plan to build a socialist state on the ashes of the old US or that they want to force us into some sort of new world socialist state. I cannot conceive of another option except possibly the efforts of Islam to destroy us. I see China as an unlikely instigator since we have become their cash cow, at least for the present.

There are similar situations related to virtually all of the listed observations. For instance, global warming has become a cash cow for many people and organizations worldwide. (There are at least a hundred web sites asking for donations to support their talking about global warming.) It has become a multi billion dollar part of the economy. Proponents have just proposed one of the most costly bills which will be a drag on our economy and will generate a huge bureaucracy whose cost and controls will have an even larger cost effect on our economy. Add all these costs to the obvious drain from purchase of foreign oil and it is plain to see that our economy is under major if not deadly attack. And it is backed, supported and even driven by the radical socialists and Marxists that have taken control of the Democrat party and most of the media.

Intoxicated by incited class envy and the opportunity to "get" those hated "business" wealthy, bosses, and imagined "masters," the sheep in the Democrat fold and other misguided members of the voting public are about to blindly "cut off their noses to spite their face. By the time they realize their error it will be too late.

Monday, June 02, 2008

A few thoughts for early June

A Hodge-podge of Ideas, Thoughts, and Observations:

Using insects as a source of oil and protein, a huge untapped renewable source, possibly far more oil than all the petroleum we have ever had.

Dubai is investing in power systems for electric vehicles and complete electric vehicles and PHEVs.

http://www.electricdrive.org It looks like they are planning for when their oil runs out.

Great Late news: The US Geological survey has just announced a huge new field of sweet (low sulfur) crude has just been surveyed in North Dakota. The Bakken Formation is larger even than the Saudi Arabian field and could be twice its size making it the largest oil field ever discovered. It has been known since 1951. The USGS did an initial study back in 1999 that estimated 400 billion recoverable barrels were present but with prices bottoming out at $10 a barrel back then the report was dismissed because of the higher cost of horizontal drilling techniques that would be needed, estimated at $20-$40 a barrel. With oil above $100 a barrel, this field can now be processed economically. It could supply all the crude America will need for as long as 70 years. (**2015 Note:** Look at what has happened since, see page 62.)

Before you start dancing in the streets, let's see how quickly the environmentalists can get Congress to outlaw drilling there. Of course, the price of fuel posted on so many street corners, infuriated motorists and truckers could mount such a force that those environmental special interests in Washington might not be able to have their way. With the current flavor of the election rhetoric against "Big oil," the new federal government could see this as an opportunity to advance socialism and put the government into the oil business to mine and distribute this oil. Considering the gross inefficiency of government in any endeavor that will probably double the end cost of that crude to refiners. I wonder who the government will hire to drill for the oil and operate the business end? China perhaps?

This brings me to another proposal for oil. Let's charge a 30% tax on all oil imports and exports with a minimum of $50 a barrel while leaving domestic oil that stays in the country tax free. We should do everything in our power to keep that money out of the hands of the politicians or bureaucrats. It should be placed in a fund in a bank and distributed in total to companies who produce useable, non fossil fuel at the rate of $.75 per gallon produced. As the volume of non fossil fuels increases past the point where the payout from the fund is greater than the input, reduce the payout to the point where input equals output. Make this adjustment on a monthly basis. This will stimulate the domestic oil industry, discourage oil imports and exports and stimulate a domestic alternative fuel industry. Nobody gets a payoff. No earmarks are used. There are no pork barrel projects involved keeping political hands out of the cookie jar. I know no legislator would propose such legislation. They would fear the fury of their lobbyists and that would injure their cash cows.

How about converting all that fat from liposuction to fuel? Centia is a new process that converts animal fats to useable fuels.

China is drilling in our backyard while we look to increase our energy costs by imposing a cap and trade system. The rest of the world must be laughing at the stupidity of the Lieberman-Warner cap and trade bill which will probably add as much as $1.50 to the price of a gallon of fuel and make many things and especially fuel so expensive we have to curtail its use or stop using it all together (unless we are very wealthy or are members of the bureaucracy or hold political office.

While we debate this ridiculous and expensive (to Mr Average American) cap and trade bill, slant drilling is enabling China and India to drill for oil that lies under our Continental shelf immediately off the Florida coast. If you want to blame anyone, blame the liberal environmentalists who have effectively driven the price of fuel through the roof by preventing American oil companies from drilling in the Gulf of Mexico and most other places with proven oil deposits. They want us all to be riding bicycles or walking to satisfy their warped sense of necessity. Of course the politicians will still be motoring and jetting around using fuel they don't have to pay for just as they do now. All of that expensive fuel will be paid for by your money.

Think about American oil companies being forbidden to drill for proven oil deposits around Florida to protect shoreline ecosystems. Sounds great, doesn't it, protecting the environment. Now that we are not drilling in these fields, the world's largest oil company, PetroChina in cooperation with Cuba is now drilling not far from Key West where American companies are forbidden to drill. Using slant drilling, they can take the oil from underneath us and, yet, we're not doing a damn thing about it. Ask any liberal what they plan to do about that. I pray none of their undersea wells blows. (as they have in a few other areas) If they do have a blowout, the Florida keys and Everglades will be irreparably damaged. PetroChina has none of the environmental controls on drilling and drilling techniques required of American oil companies. So much for our politicians protecting the environment along our shores. As far as "big oil" is concerned, last year, PetroChina overtook Exxon as the world's largest publicly traded oil company. There goes all that potential profit and billions in taxes from our shores to China. The

Chinese are laughing at our stupidity all the way to their banks. Real smart move, that. An enemy bent on destroying our economy could hardly have accomplished more.

Father Michael Pfleger received $225,000 in grants to his church from a Barack Obama earmark. This is the priest who said, "America is the greatest sin against God." and "racism is as natural as the air we breathe." Make no mistake this is all extreme racism being used to stir up blacks against white America.

This Catholic priest and the Reverend Right have made many remarks that have opened my eyes to the hatred for America being preached in some black churches. I have heard Farakahn and didn't realize how many followers of this man's hate campaign there were in the black community. This hatred is so much like the hatred being taught in Muslim madrassa schools. It makes me wonder if we haven't pushed ourselves into a very dangerous corner from which there may be no escape. I can only imagine the violent anger that will come from the inflamed black community should Hillary manage somehow to wrest the nomination from Barack at the convention. If not, there is then the general election. No matter what he says or does, McCain will be painted as a rabid racist by blacks and most of the extreme left. Any charge he levels against Barack will be called racist no matter how accurate or unrelated to race. I wonder what kind of sermons will be preached at Trinity during the campaign. I believe this will be one of the most hate filled elections America has ever seen. I have no doubt that any close finish with the decision unclear will result in a violent reaction should McCain win. I think it quite possible that it will trigger home grown terrorism and black vs white violence. If it happens you can thank those so called holy men who are inflaming their congregations precisely as the mullahs have inflamed their followers. What these so called men of God say is certainly the opposite of all Christian principals of any Christian church I have known of previously.

Interesting information on Barack Obama's background.

http://www.rollingstone.com/politics/story/13390609/campaign_08_the_radical_roo ts_of_barack_obama/3

Father Michael Pfleger quote, "Hillary thinks, 'I'm white! I'm entitled!'" I agree she thinks she's entitled, but it has nothing at all to do with her race. Of course, the father and apparently the ministers at Trinity United Church have to know their words will probably lead to violence in the streets. Their goal appears to be the complete destruction of the nation. Father Pfleger describes with the words, "America is the greatest sin against God." Either he firmly believes that and is acting on it, or is deliberately lying to promote his own agenda. In either case he is wrong

Barack Obama said Saturday he has resigned his 20-year membership in the Trinity United Church of Christ in Chicago "with some sadness" in the aftermath of inflammatory remarks by his longtime pastor, the Rev. Jeremiah Wright, and more recent fiery remarks at the church by a visiting priest. As far as I am concerned, this changes nothing. He has demonstrated who he is by how he has lived, how he voted, who his friends are, who his associates are, what he has accomplished, and especially his own words.

I am pleasantly surprised at the number of blacks I hear who describe Barack Obama as a black revolutionary and will refuse to vote for him. These are thoughtful individuals like Gale from Kentucky who said this primary battle alone has inflamed racial tensions and set back the existing black progress into main stream America at least twenty years. She says if Obama is the Democrat candidate, all this has made her to decide to vote for a Republican for the first time in her life. She also described the activist ministers as black racists.

Race hustlers have been active for many years: "There is a class of colored people who make a business of keeping the troubles, the wrongs and the hardships of the negro race before the public. Having learned that they are able make a living out of their troubles, they have grown into the settled habit of advertising their wrongs - partly because they want sympathy and partly because it pays. Some of these people do not want the Negro to lose his grievances, because they do not want to lose their jobs."   — *Booker T. Washington, 1911*

Nancy Pelosi announced that it wasn't the surge that brought about the recent successes in Iraq. It was due to Iran's President, Mahmoud Ahmadinejad's help the Iranians have given us in Iraq. Can you believe any American could make such a statement? I find it amazing and reprehensible that a member of our Congress would make such a clearly untrue statement and praise the man and nation that is supplying the terrorists with weapons and men who are daily killing Americans. Her blatant lies make those of our former Philanderer in chief almost palatable. Now it looks as though the latest efforts of our combined military forces, the surge, is having great results, and that Iraqi forces are taking over more of the burden of protecting Iraq and routing terrorists. Nancy and friends will do whatever they can to discredit or distort these facts about our nation's efforts. A victory for Iraq and expulsion of foreign terrorists is happening. For the first time ever, combined forces have retaken the port of Basra and driven the militias out of Sadr City. An Amarican/Iraqi success and complete victory would be a disaster for these leftists, and now it looks to be possible if we can finish before the left can snatch defeat out of the clutches of certain victory.

Oh yes, did you know that Barack Obama voted against a Senate resolution calling the Iraq Revolutionary Guard an Iranian creation? This in spite of the fact that they are mostly Iranians and carry arms made in or obtained from Iran and are proven to be trained and directed by the Iranian military.

I wonder if Ms. Pelosi heard her friend Mahmoud say there are no homosexuals in Iran? That's true, and the reason is **they are hanged**. You don't have to wonder, it is done publicly and the Iranians including Nancy's friend Mahmoud brag about it.

I love Governor Schweitzer of Montana who said, "we're not going to lose our gun rights in Montana. You can bet on that, but I can assure you of this: Montana will continue to take the lead to make America energy independent. We're not going to allow dictators to push us around anymore. We have an infinite supply of energy in this country. We just have a finite supply of resolve to get it right. We're already giving $2 a gallon to dictators who are trying to destroy our way of life. Look, I support the concerns that people of the world have with carbon dioxide but we have the technology right now to produce all of our energy domestically, to drive all of your cars, run of all trains and plains, light all of your light bulbs without importing oil from them and we can sequester our CO2. Right here in Montana." And he's a Democrat.

21,000 scientists have signed a petition saying human caused global warming is bunk. One of these, the President of the Czech Republic, offered to debate global warming with Al Gore. The Pied Piper of the global warming crowd refused as he has refused to debate any other of these scientists. I wonder why?

Oh yes, when we were in Glacier bay in Alaska a few weeks ago I learned that most of the glaciers that are flowing into Glacier Bay have stopped receding and are now advancing. To my knowledge, no one in the main stream media has ever reported that fact. I also learned that in 1767 the entire bay was filled with a glacier being fed by the dozen or so that remained. Most of the recession of that glacier happened between 1767 and 1850 after which it slowed and finally the feeder glaciers, all that were left, stopped around 1990 and have since been advancing. I also learned that the local natives, the Chiklit people, once lived far up in Galcier Bay. Their legends say they were driven south out of their land by a rapidly advancing glacier that advanced, "as fast as a running dog." It advanced so fast they were unable to take many of their belongings and had to abandon them and run for their lives. There are no historical records, but this probably happened When the glacier receded, they visited their former lands and found them scoured clean and not a place they could live. This probably corresponded with the time of the "little ice age" which wiped out the Norse settlement on Greenland after five hundred years of farming and raising cattle successfully during the medieval warm period. During this little ice age there was much starvation and crop failures in Europe. This also brought about the historically recorded migration of many Norse as well as Normans to the shores of the Mediterranean.

In Glacier Bay, several Park Rangers came aboard the ship to explain the glaciers for us. I met and talked with one of these Ranger, a young woman, who invited us to ask questions. I asked her why the glaciers had been advancing for almost twenty years in the face of global warming. Her reply was very interesting. She said that even though the terminus of most of the glaciers were advancing they were still shrinking by getting thinner. When I pointed out that according to recent measurements, all of the midpoints of the advancing glaciers were at least thirty to forty feet higher than they were in 1990, she didn't have an answer. That certainly doesn't indicate they are getting thinner. I don't think she knew that. Then when I commented about the black cover of the American Glacier and that the black cover must accelerate melting she said it didn't and that it was so thick it acted as an insulator. When I said that was contrary to the very well established heat transfer effect of black body radiation and pointed out that the darker sections had quite obviously melted more than the lighter, she again had no answer. Then she said that's what they taught her in her training. I said that no matter what she had been taught, the laws of physics and energy transfer are constant and immutable. I smiled, apologized for making her uncomfortable and suggested that I might not be the only on these visiting cruise ships who knew what I knew. I also suggested that she confirm what I said with her superiors.

Human caused global warming menace is a convenient myth that serves the agenda of those who hate America, hate capitalism, hate everyone who has more than they and like Howard Dean, "Hate Republicans, hate conservatives and hate Rush Limbaugh." Even accepting that global warming is as supposed and at its worst, it does not pose nearly the danger as do numerous other menaces we rarely even talk about. The destruction of tropical and temperate rain forest, overgrazing of pastures, salination of crop lands, shortage of fresh water, all of these pose much more serious clear and present danger than global warming at its worst. Of course, the threat of Islamic terrorism and imposition of Sharia law is a much bigger menace to the world than any of the others. Unfortunately, these are not politically correct, nor do they provide grist for the mills of those who would crush America as does global warming. The Lilliputians in Congress would rather joust at windmills, fill their pockets, revel in their power, and curse the things that made America great.

Quite frequently I have heard liberal friends and family members say they never listen to talk radio because its all extreme right wing lies and propaganda. Lately I have begun asking them if they had ever heard any of the conservatives on talk radio. What amazed me was that all but one of them told me they had never listened to talk radio and wouldn't ever even consider doing so. I asked them how they could pronounce judgement on those they had never heard. The answers were quite revealing. The most frequent response was that their words were all lies and hate rhetoric. When I asked them if they ever heard the words and tone of the rants of Ted Kennedy, Nancy Pelosi, Harry Reid, Howard Dean and the like, they usually replied saying something like they're just politicians, that's what they do. That was a revelation to me. These liberals firmly believed that members of their own party spoke lies and hate rhetoric—that all politicians do. They also accused the media of being biased toward the right. That makes me howl with laughter and helps me to understand why factual arguments have no affect on the sheep in the liberal fold. Suffice to say that time and time again analysis of the big three in TV has shown they all repeat negatives about Republicans many times more than similar negatives about Democrats and frequently ignore serious Democrat misconduct entirely. In interviews, they will repeatedly ask soft ball questions of Democrats while hurling high fast curved balls at Republicans. This is not just my opinion but has been confirmed by several media watch dog groups. The difference between the main stream, left wing media including the New York Times and conservative talk radio is that talk radio hosts loudly proclaim their bias while the main stream, or "drive by" media as Rush calls them, claim objectivity when they are at least as much in the liberal camp as talk radio is in the conservative one.

Oh yes, liberals have even become so brazen as to speak openly about using the so called, "Fairness Doctrine" to destroy talk radio and so silence most of the few voices of dissent. One of the major steps in developing a socialist dictatorship is to silence dissent. Hitler did it, Stalin did it, in fact all Communists nations did it as soon as they came to power. Venezuela's fat little dictator did it just recently. This brings to mind an old saying I really think is so on the monet, "Judge them by what they do and with whom they associate."

Liberals have long and often compared Nixon to Hitler, Reagan to Hitler and Bush to Hitler. Now they have decided it is wrong to make comparisons to Hitler to one leader: Iranian President Mahmoud Ahmadinejad. That makes you wonder why, doesn't it? Speaking of Hitler, I remember listening to some of his speeches when I was in school. One didn't need to understand German to feel the hate in the character and delivery of his words, the non verbal message.

Communication experts say that a major part of all verbal communication is non-verbal. To me, Hitler's speeches and those of Ahmadinejad sound the same. Both are in a language unknown to me yet the non verbal message is exactly the same, hate and anger. I hear precisely the same non verbal message of hate in recent rants from many on the left including Howard Dean, Ted Kennedy, Hillary Clinton, Sylvia Mckinney and the latest from the reverend Jeremiah Right and father Michael Pfleger. It is clear to me these are all similar communications of hatred intended to arouse and inflame to action. That action being precisely the same as the words the instigators of lynch mobs use to incite those mobs to perform their lawless violence. These are certainly not the speeches of those who would like a reasonable discussion to resolve a conflict. These are the speeches of those who want violent action of retribution for grievances often blown far out of proportion, that are imagined, or that serve the purposes of the speaker.

It seems to me that liberal Democrats with the aid of the media and supporters like George Soros hate capitalism and are planning to turn America into a secular socialist state. The old axiom **"government of the people, by the people and for the people"** will be changed to **"government of the people by the government and for the government."** Using class hatred and wealth envy to incite anger and even violence against the people who provide the jobs, create the wealth, and guide and generate the thousands of independent corporations and individual entrepreneurs that put most Americans to work. While China and other socialist nations are moving into capitalism and growing their economies at fantastic rates because of it, our country is poised to descend into the socialist misery pit. It will probably take a decade or two, but we are headed to becoming like the China of thirty years ago where one ponderous, inefficient monopoly operated everything "collectively." We are headed into the socialist gray morass where everyone is equal in poverty. Except, of course, as the pig said, "Some of us are more equal than others." It will be the sad end to an experiment in democracy which created the most free nation and the widest distribution of wealth among its citizens, of any nation, ever. Or maybe we'll become a state like our neighbor to the south, Mexico where there is no middle class only the very wealthy and the dirt poor, ruled by a government riddled with corruption and inefficiency. I wonder where our poor will be able to emigrate?

LIBERAL DEMOCRAT COWS are all multi-colored. Most are multi-racial, multi-cultural, multi lingual, and/or multi-national. 10% are homosexual, won't have calves and so never give milk. 25% are too busy going to peace rallies to have calves or give milk. 35% are on strike and refuse to give milk - The 2% Hollywood cows won't have calves because they're afraid it will ruin their career if they produce milk - 38% are feminist activists who hate bulls - 72% believe all Republicans are white bulls. The 25% who do have calves and produce milk place most of it in their family coffers and share very little with the less fortunate cows. All believe the government should guarantee them free barns, free hay and free veterinary services.

CONSERVATIVE REPUBLICAN COWS are many-colored, like bulls and believe having calves and producing milk is their main purpose in life - 85% organize into cooperative dairies and create dairy conglomerates - their cooperatives produce a milk surplus which they keep for a "rainy day" - soon 10% of the cows control 95% of the milk - they resent being forced to provide increasing amounts of their milk to non-producing cows - 72% believe all Democrats are anti-bull cows who are doing to them what the bulls usually do but without the benefits - 90% believe Democrat cows should start having calves and producing milk - 38% believe all forests should be cut down and converted to pastures - 2% control the cooperatives and are buying up all pastures to provide for themselves.

CENTRIST COWS are all pale greyish brown, don't know if they like bulls or not, and are neutral about having calves and producing milk - they are distressed by the huge dairy conglomerates, but won't do anything about them - they think all liberal Democrat and conservative Republican cows are, "out to get them" - 34% put off having calves until it's too late because they just, "can't make up their minds" - those that do have calves haven't a clue what to do with the milk they produce, but know they won't put it in the hands of the cooperatives - 97% will firmly position themselves straddling every fence with their mooer on one side and their udder on the other, "Mooudders?" - nearly all have not the slightest idea of whether they are coming or going.

Wednesday, April 30, 2008

Some Reasons for the High Cost of Oil

This is a perfect example of how governments, and in particular, socialist governments, can and do destroy the viability of any wealth creating endeavor.

Look at what is really happening to oil production in nearly all of the oil producing nations and consider why the price of crude is going to continue to go through the roof. It's a pattern that is being repeated in virtually every oil rich nation in the world. Consider the basics of oil exploration and extraction.

Exploration and discovery - It is getting more and more expensive to find new fields of oil as all the easy ones have already been discovered. Most oil fields will produce for only ten to fifteen years after which the cost of extraction increases the cost of that oil to more than the price at which it can be sold. If it costs $125.00 a barrel to extract and the going price is $115.00 a barrel, the field is shut down. Hundreds if not thousands of oil fields have already gone this way worldwide. (Of course, some of them that shut down when oil was $20.00 a barrel are being reopened like the huge fields in West Texas.) Oil exploration companies know this and are constantly searching for new fields. This costs a great deal of money, with greater and greater risk of failure. Oil exploration equipment wears out and costs a great deal to replace. These costs must come out of the profits from oil production starting with the first barrel of oil.

Extraction and transport - As oil is extracted, fields slowly give out and the cost of pumping including equipment maintenance and replacement goes up as the flow rate goes down. These costs too must be provided for out of the profits of the companies that extract and transport the petroleum.

Refining and distribution - Converting crude oil into saleable gasoline and fuel oil components is another infrastructure intensive activity necessary to turn petroleum into the end products that finally generate the money to pay for all that exploration, extraction, transport, refining and distribution. No one actually makes a dime until that fuel is finally sold to the end user. During the process from the ground to the user's tank, around a third of the petroleum is used or lost. At every level in the process a portion of the profit must be set aside to cover not only the direct costs of the three (or six) activities, but also the maintenance and replacement of all parts of the required infrastructure from seismographs and drill heads to tankers, pipelines, delivery trucks and fuel pumps. Lose any part of the whole and the system breaks down.

Unfortunately, nearly every oil exporting nation in the world is treating their petroleum as a money tree, skimming profits for the benefit of those in power and neglecting to invest profits to feed the petroleum goose that's laying the egg of black gold. Here's a quote from a Newsweek article by David G. Victor on April 17, 2008 about Mexico's oil company, Pemex.

"Pemex generates two fifth's of the Mexican government's income and is a lucrative employer, but it is ailing from neglect. For years the government has milked Pemex of cash without giving it the wherewithal to invest in and develop new sources of oil. When President Felipe Calderon proposed last week to reform Pemex and encourage more private investment in oil exploration and refining, his leftist opponents shut down the country's legislature in protest. Pemex, they claimed, is a cherished national treasure that must not be pushed into private hands."

Those lefties just can't stand to see private enterprise succeed in providing good jobs, putting people to work and taking them off of government dependency, can they?

"Mexico is hardly the only country that treats its state oil companies as ATMs for governments, unions, cronies and others who siphon the rich benefits for themselves. A large fraction of the world's oil patch is struggling with the problem that bedevils Calderon: how to make state-owned oil companies (which control about three quarters of the world's oil reserves) more effective at finding and producing oil. Venezuela's oil output is flagging. Russia's state-owned gas company, Gazprom, is on the edge of a steep decline in production. And in different ways many of the world's state-owned oil companies are struggling to keep pace with rising demand. Simply privatizing them is politically difficult, and thus most of the world's oil-rich governments are struggling to find ways to make state enterprises perform better.

"Even among state oil companies, Pemex's performance is notably poor. Used as a cash cow for the government, Pemex has never been able to keep enough of its profits to invest in exploration and better technology, the lifeblood of the best oil companies. Until a few years ago, Pemex invested essentially nothing in looking for new oil fields. It relied, instead, on the aging Cantarell field, which was discovered in the 1970s not by Pemex but by fisherman who were angry that the seeping oil was fouling their nets and assumed that Pemex was to blame. Pemex brought the massive field online with relatively simple technology. A scheme in the late 1990s extended the life of the field, but that effort has run out of steam. On the back of Cantarell's decline, total output from Pemex is sliding; some even worry that Mexico could become a net importer of oil in the next decade or two. They're probably wrong, but even the idea makes people nervous."

Mexico is but one example of how government run industries can become so riddled with corruption. Mexico's Constitution requires that its hydrocarbons be owned by the people. This translates to their being controlled by corrupt politicians who have no incentive to make the operation generate a return on investment or even become self sustaining. The end goal of virtually all politicians seems to be to take as much money as possible from wherever it can be taken by whatever means necessary to further their political careers.

Quoting David G. Victor once more, "Part of the problem is that risk taking, which is essential to success in oil, is strongly discouraged. My colleagues at Stanford, in a study released last week, have shown that a system of tough laws that control procurement make managers wary of projects that could fail. Although such laws are designed to help stamp out corruption, a noble goal, they are administered by parts of the Mexican government that know little about the risky nature of the oil business."

Government politicians, socialist leaders and dictators, despots of all kinds who run governments, and the vast majority of their subjects haven't a clue how to manage any kind of business profitably. They understand virtually none of the risks of business and the risky nature of the oil business in particular. When it comes to choosing between investing profits in their enterprise to cover risks and for benefits that may come in the future or promoting their own fortunes by sticking the cash into the public's pockets for candy and toys, you know what they'll choose. Politicians will use it to buy votes or favor. Socialist leaders will use it to satisfy the masses. Dictators will use it to control their subjects. Despots of all kinds will use it for personal aggrandizement. Virtually all government members will use it primarily to strengthen their hold on power. The concept of investing profits back into the enterprise to cover risks or for deferred gain later is as alien to them as would be little green men from Krypton. No one from the left has the slightest clue how to run and sustain an enterprise. All they really know how to do is destroy those who do. There must be an axiom here somewhere.

Look at what the left has done to our American oil industry. First of all, they have made the entire industry the focus of constant class warfare with their hate campaigns. Next, they have prohibited exploration in virtually all of the promising areas in and around the nation. They have even prevented exploration in the Gulf of Mexico while giving the green light to our good friends in China to do so together with our other good friends in Cuba. That's really a smart move that is certain to benefit the environment in the Gulf and keep oil spills from soiling our coasts. If the Chuck Schumers in our Congress have their way, the "obscene billions in profits" of our oil companies (actually a relatively small return on investment in the long run) will become obscene taxes in the hands of Senator Schumer and friends. Then they will have even more money to use in pork barrel projects and earmarks designed solely to buy votes to insure their reelection.

Teddy Kennedy's "big dig" in Boston is the champion so far. The Big Dig was a project to take a pre-existing 3.5-mile (5.6 km) interstate highway and relocate it underground. It ended up costing $14.6 billion, or over $4 billion per mile. It did absolutely nothing of what it was touted to do, but it did buy Teddy and his boys a lot of votes and other more direct benefits at the expense of federal tax payers. Any private citizen who had any part in such a monstrous boondoggle would have been vilified in the press, denounced by politicians, tried in the courts and probably have ended up in jail. But because he's liberal Democrat Teddy Kennedy he still sits in the Senate and curses others who are rank amateurs at misappropriation of public funds. And he will continue to be a champion of pork barrel projects and earmarks because he can get away with it. I guess the moral I was looking for is, Steal from a few, even a few thousand people and you will go to prison. Steal from the public treasury and if you support liberal causes, they will make you a saint. Hate campaigns and stealing public money must not bother the public much. In fact it seems to help politicians gain office. Maybe that's why there are more indicted and convicted criminals sitting in Congress than in nearly any other public group of similar size.

Thanks to the use by the left of class envy in fomenting hatred for virtually all successful businesses and industries, their friends in the media make billions by beating up on "greedy capitalists" and turning "profits" into a dirty word. They seem bent on doing to American industry what the Mexicans have done to Pemex, what Chavez is doing to the Venezuelan oil industry, and what the Russians are doing to theirs. That's certainly strangling the goose that's laying the golden eggs all because it's infinitely easier to destroy than to build. It amazes me that so many people will actually cut their own throats to spite those who have achieved more than they just because it's easy. The joy that small children seem to express by destroying sand castles and other things built painstakingly by careful hands seems natural and we usually laugh at such antics. Sadly, unscrupulous leaders whip this tendency into a political force for destruction when those children become adults without the wherewithal to build and create for themselves.

Violence is the province of those who lack: the patience to build and create, the will to control their envy, the intellect to understand the real world and the love to control their hatred. It takes skill, caring, determination, intelligence, and time to learn how to build and create anything of value. None of these are required to destroy that which we cannot equal. A classic example is the soldier who slaughtered Archimedes simply because he couldn't understand what the symbols drawn in the sand by Archimedes represented. Other examples include Czech Jan Hus (burned at the stake), the thousands killed by the Inquisition, the imprisonment of Gallileo and others like him, the demolition of ancient Buddhist statues by the Taliban, even the current flush of terrorism. All of these represent the temporary triumph of intolerance and ignorance over reason, usually through force of violence.

Friday, April 04, 2008

Lemons and Lemonade - Blending into the Culture of America

I have read Michelle Obama's Princeton theses in light of the controversy it interjected into the campaign and the attention all kinds of media have given it. Considering its source, I see nothing radical, dangerous, or even very controversial in it. I see it as a very normal expression of a young, intelligent black woman in the America of 1985. I think there is a way for the average American to understand it in the broad American culture rather than in the black culture segment within that broader culture from whence it originated. Merely replace each word white in the thesis with the word, American or even, non black wherever it refers to race and it becomes much more understandable.

America has assimilated many different ethnic and racial subgroups over the years. Many of these had to fight their way through prejudice and bigotry to become truly integrated into the American melting-pot. Yet even many of these still maintain at least part of their heritage and their culture. Many live in neighborhoods or even cities where they are with mostly others of their own ethnic background, often bound by language which tends to isolate them. In these circumstances, natural as they are, it becomes easy and convenient to blame those outsiders for many of the individual's and the group's problems. Successful members of these groups may even use the overcoming of these often imagined problems as their means to success. Unfortunately it is far easier to succumb to the temptation to blame others other than engage in the hard work of overcoming these problems in a positive manner.

There are many groups who have actually done this in America. Nationalities like the Irish, Italians, Germans and other Europeans faced with terrible discrimination and bigotry at first, then overcame it and became integrated into America, at least mostly. Of course, these were all white or Caucasian people and thus more easily integrated. I think you would find that those immigrants who came to our shores in the late nineteenth and early twentieth centuries did not see it as very easy. Look at the non Caucasian immigrants from China, Korea, Viet Nam, Cambodia, The Phillippines and elsewhere on the Pacific rim. Still in the process of integration, many of these people became highly educated and successful, some say driven by cultures that prize education, family continuity and self reliance. Few of these people used discrimination as an excuse for poor performance.

The latest cultural, ethnic invasion of America by Latinos may be creating another group to use the excuse of being denied advantages by those in the majority. This is an easy trap for those who lack the will to succeed on their own to fall into. Blaming the powerful in any venue, social, economic, ethnic, racial, and/or political, as the reason for one's failure absolves a person from any fault. The blame game has been taken to the heights of excusing one's own failure. Whether it's big business, big government, the boss, the wealthy, or even Whitey, it's the same lame and actually damaging effect. It actually keeps many so-called disadvantaged people from solving their own problems. After all, Since I am not the cause of my problems, I cannot do anything about them. As long as a person can blame those other than themselves, they have an excuse for failure in virtually any endeavor.

Misdirected and often unscrupulous leaders of these groups gather support by keeping their constituents downtrodden and so beholden to them. By virtually screaming discrimination or conspiracy and anti establishment rhetoric at every opportunity, these hate mongers and rabble rousers promote themselves and seek to control their followers. They do this by blaming the group they call oppressors, of an evil conspiracy against the helpless victims in their supporting groups. Then they call these imagined oppressors every evil name in the book as if most of their efforts were directed specifically to oppress them. This of course is right out of the NAZI play book.

All actions of these leaders, no matter how evil or outlandish is condoned or excused with, it wasn't their fault, or look where they came from. While the best known of these leaders are currently from the Black community, there are a number in the Latino community who seem to be growing in power and influence. Currently, the reverend Wright has gained the spotlight because of these actions, but he is merely one of a large group of destroyers who spout hate to rally their supporters. These are small people who take advantage of the ignorance and frustration of those they seek to lead in promoting their own agenda of hate. The lynch mob is their most prominent accomplishment. The really sad thing is that these leaders not only do great damage to those they purport to be aiding, but they help advance the efforts of their counterparts in the other groups. White supremacists, for instance, gain much credence from those leaders in minority groups who speak out with inciting, hateful charges against whites. Were it not for these minority leaders, white supremacists would have no more power than a distasteful joke.

Frequently, when members, even famous and admired members, of these disadvantaged minorities try to help their fellows by pointing out that they have the power to overcome being at a disadvantage. That by self reliance, hard work and positive effort on their part they can pull themselves up economically and socially. Even when they offer encouragement by example, effort, or pointing out that positive effort is more likely to get positive results than negative effort, they risk being condemned by many in their community to whom being a victim is their greatest asset. I illustrate with one example where all I need do is mention the name of one who is greatly admired by virtually all Americans, Bill Cosby. The response to his words of encouraging advice to his fellows was to be called by many an Uncle Tom. That was pathetic. Like the name calling done in third grade playgrounds it was childish and unworthy. His response to this attack was an indication of his greatness and humanity.

In his book, The True Believer, Eric Hoffer describes men who think so little of themselves they can only gain self-esteem by abandoning self to a cause. These true believers, as he calls them, will do anything, including committing suicide, for their cause. Following their leaders who enslave them to serve the leader's own and often undefined purpose, these are not men of free will, but true slaves of those who manipulate them. Such is the enemy free men now face.

Man has a natural instinct for enslavement. All great and small movements utilize this pack animal instinct to control masses of people as tools of opportunistic leaders. Humanitarian civilization tends to counter this instinct while mobs, movements, charismatic leaders, and fundamentalists tend to nurture and expand it.

The real power in mobs, movements, fundamentalism, and other uses of instincts to control lies in a very simple, irrefutable fact—that it is infinitely easier to damage or destroy to change things than to build or create. Only the most rudimentary skills were used by a few men to bring down the World Trade Center in just a few minutes. Contrast this with the immense effort required to design and build those same structures. In the same vein, it is far easier to make angry criticisms of ideas that differ from your own than to listen to those ideas and then make calculated judgments. Closed minds can be true agents of evil.

Of those controllable by such leaders, Eric Hoffer wrote, "People unfit for freedom—who cannot do much with it—are hungry for power. The desire for freedom is an attribute of a have type of self. It says: leave me alone and I shall grow, learn, and realize my capacities. The desire for power is basically an attribute of a have not type of self."

What is needed is for these kinds of men in any group or society to be treated for what they are, immature annoyances to society serving their own egos for their own selfish purposes. There are many of these types of leaders. Most common today are those leading the inner city gangs in the drug culture and living off of the misery of others. These are the little Napoleons with maybe a few dozen soldiers who create and destroy victims and whose lives are almost always short and violent. The romantic picture of these contemporary pirates as portrayed by our entertainment world is a far cry from the sordid realities of their lives and those of the victims of their actions. In truth these are the marauding packs of humans like feral dogs, bent on destruction and death. Why? Simply because it is far easier than being civilized. Civilization requires hard work and respect for others. Gang life disdains both as does the life of any who are slaves to the command of others rather than free men.

Benjamin Franklin said, "Those who desire to give up freedom in order to gain security will not have, nor do they deserve, either one."

James Allen said, "Before complaining that you are a slave to another, be sure that you are not a slave to self. Look within;...You will find there, perchance, slavish thoughts, slavish desires, and in your daily life and conduct slavish habits. Conquer these; cease to be a slave to self, and no man will have the power to enslave you."

What all of this says is that many people, placed at a disadvantage by any circumstance, will blame something outside of self and so be defeated from the outset. Those who realize it is up to them and so work to overcome their disadvantage often reach heights of success in spite of overwhelming handicaps. Joni Erickson Tada is one great example. Paralyzed by a diving accident at seventeen, her life was virtually over. Joni refused to be defeated and with herculean effort refocused her life and became an inspiration to thousands of handicapped people all over the world. Her books are now sold all over the world and her positive contribution to humanity is priceless.

I am reminded of an old saying I really like and try to act on. If life hands you a lemon, make lemonade. I firmly believe life has handed a lemon to many out there, but most just decry about and fight the lemon while a few add their own form of sugar, ice and water creating a delightful beverage. The individual has the power to chose between bitterness and joy.

Friday, March 28, 2008

America Needs a Mission for Energy Independence

(Excerpt from the book, Energy, Convenient Solutions)

That mission is to discover, develop and implement practical ways to save us—the United States and the world—from the ravages of the fossil fuel dragon. We should do our utmost to make everyone aware of available options for safe, affordable energy generation and use. We should also try to motivate everyone to demand we adopt these options.

We need to develop realistic solutions to the energy crisis from among the multitude of products and systems that are in use, under development, or even latent ideas in the minds of America's creative genius. We must collect and examine descriptions of fuels and energy systems—past, present, and future—and of many possible and practical ways to replace fossil fuels with renewable fuels or energy systems. All of the new systems could replace fossil fuels as the prime energy source for our nation and even the world. In the process this could lead to a carbon dioxide neutral energy system, one that adds no new CO_2 to our atmosphere. The options needed are real and practical alternatives to fossil fuels that will replace the use of petroleum and coal-based fuels with renewable, non polluting fuels and in the process:

1. build an American energy system that will stop the hemorrhaging of billions of U.S. dollars, mostly to despotic nations that preach our destruction:

2. build an American energy industry that boosts our economy and provides good jobs for many Americans:

3. stop the growth of atmospheric carbon dioxide and that possible link to global warming: and

4. accomplish most of this within just the next ten years.

There are many energy systems, sources, and conversions that comprise our total energy system. The requirements of the components of such a workable system should be judged by the following criteria:

* They should be relatively inexpensive to utilize.

* They should be developed using environmentally sound, sensitive principals

* They should be far easier, simpler and less expensive to implement than the hydrogen fuel cell system.

* They should be adaptable to our existing infrastructure with minor changes.

* They should use raw materials we already have or that can be developed here, locally.

* They should be applicable to existing vehicles with relatively minor upgrading.

* They should be useable with existing IC (Internal Combustion) engines of all types.

* They should be developed using existing, evolving technology able to be essentially complete within ten years.

* They should create a system that is a net zero contributor of carbon dioxide to the atmosphere.

* They should use an evolutionary as opposed to revolutionary change—a good start to becoming constantly improving, adapting systems driving numerous growing and improving technologies.

✳ They should be developed by America-based industry with the many resulting substantial benefits to our nation—social, political, and economic.

While the main thrust of such systems will be to provide new, better, less expensive and less environmentally intrusive systems for energy and transportation, there are many benefits other than just getting away from fossil fuels. These include direct positive effects on four of the first seven of the top twenty-two "most serious concerns of the American public" as shown in a public survey conducted by MIT and cited below.

No. 1 Terrorism—cut off the billions in oil money now going to so many despotic regimes and into funding of terrorism, chiefly to Islamic fundamentalist terrorists who plan our destruction.

No. 3 The Economy—a greatly expanded American energy industry would be an enormous boon to our economy if it only shut off the hemorrhaging of money for oil.

No. 4 Employment—thousands of high-paying new jobs would be created right here.

No. 7 Federal budget deficits—profits from new and expanded industries would pour billions into the federal treasury; money now going out overseas.

No. 13 The environment—may be far down the list of public concerns, but net carbon dioxide emissions would be greatly reduced if not eliminated. That can't be anything but good.

Even with these substantial benefits bundled into grand plans there are significant forces to be dealt with. Forces that can make a new idea work or relegate it to the ash can of history. There are real difficulties and obstacles to overcome in order for any new system to become a reality no matter how positive and/or effective that system might be. Indeed, the battle to get the most beneficial systems noticed and made a reality may require more effort than the implementation of the idea or system itself. The process, once begun, may take completely unexpected twists and turns in moving, sometimes forward and sometimes back, but always in the ultimate direction of successful implementation.

Our space program and its "put a man on the moon" goal followed just such a wandering path en route to its success. We can expect no less from our efforts to find a new fuel/energy system which certainly has a more powerful practical and obviously profitable goal. Clearly, President Kennedy's commitment to put a man on the moon in ten years and the follow-up on that commitment was a major force in making it happen. Media hype and glamorization help garner public support and enthusiasm. That was a government program operated by a government agency which was implemented mostly by private contractors according to government bid specifications. It was a process oriented solution with a single defined goal.

What we need now is leadership courageous enough to boldly state a goal such as eliminate the use of fossil fuels in ten years and then work ceaselessly toward achieving that goal. Leadership that will initiate a system oriented, broad spectrum approach to solving our growing energy crisis. This is an even greater challenge than putting a man on the moon, a serious challenge that could be instrumental in securing our very survival. We need this ten-year goal declaration to be well stated and backed by leadership with vision and the dedication to follow through. The commitment would be to develop new energy systems that will provide American-made renewable fuels or other portable energy systems and will add no more carbon dioxide to the atmosphere and do it within the next ten years. This is a much broader multiple goal than putting a man on the moon. Indeed it has many branching and interconnected avenues which could lead to a successful solution. I believe the key to final success will be found in the development of several areas of research rather than a single one. The best combination of energy sources, means of obtaining that energy, means of moving the energy from source to use point, and finally the systems of using that energy. There may be a variety of equally effective systems fitting differing needs. The result could end up a variation on the current theme where we use several types of systems in different configurations.

The attention given to new energy and fuel systems will undoubtedly involve effort into other seemingly unconnected areas. We are still deriving long-term benefits from technology developed for our space program. It would certainly be the same for any fuel/energy program. It is amazing to discover that so many of our serious problems are interrelated and how finding one solution often leads to another almost totally unrelated solution and so to the demand for another workable system.

Existing systems

Presently there are at least seven petroleum-based and mined fuels used in a variety of engines and boilers. These are in addition to coal used mostly in power plants. Use of all of these fossil fuels add carbon dioxide to our atmosphere. There are at least six non fossil-based fuels currently being used or being considered for use. Most are manufactured from plant materials and add no-net carbon dioxide to the atmosphere in use. Some do add carbon dioxide in their process of manufacture. There are a few non fossil solid fuels, mostly used for heating and cooking. There is a wide variety of harvesting and manufacturing processes used to obtain or make these fuels. Some of these manufacturing processes require more energy input than the resulting fuel can produce.

There is also the special case of nuclear fuels that use radioactivity to generate heat to boil liquids that drive turbine generators. Since these do not use combustion, they do not release carbon dioxide to the atmosphere.

The only reason we need fuel is to provide heat energy which we then convert to electricity or mechanical power. There are at least five combustion-based systems in use. The internal combustion piston engine is the most common and the most developed. Turbine engines make up the rest of the internal combustion types. Other sources of power include: piston steam engines, turbine steam engines, several types of nuclear reactors, fuel cells, and batteries. All of these power sources turn energy derived from chemical reactions or nuclear fission into electricity or mechanical energy which then powers vehicles, tools, and factories.

There are at least six types of batteries in use, some of which are very new and just beyond the development stage. These new technologies will come of age when continuing development of improved technologies lower their costs and improve their safety and efficiency.

Electric motors of many types and sizes, long important in stationary applications and semi-portable tools are growing in use in vehicles. The fastest growing application of new battery technologies is now battery-powered, cord-free tools and electronic equipment. Application of these new batteries to hybrids, plug-in electric vehicles (PHEVs), and even pure electric vehicles (EVs), is just in the beginning stages.

In the power plant segment of our energy system there are at least eight very different sources of energy we use to drive the generators that produce our electricity. Each has its own positives and negatives and all can pose serious environmental problems.

I have described all of these parts of our energy system to illustrate how complex it is. Making any major change would be a difficult and arduous task. Even deciding which changes to make—what system to develop—will be difficult. The answer could lie in a very successful technique used mostly in America for a long time, individual entrepreneurship in a relatively unfettered capitalist business environment.

The Challenge Ahead

There are literally thousands of individuals using their genius to develop new energy technologies motivated by the promise of rewards for themselves and for their organizations. We are not alone in free entrepreneurship. The powers that control China have suddenly realized its value and are now encouraging it. This has created one of the biggest economic turnarounds in the history of nations. Other nations have seen the light for some time and their economies are booming. Even India, the other Asian giant, is beginning to loosen the socialist government reins that have held their economy in check for so long. The phenomenal growth of the Irish economy is another example. Internet access to the rest of the world and primarily the free world has been a factor in these changes. Even some governments that once controlled virtually every aspect of their people's lives are now recognizing the value of free entrepreneurship, and even capitalism. Profit is no longer a dirty word in many of these nations. Tom Friedman details these changes in his recent book, The World is Flat 2.0.

Ireland is a prime example of what can happen when government frees businesses and entrepreneurs from oppressive controls and taxes. After years of wallowing in poverty in a country where government controls and high taxes on business stifled progress and discouraged investment of both time and money, the Irish took a dramatic new course. Government interference and controls of business were largely abolished. Complex reporting that bogged down management was mostly thrown out. Corporate taxes once among the highest in the world were reduced or eliminated. Government changed from being the enemy of business to being a strong supporter. The results speak for themselves.

Ireland is now one of the most vibrant economies in Europe. Business is booming like never before. There are now many high paying jobs and investment capital is flowing freely into a nation that once couldn't coax any investors. In the last twenty years more then 1,000 foreign companies have moved to or opened operations in Ireland. Local firms have also flourished and greatly expanded with worldwide impact. Employment has grown so much that Ireland now imports thousands of workers just to keep their industries running. All of this success is because of the new positive attitude of the government of Ireland to the development of business. This radical new attitude has brought on the availability of world class support services including banking, trade finance, transport systems and advanced telecommunications.

Historians like Tom Garvin are having trouble keeping score. "I have to make a mental effort to remember the Dublin of the 1950s, which was in many ways a Third World city," recalls Garvin. "Horses, no motorcars, children in bare feet, dirt everywhere, people living in slums, no television, no bathrooms - a really impoverished European country that didn't seem to be going anywhere." The picture today is almost unbelievably different: hopeful, optimistic, enthusiastic, almost ecstatic. This amazing economic outcome resulted from government working with business rather than against it and removing oppressive tax burdens rather than imposing them. What also helped was a pro-business attitude of people and even the media rather than the class hatred and anti business attitude we see so prevalent in our own country today.

The concerted effort to solve our energy problems if augmented by this kind of positive attitude and action by everyone here at home would certainly stimulate the economic growth that has sustained our economy at such high levels for so long. If our efforts at solving our energy crisis are driven by hope for substantial economic rewards we will surely succeed and hugely so. If on the other hand, those anti-business voices of doom and gloom succeed and control our government with the new oppressive regulations and taxes they have promised, our economy could will surely go into reverse and much more quickly than even the present slow down has indicated. The fall of the dollar we are currently experiencing will accelerate. Those entrepreneurs who might have solved our energy crisis will do so in Ireland, or China, or India as our stifled economy sinks into depression and our energy needs go unsolved.

How we approach and deal with this serious problem and the attitude we take toward those who have the power to solve it will ultimately decide which technologies prosper and which fall by the wayside. The steadily rising costs of petroleum fuels has made alternative systems practical that were far too expensive when oil was five dollars a barrel. One possible stumbling block to these changes could result from an effort by OPEC to increase the supply of oil and thus reduce the price. Eventually dwindling supplies of petroleum would wipe this out as a practical tactic.

There are many serious and demonstrable problems solving the energy crisis will effect right now. The biggest is the outflow of billions of dollars for oil to nations that preach our destruction. The boost to our economy alone would create a bonanza in this country like we have never before seen. New jobs, new technologies, new industries, and new entrepreneurs would flourish. Even without new taxes (what a dream that is) government revenue would soar from the increased economic activity. The demise of the oil industry would certainly be replaced by the new energy industries. Actually, those oil companies that got aboard these new technologies rather than opposing them, could use their present wealth to invest in them and grow rather than fade away.

Whether or not human contribution of carbon dioxide to the atmosphere creates global warming is actually only remotely connected to our energy related problems. If these new energy systems eliminate the wholesale use of fossil fuels, so much the better. Even if it has a negligible effect on global warming, it can do no harm to maintain the level of carbon dioxide in the atmosphere near to where it has been for a very long time. That would also satisfy the demands of the global warming proponents and opponents and redirect their energies elsewhere to other far more dangerous challenges facing humanity. Concrete benefits to the rest of the world with the exception of the oil-rich nations would also be substantial.

Thursday, March 13, 2008

Some Predictions:

After studying energy systems of so many kinds I am convinced that the future will see the greatest growth in energy generated in the form of electricity, distributed and used by a wide variety of systems. I see rapid growth in electric generating capacity primarily in nuclear, but with geothermal a close second and possibly eventually leading. I see a decline in coal fired power plants unless we find a practical technology to gather and sequester carbon dioxide, a very difficult and expensive challenge. I see wind and direct solar generation as always being too expensive and remaining minor players in contribution to the grid. Their use in small, local applications where connection to the electric grid is expensive and to home heating and providing hot water will probably be a substantial benefit and addition to the energy mix. Hydropower will not grow much as environmental concerns will make it increasingly expensive. One interesting possibility now being studied is the conversion of ocean wave action to electrical energy. Thus far, costs and practicality seem reasonable and downsides appear to be virtually nonexistent.

Vehicles will become more electric and less fuel powered as battery technology continues to improve and rapid charging systems are developed. There will always be hybrids, mostly electric vehicles with onboard charging capability, because charging capabilities may be unavailable in some places. Of course there could also be additional growth in micro turbine generators which are already being used for both remote and emergency power applications. Variety will be great at least as technologies progress and new ones come along.

There are several effective new fuel and energy systems to replace the existing system based on coal and petroleum with one that does not use fossil fuels. The benefits of such systems are many, varied, and have far-reaching positive attributes. These include immeasurable economic and political benefits for the citizens of any state or country that adopts them and environmental benefits for the entire world.

There are many innovative new products and technologies that could help us move to a new energy system with a low, or possibly zero-net carbon dioxide environmental impact. Many of these are already available and on the market. Others are soon to come. All that is needed is acceptance by the buying public and the associated development of better technologies and manufacturing capabilities. Some effective PR would provide a big boost.

Two possible direct replacements for gasoline are butanol (butyl alcohol) and 2,5-dimethylfuran (DMF). Both have been available for a long time primarily as solvents and paint thinners. Both can be used in current gasoline engines with little or no modifications. Their high cost relative to gasoline is now changing as gasoline prices rise. New manufacturing techniques have already lowered the production costs of these new fuels to competitive levels. These also have the possibility of being made out of waste plant materials by active biota. Several new techniques have already shown some success. All that is needed is further research and development of processes that can be scaled up to meet the kind of quantities required for a gasoline replacement.

One caveat regarding alternative fuels is already creating serious problems that can only grow worse. Enough corn, wheat and soy beans are being diverted from food to energy use (as ethanol and biodiesel) to bring about some major increases in the costs of these grains. Most have hit all time highs on the grain markets and no sign of a relaxation of this upward trend has yet appeared. Farmers everywhere are thrilled with this new bonanza. Increases in prices for all baked goods, meats, eggs and milk—anything that uses or requires grains—are already quite noticeable in stores.

Another concern that has quite a different but equally negative effect is the growing of palms for palm oil to be used as biodiesel fuel. Much tropical rain forest is being cut, burned and cleared to grow palms for the highly profitable oil they produce. Destruction of rain forest with its huge capacity to remove carbon dioxide from the atmosphere could more than counter any gain in the carbon dioxide balance from use of biodiesel from palm oil. I'm certain there are other problems with conversion to renewable fuels from crops.

There are many other ways to produce biodiesel that could become practical were we to pursue them aggressively. One that is well documented is the use of Algae fed nutrients from waste water or other biological waste materiels to produce useable oils. View the Internet site http://www.unh.edu/p2/biodiesel/article_alge.html. for more information on this example of just one possible process. Many of these new technologies would bear fruit if more research were provided. This would accomplish two needed goals. One would be to produce biodiesel without interfering with food crops. The second is make profitable use of waste materials that now cost money for their disposal.

Using food crops to make biofuels has already caused disruption to the food supply which is only going to grow worse. Because of this, I favor emphasis on new fuels made from non-food chain raw materials along with new battery technologies, electric vehicles and a great expansion of geothermal power generation to cover the increased energy demand. These are some of the only readily acceptable and practical options that can lead us away from dependence on fossil fuels without a major disruption of our food supply or serious damage to our environment. I see no practical development of cost-effective fuel-cell powered vehicles, hydrogen or otherwise, without a major breakthrough in technology. Although such a breakthrough is always possible, there seems to be no hint of any in the foreseeable future.

There are powerful and deeply entrenched economic and political forces all over the world that actively oppose any system to replace fossil fuels. This is because it would challenge their power and control over energy. I trust our nation will overcome this opposition and lead the world by becoming the first to adopt such a system. If we don't, I'm certain China, India and several other countries will jump at the chance to be first with new energy technology and its associated benefits.

Friday, March 21, 2008

Anecdotal Evidence Does Not an Understanding Make

All you global warming fanatics and all you anti-global warming fanatics please take note.

Just as the higher temperatures of recent years is an entirely illogical and useless indicator that we are in a period of global warming, the drastically cold weather of the 2007-2008 winter is an equally useless indicator that we are not. The opposing opinions for or against global cooling, is just as applicable. Both of these extreme positions are caused by emotional reactions exacerbated by political bias and media hype. They have very little to do with the science of climate or climate change. These opinions are used by media hypers and those with a political agenda as weapons, really brutish clubs wielded indiscriminately. Among we who analyze the facts objectively, it seems this has to be obvious to all but the dimmest of light bulbs.

For those who would like to be enlightened about what we do know about climate and also informed of the infinitely larger body of information that we do not know, there are a lot of conflicting data and wildly divergent opinions available from both good and questionable sources. Just because the word science or scientist is attached to any source of information or opinion does not make it accurate, or even honest. Ever hear of the Piltdown man hoax?

Deliberate misinformation aside, it is extremely easy for any scientist to have his opinion shaded a bit in the direction of what he hopes to be true, especially if that helps obtain a grant, gain a research assignment, get a paper published, or win a prestigious prize. (The Nobel people even bragged that it was political expediency that motivated the award to Al Gore. Is that not the ultimate height of hypocrisy?) After all, scientists are people just like the rest of us. They are certainly not immune to the temptation to shade equations and conclusions in the direction of their own desires and opinions. This is especially true where the balance point between one direction and the opposite is close to the center. They can honestly express that those close choices are one way or the other and not be condemned except by those with differing opinions or agendas.

Consider the differing pressures on scientists brought about by their position or circumstance. All are at least partially affected by the political, social, emotional, financial and hierarchical pressures of their positions in the organization, their peers, their superiors and even those who work for them. To some extent, each group described has most of the same or similar pressures of all of the other groups.

University scientists have all the pressures of the academic environment: the need to be published, the requirements to do directed research, the need to obtain grants by yielding to the desires and requirements of the grantors, the requirements to meet peer review standards, and often the need to be socially and politically correct.

Government scientists have many of the same pressures as the academics and a few different ones: The need to meet often rigid technical and mechanical government requirements, the strict hierarchy of the government bureaucracy, the annual budget submission and justification process and all the other government red tape requirements.

Private industry scientists have some special pressures: meeting profitability projections, sometimes special reporting processes, meeting company purpose or mission requirements, less job security than the others, considerable job or position competition, and more powerful superiors to deal with.

All of these pressures can affect research related decisions and the ultimate tenor of the chosen and reported results. Much data that sits on a fence is moved one way or the other by these pressures rather than by truly objective judgement.

Once in the hands of the media or politicians, information from those close choices with their many shades of gray opinions, become pure black or pure white. Remember the fable of the man who blew on his cold hands to warm them as he came in out of the cold and then blew on his hot soup to cool it? The moral is something about how can one blow hot and cold with the same breath? For media and political people, facts are rarely significant compared to the power of a position that furthers their chosen agenda. Their opinions blow hot or cold at their whim. Politization of anything is the art of creating an effective club with which to beat down and destroy competitors or rivals. It has absolutely nothing to do with finding the truth or facts in the matter, or developing a workable solution to any problem other than that of getting elected or gaining higher ratings.

If you would like to read some hopefully reasonable opinions about climate and where it might be headed, there are anumber of articles from several viewponts in earlier postings on this blog. All you need do is scroll down to find them.

For additional information in another blog goto http://hjgulfstream.blogspot.com/. The most recent article there is about geothermal energy so scroll down to the section on global warming and the Gulf Stream.

Incidently, I have a powerful personal motive for hopping onto the global warming bandwagon. As the author of a book on energy and what could be the best answer to the global warming problem, I could very easily embrace the whole global warming movement in its promotion. My book, A Convenient Solution, is about to be released and in spite of this, I still remain objectively neutral on global warming.

Friday, February 29, 2008

Global Cooling May Now Be Upon Us

http://robertd.wordpress.com/2008/02/28/some-global-cooling-updates/

Cashmere Goats are Dying by Ethel C. Fenig (see above link for complete story)

Have you noticed the absence of Al Gore (global-warming-the-sky-is-falling) in light of the unusually harsh winter across the planet? Why he wasn't even at the Academy Awards!

Meanwhile cashmere goats, and their herders, do wish Al Gore would open his mouth and spew forth some hot air about the perils of global warming instead of hiding under the cover of climate change.

At least 600 rare Himalayan goats — famed for their pashmina wool, also known as cashmere — have died and thousands face starvation after their desert habitat was blanketed with snow during the region's worst snowfall in three decades, authorities said Thursday. Over 100,000 cashmere goats have faced starvation as winter stocks of fodder ran out after heavy snow covered pastures in the remote Ladakh region near the border with China last month.

The PETA people have been unusually silent also. From American Thinker

http://www.americanthinker.com/blog

Snowfall Records Being Broken in New England

by Noel Sheppard February 28, 2008 - 10:12 ET

Remember all those articles last year about how ski resorts were going to go bankrupt, and that folks with vacation homes near such areas were going to take a bath as global warming significantly reduced snowfall levels? Well, ski enthusiasts and investors around the country should rest assured that this media hype was just as accurate as all those hurricane forecasts in 2006 and 2007. In fact, much as what has occurred across the northern US this year, parts of New England have experienced more snow than ever in history as reported by USA Today late Wednesday evening. Read the rest from NewsBusters

~ ~ ~ ~ ~ ~ ~ ~ ~ ≈ ≈ ≈ ~ ~ ~ ~ ~ ~ ~ ~ ~ ~ ~ ~ ~ ~ ~ ~ ~ ~ ≈ ~ ~ ~ ~ ~ ~ ~ ~ ~ ~ ~ ~

This La Nina Likely to Have Legs - February 28, 2008

As I mentioned in my post here about one of the satellite data sets (RSS) that showed a marked cooling globally in 2008, La Nina and PDO seem to be drivers of this change. Here is Joe D'Aleo's take on it below. - Anthony

By Joseph D'Aleo, CCM ICECAP

Evidence is growing this La Nina will be a longer term event. Most similar important La Ninas are often multi year events (1949-1951,1954-1956, 1961-63, 1970-1972, 1973-1976, 1998-2001). Though the easternmost Pacific near South America has warmed at the surface as the seasonal weakening of the tropical easterlies led to weakened upwelling, it is still cold beneath. Below you can see the latest depth-section of ocean temperatures (top) and anomalies (bottom). Temperature are in degree Celsius. Note the large reservoir of subsurface anomalously cold water (up to 4 degrees C) in the eastern tropical Pacific at 50 to 100 meters.

For the rest of the original article goto

http://wattsupwiththat.wordpress.com/2008/02/28/this-la-nina-likely-to-have-legs/

~ ~ ~ ~ ~ ~ ~ ~ ~ ≈ ≈ ≈ ~

Wednesday, February 27, 2008

Stop The Presses......What We Have Now Is Global Cooling

Call it what you will, global cooling, or "The Al Gore Effect". No you can not have your money back on all those carbon credits you just bought. What about all these efforts to stop global warming, the UN's IPCC, the Kyoto Treaty, what are we going to do?

Peter

Temperature Monitors Report Widescale Global Cooling

Michael Asher (Blog) - February 26, 2008 12:55 PM

World Temperatures according to the Hadley Center for Climate Prediction. Note the steep drop over the last year. (See graph at website link below)

Twelve-month long drop in world temperatures wipes out a century of warming. Over the past year, anecdotal evidence for a cooling planet has exploded. China has its coldest winter in 100 years. Baghdad sees its first snow in all recorded history. North America has the most snowcover in 50 years, with places like Wisconsin the highest since record-keeping began. Record levels of Antarctic sea ice, record cold in Minnesota, Texas, Florida, Mexico, Australia, Iran, Greece, South Africa, Greenland, Argentina, Chile -- the list goes on and on.

For the graph of world temperatures and the rest of the story goto:

http://petesplace-peter.blogspot.com/2008/02/stop-presseswhat-we-h ave-now-is-global.html

A compiled list of all the sources can be seen here. The total amount of cooling ranges from 0.65C up to 0.75C -- a value large enough to wipe out nearly all the warming recorded over the past 100 years. All in one year's time. For all four sources, it's the single fastest temperature change ever recorded, either up or down.

Scientists quoted in a past DailyTech article link the cooling to reduced solar activity which they claim is a much larger driver of climate change than man-made greenhouse gases. The dramatic cooling seen in just 12 months time seems to bear that out. While the data doesn't itself disprove that carbon dioxide is acting to warm the planet, it does demonstrate clearly that more powerful factors are now cooling it.

No more than anecdotal evidence, to be sure. But now, that evidence has been supplanted by hard scientific fact. All four major global temperature tracking outlets (Hadley, NASA's GISS, UAH, RSS) have released updated data. All show that over the past year, global temperatures have dropped precipitously.

~ ~

Tuesday, February 26, 2008

Verdict: All Four Major Global Temperature Tracking Outlets Release Updated Data

"For quite some time now I have been openly harping on global "warming" hysterics. Throughout my debates I have maintained that within the next 20 (or some odd) years, we will begin to see signs of the next global climate cycle - a cycle that will bring global "cooling".

It appears I was wrong.

Apparently we won't have to wait that long.

Over the past year, anecdotal evidence for a cooling planet has exploded. China has its coldest winter in 100 years. Baghdad sees its first snow in all recorded history. North America has the most snowcover in 50 years, with places like Wisconsin the highest since record-keeping began. Record levels of Antarctic sea ice, record cold in Minnesota, Texas, Florida, Mexico, Australia, Iran, Greece, South Africa, Greenland, Argentina, Chile -- the list goes on and on.

No more than anecdotal evidence, to be sure. But now, that evidence has been supplanted by hard scientific fact. All four major global temperature tracking outlets (Hadley, NASA's GISS, UAH, RSS) have released updated data. All show that over the past year, global temperatures have dropped precipitously.

Meteorologist Anthony Watts compiled the results of all the sources. The total amount of cooling ranges from 0.65C up to 0.75C -- a value large enough to erase nearly all the global warming recorded over the past 100 years. All in one year time. For all sources, it's the single fastest temperature change ever recorded, either up or down.

To read the complete article and comments goto:

http://theconservativemanifesto.blogspot.com/2008/02/verdict-all-four-major-global.html

~ ~

February 29, 2008 7:53 AM - Comment by jovial_cynic said...

And in related news: bacteria can cause rain and snow.

Check on: http://www.sciencedaily.com/releases/2008/02/080228174801.htm

~ ~

February 29, 2008 7:53 AM - Comment by HoJo...

I have quite a bit of information about new energy systems that could replace our use of fossil fuels and thus stop new carbon dioxide emissions. This would silence the global warming crowd complaining about CO2 emissions. Far more important, it would bring back home all those billions now going to nations who plot our destruction.

Check out these sites on the web.

http://hjgulfstream.blogspot.com   and   http://glowarmacs.blogspot.com

Friday, February 22, 2008

Simplifying Extremely Complex Systems - Climate

This is in response to the article, Heavy footprint weighs down U.S. empire

by Paul Hanley, The StarPhoenix spnews@sp.canwest.com

Published: Tuesday, January 29, 2008

His premise is stated in the first paragraph of the article. "Is the decline of the status of the United States a result of its heavy ecological footprint? A strong argument can be made that the fading of the American empire is fundamentally an environmental issue." To his comments about "the fading of the American empire" That reminded me of a quote from Mark Twain, "Reports of my death are greatly exaggerated."

Mr. Hanley's copyrighted article can be read at

http://www.canada.com/saskatoonstarphoenix/news/arts/story.html?id=82235e7e-e 146-4c12-af09-f6c3458cd676

This BLOG is in response to Paul Hanley's article.

The article has an interesting concept and conclusion that is a typically simplistic identification of a narrow range cause of an extremely complex system. Mostly these types of conclusions tend to promote the opinion and/or agenda of the creator. This is not intended as a condemnation, but is merely an observation by one who tends to look for the complexities in systems like the Roman Empire, the United States or even global climate. One could see the similarities of destructive effects in such factors as: the growth of government of Rome and the US and the associated increasing cost, the use of human energy, and the consumption of effort that growth requires.

Another example from another source comes from far back in history. When the 13 colonies were still part of England, Professor Alexander

See quotes on Page 91

This does not apply as closely to a representative republic, but our republic is rapidly being eroded by those who see a democracy as being more in their own best interests than a republic. This too could be an equally accurate explanation for the fall of Rome and the future of America. There are doubtless many other applicable reasons with possible equal or greater effects. Jared Diamond covers many, natural and man made in his books, Collapse and Guns, Germs and Steel.

I shall try to explain the type of problems complex systems pose for those who would try to understand them by describing one such system I have been studying. For more than ten years I have been working on answers to a very complex system or more accurately group of systems related to our use of energy. These include: energy systems we have in place, where they are headed and practical solutions to the constantly changing energy requirements and uses in the world. My book, A Convenient Solution, does not provide a single solution but it does describe many of the systems now in use, possible future systems, their practicality and how they can be implemented. I think most people would be surprised at the number and variety of energy systems in use, soon to be in use and those that could be in use in the near future. All of these systems from power plants and distribution systems to vehicles and power tools are available with existing technology. Many new concepts are already available and more are coming in the very near future. Most are being developed by independent entrepreneurs, not government. The positive effects on our economy, our environment and the well being of planet earth could be enormous.

I state in the title that freedom from fossil fuels could be accomplished in ten years. All we have to do to achieve that goal is quit spending our efforts on blaming everyone and everything we disagree with, while condemning things as they are. Then spend our energies on developing and promoting these new concepts and products. I think we have far to much use of problems as political battering rams against opponents and far too little effort at finding and implementing viable solutions. Most everyone wants a single simple answer, and by the same token many blame one or a few situations or efforts as the sole or certainly the overwhelming villain in the case. I'd like to use the current media hot button "global warming" to illustrate.

Global warming has become such a popular catch phrase it is being used as a verbal club in condemnation of many things. It has become the subject of much TV humor. Late night talk shows on TV seldom miss a chance to tell a global warming joke. Passions run high on the subject. So high that global warming has taken on almost the trappings of a religion. Certainly it rouses almost religious fervor in its believers. The truth, degree, causative factors, and ultimate results of global warming if indeed it is real, are completely lost in the passionate rhetoric from adherents and nay sayers alike.

The truth is that climate and climate change are very complex, far more complex than our best computer simulations can handle. As a result, we have great difficulty in predicting the path of a single hurricane with much accuracy. While we are getting better at it each year as more sophisticated simulations are developed we still have a long way to go before we can have as much as 80% accuracy five days ahead. A single hurricane is a far less complex system with far fewer variables than is the climate of the entire world. Change a few variables a very small amount and simulation results can be vastly different.

This is virtually axiomatic in all types of complex systems we could talk about. It is true of global climate, economics, energy, civilizations, nations, you name it=there are many extremely complex systems with almost infinite numbers of variables that are extremely difficult to understand. The question was posed and then somewhat answered in Paul Hanley's article, "Is the decline of the status of the United States a result of its heavy ecological footprint?" This is a classic example of applying a single causative system as the sole or primary reason for the behavior of an extremely complex system and then applying the same factor to another very different and also complex system. I am not saying it is not a factor, but that to explain it as the primary one is to presume a great deal. It is even possible that this factor is the effect of other factors and not a cause at all. Cause and effect often are confused in this type of situation.

To illustrate my meaning I will use climate again. It is often assumed that rising average air temperatures indicate the planet is warming. Actually, that may not be the case. The entire atmosphere holds only a fraction of the heat that the earth's liquid and frozen water holds. All of that heat is held in the planet's very thin surface skin comparable in thickness to paint on the surface of a croquet ball. Movements of ocean currents distribute far more heat energy around the planet than do air currents and thus should be a bigger contributor to climate. Indeed, it is primarily the energy from warm ocean water that powers hurricanes and we are just beginning to understand how the warm surface waters of the Pacific can affect climate over much of the globe. Discovering how changes in our atmosphere affects the oceans—actually the complex exchanges of energy between oceans and atmosphere—is an extremely difficult and complex task. Though there is much we do understand, that understanding is but a tiny portion of what is needed to design competent computer simulations. What we can project from current knowledge is a SWAG (Sophisticated Wild Ass Guess) at best.

Too often adherents to an idea will take a SWAG and run with it as a definite fact. Our media in particular tends to do this particularly if the SWAG happens to promise dire consequences for our nation or the world. Those dire predictions seem to sell newspapers and gain TV viewers. It is well known that bad news sells much better than good news. We all have a tendency to stop and gawk at an accident scene and pictures of all manner of disasters and mayhem bring many viewers to TV. The temptation to sensationalize seems far too great to keep reporters and TV news writers from emphasizing the negative aspect of virtually any situation. With all this sensationalism available it is quite difficult for any calm, objective, broadly based observations or studies to get much exposure.

Often reports of such careful observations are condemned as opposition to an accepted position or known fact. The known fact of global warming is just such a creation and is now accepted by many as axiomatic. Thirty or forty years ago many of these same individuals were treating global cooling as a known fact.

When we learn enough that we are able to predict precisely where a hurricane is going to go and how strong it will become when it is merely a disturbance off the coast of Africa—then we may be able to say whether global warming caused by atmospheric carbon dioxide is a reality with some degree of certainty. Now, no matter how you look at it, to say that the increase of atmospheric carbon dioxide is the responsible agent causing global warming in the manner it is being described by so many agenda driven spokespersons is Chicken Little at best.

The same type of observation could be made about Mr. Henley's report. I am not saying it is wrong, just that it may be an effect, rather than a cause—a symptom rather than a disease. Certainly it is worth consideration as being among countless other factors. It may be a factor, but certainly not necessarily the definitive one. There is probably not a single definitive factor at all, but rather many significant ones. To make comparison of the situation in Rome and in America today requires another stretch of the imagination and denial of countless other factors. The two systems and their complexities have far too many differences for the type of conclusion made to have more than passing interest and value. An interesting thought perhaps, but quite far from proven.

To me the concerns expressed about our lavish lifestyle and fiscal cancer are far more significant than the heavy ecological footprint. The paragraph, "The empire also needed tax gatherers and civil servants. These armies and bureaucrats had to be supported by the empire.

Expansion was also necessary to get booty and other forms of wealth, such as gold, to pay for the Roman lifestyle and the costs of expansion itself." is to me a far more significant comparison as it could be said almost verbatim of our present government. I believe Tyler's observation about democracy cited earlier in this commentary (Page 91) predicts a far more accurate and likely scenario and provides more serious concern than any ecological effects. Unfortunately, it is also a real menace that seems to interest very few Americans and certainly few politicians. Currently, this frightens me far more than any concern about

---

Monday, January 14, 2008

Mexican Drug dealer's house full of American cash. It must be seen!

Here and on the next page are pictures taken after a raid on a drug dealer's house in Mexico. Are you ready for this???

Aren't we glad that we have an open border policy between us? Just look at how well its paying off . . . for drug dealers that is.

Those are bundles of $100 bills in the closet and in the other photos.

I think allowing Mexican truckers in the U.S. is a great idea!!! Just take a look at the millions of reasons why.........

See how well these truckers are doing? What the @#@%*@ are we thinking??? Notice that nearly 100% of this money is U.S. Currency!!! Do you now wonder why the cost of living has catapulted in our country??? I don't...... Some of the illegal aliens we're letting in can afford anything at any cost!!! And for the ones who cannot......... We'll give it to them anyway!!!

And we have two border patrol agents in prison for shooting and wounding a well documented Mexican drug dealer! Who, by the way, was armed and also happens to be a convicted (by Mexico) murderer.

Makes a lot of sense, doesn't it??? Automatics, silencers...... they're all having a nice laugh about this stuff at our expense!!!

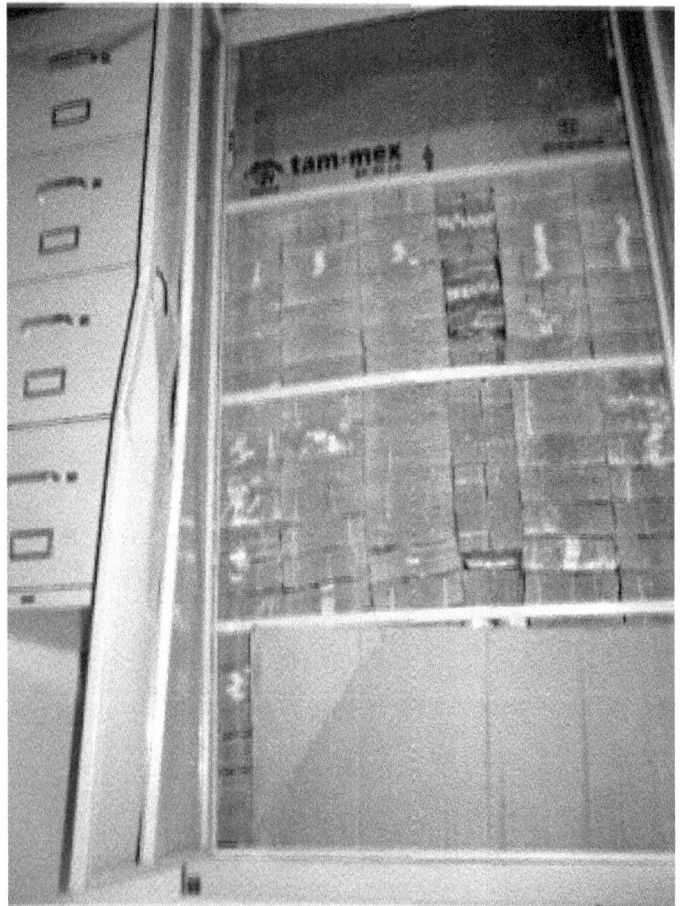

And we want to give illegal aliens amnesty and not build the border fence because of funding!?!?!? Send this to everyone, including your local representatives in Congress. Our country is bleeding from the outside in! !! Don't you think it's time we take back what we have sacrificed for over 140 years for??? I do. Build the fence higher and deeper, tighten border control, and send EVERY illegal alien home!!!

HoJo's comments:

I think you're dreaming. What good would it do to write to a bunch of idiots many of whom are probably heavy on the take as it is. I'll wager that a large portion of that cash in Mexico was scheduled to go to US Representatives and Senators either as campaign contributions or direct input into their pockets. How do you think so many of them suddenly become very wealthy after being in office for a while. I wonder how much money from similar sources found its way into the millions the Clintons have accumulated since he first gained a political office. What do you really think was the original source of all those millions in payments for speeches by our former philanderer in chief? Think about it!

I have a viable solution that will stop the illegal drug industry in its tracks, for good. Unfortunately, our Congress would never enact it because the illegal drug industry pays for so many politicians' homes, trips and elections. Why is it people refuse to believe the most obvious? Hmmmmmm?

To read about my comprehensive, solution to the drug problem that would

1. immediately make the illegal drug trade unprofitable,

2. immediately stop all the illegal activities of drug dealers,

3. immediately stop all criminal activity by users trying to get money to buy drugs,

4. immediately stop the actvity enticing people to use drugs.

5. immediately destroy the entire illegal drug industry in the U.S.

Go to http://hjdrugprb.blogspot.com.

Sunday, December 30, 2007

What Americans Really Care for - Last Post for 2007

Oh yes, regarding global warming. I take a completely neutral stance between the usual extremes of panic and denial, or hoax believers. If it is a problem I can guarantee there are many other problems that pose far greater dangers to humanity and far sooner than does global warming. Just as no one will take a serious look at any data showing global warming not to be the humanity threatening danger that fundamentalist members of the church of global warming "know" it to be, no one will even discuss these other dangerous situations. These are far more menacing, far more immediate, and far more traumatic than the worst global warming scenario the high priest of the church of global warming, Father Gore, could possibly describe.

What are these terribly serious situations? Why, the trials of Britney and Jamie Lynn and the pains of poor little Paris Hilton. Add that to the altercations of Lindsay Lohan and you have real earth-shaking events. Then there are all those bowl games and the NFL playoffs. Consider the trauma, the personal trauma that will befall those fans whose teams lose. It's enough to bring one to tears of sympathy for those poor, soon to be traumatized souls. The suicide rate will probably multiply amidst the uncontrolled screaming and ranting of those poor losing fans as their teams head for home in disgrace.

So, buck up all you who are or may be facing these traumatic events. You can survive and maybe even escape with minor wounds if you just keep a stiff upper lip. Remember, intellectuals, geniuses and others like them may lose their BSs, their MAs, and even their PhDs, but a fan goes on forever and—there's always next year or another flake to idolize.

Ho

Last Newsweek of 2007 - Lists of Newsworthy Idiots

I'm not a big fan of Newsweek for reasons that should be obvious, but the final copy of 2007 at least displays some items of interest, good and bad.

On the really sick side, their list of celebrities in their "Newsmakers Madness" section had photos of 32 individuals, most of whom are from the entertainment world and even among this nondescript group they truly represent the dregs of humanity. I am happy to say I only recognized a few names. I probably knew them only because their names and faces have been emblazoned across TV and radio news on nearly a daily basis for a number of ridiculous reasons by a fawning media that thrives on repugnant happenings of all kinds. Of the eight individuals whose names I did recognize there was only one that I know anything about beyond hearing their names tied to some completely nonsensical or ridiculous action. That most of these dismal excuses for humans seem to have much in common, at least morally, with the creature from the black lagoon is patently obvious to any sensitive mind. Fanism and celebrity worship seems to be a contagious disease now of epidemic proportions among the mindless boobs currently trying to pass themselves off as adults in our present culture.

On a much more intelligent level was their list of 34 "Famous in Life, Noted in Passing" with tiny bios. (Newsweek was gracious enough not to include any such bios about those on the newsmaker list.) This list of those who died in 2007 was a much broader and more significant group. Though still primarily from the entertainment world, most had at least something of significance in their life even if it was nastiness. Of course, celebrity status is far more apt to be granted those with attributes they were born with, money or prestige they had, often inherited, or fame garnered by outlandish public acts than any demonstration of intellect or excellence. Isn't it strange that fame is more apt to be gained by those who play-act being another person, that is being a complete fake and lie than by those they pretend to be—even some very ordinary people? Apparently, being a fake is more to be admired and valued than being the real thing. How difficult it must be for those who act to have a genuine original thought of their own without reading a script.

If you get a chance, read George Will's The Last Word at the very back of the issue. Here's the first paragraph:

In 2007, CAME THE REVOLUTION, determined to end the war in Iraq and begin the reign of justice in America, Democrats took over Congress and acted on the principal, "ready, fire, aim." They threatened to tell the Ottoman Empire (deceased 1922) that it should be ashamed of itself (about Armenian genocide) and raised the minimum wage to $5.85, which is worth less than the $5.15 minimum was worth when it was set in 1997. Onward and upward with compassionate liberalism: The Democrat controlled Senate flinched from making hedge fund millionaires pay more than a 15 percent tax rate. (**George Soros and too many of them on the Democrat side of the aisle in the Senate?**) At the year's end, there were more troops in Iraq than there were at the year's beginning. Although it was not yet possible to say the war was won, it was no longer possible to say the surge wasn't succeeding. (Harry Reid please note.) The McClatchy Newspapers, with the media's flair for discerning lead linings on silver clouds, offered this headline: AS VIOLENCE FALLS IN IRAQ, CEMETERY WORKERS FEEL THE PINCH.

George Will continues filling the page with salient bits of news the main stream media usually hides among ads in the back pages, if not completely ignoring them. Among the most significant was this story from in Seattle, USSR:

A Seattle based day-care center banned Lego building blocks because the beastly children "were building their assumptions about ownership and the social power it conveys, assumptions that mirrored those of a class-based, capitalist society." The center reinstated Legos but allowed the children to build only "public structures" dedicated to "collectivity and consensus."

Do you suppose maybe old line communist Chinese, driven from their homeland by the new business and profits movement there, have moved to and taken over Seattle? The lead article on China in this issue indicates this could be a possibility. Just a thought.

So all you liberal Democrats out there, **READY! FIRE! AIM!** or is it, **FIRE! AIM! READY!**

Thursday, December 13, 2007

Global Warming - Again! The Money Train at Work

To all you who put up with my sometimes a bit off the wall rants.

Several years ago I joined a group named The Environmental Defense Fund. Since joining I have found them to be a far left wing organization whose true agenda lies quite remote from that which they profess to support. Most of their effort seems to be to scare people about the imminent effects of anthropogenic global warming (AGW) so that they donate to the organization. What follows is but one example of exchanges we have had continually since I joined. Interestingly, not one of my emails has ever been answered. Apparently all they are interested in is getting donations for their "cause."

IMPORTANT NOTE: Whenever the AGW promoters use the phrase *Global Warming* or *Climate Change*, insert *Anthropomorphic* or *Man Made* before those phrases. *Climate change* including *global warming* and *cooling* has been going on in irregular cycles for hundreds of millions of years by natural processes and will continue long after man is extinct. AGW promoters have found a new golden calf to worship which could potentially provide them with billions of dollars. This money is being extracted from the gullible public by politicians aided by their media cohorts. This money will make many promoters wealthy, but will not and cannot make any change in the global climate. Read my book, *Climate and Much Worse Dangers We Ignore,* and learn the facts about this monstrous scam.

≈ ~ ~ ~ ≈ ≈ ≈ ≈ ≈ ≈ ≈

Dear Howard,

2008 could be a turning point in our fight against global warming.

Donate now to double your year end gift and help fight global warming.

Can you feel the tide turning? Last week's historic passage of the Climate Security Act out of a key Senate committee represents a new day for global warming action.

We are now poised to make history in 2008. But we need your help to keep up the pressure.

And to encourage your support, more than 1,000 Environmental Defense members have contributed to a Global Warming Challenge Grant to match your year end gift dollar-for-dollar.

Donate today to our Year-End Global Warming Challenge and double the value of your gift.

Your challengers are everyday people just like you. They care about our future and they helped create the Challenge Grant to help build our campaign to stop global warming.

Here are some of the things these men and woman have had to say:

Environmental Defense goes after the biggest energy problems on earth, working at the highest levels for the most significant changes. Supporting ED's efforts will allow you to have the largest effect possible in the effort to save the earth.

- Kathy R, Cambridge MA

It is our responsibility to do everything we can to save our environment. I always think of the Iroquois proverb, "In our every deliberation, we must consider the impact of our decisions on the next seven generations." What are we leaving behind for our children?

- Marjorie, Iowa City, IA

I am on board with Environmental Defense because I am concerned about my young daughter's future, and because, as a religious leader and person of faith, I can think of no greater sacred responsibility than protecting the future of life on earth. I urge people of all faiths and traditions to join in this holy task.

- Rabbi Steve Folberg, Austin, TX

Contributing to Environmental Defense is one of the few ways that an individual can hope to make a difference. If there is any hope to protect our fragile planet from being ravaged by the uncaring and ignorant, Environmental Defense will be in the forefront. We must act as stewards.

- Louise Hodges, Hanford, CA

Donate today to have your gift matched dollar-for-dollar.

In all of my years working on important environmental issues, I cannot recall a mobilization as massive and concerted as the one now underway to fight global warming. And you and I have progress to show for our efforts.

But we can't let up, not for a minute. We can't wait for the results of next year's elections. We can't hope for the sea change within American industries to continue on its own. And we certainly cannot count on Congress to pass an historic cap on global warming pollution without continued grassroots demand.

We now have serious momentum toward the kinds of changes that could lead to major global warming progress.

Please donate today to help us take advantage of this momentum and have your gift matched dollar-for-dollar.

Thanks for all you do.

Sincerely, Fred Krupp,

President, Environmental Defense

My Sincere Reply to the Solicitation:

Dear Fred:

Global warming as a result of our use of fossil fuels may be a political fact which provides many benefits for those who would control our lives for their own personal benefit, a fact in the news media since it is useful in promoting their agenda, and an economic windfall for many like yourself, who have jumped on the global warming bandwagon. It is definitely not a scientific fact.

It is a proven fact that there are at least a dozen other causes that are more likely to be responsible for any global warming rather than the increases of CO_2 in the atmosphere. In addition, the continuing destruction of forests, primarily in the undeveloped world, is very possibly responsible for more of the increase of CO_2 in the atmosphere than is the combustion of fossil fuels. I would like to see some studies of both how much CO_2 is produced by the burning done to clear these forests and the amount of CO_2 the destroyed forest no longer removes from the atmosphere. Somewhere I remember reading that a 12% increase in forests in the world would remove all the CO_2 produced annually by all the vehicles in the entire world.

I think it unconscionable that the promoters of the "global warming" panic never address these other factors, even those like forest destruction which could be controlled far easier than forcing changes in our vehicles by writing more laws. In spite of this opinion, I have written a book, A Convenient Solution, about how to change our energy system to get us away from fossil fuels and greatly reduce or stop the emission of CO_2. It will be published and released within the next few weeks. My reasons for writing the book are about problems and dangers far more challenging than any possible effects of global warming. The overpowering reason is to get us away from dependence on foreign oil and reduce the ponderous drain of billions of dollars presently leaving our country and mostly going to nations that hate us and preach our destruction.

I would even be willing to send you a copy of my book if you would like. Just let me know where. If any of the systems described in my book were to be put in effect the increase of atmospheric CO_2 would be stopped and even reversed. These changes would do far more to stop your form of CO_2 caused global warming than any of the efforts you are now making no matter how successful are those efforts.

Howard Johnson.

End of email

~ ~

PLEASE NOTE: The global warming phenomena is an artificially created, politically motivated mass movement—almost a religion—that will rarely if ever make any serious effort to really solve the problem if there indeed is one. That there are now more climate scientists questioning the CO_2 greenhouse effect than are caught up in this religious frenzy is becoming more evident. That the media and global warming fanatics completely ignore all these scientists and their evidence is increasingly evident. The reasons are simple and Fred Krup (who is a fund raiser and not a scientist of any sort) is but one example of people who are making a career out "global warming." Those reasons are simply the desire for power and money along with an anti business political agenda on the part of those who would use it to increase taxes and gain political control for themselves. I certainly would welcome a serious effort at objective examinations of data pertaining to all of the plausible global warming (and cooling) causes including the "greenhouse gas" effect of CO_2 so dear to the hearts of the left, fund raisers, and the media. The data I have seen thus far show that the greenhouse effect of CO_2 is no more the likely cause of global warming than at least a dozen other natural systems that we know quite a bit about.

I wonder just how many organizations like environmentaldefense.com are using global warming as a tool to raise money for themselves and for their political aims. I also wonder why it is these organizations have to use strictly emotional appeals and strong arm tactics to obtain their funds and promote their agendas. They capitalize on the ignorance of both the media (who haven't a clue as to the facts about "global warming") and the masses of the public who succumb to their rants of fearsome consequences. Everyone knows how the media feeds on pain and misery and will promote anything that gives them fodder for their "woe is me" attitude. In reality, the billions we spend for oil from nations who preach and plot our destruction are part of a very real and present (and rapidly growing) danger that poses a much bigger and more immediate threat to America than does global warming by even the most convoluted scenario any of the global warming crowd could possibly come up with. That is where we ought to be focusing our efforts and expending our resources and energy.

Business isn't the villain in this case, it's an enforced victim that the left and their captive media love to use as a whipping boy. Why else do you think they have made profits into a dirty word. The very profits that generate the money the government confiscates as taxes in order to feed the career bureaucrats' insatiable appetite for money and power. Global warming is merely the current tool used to obtain that power and money. What are these money grubbers going to do if they succeed in destroying American business enterprises? Where will the steadily increasing funds these bureaucrats need to run their unproductive departments come from when profits cease to exist, tax money ceases to exist, and our economy grinds to a halt?

See quotes on Page 91 for one of my favorite quotes which fits perfectly into the political scene we are now witnessing.-

In other words what is happening is that voters are in the process of killing the geese that lay the golden eggs and politicians, mostly left leaning, are handing them the ax and urging them to use it. Since it is far easier for a mob to destroy than build, that's what they will do, even though they suffer grievously in the process. They forget that the only way we can all be "equal" is if we all have nothing. As stupid as that is, it seems to be human nature. Eric Hoffer had a real good handle on these individuals and why they do what they do. In one favorite of mine he said.

"Passionate hatred can give meaning and purpose to an empty life. Thus people haunted by the purposelessness of their lives try to find a new content not only by dedicating themselves to a holy cause but also by nursing a fanatical grievance. A mass movement (like global warming) offers them unlimited opportunities for both."

You can read some of his other pertinent quotes at: **http://ehoffer.blogspot.com**

For more real information on possible causes of global warming,

goto **http://hjgulfstream.blogspot.com**

Wednesday, December 12, 2007

Liberals, Are They Genetically Haters?

In the present politically charged atmosphere of the coming Presidential race the candidates seem to be keeping most of their claws retracted under smiling faces and supposed congeniality. Even Hillary seems to be on her best behavior most of the time and that must take a lot of restraint on her part. It has been evident for some time and to virtually everyone that Hillary is an incarnation of the "Wicked Witch of the North." Her hate for all who oppose her were expressed quite accurately by Howard Dean, president of the DNC when he literally screamed, "I hate Republicans. I hate conservatives. I hate Rush Limbaugh."

I just ran across a piece I had downloaded from the Internet nearly two years ago. While reports of the nastiness of Hillary have been circulating for many years, this one comes from people with a record of being in contact with Hillary on a daily basis. I couldn't write a rant with nearly the impact of this report so, here it is:

Sunday, January 29, 2006, 22:15:58

Subject: Presidential Observations by the Secret Service - By Dave Kulow

(Shows the true character of our chief executives)

We had a neighbor when I lived in DC who was part of the secret service presidential detail for many years. His stories of Kennedy and Johnson were the same as those I heard from the guys who flew the presidents' plane

Yes, Kennedy did have Marilyn Monroe flown in for secret "dates," and LBJ was a typical Texas "good ole boy" womanizer. Nixon, Bush 41, and Carter never cheated on their wives. Clinton cheated, but couldn't match Kennedy or LBJ in style or variety.

The information below is accurate: The elder Bush and current president Bush make it a point to thank and take care of the air crews who fly them around. When the president flies, there are several planes that also go, one carries the armored limo, another the security detail, plus usually a press aircraft. Both Bush's made it a point to stay home on holidays, so the Air Force and security people could have a day with their families.

WHAT WAS: Hillary Clinton was arrogant and orally abusive to her security detail. She forbade her daughter, Chelsea, from exchanging pleasantries with them. Sometimes Chelsea, miffed at her mother's obvious conceit and mean spiritedness ignored her demands and exchanged pleasantries regardless, but never in her mother's presence.

Chelsea really was a nice, kindhearted, and lovely young lady. The consensus opinion was that Chelsea loved her Mom but did not like her. Hillary Clinton was continuously rude and abrasive to those who were charged to protect her life. Her security detail dutifully did their job, as professionals should, but they all loathed her and wanted to be on a different detail. Hillary Clinton was despised by the Secret Service as a whole.

Former President Bill Clinton was much more amiable than his wife. Often the Secret Service would cringe at the verbal attacks Hillary would use against her husband. They were embarrassed for his sake by the manner and frequency in which she verbally insulted him, sometimes in the presence of the Secret Service, and sometimes behind closed doors. Even behind closed doors Hillary Clinton would scream and holler so loudly that everyone could hear what she was saying.

Many felt sorry for President Clinton and most wondered why he tolerated it instead of just divorcing his "attack dog" wife. It was crystal clear that the Clinton's neither liked nor respected each other and this was true long before the Monica Lewinsky scandal. Theirs was genuinely a "marriage of convenience."

Chelsea was much closer to her father than her mother, even after the Lewinsky scandal, which hurt her gravely. Bill Clinton did in fact have charisma, and occasionally would smile at or shake hands with his security detail.

Still, he always displayed an obvious air of superiority towards them. His security detail uniformly believed him to be disingenuous, false, and that he did nothing without a motive that in some way would enhance his image and political career. He was polite, but not kind. They did not particularly like him and nobody trusted him.

WHAT COULD HAVE BEEN: Al Gore was the male version of Hillary Clinton. They were more friendly toward each other than either of them were towards former President Clinton. They were not intimate, so please don't read that in. They were very close in a political way. Tipper Gore was generally nice and pleasant. She initially liked Hillary but soon after the election she had her "pegged" and no longer liked her or associated with her except for events that were politically obligatory.

Al Gore was far more left wing than Bill Clinton. Al Gore resented Bill Clinton and thought he was too "centrist." He despised all Republicans. His hatred was bitter and this was long before he announced for the Presidency. This hatred was something that he and Hillary had in common. They often said as much, even in the presence of their security detail.

Neither of them trusted Bill Clinton and, the Secret Service opined, neither of them even liked Bill Clinton. Bill Clinton did have some good qualities, whereas Al Gore and Hillary had none, in the view of their security details.

Al Gore, like Hillary, was very rude and arrogant toward his security detail. He was extremely unappreciative and would not hesitate to scold them in the presence of their peers for minor details over which they had no control. Al Gore also looked down on them, as they finally observed and learned with certainty on one occasion. Al got angry at his offspring and pointed at his security detail and said, "Do you want to grow up and be like them?"

Word of this insult by the former Vice-president quickly spread and he became as disliked by the Secret Service as Hillary. Most of them prayed Al Gore would not be elected President, and they really did have private celebrations in a few of their homes after President Bush won. This was not necessarily to celebrate President Bush's election, but to celebrate Al Gore's defeat.

WHAT IS: Everyone in the Secret Service wants to be on First Lady Laura Bush's detail.

Without exception, they concede that she is perhaps the nicest and most kind person they have ever had the privilege of serving. Where Hillary patently refused to allow her picture to be taken with her security detail, Laura Bush doesn't even have to be asked, she offers. She doesn't just shake their hand and say, "Thank you." Very often, she will give members of her detail a kindhearted hug to express her appreciation.

There is nothing false about her. This is her genuine nature. Her security detail considers her to be a "breath of fresh air." They joke that comparing Laura Bush with Hillary Clinton is like comparing "Mother Teresa" with the "Wicked Witch of the North."

Likewise, the Secret Service considers President Bush to be a gem of a man to work for. He always treats them with genuine respect and he always trusts and listens to their expert advice. They really like the Crawford, Texas detail. Every time the president goes to Crawford he has a Bar-B-Q for his security detail and he helps serve their meals. He sits with them, eats with them, and talks with them. He knows each of them by their first name, and calls them by their first name as a show of affection. He always asks about their family, the names of which he always remembers.

They believe that he is deeply and genuinely appreciative of their service. They could not like, love, or respect anyone more than President Bush. Most of them did not know they would feel this way, until they had an opportunity to work for him and learn that his manner was genuine and consistent. It has never changed since he began his Presidency. He always treats them with the utmost respect, kindness, and compassion.

Please pass this on. It is important for Americans to have a true inside understanding of their President.

Hal Johnson

No wonder she's sinking in the polls. Maybe Republicans should run Laura Bush.

Monday, October 29, 2007

A Big Backfire From Liberal Democrat Actions Against Rush

I challenge any of you liberals to refute any of the facts in this BLOG. Facts, not opinions. On second thought, maybe you shouldn't read this. Your thin skin couldn't take the facts.

The beginning of the fracas, *(My commentary inserted in italics)* Harry Reid on the Senate floor:

Washington, DC—Senate Majority Leader Harry Reid made the following statement today on the floor of the U.S. Senate, urging Senators to sign a letter that calls on Mark P. Mays, CEO of Clear Channel Communications, to publicly repudiate Rush Limbaugh's characterization of troops who speak out against the Iraq war as "phony soldiers."

Below are his remarks as prepared for delivery:

"Freedom of speech is one of our country's most cherished values. Nothing sets us further apart than the countries and regimes we oppose than our belief that everyone's opinion matters, and everyone has the right to express it. That is why, when we hear things on the radio that are offensive, by and large, we tolerate them.

"But last week, Rush Limbaugh went way over the line – and while we respect his right to say anything he likes, his unpatriotic comments cannot be ignored. *(Boy, Dingy Harry, did you ever get that wrong! For one who routinely condemns the war and America, you have little authority to accuse others.)*

"During his show last Wednesday, Rush Limbaugh was engaged in one of his typical rants. This rant was unremarkable and indistinguishable from his usual drivel, which has been steadily losing listeners for years *(In your dreams, maybe! Factually incorrect* as usual. Rush continues to gain listeners and has the largest following of anyone on radio.) = until he crossed that line by calling our men and women in uniform who oppose the war in Iraq 'phony soldiers.' This comment was so beyond the pale of decency that it cannot be left alone. And yet, he followed it up with denials and an attack on Congressman Jack Murtha, a 37-year active member of the Marine Corps. (He denied the Media Matters interpretation of his words and his "attack" was to repeat Murtha's own words verbatim. Funny how liberal Democrats consider repetition of their own words as an attack on them.)

"We have been debating the Iraq war here in the Senate and throughout the country for not months, but years. *(Wrong! You, the left, and your lackeys in the media, have been condemning Bush for waging an "illegal" war, calling him and his administration "criminals," "Nazis," and launching numerous other personal attacks, twisting facts and downright lying since the war started, and strictly for political gain. You have aided and abetted our enemies and provided direct support for their propaganda machines.)* There are good, patriotic Americans who favor the war = and good, patriotic Americans who oppose President Bush's handling of it. *(There are also millions of Americans who decry the obvious assistance these bitter condemnations in your propaganda provides to these Islamic terrorists. Al Jazeera frequently uses your words verbatim in their constant attacks on our nation.)* Neither party holds a patent on patriotism. *(The liberal Democrats certainly act like they hold a patent on anti American hate speech.)* I know all my Republican colleagues would agree with that.

"Yet Rush Limbaugh took it upon himself to attack the courage and character of those fighting and dying for him and for all of us. *(He very clearly stated that he was not talking about all of those in Iraq, only those very few who were spouting the liberal Line about the war. How you could twist and mischaracterize Rush's actual words means you did not hear them yourself and are either lying about what you heard or are taking the words of some other person or organization as being correct= which they certainly are not. Perhaps you get your marching orders from 'Media Matters.')* Rush Limbaugh got himself a deferment from serving when he was a young man. He never served in uniform. He never saw in person the extreme difficulty of maintaining peace in a foreign country engaged in civil war. Yet he thinks that his opinion on the war is worth more than those who are on the front lines. *(Sounds like a description of Bill Clinton to me. See "Bill Clinton's Military Career" below.)*

"And what's worse = Limbaugh's show is broadcast on Armed Forces Radio, which means that thousands of troops overseas and veterans here at home were forced to hear this attack on their patriotism. Rush Limbaugh owes the men and women of our Armed Forces an apology. *(In the light of Rush's long standing and unquestioned support for our troops, these last statements are pure nonsense and apply more to your actions, Senator Reid. Indeed, you are the one who owes everyone an apology.)*

"On Friday, many Democrats joined me in drafting a letter to the Chief Executive Officer of Clear Channel, Mark Mays that we will send out this week. *(This may actually have been a criminal or at least illegal act. Of course, liberal Democrats are above the law, aren't they? They certainly seem to think they are.)* Here is what we wrote:"

Dear Mr. Mays,

At the time we sign this letter, 3,801 American soldiers have been killed in Iraq, and another 27,936 have been wounded. 160,000 others awoke this morning on foreign sand, far from home, to face the danger and uncertainty of another day at war. *(The same is true about just three days of the start of the invasion of Normandy in WWII.)*

Although Americans of goodwill debate the merits of this war, *(I see absolutely no evidence of goodwill on the part of any liberal Democrat in this so called 'debate.')* we can all agree that those who serve with such great courage deserve our deepest respect and gratitude. That is why Rush Limbaugh's recent characterization of troops who oppose the war as "phony soldiers" is such an outrage.

Our troops are fighting and dying to bring to others the freedoms that many take for granted. *(I can hardly believe you have admitted that, Senator Reid. George Soros, moveon.org and Media Matters will really be upset at you.)* It is unconscionable that Mr. Limbaugh would criticize them for exercising the fundamentally American right to free speech. Mr. Limbaugh has made outrageous remarks before, but this affront to our soldiers is beyond the pale. **(Compared to your 'outrageous' propaganda and hate speech about Bush and Republicans, Rush's words are mild.)**

The military, like any community within the United States, includes members both for and against the war. Senior generals, such as General John Batiste and Paul Eaton, have come out against the war while others have publicly supported it. A December 2006 poll conducted by the Military Times found just 35 percent of service members approved of President Bush's handling of the war in Iraq, compared to 42 percent who disapproved. From this figure alone, it is clear that Mr. Limbaugh's insult is directed at thousands of American service members. **(What a farce and the military knows it is. I'd like to see results of a poll comparing Rush's approval rating among all of our troops compared to yours, Senator. Try about 100 to 1.)**

Active and retired members of our armed forces have a unique perspective on the war and offer a valuable contribution to our national debate. In August, seven soldiers wrote an op-ed expressing their concern with the current strategy in Iraq. Tragically, since then, two of those seven soldiers have made the ultimate sacrifice in Iraq. *(I suppose that's why General Petraous' report was given such great support by lefties.)*

Thousands of active troops and veterans were subjected to Mr. Limbaugh's unpatriotic and indefensible comments on your broadcast. We trust you will agree that not a single one of our sons, daughters, neighbors and friends serving overseas is a "phony soldier." We call on you to publicly repudiate these comments that call into question their service and sacrifice and to ask Mr. Limbaugh to apologize for his comments.

"Just as patriotism is the exclusive realm of neither party, taking a stand against those who spew hate and impugn the integrity of our troops is a job that belongs to all of us. I can't help but wonder how my Republican colleagues would have reacted if the tables were turned – if a well-known Democratic radio personality had used the same insulting line of attack against troops who support the war. *(Your people do so all the time and there is no well known Democrat radio personality.)*

"The letter I read will be available on the Senate floor for the entire day. My colleagues on both sides of the aisle will have every chance to add their names to it, and I encourage all of us to do so. If we take the Republican side at their word that last week's vote on another controversial statement related to the war was truly about patriotism, not politics, then I have no doubt that they will stand with us against Limbaugh's comments with equal fervor.

"I am confident we will see Republicans join with us in overwhelming numbers. *(What a farce! He knows that's untrue.)* Anything less would be a double standard that has no place in the United States Senate. I ask my colleagues, Democrat and Republican alike, to join together against this irresponsible, hateful, and unpatriotic attack by calling upon Rush Limbaugh to give our troops the apology they deserve."

Hojo's Follow up Commentary: My only question is how stupid, ignorant and childish can a Senator get to concoct such a letter? The results of Reid's stupid and possibly criminal behavior triggered a response that showed without a doubt who stood where in support of our troops and just how out of touch Reid is with reality. After this completely erroneous and unjustified attack, the poise and humor with which Rush handled his actions in response certainly speaks well for the kind of a man he is. That liberals will do literally anything they can to shut down Rush Limbaugh and many others on talk radio is an accepted truth. This is because so many in talk radio are among the very few in the media who tell the truth about the liberal left and their hatred for Republicans, the military, capitalism and yes, even the America that grants them the freedom to utter their words of hatred. They particularly hate the fact that their own words are used to show their true nature and what they are after. Notice who's on the list of signers of his letter. It's a who's who among Socialist hate mongers in our Senate.

The forty Senators that signed are listed below.

Senator Harry Reid, Senator Richard Durbin, Assistant Majority Leader (D-NY)

Senator Charles Schumer, Vice Chairman, Democratic Conference (D-NY)

Senator Patty Murray, Secretary, Democratic Conference (D-WA)

Senator Daniel Akaka (D-HI)

Senator Max Baucus (D-MT)

Senator Joseph Biden (D-DE)
   Wants to be President?

Senator Barbara Boxer (D-CA)

Senator Sherrod Brown (D-OH)

Senator Robert Byrd (D-WV)

Senator Benjamin Cardin (D-MD)

Senator Tom Carper (D-DE)

Senator Bob Casey (D-PA)

Senator Hillary Rodham Clinton (D-NY)
   Wants to be President?

Senator Kent Conrad (D-ND)

Senator Christopher Dodd (D-CT)
   Wants to be President?

Senator Byron Dorgan (D-ND)

Senator Dianne Feinstein (D-CA)

Senator Tom Harkin (D-CA)

Senator Daniel Inouye (D-HI)

Senator Edward M. Kennedy (D-MA)

Senator John Kerry (D-MA)
   Wanted to be President

Senator Amy Klobuchar (D-MN)

Senator Mary Landrieu (D-LA)

Senator Frank Lautenberg (D-NJ)

Senator Patrick Leahy (D-VT)

Senator Carl Levin (D-MI)

Senator Blanche Lincoln (D-AR)

Senator Bob Menendez (D-NJ)Senator Barbara Mikulski (D-MD)

Senator Bill Nelson (D-FL)

Senator Barack Obama (D-IL)
   Wants to be President?

Senator Jack Reed (D-RI)

Senator Jay Rockefeller (D-WV)

Senator Ken Salazar (D-CO)

Senator Bernie Sanders (D-VT)

Senator Debbie Stabenow (D-M)

Senator Jon Tester(D-MT)

Senator Jim Webb (D-VA)

Senator Sheldon Whitehouse (D-RI)

Senator Ron Wyden (D-OR)

~ ~

Comments from everywhere:

For more varied comments, click on
http://www.freerepublic.com/focus/f-news/1913623/posts

I include the following few comments from bloggers:

~ ~

I don't think the shook up Dem party will appeal to the masses.

Too out there. Too socialistic, too entitlement, too anti entrepreneurship. They quite obviously try to keep the poor poor and make the rich and successful pay for it while handing power to their buddies, the super rich.

They need to work with what they have, stop the petty crap and accomplish something. Fat chance of that actually happening.

Add up Hillary's proposed trillion dollar tax increase (offered up by front man Charley Rangle) and you have a real recipe for a US financial disaster like Jimmy Carter's 20%+ interest rate debacle and the recession it caused. Are Dems really so stupid they don't realize that lower taxes equals prosperity and greater tax revenues? It happened under Kennedy, Reagan and Bush. It's just that they really aren't interested in an economy that creates wealth for so many people, only a system that puts as much money under their control as possible. How long do you think it will be until they take all your income (and property) and dole back to you (and illegals) what they decide you need.

But my question remains, why is there no press coverage on the auction? Nothing on network news, my local papers, etc. even if you hate Rush, why aren't more people disturbed? This shows strong news bias to the left. Don't you all want to hear all the news - good and bad? And why didn't all those wealthy Democrat Senators offer to match the bid as Rush did? Because they think all donations should come from your tax dollars and not from their pockets, no matter how deep.

Or do libs only want to see, hear and read good things about Dems and bad about Republicans? They seem to hate everybody that speaks the truth. In fact, hasn't unreasoning hate become their single most used method? The certainly never propose or talk about practical solutions or offer proposals for real progress.

'Today' Omits Mention of Rush's $2.1 Million Donation

By Mark Finkelstein October 20, 2007 - 13:58 ET

Given his show's modest ratings, it's unlikely that Keith Olbermann would be in a position to make a multi-million dollar donation to charity anytime soon. But let's imagine he did. Do you think that, in a segment on a related subject, NBC might find a moment to mention Olbermann's generosity?

So do I.

But "Today" managed to get through its report this morning about Rush Limbaugh's auctioning off of the Harry Reid letter . . . without mentioning that Rush has publicly pledged to match the $2.1 million winning bid. Typical main stream media "objective" reporting.

Comments from Republican Representative, Joe Wilson of South Carolina:

WILSON: Madam Speaker, last week, America's number-one radio personality, Rush Limbaugh, auctioned off for charity a letter shamefully signed by a group of 40 Democrat senators. The letter to Limbaugh's employer attacked Rush for comments blatantly distorted by Media Matters regarding persons who had lied about their service in the military. I am happy to report that the Senate letter of infamy auctioned for $2.1 million, an amount Rush says he will generously match. That brings the total to $4.2 million. The money will be donated to the Marine Corps-Law Enforcement Foundation. This charitable organization provides financial assistance to the children of fallen Marines and law enforcement officers. I wish to commend Rush for overcoming what was clearly a political ploy to chill his First Amendment rights of free speech. Rush took an abuse of power by Democrat leadership and turned it into something positive. Between Rush Limbaugh and Senate Democrats, America knows who really supports our troops.

≈ ≈

Comments from Rush on his program:

RUSH: Well, we have a winner. The auction is over. The final bid remained at $2,100,100. The winning bidder, the high bidder: Betty Casey. More about Betty Casey in due course. (Open Line Friday intro jingle) Betty Casey: $2,100,100. She now is the proud owner of the Smear Letter written by Dingy Harry Reid, read by him on the Senate floor, mailed to the CEO of Clear Channel Communications, my syndication partner. This, ladies and gentlemen -- for those of you watching on the Dittocam, this is -- the Zero Halliburton metal attaché case, and inside (I'm going to be very, very careful with this) is the letter. I am holding it up now so that you can see it, watching on the Dittocam. Here is the first signature page that contains Hillary Rodham Clinton. It also contains Senator Reid, the Senate leadership and so forth. The attaché case, the letter, and a very, very well-written and nice thank-you note from me will be included, as well as a picture of me displaying it publicly for the first time last week in Philadelphia. Now, folks, while I'm waiting on the information here to fill you in on Betty Casey, who is a noted philanthropist, I want to share with you just a couple thoughts here about this. Everything about this, the letter -- and, by the way, I have to tell you...Harry Reid in a speech on the Senate floor at 12 noon today, a little over an hour ago, attempted to horn in on all this and take some credit for it, claiming that he and I had buried the hatchet, or implying that that had been the case, and then kept using the pronoun "we" in discussing how good this was, the money going to the Marine Corps-Law Enforcement Foundation. So the Marine Corps-Law Enforcement Foundation, it's now official, is going to get in excess of $4.2 million because I am matching Betty Casey's bid on eBay -- $4.2 million. I asked Senator Reid to match and all the other senators who can afford to do so. I haven't heard from them on that. I asked Senator Reid to go on the program and discuss his discussion of me as "unpatriotic." He did not accept my offer to do that, and now has the audacity to climb aboard this, praising the effort, saying that "he" never knew that it would get this kind of money. It got this kind of money because it represents one of the most outrageous abuses of federal power in modern American history, and that is what makes it a collector's item.

This letter that Senator Reid wrote will forever memorialize him as a demagogue, and the same for the other 40 who signed it. Senator Reid will be remembered forever, here, as a disgrace. But let's put this in perspective. I think it's fascinating to see what happened here. Look at what happened. The Senate leader, the Senate majority leader, smeared a private citizen -- a private citizen, I, me, who has donated time and money to the Marine Corps-Law Enforcement Foundation. The government tried to take away my living, by sending this letter to Mark Mays at Clear Channel and asking him to confer with me about my remarks. So that was an attempt from him to take away from me my living, and, in the process, my ability to support charities like this: the Marine Corps-Law Enforcement Foundation. This is the government, by the way, that our Founding Fathers warned us about and tried to protect us from, with a Bill of Rights. As a result (and I have tingles going up my spine here, and I have had all week long), fellow private citizens took up the cause. They bid their own hard-earned, after-tax dollars -- and many of you are sending your money in small amounts and large amounts to the Marine Corps-Law Enforcement Foundation, the charity that Senator Reid indirectly attempted to damage when he smeared the charity's board member and very active donor and fund raiser. The government was used as a blunt instrument here on me, and you could almost say as a blunt instrument on people in need.

Private citizens, of their own accord -- without a government mandate, without an Algore pledge -- responded with creativity, and charity, and a sense of fun. **See, in the private sector, ideas matter, individuals care, and things get done**. I guess conservatives are compassionate after all. The winning bidder is -- and this is subject to the receipt of funds, of course -- a wonderful woman named Betty Casey. She is a trustee of the Eugene B. Casey Foundation. She gives significant sums of money to hospitals, hospices, colleges, and private schools. These include the Eugene B. Casey Diabetes Education Center at Suburban Hospital, the Eugene B. Casey Swim Center, and the Eugene B. Casey Academic Center, and the Casey Home Hospice in Rockville. She has also donated tens of millions from the foundation and her personal funds to the Washington Opera. Betty Casey has been a listener to this program since its inception. She's a huge fan. We would expect nothing else -- and we cannot thank her enough for her support in this, and I am honored, and proud, and happy to be matching her $2,100,100. We also want to give thanks to eBay Giving Works, for allowing us to break their website in the closing moments of the auction. We were trying to get the latest bid amount in the last ten seconds, and on three different computers, we got a "system down" message. We broke eBay! I don't know that anybody has ever broken eBay. As such, we have heard from south Florida lawyers, ladies and gentlemen, who suspect that there might be a hanging-chad scenario here. We, of course, are going to just flick that away as we would a Lake Erie midge during a New York Yankees game in the American League Divisional Series Playoffs. Auction Cause also is an outfit we want to thank, because they managed all of this on eBay. They were our consultant, prequalifying bidders and developing the auction. So thanks again to Betty Casey, who is a trustee of the Eugene B. Casey Foundation, a fan and listener of this program from the beginning. It's $2,100,100 for the Harry Reid letter and this attaché case from Zero Halliburton.

A demonstration of where liberal Democrats stand in their battle against America:

By Colonel Harry Riley USA ret.

Senators,

Your vote against an amendment to the Immigration Bill 1348, to make English America's official language is astounding. On D-Day no less when we honor those that sacrificed in order to secure the bedrock character and principles of America. I can only surmise your vote reflects a loyalty to illegal aliens.

I don't much care where you come from, what your religion is, whether you're black, white or some other color, male or female, democrat, republican or independent, but I do care when you're a United States Senator, representing citizens of America and vote against English as the official language of the United States Your vote reflects betrayal, political surrender, violates your pledge of allegiance, dishonors historical principle, rejects patriotism, borders on traitorous action and, in my opinion, makes you unfit to serve as a United States Senator... impeachment, recall, or other appropriate action is warranted.

Worse, 4 of you voting against English as America 's official language are presidential candidates: Senator Biden, Senator Clinton, Senator Dodd, and Senator Obama. Those 4 Senators vying to lead America but won't or don't have the courage to cast a vote in favor of English as America's official language when 91% of American citizens want English officially designated as our language. This is the second time in the last several months this list of Senators have disgraced themselves as political hacks... unworthy as Senators and certainly unqualifed to serve as President of the United States.

If America is as angry as I am, you will realize a back-lash so stunning it will literally rock you out of your pants... and preferably, totally out of the United States Senate.

The entire immigration bill is a farce... your action only confirms this really isn't about America; it's about self-serving politics... despicable at best. "Never argue with an idiot; they'll drag you down to their level and beat you with experience." ~anonymous

"If you are a liberal, you never let lack of or even contrary facts get in the way of your opinion. How you 'feel' about it is all that counts."

FOR COUNTLESS EXAMPLES: Read "I've Always Been a Yankees Fan" by Tom Kuiper and get to know Hillary Clinton like never before with this often shocking, always hilarious collection of the former-First Lady and aspiring-President's own quotes!

From claiming to be named after a famed mountaineer (Sir Edmund Hillary actually scaled Mt. Everest years after she was born), to bragging about being a lifelong Yankees fan (although she grew up in Chicago rooting for the Cubs), Hillary shows that there's no tall tale too tall to tell.

With extensive, attributed sources, including recollections from former Clinton aide Dick Morris, this is the biggest collection of Hillary quotes ever... witty with clever illustrations, and always hilarious context. Sad, but true that a US Senator and aspiring President should be such a consummate liar or have such a terrible memory. Remember these countless, "I just can't recall." statements to questions about her activities in a testimony. Do you really want such a person running the country?

The following 33 senators voted against making English the official language of America

Akaka (D-HI)

Bayh (D-IN)

Biden (D-DE) Wants to be President?

Bingaman (D-NM)

Boxer (D-CA)

Cantwell (D-WA)

Clinton (D-NY)
  Wants to be President?

Dayton (D-MN)

Dodd (D-CT) Wants to be President?

Domenici (R-NM) Coward,
  protecting his Senate seat...

Durbin (D-IL)

Feingold (D-WI) Not unusual for him

Feinstein (D-CA)

Harkin (D-CA)

Inouye (D-HI)

Jeffords (I-VT)

Kennedy (D-MA)

Kerry (D-MA)
  Wanted to be President

Kohl (D-WI)

Lautenberg (D-NJ)

Leahy (D-VT)

Levin (D-MI)

Lieberman (D-CT)
  Disappointment here.....:

Menendez (D-NJ)

Mikulski (D-MD)

Murray (D-WA)

Obama (D-IL)
  Wants to be President?

Reed (D-RI)

Reid (D-NV) Senate Majority Leader

Salazar (D-CO)

Sarbanes (D-MD)

Schumer (D-NY)

Stabenow (D-M)

"Congressmen who willfully take actions during wartime that damage morale, and undermine the military are saboteurs and should be arrested, exiled or hanged."

≈ *President Abraham Lincoln*

"Amen!"

Of course, Lincoln was one of those hated Republicans so his words now carry little weight with Congress or the main stream media.

≈ ≈

BILL Clinton's MILITARY CAREER - Dan Rather please note!

Bill Clinton registers for the draft on September 08, 1964, accepting all contractual conditions of registering for the draft. Selective Service Number is 3 26 46 228.

Bill Clinton classified 2-S on November 17, 1964.

Bill Clinton reclassified 1-A on March 20, 1968.

Bill Clinton ordered to report for induction on July 28, 1969.

Bill Clinton refuses to report and is not inducted into the military.

Bill Clinton reclassified 1-D after enlisting in the United States Army Reserves on August 07, 1969, under authority of COL. E. Holmes.

Clinton signs enlistment papers and takes oath of enlistment. Bill Clinton fails to report to his duty station at the University of Arkansas ROTC, September 1969.

Bill Clinton reclassified 1- A on October 30, 1969, as enlistment with Army Reserves is revoked by Colonel E. Holmes and Clinton now AWOL and subject to arrest under Public Law 90-40 (2)(a) registrant who has failed to report...remains liable for induction.

Bill Clinton's birth date lottery number is 311, drawn December 1, 1969, but anyone who has already been ordered to report for induction is INELIGIBLE!

Bill Clinton runs for Congress (1974), while a fugitive from justice under Public Law 90-40.

Bill Clinton runs for Arkansas Attorney General (1976), while a fugitive from justice.

Bill Clinton receives pardon on January 21, 1977, from President Carter.

Bill Clinton becomes the FIRST PARDONED FEDERAL FELON ever to serve as President of the United States.

All these facts come from Freedom of Information requests, public laws, and various books that have been published, and have not been refuted by Clinton.

After the 1993 World Trade Center bombing, President Clinton promised that those responsible would be hunted down and punished.

After the 1995 bombing in Saudi Arabia, which killed five U.S. military personnel, Clinton promised that those responsible would be hunted down and punished.

After the 1996 Khobar Towers bombing in Saudi Arabia, which killed 19 and injured 200 U.S. military personnel, Clinton promised that those responsible would be hunted down and punished.

After the 1998 bombing of U.S. embassies in Africa, which killed 224 and injured 5,000, Clinton promised that those responsible would be hunted down and punished.

After the 2000 bombing of the USS Cole, which killed 17 and injured 39 U.S. sailors, Clinton promised that those responsible would be hunted down and punished.

Maybe if Clinton had kept those promises, an estimated 3,000 people in New York and Washington, DC. who are now dead would be alive today.

THINK ABOUT IT! It is a strange turn of events. Hillary gets $8 Million for her forthcoming memoir. Bill gets about $12 Million for his memoir yet to be written. This from two people who spent 8 years being unable to recall anything about past events while under oath.

Sincerely, Cdr. Hamilton McWhorter USN (ret)

Dan Rather please note that at least George Bush reported for duty.

I wonder if any liberals read this far?

Tuesday, September 18, 2007

Bully for Australia! Their Stand Against Muslims Who Want Special Treatment

Received in an email forward:

Subject: Look what Australia is doing! Excerpts from an on going debate in Australia.

This is true and can be checked at

http://www.snopes.com/politics/religion/australia.asp

Muslims who want to live under Islamic Sharia law were told on Wednesday to get out of Australia, as the government targeted radicals in a bid to head off potential terror attacks. A day after a group of mainstream Muslim leaders pledged loyalty to Australia and her Queen at a special meeting with Prime Minister John Howard, he and his Ministers made it clear that extremists would face a crackdown. Treasurer Peter Costello, seen as heir apparent to Howard, hinted that some radical clerics could be asked to leave the country if they did not accept that Australia was a secular state, and its laws were made by parliament. "If those are not your values, if you want a country which has Sharia law or a theocratic state, then Australia is not for you", he said on National Television.

"I'd be saying to clerics who are teaching that there are two laws governing people in Australia : one, the Australian law, and another, Islamic law, that is false. If you can't agree with parliamentary law, independent courts, democracy, and would prefer Sharia law and have the opportunity to go to another country, which practices it, perhaps, then, that's a better option," Costello said.

Asked whether he meant radical clerics would be forced to leave, he said those with dual citizenship could possibly be asked to move to the other country. Education Minister Brendan Nelson later told reporters that Muslims who did not want to accept local values should "clear off. Basically people who don't want to be Australians, and who don't want, to live by Australian values and understand them, well then, they can basically clear off", he said.

Separately, Howard angered some Australian Muslims on Wednesday by saying he supported spy agencies monitoring the nation's mosques.

Quote: "IMMIGRANTS, NOT AUSTRALIANS, MUST ADAPT. Take It Or Leave It. I am tired of this nation worrying about whether we are offending some individual or their culture. Since the terrorist attacks on Bali, we have experienced a surge in patriotism by the majority of Australians."

"However, the dust from the attacks had barely settled when the 'politically correct' crowd began complaining about the possibility that our patriotism was offending others. I am not against immigration, nor do I hold a grudge against anyone who is seeking a better life by coming to Australia. However, there are a few things that those who have recently come to our country, and apparently some born here, need to understand.

"This idea of Australia being a multi-cultural community has served only to dilute our sovereignty and our national identity. And as Australians, we have our own culture, our own society, our own language and our own life style.

"This culture has been developed over two centuries of struggles, trials and victories by millions of men and women who have sought freedom.

"We speak mainly ENGLISH, not Spanish, Lebanese, Arabic, Chinese, Japanese, Russian, or any other language. Therefore, if you wish to become part of our society . Learn the language!

"We will accept your beliefs, and will not question why. All we ask is that you accept ours, and live in harmony and peaceful enjoyment with us.

"If the Southern Cross offends you, or you don't like "A Fair Go", then you should seriously consider a move to another part of this planet. We are happy with our culture and have no desire to change, and we really don't care how you did things where you came from. By all means, keep your culture, but do not force it on others.

"This is OUR COUNTRY, OUR LAND, and OUR LIFESTYLE, and we will allow you every opportunity to enjoy all this. But once you are done complaining, whining, and griping about Our Flag, Our Pledge, Our beliefs, or Our Way of Life, I highly encourage you take advantage of one other great Australian freedom, 'THE RIGHT TO LEAVE'.

"If you aren't happy here then LEAVE. We didn't force you to come here. You asked to be here. So accept the country YOU accepted."

Maybe if we circulate this amongst ourselves, American citizens will find the backbone to start speaking and voicing the same truths !

If you agree please SEND THIS TO EVERYBODY YOU KNOW! (HOORAY FOR AUSTRALIA! OUR "REPRESENTATIVES" IN WASHINGTON SHOULD TAKE A HARD LOOK AND LEARN A LESSON BEFORE WE DON'T HAVE A COUNTRY ANYMORE!

He's response:

The last comment is wasted energy. Those gutless, self-serving politicians in Washington could care less about the opinions of most Americans. They have proven themselves over and over again to place their personal ambition above the nation and above the people.

Maybe I should move to Australia. Apparently a much higher percentage of Australians love their country and culture than do Americans. It is my opinion that the "Politically Correct" and "Multi cultural" crowd in America are so full of class envy and hatred for the personal freedom, culture and economy of America that they are doing everything in their power to destroy them and bring our country to it's knees. America has done more to bring more people out of poverty than any other nation in the history of the modern world, yet the PC crowd condemns America for poverty. (Remember, their truth is that which promotes their agenda and has nothing to do with being factual.)

The degradation of our education systems and other associated systems are the result of many years of growth and control of those who foolishly believe one bloated, self-serving entity, the government, can do a better job than thousands of individual independent organizations in virtually every area. That private enterprise, capitalistic enterprise, can do anything government can do and do it better, cheaper, safer, creating more and better jobs and yes, even do a better job environmentally, there is absolutely no doubt. It has been proven time and time again. This is now especially true in our education system.

Even the Chinese have discovered this fact and look what's been happening to them. Yes they have problems with pollution, but they are also doing something about it. While our elected officials pander to powerful political and economic forces, lining their pockets and satisfying their petty egos with power, the Chinese are loosening the chains of socialism and encouraging capitalism, free enterprise and personal freedom. "Who'd a thunk it." If this continues, I can see a time in the near future where the world roles of China and the US change places. Where China and maybe others, including India, become the strongholds of free enterprise, quality education and success as they forego the dull gray life of socialism which envelops most of the rest of the western world. Can despotism and dictatorship in the west be far behind? As in Venezuela?

In my opinion the powerful and self-serving "Robber Barons" of America now sit in the halls of Congress, in bureaucratic positions in government agencies, and among the lobbyists, media and entertainment personalities. These powerful people work to impose their agendas on an American populace that has less and less to say about it's government. Though they vigorously deny it, fact is they provide aid, comfort and support to Islamic terrorists and others who would destroy us. They seem happy to sell us out to our potential destroyers just to gain power and money for themselves. That their efforts have encouraged our deadly enemies and aided greatly in their efforts to destroy us, there is no doubt. Like spoiled children that destroy toys that won't do their bidding, they work to destroy a culture and economy they cannot control.

I suggest that those America haters like Michael Moore, Sean Pann, Noam Chomsky, Susan Sarandon and the rest of the entertainment world freaks, move to Cuba or Venezuela and live under the wonderful system they are trying to foist off on America. I would suggest Europe, but before long and thanks to their European counterparts, Sharia law will be in effect there and they would be among the first to be beheaded.

Tuesday, September 18, 2007

In God We Trust - email

I recently received the following forwarded email:

"NBC this morning had a poll on this question. They had the highest Number of responses that they have ever had for one of their polls, and the Percentage was the same as this: 86% to keep the words, In God We Trust and God in the Pledge of Allegiance 14% against

That is a pretty 'commanding' public response. Therefore, I have a very hard time understanding why there is such animas about having "In God We Trust" on our money and having God in the Pledge of Allegiance!

Why are we catering to this 14%?"

Ho's comments:

We cater to the small minority because of the elitist Politically Correct crowd in the media (entertainment world). They guide and control the thoughts and opinions of the sheep and America haters among our citizens to serve their beliefs and agenda. They have those citizens who follow and support them out of habit, out of ignorance, out of class envy, out of belief systems, and out of self service.

Not to worry! If this bunch succeeds in their "hate Bush, hate conservatives, hate Republicans and hate America" campaign, the resulting aid and support for Islamic fascists and terrorists will solve that for us. They will soon replace the word "God" in the pledge with "Allah" and "In God we trust" on our coins with, "It's Allah or lose your head." I wonder how the feminists will respond to Sharia law? We'll probably see this in Europe before it gets here so if you plan to visit Europe you'd better do it soon before the Islamic fascists take over. Remember, they like to behead Americans. They've been murdering all they encounter who won't join them for a millenium and a half. Why would anyone expect them to change.

Ho

Wednesday, September 12, 2007

Reverberations from 9-11

A friend of mine just sent me the address of a website with photos of expressions of sympathy and solidarity from all over the world right after 9-11. The website is: http://www.coreykoberg.com/9-11-01. If you check it out you'll probably shed some tears.

It is so sad that the purveyors of hate and animosity have since done everything in their power including outrageous lies and ridiculous charges all laced with the vitriol of class, ethnic, racial and political hatred and envy to divide us and virtually incite mob rule. And to what purpose? That singular, self-serving purpose is political power and monetary gain for themselves. They believe they have discovered that fanning the flames of envy into unreasoning hatred among the poor and less educated will gain them the votes they need to gain power and thus money for themselves with little regard for any damage it does to our nation.

I'm quite certain those in opposition could have found a more constructive means to oppose what they believe to be wrong, but they chose instead to use the path of inciting hatred. They chose to use their followers in the media to help them launch a campaign of charges, condemnations, and even more importantly, omissions in hopes of molding public opinion and affecting elections in their favor. They acted on the known fact that it is far far easier (and cheaper) to destroy than to build. The murderous Islamic 9-11 terrorists who used planes as bombs clearly demonstrated that a few men can destroy in short order what took many men years and a great deal of money and effort to build. This old lesson has not been lost on the left.

The easy way is destruction-- the hard way is cooperation, creativity and construction. Cheap and dirty attacks are much easier than hard work, dedication, cooperation and building. In addition, those who for whatever reason are at the bottom of the income and education scales--

the underpriveleged-- the have-nots-- are easily enlisted in causes that promise the destruction of those better off than they. Enlisted by words of hatred and condemnation for those they envy for whatever reason they become a mob with mayhem and destruction their aim. How much easier to bring down those they envy than to work to raise themselves up.

In his book, "The True Believer," Eric Hoffer describes men who think so little of themselves they can only gain self-esteem by abandoning "self" to a "cause." These true believers, as he calls them, will do anything, including committing suicide for their cause. Following their "leaders" who enslave them to serve the leader's own and often ill-defined purpose, these are not men of free will, but true slaves of those who manipulate them. Such is the enemy free men now face including those within our nation as well as those elsewhere.

Here, from fifty years ago, are two of my favorite Eric Hoffer Quotes that describe these people so accurately:

"To know a person's religion we need not listen to his profession of faith but must find his brand of intolerance."

"People unfit for freedom - who cannot do much with it - are hungry for power. The desire for freedom is an attribute of a have type of self. It says: leave me alone and I shall grow, learn, and realize my capacities. The desire for power is basically an attribute of a have not type of self."

Tuesday, September 11, 2007

Copperheads, Then and Now

The more things change, the more the seem the same. A history lesson.

Although the Democratic party had broken apart in 1860, during the secession crisis Democrats in the North were generally more conciliatory toward the South than were Republicans. They called themselves Peace Democrats; their opponents called them Copperheads because some wore copper pennies as identifying badges. A majority of Peace Democrats supported war to save the Union, but a strong and active minority asserted that the Republicans had provoked the South into secession; that the Republicans were waging the war in order to establish their own domination, suppress civil and states rights, and impose "racial equality"; and that military means had failed and would never restore the Union.

Peace Democrats were most numerous in the Midwest, a region that had traditionally distrusted the Northeast, where the Republican party was strongest, and that had economic and cultural ties with the South. The Lincoln administration's arbitrary treatment of dissenters caused great bitterness there. Above all, anti-abolitionist Midwesterners feared that emancipation would result in a great migration of blacks into their states.

As was true of the Democratic party as a whole, the influence of Peace Democrats varied with the fortunes of war. When things were going badly for the Union on the battlefield, larger numbers of people were willing to entertain the notion of making peace with the Confederacy. When things were going well, Peace Democrats could more easily be dismissed as defeatists. But no matter how the war progressed, Peace Democrats constantly had to defend themselves against charges of disloyalty. Revelations that a few had ties with secret organizations such as the Knights of the Golden Circle helped smear the rest. The most prominent Copperhead was Ohio's Clement L. Vallandigham, who was a vehement opponent of President Abraham Lincoln's policies. During the American Civil War (1861-1865), he headed the secret antiwar organization known as the Sons of Liberty.

At the Democratic convention of 1864, where the influence of Peace Democrats reached its high point, Vallandigham persuaded the party to adopt a platform branding the war a failure, and some extreme Copperheads plotted armed uprisings. However, the Democratic presidential candidate, George B. McClellan, repudiated the Vallandigham platform, victories by Maj. Gen. William T. Sherman and Phillip H. Sheridan assured Lincoln's reelection, and the plots came to nothing. With the conclusion of the war in 1865 the Peace Democrats were thoroughly discredited. Most Northerners believed, not without reason, that Peace Democrats had prolonged war by encouraging the South to continue fighting in the hope that the North would abandon the struggle.

Copperheads were the "Peace" faction of Democrats in the North who opposed the American Civil War, wanting an immediate peace settlement with the Confederates. They were also called "Peace Democrats" and "Butternuts" (for the color of the Confederate uniforms). The Copperheads nominally favored the Union but strongly opposed the war, for which they blamed abolitionists, and they demanded immediate peace and resisted draft laws. They wanted Lincoln and the Republicans ousted from power, seeing the president as a tyrant who was destroying American republican values with his despotic and arbitrary actions. (Sound familiar?)

Some Copperheads tried to persuade Union soldiers to desert. They talked of helping Confederate prisoners of war seize their camps and escape. They sometimes met with Confederate agents and took money. The Confederacy encouraged their activities whenever possible. Most Democratic party leaders, however, repelled Confederate advances.

Some historians, such as Richard Curry, have downplayed the treasonable activities of the Copperheads, arguing that they were simply people who fiercely resisted modernization and wanted to return to the old ways.

Media Supporters

The Copperheads had numerous important newspapers, but the editors never formed an alliance. In Chicago, Wilbur F. Storey made the Chicago Times into Lincoln's most vituperative enemy. The New York Journal of Commerce, originally abolitionist, was sold to owners who became Copperheads, giving them an important voice in the largest city. A typical editor was Edward G. Roddy, owner of the Uniontown, Pennsylvania Genius of Liberty. He was an intensely partisan Democrat who saw black people as an inferior race and Abraham Lincoln as a despot and dunce. Although he supported the war effort in 1861, he blamed abolitionists for prolonging the war and denounced the government as increasingly despotic. By 1864 he was calling for peace at any price.

John Mullaly's Metropolitan Record was the official Catholic paper in New York City. Reflecting Irish opinion, it supported the war until 1863 before becoming a Copperhead organ; the editor was then arrested for draft resistance. Even in an era of extremely partisan journalism, Copperhead newspapers were remarkable for their angry rhetoric. "A large majority [of

Copperheads]," declared an Ohio editor, "can see no reason why they should be shot for the benefit of niggers and Abolitionists." If "the despot Lincoln" tried to ram abolition and conscription down the throats of white men, "he would meet with the fate he deserves: hung, shot, or burned."[2] Through the 1864 election, Wisconsin newspaper editor Marcus M. Pomeroy called Lincoln "fungus from the corrupt womb of bigotry and fanaticism" and a "worse tyrant and more inhuman butcher than has existed since the days of Nero... The man who votes for Lincoln now is a traitor and murderer... And if he is elected to misgovern for another four years, we trust some bold hand will pierce his heart with dagger point for the public good."

Copperhead Resistance

The Copperheads sometimes talked of violent resistance, and in some cases started to organize. They never actually made an organized attack, though. As war opponents, Copperheads were suspected of disloyalty, and Lincoln often had their leaders arrested and held for months in military prisons without trial. Probably the largest Copperhead group was the Knights of the Golden Circle; formed in Ohio in the 1850s, it became politicized in 1861. It reorganized as the Order of American Knights in 1863, and again, early in 1864, as the Order of the Sons of Liberty, with Clement L. Vallandigham as its commander. One leader, Harrison H. Dodd, advocated violent overthrow of the governments of Indiana, Illinois, Kentucky, and Missouri in 1864. Democratic party leaders, and a Federal investigation, thwarted his conspiracy. In spite of this Copperhead setback, tensions remained high. The Charleston Riot took place in Illinois in March of 1864. Indiana Republicans then used the sensational revelation of an antiwar Copperhead conspiracy by elements of the Sons of Liberty to discredit Democrats in the 1864 House elections. The military trial of Lambdin P. Milligan and other Sons of Liberty revealed plans to set free the Confederate prisoners held in the state. The culprits were sentenced to hang but the Supreme Court intervened in Ex parte Milligan, saying they should have received civilian trials.

Most Copperheads actively participated in politics. On May 1, 1863, former Congressman Vallandigham declared that the war was being fought not to save the Union but to free the blacks and enslave Southern whites. The Army then arrested him for declaring sympathy for the enemy. He was court-martialed and sentenced to imprisonment, but Lincoln commuted the sentence to banishment behind Confederate lines. The Democrats nevertheless nominated him for governor of Ohio in 1863; he campaigned from Canada but was defeated after an intense battle. He operated behind-the-scenes at the 1864 Democratic convention in Chicago; this convention adopted a largely Copperhead platform, but chose a pro-war presidential candidate, George B. McClellan. The contradiction severely weakened the chances to defeat Lincoln's reelection.

Profile of the Average Member

The sentiments of Copperheads attracted Southerners who had settled north of the Ohio River, conservatives, the poor, and merchants who had lost profitable Southern trade.[3] Copperheads did well in local and state elections in 1862, especially in New York, and won majorities in the legislatures of Illinois and Indiana.[3] Copperheads were most numerous in border areas, including southern parts of Ohio, Illinois, and Indiana (in Missouri, comparable groups were avowed Confederates). The Copperhead coalition included many Irish American Catholics in eastern cities, mill towns and mining camps (especially in the Pennsylvania coal fields). They were also numerous in German Catholic areas of the Midwest, especially Wisconsin.

Historian Kenneth Stampp has captured the Copperhead spirit in his depiction of Congressman Daniel W. Voorhees of Indiana:

"There was an earthy quality in Voorhees, the tall sycamore of the Wabash. On the stump his hot temper, passionate partisanship, and stirring eloquence made an irresistible appeal to the western Democracy. His bitter cries against protective tariffs and national banks, his intense race prejudice, his suspicion of the eastern Yankee, his devotion to personal liberty, his defense of the Constitution and State's rights faithfully reflected the views of his constituents. Like other Jacksonian agrarians, he resented the political and economic revolution then in progress. Voorhees idealized a way of life which he thought was being destroyed by the current rulers of his country. His bold protests against these dangerous trends made him the idol of the Democracy of the Wabash Valley."

Today:

The Bush haters, capitalism haters, organized far left (read liberals, progressives, socialists, and communists), anti war activists, and others, all of whom seem to be walking in lock-step with Al Queda and our other totalitarian enemies, have much in common with the Copperheads. The only difference is that the war in question is not over. They are invested in our defeat and humiliation in Iraq and are doing everything in their power to bring about that defeat. Their current ridiculous pre condemnation of Gen. David Petraeus's report is just one more activity orchestrated by moveon.org and/or the New York Times. It's hard to tell who's calling the shots, but hearing precisely the same words of condemnation from so many Democrats and media reporters makes it clear their mantras and marching orders come from a single source.

Remember the plethora of "gravitas" statements a while back? It is impossible for these repetitions of words and phrases to be accidental. It remains to be seen if we will win in Iraq as we did in the civil war and thus relegate the Democrats to relative political obscurity or give in to the efforts of the left and go down to defeat and humiliation and thus relegate Republicans to political obscurity.

See quotes on Page 91

It is quite clear that this describes today's America precisely. Historically, collapses are quite sudden and unexpected and happen when a nation is at its peak. Debt and liberalism are sure to destroy America in the very near future. We have neither the guts or determination to do the things that will save us from destruction. The far left should be ecstatic, albeit for a very short time until the despots take over and murder and mayhem become the prime political control activity. I wonder how many main stream media personalities will be left alive after the fall.

Thursday, July 19, 2007

Words to go - How Word Meanings are Changed

The phrase, "a gay young man" has a totally different meaning today than it did a hundred years ago. Then it was a phrase describing a happy, maybe frivolous, but certainly pleasant young man- a compliment mostly. In fact, the word "gay" has been hijacked from our language and turned into a word bearing no relationship to its earlier, corporeal meaning. Its usage in the previous sense has been entirely eclipsed by this new meaning and the old one has completely disappeared from use. I doubt there is a person under fifty in the US who has ever used "gay" in any way other than to describe sexual orientation. There are several other words that have been drastically changed in meaning, good or bad, by the"sexual revolution."

"Prostitute" is one that used to hold a very bad, negative connotation and has now become almost complimentary– at least in the entertainment world– and that includes sports, media news, and even politics. Of course, the entertainment world, now so revered by the public, traces its origins back to the camp followers and dancers who followed armies and provided sex for money. In fact, the synonymous word "hooker" originated as a description of a member of "Hooker's army," the large and well organized camp followers and sexual slaves General Hooker supported for his troops during the Civil War. With literally millions of "teeny boppers" adopting the dress, makeup and often the actions of prostitutes how long will it be before the word will be applied to any young girl and become synonymous to "young girl"?

After all, word usage, moral codes, dress standards, "normal" accepted behavior, even pejorative intents, change as meanings and peer acceptance or demands change. The media, all kinds of media, has become a powerful tool for this to the dismay of many and the joy of those media personalities who look for more and more shocking language and word usage to influence public actions, language and morals. The good or bad of this depends on where each individual stands in the moral or social spectrum at any given time. Those who decry our current "moral decay" and "destruction of family values" are merely reacting to these changes which are, like unruly children, pretty much out of their control. "Shock jock" Iiames was pretty much a victim of this ongoing conflict when he stepped just slightly over current bounds. Incidently, these boundaries are the opposite of fixed in any sense. They are constantly changing like edges of shapes in snow or desert sand by fickle, agenda driven winds from varying directions and force. Heaven help the individual who treads these amorphous shapes and happens to step on the wrong side of an edge at the wrong time. The media will glorify or condemn such actions at a whim or as moved by the direction of the winds of contemporary political agendas. These winds are driven and controlled almost entirely by someone's or some group's lust for power, money, or both. The vast majority of the common folk blow in these winds and exert little effort to change or resist them. Those in power count on this non-thinking, non-involvement to hold on to their positions of power.

Political labels are also changing as different groups of power brokers exert more or less influence. Those power brokers of the nineteenth century we dubbed "Robber Barons" are long gone, but their legacy lingers on, haunting all successful business people with strong negative images in a mostly media driven culture riddled with class envy and that describes "profits" as evil and depicts "businessmen" as dictatorial oppressors of the masses. "Governmentalists," my term for the whole spectrum of "let the government do it" proponents come from a long history of anti-capitalist, anti-business, anti-establishment movements variously called, socialist, communist, populist, fascist, and even democratic. They gain their popularity by use of a human trait we could call "the Robinhood syndrome" or "take from the rich and give to the poor." This, of course, is driven by envy and jealousy and exhibited by anger of the poor toward the rich. This force, variously named class envy or some other form of group envy, is evident where those that have the least are pitted against those who have the most, regardless of how either came to be in that stage. This pitting of the haves against the have nots, the rich against the poor, is often promoted with loud condemnation by the powerful and influential (and very wealthy) entertainment world in movies, TV shows, news broadcasts and such. Their animosity toward successful capitalists and industrialists and their portrayal of them as greedy oppressors is legion. Many very wealthy politicians use the same tactics to gain votes from the "poor and oppressed." The truth is that in our country, those greedy individuals and organizations are the main source of revenue for all levels of government either directly through taxes or indirectly through wages paid to employees and then taxed by governments. This includes all payments for government services including social services and social security. The wealthiest five percent of our nation provide a hefty fifty percent of tax revenue mostly from gross profits of these businesses and industries.

Those media personalities and politicians who protest loudly at evils committed by the likes of the Enron crowd or the mischief of the dot com manipulators are not nearly as vocal about similar activities of wealthy members of the media, the legal profession, politicians mostly of the left and in particular, those with extreme wealth who support leftist policies and causes. Several studies have been conducted on the behalf of business organizations showing that business on both the personal and corporate level has a much lower incidence of dishonesty and criminal activity than does virtually any other major component of our nation including government, the professions, unions, the entertainment world including sports and media, and in particular, our elected officials who happen to have the worst record of any group examined. Of course, these studies are suspect since they were done by organizations that are not strongly anti-business. Surprisingly, university studies of the same subject seem to bear this out in spite of the strong anti-business, anti-capitalist leanings of the university environment. The realities of this do not at all indicate any innate honesty among members of the business community, but rather are the result of laws, controls and reporting requirements enacted to correct past abuses by those "robber barons" of earlier times. This body of business control legislation has been growing steadily for more than a hundred years. Very little such legislation encumbers or limits the activities of most other groups including labor unions and of course, our legislators who write such laws and determine such controls.

The legal profession is a special case because of their unique relationship with the body of law. Their members are an overwhelming majority in all legislative bodies, writing virtually all laws and then sitting on the judicial benches in judgement of those who are suspected of violating those laws. This gives them ample opportunity to provide "wiggle room" for legal maneuvering in much legislation providing long range benefits including "job security" for their colleagues. I'll only mention in passing all the very special and expensive (to taxpayers) perks and privileges they are constantly granting themselves. Things like their own special and very generous health and retirement plan, virtually unlimited travel expense accounts, multi-million dollar well staffed luxury offices and then there's all that pork and well hidden graft written into so much legislation for the sole purpose of buying votes. Of course, they have seen to it that such activities are all legal.

Is it any wonder that the latest polls show lawyers as one of the least trusted professions? How is it we tolerate our congressional public servants= that's sure an oxymoron= who have the lowest approval rating ever recorded for Congress. Do you wonder why the media constantly harps on the President's low approval rating but never mentions the much lower rating of Congress? The truth is obvious to all but the dullest and most prejudiced minds, and you know just who you are. Yes, words are changing just like everything else and many carry meaning with far more political impact than fact. I will finish this by mentioning a few.

Just a few in addition to those mentioned include: abortion, anti-war, bio-anything, criminal, Christian, endangered species, environmental, freedom, global warming, hunger, illegal immigrant, Islam, labor union, left wing, Muslim, nuclear, politically correct, politician, profit, protest, right wing, sexual orientation, socialist, terrorist, welfare, wetlands. There are thousands more.

Like many writers, I have a large vocabulary and in general, like most people, use not even a fraction of it on a daily basis. Quite frankly, most people don't really care about vocabulary. We live in a society in which words aren't used, they are made up or changed to new and different meanings. I'm always curious about them though. I often get excited when I happen across old meanings of words that have very precise connotations in present day. For instance, I think it's fascinating that the word virgin once simply meant an unmarried woman. It had nothing to do with a Hymen being intact as it now means. Virgins were often mothers, had partners as she chose (Hollywood virgins???) and may have been warriors.

Obviously, if a word challenges my vocabulary, then I'm curious enough to look it up. One word I recently looked up was 'polymath'. New one on me. It means a person of great learning in several fields of study. It is something or someone I would strive to be or emulate= like someone with a PhD about a number of subjects. I had instilled in me at an early age a hunger for knowledge, for information, for understanding= logical understanding. Trying to satisfy this hunger has taught me one significant thing. The more I learn, the more there is I realize I don't know and might never be able to know. I guess that's just the natural progression of things. My how things do change.

Monday, June 18, 2007

Rising Fuel and Food Prices

Leesburg Indiana - HoJo Press

I am also emailing this to my entire address book.

The food/energy crunch is upon us. Evidenced by the immediate prospect of four dollar per gallon gasoline and five dollar per gallon milk (and the promise that both will continue to rise) Americans are becoming aware of something this writer wrote and spoke about at least twenty years ago. I did not think then it would happen so soon, predicting the crunch for somewhere around 2040. Increasing shortages of petroleum, a limited resource, has combined with increasing use of biofuels, another limited resource, as promoted by the President (and many politicians and environmental activists) to create a major crisis in both the energy and food industries.

This article is mainly about oil companies and refineries and, as usual, politicians are taking pot shots at oil companies and threatening punitive and corrective actions. Haven't those politicians and their buddies in the media done enough damage to that industry already? First, they impose massive controls and restrictions on refining and prospecting for oil which is the real cause for much of our dependence on imported oil and lack of new refineries. Wasn't that their real goal in the first place– to punish Big Oil for making impacts? Or do they and their co-conspirators in the media merely play the blame game and do it specifically to divert attention from their own miserable, self-serving actions. (Check out some earlier postings in this BLOG >)

I'm no fan of Big Oil, but doesn't it seem logical to suppose that a for profit company of any kind would then do those things that made for high profitability and not make the huge investment required to build refineries? The monumental effort and investment they did make was in internal expansion of existing refineries. If not for that we would certainly now be importing most of our gasoline at world prices far above what we now pay. Add to that the very real threat our government makes to soon have 20% of our gasoline replaced by biofuels and you have a force that is a real threat to the profitability of adding refinery capacity. I doubt any of you would buy a home where there was a very real threat to reduce the value of that home by twenty percent in the very near future. Unless for charity, you wouldn't go to work for anyone without pay (or profit). Also, you would not take a job you knew would soon be replaced. So why would you expect any company to do so? Those companies are made up of people just like you.

There is another force acting in this energy equation that will negatively impact everyone's pocketbook. Not so obvious, but very real nevertheless, is the sharp boost in food prices brought about by just the threat of the increasing use of biofuels. About thirty miles south of me a huge plant is rising out of the cornfields along I-15. No, it is not an ethanol plant like at least twelve now built or being built in our state. It is a biodiesel plant which will convert soy beans into diesel fuel. The big difference between biodiesel and ethanol is that it can go directly into the fuel tanks of virtually all present diesel vehicles with no modification! Also, a soy bean oil plant is much simpler and cheaper than an ethanol plant, uses less energy per energy equivalent of ethanol, doesn't produce carbon dioxide as a by product, and gives off fewer pollutants. This huge plant, scheduled for opening late in the year, will use as much as thirty percent of Indiana's soy bean crop. I have no idea if they are on schedule but looking at the plant as I passed it yesterday, I seriously doubt it.

Already, soy bean futures are climbing along with corn futures. That's great for Indiana farmers– farmers in all grain producing states– but does not bode well for food producers and the buying public. With milk soon to pass five bucks a gallon and other food products also on the rise, the public, and especially those governmentalists who look to the government for solutions to every problem, will soon be shouting, "Do something!" It's already been noted by the media with their usual predictions of doom and crisis.

I am beginning to wonder about existing grain supply contracts with China and many other nations who cannot produce enough food for their people as it is. Because of population growth, many once food exporting nations have become food importers in recent years. How do you suppose diverting 30% of our raw food production into fuels will affect the completion and renewals of food export contracts. I'll wager China will not be very happy– in spades! If five buck a gallon milk is here now, how soon do you suppose two dollar a dozen eggs will be a common reality? How about five bucks a box cereal?

OK, so I've described the problem. How about a solution? Well, I've been working on not one, but a whole complex of interwoven solutions. This is not a simple problem. It has many tentacles reaching into many aspects of our economy and our lives. You all know of what I speak. My book, *Energy, Convenient Solutions* should be published by year's end. (nfo revised 2-7-11)

(for info, click on **http://ecsreview.blogspot.com**

or, **http://ecsindepend.blogspot.com**

No, it is not really a solution, but it is a collection of facts that could lead to several. The best thing government could do is to encourage private enterprise to work on it, grease the skids for as many of the proposals as could come out of it, not waste money on dead ends for political purposes, and just get out of the way. American ingenuity and can do spirit will provide the practical solutions, make a little profit (or maybe a lot), put many Americans to work in high paying jobs, boost our real economy and, as long as taxes stay low, provide a huge boost to tax income. In fact, this is already happening. (See the new innovations I found out about and recorded in the last portion of my book.)

I wonder why the media hasn't been shouting about the fact that all but a few states are not only in the black, but are now having huge and growing surpluses– a very new thing. Thank you George Bush for those tax cuts. (Democrats insisted they would wreck our economy, remember? They were wrong as usual) Now these Democrats promise to demolish this economic miracle with huge new taxes. No wonder Congress has an approval rating far lower than Bush. Why doesn't the media ever mention that? They shout about Bush's low rating but never mention the dismal record and even worse approval rating of the Democrat controlled Congress. Harry Reid and Nancy Pelosi each have ratings even lower than all of Congress. Hmmmmmmmm?

I'll be interested to receive responses. Does anyone even care?

Happy father's day!   Ho

Saturday, June 16, 2007

Another Destroy America Bill?

The mounting expressions of hatred and remarks and efforts I see as anti-American aimed to demean and damage our nation all in the cause of political expediency. Actually, this is just one factor among many self-serving ones that completely ignore the will of the people. Coming from so many politicians and media people, it causes me to seriously wonder about their intelligence, motivation and honesty. Why? The general public is so turned off by this that the President's approval ratings have sunk to new lows. This is regularly and gleefully reported by the main-stream media (Rush describes them accurately as "the drive-by media"). Of course, that same media somehow neglects to mention that the Democrat controlled Congress has an even lower approval rating and that Harry Reid and Nancy Pelosi have ratings even lower still. Now why would they not want us to know that? Hmmmmmmm?

The impending legislation supposedly aimed to stop illegal immigration is a sad example. Have we reached a point where we write laws and then refuse to enforce them? Why are we turning our border guards into the bad guys while describing illegal aliens, criminals actually, into heros? What is the real motivation of people like Ted Kennedy whose pronouncements about the last amnesty bill were out-and-out lies. (By his own words) Why is this bill actually described by that same Ted Kennedy as, "Too complex for anyone (but we in the Senate) to understand." To me that is a clear indication that Senators consider themselves and their work as far beyond the understanding of the masses. Apparently we should bow to their superior abilities and do as they want. Or are they merely afraid that the people will discover the mischief they are actually up to.

None of the desires of the vast majority of Americans (by almost any poll numbers you can find) have the remotest chance of being part of that bill. They (The President and Senators) want to ram it down our throats over any and all objections, and without explaining why. I'd certainly like to know the real reason why? What motivates these people who so demean, flaunt and refuse to enforce the desires of such a vast majority of our people. Maybe they just want to bring in more people who hate America and will work to divide and destroy us.

The government refused to enforce the last law and as a result we now have at least four times as many illegal aliens as we had before the last law that was supposed to stop illegal immigration. Of course, all those who so opposed the last immigration law, the majority of Americans, said that it would only encourage more illegal entries. They were absolutely right while Ted Kennedy and his buddies were dead wrong. (I'm sure they knew they were misleading us) As far as I can see this will be a repeat of the last law. The gates will open up to an even greater invasion as illegals take advantage of the provisions in the law that favor them and our government will once more refuse to enforce any of the controls. I believe actions speak much louder than words and what happened after the last law was not enforced will be even worse when the new law goes into effect and its provisions remain unenforced.

That brings up a really big question. Have we reached a point at which criminal law is no longer being adequately enforced? You can find evidence of that everywhere. Statistics show that even hardened criminals including murderers, are only convicted about 15% of the time when they are apprehended. Early release of some criminals, even violent ones, has become rampant. Police departments in many cities are now ordered not to apprehend or detain illegal aliens for virtually any reason. No wonder so many now flaunt our laws with impunity. That is becoming a motivator of vigilantism, but of course, such action will be punished with vengeance. Just who is in charge and how far are we now from total anarchy? I wonder! Do you wonder?

Thursday, May 17, 2007

Free Men and G-men - Freedom of Speech

This is a response to the increasing number of specific threats to the freedom of speech and talk radio in particular. Republican Trent Lott has now joined the numerous liberal Democrat voices in calling for muzzling talk radio. So much for freedom of speech.

I am terribly disappointed in our present crop of politicians and main stream media personalities. I am particularly disappointed in the Republican party who's members seem now to be taking the same kinds of self-serving actions the Democrats have so mastered and practiced for so long, spending and expanding government power and control. Now they are even beginning to appear among the ranks of those who want to shut down talk radio, the one voice of many people, previously without a voice, pointing out the excesses of government= politicians, bureaucrats and other so-called public servants. Is "public servant" ever a misnomer. Many have become self-servants acting as if they were saying, "the public be damned." It is no wonder they rant against the restraints of our Constitution and twist its meaning beyond recognition= that marvelous document designed specifically to protect the people from them, and would be tyrants like them= those who "know what's best for the masses." I lump all these people: Democrats, Republicans, Independents, Conservatives, Liberals and media personalities, into one group I call "Governmentalists" or "G-men." They are the G-men (and women) of the current age. They have perverted the old saying about government to, "That government governs best that governs most." They ultimately admire, support or become Vladimir Lenin, Hugo Chavez, Mao Tse Tung, Fidel Castro or Saddam Hussein. Their answer to virtually every problem is, "The government should do something about that" and then try to devise ways they can use that problem to gain power and money for themselves.

It looks as if the main body of real Americans, those I call "Individualists" or "Freemen" are now restricted mostly to the heartlands. For all intents and purposes, they have been completely rejected, reviled and frequently "dissed" by G-men. They are the self-starters and creative geniuses who built this country and made it a magnet for people from all over the world. I don't believe I need to repeat the words engraved on the Statue of Liberty here= most of you, except those who graduated from public schools in the last thirty years, know them. Despite a huge invasion of criminals and political efforts to turn us into a gray, socialist state, this is still the safest, freest, most secure country in the world. It is not, as G-men would have you believe, the source of all evils and world problems and is undoubtedly doing more positive environmental effort than any other nation= we do while others discuss. And free enterprise capitalists among freemen do far more for the environment than do government bureaucrats. Sure there are some stinkers and criminals among them who do bad things, but I'll wager they are a much smaller percentage than stinkers criminals among G-men.

The real evil doers who twist and interpret our Constitution to seem to mean the exact opposite of what it really says and means are found among those who seek to destroy our country= who speak against it at every opportunity. They are the Cindy Sheehans, Michael Moores, Cynthia McKinneys, and even Ted Kennedys among us that the media so loves to quote. They include the PC imposers and others who seek control and call it freedom. They verbally oppose slavery but work to make us all slaves of the state. They give active aid and support to Islamic terrorists and their Islamo-fascist leaders who almost daily announce their determination to exterminate us. I can't believe those G-men I mentioned do not understand the Islamo-fascists fully intend to exterminate them and probably at the first possible moment.

OK! So maybe I am a bit worked up. I doubt I will live long enough to see my nation destroyed, but my children and grandchildren may and that's why I'd like to wake up those who's minds have been clouded by hatred and prejudice for anything or anyone who expressed a differing opinion. Have G-men their own definition of freedom of speech? It seems they believe only speech that supports their agenda should be free.

Here's a list of what I see as the difference between G-men and Freemen - as defined in the previous paragraphs - at least most of them. Not all people can be painted with such a broad brush so exceptions are many.

✳ Freemen believe the rest of the world should be more like America.

✳ G-men believe America should be more like the rest of the world.

✳ Freemen believe we are fully capable for doing most things for ourselves and making our own decisions.

✳ G-men believe the government should do many things for us because we can't take care of ourselves or make our own decisions.

✳ Freemen believe we are far better at handling our money than is the government.

✳ G-men believe government bureaucrats (read G-men politicians) are better equipped to handle our money than we are.

✳ Freemen believe the existing free enterprise capitalistic system is the best system for America and the American economy. (It's what makes America a world leader and angers the despots of the world.)

✳ G-men believe European style socialism leading to dictatorship (ala Venezuela) with them in charge is best for them and who cares about Americans or the American economy. Besides America needs to be taken down a notch or two.

✳ Freeman version of an old Chinese saying: "If you give a man a fish, he has food for a day. If you teach him to fish, he had food from then on."

✳ G-man version of the same saying: "If you give a man some fish, he has food for some time. If you continue giving him fish, he will become totally dependent on you. Don't ever let him learn how to fish.

✳ Freemen support our military, join our military, respect our military and view them as our guardians against evil countries and despots.

✳ G-men despise our military, use all means possible to discredit our military and view them only as tools of American imperialism.

✳ Freemen believe our military is supposed to break things and kill people.

✳ G-men believe our military is supposed to be a tool for social action and food distribution.

✳ Freemen believe laws should be enforced and criminals punished.

✳ G-men believe laws one doesn't like should not be enforced or obeyed. And that criminals are only misguided victims of troubled childhoods and should not go to jail.

✳ Freemen attract and support: the successful, the hard-working, the entrepreneurs, capitalists, the privately employed, concerned Americans, and those who value freedom and individual enterprise.

✳ G-men attract and support: the unemployed, the unemployable, criminals, free loaders, government employees, entertainment world types (celebrity status automatically makes them experts on everything), professional activists, trial attorneys, illegal aliens, Muslim extremists and those who hate America.

✳ Freeman definition of truth: That which is not false or lies or fabrications. (Almost completely absent from political speech.)

✳ G-man definition of truth: Any thing that agrees with the G-men agenda regardless of its veracity as long as it is spoken by or agrees with the G-men agenda.

✳ Freeman definition of false: That which is not true, lies or fabrications.

✳ G-man definition of false: Any thing that disagrees with the G-men agenda regardless of its veracity as long as it is not spoken by or disagrees with a G-men. Any thing uttered by a Freemen.

✳ How do Freemen keep from hearing anti Republican, liberal and anti America news? Turn off their TV and listen to talk radio.

✳ How do G-men keep from hearing the truth about Democrats, Conservatives and America? Turn off their radios and watch TV news.

✳ Freeman news, anything that's good about of for America.

✳ G-man news, anything that's negative or bad about or for America.

✳ Freeman definition of freedom of speech: The freedom to express one's opinion in public regardless of the content. Vulgarity and shouting "Fire" when there is non is frowned upon.

✳ G-man definition of freedom of speech: The freedom to express ones opinion in public as long as it agrees with the G-men agenda. Speech that disagrees with G-men principles and ideas is strictly forbidden.

✳ Freeman opinion of the "Fairness Doctrine." We certainly don't need it.

✳ G-man opinion of the "Fairness Doctrine." We desperately need it to silence talk radio.

✳ Freeman opinion on illegal aliens. "They should be rounded up and deported, criminals should be prosecuted, A sound registration with ID cards is required. Those who disobey the existing laws should be charged and prosecuted."

✳ G-man opinion on illegal aliens. "Open the borders! Let them all in! Let them all vote as we know they will vote for us."

✳ Freeman opinion on Islamo-Fascist terrorists. They should be fought and either incarcered or killed as they pose a serious threat to America and Americans. Witness all the terrorist acts against Americans including 9/11.

✳ G-man opinion on Muslim "freedom fighters." They're merely expressing their religious beliefs and we should respect that. Maybe if we act nice toward them they will leave us alone. Don't do anything to upset them or they might not like us.

* Freemen heros: George Washington, Abraham Lincoln, Dwight Eisenhower, Ronald Reagan, Rush Limbaugh, those who died in our wars.

* G-men heros: Eugene V. Debs, Karl Marx, Fidel Castro, Hugo Chavez, Dan Rather, and those who dodged the draft and refused to serve in the military.

* Women admired by Freemen: Molly Pitcher, Jacquelyn Cochran, Elizabeth Dole, Condelezza Rice, and Dolly Parton (I don't even know her politics)

* Women admired by G-men: Eleanor Roosevelt, Princess Di, Helen Gurley Brown, Paris Hilton (I don't know her politics either) and the smartest, sweetest, kindest, most honest darling of them all, Hillary

* Freeman weather: sunny, bright, warm and pleasant.

* G-man weather: gloomy, gray, cold and unpleasant.

* Organizations supported by Freemen: Churches, Boy and Girl Scouts, Chambers of Commerce, private schools, most pro American organizations.

* Organizations supported by G-men: Mosques, the ACLU, Labor unions, Teachers union, MECHA (look it up), failing public schools, most anti American organizations.

Wednesday, April 04, 2007

Education - A Comment and Responses

Uncle Mike,

I almost can't read all of the information that you so eloquently share. But, on education... I was interested. After all, it is my field for 30 + years. I did read that latest Blog. I agree that our students need a "kick in the pants" and that the sports, music, and entertainment idols have taken over many of our youth. To whom do most look up? See above... But my thought is this: Why can't we all work together...all countries. I know competition inspires, but cooperation could help the world. I don't know if we will ever get there, but in my small corner of the world (two elementary schools) I will continue to push for cooperation vs. competition as the way to go. If all the Chinese and American scientists could cooperate, the world would be a better place. My view is somewhat simplistic, but it is too bad that it can't work.

Carole

Dear Carole:

Thank you so much for your thoughtful response. Please read my following words not as condemnation, but admiration for those brave souls like yourself who hope and work for a better world where we all work together in peace and harmony. That would indeed be a wonderful world. Among idealists and dreamers— those positive, hopeful souls that want a truly benevolent world— indeed all who deal in hopes and promises for everyone— there are those dedicated souls who "know" there is always the possibility that by some miraculous action we can all work together for the common good. "The Impossible Dream" from 'The Man from LaMancha" is one heart rending musical plea for the Don Quixotes of our world. It is a powerful emotional appeal which touches many of us, mostly because it seems so hopeless. Believe me, I have felt its grip.

Unfortunately, the real world is just not such a place. There are truly many evil and malevolent people who, in varying degrees, would and do gladly use such appeals to further their own cause or belief system to their own or their groups imagined benefit and to the detriment of others. Their appeals seem just as worthy and emotionally compelling as any other, often more so as they are not bound by morals or truth. The reality of the existence of these kinds of people, even if they were in a tiny minority of say one in a thousand, would and does of itself, counter or destroy virtually any unprotected positive effort. Sadly, they are not a tiny minority. Those self serving actions seem to come from a dominant human nature in virtually any culture. The honor system works only if used on a very small scale, in a controlled arena or with a particular group with at most very few outsiders. That the poor boxes in churches have so often been robbed is an old and classic illustration. They only work where they are constantly watched.

Even the best motivated professionals, including scientists, compete with each other individually and in groups, sometimes viciously, but sometimes also in a friendly rivalry. The men who worked on the human genome project are a pretty good example of both. There certainly was friendly rivalry but there was also some extremely vicious and acrimonious responses to ideas espoused by some and despised by others. One man working with his small private group and in defiance of government instruction, developed a very successful, quick and accurate method of discovering and recording genetic code. His procedure cut the time (and the cost) for project to less than half of that projected. That complete story is a perfect example of intelligent and well meaning scientists who should have been cooperating, but instead were sometimes almost at each other's throats like schoolboys fighting in a playground disagreement during a game. Fortunately, one of the major combatants backed down to quell the conflict. Sadly it became his reputation that was sullied in that tight little scientific community even though the concept he developed was subsequently adopted by everyone in every group involved. He was the one who was right, yet he was the one who suffered merely because he went against the consensus and associated peer pressure to develop his own system.

Conflicts of this type are inevitable between individuals, groups, families, tribes, cultures, nations, clans, races= any identifying characteristic, cause, idea, concept, action or other difference becomes the dividing factor. In their best state, they become friendly rivalries, often very motivating, quite fruitful and rewarding to all sides. In their worst state, they ultimately develop into warfare on many scales and with the resulting death and destruction. The "space race" was one rivalry between nations that was about as "friendly" as one could imagine between two powerful nations possessing the capability of blowing each other to smithereens. Perhaps MAD did work? With luck, this is the kind of rivalry and competition we will experience with the Chinese, Indians and others, particularly in the new e-world where anything that can be digitized is instantly transported to the entire globe.

Make no mistake, education, specifically the education of the very young, will be a major deciding factor in the results of this competition. Not only in who wins, but in the direction the entire lot of humanity takes– how the winner shares that success with the rest of the world– how the results affect our lives and the environment– the attitude of those involved in the competition– plus a thousand other factors of great significance to individuals and groups. We really need a strong, positive force educating those leaders of tomorrow while they are young and malleable.

Whether we like it or not, the Chinese, as a nation, have chosen deliberately to out educate, out produce, out innovate, out create, out wealth and out wit us and delegate our nation to second place on the world scene. Whether this develops into friendly rivalry or bitter warfare is up to the leadership of those nations as guided by circumstance or the will of the people. The sudden emergence of the e-world carries with it wonderful possibilities that the will of the people will become an increasing force for the positive. It is intriguing that Chinese leadership has chosen to abandon much socialist doctrine and emphasize profits, individual enterprise and almost laissez-faire capitalism as their tool to do the job. There are numerous others in the wings, working and driving, some with varying degrees of malevolence toward us. Read Tom Friedman's book, "The Earth is Flat 2.0" for a much more in-depth explanation of that to which I'm referring.

Quite the opposite of the emerging nations, the Islamic world is and has, for at least fourteen centuries, chosen the route of hatred and warfare as virtually their only means of competing. That they've been at it consistently for fourteen hundred violent years sumarily disputes those who now blame us for their recent acts of violence. With madrassas and imams teaching the very young nothing but hatred for all who disagree with their rigid way of life, Islam chooses murder, mayhem and warfare as their tools for competing. This is true not only for their efforts against all "outsiders," but even against other sects within Islam itself. They are as much an enemy of the Chinese, Indians and others as they are of the West and specifically, the US. They are a powerful menace to humanity with which we will have to deal one way or another. Either we defend ourselves, join their regressive religion or die by their hands. They, not we, made that choice centuries ago. Short of all out war, the only way to deal with them is to choke off their money supply by finding an alternative to petroleum as our major energy source. That is the major thrust of my book and I believe it can be done within ten years or even less. Incidently, I truly believe their leaders, even American Islamic leaders, when they say they want the entire world governed by Islamic Sharia law. I also believe their current rapid infiltration of Europe will soon result in at least one European nation under Islamic law, probably France.

The education essay was but a small part of my book, "SOLUTIONS!" which I have been developing and researching for the last five years and which I hope to have published this year.

For your information, the main effort of the book is addressing the energy/oil crisis, but that actually affects most of the other problems covered in the book. Here's my latest, description of this positive book:

A ten year plan to put America back on top by regaining the lead in energy, education, science, engineering, economics, the environment and much, much more.

I'll bet you didn't even know we lost it, did you?

Well, if we haven't already lost it, we are about to unless we reverse course quickly.

The purpose of the book - -

- - it is to propose timely, affordable and practical solutions to several of the serious problems facing our nation including:

1. Our growing consumption and dwindling supply of increasingly expensive petroleum based fuels.

2. Our continuing addition of carbon dioxide to the atmosphere and its possible link to global warming.

3. Our increasingly dangerous transfer of huge amounts of money from the US (and many other free-world countries) to totalitarian regimes that threaten, indeed promise, our destruction while helping tyrants stay in power.

4. The vagaries and complexities of an inconceivable complex web of federal and state income tax laws.

5. The national security crisis including the growing illegal alien invasion of our nation.

6. A huge, money making drug problem that fosters murder and other law breaking by competing drug organizations as well as unscrupulous individuals.

7. An education system that is rapidly destroying our leadership position in the

world, primarily in science and engineering innovation, but in other areas too.

8. An information media that values celebrity over substance, sensation over excellence, sex over morality, bias over objectivity, and dollars over honesty.

9. A Social Security system on the verge of bankruptcy which no one seems willing to address creatively.

And there are others. . . .

Saturday, March 31, 2007

Education -- a matter of concern

Why Is Our Education System Asleep?

WHAT CAN WE DO TO AWAKEN IT TO DEAL WITH THE E-WORLD?

Think about this: many students in the developing nations are working many hours a day– ten, sixteen, even twenty– to learn enough so they can get a good job or get into a prestigious university. Consider how much time these dedicated young people would spend watching the antics of "prostibimbos" like Britney Spears and Paris Hilton on TV. That should give you some idea of the huge gap between where those young people are going and where our young people are headed and how that portends the future of their nations versus ours. Kinda scary, huh?

The unprecedented and growing shortage of scientists and engineers in our nation is balanced by unprecedented growth of graduates in law and the social disciplines. (The US is by far the most litigious nation on earth.) Couple this with the rapidly declining skills in language, math and science of our high school graduates and we find that there is a huge crisis in education that threatens to soon bury us in a sea of technological advances from the developing nations. In fact, many experts feel that we have fallen so far that recovery will now be virtually impossible. The bulk of basic research and development is now moving to centers and universities in China, India and Russia where it costs much less than in the US. The e-world with its ability to instantaneously transfer information= huge quantities of information= to virtually any place on the globe for study, manipulation and publication, has moved much of the dog work of science and engineering out of the US to many places where it can be accomplished faster, cheaper, and with better accuracy.

In addition to foreign students now more likely to return home after completing their studies at US Universities in both China and India, universities in those countries are now turning out far more science and engineering graduates and post graduates than we are. This is resulting in a substantial "brain drain" that we can ill afford. Now it is the dog work that is going overseas, but how long will it be before the much larger and better motivated pool of Chinese scientists and engineers combine with government supported entrpreneurial effort to move the bulk of new and creative technology as well as the leadership thereof from the US to China. And there are numerous other nations trying to take the same or a similar path. And remember, every one of those scientists and engineers is able to communicate with and exchange information with every other scientist in the world, almost instantaneously. In the e-world, everything that can be digitized and that needs work will soon be moved to that place where the work strikes the best combination of speed, excellence, and cost. An office around the world is just as easily accessed as the one on the other side of the wall.

For these reasons= because of the Internet, e-commerce, e-science and email= we have serious and rapidly increasing competition in the fields of science and engineering from many parts of the world now including China, India, South Korea, and much of the Pacific Rim nations in addition to Europe including the Eastern Block, Russia and other parts of the old Soviet Union. With foreign students sometimes outnumbering Americans in science and engineering courses and especially in graduate schools at many of our prestigious universities we are producing far fewer of these important individuals than the growing need of our own science and industry. Until recently, the shortfall in scientists and engineers has been made up by foreign students who choose to stay in America and take positions here, but that is no longer the case. Many foreign students, especially Chinese and Indians now find they can obtain really good jobs at home so choose to return there rather than stay here to work. As a result, many tech jobs in America now go unfilled for lack of applicants with the needed skills, primarily in science and engineering. It's all because of the e-world revolution= things have changed, dramatically.

With their booming economies, China, India and numerous much smaller countries are now building universities= high quality universities= primarily for science and engineering students. Secondary schools, even primary schools are increasingly concentrating on science and engineering curricula in order to prepare students for the rigors of jobs in the tech sector or further education in science and engineering. Unfettered with political or traditional limits and encouraged and supported by governments that now realize the huge potential to be gained by encouraging education and business entrepreneurship, these new universities are positioning their nations to succeed in an 3entirely new and different world. The e-world no longer divided by mountains or oceans= the e-world where distance and time have disappeared= are no longer a factor in the transfer of information.

Look at the leadership of these nations. Many are scientists and engineers who understand, who "get" the e-world and its many ramifications. In China, India and in numerous other "progressive" nations, science, engineering, business and industry are greatly admired and increasingly promoted. Those who succeed in business are treated with respect and honor. Entrepreneurs are supported by the leaders, in the media and in the public eye. They are rewarded for their service to improve the growth of their nation's economy, prosperity and reputation in the world.

Look at the contrast with many nations and leaders in the developed west. Most are lawyers or social activists, politicians who are so wrapped up in the past and past dogma they don't "get" much if anything about the e-world. These politicians haven't a clue about what has changed in the last ten years and what will change in the next ten. They, the media and the rest of the entertainment world of western developed nations, often resort to the use of class warfare as weapons of politics and cultural division, denigrating business and treating entrepreneurs as if they were nineteenth century "robber barons." For the most part, western democracies load down businesses with restrictive laws, punitive taxation, huge reporting requirements and in some cases, labor laws making it almost impossible to fire an employee. Labor unions promote and expect counterproductive, "make-work" practices that favor their members and raise the cost of products. Classic example: the American auto industry.

Not a few poor socialist nations are moving into the capitalist, entrpreneurial realm of the e-world with astonishing economic success. Several, China, India and Ireland for example, are doing so quite rapidly. The key to their success: their leaders are capitalizing on educating scientists and engineers, promoting entrepreneurial freedom, arranging laws about business startups and new industries that promote rather than hog-tie the initiative of business While there could be many pitfalls in the road from the gray, regressive world of socialism to socially conscious capitalism and the immense personal freedom and opportunity of the e-world, the rapid advancement of major parts of these nations in the throes of this change is quite evident to those who choose to see= to "get it." The very speed with which the world is changing has already left behind numerous nations that didn't adapt to the new rules quick enough. At the same time, some of the present leader nations, including the US, seem to be poised for a possible plunge into the gray fog of hedonistic, anti-creative socialism. With news media more engrossed in sensationalism, sex and celebrity than with real news and a public more fascinated by the antics of "prostibimbos," than statesmen or scientists, and a public that values and idolizes sports figures over businessmen (and women) scientists and engineers, is it any wonder that our young people in their music, worship crime and brutality while completely ignoring the positive, enriching things of life? The "politically" correct crowd would have us ultimately ignore all human failings or achievement and condemn us to the slow death of submergence in a gray mud of anti-exceptional humanity with no high achievements or low degradations.

Is there any good news out there for the western developed world, or are we doomed to fall on the trash heaps of history like Carthage and Rome? In a word, yes. In spite of all the anti business sentiment from the entertainment world– media news is now firmly a part of this, entertaining even more than informing– there are still successful entrepreneurs building e-world enterprises In a business world almost without borders. Our universities are still graduating exceptional scientists and engineers and even multi national companies are still hiring American scientists and engineers. We can build on that by finding ways to encourage more bright American students to choose an education and career in science and/or engineering. Even business degrees should be encouraged– in spite of debacles like Enron and the dot-com shenanigans. Fortunately for America, those kinds of "business" people are actually few and far between.

More good news: the concerted effort to "dumb down" the products of our primary education system seems to have run its course. The increasingly challenging demands of the job market with its surplus of unskilled workers, many of whom are barely literate, and shortage of those equipped with marketable skills complained of by employers for years, is having an effect on educators, the public, and even a few politicians. With many secondary school graduates unable to handle math, English or social requirements of entry level jobs, employers are now demanding schools do a better job on the basics. Parents, alarmed at this situation are organizing and becoming more demanding of their children's schools. Even those who wouldn't dare to comment about the poor parenting of many minority students for fear of a racist label are beginning to speak out about this serious problem while now actively seeking remedies, even painful ones. Thank you Bill Cosby! Making those comments took real courage.

It's about time the various and sometimes feuding elements and cultures in our country quit bitching about each other and start looking in the mirror for answers and solutions. The only person whose attitude anyone can change is their own. The only way anyone can become convinced to change their own attitude is with positive leadership willing to bite the bullet and look inward for solutions. The only way we will find those leaders and give them the power to succeed is to quit demonizing the very business and industry that provides the jobs, income, and taxes that make our education system possible. It's a about time Americans stopped treating profit as a dirty word and begin applauding it.

That's exactly what Chinese leaders did that broke the yoke of poverty for many Chinese and started their unprecedented economic expansion. They reversed the long standing socialist/communist hatred for business and profits and said aloud, "Business is beautiful. Profits are beautiful. Capitalism is beautiful." And they have yet to look back. Sure, they are a long way from laissez faire capitalism, and they may yet stumble because of political roadblocks or upheavals, but . . . but! They might also become the worlds biggest, best and most free capitalist nation, considering they have just freed a people who have been in virtual slavery for thousands of years. For an energetic, hard working people, suppressed for so terribly long, even in a nation so large, this could be very heady stuff.

I only wonder, is it possible we are in the throes of doing the exact opposite with our socialist activists in Hollywood, Washington and New York calling the shots– the constant stream of hatred for business, profits and capitalism? In contrast, consider the constant stream of adoration for entertainment world celebrities including the news media and sports– people who are performing in the public eye, play acting or playing sports– and this adoration continues virtually regardless of any degrading activity it is in which they choose to engage. In the e-world this is not leadership, but self destruction.

To get our education on track we need to remove ourselves from the nineteenth century condemnation of "robber barons" and all they represent. They have long been gone, destroyed by their own concentration on self-service. Maybe they all became politicians or socialists. We need to stop beating that dead horse. Today's business, now mostly dominated by technology, is a completely different animal, living in a fish bowl. The transparency of the e-world is making it increasingly difficult to hide anything, good or bad from anyone. And because of the e-world, one bad move and everyone on the globe knows about it or soon will. With twelve billion eyes looking and twelve billion ears listening and most each of those able tell it to the entire world instantly, it is becoming extremely difficult for anyone to hide anything. Couple that with the fact that of those six billion, many are holding and using video cameras creating video that can quickly be posted to the Internet and you have a virtual earth-scale fish bowl with all of our activities viewable through the transparent sides. Indeed, big brother may be watching, but the entire world is watching big brother at the same time.

The twenty-first century will be the century of education and technology, even more so than the last. Education will be absolutely essential for virtually everyone. The e-world will eventually make it practical for everyone to learn as much as their brains can hold and as quickly as their brains can take it in. Instant access to all information will make that not just possible, but necessary. All work and creativity will quickly gravitate to those able to understand what is needed and accomplish it, wherever in the world they may be. That goes for teaching and learning as well. The nation that provides the best and quickest Internet access to the most of its people however that is accomplished, will have the potential to lead. Real leadership in the real e-world will go to that nation, people or culture that best motivates its members to use this instant access to expand their minds, to learn, to train and to teach and train others, to teach those basic skills to those who didn't have them.

Some significant quotes on the subject:

...the generation of scientists and engineers who were motivated to go into science by the threat of Sputnik in 1957 and the inspiration of JFK are reaching their retirement years and are not being replaced in the numbers that they must be if an advanced economy like that of the United States is to remain at the head of the pack. — The World is Flat

...math and science are the keys to innovation and power in today's world, and American parents had better understand that the people who are eating their kids' lunch in math are not resting on their laurels. — Still Eating Our Lunch: Singapore, New York Times.

— Thomas Friedman, 2005

America's high schools are obsolete. By obsolete, I don't just mean that our high schools are broken, flawed, and under-funded—though a case could be made for every one of those points. By obsolete, I mean that our high schools—even when they're working exactly as designed—cannot teach our kids what they need to know today…This isn't an accident or a flaw in the system; it is the system.

—Bill Gates, 2005

The critical lack of technically trained people in the United States can be traced directly to poor K-12 mathematics and science instruction. Few factors are more important than this if the United States is to compete successfully in the 21st century.

—National Academies, 2005

We know—and this report demonstrates—that there is a need to make drastic changes within the Nation's science and mathematics classrooms. If not, our Nation risks raising generations of students and citizens who do not know how to think critically and make informed decisions based on technical and scientific information.

= NSF Report February 2006

America's competitive edge in this "flat world," its strength and versatility, all depend on an educational system capable of producing young people and productive citizens who are well prepared in science and mathematics. We know—and this report demonstrates—that there is a need to make drastic changes within the Nation's science and mathematics classrooms. If not, our Nation risks raising generations of students and citizens who do not know how to think critically and make informed decisions based on technical and scientific information. Nor will they have a firm grasp of academic language necessary to advance into STEM careers and produce the innovation and discovery necessary to maintain our Nation's prosperity for the future.

= Conclusion of NSF Report, February 2006

For more information on the subject, here are links to some specific articles on the Internet.

Related Websites

Science and Engineering Indicators 2006:
http://www.nsf.gov/statistics/seind06
S & E Indicators 2006 (Excerpts):
http://www.nsf.gov/news/news_summ.jsp?cntn_id=105858
S & E Indicators 2006: Global R&D Landscape (Fact Sheet):
http://www.nsf.gov/news/news_summ.jsp?cntn_id=10585
America's Pressing Challenge (Full Text)
http://www.nsf.gov/statistics/nsb0602
America's Pressing Challenge (Fact Sheet):

http://www.nsf.gov/news/news_summ.jsp?cntn_id=105859

National Science Board: http://www.nsf.gov/nsb

The National Science Foundation (NSF) is an independent federal agency that supports fundamental research and education across all fields of science and engineering, with an annual budget of $5.58 billion. NSF funds reach all 50 states through grants to nearly 1,700 universities and institutions. Each year, NSF receives about 40,000 competitive requests for funding, and makes nearly 10,000 new funding awards. The NSF also awards over $400 million in professional and service contracts yearly.

Receive official NSF news electronically through the e-mail delivery and notification system, MyNSF (formerly the Custom News Service). To subscribe, visit www.nsf.gov/mynsf/ and fill in the information under "new users".

Useful NSF Web Sites:

NSF Home Page: http://www.nsf.gov

NSF News: http://www.nsf.gov/news

For the News Media: http://www.nsf.gov/news/newsroom.jsp

Science and Engineering Statistics: http://www.nsf.gov/statistics

Awards Searches: http://www.nsf.gov/awardsearch

How do we accomplish this momentous and challenging task before us?

How do we do this? It will require a major change of direction for many people and a completely new kind of education system. It will require educators to think outside-the-box. Here is just one idea I have come up with that could accelerate our education system in K-12 grades.

I have one suggestion for a radically new system designed for rapid growth and high achievement for students. First of all, lets quit forcing people to go to school= leave that up to parents. Once people see education as a privilege and opportunity rather than an obligation, it puts a whole new factor in play. Second, let's disconnect education from chronological age. An entrance exam requiring passage of basic social and communication skill requirements to start school could be administered several times a year, say anytime parents feel their child is ready. Those who passed would start school. Those who failed wouldn't start and would be given a report describing what they needed to learn of basic social and communication skills. There could even be "prep" schools available

How about a completely new system for education from K through 12. The basic system, infrastructure, grade levels and teaching methods will obviously have to be considered for change and improvement. The use of classroom teaching may be modified as teaching via the Internet could even be found advantageous for some students and/or subjects. But there is one concept concerning advancement through the system that I would like to see changed drastically. That is the way students are advanced through the various grade levels. As it is presently, some students learn so quickly they can become bored for lack of challenge. At the other end of the spectrum there are those who have a difficult time keeping up. This is also often quite different as subject matter varies. One student may learn math very quickly while the same student may be relatively slow in English or another subject.

To provide for all kinds of students, each subject should be broken up into sections much smaller than semesters or quarters. Lets start with two week "chunks" of learning a part or several parts of a subject. These "chunks" would progress directly from one to the next in a sequence keyed to the fastest learners- the ones who "get it" the quickest. An evaluation test would be administered at the end of the two week "chunk" which could be graded and if a certain test score is reached, the student advances to the next "chunk" with the grade earned going into his record. Those who did not advance would simply repeat the last "chunk" without the stigma of failure. After the second time through the process would be repeated, a test score would be issued and the student would advance to the next "chunk" in that particular subject or again repeat it once more. The grade of record would be based on the test scores and performance over the entire "semester" of eight "chunks" or "quarter" of six "chunks." This would leave two weeks for vacation and holidays each year. That is of course considering going to school year 'round. Use of two "semesters" or three "quarters" each year of mandatory attendance would provide time for summer vacations for those children and for those areas where it was important for any reason.

In action this program would probably see most students varying between taking each "chunk" once or twice. Some would breeze through only needing single "chunks" for one subject while other subjects might require mostly two "chunks." There would naturally be a strong incentive to excel and require only single "chunks" or one-time-through each for many students. In a single subject, some students might require two or more "chunks" to master some parts of a subject while other parts would be completed in but one with ease. With a broad enough curricula including English, math, science, history, languages, the arts, shop, athletics and others, every student would have a broad opportunity to excel in at least one or more subjects. Certainly there would be some stigma for some slow learners, but as in the present, special help could be used along with guidance into the best path for achieving a career.

Of course there would be inequalities. There are always inequalities. All schools are not the same. Some have better funding than others. Some are in areas where frequent damage makes maintenance expensive. Some teachers are better in many ways than others. Some school organizations are better than others. Some legal requirements are more restrictive or expensive than others. There are any other differences, even among students and their families. Some families and cultures place a lot more emphasis on education than others. Personal prejudices of many kinds can seriously damage a school's ability to get their message across to some students. Anti-intellectualism of many kinds can instill animosity and/or fear in some students. Peer pressure can be either a positive boost or a negative downer on a student's attitude toward school and educators.

Parents, their attitude toward schools and their students, the importance they place on education at home, their level of education and amount of personal pride and good self image, all of these can be of paramount importance to the desire for learning and school in every child. Parents, their own educational level and the culture they come from, is probably the most significant factor in motivating their children to be hungry for learning. This is so very evident in the achievement level of the children of so many immigrants. Those parents that come from cultures that place great value on education usually have children that excel in school. Those that come from poor or backward cultures may have a dim view of education, sometimes even fearing it will harm their children. Certainly many place little value on education and instill that value system in their youngsters. The task we face is educating parents not just to the value of an education, but to help the natural curiosity of the young flow into the constructive paths of a formal education.

The media, electronic and print, could do a much better job of guiding young people in a better direction than promoting the worshiping of useless prostibimbos, play actors, musicians and sports personalities. It's gotten so the main stream media does far more reporting about the antics of these entertainment world celebrities than they do about all but the most serious issues facing the world. The sound bites of these people and of the latest spotlight seeking politician vie for their ten or twenty seconds of attention while in depth reporting about serious issues is relegated to special TV shows, cable channels and talk radio. Even there it is often sensationalized or highly biased. It's really a sorry state when the news media gets so into the bottom line or promoting a political agenda that objectivity and honesty goes out the window. Of course the public will have to demand this and in a substantial fashion before it changes so don't hold your breath.

Thursday, February 15, 2007

Why? A Non political Rant on the Hydrogen Economy

This is not meant as a criticism of anyone, just a question about interest. Are any of you really much interested in the overall energy problem and global warming or do you just think nothing can be done about it so why bother trying?

I've not been overwhelmed by replies to my request for help at: http://hjshee.blogspot.com. I know it's only been a few days, but I thought surely someone would have something to say by now. Hopefully, there are those among you who may yet reply if only to say, "I'm considering!" If you are, take the time to click "reply" to the email that took you here now and enter, "I'm thinking" and send it off. Then I will at least know you received my emails. Maybe it's just that many of you have been turned off by my political rants. I'm sorry if that is so as this is certainly not political, but how are you to know, right? I received but a single reply and that was because my HTML link didn't work on non HTML emails. This prompted me to send out a follow-up letter with the info in non-HTML language.

Am I the only one who has any interest in solving what I see as one of our most pressing national problem, or is it just not that important to most? Would it get your attention if gasoline were suddenly five bucks a gallon? How about if our economy suddenly went into another great depression? I know interest has lagged since gas has dropped to just above two bucks in much of the country. Even at that price, billions of dollars are still going from us to nations that actively seek our destruction. That still doesn't seem to frighten anyone. I guarantee it will when our economy crashes as our enemies promise it will, and they have a great deal of control over that. Just imagine a Taliban type government in Saudi Arabia and Iraq controlled by Iran. (Which will certainly happen as soon as we withdraw) Those in control there scream now for our destruction and that would put their hands in control of the oil spigot. You think that fat little dictator in Venezuela wouldn't join in shutting off our oil if he thought it would destroy our economy? I personally believe all those enemies mean it when they say they want to destroy us. Close down the oil supply from Islamic countries and Venezuela, and one bomb each on the Alaskan and Russian pipeline and the West would be virtually without oil. You think we wouldn't have a huge economic collapse then? Teheran, Damascus, Caracas and Moscow would celebrate in the streets while Israel would disappear.

This is not about bashing anyone and is equally valuable to those who do and who don't see carbon dioxide driven global warming as a problem. I've had a singular lack of success with probably fifty or more inquiries sent to environmental groups and public service agencies, private and governmental. Likewise to my Congressional representatives on a state and national level. I received but two replies, from Rep Mark Sauder and Senator Dick Lugar, but neither one understood what I was trying to explain to them. Their staff saw the words, "Hydrogen Economy" and immediately assumed I was writing in support of the hydrogen fuel cell - which I am very much against for reasons explained in my book. Their responses were a verbal pat on the back for my support to something I am actually very much against. My follow up letters with corrections have not been responded to. None of the "public interest" and environmental groups even acknowledged my correspondence. By the way, I sent it both by email and by snail mail through the USPS.

I have written to about thirty other public figures (including Al Gore) who are quite vocal about the environment and global warming and received not a single reply or even acknowledgment. I have received responses from several talk-show hosts including one who put me on his program for about fifteen minutes a year ago. I have also received a phone call from a man who said he was a representative of the Communist Chinese government. He seemed very interested and asked for a copy of my book. I have not heard from him since sending him a copy.

Then I sent my request for help to my entire email address book, yourself included. Apparently most all of you don't see my effort as worth a response or are too busy - that I can understand. Most people remain quite disinterested in real solutions or are so overwhelmed with media hype they have lost all interest due to overkill and burn-out. Maybe folks just don't believe all the hoopla in the increasingly doomsday media that inundates us with dire warnings on a daily basis. Doesn't it all sound like a constant "Cry Wolf" story?

It's frustrating to one who is very fearful about the future in this area based upon his own solid knowledge and not on any media or political hype. Maybe I should just give it up and go back to writing science fiction. Maybe I would be able to better get the message across in that way. Certainly, my 30 or so SFnovelist buddies are far more interested than any of the others I have contacted. I got more responses - good responses - from them including the scientists, college professors, publishers and all, both male and female among them, than all other sources combined. They also asked some very pointed questions and contributed some great additional ideas.

Apparently, politicians have no interest in anything that doesn't contribute directly to their next reelection and environmental activists are so busy seeking contributions to their causes they haven't time to look at independent ideas or solutions for the problems that drive their causes, particularly coming from a total unknown. Most individuals are so wrapped up in their jobs and in securing food, clothing, shelter and providing for children they have little time to consider even those things they see as dire needs or pressing problems if those things don't affect them directly or immediately. The problems of overall humanity and the planet are just too daunting to even think about. Easter Island was a prime example of how that works and I am quite certain in my own mind that we are headed that way inexorably, and soon. Soooo....Why worry? Be Happy!

Tuesday, January 23, 2007

Writing, Global Warming and Some Politics

I know, I write a lot and some of what I write (mostly re: politics) angers and upsets some of you. Well, some of what you express can anger and upset me, but mostly it's your gross misunderstanding of my meaning and intent. I find that anger is not nearly as strong as it used to be. No, I am not changing under pressure. In fact, if you know me at all, pressure applied will meet an equal or greater resistance to that pressure. (One of HoJo's laws) Maybe it's because my writing gives me an outlet for those energies as I tell the world what to do and how to go about it even if no one listens or reads. I am trying to be less strident in my words, but those know-it-all, self serving politicos (from all points of the political compass) are becoming more and more strident. Maybe I'm just becoming more mellow in my old age. Maybe my years with Barb toned me down a bit. She was an Irish liberal Democrat and we had great political discussions = emotional, but not angry. I don't know how we managed that.

Now, guess what? I'm involved with another Irish liberal Democrat, Daphne. How could I be so lucky? I wonder, could the Irish be genetically Democrats? So far no political sparks = a few little rubs here and there, but nothing remotely angry or confrontational. She has requested, "Be a bit less strident in your wording, just to lessen the possible anger of readers." She may be right so I am trying = not to change my positions = just to soften my rhetoric. I'm certain to ramble about quite a bit in this writing which is opinions, not news so feel free to buzz off at any time.

Incidently, I have decided that politics is a purely emotional thing with little or no logical, rational or reasoning vector. I have also decided that politicians never appeal to logic or rational thought, only emotions or instincts. How else could you explain the differences between what they promise before elections that virtually all of even their supporters recognize as a pack of lies. Contrast that with their performance after being elected when most of what they actually do is not remotely related to their promises, but mostly amounts to payoffs for money and support during the latest election. There is no rational component to that, at least not to the voter.

I have a well developed plan which, among other benefits, cuts off a great deal of the ability to "pay off" supporters with money and privilege. Of course, no politician in his or her right mind would support such a plan because it provides direct benefits to the people and not the politicians. It would also prevent much of the now overwhelming power of buying votes with public money.

It has become my opinion that Republicans are just as self-serving in this as are Democrats. It's just that it is still fairly new to them and so Democrats, with their many years of full control, are far more experienced and thus much better at fleecing the public than Republicans. Besides, the main stream media are virtually all firmly in their pockets for whatever reason. One slight slip by a Republican and the wrath of the media immediately descends in vast numbers. Said individual usually is relegated to the political trash heap. Similar or even more serious actions by a Democrat and excuses are provided, explanations are given, hidden virtues are suddenly brought to the fore and even prison sentences are pardoned. Said individual either continues to hold his office or is provided another well paying and often influential position. Examples of both are so numerous, a listing would be meaningless, but one typical one is provided in the next few paragraphs.

I am appalled at the main stream media and at liberal Democrats for their constant expressions of hatred and demonstrated hypocrisy, especially in things like the Foley case. I have several friends who are gay. Their lives do not revolve around their sexuality any more than mine does. Yes, it is an important part of who they are, but they have families and friends they love and care for just as I do. Sex has nothing to do with those relationships.

The main stream media - ABC, CBS and NBC have aired about 150 comments and reports on Foley and he has merely been accused of sexual comments in private Internet exchanges with an underage individual. From these comments and reports you would think Foley's sexual activities were the only thing he did or thought about.

The New York Times (Liberal Isvestia) lead the charge in defaming Foley. He then resigns his seat in Congress in shame and continues being the subject of critical reports by the main stream media. The Republican party severely chastised Foley who had not been convicted of anything. The liberal main stream media continue bashing the Republicans with Foley.

Typically, when Democrats do far worse, there is no such flurry in the media. Consider Representative Mel Reynolds of Chicago who in 1995 was convicted of having actual sex, (not Internet sex) with an underage campaign worker and sent to prison. He kept his Congressional seat up until he went to prison. He was treated to a mere twenty reports by NBC, and CBS combined. He was never mentioned by ABC who had earlier in the year touted him as a "Person of the Week" and praised him for his work with young people. In 2001 he was pardoned by President Clinton.

The following describes the essence of how liberals and their friends in the media treat criminal liberal Democrat politicians like Mel Reynolds who spout their agenda: "Jessie Jackson has added former Chicago democratic congressman Mel Reynolds to Rainbow / PUSH Coalition's payroll. Reynolds was among the 176 criminals excused in President Clinton's last-minute forgiveness spree.

"Reynolds received a commutation of his six-and-a- half-year federal sentence for 15 convictions of wire fraud, bank fraud and lies to the Federal Election Commission. He is more notorious; however, for concurrently serving five years for sleeping with an underage campaign volunteer. (Apparently OK if you are a Democrat.)

"This is a first in American politics: An ex-congressman who had sex with a subordinate, won clemency from a president who had sex with a subordinate then was hired by a clergyman who had sex with a subordinate. His new job? .....Youth counselor."

Once again the Main stream media will never report on this, certainly not just before an election.

Quite obviously is much better to be a liberal Democrat if you are a criminal or evil doer. Republicans punish members merely accused of wrong doings. Democrats applaud and support members convicted even of major crimes. Yes! There is a difference.

The blatant efforts by the media to unseat Republicans and replace them with Democrats is obvious to all but the most feeble minded. Just before the election a report was leaked describing a meeting between media supporters and high ranking Democrats. The purpose of the meeting was to coordinate efforts in the media to aid Democrats and defeat Republicans in the upcoming elections. The media were livid about this disclosure of their true nature.

It is obvious Democrats are frequently and effectively promoted by the media while Republicans are lambasted at every opportunity. It is easy for them to do this by repeated reporting of (or creating) Republican negatives and Democrat positives. Besides things like the Foley incident, look at two others:

1. The economy. Remember "It's the economy, stupid?" Clinton ran on and was supported in the media for "the best economy ever." Report after report on the booming economy came from the media. Now when virtually every economic indicator shows we truly do have "the best economy ever," with most statistics far better than the best during the Clinton years, the media is virtually silent about it. Rest assured you will see none of the constant praise for the economy like that heaped on Clinton by his fawning media. Any media reports will minimize any and all good economic news, of which there is an overwhelming number at the present. Let a single possibly negative report come out it will be reported and analyzed ad nauseum by these so called "objective reporters."

2. Then there is the price of gasoline. Once more, during the election, numerous Democrat operatives and candidates accused Bush of manipulating gas prices to help Republicans. This was frequently reported in the media. How many times did that same media point out the facts about gasoline pricing? -- 0 -- What partisan chicanery! Does Bush control OPEC or the world prices of crude? Or do the American oil companies? This is complete nonsense and highly inflamatory, but many of the American electorate are either so stupid or ill informed they believe it. Once again it is the media's fanning of emotional fires that works while facts are totally ignored or misrepresented.

I wonder how the election would have gone down if the main stream media actually did report things objectively?

So I shall continue writing, and probably continue irritating those I have irritated in the past with (hopefully) factual information. It seems factual information (like my latest bit about global warming, or the above few paragraphs about Foley and Reynolds) is most irritating to those driven to the left by their hopeful, but irrational feelings. Many on the left are like rabid sports fans providing great adoration and emotional support for the objects of their adulation and hatred and animosity for those on the opposing team regardless of facts about either. I have come more and more to believe that reason and logic have absolutely nothing to do with these emotional attachments, either fans for sports heros and their teams, or voters (primarily of the left, but many from the entire spectrum) for politicians and their parties. Both have a large component of complete irrationality and defy all reason and logic: "Don't bother me with the facts, my mind's made up."

I only hope the movie that prompted all this isn't thinly disguised anti-establishment crap like so many of this type of movie tend to be lately. I have become so suspicious of any movie with a message. I don't mind obvious messages, even political ones. That's what most creative writers do, give wings to their opinions. What I do mind and what really ticks me off are message films (or writing) that pretend to address a usually popular theme and then spend most of the film promoting or berating some political or social group or idea often in an almost subliminal fashion. I certainly despised both the method and the message of "Farenheit 911," but it was at least honest about its promotion of socialism and message of hate for conservatism and capitalism and I respect that, the only honesty connected with the movie.

I can't think offhand of a simple example of the other kind as, most often, the propaganda comes through in little vignettes or comments buried in the film so as to be impressed on the watcher (or reader) while not being noticed. These subliminal agenda promotions are much the same as hidden advertising: the Coke can on the kitchen counter, the cigarette in the glamorous actress's hand (now long gone), the flashy new car with prominent brand pronouncement. Movie sets are a treasure trove of hidden advertising opportunities for which companies pay huge amounts of money.

Al Gore's book and movie about global warming is a classic example of a major complex example of political propaganda. It is clearly a political message and agenda thinly hidden within a very myopic view of climate and climate change. Based largely on anecdotal information of very limited scope, even his accuracies are thin as he deals solely with the greenhouse effect of man-made CO_2 on climate, ignoring all other factors. Many of these other factors: ocean currents (move far more heat energy than the atmosphere), atmospheric dust particles, variation in cloud cover (both dust and clouds reflect the sun's heat), variations in solar energy output, variations in the earth's position and attitude relative to the sun, may easily out shadow the greenhouse contribution to warming by factors of as much as ten or even more.

It's interesting to note that as recently as the 1970's the same groups now so concerned with global warming were expressing the same kind of concerns about global cooling and what were we to do about another eminent ice age. (They have been coming on after about ten thousand year warm periods for a very long time and we are now more than ten thousand years past the end of the last ice age.)

Climate and weather form an extremely complex system about which we still understand but a tiny part. Weather predictions of a few days are fraught with inaccuracies that grow exponentially with time. A carefully considered forecast for the tenth day in the future has

Ho's Rants - BLOG, 2005 to 2015

roughly the same degree of accuracy as a dart board throw at a collection of the weather reports for past days at or near the same time and location of other years. (Actually, one comparison of just such predictions gave a slight edge to the dart board.) World climate is at least several orders more complex than weather. When we can predict when and where a hurricane will strike before it forms, then we may begin to have an accurate and realistic understanding of climate.

The man-made increase of atmospheric carbon dioxide (CO_2) effect on climate, even if it is enough to tip a precarious balance, may much more be brought about by the destruction of forests than by the burning of fossil fuels. The known annual cycling of CO_2 in the atmosphere is due to increases and decreases of active plant growth in the northern hemisphere each summer. (Because most land lies in the northern hemisphere.) This powerful CO_2 engine, tipped by forest destruction (a human activity), may have changed enough to be the major cause of the steady increase of CO_2. The contribution of fossil fuel consumption could be corrected by enough increase in forest, the largest force in removing CO_2 from the atmosphere.

One other important consideration, other greenhouse gasses like water vapor and methane could be major factors affecting atmospheric temperatures. Dust particles in the air and clouds can cause a cooling of air temperatures as they reflect sunlight and heat out into space. Another factor about forests is that they absorb enough heat energy from sunlight to have a substantial effect on both the air temperature above them and the amount of moisture in that air. The disappearing snow on Mt Kilimanjaro was directly linked to the cutting of the forest around the base of the mountain as the new drier, warmer winds blowing up the slope resulted in much less snow. That particular situation was more a contributor to global warming than a result of it.

None of these factors are even mentioned in Gore's work, primarily because they would work against his particular agenda. They are also completely ignored by the media who like to attack entities (like the oil companies) which they can paint as evil, greed driven monsters and so divert attention from their substantial failings while promoting their own, self serving agenda and attempting to preserve their so called "objective" stance.

I could go on, but I urge those who want to know the truth about what most knowledgeable scientists think about climate change and global warming look for some unbiased opinions. Nigel Calder describes many of the conflicting theories about climate change and how and why it happens in his book, "Magic Universe." This is a collection of short articles on things like the carbon cycle, ocean currents, biosphere from space, ice-rafting events, earth systems, plate motions, earthshine, the sun's interior, solar variability, the gravitational disturbances caused by the planet Mercury, volcano explosions and other forces and events that all can have an effect on the earth's climate and can contribute to global warming and cooling. There are many other studies of the earth's climate forces that provide truly objective insights into our future weather and without a political objective. Of course, those serious studies don't sell like the catastrophic predictions of a national politician who gets lots of media coverage. Maybe we should hear Paris Hilton's opinions on global warming. I'm sure the media would cover that, probably on the front page.

Why the Minimum Wage delivers the opposite of what it promises

Saturday, January 20, 2007

The new minimum wage law, job opportunities destroyed by Democrats

I know it is almost sacrilegious to be against raising the minimum wage in America, but I am and here's why:

Emotionally, it sounds great to be for higher pay for the lowest paid workers - that no one can raise a family on minimum wages - that those wealthy (and greedy) companies should be able to pay their lowliest workers more. It's what politics runs on—pure emotion. A rational thought rarely comes from the lips of any politician. It's always: "kissing babies" or "helping seniors" or "providing a living wage" or "fighting those greedy big companies" or a thousand other emotional appeals to class envy and class hatred.

As is almost always the case, the emotional appeal of political rhetoric is long on passion and short on reality, reason or logic. Of course, if there is enough political capital (or donations to the party) to be had to making exceptions that defy the logic of the main course, those exceptions will be made. The latest minimum is a classic example of both such a law and such an exception.

First of all, in September of 2005 I proposed a change in the minimum wage law to make it more suitable for a nation with regions of highly variable living costs. It applies even more today than then with the proposed change to $7.25 an hour. There is no question that this increase will move many more jobs from low economic areas to more affluent ones. More thousands will leave rural areas and move to cities as jobs worth less than $7.25 an hour will disappear. Many in depressed areas will simply will have no jobs at all.

Now about the exception I mentioned: how is it that our compassionate legislators can specify an exception in Samoa where, for the benefit of tuna canneries, the minimum wage was set at $3.25 an hour, four dollars less than elsewhere in America? Could it be that the tuna canners donated a little money to the Democratic cause? Tell us about it Nancy? Why? How about making an exception to say, South Dakota, or Mississippi, or Indiana?

The cost of living as shown by household expenditures in the rural areas of these states is about $20,000, a fraction of the $70,000 that it is in Boston, for instance. Anyone with half an ounce of brains can see that disparity and understand the damage the "one size fits all" minimum wage does to those rural areas. Of course, who ever accused politicians of having more than half an ounce of brains. Lots of rhetoric, lots of brass, lots of crocodile tears, (how about it Teddy?) but brains???? Only in the "I want power and money" sense do any politicians have brain power. If you think about it, they usually create more problems than they solve. The latest minimum wage law is a classic example. It will do great damage to those in the poorest areas and nothing to those in the wealthiest. Read my proposal - the third post in this BLOG for a real answer that would make the minimum wage law an effective tool that would help rather than damage the poorer areas of our nation.

Sunday, August 13, 2006

Minimum Wage - popular political promise that delivers only job losses

Why the minimum wage, like price controls, will always work against the welfare of most workers.

This is in part a response to the remark from "anonymous" who sees the minimum wage as too low to provide for a family.

If you want to be paid far more than your job is worth, go to work for government. Every other job in a free society has a value dependent on what the job produces. When you place a floor or minimum on wages, all you do is eliminate all opportunities to work for less than that minimum. When any employer finds jobs that are costing more than they are producing, those jobs are changed, outsourced or eliminated one way or another. "Downsizing" is another result of this and is just another effort for employers to survive. Jobs are available as they offer employers opportunities for profit. Jobs that are not profitable to employers for any reason are nothing but employer paid welfare. They will be eliminated by the employer cutting the job or eventually going bankrupt.

Recently, politicians in one American city decided to raise the minimum wage in their city to $10.00 an hour. Fortunately, for the citizens of that city, the proposal was defeated. Current efforts of our national Congress to raise the federal minimum wage may be successful to the benefit of only those politicians who can boast of their efforts "to provide a living wage for all Americans." That statement, like so many others from our politicians, waves a popular flag of helping the little guy (the almost totally ignorant poor) while actually slashing available jobs particularly for poor young people. All any minimum wage law does is eliminate all job opportunities whose benefits to an employer are lower than that minimum.

It sounds so appealing to say, "I'm raising your pay by raising the minimum wage." or, "Every American who wants to work should be paid a living wage." or, "How can anyone raise a family on a minimum wage?" Politicians promise much which eager voters eat up, but what they deliver is often exactly the opposite of what they promise. With the federal minimum wage now far below the previous percentage of the average wage, Americans are enjoying a booming economy with entry level jobs mostly starting above minimum wage standards. This means there are jobs available for part time or young and student workers where they can supplement family incomes and gain work experience. These are the jobs that disappear when the minimum wage is raised. Examples are legion and have even decimated the economies of entire cities and areas.

What the politicians who want to raise the minimum wage should really be saying is, "I'm eliminating all chances for employment that pays less than the minimum wage." or, "All jobs that are worth less than the new minimum wage to employers are hereby eliminated." or, "The higher I can raise the minimum wage the more job opportunities will be eliminated." or, "If your children are willing to supplement the family income by working for less than the minimum wage, I won't let them have a job." Of course to do so would be political suicide so this truth is never uttered by politicians.

Price controls, like minimum wages get occasional mileage from politicians, often with disasterous results including shortages, black markets with high prices and lack of sufficient production. Price controls, like other government restrictions, often drive producers out of business by making it unprofitable. A recent, almost tragic example is the shortage of flue vaccine last winter. Price restrictions placed by our government (and I believe several others) on flue vaccines combined with the possibilities of costly litigation, drove all American producers out of the vaccine business. The potential profits were so small and the risks so great as to make manufacture of the vaccine unatractive. Then, when a problem arose with one of the few remaining foreign suppliers, a huge and dangerous shortage was immediately created. Canada is now experiencing shortages of many critical drugs and have modified their price controls to allow some degree of flexibility. Negotiated prices are fine and while they may create some of the same problems as price controls, those problems are usually limited and frequently, the negotiated price is supplemented by the agency doing the negotiations. In this instance, someone still pays for the higher price, government (us) or the agency.

Wednesday, September 28, 2005

How the Minimum Wage must be changed

If we must have a minimum wage, it certainly needs some tweaking

The present federal minimum wage is a one-size-fits-all law that is extremely unfair to both prosperous locales and poor ones. In prosperous areas, there is no chance that anyone will work for the current minimum wage so it is practically useless. In lower income areas it costs jobs that some people might like to have. A single person in an area where it costs $1,200 a month for bare essentials would need at least, $8.00 per hour to survive. A young person living with parents in rural Wyoming might be able to get by at the same comfort level for $350 a month or $2.20 per hour and get by famously for $5.00 per hour. Yet those jobs below $5.75 per hour do not exist. They have either been replaced by automation or shipped overseas because of government edict. That young man living at home must head for a big city where there are jobs available at and above the minimum wage and he won't be able to live nearly as well as he could have out in the country for much less money.

This prevents many industries from expanding into depressed areas where they are needed most. It also prevents industries from being successful in areas where high local wages combined with high living costs, make investment unprofitable. This economic pressure steals workers from low cost areas further depressing their economies. An example of what this standard national minimum wage does to many rural areas occurred shortly after the last increase in the minimum wage. I have been unable to find the source of the information so the example will be representative of what actually happened.

The ABC company manufactured widgets at their plant in a small Kansas town about seventy miles from Kansas City. They employed about three thousand assemblers, mostly women who hand assembled the widgets from parts manufactured elsewhere and shipped to the plant. These assemblers were housewives, teenagers and people who otherwise would not have a job for various reasons. Many worked part time. They came mostly from three small nearby towns and the surrounding rural area. They were all paid the minimum wage, five dollars an hour. At this pay rate the widgets cost $2.50 each out the door. Because the cost of living in the area was quite low, five dollars an hour provided a living for some and augmented pay earned by other members of the household or family. The employees were happy to have their jobs and there was always a waiting list of job applicants.

When the national minimum wage was raised to $5.75 per hour, the factory owners were faced with a troubling decision. This change immediately raised their cost for a widget to $2.88, eight cents more than their previous selling price. They had a competitor in Chicago who used an automated system to make the exact same widgets for $2.75 each and were selling them for $3.10. Their costs were not affected by the increase in the minimum wage. After they were denied an exception asked for in a letter signed by almost all of the employees, the owners realized that even if they raised their price to $3.10 and could maintain their customer base there would not be enough gross profit to cover their expenses and they would lose money. There was no way they could raise their price to $3.26, the price needed to maintain profitable operation of the plant.

The closing of the plant cost 3000 people their jobs and took more than half a million dollars out of the local economy each month. This was an economic disaster for the community and for many people who lived there. All the local businesses took a major hit with many having to close their doors putting still more people out of work. Sure, that money merely moved to Chicago so the overall economy never missed a beat. Unfortunately, the proponents of the one-size-fits-all minimum wage never consider that there are those in our nation who would be well served to have a job paying less than the federal minimum.

There are many areas in our country where the cost of living is several times what it is in other areas. Try to live in New York City for what it costs to live in rural Indiana for example. Yet the minimum wage is the same everywhere. Why not adjust the minimum wage to account for the cost of living variations due to location? Exemptions from the minimum wage could also be granted certain age groups or depressed localities. This could be done on a city by city, cost of living basis.

The cost of living standard based on a national average of 100 is as low as 70 in some rural areas and as high as 200 in New York City and 179 in Boston. Interestingly, Buffalo, NY is 86.7. Rural Indiana areas go as low as 76, rural Mississippi and South Dakota as low as 70. These are actually for small towns in rural areas. Using another basis, household expenditures are as high as $70,000 in Boston and as low as $20,000 in rural South Dakota. It is interesting to note that in spite of the high cost of living, New York City households spend only about $45,000 per year, much less than in Boston.

Should the minimum wage be pegged to the cost of living index at $5.75 for the national average of 100 the result would be as follows. In New York City the minimum wage might be set at $11.50 per hour while in rural Nevada it might be as low as $4.00 per hour. I feel certain you could find more workers at $4.00 per hour in rural Nevada than for $11.50 per hour in New York

City, at least on a percentage basis. In Boston the minimum wage would go up to $9.45 per hour and In Indianapolis it would be near the national average at $5.88 per hour. This might even tempt businesses who are shipping jobs overseas to invest in depressed areas with low minimum wages. Liberals and unions would have a fit, but lots of young people who would like to work near their rural homes might stay there and work if they knew they could earn enough for a basic lifestyle.

If the minimum wage were pegged to the average household expenditures the story would be quite different. In New York City the minimum wage might be set at $6.50 per hour while in rural Areas around the country it might be as low as $3.00 per hour. I feel certain you could find more workers at $3.00 per hour in rural areas than for $6.50 per hour in New York City, at least on a percentage basis. In Boston the minimum wage would go up to $10.65 per hour and In Indianapolis it would be higher than NYC at $7.45 per hour.

Perhaps a mix of the two in some proportion would be a better basis for a variable minimum wage. Certainly, the minimum wage is a detriment to a large portion of the nation. Where it is too high it helps drive business and industry away. Where it is too low it helps create a labor shortage.

Monday, November 13, 2006

Reproduction of an Email About the 2006 Election and My Follow up to One Response.

I sent the following email to my entire mailing list of fifty-three immediately after the election. I received a few favorable responses and one unfavorable, probably about the ratio of right leaning and left leaning individuals on my list. I am including this and my response among my rants rather than using email so those who really don't want to read it won't be bothered.

~ ~

Hi All!

Sure, I'm disappointed by the results of the election but I've been quite convinced that was going to happen for at least the last year. I wrote the following shortly after the election while the Senate was still in doubt:

Joyful Democrats: Ah, there's good news for all you leftists, tyrants and Muslim fundamentalists of the world. Nancy Pelosi is wearing a permanent Cheshire cat grin and rubbing her hands together in anticipation. The hated Republicans have lost the US House and your guys are now in control. Liberal Democrats are happy, trial lawyers are happy, European Socialists are happy, Muslim terrorists are happy, Hugo Chavez is happy, Illegal immigrants are happy, bin Laden is happy, Abortionists are happy, atheists are happy, Mexicans are happy, Fidel is happy, and Communists everywhere are happy. (China, Cuba, N Korea, Indonesia, etc.) Are there no sad and solemn faces? Al Queda, Iranian, Shiite and Taliban leaders and mullahs are ecstatic. Members of the coming Caliphate are rubbing their hands in joyful anticipation of our withdrawal (and military defeat) in Iraq.

(Added to this paragraph today for this blog: The amazing thing is that during the days that followed the election there were news reports and quotes from almost all of those mentioned confirming the accuracy of my statement.)

The world is now indeed much safer and in a more compassionate state. The ills of the world caused by those greedy, war mongering capitalists and their buddies in the Bush administration will soon fade into nothing and we can all rely on the US government to fulfill our every need. Our armies will all now lay down their arms and go home, terrorists will become peace loving peasants once more and everyone will live in glorious peace and harmony. Yeah! Right!

What amazes me is that Republicans ever managed to gain control of the legislature in the first place. With the mixture of rampant vote buying, hate speech, class warfare and promises of governmental nanny treatment of all non-wealthy Americans combined with the results of an education system that continues to dumb down America and a main stream media who will report no wrong in liberal Democrats and no right in conservative Republicans, it is a wonder Democrats don't get all the votes.

Now we can see rescinded those evil tax breaks for the wealthy. (According to liberal pundits that's anyone with a job) And what will the Dems do when the effect on our economy finally results in lower tax revenue? Why raise taxes again, of course. Reality is always trumped by ideology in their minds. Our troops will soon be exiting Iraq in defeat and disgrace much as they did Viet Nam. Instead of a wall, an eight lane highway will be constructed into Mexico for illegals and terrorists alike. (I hope that's a symbolic joke and not a prophecy.)

I know it's against liberal law to read anything that doesn't follow the edicts of the New York Times, or view anything not on NBC, CBS, or ABC, but if you would like to read some opinions that you will never see or hear in the highly biased main stream media, try this link - really, it won't hurt - much. Or are you afraid to read something that might pollute your mind?

Click on http://houstonconservative.com/. It's probably as accurate assessment of the situation as I've read. It points out what most conservatives have known for a long time - GW is not a conservative and should have no trouble getting along with the Dems in Congress. The war and tax reduction are about their only points of significant difference. Certainly, spending and government growth is not.

If this seems a bit strident to you or upsets you then you are experiencing the feelings I have when reading or listening to all that PC BC on ABC, NBC & CBS. (If you can't figure out what that means then you are doubtless a true product of our education system.)

Oh yes, someone once told me, "Smile, things could get worse." so I smiled, and sure enough, things got worse. And I am an optimist.

~ ~

I received a response from a (presumed) liberal source I hold in high esteem and who shall remain nameless. Like many reporters, I will go to prison rather than reveal my sources. Here is my answer to that response:

Dear Anonymous:

I want you to know how much I appreciate your comments - really and deeply appreciate them. I know they come from the heart. I hunger for real opinions different from my own and the opportunity to at least be heard, if only in part. Your mind is far more open than many who share your opinions and philosophy. Please don't stop communicating.

My Barbara was a liberal Democrat who actually understood and patiently listened to my commentary. We didn't always agree, but she understood where I was coming from. She was also very disappointed in the preponderance of hate and personal condemnation coming from Democrat politicians and recognized the bias and partiality of the main stream media. We never had a single political argument, believe it or not - disagreements, many, but no arguments. There was no question that I had voted for many more Democrats than she had Republicans.

My new lady, Daphne, is also a liberal Democrat and we seem to be traveling a similar path in political discussions. She has urged me to be less strident in my political rantings and I am trying to do so, particularly where family members are concerned. She and Barb both are of Irish descent and I have commented in jest that the Irish seem to be genetically liberal Democrats. Now I read a report from some British university that says political bias may indeed be partially controlled by our genes. In part of the study of identical twins, the results indicating genetic bias were very specific. I wonder if that's why one part of our family is so liberal?

I question only one statement in your email, "What amazes me is the volume of assumption and insult that fill this email."

First of all, that statement precisely describes how I see virtually all verbiage coming from the left, including politicians, supporters, most media commentary and some responses from liberal friends and members of my family. Of course, I would add hatred and downright prevarication to my comments about words from the left.

Secondly, I will admit to frustration, sarcasm, parody and dire prediction, but insult??? Maybe you consider comments that are at odds with your core beliefs as insults of some sort. (not a slam or sarcasm, but a real concern) I fail to see any. Also, one person's assumption is another person's opinion and yet still another person's facts. We all have the right to be right, wrong, or partially both. Or maybe I should say, enjoy the probability of so being. Please remember as well that one's position in this venue is a very individual thing. - one person's right can be another's wrong. My favorite example: Right and wrong have very different meanings for a lion than for a lamb. That's one place where I find some agreement with liberal philosophy - at least espoused liberal philosophy, the part about right and wrong being quite ephemeral. Absolutes are for the fundamentalists of this world.

Third - Joyful Democrats paragraph: When I wrote that I didn't realize how accurate it would turn out to be. One look at Nancy Pelosi's face in media photos confirms my first statement. I even wrote: "(Added to this paragraph today for this blog: The amazing thing is that during the days that followed the election there were news reports and quotes from almost all of those mentioned confirming the accuracy of my statement.)" That is an absolute fact as reported by numerous media sources - Reuters, MSNBC and Associated Press that I know of. The paragraph that follows that was pure parody which, if it came true, (the last part anyway) would bring unbounded joy to myself and all of humanity.

The next paragraph, "What amazes me . . ." Sure! It's an opinion! But think about this: Where are all the Republicans and their teams of lawyers yelling "vote fraud!" and "recount!" and promising to tie up numerous state and local elections as promised by many Democrats before the election? How about the many big city Democrat machines some of whom even brag about "stealing" elections like "Boss" Daly of Chicago. Some precincts in Cook county and in St Louis actually reported more Democrat votes than they had registered voters. Where are all the investigative reporters hot after these stories? Hmmmmmmmmm! "Vote early and often." a common joke around Chicago, may (sadly) be quite true. I voted in Cook County and know how difficult it was (and probably still is) to vote Republican there.

Several comments regarding the paragraph starting about taxes: Rescinding the Bush tax reform is one of the announced priorities of the Democrat Congress. I didn't say it - Charley Rangle did and he will head that committee in the next congress. No matter how you describe it, doing nothing about the law that will soon expire, is still raising taxes and by a substantial amount at that. This will be done in spite of the overwhelming evidence that lower taxes produces increased tax revenue because of the stimulating effect it has on the economy. Democrats adhering to true party dogma promise to raise taxes by killing the Bush Tax cuts. The real meaning of that dogma? "We can better spend your money than you can" Oh yes, these "tax cuts for the wealthy" when rescinded will raise taxes on the average American family taxpayer by $1,500 to $2,500 per year. Is this what Dems call helping the middle income American? Who's kidding who? They'll probably end up blaming Republicans for increasing taxes. It surely wouldn't be the first time Democrats blamed Republicans for bad things resulting from Democrat actions. This whole scene is obviously the use of active class warfare to create hatred in the hearts of the so called, middle (and lower) income Americans for those who earn more than they.

The very first thing on the agenda of Democrats looks to be to raise the minimum wage. Class warfare comes to the forefront as a tool for this economically destructive policy that costs so many people productive jobs in the poorer sections of our economy and boosts the pressure for illegals to enter our country seeking jobs. Many jobs unskilled illegals take are not covered by the minimum wage. Listen to the arguments of those favoring this. If what they say is true, why not raise the minimum wage to $20.00 per hour - or $50.00? If their rational is correct, that would raise the pay of wage earners well into the "living wage" category and we would all benefit greatly. The real reason is strictly the propaganda value of raising the "partial wage floor," a far more accurate name for the process and to buy votes! To learn more about this and to hear a thoughtful and workable solution, Click Here to see one of my "solutions" to one of our knotty problems. Unlike many politicians of all persuasions, I don't just condemn or support blindly, I seek to create possible solutions outside party politics. Some of you ought to try that some time - instead of simply belly aching, think about and then write about a solution. Of course, that requires real work and effort and maybe a few less hours in front of the boob tube.

Iraq: Again, Democrats are in a perfect position to do what ever pleases them and blame all the problems on Republicans and the Bush administration. Don't be too surprised if Democrats directly bring on a withdrawal from Iraq in defeat and disgrace similar to Viet Nam and blame that on Republicans. They cannot afford for Iraq to become a success. They see the same long range benefits for our failure in Iraq as the Muslim terrorists. Oh yes, look for a change in the reporting about Iraq in the main stream media. I predict it will slowly move from negative to positive as Democrats are in control long enough to claim any success there as due to their efforts. They are in a win-win situation. If things go badly, they can and will blame it on Bush and Republicans. If things go well they can and will take credit for success and their media lackeys will affirm whichever position they decide to take. They did it before and will surely do it again. Also, look for them to make nice with the Iranians and possibly bring them in to help our withdrawal from Iraq. Israel will probably soon be dead meat.

The highway to Mexico is of course a parody that predicts the future for Illegal aliens of whatever stripe. If you think we have lots of them now, just wait 'til the next amnesty. Bankruptcy of Social Security anyone? (I do indeed hope that's a symbolic joke and not a prophecy, but I fear the immigration flood gates are about to be opened.) Will Spanish become our national language in a few decades?

"I know it's against liberal law . . ." For those who take my words literally, this is a bit of sarcasm with some basis in fact. For those who might not fear a very different view than the highly biased one promoted by the New York Times et al, try http://houstonconservative.com/. It's probably as accurate an assessment of the situation as I've read and is certainly no more right leaning than the Times et al are left leaning. It points out what most conservatives have known for a long time - GW is not a conservative and should have no trouble getting along with the Dems in Congress. The war and tax reduction are about their only points of significant difference. Certainly, spending, illegal immigration and government growth is not.

About all that PC BC on ABC, NBC & CBS. (If you can't figure out what that means then you are doubtless a true product of our education system.) Read John Stossel of ABC, Bernie Goldberg of CBS or several other "liberal media people" who freely admit the liberal bias of their media cohorts. These are not Rush Limbaugh followers, but genuine credentialed liberal media people who have the courage and honesty to describe what most in the media work so feverishly to hide and deny. I applaud them for the courage to admit who they are and that they have biased views. Did you notice that Dan Rather still insists those falsified papers - **proven and admitted falsified papers** - that he presented as real are actually real! He's either delusional, demented or living in a very different reality. The sad commentary is that there are actually people who still believe him. **Damn the facts, it's our agenda that counts!**

Oh yes, someone once told me, "Smile, things could get worse." So I smiled, and sure enough, things got worse. I note nearly all liberals do not want to be called liberals, (or anything else) they do not want any label describing who and what they are or believe in. They would have you believe they represent the vast majority of "average Americans." Are they in truth hiding their political beliefs? In contrast, most conservatives I know, freely call themselves conservative and like being though of as such. I find myself far too conservative for my liberal friends and family, while at the same time I seem far to liberal for many of my conservative friends.

I stand on predictions I made some time ago in several lectures and the associated papers on the subjects therein.

Wednesday, November 08, 2006

Joyful Democrats and the Happy Spawn of Their Success

Ah, there's good news for all you leftists and Muslim fundamentalists of the world. Nancy Pelosi is wearing a permanent Cheshire cat grin and rubbing her hands together in anticipation. The hated Republicans have lost the US House and your guys are now in control. Liberal Democrats are happy, trial lawyers are happy, European Socialists are happy, Muslim terrorists are happy, Hugo Chavez is happy, Illegal immigrants are happy, bin Laden is happy, Abortionists are happy, atheists are happy, Mexicans are happy, Fidel is happy, and Communists everywhere are happy. (China, Cuba, N Korea, Indonesia, etc.) Are there no sad and solemn faces? Al Queda, Iranian, Shiite and Taliban leaders and mullahs are ecstatic. Members of the coming Caliphate are rubbing their hands in joyful anticipation of our withdrawal (and military defeat) in Iraq.

The world is now indeed much safer and in a more compassionate state. The ills of the world caused by those greedy, war mongering capitalists and their buddies in the Bush administration will soon fade into nothing and we can all rely on the US government to fulfill our every need. Our armies will all now lay down their arms and go home, terrorists will become peace loving peasants once more and everyone will live in glorious peace and harmony. Yeah! Right!

~ ~

If anyone would like to know why I am not a liberal Democrat (or right wing conservative for that matter) click on **http://hjnonlib.blogspot.com**. I wonder why Liberals almost never say what they are for, only what they are against? Speaking of being for something, I am working on a book called simply, "Solutions!" which offers solutions, viable, creative, innovative solutions, to a number of other serious problems including the drug problem, income taxes, illegal immigration and personal identity among others.

I hear lots of angry denunciations, condemnations, accusations and downright nasty personal attacks, aired and shouted in the present political campaign from members of all sides. I rarely hear any reference to any kind of solutions to the problems cited. Certainly there has been almost no issues dealt with positively. Apparently, anger, hatred and condemnation reach and influence the American electorate and substantive, rational treatment of issues does not. Add to that the vast lack of knowledge and understanding of all but the most trivial matters that dominates and controls the minds of so many Americans and you have a formula for disaster.

Unfortunately, my "Solutions" would strip politicians of much of the lucrative control they now wield and prompt them to serve those main stream Americans they now so ignore. Powerful monied groups, corporate, union and professional, would do their best to stop implementations of many of my "Solutions" because they would rob those groups of much of the money and power they now enjoy because of the problems. (Illegal aliens for instance) It might surprise some of you to know how much I despise these kinds of people in corporations large and small. Of course, the same kinds of individuals in government, labor and trade unions, universities and the professions which I despise equally are considered acceptably decent by the left. Should you want to read about some of my non-partisan solutions, click on one or more of the following links:

Drugs - A Real Answer to the Drug Problem - - Page 499XXXX

Taxes - The Johnson Tax Code - - - - - - - - - - Page 200 - - - - **http://jtax.blogspot.com**

There are several more in process. These are excerpts as the full text is in process of being incorporated into my book and will soon be submitted to a publisher.

Of course, most of those on the political left would never expose themselves to such new and novel ideas because they know that anything that is not fed to them by fellow leftists must be a plot by the religious right. I know because I have been accused of that very thing (following the extreme fundamentalist Christian right in ignorance) by some family members from the left. Apparently, they view any idea or opinion that is not in lock-step with the mantras of the left as being stupid, impossible, useless or even worse, coming from the religious right. If that isn't a demonstration of their being extremely closed minded, what would you call it? One thing most liberals and leftists are definitely not is open minded.

Tuesday, November 07, 2006

I Voted!

Well! I voted! It was an interesting experience considering the contentiousness of this election with Democrats and their mouthpieces in the main stream media on one side shouting hate and "foul" and the Republicans and their mouthpieces in talk radio on the opposing side shouting "stay the course" and praising the economy. Neither party seemed to have anything to say regarding the issues as character assassination and negative ads crowded the airwaves.

I live in an interesting county and state. You liberal Democrats would be shocked to know that by voting a straight Democrat ticket on the partisan ballot you would only be voting for three candidates out of twenty-three. The first of the three were for house district 3 where my neighbor, Tom Hayhurst, was the Democrat opposing Mark Souder. Mark Ruppel was the Republican running against an unknown Democrat (at least I never heard of him before). The third and last Democrat on the ballot was running for Sheriff

There was no Democrat in the race for the US Senate as Dick Lugar was unopposed. All of the remaining twenty candidates for the state, county and township offices were Republicans running without Democrat opposition. As a matter of interest there were five Libertarian party candidates on the ballot in the state including Dick Lugar's only opposition. There are, in fact, two Libertarian candidates in the state who have a realistic chance of winning. Both are running against both Republican and Democrat candidates. It rather made voting simple, at least for Republicans.

With most voters offered only a choice between the lesser of two evils and the two media extremes digging up and inventing dirt while calling each other names it is no wonder the country is in a political morass. Such is the testimony to the dwindling intelligence of the American public in this one's opinion. Also in my opinion, American voters will indeed get what they deserve and that will have virtually nothing to do with what the vast majority of candidates have said during the campaign. Apparently Americans are more likely to be swayed by hate filled damning rhetoric than by even a hint of attention to the huge problems facing our nation. I see us as playing political Russian Roulette and our real enemies have loaded all barrels of the gun.

I'm reminded frequently of the following quote:

See quotes on Page 91

There is no doubt in my mind that Republicans are equally at fault in trying to buy votes by handouts "from the public treasury." They learned to do this from Democrats. We are becoming a nation of self-serving dependents expecting the government to fulfill the extravagant promises of gifts from the public treasury. One blip, probably a major oil crises which I believe will come upon us soon, and our economy will collapse and make the great depression look like a tea party. We are certainly now moving 'From Apathy to Dependency." Can bondage be far away? I see bondage as a Socialist dictatorship and our nation as much closer to bondage than you can imagine.

I often hear the question asked, "Why so much negative campaigning and character assassination during the campaign?" One quick look at human nature and emotional response provides a very telling answer. It is so very much easier to destroy than build. The emotional release from hating and venting is far more motivating than rational discussions of issues and ideas. There is an old question that asks, What is the difference between the men you would hire to tear down a house and those you would hire to build a new one. 9/11 gives us a dramatic example of this difference. Contrast the very few men who brought down the twin towers, crashed into the Pentagon and were trying to destroy the Capitol all in a few hours, with the huge numbers of men, vast expenditure of capital, and years of effort required to conceive of, design and build those buildings. Years of hard work by many skilled men can be destroyed in a few minutes by a few rough men. Character assassination, even if untrue can move far more voters than the best presentation on issues. The use of class warfare is the constant tool of those inept souls who can and would destroy, but have little skill to build.

Statesmen build! Politicians destroy! The public suffers in unthinking, ignorant control of their emotions!

I'll Soften My Words. Will Kennedy, Pelosi, Dean et Al Soften Theirs?

My lady, Daphne, tells me my words in political commentary (HoJo's Rants) sound as if I think I "know it all" and thus elicit anger from those with opposing views. She is probably right. I'm sorry if I come across that way. It is definitely not how I think. In fact, nothing could be farther from the truth. These are my O P I N I O N S ! Just like all political views of every other person , they are the OPINIONS of those individuals. I believe I have the right to my opinion and also the right to be wrong. Likewise, I believe those who disagree with my opinions also have the right to be wrong. Also, I don't see things as two opposing views - as black and white, right and left, Republican and Democrat. I rather try to view both positives and negatives of each view and make my decision and opinion accordingly. This is quite difficult when views that oppose my basic ideas elicit a strong opposing reaction. I am especially moved in these directions by those who see their opinions as the only proper or correct ones.

I have never verbally abused or questioned the sanity, intelligence or loyalty of those in my family and among my friends, at least not in many years. In contrast I have been cursed and had my sanity, intelligence and religious views called "unbelievable, disastrous, ridiculous, stupid" and a few other choice invectives by those who cannot understand how I can possibly not see things or believe as they do. While I have been told my opinions are not welcome by several who oppose my views, I listen with respect to the words of these same people, mostly without comment, just to prevent angry responses. Mostly, I try to present facts in contrast to the emotionally charged views of others. I try to at least get others to examine all the facts as well as my opinions and consider opposing views.

I have even been accused of supporting and even being a fundamentalist Christian. Anyone who believes this knows very little about who and what I am or what I believe. I argue against and have little respect for fundamentalism of any kind from as far back as I can remember. That includes political fundamentalism. Eric Hoffer expressed my views about fundamentalism (he didn't call it that, but the similarity is obvious) as well or better than I could myself.

"Passionate hatred can give meaning and purpose to an empty life. Thus people haunted by the purposelessness of their lives try to find a new content not only by dedicating themselves to a holy cause but also by nursing a fanatical grievance. A mass movement offers them unlimited opportunities for both."

Maybe I should pose my commentaries as questions. Hoffer had something significant to say about that.

"Language was invented to ask questions. Answers may be given by grunts and gestures, but questions must be spoken. Humanness came of age when man asked the first question. Social stagnation results not from a lack of answers but from the absence of the impulse to ask questions."

I have some commentary to add to something my sister sent me. What she sent was quite true and well said. My words are added (in italics) not as a rebuttal, but as an addition, a respectful addition which might indicate a very different perspective. My premise (opinion) for these additions is that fundamentalist Islam presents a menace at least as great as, though quite different from, that the NAZIs did about the time of the Munich agreements. Besides, Islam has more than a millennium of history of death and destruction wherever they went. They clearly express their intentions and back those declarations with action. They've been hacking the heads off of unbelievers for most of their existence. Only now do they have the resources to take on and enslave the world. Why is it so many Americans refuse to see the danger?

It's ludicrous to blame America's actions and presence in the Middle East for the animosity of so many Muslims. That animosity (for Western civilization) has been around for at least a millennium. (I don't see George Bush as having been around that long.)

Certainly I believe my ideas to be right! So do each and every one of you who read these words. We all do that or else abdicate our personal responsibility and self respect. Here's the item from my sister with my comments in italics.

"Make Love Your Aim." 1 Corinthians 14:1

Some Comments About Iraq

Yesterday 10 more U.S. soldiers were killed, making October one of the deadliest months on record for the U.S. (Only in the Iraq war) We are fast approaching a tragic 3,000 U.S. soldiers dying in the streets and sands of Iraq .

NOTE: Put those statistics in perspective. Between December 19 and January 25 - 37 days - American forces had 81,000 casualties. 24,000 Americans were captured and 19,000 were killed in a forest near Ardennes, France. That was one battle in WW II. How many of those who died in German concentration camps would you blame on the actions of American forces? I have no figures on civilian deaths caused by American forces, but I'm sure there were some. Also, Iwo Jima: 35 days, 26,000 casualties and 6,800 dead. Guadalcanal: 183 days, 19,000 casualties and 7,100 dead. Big as they were, these were only a few of the many battles of WW II.

I know many readers see this current action as minor and no long range threat. You are certainly entitled to your opinion. I however, view it as much more. Islam has always been at war with all who believe differently from them. United, even under the leadership of numerous feuding leaders, they could soon control most of the world's petroleum. Certainly you can see they will then do everything in their power to destroy the economies of the Western World. Once Pakistan is under their control there will be two nuclear powers willing and able to loose the atomic genie. Once they do this, the rest should be easy.

Last week an independent report revealed that more than 655,000 innocent people have died in Iraq as a result of the U.S. invasion. *(Technically correct except that most of those deaths were caused by Islamic terrorists.)* Just today the Brookings Institution reported a half-million people have been displaced since February - an estimated 100,000 of them children. One report puts the total number of displaced persons at 800,000. *I wonder about the agenda of those making the reports mentioned. Clearly the crisis is spiraling out of all control. Wrong! It is completely under* control of the Islamic terrorists, insurrectionists who are being encouraged and emotionally supported by liberal Democrats and the main stream media. That the propaganda from the terrorists is mainly a repeat, often word for word, of things being said by many Democrats in the media, must be obvious to all but the most prejudiced.

Today when asked about the President's reaction to the mounting death toll, the White House Press Secretary responded that "his strategy is to win." Winning, in his terminology means helping create a free, democratic and independent Iraq able to defend itself and take care of its people.

When is winning losing? Jesus asked, "What does it profit them if they gain the whole world, but lose or forfeit themselves?" (Luke 9:25) Most people of faith believe in a different kind of winning. Just as wars kill, words can heal. Just as hate destroys, love strengthens. Bonds of understanding and goodwill ? whether between persons or nations ? are made not with clenched fists, but open hands. Speaking of hate, have you listened to the hate speech of so many powerful Democrats for the last three years?

Our hearts are broken by the violence and our nation diminished by pouring U.S. troops and treasure into the middle of what amounts to a deadly civil war, causing untold misery and fueling the very fire that terrorists have been hoping for. Equally tragic is the fact that the majority of representatives in the U.S. Congress have allowed this to happen. That is why your vote this November is more important than ever. It most certainly is not our efforts that fuels the terrorists as much as does the verbal support and encouragement being given to them from those in our country who seem to want our defeat, humiliation and economic collapse. Apparently, they think they will gain power if this happens.

≈ ≈

Some predictions: Should the Democrats gain control of Congress and pull our troops out of Iraq as they want, (Republicans may be forced to do the same thing eventually) I believe the following events will happen, and quite soon:

1. The terrorists (including those in control in Iran, Syria, Somalia and a few other Islamic nations) will soon control the entire Middle East, including Iraq, Saudi Arabia, Kuwait and the rest of the Arabian peninsula.. This eventuality may be delayed as they fight among themselves to find out who will be in charge. Oh yes, during this series of events, Israel will be annihilated and Afghanistan, Pakistan and many other Muslim nations will join rather than fight the fundamentalists.

2. Once in control, they will turn off the oil spigot and watch as the western world economies collapse and burn. Europe, with it's 35% Muslim population will fall first in the following order; Spain, France, The Netherlands, and Germany. England, the Scandinavian countries and Russia will resist the longest but will probably succumb to nuclear blackmail. There will be millions of dead bodies to dispose of.

3. The American and far eastern economies will take the longest to collapse even with several terrorist nuclear attacks. Weakened America will be invaded from the south. China will stand by

and cheer as America and Europe go down. They will finally do battle with Muslims with atomic weapons and who knows where that will lead.

I predict this will happen quite rapidly and quite soon - within the next ten or twenty years. I see no way it can be avoided considering the advance comments of those who may soon be in power in this country. And remember, I'm an optimist.

Please remember, I do not feel like a clairvoyant, nor do I see my opinions as unchangeable. These are merely my opinions under the present, known circumstances. Just try to consider these things rationally and not emotionally. I realize it is difficult, (It is for me as well) but rather than close your mind, think about what I have said.

Monday, October 23, 2006

Lou Dobb's new book: "The War on the Middle Class"

Lou Dobbs says about his new book: "The government, big business, big labor and many other special interest groups and politicians from both parties are enriching themselves at our expense. Now more than ever, we're finding ourselves at the mercy of those individuals and organizations that control jobs, provide goods and services, and wield power... The middle class is being picked apart and its future mortgaged for the benefit of a small group of powerful American interests."

More on: "The War on the Middle Class"

Through his nightly CNN show, "Lou Dobbs Tonight," his syndicated radio program and his monthly columns in Money magazine and U.S. News and World Report, Dobbs has become one of America's most visible, popular, and respected voices on business and financial matters. With his upcoming book, "War on the Middle Class: How the Government, Big Business, Big labor, Powerful and wealthy professionals and other Special Interest Groups are Waging War on the American Dream by controlling members of both parties. He also describes How to Fight Back," Dobbs tackles the issues that are on the top of so many American's minds, including: the deplorable state of our health care and public education systems, corporate outsourcing of jobs, immigration and border patrol, and of course, the state of our nation in general under the current political administration. In particular, Dobbs takes an impassioned and rousing stance on the all-out class war that is turning the American dream into a nightmare, particularly for our dwindling middle class, and proposes a series of measures to resolve each issue he brings to the fore and incite people to preserve their rights and dreams. "War on the Middle Class" is provocative, incendiary, and bound to be widely discussed—the perfect book to establish the terms of debate in this year's midterm elections.

End of CNN commentary

≈ ~ ≈ ~

In the interview, Lou mentioned several other powerful and influential groups including, government employees, trial lawyers, and the media and entertainment complex along with a few others I can't remember. The common denominator is the billions spent by these groups to get preferential legislative treatment on laws that benefit them. These billions pay for laws advantageous to those providing the money. Powerful examples include

The Enron debacle - the Clinton pardons, especially Mark Rich - the Abramoff scandal - and many others that cut across party lines. Both major parties are being bought and paid for by powerful and wealthy lobbyists.

Then on a smaller scale there are the personal enrichment schemes like Senate Minority Leader Harry Reid who is now being asked to step down from his leadership position right now and undergo a full investigation of his activities. Once again it seems the media is mostly turning a blind eye to what is clearly a probable case of buying influence by kicking back profits to a Senator who pushed legislation and peddled his influence in ways that helped create the profits he received. (Click on the above link for details) The fact the connection between Reid and the land developer he assisted was covered up in an UNDOCUMENTED (and therefore theoretical) business deal is what makes this look like a story of covering up (instead of whatever lame excuse Reid and Brown are trotting out). This type of chicanery is rampant in both parties.

The result is transferring billions from the pockets of ordinary Americans (average yearly income about $30,000) and into the pockets of the increasingly wealthy: professionals, investors, Congressmen, business leaders, union leaders, etc. Make no mistake, this is all supported and implemented by both political parties.

I am working on a book called simply, "Solutions!" which offers a good way out of this destructive practice along with solutions, viable solutions, to a number of other serious problems including the drug problem, income taxes, illegal immigration and personal identity among others. I hear lots of angry denunciations, condemnations, accusations and downright nasty personal attacks, aired and shouted in the present political campaign from members of all sides. I rarely hear any reference to any kind of solutions to the problems cited. Certainly there has been almost no issues dealt with positively.

Apparently, anger, hatred and condemnation reach and influence the American electorate and substantive, rational treatment of issues does not. Add to that the vast lack of knowledge and understanding of all but the most trivial matters that dominates and controls the minds of so many Americans and you have a formula for disaster.

Unfortunately, my "Solutions" would strip politicians of much of the lucrative control they now wield and prompt them to serve those main stream Americans they now so ignore. Powerful monied groups would do their best to stop implementations of any of my "Solutions."

Should you want to read about some of my solutions, use one the following links:

Drugs - A Real Answer to the Drug Problem - - **http://hjdrugprb.blogspot.com** - Page 499

Security - Solution to the ID Problem - - - -- - **http://hjidsecurity.blogspot.com** - Page 206

These are excerpts as the full text is in process of being incorporated into my book and will soon be submitted to a publisher.

Why I am not a Liberal, Socialist or Communist

Tuesday, October 17, 2006

I look at all politicians with a great deal of suspicion. Many are power hungry control freaks who abuse the trust given them and serve themselves before and above the voters who put them in office. Politicians are not the only ones fitting this mold. There are many individuals and groups that wield power and influence over others on virtually every scale. These are the mighty, the rich and famous in both public and private pursuits. In addition to politics they include: business, law, media, entertainment, finance, education, sports, and even religion. Most have huge, self-serving egos. Their goal in life seems to be focused on gaining money, power and fame for themselves. Like Monkey Kings, they wield their power, fame and money to aggrandize themselves and gain influence and control.

I can understand these people far better than most. Some I know as really decent, caring individuals who nonetheless spout the hatred and vitriol coming from many politicians on the left. A few instances illustrate my point. Recently I was riding in a vehicle with several people I knew to be rabid liberals. They assumed me to be just as rabid a right wing Christian fundamentalist. (Far from the truth by any measure) Knowing their views from the extreme left I can see why they think that way. In fact, while they view me as an extreme right winger, my conservative friends see me as far too liberal politically for their tastes. One in the vehicle launched a diatribe against George Bush citing his support for Ken Lay and other capitalist crooks, the war in Iraq and several other statements condemning Bush, Cheney and Republicans in general. I thought of mentioning that Ken Lay was as much a friend of the Clintons as of GW, but decided to keep still and let it pass. In a similar situation earlier I had replied that I heard only hatred, vitriol and condemnation coming from liberals and quoted Howard Dean's "I hate Republicans! I hate Conservatives! And I hate Rush Limbaugh!" as an example. I was greeted only with a stream of expletives with no sound reasons why they felt that way, no defenses of their champions, and certainly no proposals about any solutions to any of the problems. It was quite evident they never listened to anything or anyone who had opposing views.

Several times I had tried to discuss possible solutions, workable solutions, to some of our most pressing problems. The best response I have received to these solutions is a condescending silence. No discussion, no looking at the solutions, only words similar to Dean's famous remarks. Apparently these liberals treat their political beliefs as a religion and they are fundamentalists, following edicts and mantras passed down from the powers that control the movement. I have described those people "Feudals" after the feudal system that came out of the dark ages in Europe where Lords literally "owned" the serfs that lived in their territory. Socialism/communism is the modern version of feudalism where the "state" controls every aspect of the lives of common folks (serfs) and where government and government officials take the role of "Lords" and control them.

Why do I say this and why do I feel so strongly about the dangers to our nation posed by liberals and their media supporters?

The predictions of liberals are almost always wrong.

1. When sweeping changes in welfare requiring recipients to work were put into law, liberals predicted thousands would be unable to survive and there would be a major crisis. They were dead wrong. Former welfare recipients went to work in unprecedented numbers and removed themselves from welfare roles. Of course, you didn't see that reported by the main stream media. Republican version of an old Chinese saying: "If you give a man a fish he has food for a day and will be back the next day for another fish. If you teach him to fish he has food from then on and will rely on his own efforts." Liberal Democrat version of the same saying: "If you give a man a fish he has food for a day and will vote for you as long as you keep giving him fish. So take fish away from those who catch them and keep giving them out. If you teach him to fish he has food from then on and will not be beholden to you for anything so make him angry with all those who have fish and whatever you do don't teach him to fish."

2. When Republicans lowered taxes, liberals predicted huge deficits and lowered tax receipts. They were dead wrong! Deficits have been cut in half and tax receipts are now higher than ever in history. Of course, you didn't see that reported by the main stream media.

3. When George W. Bush promised the deficit would be cut in half by 2009, liberals ridiculed him as "stupid" and "unrealistic" and that the deficit was going through the roof. Bush was right and the liberals were dead wrong! Deficits have been cut in half this year, three years ahead of the promised date. Of course, you didn't see that reported by the main stream media.

4. After 9-11 liberals predicted the economy (the worst since the great depression according to their leaders and the media) was going into the tank. They were dead wrong! Bush's tax cuts spurred the economy to heights far above the .com boom of the Clinton years and shows no sign of slackening any time soon. This despite years of predictions to the contrary by liberal main stream media pundits.

Differences in media treatment of Republicans and Democrats in trouble.

There are many examples. I will use only one.

Republican inappropriate sex - Representative Mark Foley of Florida who is accused of sexually explicit Internet communication with a page is blasted by the media with a total more than 150 negative reports by ABC, NBC and CBS combined. The New York Times (Liberal Isvestia) lead the charge. Foley resigns his seat in congress in shame and continues being the subject of critical reports by the main stream media. The Republican party severely chastised Foley who had not been convicted of anything. The liberal main stream media continue bashing the Republicans with Foley.

Democrat inappropriate sex - Representative Mel Reynolds of Chicago who in 1995 was convicted of having actual sex, (not Internet sex) with an underage campaign worker and sent to prison was treated to a mere twenty reports by NBC, and CBS combined. He was never mentioned by ABC who had earlier in the year touted him as "Person of the Week" and praised him for his work with young people. In 2001 he was pardoned by President Clinton.

The following describes the essence of how liberals treat criminal politicians like Mel Reynolds who spout their agenda:

"Jessie Jackson has added former Chicago democratic congressman Mel Reynolds to Rainbow / PUSH Coalition's payroll. Reynolds was among the 176 criminals excused in President Clinton's last-minute forgiveness spree.

"Reynolds received a commutation of his six-and-a- half-year federal sentence for 15 convictions of wire fraud, bank fraud and lies to the Federal Election Commission. He is more notorious, however, for concurrently serving five years for sleeping with an underage campaign volunteer.

"This is a first in American politics: An ex-congressman who had sex with a subordinate, won clemency from a president who had sex with a subordinate then was hired by a clergyman who had sex with a subordinate. His new job? .....Youth counselor."

Once again the Main stream media will never report on this.

Quite obviously is much better to be a liberal Democrat if you are a criminal. Republicans punish members merely accused of wrong doings. Democrats applaud and support members convicted even of major crimes. Yes! There is a difference.

Liberals and al Qu'ida - the unholy alliance

Why is it that so many al Qu'ida spokesmen repeat the exact same condemnations of America and the Bush administration as liberal hate mongers like Howard Dean, Ted Kennedy and Nancy Pelosi? It's really quite simple - both groups want the same things: America out of the Middle East, America to lose in Iraq, America humiliated and defeated, the American economy in a shambles. The reason?

1. If Bush's America wins in Iraq and turns Iraq into a viable democracy, all four of these plans of the Islamic terrorists and liberal Democrats will be thwarted. This will deal a savage blow to both Islamic terrorists and liberal Democrats. If America loses they both win. If America wins, they both lose.

2. If the economy continues as it has, stimulated by the Bush tax cut, Democrats will have another huge hurdle to get over, "It's the economy, stupid!" That's why liberals and their media supporters are constantly saying how bad the economy is in spite of realities to the contrary in virtually every single economic indicators. Remember, "The worst economy since the great depression." How anyone could believe that in the face of what they can easily see every day in mind boggling, but some do. Go figure!

Hate filled zealots have hijacked the Democrat party.

The attitude of elitist liberal zealots is: "I know I'm right - I won't listen to anyone who disagrees with me - My agenda defines truth and reality - no ideas other than mine have any value, all are evil." This superiority complex attitude is confirmation of Eric Hoffer's insightful words as applied to the current liberal Democrat party. He said,

"Passionate hatred can give meaning and purpose to an empty life. Thus people haunted by the purposelessness of their lives try to find a new content not only by dedicating themselves to a holy cause but also by nursing a fanatical grievance. A mass movement offers them unlimited opportunities for both."

"All mass movements avail themselves of action as a means of unification. The conflicts a mass movement seeks and incites serve not only to down its enemies but also to strip its followers of their distinct individuality and render them more soluble in the collective medium."

"There is apparently some connection between dissatisfaction with oneself and proneness to credulity. The urge to escape our real self is also an urge to escape the rational and the obvious. The refusal to see ourselves as we are develops a distaste for facts and cold logic. There is no hope for the frustrated in the actual and the possible. Salvation can come to them only from the miraculous, which seeps through a crack in the iron wall of inexorable reality. They asked to be deceived."

"The uncompromising attitude is more indicative of an inner uncertainty than a deep conviction. The implacable stand is directed more against the doubt within than the assailant without."

There is no doubt the liberal who now control the Democrat party concentrate on passionate hatred. It has become their main if not sole tool in elections. Just listen to their campaign speeches, their declarations, their campaign ads, their passionate lies about the economy and their dire predictions about how terrible everything is from the environment to fuel, to poverty, to employment, to the Iraq war to virtually every facet of our nation's activities. Leadership of the Democrats has made them become the party of passionate hatred impugning every opponent with hate filled diatribes and emotion and completely ignoring even the hint of attention to any of the very serious issues facing the American people. Since they know they can not win with ideas of how to deal with the issues they rely on hatred and inflaming the mob emotionally beyond all reason.

Unfortunately, the highly biased main stream media has a powerful influence on unsophisticated individuals. Many of these occasional voters know far far more about the private lives of Paris Hilton and other pop-culture idols than even the names of important public officials. Surveys and man-on-the-street interviews prove this without a doubt. Sad, but true. It is no wonder so few of them ever vote, but maybe that's better for the nation. The continuing dumbing down of the nation provides masses easy to influence with emotion rather reason. Unfortunately for the left, those individuals do not vote in significant numbers.

Predictions - what I see in our future if liberal Democrats win in November.

International:

1. Iraq: After our withdrawal, the Iraq civil war will grow until the entire nation is in chaos. Soon the Shia governments of Iran and Syria will move in. There will be massive genocide in the Kurdish and Sunni sections as the Iranians consolidate their control. Iraq will become a fundamentalist Islamic client state of Iran.

2. Afghanistan: Shortly after we abandon Iraq in defeat, we will withdraw from Afghanistan. Soon after the Taliban will return, take over and pick up where they left off.

3. Kuwait, Saudi Arabia, Bahrain and the Arabian peninsula: Islamic terrorists will move in and subvert the entire area eventually setting up a fundamentalist Islamic state or states with Sharia law.

4. Pakistan: Musharif will be overthrown, probably murdered, and Islamic fundamentalists will take over creating another Islamic state with Sharia law.

At this point the entire middle east surrounded by Turkey, Russia, China and India, will be under Sharia law and controlled by fundamentalist Muslim mullahs. Israel will have been eradicated. The Caliphate will be complete and in control. Most of the world's oil will be under their control. With money for oil coming in from China and India, oil shipments to America will be shut off - our economy will collapse.

At some time in the next twenty-five years, Muslims will take over most of Europe.

Domestic:

1. One of the liberal government's very first actions will be to silence talk radio by invoking the so-called "fairness doctrine." They will also revoke the license of Fox news under some pretense. At this time the liberals will be in firm control of all means of communications and opposition will have no voice. This is already true at most college campuses and it will be easy to then impose on the entire nation.

2. The Bush tax cuts are revoked - taxes go up - gas prices go through the roof - the economy falls - tax receipts drop precipitously and the deficit explodes.

3. With the economy in free fall, the federal government will begin nationalizing private industry and the US will become a Socialist state. The liberals will have achieved their goal.

4. Social Security will be bankrupt and will be replaced by a new socialist welfare program with an infinite number of controls.

5. A government healthcare system will be put in place and within a year and very soon thereafter it will take a year to get an appointment with a doctor, even for some major problems. Many individuals will have serious problems with the long waits for healthcare.

Thursday, October 19, 2006

The Unbelievable Hypocrisy of Liberals and the Main Stream Media

I am appalled at the main stream media and at liberal Democrats for their constant expressions of hatred and demonstrated hypocrisy, especially in things like the Foley case. I have several friends who are gay. Their lives do not revolve around their sexuality any more than mine does. Yes, it is an important part of who they are, but they have families and friends they love and care for just as I do. Sex has nothing to do with those relationships.

The main stream media - ABC, CBS and NBC - have aired about 150 comments and reports on Foley and he has only been accused of sexual comments in private Internet exchanges with an underage individual. From these comments and reports you would think Foley's sexual activities were the only thing he did or thought about.

The New York Times (Liberal Isvestia) lead the charge in defaming Foley. He then resigns his seat in Congress in shame and continues being the subject of critical reports by the main stream media. The Republican party severely chastised Foley who had not been convicted of anything. The liberal main stream media continue bashing the Republicans with Foley.

Previously, when Democrats do far worse, there is no such flurry in the media. Consider Representative Mel Reynolds of Chicago who in 1995 was convicted of having actual sex, (not Internet sex) with an underage campaign worker and sent to prison. He kept his Congressional seat up until he went to prison. He was treated to a mere twenty reports by NBC, and CBS combined. He was never mentioned by ABC who had earlier in the year touted him as "Person of the Week" and praised him for his work with young people. In 2001 he was pardoned by President Clinton.

The following describes the essence of how liberals treat criminal politicians like Mel Reynolds who spout their agenda:

"Jessie Jackson has added former Chicago democratic congressman Mel Reynolds to Rainbow / PUSH Coalition's payroll. Reynolds was among the 176 criminals excused in President Clinton's last-minute forgiveness spree.

Reynolds received a commutation of his six-and-a-half-year federal sentence for 15 convictions of wire fraud, bank fraud and lies to the Federal Election Commission. He is more notorious; however, for concurrently serving five years for sleeping with an underage campaign volunteer. -

This is a first in American politics: An ex-congressman who had sex with a subordinate, won clemency from a president who had sex with a subordinate then was hired by a clergyman who had sex with a subordinate. His new job? ..... Youth counselor."

Once again the Main stream media will never report on this because he is a liberal Democrat.

Quite obviously it is much better to be a liberal Democrat if you are a criminal or evil doer. Republicans punish members merely accused of wrong doings. Democrats applaud and support members convicted even of major crimes. Yes! There is a difference.

The blatant efforts by the media to unseat Republicans and replace them with Democrats is obvious to all but the most feeble minded. Recently a report was leaked describing a meeting between media supporters and high ranking Democrats. The purpose of the meeting was to coordinate efforts in the media to aid Democrats and defeat Republicans in the upcoming elections. Doesn't sound like objective reporting to me.

It is obvious Democrats are frequently and effectively promoted by the media while Republicans are lambasted at every opportunity. It is easy for them to do this by repeated reporting of (or creating) Republican negatives and Democrat positives. They also ignore good news about Republicans and bad news about Democrats. Besides things like the Foley incident, look at two others:

1. The economy: Remember "It's the economy, stupid?" Clinton ran on and was supported in the media for "the best economy ever." Report after report on the booming economy came from the media. Now when virtually every economic indicator shows we truly do have "the best economy ever," with most statistics far better than the best during the Clinton years, the media is noticebly silent about it. Rest assured you will see none of the constant praise for the economy like that heaped on Clinton by his loving media. Any media reports will minimize any and all good economic news, of which there is an overwhelming number at the present. Let a single possibly negative report come out it will be reported and analyzed ad nauseum by the media.

2. Then there is the price of gasoline. Numerous Democrat operatives and candidates are accusing Bush of manipulating gas prices to help Republicans. What partisan chicanery! Does Bush control OPEC or the world prices of crude? Or do the American oil companies? This is complete nonsense, but many of the American electorate are either so stupid or ill informed they believe it.

I wonder how the election would go down if the main stream media actually did report things fairly, objectively and without their obvious prejudice?

Sunday, August 13, 2006

Failures and Collapses of Societies

Professor Jared Diamond Asks: "Will tourists someday stare mystified at the rustling hulks of New York's skyscrapers, much as we stare today at the jungle-overgrown ruins of Maya cities?"

I met a traveler from an antique land
Who said: "Two vast and trunkless legs of stone

Stand in the desert. Near them, on the sand,
Half sunk, a shattered visage lies, whose frown,
And wrinkled lip and sneer of cold command,
Tell that its sculpture well those passions read,
Which yet survive, stampt on these lifeless things,
The hand that mockt them and the heart that fed:
And on the pedestal these words appear:
'My name is Ozymandias, king of kings:
Look on my works, ye Mighty, and despair!'
Nothing beside remains. Round the decay
Of that colossal wreck, boundless and bare
The lone and level sands stretch far away."

"Ozymandias." by Percy Bysshe Shelley (1817)

Examples of total failures of societies leaving substantial ruins, but virtually no survivors:

1. Those total collapses we know virtually nothing about:

   a. The Dorset people of the arctic
   b. The Cahokia people (St Louis)
   c. The Anasazi in our southwest
   d. Mohenjo Daro ruins - Pakistan
   e. Machu Pichu and Tiwanaku in South America
   f. Great Zimbabawe in Africa
   g. Angkor Wat and Harappan Indus Valley in Asia
   h. Easter Island in the Pacific

2. Those collapses we do know some details about.:

   a. The Maya in middle America
   b. The Norse in Greenland
   c. Rwanda in Africa
   d. Pitcairn and Henderson Islands

3. Societies with difficult situations that are still thriving:

   a. Iceland
   b. Tikopia (small Pacific Island)
   c. New Guinea Highlands
   d. Tokugawa Japan
   e. Dominican Republic compared to Haiti
   f. China
   g. Australia
   h. Netherlands

Reasons for the collapse of societies and civilizations: Few collapses were due to a single factor as most were destroyed by a combination of these factors, all aggravated by expanding populations.

1. Environmental changes - fragility (susceptibility to damage) and resilience (potential for recovery)

   a. Deforestation
   b. Soil depletion and salinization
   c. Water depletion
   d. Wild food sources
   e. Domestic food sources
   f. sources for non-food goods

2. Climate change

   a. temperature
   b. rainfall
   c. sunlight

3. Hostile neighbors (competition for resources)

   a. wars
   b. fighting and murder

4. Friendly trade partners

   a. difficulty in transporting goods
   b. availability of goods to trade
   c. willingness to trade

5. The society's responses to the first four

   a. Population pressures
   b. Power of the rulers
   c. Willingness to cooperate.
   d. Willingness to defend oneself from attack

My questions and possible subject for several other discussions is this:

How close is humanity to a total collapse (These collapses always happen - and usually very suddenly - immediately after great heights of material and cultural success are reached.) When will it happen? What signs and indications are already with us? How can it be prevented? (Steps and solutions)

Suggested reading: *Collapse* by Jared Diamond.

~ ~

There are many factors in the collapse and demise of isolated populations - usually on lands isolated by geography such as islands - or the earth, an island in space. What humans have done in the past to exterminate themselves and continue to do on a global scale. These factors are not listed in any particular order, but some are directly linked to others and all are accelerated and expanded by population pressures.

1. Elimination of large animals, predators first (they compete with us for food) prey animals later.

Examples: North America - bear, cougar, wolves, buffalo, deer. (I know, some of these have come back, but how much predation of humans by large predators will we be willing to tolerate?) Pacific islands - land birds, sea birds, large mollusks, fish, etc. Specific examples: the moa - New Zealand, the dodo - Mauritania, the passenger pigeon US, the giant palm - Easter Island, many land birds - Pacific islands. Easter islanders eliminated virtually all land animals, birds and near shore sea life. Their only remaining source of animal protein was chickens which they carefully maintained. The man eating tigers of the Zondervan in India are still preying on humans as the people there have decided to accept an amount of predation on local people rather than exterminating them. How much predation on American citizens would we be willing to accept in order to live with predators like grizzly bear and cougar?

2. Deforestation - A major factor in nearly all societal collapses, deforestation inevitably leads to some or all of the following: lowered rainfall, loss of habitat for wild food animals and birds, soil erosion and loss of agricultural viability, soil depletion, desertification and even climate change. Virtually all island collapses included the complete elimination of trees. Easter Islanders eliminated the largest palm tree on the planet as well as all woody growth more than ten feet tall. The Anasazi eliminated all trees in Chaco Canyon resulting in greatly lowered rainfall, crop failures and subsequent abandonment after many hundreds of years of successful occupation. Worldwide deforestation (now well underway) would lead to major climate change, probably far more devastating than the currently popular, global warming scenario.

3. Unsustainable harvesting of wild seafood - Over harvesting of wild food populations was a major factor in all Pacific Island collapses. The largest and most easily harvested disappeared first until finally, only very small shellfish remained. Currently, all ocean fisheries, except the Indian Ocean, are declining. In fact, the North Atlantic area fisheries have collapsed and will take many decades, perhaps centuries, to restore. The use of new technologies has enabled commercial fishermen to decimate the most productive fish populations with uncontrolled harvesting. While there is a tentative world accord aimed at this problem, the worst offender nations have not signed the accord and continue to plunder the oceans with ever expanding fishing fleets harvesting far more than the fisheries ability to renew the resource. A byproduct of this gross harvesting of wild fish for food is the destruction of sea floor habitats by heavy bottom nets and the killing of millions of tons of non-food sea creatures. Add to this the destruction of many areas where ocean fish spawn and their young can grow, protected from predation. Our wild ocean food source is declining at an accelerating rate with many popular species already virtually non-existent. Without a concerted effort at managing this dwindling resource it will be virtually gone in another thirty or forty years.

4. Soil depletion, desertification, and salinization

a. SOIL DEPLETION

This is a problem for every highly used agricultural area. Every crop grown removes some essential elements from the soil and even from ocean water. Repeated growth of the same crop exacerbates the problem. It is addressed by two methods, crop rotation and/or fertilizers. Neither is a complete solution and in some cases the so takes many years to become productive again. This is particularly true where slash and burn agriculture is practiced as in the Philippines. Five or six years of cultivation is all it takes to deplete the soil of nutrients after which it is unproductive for six to ten years.

In the US and other highly productive agricultural areas, chemical fertilizers are used extensively to keep fields productive for many years. Even then, some trace elements are gradually removed and must be replaced to keep the soil productive. Three eruptions of the Yellowstone super volcano over the last two million years spread ash over most of the central and western US. This ash fall enriched the soil from Montana and the Dakotas to Louisiana, Texas, and Southern California. It is the main reason the soil in this area is so productive. Many of the essential elements in this soil are gradually removed by intensive farming and irrigation and must be replaced. This is not inexpensive.

b. DESERTIFICATION and SALINIZATION

In many areas there is not enough rainfall to grow crops on otherwise fertile and productive soils. Water is mined with deep wells and the land is irrigated. Since much of the irrigation water evaporates and does not flow away from the land, dissolved salts accumulate in the soil. This increase in salinity eventually makes the land unsuitable for crops. The land becomes in affect a desert where irrigation does not work. There is no practical way to reverse this process. Rainfall in sufficient quantities to wash the salt out of the soil cold reverse the salinization, but it would take many years to do so.

Monday, July 31, 2006

John Stossel - a fellow non-liberal?

I have just completed reading *Myths, Lies and Downright Stupidity - Get Out the Shovel - Why Everything You Know Is Wrong* by John Stossel - member of ABC's 20/20. This is the second book by John that I have certainly enjoyed. Not since Eric Hoffer have I found so much in concert with an author of social/political information and ideas.

His first book, *Give Me a Break*, was an enjoyable romp over the writhing carcases of pompous politicians, media personalities and others who seem to think their ideas to be sacrosanct. John tells it as he sees it. It was a truly refreshing and candid reporting of observations from one in the "holy" media who can see through the smoke and mirrors and define the real truth for all willing to read and see.

Myths, Lies and Downright Stupidity is a thought-provoking sequel to his first effort. The several comments below from the back cover are timely and echo my own opinion.

"Proving that learning can indeed be fun, John Stossel flays conventional wisdom with startling research and straight talk. Reading *Myths, Lies and Downright Stupidity* will make you immediately smarter than your friends. And that's no lie."

Bill O'Reilly, Anchor, Fox News Channel

"If John Stossel weren't such a troublemaker, he'd be considered a national treasure. But he is an equal-opportunity offender [A phrase I have used to describe my own writing for at least the last seven years.], sticking thorns in the side of whoever happens to deserve it at the moment. *Myths, Lies and Downright Stupidity* is Stossel at his very best: blunt, brilliant, counterintuitive—and, best of all, brutally impatient with the droners, yes-men, and hustlers who try to hide the truth from us.   *Stephen J. Dubner, co-author, Freakanomics*

Start of the blog

Meanings long lost:

Liberal - conservative, right-wing - left-wing, Democrat - Republican, socialist - capitalist, black - white, Muslim - Jew - Christian: thanks to the omnipotence of the omnipresent media, these terms have become virtually meaningless and are now almost always used to transfer the blame for political, religious and social evils from oneself to another group of "evil" people. "They are responsible!" is the phrase that comes to mind. It really doesn't matter much who "they" are as long as "they" are some ones other than ourselves and preferably some group to which some manner of evil stigma can be attached. The truth of it matters not as long as you can get enough people to complain about it loudly enough and with enough force of numbers - primarily vocal numbers, and even violence, or those efforts that appeal to the protestations of the media/entertainment world. These primarily, non-thinking, like minded sheep, will dedicate mindless effort to the condemnation and destruction of virtually any thing, system, person, promotion or purpose that is not in concert with their particular belief system. They will do so even to the extent of much violence and their own destruction. They rarely even attempt any really constructive effort. They are destroyers, not builders, and they are winning the minds of millions all over the world. Hate really does work Ask Hitler, or Pol Pot, or Stalin, or any of the many kinds of terrorists now ravaging the planet, and even many "peace" protestors.

Until recently I believed there were only a very few people who recognized any of these facts at all other than men like Eric Hoffer, Phillip Wylie, my father and a very few others even less known. I am now able to add another voice to this astute group, that of John Stossel of ABC's 20/20. In his most recent and quite unusual book of mundane yet powerful observations, Myths, Lies and Downright Stupidity. John reports the results of his research into many of the commonly held and almost "sacred" opinions that are so very wrong.

John makes some enlightening statements in his introduction, he says:

"MYTH-BUSTING is fun. I wound up doing it by accident: Researching consumer stories, I discovered that much of what I thought to be true was nonsense.

"On the other hand, "myth" doesn't necessarily mean "false"—it can also mean "a popular belief or tradition." Occasionally, just as we were ready to shovel the nonsense away, a myth would turn out to be true."

The balance of the Introduction will be entered here when I receive permission.

He hits one of my favorites on the first page of the first chapter entitled, "Clueless Media." I quote:

"MYTH: *The media will check it out and give you the objective truth.*

"TRUTH: *Many in the media are scientifically clueless, and will scare you to death."*

The information between that revelation and his final conclusion is positively brutal, wonderfully refreshing and deadly accurate. Should you read his book and my commentary, I hope you will understand why the liberal wing of my family considers me a right wing extremist and my moderately conservative mid-western friends see me as far too liberal for them. The following is a quote of his entire conclusion: [Bracketed words in italics are mine.]

MYTH: *John Stossel is a conservative*.

TRUTH: *I'm a libertarian.*

PEOPLE CALL ME A CONSERVATIVE.

I understand why. The publisher of my last book called me the "scourge of the Liberal Media" on the cover. Liberal writers call me "that conservative on ABC." Not that they actually know what the word means—to many on the mainstream media, "conservative" seems to mean anyone they don't trust or don't like. They even call extreme leftists. Like Soviet and Chinese Communists, "hard-line conservatives."

I want the word "liberal" back! Today's liberals stole it and perverted it. They've changed it into a philosophy that advocates health police, high taxes, and speech codes [PC anyone?] and despise the creative liberalism of free markets. "Liberal" doesn't mean liberal anymore. [How true! How true! How true!]

In the eighteenth century, libertarianism or liberalism, was a reaction against monarchy, the aristocracy, and established religion. The limits on state power embodied in the Declaration and the Constitution offered a liberal alternative to the dictatorship of the central planners. [A perfect description of the bureaucracy that now controls our lives.] It affirmed that we had "unalienable rights."

The founders' vision of limited government encouraged Americans to voluntarily join with others to help their communities and themselves. It led us to create a nation that is prosperous, free, and peaceful. We have done it not because we were compelled, but because we were free to do so. Believe that the best thing about America is free people exercising the unalienable rights the Founding Fathers affirmed: having families, forming communities, and working together—mostly without government.

It's a very old, very liberal idea.

End of John Stossel's Conclusion.

I would go one step further than John Stossel and have renamed today's liberals as "feudals" in my book The Feudals. Feudals are the opposite of true liberals as they openly advocate an authoritarian socialist dictatorship with their leaders as the intellectually superior ruling class controlling every action of the common people or "serfs." All ideas, systems and philosophies that do not submit to their "superior authority" are to be silenced and suppressed. If they succeed, Americans will become subject to the authoritarian, autocratic rule our founding fathers left Europe and fought and died to escape. Today's liberalism is yesterday's feudalism in modern clothing. It is the enemy of all kinds of freedoms, individual enterprise, capitalism and certainly will enslave and become the nemesis of the common man.

Howard Johnson July 31, 2006

Monday, June 19, 2006

The Party of Doom, Gloom and Hate

John Murtha: The currently anointed liberal Democrat attack dog from the house has made himself judge, jury, prosecuting attorney and jailer of several young marines on the basis of accusations from our enemies. These marines are now spending at least part of their time in shackles and chains at Camp Pendleton. I thought liberal Democrats always espoused treating the accused as "innocent until found guilty." Ignoring even the word, "alleged," Murtha speaks as if they have been proven guilty and, in effect, accuses the entire Marine Corps of being terrorists. Apparently anything immoral, extralegal or evil, is perfectly acceptable when it promotes the anti-American agenda of liberal Democrats. Of course, he proudly announces he was a Marine. Big deal! So was Lee Harvey Oswald.

The hate America crowd: Murtha has joined the cadre of liberal Democrats who will deliberately say and do anything that will cause damage to our country if there is the remotest possibility it can be used to discredit Republicans. Liberal Democrats and their leftist media lackeys are the best allies Al Queda has. The reason is quite obvious. Al Queda and liberal Democrats have the same agenda for America, destruction and defeat. If we succeed in Iraq it will sink the Democrats who have bet their whole political capital on our defeat there. Virtually everything they say or do works against our success and gives aid and comfort to one of the vilest enemies we have ever faced. The war in Iraq is their centerpiece and must be lost. They want another Viet Nam debacle and are doing everything they can to bring it about. Why else would they promote withdrawal with such vehemence.

Silence about the economy: They have finally, and for obvious reasons, grown mostly silent in their constant harangue about "the worst economy since 1930." There are numerous other truly needed and promising Republican efforts they are doing everything possible to block and scuttle. This includes proposals on taxes, health care, the military, immigration and border protection among many others. They denounce and work constantly to obstruct and destroy any of these proposals. They are so consumed with regaining power, they want no Republican proposals to pass that might benefit the nation and conceivably put the Republicans in a good light. They don't give a damn about the nation or the people. Their singular and focused attention is on regaining power by any means possible, no matter how their efforts damage the American people. I can't believe the American people will support the politicians of this party which has become the party of hate and animosity.

On the petroleum issue: The United States is the only oil producing nation in the world that has not increased its production of petroleum in recent years. Virtually every other nation on earth with petroleum reserves has increased production from 5% to 20%. On the other hand, our production of petroleum is steadily shrinking. Soon Cuba will be drilling for oil off our southern coast precisely where American oil companies are prohibited from drilling. I wonder why???

Monday, June 12, 2006

Memorial Day - a Different Meaning

Monday our quartet, The Willows, sang at the Leesburg Memorial day services at the cemetery after the annual parade. It was something our quartet has done for many years. It was a very teary day for me for several reasons. Barbara sang with us the first few times we were in the service and May twenty-ninth this year was our thirteenth anniversary. One more emotional milestone. We sang "I'm Proud to be an American," a very inspirational and patriotic song.

CAUTION! This paragraph is not politically correct! The parade, the memorial service and our song reminded me I am still very proud to be an American. This in spite of all the anti-American rhetoric from the main-stream media and the political left with their messages of hate created to attempt to divide us and degrade our image in the world. This effort is all because of their insatiable appetite for money and power. That small town parade and Memorial service is what America is to me. Fly over country is where the real Americans are who are willing to work for freedom for all people. The elitists of the left look down their upturned noses at these Americans and their "misguided attitudes" and "right-wing religious dogma." With their "holy" dogma and corruption of our Constitution, they cannot understand the heart and soul of the increasing numbers of real Americans who are starting to take our nation back for real freedom and prosperity. They can't stand it that our economy is doing so well and that we are fighting for real freedom. They are doing everything in their power to scuttle and destroy our economy and our efforts for freedom no matter how damaging those efforts are to the nation. They've lost on the economy so their only hope to regain power is for us to fail in Afghanistan and Iraq. Should our efforts there result in successful democratic governments, they will lose a great deal of political capital and be out of power for a long time to come. For this reason they have become defacto supporters of our enemies, working and hoping for our defeat and humiliation in the middle east. I call that treason!

I've never figured it out - are those politicians from the liberal left pawns of the leftist main-stream media, or are the main stream media simply the voices of the liberal left? Maybe they are all merely the property of George Soros. Now, down from my soap box.

Sunday, April 30, 2006

Letter to Senator Frist About Illegal Aliens

This letter sent to Senator Frist from a retired border patrol agent has more common sense than all the bull being spewed from the Senate, with the exception of a few sensible representatives. Anyway, this guy has it together and shows the rhetoric for what it is.

Dear Senator Frist:

There is a huge amount of propaganda and myths circulating about "Illegal Aliens", particularly "Illegal Mexican, Salvadorian, Guatemalan and Honduran Aliens".

1. "Illegal Aliens" generally do NOT want U.S. citizenship. Americans are very vain thinking that everybody in the world wants to be a U.S. citizen. Mexicans, and other nationalities want to remain citizens of their home countries while obtaining the benefits offered by the United States such as employment, medical care, in-state tuition, government subsidized housing and free education for their offspring. Their main attraction is employment and their loyalty usually remains at home. They want

benefits earned and subsidized by middle class Americans. What "Illegal Aliens" want are benefits of American residence without paying the price.

2. There are no jobs that Americans won't do. "Illegal Aliens" are doing jobs that Americans can't take and still support their families. "Illegal Aliens" take low wage jobs, live dozens in a single residence home, share expenses and send money to their home country. There are no jobs that Americans won't do for a decent wage.

3. Every person who illegally entered this nation left a home. They are NOT homeless and they are NOT Americans. Some left jobs in their home countries. They come to send money to their real home as evidenced by the more than 20 billion dollars sent out of the country each year by "Illegal Aliens". These "Illegal aliens" knowingly and willfully entered this nation in violation of the law and therefore assumed the risk of detection and deportation. Those who brought their alien children assumed the responsibility and risk on behalf of their children.

4. "Illegal Aliens" are NOT critical to the economy. "Illegal Aliens" constitute less than 5% of the workforce. However, they reduce wages and benefits for lawful U.S. residents.

5. This is NOT an immigrant nation. There are 280 million native born Americans. While it is true that this nation was settled and founded by immigrants (Legal Immigrants), it is also true that there is not a nation on this planet that was not settled by immigrants at one time or another.

6. The United States is welcoming to "Legal Immigrants. "Illegal Aliens" are NOT immigrants by definition. The U.S. accepts more lawful immigrants every year than the rest of the world combined.

7. There is no such thing as the "Hispanic Vote". Hispanics are white, brown, black and every shade in between. Hispanics are Republicans, Democrats, Anarchists, Communists, Marxists and Independents. The so-called "Hispanic Vote" is a myth. Pandering to "Illegal Aliens" to get the Hispanic Vote is a dead end.

8. Mexico is NOT a friend of the United States. Since 1848 Mexicans have resented the United States.

   a) During World War I Mexico allowed German Spies to operate freely in Mexico to spy on the U.S.

   b) During World War II Mexico allowed the Axis powers to spy on the U.S. from Mexico.

   c) During the Cold War Mexico allowed spies hostile to the U.S. to operate freely.

   d) The attack on the Twin Towers in 2001 was cheered and applauded all across Mexico.

   e) Today Mexican school children are taught that the U.S. stole California, Arizona, New Mexico and Texas. If you don't believe it, check out some Mexican textbooks written for their schoolchildren.

9. Although some "Illegal Aliens" enter this country for a better life, there are 6 billion people on this planet. At least 1 billion of those live on less than one dollar a day. If wanting a better life is a valid excuse to break the law and sneak into America, then let's allow those one billion to come to America and we'll turn the USA into a Third World nation overnight. Besides, there are 280 million native born Americans who want a better life. I'll bet Bill Gates and Donald Trump want a better life. When will the USA lifeboat be full? Since when is wanting a better life a good reason to trash another nation?

10. There is a labor shortage in this country: This is a lie. There are hundreds of thousands, if not millions, of American housewives, senior citizens, students, unemployed and underemployed who would gladly take jobs at a decent wage.

11. It is racist to want secure borders:

a) What is racist about wanting secure borders and a secure America?

b) What is racist about not wanting people to sneak into America and steal benefits we have set aside for legal aliens, senior citizens, children and other legal residents?

c) What is it about race that entitles people to violate our laws, steal identities, and take the American Dream without paying the price? For about four decades American politicians have refused to secure our borders and look after the welfare of middle class Americans. These politicians have been of both parties.

A huge debt to American society has resulted. This debt will be satisfied and the interest will be high. There have already been riots in the streets by "Illegal Aliens" and their supporters. There will be more. You, as a politician, have a choice to offend the "Illegal Aliens" who have stolen into this country and demanded the rights afforded to U.S. citizens or to offend those of us who are stakeholders in this country.

The interest will be steep either way. There will be civil unrest. There will be a reckoning. Do you have the courage to do what is right for America? Or, will you bow to the wants and needs of those who don't even have the right to remain here? There will be a reckoning. It will come in November of this year, again in 2008 and yet again in 2010. We will not allow America to be stolen by third world agitators and thieves.

David J. Stoddard = U.S. Border Patrol (RET) = Hereford, Arizona

Monday, April 17, 2006

The Hypocrisy of Outspoken Liberals

Liberals and leftists say one thing and do another=surprise!

Best selling author Peter Schweizer tells the real story of how big time liberals talk like liberals, but actually do so many of those hated conservative, capitalists things they so vitriolically decry. When it comes to their personal lives, these liberals are right in there with the worst of those they so condemn.

Just a few extensively documented examples:

John Kerry

Says: The "super-rich" are not paying their fair share of taxes.

Does: Pays less than 15% of income in taxes. Although along with his wife he is worth in excess of $700 million.

Al Franken

Says: Conservatives are racist because they lack diversity and oppose affirmative action.

Does: Has hired less than 1 percent African-American employees over the last fifteen years.

Ralph Nader

Says: Unions are essential to protect worker rights.

Does: Fired his employees and changed the locks when they tried to form a union.

Barbra Streisand

Says: Americans need to cut back on their conspicuous consumption and protect the environment.

Does: Spends $22,000 a year to water her lawn; maintains a 12,000 square-foot air-conditioned barn.

Senator Hillary Clinton

Says: "Thirteen-year-old girls are capable of deciding to have abortions without parental [or paternal] consent. "

Does: Prevented Chelsea, then 13, from getting her ears pierced because she "wasn't ready for them."

George Soros

Says: The wealthy should pay higher, more progressive tax rates.

Does: Holds the bulk of his billions in tax free overseas accounts in Curaco, Bermuda and the Cayman Islands.

Nancy Pelosi

Says: I pride myself in being a liberal and fighting for labor unions.

Does: Owns upscale vinyards, restaurants and hotels that hire only non-union workers.

Noam Chomsky

Says: America is the modern NAZI Germany and the Pentagon is the most hideous institution on earth and constitutes a menace to human life.

Does: Signed on with the Research Laboratory of Electronics, funded entirely by the Pentagon and has cashed checks totaling millions from his work there.

Senator Ted Kennedy

Says: I demand that America take immediate action to reduce global warming by shifting to alternative energy sources

Does: In addition to huge personal profits from oil, he fiercely opposed erection of wind turbines off the coast of Massachusetts that would have replaced a polluting coal-fired power plant operating near Boston. His reason? Some of those turbines would be placed in areas where he liked to sail.

Michael Moore

Says: I've never owned a share of stock in my life and anyone who says otherwise is a liar.

Does: Examination of federal tax forms clearly show that Moore bought and sold shares in Halliburton and a number of other *vicious, evil* corporations.

View Schweizer's web page and order his book, *"Do as I Say, Not as I Do!*

Monday, April 17, 2006

Our Constitutional Protection, Going, Going, Gone?

In preface I would like to explain my definition of a few terms often misinterpreted:

The left, or far left - This relatively small, but noisy and very activist group includes mostly old Marxists, radical socialists, fascists, communists and all who are caught in the antiquated, often evil and always unworkable ideas of government as the best answer to every problem. All of this is merely the feudalism of the middle ages dressed up in new garb and with bigger units of control. They want the entire world, no exceptions. Their counterparts on the right include the extreme religious right. Both are fundamentalists and would impose their will by force if necessary. Each views everyone outside of their tiny group as being part of their opposite group. Like any group of "believers" they can be rabid and violent.

Liberal (noun) - a label generally attached to those who are to the left side of the political spectrum. A much larger segment of the public than either lunatic fringe, They are mostly civil and accept far more variation in plans and purpose than the far left. Unfortunately, they seem to be unduly influenced by the lunatic fringe of the far left. The hate rhetoric of the far left seems to be influencing them unduly. In spite of rabid protestations against the evils of religion and capitalism, most "liberals" respect religious beliefs and offer some support to capitalism. They tend to want government to solve all problems.

Liberal (verb) - free and generous, tolerant of different ideas and concepts; broad minded, democratic or republican forms of government (representative) as opposed to monarchies, aristocracies or dictatorships, favoring reform or progress.

Centrist - One who sits politically somewhere in between liberal and conservative. Sometimes they seem not to have an opinion, but vacillate from one side to the other, "as the wind blows." They frequently will follow the polls rather than any ideology.

Conservative (noun) - a label generally attached to those who are to the right side of the political spectrum. A much larger segment of the public than either lunatic fringe, They are mostly civil and accept far more variation in plans and purpose than the far right. Unfortunately, they may be unduly influenced by the lunatic fringe of the far right. In spite of rabid protestations against the evils of atheism and socialism, most "conservatives" respect all religious beliefs and some limited government programs. They give the bulk of their support to capitalism. They tend to want problems solved by individual initiative in a free enterprise system rather than government.

Conservative (verb) - Certainly different than, but not the opposite of "liberal." Conserving or tending to conserve things and ideas as they are. "If it ain't broke, don't fix it." Tending to oppose changes, to keep traditions and institutions in place. Environmentalists are those who would "conserve" the environment. In spite of being "conservative" on the environment, environmentalists tend to be in the liberal political camp.

Radical - person or action far from the norm or average in any direction. Idea, action or person vastly different from those generally or loosely accepted.

Religious right - Actually a very small minority with rather extreme views based on their religious views, usually fundamentalists. These are Christians in the Americas, Europe and often Muslims in the rest of the world. They want the entire world, no exceptions. Their counterparts on the left include the extreme atheist left. Both are fundamentalists and would impose their will by force if necessary. Each views everyone outside of their tiny group as being part of their opposite group. Like any group of "believers" they can be rabid and violent.

Political parties are not defined as they usually include pressure groups with varying agendas and opinions. While the range of the above definitions can often be found in both American political parties, Republicans tend more to be more to the right side while Democrats tend more to the left. Both lunatic fringes tend to exert more than their proper share of influence. While the far left seems virtually in control of the Democrat party. The influence of the far right on Republicans has waned considerably in recent years.

End of preface and definitions, start of essay.

Why is it so many on the left believe that any person, word or concept that doesn't agree precisely with their "holy" and "sacrosanct" opinions is inherently passé, evil, or driven by the agenda of the evil religious right? Why is it they have the right to act on the belief that killing a baby in a mother's womb for the mother's convenience is acceptable while those whose beliefs are different and who believe that doing so is evil, do not have a right to act on their beliefs? Why is it they have the right to ban any and all religious symbols and words from virtually every public venue and so impose the religion of secular humanism or atheism on us as the state religion of America in direct defiance of the first amendment which strictly forbids it?

When will the left, send the ACLU to demand that all the statuary, building decorations, monuments and printed word depicting Judeo-Christian law and history that was the foundation of our nation be demolished or otherwise removed from all public places? Certainly the visage of Moses holding the ten commandments is far more damaging and offensive to the psyche of an atheist than a Christmas carol or the greeting, "Merry Christmas" is to an atheist child in a public school. These type of actions orchestrated by the left and forced on an intimidated public by the ACLU and idiotic judges certainly sound exactly like the efforts of the Taliban in Afghanistan, particularly when they blew up those Buddhist statues. If this is not the evils of dictatorship then Hitler was a benign ruler.

For 200 years our Constitution has worked to protect the people from vicious, dictatorial practices of government. That is precisely what the framers intended and it succeeded for a time. Now the Left seeks to remove those protections, not by law and representative amendment as proscribed in that Constitution, but by judicial decisions and opinions in which the people have no say whatsoever. If that is not dictatorship and denial of representative democracy then there has never been a dictator on the face of this earth.

An example of one member of the judiciary, Ruth Bader Ginsberg, who is not protecting our Constitution but seems to want to subvert it to foreign laws follows:

About those Foreign Laws by: Robert Morrison

Justice Ruth Bader Ginsburg has come in for a knuckle-rapping from, of all people, the editorial writers of The Washington Post. That's a bit like L'Osservatore Romano criticizing the Pope.

The Post's editors found Justice Ginsburg's speech in South Africa out of line. Apparently, she not only has the wrong ideas about incorporating foreign laws into her Supreme Court opinions, she is also exporting her errors. She started off titling her speech "A Decent Respect to the Opinions of [Human] kind." She took her title from the majestic opening lines of the Declaration of Independence, but she couldn't resist improving on Mr. Jefferson's prose. Justice Ginsburg: Surely you must know that "mankind" to the Founders included women; it meant humankind.

From that unpromising start, it got worse. Had she read a little further, she might have stumbled upon some phrases like "endowed by their Creator," "certain inalienable rights," and "life, liberty, and the pursuit of happiness." She might also have noticed that it was a declaration of independence they had approved.

Justice Ginsburg distinguished her views of constitutional interpretation with those of the "frozen in time" old fogeys like Justice Antonin Scalia. As she proudly noted, she saw the Constitution as belonging to "a global 21st century, not as fixed forever by 18th-century understandings." Who'd have thought Ginsburg would actually come out in favor of constitutional global warming?

Of course, Justice Scalia does not think the Constitution is frozen in the 18th century. He recently praised the 20th century amendment that gave women the vote. The Nineteenth Amendment was delayed some fifty years by the opposition of congressional Democrats. Would Justice Ginsburg respect it less if it had been passed in 1870? Or in 1790? Scalia told a New Hampshire audience he had to question the label "moderate" when it comes to constitutional interpretation. What is that? Halfway between what the Constitution says and what you want it to say?

Ginsburg told her South Africa audience that under her more fluid interpretation, "every generation can invoke its principles in their own search for greater freedom." Indeed they can. By amending the Constitution, Suffragettes labored for a century to win the right to vote for women. It should not have taken so long, but by the time the Nineteenth Amendment was ratified, no one questioned the right of women to vote. Nor has anyone seriously questioned it since.

Justice Ginsburg herself has argued that Roe v. Wade "short-circuited" a process of abortion law liberalization. No small part of the opposition to Roe comes from the deeply held conviction of millions that it was illegitimately thrust upon us. The Roe court overturned the abortion laws of all fifty states. The editors of The Post took Justice Ginsburg to task for her attacks on congressional critics who deplore her selective use of foreign law. The editors said it was wrong for her to charge her critics with inciting a dangerous "fringe" that threatened the lives of Supreme Court Justices.

Here's a thought, though. Maybe we should tell those would-be assassins that killing judges is morally wrong. Maybe we can persuade them by posting some Commandments in our schools and public buildings: "Thou shalt not kill" would be a good start. And we might even get Justice Ginsburg to approve: Let's tell her they came from Mount Sinai and they're foreign law.

Iraq - An instructive exchange with a bright young man

When I recently published a letter from Congressman Murtha along with my rebuttal, I soon found myself engaged in an enlightening battle of words with a bright and idealistic young man. I only hope he learned as much from the exchange as I did.

Saturday, April 15, 2006

Apparently those supporters of Congressman Murtha's position on Iraq can find nothing to say other than rant and rail against the Bush administration. Thoughtful discourse seems not to be their forte. They might do well to consider the following from the Free Muslim Coalition. This may be a very different view than that of the terrorists, their supporters and their sympathizers.

FMC Blog

It is interesting to note the comments of blog readers, both those who agree and those who disagree. It is also easy to see those replies motivated by unreasoning hatred and those form concerned, thinking individuals. I leave it for the reader to decide which opinion has the upper hand. The same could have once applied to Neville Chamberlains, "Peace in our time" speech when world domination was in the offing.

Should the U.S. Leave Iraq?

When Rep. John Murtha said that the United States must leave Iraq immediately he ignited a national debate on whether the U.S. should leave Iraq. Normally, such a statement would not have been noticed, but because Congressman Murtha is a retired Marine colonel who earned a Bronze Star and two Purple Hearts for his service in

Vietnam Washington listened. In response to Congressman Murtha, the White House stated: "The eve of an historic democratic election in Iraq is not the time to surrender to the terrorists."

Unfortunately, the debates that followed congressman Murtha's statement were often misguided and off-point. Most of the discussions that followed dealt with whether the U.S. should leave Iraq. However, whether the U.S. leaves Iraq is not an issue. Most American politicians, including President Bush want to leave Iraq. The real issue is when should the U.S. leave and under what conditions?

In calling on President Bush to withdraw American troops from Iraq, Congressman Murtha justified his statement by concluding that the Bush administration's management of the war effort is based on "a flawed policy wrapped in illusion," and said the continued presence of U.S. troops in Iraq is "uniting the enemy against us."

So is Congressman Murtha's conclusions correct? Is the Iraq war effort a failure? We at the Free Muslim Coalition Against Terrorism don't think so.

Clearly, the conditions in Iraq are not ideal. More than 2000 American troops and tens of thousands of Iraqis have been killed; explosions occur on a daily basis and the country may be more divided today than it has ever been. Despite these facts, the war effort in Iraq is a huge success. Iraq has been transformed into an open democratic society and there is no going back.

Let's not forget that Iraqis for the first time in recent history elected their government, voted on a constitution and in the coming days will again elect a new government. Despite their many challenges, Iraqis today freely and publicly criticize their government and are free to change their government any time they feel their government is not doing a good job. This puts Iraqis in a unique position in the Middle East. They are holding their government accountable which suggests that Iraq will never again have another authoritarian government. Indeed, Iraq has been transformed and there is no going back.

However, the U.S. should eventually leave Iraq but not now. The United States cannot leave Iraq immediately nor can the United States set a timetable for withdrawal. If the United States sets a fixed timetable the insurgents could merely wait until the U.S. leaves and then redouble their efforts to overwhelm the government of Iraq and/or attempt to create a civil war. This cannot happen under any circumstances. No matter whether one supported or opposed the Iraq war the entire world and all Americans must now put the past behind them and do whatever it takes to make Iraq a successful, united and prosperous state.

We, the Free Muslims, have stated in the past that a democratic, secular and prosperous Iraq can positively transform the Middle East like no war or any amount of money can. This is why Iraq must succeed and all Americans must unit behind their government to make sure that Iraq succeeds.

Having said this, the United States should give serious consideration to moving U.S. forces outside of Iraq's cities and population centers as soon as possible. The U.S. military should be far enough that the average Iraqi feels he lives in an independent sovereign country but close enough that they can return in case of an emergency. There are many benefits to stationing American troops outside of Iraq's population centers. The most important reason is that the new Iraqi government will understand that American troops will not always be there to protect them and thus, they will have to do a better job of reconciling with all Iraqis, including Arab Sunnis. At the end of the day, the new Iraq must be the home of all Iraqis without even the appearance of being lead by a sectarian government. This is where the existing Iraqi government has failed.

For example, the first election was boycotted by Sunni Arabs and the overwhelming majority of the Sunni Arabs voted against the constitution. This is not a healthy situation. Iraqi Kurds and Shias must do a better job of compromising with Sunni Arabs if Iraq is to become a stable, democratic and prosperous nation. The degree of compromise and reconciliation necessary to stabilize Iraq may not occur if Shias and Kurds feel that the United States is there to protect them whether they compromise or not.

In conclusion, the United States must make it clear to all Iraqis that it is not an occupying power and that it will leave Iraq one day after it becomes stable. The U.S. government must plan for the eventual withdrawal from Iraq by removing American troops from Iraqi cities and stationing them in unpopulated areas as soon as possible.

The U.S. military must rely on the Iraqi military and other security forces to protect Iraq. This Iraqi military is now in a better position to take more responsibility. Since July, 2005, 22 new battalions and 5,500 Police Service personnel have been trained and equipped (as have some 2,000 Special Police commanders). Coalition senior officers report that Iraq now has approximately 130 battalions.

Moreover, the U.S. military must not rush to assist the Iraqi military and Iraqi security forces every time they face difficulty. The more difficulty Iraqi forces experience, the more likely it is for the existing leaders of Iraq to reach out and compromise with Iraq's dissenters who are mostly Sunni Arabs. All parties must understand that unless Sunni Arabs feel that they are equal partners in today's Iraq there will never be peace in Iraq nor will Iraq stabilize. Once Shias, Kurds and Sunni Arabs reconcile, the insurgency will die and the terrorists will find themselves in a lonely and hostile place.

Thursday, February 02, 2006

Islam, Terrorism, Liberals and more

The following is a series of responses and comments prompted by the second post to this blog which can be read at the end of this one. I chose this method rather than just adding another comment as I have a lot more to say and would hope for readership. The first section is a series of comments and my responses. The last response is lengthy and detailed and is the reason for my posting the entire series.

John Burgess said...

Nice piece!

I'd only note that the term "Wahhabi" tends to get misused. The majority of Wahhabis are not terrorists, nor are they sympathetic to terrorists.

The term that seems to be gaining momentum--due largely to Anthony Cordesman at the CSIS--is "neo-salafist". This correctly encompasses the violent extremists while excluding the Wahhabis who are, actually, rather quietist in their outlook.

10:06 AM

HoJo added, "My understanding of Wahhabis is quite different. I shall research this information and make appropriate adjustments."

Ian said...

America is already weak. America is already ineffective. The actions taken by our president and his subsequent approval rating show little confidence from the country in our leadership. This shows weakness. Bush shows weakness.

It is insulting for you to compare Iraq to WWII... completely and utterly insulting. In the Iraqi war, we are the aggressors. We made the invasion. Germany and Hitler were the invasive party in WWII. The anniversary of Pearl Harbor was 4 days ago... I don't think I need to remind you who was the aggressor there.

It is often interesting to see the injustices that are perpetrated for no reason, to see the people stand idly by and watch the deterioration of a nation and morality because they are too afraid to be shut up by propagandists and overbearing, dangerous nationalists.

Terrorism is the product of stubbornness, elitism and pigheaded foreign policy. The path to the heart of our "enemies" lies not in bombing their cities. Surely you can see this.

7:03 PM

HoJo said...

Ian:

Pardon me, but your indoctrination into leftist philosophy is showing. In many respects you are quite accurate when you say America is weak. The consummate destruction of morality in our nation that has been promoted by the left for so many years has substantially weakened us. Your President, "Slick Willy" clearly demonstrated that with his direct lies and redefinition of sex. Your great and honorable leaders like Teddy Kennedy and Robert Byrd also demonstrate that almost on a daily basis.

I will stand on my statements about WWII. I think it insulting to say we were the aggressors in Iraq. If that be true then surely we were also the aggressors in Germany and Japan. There is no question, Saddam Hussein was precisely the same kind of despotic dictator as Hitler. The similarity of his treatment of the Kurds to Hitler's treatment of the Jews is inescapable. The only difference was that we stopped Saddam Hussein before he became powerful enough to be a major world threat. How much of a threat would he be now if he accomplished what he clearly stated was his intent and taken over the entire Arabian peninsula? Think about it.

Some time back I watched a Peter Jennings special on our dropping of the atom bomb. The way it was presented one would have thought that we were the evil aggressors against the poor Japanese. This special was clearly meant to rewrite history and paint America as evil. The main stream and very liberal media still seem to try their best to paint our nation as an evil aggressor virtually everywhere. Surely you get all your news from the liberal triplets. I doubt you ever listen to or read any information that differs from your own views. My sister, whom I love dearly, once wrote me, "You have such a fine mind, I cannot fathom why you waste your attention on such persons as Rush Limbaugh and George Bush and the Religious Right." That was after she wrote that I was the only person she knew who voted for George Bush. All that demonstrated to me was that she hadn't a clue who I really was or what I thought. Simply because I was not in complete accord with her liberal views I was lumped in with all those "stupid, ultra conservative, fundamentalist Christians from fly-over country." That is as much prejudice as, "all blacks are . . ." Should you want to learn something of this kind of political prejudice, read Eric Hoffer's "The True Believer." I see you like many young people as caught up in a political belief system that controls your thoughts, shutting out absolutely everything that does not agree with the "holy" liberal agenda.

I like your paragraph about injustices and agree almost completely. I would merely replace your word "nationalists" with "liberal one-worlders." Europe stood by and did precisely what you described as Hitler's power grew. I would suppose that you would have us stand by now and let tyrants and world conquerors like Saddam Hussein grow in power in the same way.

Your words on terrorism: I see you following the mantras of the left in blaming America for terrorism and describing our actions as, "bombing their cities." Would you then also blame America for causing the Japanese attack on Pearl Harbor? Many people did, you know. The Japanese went to war with us because we shut off vital materials we had previously been providing. I doubt you know that. I realize it would go against your belief, but try substituting the words, "liberating their cities" for "bombing their cities" and you get an entirely different slant.

You might be surprised to know that I disagree strongly with many of the Bush administration policies. Read the comments on my blog about the environment as the blog itself may not make that clear. I like to think I have a mind open to all kinds of information from all kinds of sources. I have an idea that you and I would have more agreements than disagreements. Our big differences would come in the methods we would choose to achieve those goals.

I certainly would not be condescending in my comments because I know you are a very bright, thoughtful, idealistic young man. I would only suggest that you consider the possibility that your deeply ingrained prejudices may be guiding your emotions and anger. There really is a possibility you could be at least partly wrong, you know. I will readily admit to being wrong a few times myself. Peter Abelard said, "By doubting we are led to inquire. By inquiring we perceive the truth." As I suggested, read Eric Hoffer if you can find his work. His views are very down-to-earth and quite enlightening. Incidently, in his time he was considered to be quite liberal.

Cordially, Uncle Mike

6:10 AM

Fish said...

Uncle Mike,

It's pretty difficult to respond to most of the things that you say and I think it's pretty evident that there is a great deal of futility in my even trying to do so. But you made some pretty large mistakes in your response to me.

First of all, I have been indoctrinated into nothing. I am a thinker who sees alternate points of view, has heard numerous opinions and has chosen what he believes to be the right one. I don't associate with a political party or an ideological category. I have my own conceptions of right and wrong, my own analysis of morality. I am a philosophy major at Reed College who is deeply intrigued by ethics and morals. These issues cannot be invaluated in a philosophical manner by one who is "indoctrinated".

Obviously, your sense of morality and mine are vastly different. While we may both share concepts of right and wrong that are similar, I can't believe anyone would fault a president for sexual indiscretions more than a president who has led a war that has killed innocent people both in America and in the Middle East.

Your President, "Slick Willy" clearly demonstrated that with his direct lies and redefinition of sex. Your great and honorable leaders like Teddy Kennedy and Robert Byrd also demonstrate that almost on a daily basis.

Here's where you make a huge error that shows your rush to judgement and, unfortunately, an inability for critical evaluation. Bill Clinton is not "my president" exclusively by any means. He is not the exclusive president of the liberals, the democrats, the radical leftists or the sexual transgressors. For 8 years, he was the President of the United States and all its citizens. I never voted for him (I was 11 when he was elected for the second time), but he was my president. As much as I hate to say it, George Bush is my president in the same respect. I didn't vote for him, but I live in this country and he is my president. And that is precisely the problem. He doesn't represent my sense of right and wrong and certainly doesn't represent the concerns of people who hold similar opinions to me. This is why he is a bad president at the very root of all things.

Mostly, I am taken aback that you say "Teddy Kennedy and Robert Byrd are" my leaders. These two men are not my leaders. I am a leader. I believe what I believe. I have my sense of right and wrong, my conceptions of how the country should be run, and my ideas for making the world better. I certainly don't believe that Teddy Kennedy and Robert Byrd are leading me in any direction. I'm leading myself to my own conclusions, critically evaluating everything that I hear from every source--Democrat or Republican.

I have no great admiration for the Democratic party of late. It's not liberal enough. It doesn't truly advocate what is right and what is wrong. They are spineless individuals who are more concerned about earning the vote than doing the right thing. I represent myself; I don't buy in to what my "leaders" say just because they say it.

And you should do the same with regards to Bush. You voted for him. He's your leader. He's mine too. But part of living in a democracy means questioning the wrongdoings of our leaders when they take the wrong step with regard to policy, even if it isn't socialy acceptable to do so.

I don't know that I want to get into WWII and Iraq except to say this: Hitler systematically killed Six Million Jews. It became a science. A low-cost effort to eliminate a people from the world. To compare Hitler to Saddam Hussein demonstrates your inability to look beyond Bush's rhetoric.

Hitler had the tools, the power and he implemented them. A "what if" argument is unsound and fallacious. What if Saddam Hussein actually had nuclear weapons? Then maybe Bush would have had cause to go to war.

But alas, he didn't. And so... he didn't.

It is an unjust war. Nearly all wars are. I haven't been fed this by the "leftist" media (the people at Fox News sure are a bunch of tree-huggin' hippies!), but have realized it on my own in my nearly 21 years of life.

Ian

Ian:

You said, "It's pretty difficult to respond to most of the things that you say and I think it's pretty evident that there is a great deal of futility in my even trying to do so. But you made some pretty large mistakes in your response to me."

I could say the same to you, but won't. My mistakes, as you call them, seem to me to be differences of opinion. Of course, I have observed that any disagreement with the absolutely politically correct positions with those on the liberal left (and Christian fundamentalists of the right) are considered mistakes or errors by those self-same individuals. I still contend that your "objective" education has helped instill in you certain beliefs about what is right and what is wrong. You are, even as I am, a product of genetics plus all the input from others present and involved in your upbringing, education and personal discovery. These influences determine who and what you are, your moral standards, your belief systems, even your likes and dislikes. Some of these inputs you will accept, some you will rebel against, some you will ignore. No one is exempt from these influences. It is how we become who we are. When we describe this about ourselves we call it independent personal choice. In others we call it indoctrination or prejudice.

Virtually everything you have learned thus far in your life you learned from another human in one way or another. There is extremely little chance that personal, unaided discovery has contributed much to who you are. I'm sure your parents did all possible to teach you to think for yourself=to be your own person=to be a leader and not a follower= to make up your own mind. I know I did that for all five of mine as best I could. Since you valued your parents and their thoughts and beliefs it is quite natural for these to have had a major effect on you. Even so, I will also wager there were times when you disagreed with them=even argued your case forcibly. I know my gang were never afraid to oppose me when they thought differently. This is the natural course of human events.`

Your grandmother and I were brought up in virtually the same home environment yet we view many things quite differently. Differences became much stronger after college where she and I took paths of significant differences. She studied drama and the humanities; (the touchy-feely world of emotion, hopes and human behavior) I studied science and engineering. (the pragmatic world of facts, mathematics and realistic solutions) As a result of our nature, our home experience and our formal education we came to view things from very different vantage points. I seriously doubt you (or she) ever seek out and listen to or consider seriously opinions, thoughts, principals or "morals" that are not in concert with your own regardless of where you actually stand. You "knew" those people are wrong, misguided, stupid or ignorant simply because they don't agree with you.

Yes, technically, Bill Clinton was indeed "my" president. Common treatment of language includes a rather broad definition of this term and I claim the right to use it in a general term. He was most certainly not my choice for President in the same way George Bush is certainly not your choice. When technicality serves to prove a point it is used. When generality serves, that is used. Come on Ian, you knew precisely what I meant, or do I need spell it out for you?

You wrote, George Bush is my president in the same respect. I didn't vote for him, but I live in this country and he is my president. And that is precisely the problem. He doesn't represent my sense of right and wrong and certainly doesn't represent the concerns of people who hold similar opinions to me. This is why he is a bad president at the very root of all things.

I am to take it from this that you believe Bush is a bad President simply because you and those "who hold similar opinions to me." believe so and disagree with him and his policies? In other words, anyone who disagrees with you is bad? Is that not a very arrogant statement? I hear similar statements from so many liberals–they are just right and anyone who disagrees with them is stupid, ignorant, evil, mislead, etc... Maybe they (and you) are just incredulous that anyone would question the "holy" opinions or agenda of the liberal. I haven't a clue!

About your references to this "illegal" war and how incorrect it is to compare Hitler and Hussein. That is merely an opinion, not a fact. Had the free world (or any part of it) stopped Hitler in the mid 30s when "Peace in our time" was the rule of those who refused to act against an obviously growing menace, the organized murder of millions by the NAZIs would never have come to fact. Possibly even the several times as many millions murdered systematically by the Bolsheviks in Russia could have been prevented. Of course there is no way to predict where Saddam Hussein would have gone had he not been stopped. If you deny that possibility then technically, you are once more correct. I certainly do not agree.

Hitler in nineteen–forty–one was a vastly different threat than Hussein in 2001. You are once more correct, technically. However, Hitler in 1933 was even less of a menace than Hussein before the first Gulf War. The difference is that no one stopped Hitler. Would you have considered a war to prevent Hitler from building his juggernaut of death another illegal or immoral war? Would you have called illegal, a war to stop or prevent the murders of millions just because you are opposed to war? And on what would you base your opinion?

Once more, the conclusion to follow is a projection, and not an actual fact, but from existing records, twice as many Iraqis were killed by Saddam Hussein's government each year before the "liberation" (to you, occupation) of Iraq by coalition forces than have died in any of the years since. That means the "illegal" and "inhumane" war has saved as many as 35,000 net lives in Iraq. Of course, Hussein could have lowered his rate of killing in response to appeals from American peaceniks. What do you think?

Another report by a British research group for the year 2005 reported 900 coalition deaths from all causes in 2005. They also reported 4200 Iraqi deaths during the same period. 2100 were terrorists killed by coalition action.1700 were civilians killed by the actions of terrorists. 400 were non–combatants killed by coalition forces during actions against terrorists. It is interesting to note that during all of 2005, about twice as many young men were killed by gun violence (700) in Chicago as in Bagdad, (348) a city of twice the population of Chicago. Statistics in the rest of Iraq average out to about the same, including terrorists killed in military action. Extended to the rest of the US at half the rate of Chicago to be safe, internal, home grown terrorism right here in the US is at least twice as deadly as in Iraq. We have a far bigger body count here at home, even on a percentage basis, than we do in Iraq and other than the most sensational murders or accidental shootings, it is rarely even mentioned in the media.

In one of your comments you said, "Terrorism is the product of stubbornness, elitism and pigheaded foreign policy. The path to the heart of our 'enemies' lies not in bombing their cities. Surely you can see this." I suppose you mean that American imperialism was responsible for all thirteen hundred years of Islamic terrorism including the anti-Hindu terrorism in India, the anti Buddhist terrorism in most of Asia, the conquering of Christian Constantinople by Sulemon the Magnificent, the sacking of the library in Alexandria and all the other wars and terrorism visited on people by Islamic armies and terrorists. Apparently you would agree with Samiul Haq described in the following quote from an article about Islam.

"In the 1980s the Soviet Union epitomized, for fundamentalist-minded Muslims, the abode of war. Today it is the United States that symbolizes the dar-al-harb. How this came to pass, how America, which supported -- created, some would say -- the jihad movement against the Soviets, came to become the No. 1 enemy of hard-core Islamists is one of the more vexing questions facing American policy-makers and the leaders of a dozen Muslim countries today. One school of thought, Samiul Haq's school, says it's the Americans' fault: American imperialism and the export of American social and sexual mores are to blame." (This could indeed be considered an indictment of the Hollywood liberal left's effect on sexual mores?)

"The other school of thought holds that Islam, by its very nature, is in permanent competition with other civilizations. This is the theory expounded by the Harvard political scientist Samuel Huntington, who coined the term "Islam's bloody borders" -- a reference to the fact that wherever Islam rubs up against other civilizations -- Jewish, Christian, Hindu -- wars seem to break out. Men like Haq deride this view, and yet, in their black-and-white world, Islam stands alone against the world's infidels: Christians (or "Crusaders," in the fundamentalist parlance) to be sure, but Jews and Hindus especially. In Haq's view, the West is implacably hostile to the message of Islam, and so the need to prepare for jihad is never-ending."

Listen to the rhetoric of these fundamentalist Muslims. They are totally intolerant of any views other than their own very narrow, fundamentalist doctrine. Listen to the voices of those who support their goals. They are bringing their seventh century mentality and literal hate message of the Koran into the present as they have since Mohammed first brought the Koran to them. Any truce offering they make is specifically made to enable them to build up their forces, weapons and fighters for the next attack. To not respect their expressed and written words is suicidal folly. They not only want the extermination of the Jews, but the extermination of

Christians, Hindus, Buddhists, and all other religions including even some Muslims who don't agree with them. They base this on the literal wording of the Koran. Their goal? Subjugation of all the peoples of the world by a Taliban-like world government and murder of all who don't accept and convert to their satanic belief system. Those are their own pronouncements, not my opinion.

Another absolutely necessary action: That action is to immediately develop useable, non-petroleum fuels to cut off the economic destruction of the west. The Islamic world and all petroleum financed dictators would soon be destitute and without resources were we to implement such an action. This would be the cheapest and safest way to destroy Islam-bankrupt them. Combine their massive population growth, removal of oil revenue would bring them to their knees economically and militarily. I have outlined a workable plan to solve not only our dependence on foreign oil, but to take giant steps to reversing CO_2 emissions and the purported concomitant global warming. This a plan. Something I see almost noone of from the ranks of liberals. I saw lots of condemnation in your words, but where is your plan? I realize it is much easier to destroy than to build. Are liberals just not up to the hard work of building, but must concentrate on hate and destruction?

I realize the chances of our taking these steps is very remote. The left would rather commit suicide and probably will and could even take all of us with them when they do. Didn't some one say, "All that is needed for evil to triumph is for good people to do nothing." Of course, Islamic terrorists, Fidel Castro, Caesar Chavez and most American Liberals view conservatives and Republicans as the evil Satan. Come the Islamic take over, they will be the first to be beheaded, but liberals, you will be next! As models, look at the French revolution and the Bolshevik revolution. Remember, there was no such blood bath in our own revolution because those involved had little taste for blood, but a real thirst for freedom.

The Moslem world is mostly either under the totalitarian fist of oppressive dictators or the chaos of anarchy. Their chosen enemies are all free men everywhere. Their supporters are those who believe their rein of absolute power will be fulfilled if they support and help these angry men. Financed by money from the west's thirst for petroleum products, Islam is posing an increasing menace to the US and free men everywhere. By using the power of class, ethnic, cultural, racial and religious hatred, to incite violence and terrorism against the United States, these truly evil men are uniting the poor and ignorant of the world as pawns in their thirst for dictatorial power. Their word is hatred, their mantra is envy, their message is death and destruction, and their appeal is to those who have little or nothing to lose. This is almost precisely the carefully hidden agenda of the American liberal left. Hunger for power makes for strange bedfellows.

Heros: We all have heros of one sort or another. These are usually people we look up to and respect for a variety of reasons. Sometimes we seek to emulate them. I have a number of people I consider my heros. My parents, my sisters, (yes, your grandmother is one of my admired heros) Even my children and grandchildren I consider heros of a sort. I know I can always learn from them. Most of my other heros are those whose words and actions I respect and admire even though I don't always agree with them. All are strangers in a personal sense as I have never met any of them. In no particular order they include: Talbot Munday, Helen Keller, Mother Theresa, Albert Einstein, Andrei Sakharov, Mohandas Gandhi, Edwin Hubble, and two with web sites,

Stephen Jay Gould - **http://www.stephenjaygould.org**

Eric Hoffer - **http://www.erichoffer.net**.

I know there are others but none come to mind immediately. Incidently, should you google Talbot Munday you will see a reference to one of my blog sites about the fourth listing down. You might want to take a look at **http://2therealworld.blogspot.com**, a lecture I have given to several groups of young people that was quite well received.

You'll notice there are no politicians included among my heros. I have little respect for most politicians with their duplicitous words and devious motives. They may spout meaningless pap to the public, posture mightily, make ridiculous laws, send our men to die in foreign lands, spend our money lavishly and often foolishly, feather their nests from the public treasury and a thousand other significant actions serving self rather than the nation, and promise many things while doing just the opposite, yet we are stupid enough to continue electing them time and again. I often wonder, how many public serving statesmen our nation has actually held in office the last two hundred and twenty some years. I'll wager there weren't many. I'll also wager there are more true and honorable public servants reporting to the board rooms of America than walking the halls of Congress and other public buildings in Washington.

So Ian, do you have any heros? If so, who are they? Who would you describe as a statesman serving the public rather than self?

Leadership: So, where is your leadership into the brave new world of liberal freedom and peace? According to your words, you are a leader. A leader of one? Who are your followers? Who will implement the grand plans you have for changing this evil world? And, by the way, I don't recall reading about any plans. Do you have any? I see lots of condemnation–lots of anger–lots of "anti" words coming from you. How about the positive=the constructive–the building–the solutions? You despise Bush, but offer no creative thought about solving the problems facing our nation. It's quite easy to condemn the actions of other, but quite a different thing to propose practical, productive solutions to the problems with which they are dealing.

A favorite quote of mine: "Choose, and take the consequences. Choose to command, and learn the pain of the barbed treachery of envy. Choose to obey, and learn how soon obedience begets contempt. Choose the philosopher's life, and learn the famished waste of thought that, like a barren woman, lusts unpregnant. Choose . . . or become the victim of others' choosing." by Talbot Munday

To me, leadership is not walking alone into the future, but leading individuals into productive effort for a worthwhile constructive cause. Leadership is bringing people together and helping them to achieve as a group, far more than the total the group could achieve with individuals going it alone=synergy if you will. Leadership demands a practical plan aimed at a goal, a real goal. To that end I have written and continue to add to a book titled, "Solutions." It is a collection of workable plans to solve some of our most vexing problems=national and world=wide. To date I have addressed revision of our ridiculous tax structure, welfare, health care, global warming, atmospheric pollution, our dependence on foreign petroleum, the drug problem=and several others. I have also listed numerous other problems I plan to address in the future. Here are links to those plans I have posted to date.

Taxes & welfare - The Johnson Tax Code - **http://jtax.blogspot.com** Page 200

Fuels - Gasoline and diesel alternatives - **http://cheapfuels.blogspot.com**

Drugs - A Real Answer to the Drug Problem - **http://hjdrugprb.blogspot.com** Page 499

Security - Solution to the ID security Problem - **http://hjidsecurity.blogspot.com** Page 206

What concrete plans do you have for our nation in the next fifty years? I'd certainly be eager to read them. Or are you, like so many liberals, so caught up in anti-Bush, anti-war, anti-capitalism, anti=whatever effort you have no time for creative, productive, positive efforts at building? I realize these are questions you don't really want to answer so I will consider your silence an admission that you have no plans. You call that being a leader?

With kindest personal regards, Uncle Mike   (No reply was forthcoming)

Letter from Democrat Congressman John Murtha

Friday, December 09, 2005

I received the following from one of the more liberal members of my family and inserted it here as it is what prompted the current exchange. It's a letter from Congressman Murtha asking for donations. I suggest that to understand what the congressman is saying you substitute the words, "Have an Honest Debate over How to Raise the White Flag of Defeat and Surrender," when he says, "Have an Honest Debate For the Safety of Our Troops." That's actually what he means.

The letter begins:

"America wants and deserves real answers on Iraq: What is the clear definition of success? Is there a plan? How much longer and how many more lives? In short, what is the end game? Because we in Congress are charged with overseeing the safety of our sons and daughters when the president sends them into battle, it is our responsibility, our obligation to speak out for them. This obligation has not been met. That's why I am speaking out now. I offered a concrete plan to get our troops out of harm's way, where they have become the target. I don't expect every member of Congress to agree with my specific proposal in this debate - but I do expect them to take part in that debate, not to squash it. I am asking you to join me in demanding a real discussion of the war in Iraq from the U.S. House of Representatives. Tell Congress to Have an Honest Debate For the Safety of Our Troops.

For too long Congress has counted itself out of any real debate on Iraq policy. We didn't talk about troop levels, even after the White House fired General Shinseki because he complained the levels were too low. One problem we encountered was the lack of proper training for our troops; service members were placed to guard the prisons but weren't trained; consequently we had Abu Ghraib, and no action from Congress. And if you look at the casualties, they have doubled since then. It's time to change our course - we can't just sit back any longer. I've taken a lot of trips to Iraq. When I came back from my last one, I had become convinced we were making no progress at all. This can't be Republican and Democrat. It can't be recrimination one way or the other. We have to work this thing out, and we can't let a real solution get caught in the crossfire of an understandably heated political fight. It's time for a serious conversation, not more rhetoric. Tell Congress to Have an Honest Debate For the Safety of Our Troops.

The past few weeks have had a lot of firsts for me. I have never sought out the spotlight, or even taken the lead in a House floor debate the way I did a few weeks ago. And I've never signed an email like this before. But I see the beginning of a debate that is long overdue, and we can't afford to let it get overtaken by talking points or the news cycle. I'm offering this petition, which will be delivered to Speaker of the House in order to keep our Congress focused where it should have been all along. I hope you'll sign if you agree.

Congressman John Murtha

Monday, December 12, 2005

My Response

No Congressman Murtha, I don't agree. Congress has a sworn duty to focus on winning both the war and the peace in Iraq with a resounding victory. By your own words, you want us defeated. This is but one more of thousands of efforts by liberal Democrats - the ones I call the Feudals - to bring this country to its knees in another humiliating defeat like Viet Nam. And, no! I was not in favor of the Viet Nam war. I didn't think the whole of Southeast Asia was worth the sacrifice of a single American life. We would have won that war easily and with a lot less loss of life on both sides were it not for the fact that liberal politicians micro-managed the war for political gain in America. I can absolutely guarantee if politicians like Murtha, Ted Kennedy, Barbara Boxer, Nancy Pelosi and the other liberal self-servers were in power at the time of the first Gulf War that Saddam Hussein would now control not only Kuwait but Saudi Arabia and the entire Arabian peninsula. These politicians are now trying desperately to help our enemies by encouraging insurrection and terrorism. All I can conclude is that they hope to regain power by bringing our nation to defeat and retreat in the Middle East. They will gain as they blame this defeat that they will have helped engineer on Bush and his administration.

All you have to do is listen to the propaganda from al Gazeera and al Queda to hear the same words as come out of the mouths of liberal Democrats. I like to think these liberals are just too stupid to realize how much they are helping and encouraging our enemies. The alternative is too frightening to consider. These enemies are also the enemies of free Iraqis as well.

The brutal dictators of the world are in a huge majority in the UN. The freedom Americans have always espoused and supported strikes fear into the hearts of these despots. That's why the majority of nations hate America - their tyrants fear for their lives. The common people don't, but they have little effect on the state press in so many oppressed nations and the liberal press elsewhere.

If the policies that liberal Democrats now propose and efforts they now oppose were in power during World War II, I guarantee you that Japan would have occupied western America and Germany would have occupied the eastern half. If they had merely been in control when "The Bomb" was proposed, it wouldn't have been dropped and a million more Americans and several million more Japanese would have died.

France is just beginning to feel the effects of a Muslim invasion that has been going on for decades. Up until now they have been able to sweep much of these troubles under the carpet. I predict things are going to get much worse in France and Germany will soon follow. All you have to do to understand what us going to happen is to read what Bin Laden and other Wahabi Muslims are writing. Iraq is the keystone. Bin Laden even says so. We didn't believe his threats of terror and warfare before 9-11 and apparently liberal Democrats have gone back to considering he, al Queda and the terrorists (freedom fighters to liberal Democrats) no longer pose a threat. I would prefer we lose two-thousand, three-thousand, or even more in Iraq then two or three hundreds of thousands in American streets.

Have any of you ever read or listened to George Bush's plan for victory in creating a democratic Iraq? It was published on the Whitehouse web site more than two years ago. Probably not. That way you can continue to say he has no plan. The liberal Democrat plan is to provide al Queda and other Muslim terrorists a specific timetable for the withdrawal of our troops so they can plan their takeover as our troops leave. How can any human being who doesn't want to ensure our total defeat possibly make such a proposal. I like to think it is merely stupidity, but fear there is a far more sinister purpose. The truth of the matter is that if America perseveres and does create a free and democratic Iraq, it will be a huge blow to Muslim extremists. That's why these despots are trying so hard with murder and mayhem toward innocents. A free Iraq would also spell the death knell for liberalism in America for a very long time. That's why you don't want us to succeed!

Remember the fiasco in Mogadishu with American bodies being dragged through the streets? Weren't liberals in control during that action? And how about the blunder in the desert when we were supposed to be rescuing the hostages from Iran? By what effort and at whose direction did those hostages finally come home? Congressman Murtha, if you want lots of people to die and America to look weak and ineffective, turn the military over to liberals. If you want the least number to die and real freedom for the peoples involved, count on good old conservative Republicans. I suppose you will continue to propose we wave the white flag of defeat and surrender so the despots of the world will be assured they have nothing to fear from America. Then, the "shot heard 'round the world" will have been effectively silenced. Perhaps you want the world to forget completely what we Americans started at Lexington and Concord.

Howard Johnson

Monday, April 10, 2006

Some Folks Get Angry at My Blogs

I recently received an angry totally emotional response to this blog. I thought it quite immature = a purely schoolboy curse with no redemptive value. It so surprised me I reeled off a curt response. I have received responses of a similar nature before, but have never adopted a policy to deal with them. I now have such a policy.

I cannot prevent anyone from reading my blogs so you folks who don't like to read things that disagree with your "holy" opinions will just have to not read my blogs. As far as I can tell, freedom of speech has not yet been repealed in this country. What I can and will do is remove the email address of those who send me such emails from my address book and from my list of those from whom I accept emails. This will protect both of us from feeling angry, insulted or intimidated. I have already done this for those few individuals who call those who happen to have a view different from their own an "idiot" or "---hole." It will also prevent me from having the strong desire to respond in kind.

Please note! This applies only to purely angry, cursing, irrational responders. Strong even emotional disagreements are certainly welcomed. I ask only reasonable restraint in describing what should be done with certain parts of my anatomy. Ah civility--where has it gone? Replaced, perhaps, by the political correctness of the extreme left who seem to have sunk to pure name calling and expressions of hatred for any and all who disagree with their "sacred" opinions?

For those of you, who for any reason, would like to be removed from my email address books, Click here, send me an email with the word "remove" and it will be so.

Saturday, April 15, 2006

Illegal immigrants -- an opportunity to do right by all

The operative word here is "illegal!" For those of you who do not understand American English that means "law breaker," "criminal," "outlaw," "crook," "dishonorable," "felon," "immoral," "condemnable," "reprehensible," "felonious," "at fault." (Other language words for criminal) Are you beginning to understand? The idea of rewarding these criminals with amnesty and even citizenship is repugnant to me and to all decent, law abiding Americans. That is except for emotional idiots who feel guilty about everything and those selfish individuals who use the misery of others for personal gain or to promote their own agenda.

I have a series of proposals which would turn the current "foreign invasion" of our country into an economic and social advantage. It would provide a legal status for most of those now in our country illegally and the same for those who want to come here. It would not provide amnesty or grant any level of citizenship to illegals. These proposals would address the many gross insults and injustices now imposed on our country by the millions of illegals already here and those trying to get here.

Step 1 - Identification: Require the registration of every immigrant with a digitized photo and fingerprint ID card. Click here to read about a proven system that could be adapted to handle "guest workers," (GWs). A sub-system of the Internal Revenue Department could handle the administration and the taxes that would be collected. Instead of a Social Security number, Gws would receive a GW number with letter codes instead of numbers in the form XXX-###-### where the Xs represent letters and #s represent numerals. This would preclude confusion with the all numeral SS number.

Step 2 - Citizenship: Amend the Constitution and remove the antiquated wording that grants automatic citizenship to anyone born on American soil. Change it to require that the mother be either an American citizen or a legal immigrant in the process of becoming a citizen. Deny granting citizenship in all other cases. Specifically deny citizenship to anyone born to a mother illegally in the country or having Guest Worker status.

Step 3 - Welfare: Specifically deny welfare benefits, healthcare, education and any other social services to anyone who is not registered and does not have a GW card. Not to do so threatens the overburdening and destruction of the entities now providing these services. This is happening in many areas of our country right now and will only get worse.

Step 4 - Paying for it: I propose a multi-tiered method of paying for welfare and other benefits provided for GWs. This would be a pay-as-you-go system designed so that GW s would at least in part, pay for the benefits they receive.

A. Income tax: A flat tax of 25% on all income, deducted from all wages by employers using the same system the IRS now uses. No deductions, no exceptions. A flat 25% tax on those who are self employed using the Current IRS tracking of this type of income. This tax to be kept in a separate account for use in the GW program only and not deposited into the general fund.

B. Tariff: Registration of GWs will include their country of origin. I propose a floating tariff or duty on all goods imported into the US from each country. Such duty will be applied to the country of origin of the goods, not the country from which it is imported. The percentage being determined by the actual number of GWs registered from each country. Special punitive tariffs could be imposed in situations like in Venezuela where a national policy of anti-American activity does financial and other damage to our country. Using Venezuela as an example, I propose we impose a punitive tax of 10% on all imports, including oil, coming from or originating in, Venezuela until and unless financial support for anti-American activities ceases.

C. Registration fees and services payments: I propose a twenty dollar charge for registration to pay for the card. This payment can be deferred until the applicant actually has a job, but is to be deducted out of the very first month's pay by the employer. I propose a minimum cash payment by every GW of $10.00 for each and any social or health services including emergency room treatment. This will discourage abuse of the system by those with very minor ailments or problems. Payment will go directly to the agency or healthcare facility providing the service.

Step 5 - Enforcement: The bugaboo of all laws and in particular with respect to illegals, enforcement would have to be strict and swift. I propose a system of fines and criminal actions against any employer who hires without a social security or GW number check. The flat tax would remove any incentive to use single SS or GW numbers for multiple individuals. Criminal actions against record falsification, illegal hiring or non-tax payment are already on the books and only need to be enforced. With most of the advantages of illegal hiring gone, employers would be encouraged to edhere to the law and keep records accordingly. Of course there would be abuses. There are many abuses of the IRS laws right now without much enforcement. Plugging loopholes would have to be an ongoing effort.

Step 6 - implementation: Once the new law is in place, it would take a number of months to register GWs and get the control and enforcement systems in place. I see no possibility of avoiding problems during that time of changeover. I suggest a period of six months to register most GWs. It may take longer, but that depends on how swiftly and well our registration system is set up.

A. Employers: The obvious first need is that employers comply with the new law immediately. They would have to provide lists of all undocumented workers and possibly even pre-register each one. Sanctions and even criminal actions against employers would have to be the very necessary first step. The system which would best serve this purpose would reward the employer for compliance and punish for non-compliance. This part of the law would have to be carefully written with room for adjustment once problems arose.

B. Tax collection: As an incentive to register without penalty, no taxes would be collected or deducted until the six-month signup period is over. Wages would be recorded by employers, but deduction of the 25% flat tax would not begin until the end of the six month startup period. Yes, this might create a problem for many GW s as their pay would suddenly be reduced by a fourth, but detailed explanations could help. The way the non-system is now working, there is no tax. Of course, what is going on now is illegal criminal action by both workers and employers. Enforcement of existing laws and associated punishments would be far harsher than this proposed system, taxes and all.

C. Social services and health care: As it is now, private firms and governments at all levels have to pay for services provided gratis to illegals. With small cash payments required for each service provided, there would be an incentive to limit accessing these services except where truly necessary. It would even be possible to set up a system of automatic payments using an account accessed via the GW ID card much like a credit card. Any amount debited to the ID card account would be automatically deducted from the individual's next pay. There will be more added to this later.

What is really driving this attack on America:

1. The government of Mexico is actively promoting and aiding the movement of their criminals, and the poorest and least educated of their citizens. This is not an opinion. But a demonstrable fact from speeches by government officials, news sources and released documents.

2. Overburdened with one of the highest birthrates in the world, Mexico and many other South and Central American nations are exporting the absolute worst of their surplus population to the United States. This has become well known government policy.

3. Many other nations including China, Pakistan, India, Bangladesh and most overpopulated Muslim nations, as well as the whole of Africa are now using Mexico and our porous southern border as a conduit for their poor, their criminals and their terrorists. The northern border is also being used increasingly.

4. There are numerous highly organized and well financed "underground railroads" leading to virtually every state to hide, aid and disperse illegals to every corner of the US. They are also aided in their efforts by the ACLU.

5. Organizations like MEChA and LaRaza actively promote the political takeover by a Latino majority as soon as possible. When this majority takes control they plan to act on the secession of a large portion of the Southwest and the formation of a new nation, "Atzlan" with Spanish as their national language and the motto, "Yanqui get out!" If you doubt this, Click here or even go to their own websites LaRaza and MEChA and read what they are saying. Try to find and read the Spanish language version as it is far different and more obvious than the "doctored" English language version.

6. The recent highly organized protest marches and rallies against immigration reform have been organized by groups financially supported by the Mexican government through "arms length" organizations. Many of these are organizations with world Communist backing, often receiving money from Venezuela's strongman and virtual dictator, Hugo Chavez. After the initial protests backfired a bit because of the shouting of anti-American slogans and waving of Mexican and other flags, the organizers quickly ordered their "troops" to hide those flags, wave only American flags and shout pro American slogans. TV footage and photos of the protesters before this order went out and after demonstrate this clearly. The disingenuousness of those who organized the protests should be obvious to all but the most prejudiced and ignorant.

7. The enemies of America, whatever their motives, are working feverishly to bring down America. This is because our nation's success, high living standards, philanthropy, generosity, help to humanity–driven by free and responsible people using free-enterprise capitalism–puts the lie to virtually everything the far left stands for. Unfortunately, many well-meaning, idealistic

Americans, motivated by misdirected emotional appeals are providing aid and support to these enemies who would destroy our nation.

On illegal immigrants - Teddy Roosevelt & others,

Amen to this! 99 years later.

Theodore Roosevelt's ideas on Immigrants and being an AMERICAN in 1907.

"In the first place, we should insist that if the immigrant who comes here in good faith, becomes an American and assimilates himself to us, he shall be treated on an exact equality with everyone else for it is an outrage to discriminate against any such man because of creed, or birthplace, or origin. But this is predicated upon the person's becoming in every facet an American, and nothing but an American... There can be no divided allegiance here. Any man who says he is an American, but something else also, isn't an American at all. We have room for but one flag, the American flag... We have room for but one language here, and that is the English language... and we have room for but one sole loyalty and that is a loyalty to the American people."

Wednesday, April 12, 2006

If you are ready for the adventure of a lifetime, TRY THIS:

Enter Mexico illegally. Never mind immigration quotas, visas, international law, or any of that nonsense.

Once there, demand that the local government provide free medical care for you and your entire family.

Demand bilingual nurses and doctors.

Demand free bilingual local government forms, bulletins, etc. Procreate abundantly.

Deflect any criticism of this allegedly irresponsible reproductive behavior with, "It is a cultural U.S.A. thing. You would not understand, pal."

Keep your American identity strong. Fly Old Glory from your rooftop, or proudly display it in your front window or on your car bumper.

Speak only English at home and in public and insist that your children do likewise.

Demand classes on American culture in the Mexican school system.

Demand a local Mexican driver license. This will afford other legal rights and will go far to legitimize your unauthorized, illegal, presence in Mexico

Drive around with no liability insurance and ignore local traffic laws.

Insist that local Mexican law enforcement teach English to all its officers.

Good luck! You'll be demanding for the rest of time or soon be dead. Because it will never happen. It will not happen in Mexico or any other country in the world except right here in the United States, Land of the naive and stupid, idiotic politically correct politicians.

Angst and Humor about Illegals

MR. PRESIDENT, I'M HEADED TO MEXICO

David M. Bresnahan April 1, 2006 NewsWithViews.com

Dear President Bush:

I'm about to plan a little trip with my family and extended family, and I would like to ask you to assist me. I'm going to walk across the border from the U.S. into Mexico, and I need to make a few arrangements. I know you can help with this.

I plan to skip all the legal stuff like visas, passports, immigration quotas and laws. I'm sure they handle those things the same way you do here.

So, would you mind telling your buddy, President Vicente Fox, that I'm on my way over? Please let him know that I will be expecting the following:

1. Free medical care for my entire family.

2. English-speaking government bureaucrats for all services I might need, whether I use them or not.

3. All government forms need to be printed in English.

4. I want my kids to be taught by English-speaking teachers.

5. Schools need to include classes on American culture and history.

6. I want my kids to see the American flag flying on the top of the flag pole at their school with the Mexican flag flying lower down.

7. Please plan to feed my kids at school for both breakfast and lunch.

8. I will need a local Mexican driver's license so I can get easy access to government services.

9. I do not plan to have any car insurance, and I won't make any effort to learn local traffic laws.

10. In case one of the Mexican police officers does not get the memo from Pres. Fox to leave me alone, please be sure that all police officers speak English.

11. I plan to fly the U.S. flag from my house top, put flag decals on my car, and have a gigantic celebration on July 4th I do not want any complaints or negative comments from the locals.

12. I would also like to have a nice job without paying any taxes, and don't enforce any labor laws or tax laws.

13. Please tell all the people in the country to be extremely nice and never say a critical word about me, or about the strain I might place on the economy.

I know this is an easy request because you already do all these things for all the people who come to the U.S. from Mexico. I am sure that Pres. Fox won't mind returning the favor if you ask him nicely.

However, if he gives you any trouble, just invite him to go quail hunting with your V.P.

Thank you so much for your kind help.

Sincerely,

Mexican Standoff

I don't know how everybody else feels about it, but to me I think Hispanic people in this country, legally or illegally, made a huge public relations mistake with their recent demonstrations.

I don't blame anybody in the world for wanting to come to the United States of America, as it is a truly wonderful place. But when the first thing you do when you set foot on American soil is illegal it is flat out wrong and I don't care how many lala land left heads come out of the woodwork and start trying to give me sensitivity lessons.

I don't need sensitivity lessons, in fact I don't have anything against Mexicans, I just have something against criminals and anybody who comes into this country illegally is a criminal and if you don't believe it try coming into America from a foreign country without a passport and see how far you get.

What disturbs me about the demonstrations is that it's tantamount to saying, "I am going to come into your country even if it means breaking your laws and there's nothing you can do about it."

It's an "in your face" action and speaking just for me I don't like it one little bit and if there were a half dozen pairs of gonads in Washington bigger than English peas it wouldn't be happening.

Where are you, you bunch of lilly livered, pantywaist, forked tongued, sorry excuses for defenders of The Constitution? Have you been drinking the water out of the Potomac again?

And even if you pass a bill on immigration it will probably be so pork laden and watered down that it won't mean anything anyway. Besides, what good is another law going to do when you won't enforce the ones on the books now?

And what ever happened to the polls guys? I thought you folks were the quintessential finger wetters. Well you sure ain't paying any attention to the polls this time because somewhere around eighty percent of Americans want something done about this mess, and mess it is and getting bigger everyday.

This is no longer a problem, it is a dilemma and headed for being a tragedy. Do you honestly think that what happened in France with the Muslims can't happen here when the businesses who hire these people finally run out of jobs and a few million disillusioned Hispanics take to the streets?

If you, Mr. President, Congressmen and Senators, knuckle under on this and refuse to do something meaningful it means that you care nothing for the kind of country your children and grandchildren will inherit.

But I guess that doesn't matter as long as you get re-elected.

Shame on you.

Pray for our troops.

What do you think?

God Bless America

Charlie Daniels

American by birth! Montanan by the grace of God! Christian by choice!

Forced to live under a Godless government by far left courts.

Friday, March 31, 2006

Iraq Is the Right War, at the Right Time

A University of Hawai'i political science professor explains why he thinks Iraq is the right war, at the right time.

Was Bush Right? By R. J. Rummel Ph.D.

I have been increasingly disappointed with the poll results on our war in Iraq. In December 2003, 63% of people in a CBS/New York Times poll thought the war was the right thing to do when asked, "Looking back, do you think the United States did the right thing in taking military action against Iraq, or should the U. S. Have stayed out?" Only 31% thought we should have stayed out.

However, in December 2005, just before the Iraqi election, the split was down to 48 to 48. By then, Democrats were turning against continuing the occupation, with Democrat National Committee chairman Howard Dean saying thet the "idea that we're going to win in Iraq is an idea which is just plain wrong." Other notable Democrats called for either immediate withdrawal or a timetable for withdrawal. (See HJ Commentary 1)

The urge to end the war is powerful and understandable. People look at the cost of trying to nurture a democracy in Iraq and naturally ask, "What's in it for us?" "What does this have to do with American security?" "Is it worth the deaths of more than 2,2000 American soldiers?"

By now some 10,000 military personnel fromHawai'i have served in Iraq. More than 1.000 are there right now. This August. About 7,000 more soldiers will deploy to Iraq. These very questions keep many of us in the islands up at night.

Why am I disappointed by the steady decline in support for the war? Because I believe President George W. Bush is right to stay the course in Iraq. My views come from a lifetime of studying totalitarian regimes—of which Hussein's Iraq was certainly one—and the profound ways in which they threaten humanity. Success in Iraq would have equally profound and positive benefits for the world. This is omething I wish more people understood, and what I hope to explain here.

THE DEMOCRATIC PEACE

It has been three years since the United States invaded Iraq—with the support of 49 nations, with specific Congressional approval, and under UN Security Resolution 1441—to eliminate the threat posed by Hussein. No one has forgotten that the administration based its urgency for the invasion on the belief that Hussein possessed, or could easily assemble, weapons of mass destruction which could threaten the region. (See HJ Commentary 1)

Because these weapons have not been uncovered, manycritics of the war have come to see America's attempt to foster democracy in Iraq as a post hoc justification for the war. This view disregards that liberating the Iraqi people was always a central component of Bush's plan (just one more of many components), second only to thwarting Hussein's weapons of mass destruction ambitions. In his speech on the eve of the March 20, 2003 invasion, Bush spoke repeatedly of "helping Iraqis achieve a united, stable and free country," of "restoring control of that country to its own people.

Nor is Bush's interest in democratization limited to Iraq. Speaking to reporters in 2004 about his insistence that the Palestinian authority also become democratic, Bush explained, "The reason why I'm so strong on democracy is democracies don't go to war with each other ... I've got great faith in democracies to promote peace."

In other words, he had faith in what is called by students of international relations the democratic peace. Secretary of State Condoleezza Rice made this connection explicit in her December 11, 2005, Washington Post article, "The promise of Democratic Peace."

This is the goal worth pursuing, that one makes Iraq the right war, at the right time. The long-term benefits of a democratized Iraq are inherently beneficial, to the Iraqi people, to the region and to us. This is because the theory of democratic peace simply works.

International Wars 1816-2005

BELLIGERANTS	WARS (AT LEAST 1,000 KILLED)
Democracies vs. Democracies	0
Democracies vs. Nondemocracies	166
Nondemocracies vs. Nondemocracies	205

Sources: Melvin Small and J. David Singer, SIPRI, PRIO, Monty Marshal, R. J. Rummel.

We know from research done over the last three decades that this is true. The table above shows that, since 1816–the end of the Napoleonic Wars–there have been no wars between two democracies, although there were 371 bilateral wars.

Since 1816, there have been only three cases of violence between democracies that ended in deaths. Two of these involved Peru and Ecuador. In 1981, Peru was only marginally democratic, as was Ecuador, but less so. This was also true of Peru and Ecuador in 1984. The only other case of violence over these nearly two centuries was marginally democratic Ecuador (initiator) vs. the United States, in 1954. Only three cases and none since 1984, despite there being122 electoral democracies today, 89 of them liberal democracies whose people have civil liberties and political rights.

There is much more to the democratic peace than avoiding war or international violence. Democracies have been involved in many wars, some they launched themselves (America's invasions of Afghanistan and Iraq being the most recent examples). However, by an order of magnitude or more, democracies fight the least severe wars, in terms of numbers killed, compared to authoritarian or totalitarian regimes.

Moreover, on the average, democratic nations are the most internally peaceful–they have the least violence in numbers killed in rebellions, civil wars, civil unrest, anti-government riots, violent strikes and coups.

Perhaps most importantly, democracies seldom murder their own citizens. Democide (genocide and mass murder) is an evil of militarism (as in Burma), monarchism (Russia's Peter the Great), theocratism (Iran), fascism (Hitler), and communism. (The last two are typical examples of socialist dictatorships) Over the whole 20th century, governments–almost all nondemocracies–murdered about 262 million people, eight times the number killed in combat in all the last century's international and domestic wars.

In stark comparison to this horrible cost of dictatorships, no liberal democracy has systematically murdered its own people.

Saddam Hussein is up among the mega-murderers. He murdered close to a million Kurds, Sinnis and Shiites, and launched a war against Iran in which probably a million more died. Hussein and his form of government, regardless of its armament, were themselves threats to peace and security, and a proven disaster for the people of Iraq.

Building the Democratic Peace in Iraq

Of course, the democratic peace doesn't just happen on its own. It takes hard work. Although baghdad fell to coalition forces within three weeks of the 2003 invasion of Iraq, and Hussein himself was captured in December of that year, the path to democracy and stability in the country has been a long complicated one.

As the Bush administration did in Afghanistan, in Iraq it helped Iraqis rebuild and develop their country economically, and create from scratch a new army and security force. The United States has also helped them democratize, as it successfully did with

Germany and Japan after world war II. Here are the four major events in that peace process thus far.

1) On June 28, 2004 Bush transferred sovereignty to an interim Iraqi government which prepared for a national election of a transition government whose onmly purpose was to write a constitution.

2) In January 2005, the Iraqis voted this government into temporary power and, with much conflict, bargaining and negotiation, it wrote a constitution.

3) In an October referendum, Iraqis approved this constitution.

4) In December, under the new constitution and for the first time ever, Iraqis voted in a national, competitive election for a democratic government.

About 70% of iraqis turned out to vote and, according to foreign election observers and the United Nations, it was a fair election meeting international standards.

When you and I vote, we drive to a local elementary school, then safely and easily mark our choices. No one assassinates election workers, or threatens to murder voters simply for showing up. This hasn't been the case for ordinary Iraqis, who have taken great risks to hold and participate in elections. Throughout Iraq's pursuit of the democratic peace, there has been bloody opposition by foreign terrorists, who saw the American occupation of iraq as an opportunity to defeat American power, and who especially understood that a Muslim democracy in the Middle East threatened their ambitions to spread a fundamentalist theocracy.

Even more powerful opposition ha scome from Sunni insurrectionists, those who had most benefitted from Hussein's rule (he is a Sunni himself). Every one of their roadside bombs directed against American forces is specifically meant to make those of us at home second guess our presence in Iraq in support of democratization. Judging from the poll results I opened with, the attacks have indeed taken their toll on our will to see through the reconstruction of Iraq as a functional democracy.

Nonetheless, Bush has refused to withdraw. He is convinced of the rightness of what he calls the Forward Strategy of Freedom and this war as I am.

Iraq in the Big Picture

On November 6, 2003, in a speech to the National Endowment for Democracy, Bush proclaimed his Forward Strategy of Freedom. Although focused on the Middle East, it was general in tone. He stated that, "As in Europe, as in Asia, as in every region of the world, the advance of freedom leads to peace." He emphasized that, "There are ... essential principals common to every successful society, in every culture.

"Successful societies limit the power of the stste and the power of the military–so that governments respond to the will of the people, and not the will of an elite.

"Successful societies protect freedom with the consistent and impartial rule of law, instead of selectively applying the law to punish political opponents.

"Successful societies guarantee religious liberty–the right to serve and honor God without fear of persecution.

"Successful societies privatize their economies, and secure the rights of property. They prohibit and punish official corruption and invest in the health and education of their people. They recognize the rights of women.

"And instead of directing hatred and resentment against others, successful societies appeal to the hopes of their own people."

These principals provide the foundation for the president's new foreign policy–new in the sense that he had not so clearly articulated it before. He committed the United States to promote and foster freedom, and he put dictators on notice that they will no longer be "excused and accommodated."

Two days after the speech, as if to double underline it, the president issued a proclaimation naming November 9 World Freedom Day. He proclaimed: "Fourteen years ago, freedom-loving people tore down the Berlin Wall and began to set a nation free from Communist oppression. On World Freedom Day, the United States joins with other countries in commemorating that historic day. The United Dtates is committed to liberty, freedom and the universal struggle for human rights. We strive to advance peace and demoracy and to safeguard these ideals around the world."

So, why are we fighting in Iraq and fostering democratic freedom there and elsewhere? The answer is to promote an end to war, democide and famine, and to minimize internal political violence. In other words, it is to foster global human security.

Surely, creating a world in which there will never be a war or democide is in the American national interest, the vital interest of our children, and is worth fighting and dying for.

R. J. Rummel Ph.D. is professor emeritus of political science at the University of Hawai'i at Manoa. He has published 32 books, received a number of awards for his contributions, and has been frequently nominated for the Nobel Peace Prize. His Web site is at **www.hawaii.edu/powerkills** and he keeps a daily blog at **http://freedomspeace.blogspot.com**.

Closing comments by Howard Johnson:

This factual presentation (provable facts) is in stark contrast to the constant emotionally charged stream of non-facts being presented to the American people by the likes of Howard Dean, Nancy Pelozi and Ted Kennedy along with their dupes in the media who revel in their power to sway ignorant people to follow their agenda. I believe the real reason Democrats are so vocal against the war and blame every national problem (including natural disasters) on George Bush is twofold. First and foremost, American success in creating a democratic Iraq would so enhance Republican prestige and so damage Democrats and liberals in particular that a major shift to Republican political power would result. Democrats will do anything to prevent that from happening including scuttle America and aid totalitarianism in the world. Liberal Democrats are working diligently to destroy every valiant effort made by those who founded this country to promote freedom and democracy and protect us from our own government including our Constitution.

HJ commentary 1: This was a purely political effort aimed at discrediting America and the Bush administration in order to gain political advantage and power. Democrats seem to want to do as much damage to America and the cause of freedom and democracy in the world as is possible by blatant lies and deceptions. Aided by their biased, liberal, "drunk with power" fellow travelers in the media, liberal Democrats have mounted an unprecedented hate campaign of destruction against everything good America has stood for in the world including being the champion of democratic freedom and the "Guardian of Democracy." Apparently they believe they can regain power by working to destroy America and obliterate our influence in the world. They have done more to aid Al Queda, despotism and dictatorship in the world than those forces could possibly have done by themselves. This is to me a concentrated effort to destroy freedom and democracy and prevent peoples all over the world from enjoying peace and freedom. Hitler's NAZIs and Stalin's NKVD were far less effective if a bit more brutal.

The Bush message the media has forgotten or deliberately ignored are the numerous points (I believe there were seventeen) submitted to the United Nations in the original request for action against Saddam Hussein. The only one of those points ever mentioned in the media and the centerpiece of Democrat hate rhetoric is the WMDs mantra. Occasionally they mention one other point, his support and aid for Al Queda, but that one has pretty well been proven accurate by now. As to the lack of discovery of WMDs, why did the media ignore the discovery of MIG 25s buried in the desert sand? These advanced Soviet aircraft are clearly effective weapons of Mass destruction. All other WMD evidence discovered was either declared invalid, inconclusive or was completely ignored by our "objective" news media.

Consider what might have become of Iraq if liberals had not done everything they could to scuttle our efforts there. They effectively destroyed nearly all of our positive efforts knowing that if America succeeded in Iraq it would provide a huge benefit to the Republican party. This destructive effort was made strictly fo political purposes. They didn't give a damn what happened to America, our armed forces, or the people of Iraq

Some Additional HJ Commentary Not Directly Related:

The intellectual elite who arm themselves against any thought that differs in direction or intent from their own tightly held beliefs are the blind driving force behind the "anti-war" crowd. These closed minds ignore the hundreds of millions slaughtered because of reluctance to engage in or even accept "constructive" or "preventive" wars against tyrants. They are like Neville Chamberlain who on September 30, 1938 reported on the Munich agreement saying, "My good friends this is the second time in our history that there has come back from Germany to Downing Street peace with honor. I believe it is peace in our time." How wrong he was then and how wrong the anti-war forces are now in precisely the same vein regarding Iraq. Should we pull out of Iraq now without establishing a democracy will the Muslim hordes do to Europe and America what they repeatedly did in India and what they promise to do now in all their rhetoric? History will provide the answer.

Some Loosely Related Quotes from Stephen Jay Gould and Erc Hoffer:

The most erroneous stories are those we think we know best - and therefore never scrutinize or question.

Nothing is more dangerous than a dogmatic world view - nothing more constraining, more blinding to innovation, more destructive of openness to novelty. —*Stephen Jay Gould*

These quotes of Eric Hoffer from many years ago still ring true and surely will always:

What the intellectual craves above all else is to be taken seriously, to be treated as a decisive force in shaping history. He is far more at home in a society that weighs his every word and keeps close watch on his attitudes than in a society that cares not what he says or does. He would rather be persecuted than ignored.

Every extreme attitude is a flight from the self.

The untalented are more at ease in a society that gives them valid alibis for not achieving than in one where opportunities are abundant. In an affluent society, the alienated who clamor for power are largely untalented people who cannot make use of the unprecedented opportunities for self-realization, and cannot escape the confrontation with an ineffectual self.

There are many who find a good alibi far more attractive than an achievement. For an achievement does not settle anything permanently. We still have to prove our worth anew each day: we have to prove that we are as good today as we were yesterday. But when we have a valid alibi for not achieving anything we are fixed, so to speak, for life. Moreover, when we have an alibi for not writing a book, painting a picture, and so on, we have an alibi for not writing the greatest book and not painting the greatest picture. Small wonder that the effort expended and the punishment endured in obtaining a good alibi often exceed the effort and grief requisite for the attainment of a most marked achievement.

—*Eric Hoffer*

A Black Minister Tells it like it is

By Rev. Jesse Lee Peterson

c 2005 WorldNetDaily.com

Say a hurricane is about to destroy the city you live in. Two questions:

What would you do? What would you do if you were black?

Sadly, the two questions don't have the same answer.

To the first: Most of us would take our families out of that city quickly to protect them from danger. Then, able-bodied men would return to help others in need, as wives and others cared for children, elderly, infirm and the like.

For better or worse, Hurricane Katrina has told us the answer to the second question. If you're black and a hurricane is about to destroy your city, you'll probably wait for the government to save you.

This was not always the case. Prior to 40 years ago, such a pathetic performance by the black community in a time of crisis would have been inconceivable. The first response would have come from black men. They would take care of their families, bring them to safety, and then help the rest of the community. Then local government would come in.

No longer. When 75 percent of New Orleans residents had left the city, it was primarily immoral, welfare-pampered blacks that stayed behind and waited for the government to bail them out. This, as we know, did not turn out good results.

Enter Jesse Jackson and Louis Farrakhan. Jackson and Farrakhan laid blame on "racist" President Bush. Farrakhan actually proposed the idea that the government blew up a levee so as to kill blacks and save whites. The two demanded massive governmental spending to rebuild New Orleans, above and beyond the federal government's proposed $60 billion. Not only that, these two were positioning themselves as the gatekeepers to supervise the dispersion of funds. Perfect: Two of the most dishonest elite blacks in America, "overseeing" billions of dollars. I wonder where that money will end up.

Of course, if these two were really serious about laying blame on government, they should blame the local one. Responsibility to perform legally and practically fell first on the mayor of New Orleans. We are now all familiar with Mayor Ray Nagin the black Democrat who likes to yell at President Bush for failing to do Nagin's job. The facts, unfortunately, do not support Nagin's wailing. As the Washington Times puts it, "recent reports show [Nagin] failed to follow through on his own city's emergency-response plan, which acknowledged that thousands of the city's poorest residents would have no way to evacuate the city."

One wonders how there was "no way" for these people to evacuate the city. We have photographic evidence telling us otherwise. You've probably seen it by now the photo showing 2,000 parked school buses, unused and underwater. How much planning does it require to put people on a bus and leave town, Mayor Nagin?

Instead of doing the obvious, Mayor Nagin (with no positive contribution from Democratic Gov. Kathleen Blanco, the other major leader vested with responsibility to address the hurricane disaster) loaded remaining New Orleans residents into the Superdome and the city's convention center. We know how that plan turned out.

About five years ago, in a debate before the National Association of Black Journalists, I stated that if whites were to just leave the United States and let blacks run the country, they would turn America into a ghetto within 10 years. The audience, shall we say, disagreed with me strongly. Now I have to disagree with me. I gave blacks too much credit. It took a mere three days for blacks to turn the Superdome and the convention center into ghettos, rampant with theft, rape and murder.

President Bush is not to blame for the rampant immorality of blacks. Had New Orleans' black community taken action, most would have been out of harm's way. But most were too lazy, immoral and trifling to do anything productive for themselves.

All Americans must tell blacks this truth. It was blacks' moral poverty not their material poverty that cost them dearly in New Orleans. Farrakhan, Jackson, and other race hustlers are to be repudiated they will only perpetuate this problem by stirring up hatred and applauding moral corruption. New Orleans, to the extent it is to be rebuilt, should be remade into a dependency-free, morally strong city where corruption is opposed and success is applauded. Blacks are obligated to help themselves and not depend on the government to care for them. We are all obligated to tell them so.

The Rev. Jesse Lee Peterson is founder and president of BOND, the Brotherhood Organization of A New Destiny, and author of "Scam: How the Black Leadership Exploits Black America."

Monday, February 20, 2006

HUD promotes Racial Bigotry

The following Letter was inspired by and in response to a series of radio ads now running here in California and probably the rest of the country. In the ad, three men call about an ad in the newspaper for an apartment and are told the apartment is no longer available by an ethnically neutral female voice. The three include an obvious Latino, an obvious Indian American, and an obvious African-American. When the fourth man calls and gives his name as Graham Wellington, in an obvious English-American voice, he is told the apartment is still available. This is one of the most conspicuously bigoted and highly discriminatory ad of any kind I have heard in a very long time. In response I sent the following letter. I couldn't find an email address to use so it went out snail mail. I suppose all you bleeding hearts out there think this ad is perfectly OK.

San Francisco Regional Office of FHEO
U.S. Department of Housing and Urban Development
600 Harrison Street, 3rd Floor
San Francisco, California 94107-1387

I am incensed at the recent series of radio ads about housing discrimination which are apparently coming from your organization. These ads are a blatantly obvious attempt to smear Caucasian, English-Americans and incite anger toward them by Latinos, Indian-Americans and African-Americans. These ads are highly discriminatory and would never be used in another venue with a reverse implication castigating equally any minority other than Caucasian, English-Americans. Graham Wellington indeed–your intent is blatantly obvious and it is most certainly not to promote fair housing. To be truly fair–a word I seriously doubt anyone in your organization really understands–you would run four ads with each of the ethnic groups used, winning in turn the apartment in preference to the other three. This would be "fair."

The "Graham Wellingtons" of our country have become part of the most discriminated against group by virtually every government agency, media mouthpiece, news reporter, and politician in the country.

Unfortunately, should your bigoted ad actually be run with any of the other three groups being accepted by the apartment owner, the ACLU and dozens of other similar organizations would be filing law suits the first day the ad ran. How about leaving the ad as is but replacing, "Graham Wellington" with Harvey Goldberg, Sean McGinty, Antonio Sabartini, Franz Shultz, or Hillary Swank? You could even make more of an impact for your agenda by changing the African American's voice to that of a homosexual and making the Indian American a woman.

You people are most certainly not against discrimination, but strongly support it when it is turned against groups of any kind other than those you favor. Pardon me, but your supposedly hidden agenda is showing clearly and it surely isn't equal treatment for all. Replacing bigotry against one or more ethnic groups with bigotry against another is replacing one evil with another. This is clearly what your ad is doing. How about a change to real fairness?

Cordially,

Howard E. Johnson

Wednesday, February 15, 2006

The Enemy We Grossly underestimate
The power and menace of the enemy sworn to destroy us.

This is the real reason the Bush administration went to war in Iraq and why we will probably fail and waste the 3000 dead American service personnel while forgetting the other 3000 that died in the 9/11 attacks. I have no particular love for GW, but I do understand at least part of his real reasons for the Iraq war, the goals if you will. He wants to stop the spread of fundamentalist Islam's growing power and control in the middle east and eventually Europe. I agree with his goals, but don't believe we have the slightest chance of achieving them for several reasons. I believe Europe will soon be under the domination of Islam - within ten to thirty years. I believe we will see Taliban type Islamic governments in Spain and France first, driven by the same force that once controlled Spain and the Ottoman empire, and has continued invading and subverting India since the 700s. My only hope for our survival is that their various factions succeed in destroying each other, a very significant possibility.

1) I firmly believe Islamic fundamentalists will triumph and place virtually the entire middle east and eventually Europe under Taliban type governments. With the liberal press and politicians providing substantial support for Islamic terrorists, it is only a matter of time until we abandon the only action now under way to stem this tide of terror and murder.

2) Unless we find a way to cut off the huge flow of oil money into Islam - money paid for petroleum products - unless we find alternatives to petroleum almost immediately, America will

fall into economic disaster and political chaos. Increases in atmospheric carbon dioxide and global warming will pose even more serious problems for a rapidly degrading environment. Islamic fundamentalists by their very dedication to their religion have absolutely no concern about the environment. Death and destruction is their universal answer to all problems.

3) All one has to do is read the writings and pronouncements of Osama bin Laden to know what is coming. I believe him when he says in one of his statements. "America will soon collapse into oblivion. All we have to provide is a tiny bit of terror every year or two. It will fan their internal flames of hatred and disturb their already precarious internal power balance. They will soon destroy each other. Islam will then march triumphant over the rotting corpses of these satanic monsters. Their passion for things of the flesh and not of the spirit will surely destroy them." Read "of the spirit" as "of my version of Islamic law." I pray this is not prophetic, but fear that it is.

I believe the present administration has some true visionaries who understand the growing menace we face from Islamic fundamentalists. I believe they are opposed by a strange cabal of raw idealists, power hungry despots, ignorant peace activists, hopeless Communist losers, and brazen traitors, all of whom are willing to see American power and influence destroyed in order to gain or regain influence and political power for themselves. Overtly, they seem to see no threat whatsoever from a growing menace that uses mass-murder of non-combatants as a tool of intimidation and fear to eviscerate all who do not accept the supremacy and absolute control of their religious law. How these brain-dead sub-humans can see the dangers as "criminal" problems requiring "police" responses and the terrorists as deserving of the full force of America's criminal court system is obvious when you think about the agenda of the ACLU and the National Lawyers Guild. These two groups are dedicated to the degradation of America and the destruction of American capitalism. A look at the origin of the NLG says a lot about both organizations.

The National Lawyers Guild:

- Is a radical organization of lawyers, founded in 1936 by the Communist Party USA

- Is an active affiliate of the International Association of Democratic Lawyers, which served as a Soviet front group during the Cold War

- In the post-Communist era has continued to embrace its Communist heritage

- Has sought to legally represent individuals and groups that have attacked the U.S.

- Is at the forefront of efforts to weaken the nation's intelligence-gathering agencies

- Named as a key member of the Open Borders Lobby in the pamphlet "The Open Borders Lobby and the Nation's Security After 9/11," written by William Hawkins and Erin Anderson

To read more on this subject click on, http://www.discoverthenetwork.org

Islamic fundamentalists have announced and will continue to use the following method to destroy us. The violent 9-11 attack was followed by furious government activity in response. Huge expense and overpowering concerns followed. The lack of any terrorist attack in the US for some time is a calculated tactic of bin Laden and al Queda! Next, they will mount another violent and deadly attack, viz a viz 9-11, possibly on a seven or twelve year cycle. Then once more they will wait for the resulting furor to die down and morph into criticism and internal squabbles as we frantically prepare for another attack. They can merely sit back and wait while we quarrel with each other about how to deal with terrorism. This will lead to disunity between opposing factions in our government and distract us from preparedness. They have already offered us a truce which is an old arab ruse to give them time and opportunity to rearm, and to train and build up their militants once more. Then as we bicker and let down our guard another major attack, deadlier than the first will be mounted. Perhaps a deadly bomb at a huge sporting event or a dirty suitcase bomb in one or more of our cities. Once more we will struggle furiously to avert another attack while they merely sit and wait for the furor to die down. They are using western freedom and our adversarial based democratic political system to destroy us. We are not only letting them, but are willing partners in our own destruction. I predict that unless drastic steps are taken soon, Europe will fall to the sword of Allah within the next two decades and America will follow soon after. When that happens there will be no more peace marches or protests–indeed all who would do so will be in their graves along with all American liberals, conservatives, moderates, Christians, Jews, and non-Muslims. Islamic fundamentalists are not squeamish about beheading any and all who oppose them.

There is one place where I agree with many liberals, but for totally different reasons. Oil companies are not our friends. Their promotion of huge expenditures of government funds (read your tax dollars, not their own money) for research and development of the hydrogen fuel cell and the so-called "hydrogen economy" is a complete fraud. It has been foisted off on us as the ultimate answer to our energy needs and it will never become economically feasible for a large number of very valid reasons. It is a deliberate smoke screen designed to prevent us from developing alternative fuels and power systems so those same oil companies can continue to reap huge profits and send vast amounts of cash into the coffers of the most virulent enemies we have.

There are real good, valid, practical means of our becoming energy independent in less than ten years and though some are gaining attention, none have received more than a small fraction of the government money being sent down the hydrogen fuel cell rathole. I am in the process of rewriting a book on the subject titled "The SUPER Hydrogen Economy" which describes many promising systems and shows the hydrogen fuel cell for the dead end it really is. New York Times reporter, Mathew L. Wald, in an article in the May 2004 issue of Scientific American, writes, "Despite the technological and infrastructure obstacles, a hydrogen economy may be coming. If it is it will more likely resemble the perfume economy, a market where quantities are so small that unit prices do not matter. It will appear in items like cellular phones and laptop computers."

If we move quickly and switch from petroleum fuels to full dependence on renewable fuels with proven reliability and requiring little change in our infrastructure the flow of American billions out of the country will cease. That change alone could reverse our teetering balance of trade from huge negative numbers to positive. The technology is ready now to make this changeover. It would not only be a monstrous boost to our economy, but would encourage vast new manufacturing investment and place us in the lead in supplying the world with environmentally friendly energy that could even halt global warming. I suppose the "hate

America" crowd will do all in their power to find some ridiculous reason to prevent this from happening.

If as I suspect, we do not do this, I see China as possibly the only hope to prevent the entire world from entering a new dark age of hideous pain and torture for most people. This under ruthless and evil Taliban style governments following the most oppressive form of Islamic law. They will eventually be armed with European and American weapons and nuclear bombs which they will not hesitate to use. By the time Liberals in Europe and then America get unstuck from stupid and realize what is happening it will be far too late. The Chinese, having no lay-down-and-die philosophy will meet Islam head on in an all-out nuclear war if they can control their sizeable Muslim population in their eastern regions

Fundamentalist Islam is a real threat and is gaining the power to do to the entire world what it did in the past in India and to all who opposed them. The appeal of Islam to the disenfranchised poor males of the world is unmistakable. Their message is destroy–get even–hate–kill–murder–chop off the heads of any who won't bow down. They are an angry, vengeful, male dominated mob of huge proportions, incited by religious fanatics who don't give a damn if they destroy all of humanity to the last man as long as they can obliterate any who disagree with them. Envision Ghengis Kahn with millions of troops, modern weapons and nuclear bombs.

Eric Hoffer wrote two descriptions of the likes of these mad-men, but didn't anticipate the depth or power of their hatred:

"All mass movements avail themselves of action as a means of unification. The conflicts a mass movement seeks and incites serve not only to down its enemies but also to strip its followers of their distinct individuality and render them more soluble in the collective medium."

"Passionate hatred can give meaning and purpose to an empty life. Thus people haunted by the purposelessness of their lives try to find a new content not only by dedicating themselves to a holy cause but also by nursing a fanatical grievance. A mass movement offers them unlimited opportunities for both."

From a pure numbers standpoint the Islamic world poses serious threats. Their nations and peoples exhibit the highest birthrate in the world that promises to more double their numbers every generation. Their total disregard for human lives of even their own people promises annihilation on a massive scale. What Cortez did to the Aztecs, Islam will do to humanity. Just imagine a Cortez, a Genghis Kahn, or a Hitler with nuclear bombs, modern military hardware and an unlimited supply of fanatical warriors and you'll see what we're facing. Actually I don't see Osama bin Laden as near the threat as others in or near his command. These men are certainly as ruthless as was Genghis Kahn and may soon have nuclear weapons in their arsenal if not already. They will use them freely when it suits them.

In spite of these known facts, liberals want us to pull out of Iraq now and turn the middle east over to this man and his followers? That is stupidity, suicide, and absolute madness, all wrapped up in the same package! It is an accepted fact that Iraq is now in the throws of a civil war. As soon as our troops leave, Iraq will be an even bloodier battleground and whoever wins will do so under a leader of intense cruelty. He'll make Saddam look like a Mother Theresa. The only possible course of defense when that happens is a massive nuclear threat with teeth and the Chinese and the liberal left in this country would never permit that.

Here's a bit of history of those peaceful Moslems:

Alain Danielou (1907-1994) son of French aristocracy, author of numerous books on philosophy, religion, history and arts of India, in his book, Histoire de l' Inde writes:

"From the time Muslims started arriving, around 632 AD, the history of India becomes a long, monotonous series of murders, massacres, spoliations, and destructions. It is, as usual, in the name of 'a holy war' of their faith, of their sole God, that the barbarians have destroyed civilizations, wiped out entire races." Mahmoud Ghazni, continues Danielou, "was an early example of Muslim ruthlessness, burning in 1018 of the temples of Mathura, razing Kanauj to the ground and destroying the famous temple of Somnath, sacred to all Hindus. His successors were as ruthless as Ghazni: 103 temples in the holy city of Benaras were razed to the ground, its marvelous temples destroyed, its magnificent palaces wrecked." Indeed, the Muslim policy vis a vis India, concludes Danielou, seems to have been a conscious systematic destruction of everything that was beautiful, holy, refined." Remember the statues of Buddha in Afghanistan?

Dr. Babasaheb Ambedkar Writes:

"The first Muslim invasion of India came from the north-west by the Arabs who were led by Mahommad Bin Qasim. It took place in 711 A.D. and resulted in the conquest of Sind. This first Muslim invasion did not result in a permanent occupation of the country because the Caliphate of Baghdad, by whose order and command the invasion had taken place, was obliged by the middle of 9th century A.D. to withdraw its direct control from this distant province of Sind. Soon after this withdrawal, there began a series of terrible invasions by Muhammad of Ghazni (the idol breaker) in 1001 A.D. Muhammad died in 1030 A.D., but within the short span of 30 years, he invaded India 17 times. He was followed by Mahommed Ghori, who began his career as an invader in 1173. He was killed in 1206. For thirty years Muhammad of Ghazni ravaged India and for thirty years Mahommad Ghori harried the same country in the same way.

Then followed the incursions of the Moghul hordes of Chenghiz Khan. They first came in 1221. They then stayed on the border of India but did not enter it. Twenty years later, they marched on Lahore and sacked it. Of their inroads, the most terrible was under Timur in 1398. Then comes on the scene a new invader in the person of Babar who invaded India in 1526. The invasions of India did not stop with that of Babar. There occurred two more invasions. In 1738 Nadir Shah's invading host swept over the Punjab like a flooded river "furious as the ocean". He was followed by Ahmad Shah Abdali who invaded India in 1761, smashed the forces of the Marathas at Panipat and crushed for ever the attempt of the Hindus to gain the ground which they had lost to their Muslim invaders.

These Muslim invasions were not undertaken merely out of lust for loot or conquest, but also to strike a blow at the idolatry and polytheism of Hindus and establishing Islam in India.

Muhammad of Ghazni also looked upon his numerous invasions of India as the waging of a holy war. Al'Utbi, the historian of Muhammad, describing his raids writes:

"He demolished idol temples and established Islam. He captured ......cities, destroyed the idolaters, and gratifying Muslims. He then returned home and promulgated accounts of the victories obtained for Islam........and vowed that every year he would undertake a holy war against Hind."

(source: Dr. Babasaheb Ambedkar Writings and Speeches. Reprint of Pakistan or The Partition of India. Education Department. Government of Maharashtra 1990 Vol. 8. p. 53-66)

For more information on conflict with Hindus, click
http://atributetohinduism.com/Islamic_Onslaught.htm

For information on modern conflicts with Christians: Click
http://www.falange.us/xtian-225.htm

Wednesday, JANUARY 10, 2007 08:33:34 -0600

A VERY RECENT EVENT OF SIGNIFICANCE:

Once more we are sleeping!

What Thomas Jefferson learned from the Muslim book of jihad - By Ted Sampley

U.S. Veteran Dispatch - January 2007

Democrat Keith Ellison is now officially the first Muslim United States congressman. True to his pledge, he placed his hand on the Quran, the Muslim book of jihad and pledged his allegiance to the United States during his ceremonial swearing-in. Capitol Hill staff said Ellison's swearing-in photo opportunity drew more media than they had ever seen in the history of the U.S. House. Ellison represents the 5th Congressional District of Minnesota.

The Quran Ellison used was no ordinary book. It once belonged to Thomas Jefferson, third president of the United States and one of America's founding fathers. Ellison borrowed it from the Rare Book Section of the Library of Congress. It was one of the 6,500 Jefferson books archived in the library.

Ellison, who was born in Detroit and converted to Islam while in college, said he chose to use Jefferson's Quran because it showed that "a visionary like Jefferson" believed that wisdom could be gleaned from many sources.

There is no doubt Ellison was right about Jefferson believing wisdom could be "gleaned" from the Muslim Quran. At the time Jefferson owned the book, he needed to know everything possible about Muslims because he was about to advocate war against the Islamic "Barbary" states of Morocco, Algeria, Tunisia and Tripoli.

Ellison's use of Jefferson's Quran as a prop illuminates a subject once well-known in the history of the United States, but, which today, is mostly forgotten - the Muslim pirate slavers who over many centuries enslaved millions of Africans and tens of thousands of Christian Europeans and Americans in the Islamic "Barbary" states.

Over the course of 10 centuries, Muslim pirates cruised the African and Mediterranean coastline, pillaging villages and seizing slaves. The taking of slaves in pre-dawn raids on unsuspecting coastal villages had a high casualty rate. (IMPORTANT, see NOTE: at the end of this paragraph) It was typical of Muslim raiders to kill off as many of the "non-Muslim" older men and women as possible so the preferred "booty" of only young women and children could be collected. Young non-Muslim women were targeted because of their value as concubines in Islamic markets. Islamic law provides for the sexual interests of Muslim men by allowing them to take as many as four wives at one time and to have as many concubines as their fortunes allow.

NOTE: In February 1982 I was working in San Miguel, the Communications Center for the Navy in the Philippines. The comment about raids on coastal villages reminded me of a troubling experience I wrote about in a letter home on that date. This is from that letter:

"A rather chilling experience happened the night before last. I walked down to the beach just a quarter mile from here to eat my supper and watch the sun set. It was a beautiful sunny day in the eighties and the long sandy beach was deserted. Less than half a mile from where I sat on the beach was a small fishing village with twenty or so boats and a few shacks just beyond the fence that marked the edge of the military reservation.

"I had been there nearly an hour, finished my sandwich and was preparing to watch the sun set on the ocean when the unmistakable click of a shell being chambered in a rifle came from right behind me. I turned to see two Marines approaching from the base. They stopped and put their rifles at ease when they recognized I was an American. Somewhat unnerved, I asked what was going on. One asked if I had noticed any fast moving boats on the horizon. When I said one went by, turned around and headed back the other way he suggested I get off the beach immediately. That the boat was probably a Muslim pirate who may have spotted me on the beach and could be preparing to attack.

"Just a few months before, these pirates had attacked the nearby fishing village, killed several men and carried off everything of value, as well as two young women from the village. With their fast boats, actually long narrow boats with outriggers and pivot engines on the back, they could come from the horizon to the beach in less time than it would take me to run through the sand to safety. They would probably shoot me as soon as they hit the beach and then plunder my body, including knocking all the gold from my teeth and be away in their boats in about five minutes. It had happened before on this very beach. That's why they patrol the beach every morning and evening. The South China Sea is famous for mostly Muslim pirates to this very day. I thanked the Marines for the warning and viewed the beautiful beach in a very different light."

I didn't mention it in the letter, but the marines told me the women they abducted from the village would probably be sold as slaves in Indonesia or another Islamic country. It seems things have not changed very much since then - Muslim slavers were still at their trade, at least in that part of the world. - End of note - quote continues,

Boys, as young as 9 or 10 years old, were often mutilated to create eunuchs who would bring higher prices in the slave markets of the Middle East. Muslim slave traders created "eunuch stations" along major African slave routes so the necessary surgery could be performed. It was estimated that only a small number of the boys subjected to the mutilation survived after the surgery.

When American colonists rebelled against British rule in 1776, American merchant ships lost Royal Navy protection. With no American Navy for protection, American ships were attacked and their Christian crews enslaved by Muslim pirates operating under the control of the "Dey of Algiers"--an Islamist warlord ruling Algeria.

Because American commerce in the Mediterranean was being destroyed by the pirates, the Continental Congress agreed in 1784 to negotiate treaties with the four Barbary States. Congress appointed a special commission consisting of John Adams, Thomas Jefferson, and Benjamin Franklin, to oversee the negotiations.

Lacking the ability to protect its merchant ships in the Mediterranean, the new America government tried to appease the Muslim slavers by agreeing to pay tribute and ransoms in order to retrieve seized American ships and buy the freedom of enslaved sailors.

Adams argued in favor of paying tribute as the cheapest way to get American commerce in the Mediterranean moving again. Jefferson was opposed. He believed there would be no end to the demands for tribute and wanted matters settled "through the medium of war." He proposed a league of trading nations to force an end to Muslim piracy.

In 1786, Jefferson, then the American ambassador to France, and Adams, then the American ambassador to Britain, met in London with Sidi Haji abdul Rahman Adja, the "Dey of Algiers" ambassador to Britain.

The Americans wanted to negotiate a peace treaty based on Congress' vote to appease. During the meeting Jefferson and Adams asked the Dey's ambassador why Muslims held so much hostility towards America, a nation with which they had no previous contacts.

In a later meeting with the American Congress, the two future presidents reported that Ambassador Sidi Haji Abdul Rahman Adja had answered that Islam "was founded on the Laws of their Prophet, that it was written in their Quran, that all nations who should not have acknowledged their authority were sinners, that it was their right and duty to make war upon them wherever they could be found, and to make slaves of all they could take as Prisoners, and that every Musselman (Muslim) who should be slain in Battle was sure to go to Paradise."

For the following 15 years, the American government paid the Muslims millions of dollars for the safe passage of American ships or the return of American hostages. The payments in ransom and tribute amounted to 20 percent of United States government annual revenues in 1800.

Not long after Jefferson's inauguration as president in 1801, he dispatched a group of frigates to defend American interests in the Mediterranean, and informed Congress.

Declaring that America was going to spend "millions for defense but not one cent for tribute," Jefferson pressed the issue by deploying American Marines and many of America's best warships to the Muslim Barbary Coast.

The USS Constitution, USS Constellation, USS Philadelphia, USS Chesapeake, USS Argus, USS Syren and USS Intrepid all saw action. In 1805, American Marines marched across the dessert from Egypt into Tripolitania, forcing the surrender of Tripoli and the freeing of all American slaves.

During the Jefferson administration, the Muslim Barbary States, crumbling as a result of intense American naval bombardment and on shore raids by Marines, finally officially agreed to abandon slavery and piracy.

Jefferson's victory over the Muslims lives on today in the Marine Hymn, with the line, "From the halls of Montezuma to the shores of Tripoli, we will fight our country's battles on the land as on the sea."

It wasn't until 1815 that the problem was fully settled by the total defeat of all the Muslim slave trading pirates.

Jefferson had been right. The "medium of war" was the only way to put and end to the Muslim problem. Mr. Ellison was right about Jefferson. He was a "visionary" wise enough to read and learn about the enemy from their own Muslim book of jihad.

* * * End of Ted Sampley Commentary * * *

We would do well to heed Jefferson's wisdom, but I doubt we now have the stomach for it. We'll probably just die!

Eric Hoffer closed his mid-sixties book, "The Temper of Our Time" with a discourse on the American intellectual. His words seem almost prophetic in the atmosphere of today's world. Here are those closing words:

"The American intellectual rejects the idea that our ability to do things with little tutelage and leadership is a mark of social vigor. He would gauge the vigor of a society by its ability to produce great leaders. Yet it is precisely an America that in normal times can function well without outstanding leaders that so readily throws up outstanding individuals. When you talk to an American intellectual about common Americans it is as if you were talking about a mysterious people living on a mysterious continent. [People from fly-over country perhaps?]

"Yet when all is said about the intellectual's preposterous stance there remains the incontestable fact that his chronic militancy and carping have been a vital factor in the Occident's social progress. The blast of the intellectual's trumpets has not brought down or damaged our political and economic institutions. Napoleon predicted that ink would do to the modern social organization what cannon had done to the feudal system. Actually, in the Occident, ink has acted more as a detergent than an explosive. It is doubtful whether without the activities of the pen-and-ink tribe the lot of the common people would be what it is now.

"The events of the past fifty years have sharpened our awareness of the discrepancy between what the intellectual profess while he battles the status quo, and what he practices when he comes to power, and we are wont to search for the features of a commissar in the face of impassioned protest. Actually the metamorphosis of militant intellectual into commissar requires a specific cultural climate and, so far, has taken place mainly outside the Occident. It is easy to underestimate the part played by Russia's and China's past in the evolvement of their present Marxist systems. A century ago Alexander Herzen predicted that Russian Communism would be Russian autocracy turned upside down. In China, where Mandarin intellectuals had the management of affairs in their keeping for centuries, the present dictatorship of an intellectocracy is more a culmination of, than a rupture with the past.

"In Western Europe and the USA, where tradition of individual freedom has deep roots in both the educated and the uneducated, the intellectuals cannot be self-righteous enough nor the masses submissive enough to duplicate the Russian or Chinese experience. Thus in the Occident the militant intellectual is a stable type and a typical irritant; and whenever the influence of the Occident becomes strong enough the chronically disaffected intellectual appears on the scene and pits himself against the prevailing dispensation, even when it is a dispensation powered by his fellow intellectuals. We see this illustrated in the present intellectual unrest in Eastern Europe and Russia, and it is beginning to seem that dominant Communist parties have more to fear from a Western infection than the Occident has to fear from Communist subversion." [Is not the current hate America campaign from the left evidence of this as an accurate, factual prediction?]

"Stalin's assertion that "no ruling class has managed without its own intelligentsia" applies of course to a totalitarian regime. A society that can afford freedom can also manage without a kept intelligentsia: it is vigorous enough to endure ceaseless harassment by the most articulate and perhaps most gifted segment of the population. Such harassment is the "eternal vigilance" which we are told is the price of liberty. In a free society internal tensions are not the signs of brewing anarchy but the systems of vigor—the elements of a self-generating dynamism. Though there is no unequivocal evidence that the intellectual is at his creative best in a wholly free society, it is indubitable that his incorporation in, or close association with a ruling elite sooner or later results in social and cultural stagnation. The chronic frustration of the intellectual's hunger for power and lordship not only prompts him to side with the insulted and injured, but may drive him to compensate for what he misses by realizing and developing his capacities and talents."

* * * End of Hoffer quote * * *

A classic example of liberal incompetence and distortion of the facts is demonstrated by an up-to-the-moment comment regarding the media frenzy some time ago over Dick Cheney's accidental shooting of a friend. In this instance, liberal politicians and media personalities asked questions that had already been discharged by the facts. Their questions were formulated strictly to impugn their hated enemy, not gain meaningful information. Almost every conceivable evil by Dick Cheney was proposed in these questions by one or more members of the media since the incident occurred. There is no need to recount them here. Several reporters actually suggested almost gleefully that his shooting victim might die. I can not imagine the mind that could make a more evil, ghoulish comment.

I have but one question to pose to these media ghouls. Why were there virtually no evil suggestions made as questions of Teddy Kennedy after the accident that took the life of Mary Jo Kopeckni at Chappaquiddick? Or after the supposed suicide of Vince Foster. The answer is quite obvious. Liberal elitists hold themselves and their fellow leftists to a vastly different and drastically lower standard of behavior than any opposing individuals. Real facts seem to be the enemy of the left in virtually every situation. Completely void of constructive programs or ideas and mouthing mantras of false information and imponderable suggestive questions, they are reduced to shouting virtual obscenities and gross distortions of facts. Only the most fanatical blind followers, vast conspiracy believers, political hangers on and self-disenfranchised dissidents could possibly support these outrageous statements, let alone actually believe them.

That they are actively aligning themselves with fundamentalist Muslim extremists to gain political traction is a fact that will eventually make them even more sorry caricatures of a human beings. The sad thing is that so many hate filled cultural, economic, racial and social minorities actually join and blindly support them because it is easier for them to destroy and bring others down to their pathetic level than to build and raise themselves up to any state of higher self esteem. It is no wonder that the left's raw hatred appeals to all the unsuccessful poor, the dregs of humanity, criminals, mentally deficient–those with nothing to lose who have abandoned society and civility.

The Feudals - Tuesday, February 07, 2006

This Essay and the book, "The Feudals" which contains it, are now six years old. So much of what happened in those six years is an extrapolation of these words. The Left is screaming hatred at many long held American traditions and principals. Will they win?

ESSAYS on THE "FEUDALS"

A FEW DEFINITIONS THAT MAY PROVE USEFUL IN THIS SECTION:

conserative - cautious, prudent, moderate. - opposed to great or sudden changes, supporting the existing regime, believing in established principles, not taking risks.

conservation - the act of preserving resources from loss, decay or injury.

idealist - believing in reality as perception, seeing things as they wish they were rather than as they are, striving for perfection, a dreamer, an impractical person.

liberal - progressive in thinking or principles - open handed, generous, broad minded, especially in religion or politics.

libertine - given to lewdness, free from moral restraint. (The Clintons?)

pragmatist - dealing with events as to show their relation; practical, springing from experience, not theory; officious, meddlesome, opinionated.

reactionary - wishing to return to the real or imagined ways of the past, rejection of the present ways, wishing to go back to a previous state of affairs. (The Amish?)

realist - dealing with things as they actually are, as opposed to idealism or romanticism - emphasizing what can be done with things as they are.

Be not the first by whom the new are tried, Nor yet the last to lay the old aside.

— *Alexander Pope, An Essay on Criticism, 1711*

Beware the Liberals Who Are Feudals - June 20, 2000 -

As a long time listener to Rush Limbaugh I enjoy hearing him whenever I can. This worries the more liberal members of my family who won't listen to him, but do listen to the even more prejudiced main stream media. No need for them to worry! I find his positions on many subjects as myopic and prejudicial as those of the media. I like him because he blatantly admits to a prejudicial position and is proud of it. I despise the media when they claim to be objective and just "report the news!" That they color their reporting to suit their own agenda is patently obvious. Of the two, my experience tells me Limbaugh is far more truthful than the main stream media.

I remember a time in Cleveland when I frequently had lunch with a reporter from the Cleveland Press with whom I had major differences of opinion on most of his articles. During one heated discussion about something in the paper that was obviously in error, he stated emphatically, "We don't report the news! We create it!" That statement has stuck with me through the years and I believe it has become the typical attitude of many in the media. I thought about it during one Peter Jennings special on our war with Japan and the dropping of the A-bomb. The essence of this so called "documentary" was how brutal we were to the poor Japanese. To one who didn't know the truth, it painted the US as the aggressor against the poor defenseless Japanese. The attack on Pearl Harbor, the Bataan death march, the use of American POWs as slave labor in places of great danger, the rape of Nanking - none of these were ever mentioned during the program. I have never even heard of such a blatant rewriting of history while so many were still alive who lived through it. The thing about it that makes my hair stand on end is the question, what is the agenda of those in the media who perpetrate such blatant frauds? Also, who is pulling the strings of this Canadian school dropout with the pretty face and smooth vocal ability?

The more highly slanted and even downright false "news" like the previous example, I hear from the main stream media, the more nervous I am about the forces behind it. I see more and more hate campaigns being mounted in the media against any and every obstacle to the control of the individual and his freedom by the state. These campaigns are mounted with fiercely emotional diatribes and name calling against any person or group that disagrees. Facts are grossly distorted or ignored and mantras are developed that are repeated over and over again, word for word by controlled liberal politicians and so-called journalists. Any question that might have a negative answer asked of our current administration by any of the very few honorable journalists will elicit a jumble of meaningless words or be completely ignored with statements totally unrelated to the question. I myself have heard this time and time again so it isn't second hand information. If they can't silence any opposition by force, ridicule or coercion, and particularly if the general public begins to understand the truth, they will mount these highly organized and cleverly orchestrated hate campaigns to sway public opinion. In all fairness I can't call these people "liberals" for they have usurped an honorable title and perverted it into a cause for amorality, hatred, and perverse ideals which destroy the individual and substitute subjects for their complete control and domination. To call these would be world dominators with their new world order "Liberals" would dishonor those dedicated souls who started this country for freedom and respect of the individual. These patriots, another word the new world order despises, were called liberals and were truly so as they destroyed the bonds of totalitarianism and started a new nation based on representative government.

A new, more fitting name for these people is "Feudals." I have coined the term "Feudals" to designate those who have taken control of the liberal wing of the Democrat party and who manipulate most of the media. This, because they are actually reactionary and seek to return us to a form of feudalism where the all-powerful state controls every aspect of the lives of the general public. Recognizing there are many decent, concerned "liberals" like my sister, her husband and my wife, Barbara, "Feudals" seems to fit. It seems unfortunate to me that many of the few true liberals feel they must to go along with (and vote with) the Feudals who are so obviously in control. These Feudals have perverted the Constitution and promoted numerous emotional hate campaigns to destroy the moral fabric of our nation in order to gain control over the general public. While professing to be for oppressed people they use and promote bigotry and hatred to keep and strengthen their control over many groups.

A classic example of this is the hate campaign being waged against the NRA by the Feudals. I understand there is a group trying to block the NRA from opening a restaurant in New York's Times Square. Hate posters and protests are certain to follow should the restaurant be opened. No action seems beyond use by these people in their efforts to silence and destroy any dissenting opinion. They do not want to debate, just shout hate mantras. Could it be their opposition has no basis in fact? As long as the current Constitutional guarantee of freedom of speech stands and is interpreted as it is now, unreasoning hate and emotional diatribes will be used by the Feudals and their lackeys to silence any voice that dissents from their "holy" view.

To better understand the deceptions, infringements and subversions, every concerned citizen and serious student should thoroughly read and study "Our Enemy, The State", the classic and brilliant critique distinguishing "government" from "STATE" by Albert J. Nock, and "The Law", by Frederick Bastiat. See also "Feminist Follies" elsewhere in this section.

The second amendment says, "A well regulated Militia being necessary to the Security of a free State, the Right of the People to keep and bear Arms shall not be infringed."

The Second Amendment Stands as the Guarantor of All other Rights and of the Defense of the Constitution itself.

Let's continue describing the current, cleverly orchestrated attacks on the 2nd amendment. I am not a member of the NRA nor do I intend to become one. However, I certainly stand with them rather than against them in their current battle with the Feudals. The second amendment was put into the Constitution for the expressed purpose of protecting the individual from an overpowering government. So far it has worked quite well, all things being considered. There are already many federal, state and local laws controlling gun ownership and use. Gun registration has already wrought havoc in several countries including South Africa, Canada and Australia where gun registration was followed by the outlawing of some weapons and then their confiscation from owners who registered them. In other words, the guns were confiscated from law abiding citizens only.

Since few criminals registered their guns, this left only the criminals and the government in possession of weapons. In South Africa, home invasions and gun murders have skyrocketed. People there with the means have turned their homes into fortresses to keep the criminals out. Police are frequent victims as they are viciously attacked and murdered by criminals who steal their guns and ammunition. In both Canada and Australia, where not all guns are yet outlawed, gun crimes are on the rise as criminals realize their victims are less able to protect themselves. The Feudals will do everything in their power to keep you from learning about this and about similar statistics in our own country.

Federal government statistics, published by the NRA show that with few exceptions, those parts of our country with the fewest gun control laws also have the lowest gun crime rate and those with the most stringent laws have the highest. When our Philanderer in Chief was asked about this at a televised interview session, his answer was typical and quite telling. He refused to acknowledge this information from the records of the federal government saying, and I paraphrase, "Setting that aside, lets talk about the gunshot deaths of children." In the ensuing comments he neglected to mention that the NRA program of educating children about guns has substantially reduced the number of accidental gunshot deaths of children in the school systems where it has been implemented. He also neglected to mention that most of the gunshot deaths of children (all people under the age of twenty are considered children in these government statistics) were not accidental, but were from acts of inner city criminals under the age of twenty.

Could it be that the criminal element in this country and the billions in drug money is the force behind these attacks on the use of guns and the NRA? With illicit drugs as one of the largest sectors of our economy, it stands to reason that there is a great deal of money available to buy politicians and public officials. It is my contention that drug money supports all anti-gun and anti-drug campaigns. Keeping drugs illegal, drives the price through the roof, benefitting those drug moguls with a seller's market. Since interdiction catches only a small part of the drugs being distributed, the so-called "War on drugs" should be called the "War for drug profits." Did we learn nothing from prohibition? The real answer for this would be a Federal system to deliver drugs free to anyone who wants them in a controlled environment. This would cost far less than present interdiction efforts and put all drug criminals out of business, stopping all drug related crimes instantly! It would also provide a system to treat drug addicts rather then make them criminals. The details of this is described in another essay in my book, "Thoughts on the Cultures of Today." Unfortunately, money from the illegal drug trade going through Feudal politicians and the media would fuel a hate campaign of unprecedented proportions to stop any such challenge to their lucrative illegal business. They want it to stay illegal and will do anything to keep it so!

Making guns illegal would do the same things for guns. The criminals would then have another business to syphon money into their coffers. The organization to handle illegal guns is already in place. Few criminals need more than fifty to a few hundred dollars to obtain an illegal gun right now. Imagine the situation that would exist after the Feudals passed universal gun registration and then confiscation. The criminal organization to supply guns would become a major source of new revenue and honest, law-abiding citizens would be disarmed.

It is imperative to recognize that the registration of guns followed by the confiscation of guns would leave a citizenry disarmed and facing a growing army of heavily armed criminals! That is the reality! It has happened in South Africa and is happening in Canada and Australia where efforts are now being mounted to reverse the new gun laws. It is the rule in many parts of the world. Remember the War Lords in Somalia and their Jeep mounted machine guns?

It is apparent the Feudals plan to repeal the 2nd amendment. Let's not permit the US to slide down this dangerous path. Concentrate on taking weapons away from criminals, not from honest, law-abiding citizens! Let us not erase or subvert our precious second amendment rights. An armed citizenry is proven to be the best defense against criminals and gun crimes throughout the world! The Feudals would remove that protection and leave guns in the hands of criminals. Did you ever wonder why they are so adamant and determined to remove your right to protect yourself? Think about it! Increased theft, including home invasions, provides income for the illegal drug business as money from many crimes are used to pay for drugs. The drug criminals will realize greatly increased income from this increase in business. Powerful anti gun legislation like anti drug legislation will move much more money into the hands of the drug criminals. For them it is a business decision and a very powerful one to support such legislation and to do what harm they can to those like the NRA, who support the second amendment. True, the NRA is a powerful lobby, but they are up against a powerful, secret lobby backed by billions of dollars from illegal drug sales. These criminals can buy many politicians while the NRA can only try to persuade with the comparatively puny funds they have. The Hollywood Feudals frequently glorify drugs and criminals in their movies and TV shows while demonizing the NRA and other honest and legal groups. Are they also the beneficiaries of this illegal drug money? They are certainly the hotbed of drug use, so why not also the recipients of drug money?

I have proposed a revolutionary progam to eliminate much of the drug problem and its associated criminal activity. To view this unique, workable solution, Click Here!

Political use of the death penalty: Another example of the methods used by the Feudals to obtain control surfaced during the Bush/Gore campaign and was noted by Rush Limbaugh on his radio program. He commented on several current articles in the media about the death penalty. The articles subtly linked Governor Bush with the death penalty. Rush said he smelled a concentrated effort to mount an attack on Bush in the media by linking his name with articles on the death penalty. This was quite obviously to boost the lackluster performance of Gore by pumping up an issue that would affect a governor but not a vice president. He predicted a flurry of articles on the death penalty in the printed media followed by comments in the electronic media. All would use the same mantra he predicted of tying George Bush and the death penalty together. Within a month of that prediction numerous articles appeared in many newspapers and then Time and Newsweek with a cover story in Time of June 12 entitled "Death on Hold - Bush Ponders the Penalty." I can't remember how many times Rush has made similar predictions. If he is correct, we will be pounded by death penalty articles and coverage on TV right up until election time. The Feudals have created a controversy involving Bush that Gore is immune to. Hitler's propaganda minister Goebbels would have fit right in with the Feudal's arrogant propaganda organization. His, "If you tell a lie often enough and without apology, people will begin to believe it." is obviously the basis for their efforts. It will be interesting to see how well this plays. It could backfire on them since polls indicate the overwhelming majority of Americans favor the death penalty. Should this prove to be the case in the polls, this propaganda push will be dropped like a hot potato and will quickly disappear from the scene. The old "Poisoning our waters, starving our children and taking from our elderly" mantra will probably be wheeled out in its place. Time will tell.

Think about one more thing. Those who are fighting against new gun control legislation are not pressing for laws to force you to have a gun. Anyone who so chooses can remove all weapons from their home and many do. You now have freedom of choice about this. Those Feudals, who promote new gun control legislation, plan to take this freedom from you. This voluntary personal choice is one of the foundations of our democracy and tenets of our freedom. With freedom comes the responsibility for our own actions and accountability for their effects as well. As a nation, we won the cold war by being armed against an evil that would destroy us and our freedom. There were those among us, well-meaning people, who would have unilaterally disarmed our nation in the name of pursuing peace. History still tells us that would have been a grievous mistake. I firmly believe that a disarmed citizenry would fall victim to an overwhelming criminal conspiracy. That is the path that Hitler's Germany took in the thirties. After guns were taken from all citizens, the NAZI criminals held free reign and look what happened then. When both criminals and government have nothing to fear from the citizenry they will merge into one overwhelming force. We're closer to that than you may think!

The New Feudalism - June 2000 -

The feudal system of the middle ages is my model for what I believe the new form of liberalism will do to America. For this reason I have coined the term "Feudals" to be used in place of "Liberals" for those entertainment world activists and their cohorts who most definitely do not follow the old idealistic "Liberal" concepts. They are much more like Fascists and others of the extreme right than like the idealistic left. Make no mistake, their political goal is for government to control every aspect of our lives and they intend to control that government. They intend it to be, Government of the people, by the Feudal Lords and for the benefit of the Feudal Lords. Read also my essay, "Beware The Liberals Who are Feudals."

The Feudals hate any form of personal freedom or individuality as they steal for themselves more and more decisions from the individual. At the same time, they mouth their mantras about the poor and downtrodden multitudes as they seek to enslave them. Ignorance is their ally, emotion is their tool and reason is their enemy. Mass hysteria is the tool they use to manipulate those who have lost the ability to reason. They have adopted this tool and the other tactics that Herman Goebbels used so effectively to enslave Nazi Germany for Hitler. This is nothing new.

See quotes on Page 91

This explains the effectiveness of the Feudal's vote getting powers. Their "Tax and spend" philosophy is based in this reality. By pledging more and more money to more and more people, the Feudals are buying votes primarily from the poor, the weak, the helpless and anyone else looking for a handout. In spite of their "help for the downtrodden" rhetoric, they are not really interested in helping these people. They just want their vote, their blind obedience and political enslavement, promising anything to get it.

The Feudals will do anything to control their people, even evil things they constantly accuse their opposition of doing. While eschewing racial bigotry, they practice political bigotry on a massive scale. If you are pursuing a career in the entertainment world you had better speak like the Feudals or you will go nowhere. One conservative comment, or any statement in conflict with Feudal ideals and you will be black-balled. Many an aspiring actors has been dumped after making a conservative political comment. They are constantly being told by fellow aspirants never to speak their conservative political views or they won't get work.

The only conservatives in the entertainment world, are those who achieved high position before their political positions were known or who became conservative after they achieved stardom. Even they are subject to ridicule which grows more vocal as the Feudals gain power.

Charlton Heston is one example. Since speaking out for conservative causes, he has become the brunt of vicious jokes and ridicule from countless comedians and TV news people. Dan Quail and the "potato" incident is another example of how the Feudals use ridicule to destroy an adversary's credibility, even when it is trumped up. Actually, the word Dan understood he was spelling was "potatoes" and he was interrupted before he had a chance to add the s. That was never mentioned in the media. Here is a talented, highly educated man being repeatedly called "stupid" by the media for the purpose of silencing a voice speaking out in favor of things they oppose.

A Feudal attack tool: This tactic of calling Republicans stupid or disparaging their intelligence is a tool the Feudals have used effectively for years. It first came to my attention with the totally unwarranted attacks on Gerald Ford. By both innuendo and direct statements he was called stupid and confused by many in the media. I heard one commentator say, "Ford took too many hits in the head when he played football." In truth, Gerald Ford was and is a very intelligent man who was an effective congressman and republican leader in the house. I have never heard any media commentator question the intelligence of any Democrat. It has happened with every single Republican President from Ford to the present. In the current Presidential election Feudals have repeatedly impugned George Bush's intelligence while insinuating near genius status to Junior Gore. In fact, Bush's educational performance and accomplishments are far greater than those of Gore who dropped out of both law school and divinity school because he couldn't make the grade.

Feudals never let facts stand in the way of what they say. These false accusations are constantly used by the Feudals to condemn and vilify opponents and their positions. Nearly all voices in the media are party to this vicious and untrue activity. Jay Leno of the Tonight Show is one rare exception. I have no idea what his political leanings are, but the effect of his political jokes fall fairly equally on all. In contrast, Roger Miller, the clown who displays his ignorance each week on the Monday night football TV show, is positively vicious in his attacks on any who are not firmly in the Feudal camp. He frequently repeats the Feudal mantras about poisoning the water supply, starving the children, stealing from senior citizens and other false and ridiculous charges that were used so effectively in the last few National elections. Maybe he's a reincarnation of Goebbels or at least one of his students. He certainly speaks the same language, the language of class warfare and hate. Many popular comedians do the same thing. This constant hate barrage fired against conservatives and conservative values has taken its toll. As Goebbels said, "Tell a lie often enough and people will believe it." The Feudals most certainly use that and most effectively.

What do the Feudals want "for the good of the people?" Check the following list:

1. Killing of babies - abortion on demand, Government paid
2. Unrestricted sex for all ages (sex with children is coming)
3. Promotion of homosexuality as normal, is bestiality next?
4. Teaching of all kinds of sexual activity in schools
5. Elimination of truly free speech. (Unless it agrees with them)
6. Unlimited immigration (more votes for them)
7. Silencing of all views that differ from their own
8. Free government controlled healthcare for all

(regardless of cost - the government will determine who gets what care)
9. One person, one vote (including criminals, the mentally ill, the incompetent, and possibly even a few dead folks)
10. No moral standards for holding office (except for conservatives)
11. Complete registration and Federal control of all guns
12. Bigger, more powerful labor unions and government
13. Bilingual everything (they want the Latino vote)
14. Lowered education standards
    (ignorance makes people easier to control and manipulate)

What can we look for as their goals for the future? Maybe:

15. Incorporation of our military into the United Nations
16. Destruction of all organized religion (Christianity first)
17. Subordination of our laws to International law
18. Confiscation of all guns in private hands
19. Repeal of the second amendment
20. Sex between children and adults OK
    (its already on the agenda in a national libraryassociation and NAMBLA)
21. Complete amoralization of the public
22. Increased taxation to "spread the wealth more equally"
23. Complete amnesty for illegal aliens.
24. Complete healthcare and welfare for illegal aliens
25. Federal control of the entire education system
26. Removal of all personal responsibility for actions

What the Feudals are against

1. States' rights (counties', cities', even individuals' rights)
2. True freedom of speech - they want to suppress dissenting views
3. The 2nd amendment to the Constitution
4. Big or small business and corporations
5. Any kind of successful business or responsible organization
6. Personal wealth (except for themselves)
7. Individual liberty and initiative
8. Family values, especially Christian
9. Christianity
10. Religions of all kinds other than Atheism
11. Sexual morality
12. Marriage (except for same sex)
13. Responsible fathers (men are unnecessary after conception)
14. Personal responsibility (environment is the cause of . . .)
15. Honor of any kind
16. The US Military

17. The Police
18. Innovative school principles, teachers, board members
19. The NRA and any other organization that doesn't agree with their agenda
20. Any kind of power in the hands of a Non-feudal
21. Conservatives, Libertarians and their ideals
22. Rules or laws that don't agree with their philosophy
23. Rules or laws that interfere with anything they want to do
24. Unbiased courts, reporters, judges, or politicians
25. Any person or thing that doesn't agree with them

The Feudals strive to change many words from good to evil, thus destroying historically good character traits. See how often these words are used in derision, sarcasm, misuse or branded as obsolete by the Feudal Media: patriotism - loyalty - honor - decency - reverence - fidelity - respect - responsibility - kindness - marriage - affection - diligence - tradition - beauty - honesty - trust - charity - friendship - friend - morals - glory - plus many more. If you believe most of what the Feudals say about these kinds of words, they are signs of weakness or evil. They even twist the language to suit their views. There is nothing as insidiously evil as to call the movement that promotes the killing of human babies in the womb, "Freedom of Choice." The baby being killed certainly has no freedom of choice. It is merely butchered to satisfy the needs of some floozy who helped create it and then didn't want it. Is this female so different from the one in Texas who recently drowned her four small children because she didn't want to have to take care of them anymore? The only difference is the age of the infant. Maybe we should let mothers kill their babies under a year old. That would provide more "Freedom of Choice."

The Feudals do not want, or believe in democracy. They want a dictatorship with them as dictators. Raw power is their goal so that each and every one of us will do their bidding every day of our lives. Every single factor that promotes individual freedom is currently under some form of attack by the Feudals. Some are very subtle, but other are being brought more and more into the open. These attacks are more open because the Feudals are winning. At each new victory they become more brazen with their attacks on personal values and responsibility which are the foundation of true freedom. While overtly praising and promoting diversity, they soundly condemn any who disagree with them. Angry, hate-filled words are used to promote laws to punish those who have principles and ideals that differ from their own. Make no mistake! The media use ridicule and promote hate for any who disagree with them. There are very few voices raised in opposition to this one-sided monster of political misinformation.

The elitist, intellectuals who lead and support the Feudals, see themselves as above the rules that govern the masses. Armed with vast wealth and teams of like minded and frequently unprincipled lawyers, these power-hungry demagogues seem able to get away with murder. They will viciously attack opponents with the willing aid of the media, holding them to account for actions far less damning than what they themselves have done and then escaped punishment. They are held to a far lower accounting than conservatives in every venue, particularly in the media.

Examples are legion. I will sight only a few. Richard Nixon was severely criticized, even vilified by the press and many others when a single FBI file was found in the White House. When over 700 missing FBI files mysteriously appeared on a table in the Clinton White House it was treated like an every day occurrence and there was almost no criticism and certainly no vilification by the media. There is no doubt that those files were used to find out about GW Bush's DUI of the far distant past. This was then provided to the press at the most damaging moment. I see it as a testimonial to the integrity of Bush's past that they couldn't find anything else. Undoubtedly these files were used by the Feudals to search for information which they could use to control or wound opponents and even to control and manipulate their own members. Why no media outrage?

There is no doubt about the use of these files on Newt Gingerich in concert with the so-called accidental (and very illegal) taping of one of his private cell-phone conversations the Feudals managed to obtain. If Republicans had done such a despicable thing, the media would have had a field day of crucifixions. Since it benefitted the Feudal Democrats by destroying an extremely effective Republican, it was OK according to the media. I wonder just how much those who now pull the strings of Junior Gore have gleaned from those FBI reports since their mysterious appearance.

The Feudal Whitehouse: The travel office affair, Monica Lewinsky and all the other women who were groped, fondled and who knows what else by our Philanderer in Chief are but the tip of the iceberg in a White House sea filled with many other invisible icebergs virtually unmentioned by the Feudal media. In comparison, look at the treatment of Senator Bob Packwood who certainly was guilty of far less than Clinton. He was vilified in the Feudal media and crucified by the "feminazis" while the attitude toward Clinton was, "His private life didn't interfere with his ability to govern." Clinton was let off with a press attitude of "Boys will be boys" rather than the hue and cry for blood that the Packwood incident created. The complete silence of the "Feminazis" on Clinton's many dalliances displayed their monstrous hypocrisy. They have become merely another group politically enslaved by the Feudals.

How Clinton gets the female vote. It is a known fact that many women are fascinated by men who are rogues. Young women are overwhelmingly fascinated by young men who are less than decent. Guys just over the edge , who lie to, cheat on and mistreat women, seem to hold a fascination for many of them. Remember the Fonz on the TV program "Happy Days?" He was a caricature of the guy from highschool who was so fascinating to so many girls. Just over the moral, legal, ethical and honest edge, these boys danced with danger, mocked authority and almost always attracted a number of giddy female followers. Often, the farther they were from decent, honest boys, the more girls they attracted, the more that would sneak out to be with them. These guys were the ones with whom most girls first had sex. They fathered the most babies in most high schools and would brag about cheating on their girlfriends and later, their wives.

Behavioral scientists who study Chimpanzees say this is common behavior among our nearest relatives. Female Chimps will frequently sneak away from their group to meet rogue males for sex. These males skirt the edge of the female's territory looking for females from family groups other than their own. This has the effect of broadening the gene pool of the group and thus promotes diversity and prevents inbreeding. As many as half the offspring in any group may be sired by these rogue males.

Bill Clinton certainly fits the description. Since so many females make decisions based on emotion which is in fact genetically controlled instincts, it is not surprising that he appeals to so many of them. No logical argument will sway them. No despicable act he has committed has yet turned them off; they still love him, not in spite of his actions, but because of them. They are genetically programmed to behave in just such a manner. They just can't help themselves. When I hear four well known females in a TV talk session laughing coquettishly while talking about the really despicable acts of Bill Clinton and referring to him as a "naughty boy" it makes me realize just why the women vote so overwhelmingly for him. His sexual dalliances and misconduct didn't hurt him with women, they helped him! "Who cares that he's an admitted liar, cheat and womanizer? That's what we like! No goody two-shoes nerd for us!" These females still love that paragon of morality, Ted Kennedy don't they?

How about Judges Bork and Thomas? Both were vilified because they held different opinions from the Feudals. Those arrogant, self-righteous, self-serving media critics vilified both Bork and Thomas simply because they held conservative views. Again, anyone who disagrees with their divinely ordained views will be subject to the worst kind of emotional diatribes. Hate-mongering at its worst is a constantly used tool of the Feudals!. The hate campaign against Judge Bork succeeded, but when it appeared to be failing against Judge Thomas, two old Feudal war lords got together to trump up sexual harassment charges. Ted Kennedy, an exemplary moral man, joined Ohio senator Howard Metzenbaum in a smear campaign. Together they convinced Anita Hill to make charges against Judge Thomas while his confirmation was before the Senate. Isn't it amazing that she came forward after all those years and at just this time?

How about the aspiring first female president, Hillary? She has been held virtually innocent by the media of the many known lies, vilifications and "I just can't recalls" emanating from her and her cohorts. Newt Gingerich was demonized and virtually crucified by the Feudals and their darlings in the media for his four million dollar, two book advance a few years ago. In stark and obvious contrast, Hillary Rodham Clinton's eight million dollar, single book advance is apparently OK with the same people. The media hounds vociferously claimed possible mischief and conflicts of interest from Newt's book deal. Those are small potatoes compared to the same possibilities inherent in the book deal of the new Feudal Senator from New York. While Newt stood down on his book deal and took only a one dollar advance in response, it was a genuine deal and is being consummated. In stark contrast, there is no chance Hillary will stand down since the voices of the media will only support this obvious payoff which has virtually no chance of making money for her publishers even if she does write the book. I seriously doubt this "marvelous" book will ever be written, certainly not for many many years if it is, and it will have to be the best selling book ever for the publishers to make any money. I recently received the following via an email, "Bill Clinton is getting $12 million for his memoirs. His wife, Hillary, got $8 million for her memoirs. That's $20 million for memories from two people who for eight years repeatedly testified, under oath, that they couldn't remember anything"

Unfortunately there are a lot of decent, caring liberals who seem to have to accommodate their evil, Feudal comrades. I wonder how their conscience handles these kinds of increasingly frequent occurrences? These kinds of frauds must be obvious to all but the most dull-witted, even in the liberal camp. There are none so blind as those who will not see. I fear many feel the end justifies the means and any activity that promotes their cause is therefore OK. Didn't things happen in just that way in Hitler's Germany? How many decent Germans closed their eyes to NAZI evils in exactly the same manner? How many American Liberals are doing precisely the same thing now? Who are those being demonized by Feudals in precisely the same way Jews were demonized by the NAZIs? NAZI-like hate speach is more and more coming from the mouths of the Feudals. Though they don't call directly for violence, many like Jesse Jackson, repeat impassioned calls for their people to take to the streets when they don't get their way. If that isn't a call for violence then Hitler was a benevolent dictator.

The feudal view of reality: I recently held a rather heated discussion with a liberal female friend about our growing government and how the erosion of personal freedom concerned me. She countered by saying how much the evil people in big corporations control our lives by hiring and laying off at will and demanding overtime and the like. It was the typical class warfare theme of the little people against the all powerful corporations. I had just heard a talk by a Silicon Valley billionaire entrepreneur about what he did with all his money. In the last ten years, the investment of his money into his company provided good incomes for more than three thousand families. Those families had been able to send several thousand students through college, buy homes, take vacations and support the community themselves. He had paid millions in local taxes to support the community and even more millions to the federal and state governments. This "evil" capitalist, in her view, was providing the livelihood for thousands directly and tens of thousands indirectly in the surrounding communities. His genius and hard work were raising the living standards of the area far more then any government welfare could possibly do. He was using his wealth to create wealth for himself and many others. There are thousands just like him all over our country. These are the men and women who do the most to raise the living standards for everyone, not the government.

I'm sure there are evil corporate people at all levels. I am equally certain there are at least the same percentage of equally evil government people. It has been proven time and time again, by business managers from as far back as Henry Ford, that genuine concern for the health and welfare of employees is essential to the long term success of business. Sooner or later evil management will cause a business to fail just as surely as poor management. In contrast, government can hide evil and ineffective people as they have no bottom line to meet; business cannot. All that any government agency needs to do to survive and grow is please the politicians who vote the funds for their operation. When they are a tool for the reelection of those same politicians, the incentive for evil cooperation is monstrous. Why do you suppose the vast majority of government employees vote for the Feudals? Like Tyler's comment, they are voting themselves money from the public treasury. Only government employees can do that directly.

American business profits pay the entire cost of the government with taxes they pay directly and those paid by their employees. And just who creates the wealth that pays for this bloated, wasteful government? In fact, Privately owned business and creative professionals generate all wealth in this country. Every penny the City, County, State and Federal governments spend comes ultimately from private business of some sort including individual enterprise. Governments create no wealth, they only consume wealth. Every penny comes from the pockets of businessmen, professionals and their employees. The average American currently works about a third of each year to pay taxes. The wealthy can work as much as two thirds of the year to pay their taxes. Those taxes feed our bloated government

The three groups who are involved with wealth are, producers, consumers, and organizers. Of these three groups, producers are the only ones who actually create wealth. Organizers help in the creation of wealth by increasing the efficiency of the producers. Consumers do just that, they consume what wealth the producers create. Money has no value of itself. It is merely the agent used to facilitate the transfer of goods and services between individuals and organizations. Without the medium of money, barter and trade would have to be used in any exchange of goods and/or services. The "private sector" consists of producers, organizers and consumers. Government consists mostly of consumers with a very small number of organizers. Taxes are the means government uses to remove money from the "private sector" and place it under the control of bureaucrats. A large portion of this money is needed just to pay for the bureaucrats and attorneys. The amount left over is divided between national defense, infrastructure, welfare and Social Security. In a manner of speaking, all of this money is used to "buy" votes In other words, to provide money from the public treasury to voters. (See Tyler quote, Page 91)

At the present time, this money amounts to 31% of the Gross National Product. In other words, 31% of what the producers create with the help of the organizers is diverted into the treasury controlled by the various government agencies and bureaucrats. This steadily growing amount of money buys many votes including those of workers in the many government agencies and bureaucracies. They vote to keep their jobs. Certainly those receiving welfare of any kind as well as other handouts for any purposes will vote for those who promise to continue or increase the handouts. Government subsidy programs buy many more votes as do the many contracts issued for products and services requested by all sectors of the government. As laws grow more complex, attorneys' votes are bought by the promise of growing need for legal services by, for, because of and against government. Many professional services fall into this same category as government growth increases the need for all kinds of services both by government and by those who must battle with or comply with growing red tape. I would like to know just what portion of support for Democrat candidates comes from these bought and paid for voters. My guess is it adds up to at least half of Democrat votes, maybe more.

It wouldn't be so bad if government payrolls were not so bloated. A number of years ago a friend of mine from a university managed a test program in one of the US Navy departments. This particular department dispersed the checks for all naval veterans. The purpose of the test was to determine the fewest number of people who could handle the load of creating, organizing and distributing monthly checks for the entire country. They made records of all traceable activities and supplies for a two-month period before making any changes. They then reduced the total work force of 320 by forty to 280. These people were moved to other jobs or chose to retire. No one lost their job.

After a month to adjust to the new arrangement, things settled down to routine and all the checks went out on time. Again records were made for two months as before. The employees were told there were to be several adjustments to the workforce during the following year, but nothing else. Only the manager and my friend who was acting as the assistant manager knew what was happening.

At the end of the two-month record period the workforce was again reduced by forty people. The same sequence of events occurred. Again there was a month for adjustment followed by a two-month period of careful record keeping. Similar reductions continued until the workforce was reduced to a scant sixty people which they found could not handle the load. At this point the last forty people were returned to the group. The workforce was retained at that level, 100, doing the work that previously was being done by 320.

Research statistics of the study showed only one significant change. While there was some small reduction in paper and other office supplies, the reams of "Inter Office Memos" previously required was reduced to a few pads. Communications had changed drastically. In spite of the increased workload for each individual, morale was better than it had been when the test began. The employees were very proud of their ability to get so much done with so many less workers. To my knowledge, none were told about the experiment.

If you applied that same effort to all government departments, the payroll would probably be cut at least in half. That will never happen as long as the Feudals control the bureaucracy. Most of those excess people vote for the Feudals since they know they are voting for their jobs. When you hear politicians crying for money for "the schools," "the poor," or any other seemingly benevolent program, remember, most of that money goes to pay for the people used to administer and police the program. It's a wonderful way to buy votes with public money. Those bureaucrats and their political mentors want bloated payrolls. The bigger they are, the more votes for them.

Republican threats to reduce the size of government and eliminate many jobs must mobilize many government workers to work hard for the election of Democrats with their continuing efforts to grow the Federal Government in particular. My guess is that among those who are private sector producers and organizers, at least 70% and maybe as much as 80% vote Republican. It is amazing that Republicans get as many votes as they do considering the huge number of bought and paid for votes combined with the labor unions and minorities adding to the Democrat totals. Add the effects of the extreme bias of the main stream media on a vulnerable public and the amazement grows. The one bright spot for Republicans is that the public is increasingly skeptical of the main stream media as their bias grows more desperate and thus obvious to all but the most dull-witted. Thinking people increasingly doubt the truth of network TV news and search elsewhere for information, particularly political information. Growth of cable news programming is burgeoning, particularly those channels showing less liberal bias.

This bias appears in many ways exemplified by the following story after the Supreme Court ruling in the Florida Election case. In the first report after the decision, Dan Rather referred to the court as "The Republican Supreme Court" several times. An enterprising radio news man counted the times this term was used on network TV broadcasts and came up with 48 including the three by Dan Rather. During the same period, the Florida Supreme Court was referred to at least fifty times without mention of any party affiliation. No one called it the Democrat Florida Supreme Court! There are seven Republican appointees on the Supreme Court and five Democrat. The Florida Supreme Court consists of six Liberal Democrats, a Liberal Independent and no Republican appointees at all. The media does not miss an opportunity to word things to Liberal Democrat advantage.

There are so many examples of this bias and so many complaints it is taken for granted by most thinking people. Most of our media has become as one-sided and inaccurate as all but the most blatant NAZI and Communist propaganda in the political arena. For more in-depth information on this read, "Bias" by Bernard Goldberg.

My liberal friend could not see any of this and saw no media bias. Neither could she see the difference between a businessman seeking wealth to invest to create more wealth and a politician seeking control of wealth to dispense as he wishes to enhance his power. To her, the businessman was a greedy capitalist and the politician a dedicated servant of the people. Actually, the businessman gains power and wealth for himself while providing wealth and freedom for his workers. At the same time he must comply with endless regulations and red-tape which take a lot of money out of the pockets of his workers and transfers it to lawyers and accountants. The politician gains power over the people without creating anything. At his best, he takes some money from the haves and gives it to the have nots. At his worst he becomes a Rostenkowski or other crooked product of a corrupt political machine. Sadly, the vast bulk of this money goes to government paper pushers, investigators, attorneys and accountants who must pore through endless forms and investigate endless applicants, to determine who gets the remaining money and how much. One provides a net gain, the politician, a net loss. You only need look as far as the lavish offices and lifestyles of the two Clintons to view examples of the total, selfish disregard for the money American workers pay into the public treasury. Nicholas and Alexandra couldn't have done better. These Feudal "Royals" believe it to be their due.

The Feudals have a real attitude problem with business people. For some reason, they express the view that all business types are heartless crooks while government people are dedicated public servants and the entertainment elite are gifted performers with hearts of gold. If there is a difference between business people and these other two groups it is that business types and their employees, tend to be self-reliant, hard working and more independent. Many are quite willing to risk new ideas and new ventures. Obviously Feudals hate anyone displaying independence and initiative over whom they have little or no control. Government types tend more to be dependant and in need of long term security. That's why they work for the government, security. The entertainment elite, are self centered, self serving, egotistical role players without a clue about real people in the real world. In contrast to the expressed views of the Feudals, I doubt there is much difference between the business and public types in their basic greed, intelligence or moral character. Character tests have indicated a slight difference in honesty between the groups favoring the private sector workers over the public sector. I see the results as so close there probably is very little real difference although my instincts tell me the test is right. The entertainment, elite are a completely different story. With their fiction, glamour and fan adulation, they come from a totally fake world and have little grasp of reality.

When you look at those in power among the Feudals it is an entirely different story. Contrast the darlings of the Feudals, Bill and Hillary Clinton with George and Barbara Bush. When it comes to integrity there is no contest. The goings on in the Clinton White House make even Richard Nixon look like a saint. As long as you are a Democrat, lying, cheating, maybe even murder is acceptable behavior. Bill has not only redefined government, but adultery, perjury, honesty and the functions of the oval office as well. No republican could possible get away with the lies and unconscionable actions of Bill and Hillary, and the rest of their unsavory bunch. They have honed escape from prosecution to a fine art. The phrase, "I just can't recall." was spoken many times by poor little Hillary when she was questioned about so many recent happenings. This stands in stark contrast to her perfect memory of other things that happened many years ago. Perhaps she is a victim of selective memory loss.

I guess it must be true that Republicans are held to much higher ethical and moral standards than Democrats. Certainly this is true with the media.

Where are the Feudals leading us? As more and more of the people's money is taken in taxes, this money is given, with strings, to more and more people. Total control is their aim. They seek to expand their power over everyone by punishing those who are hard-working and successful while rewarding those who are not. Clinton's multitude of last minute pardons and executive orders were clearly payoffs and deliberate policy traps for the following administration. The media did question a few of the most blatant, but there was certainly no hue and cry. He certainly got away with it with only minor repercussions, didn't he? At least so far.

See quotes on Page 91

The Feudals' War on God and Religion

Indeed, there is a war going on right now for your soul and you are losing. With prayer, God, the Ten Commandments and any kind of religious expression removed from all public places, the Atheist arm of the Feudals has already succeeded in its first major effort. That goal is to make Atheism the state religion of the new order. Make no mistake, Atheism is a belief system and thus is truly a religion. The Feudals will not rest until they have destroyed all other religions and America is Atheist. Other religions are an anathema to their control. Their desire to be the supreme power leaves no room for a God of any kind more powerful than they. They are the primary reason for the Muslim world's hatred for us.

The first steps taken here are the same exact steps taken by the NAZIs in Germany. Step one is to destroy all religion and the individual family along with it. Then take the children away from their parents and place them in youth camps. The state will then become their parents. This process is well underway in our country right now. The Feudal media attacks religion at every opportunity. Religious values, indeed even morals, are held up to furious ridicule. Anyone who speaks out in opposition to this effort will be attacked unmercifully, both directly and subtly. If you doubt my words, read on.

A few weeks back I was watching "The West Wing" TV program. Perhaps it should be renamed "The Left Wing." During one ten minute section of the program, the "President" was to meet with a group of radio talk show hosts. The meeting had nothing to do with the story line and I was curious as to where it was going. Leading up to the meeting there were a number of side references uttered by members of the staff, phrases like "Is she here?" and "There she is." followed by a fleeting glimpse of a fortyish, blond woman walking by. This was followed by, "I see she has a new hairdo." I was beginning to suspect a spy or assassin was in the White House.

Finally the "President" was ushered in to meet the group of ten or twelve radio talk show hosts. It was completely out of context of the story and I was mystified. The blonde woman stood in the center of the group and as the scene progressed its purpose became obvious. It was a direct personal attack on Dr. Laura Schlesinger, a real talk show host who is a strong spokeswoman for religious ideals, the family, individual responsibility and some of our most sacred personal values. The intent of the piece was unmistakable. The blonde woman was Jewish, a PhD and not a medical doctor, and had recently changed her hairdo just like the real Dr. Laura. The "President" proceeded to use the typical Feudal mantra, first ridiculing her use of "Dr'" which is quite legitimate, with the phrase. "You are not a real doctor are you?" He then proceeded with a vicious diatribe against her use of the Bible, citing as many conflicting passages in the Bible as he could in the several minutes the scene took. Particular emphasis was made of her calling homosexual behavior a sin by citing the Bible. Unlike the real Dr. Laura, the blonde in the scene just stood there looking beaten and with no response. I would love to hear the real Dr. Laura's response. Her efforts must be getting to some of the powerful Feudals. So much so they had to strike back overtly.

This was not just an attack on Dr. Laura. It was a highly organized, well written diatribe against religion and the Bible which had absolutely nothing to do with the story line of the program. Most of these attacks lie well hidden within a script and are quite subtle. Using these kinds of tools, Hollywood has worked diligently to erode the moral character of our country. They have refined the promotion of sex, drugs and violence to a high art, usually in a more subtle fashion than in this show.

Atheism, the new state religion: Not only have the Feudals worked to establish Atheism as the official state religion in the US, but they are in the process of stamping out Christianity completely. Recently in Lawrence Kansas, the High School banned anything to do with Christmas from the school. No Christmas tree, no Christmas Concert, no Christmas Carols, children are even forbidden to wish each other Merry Christmas or exchange Christmas cards. December 25th is not referred to as Christmas day. It is no longer Christmas vacation. It's now called Holiday vacation. What will they call it when they realize "Holiday" means Holy Day? Decorations are inspected for any possible Christian content which must be removed. Calendars do not even list Christmas. In a blatant display of animosity against Christians, Halloween and Quanza are still shown and there is no effort to remove their symbols. Check any new calendar you may have. A Catholic school recently purchased several hundred calendars for use in the school. While both Quanza and Halloween were on the Calendars, Christmas was not, and this was a religious calendar for a Catholic school. In contrast to Christmas, Halloween is celebrated in the Lawrence Kansas Highschool with all the usual devil worship icons and symbols. Apparently this is quite all right since it is anti-Christian.

When I was in highschool, the student body was about half Christian and half Jewish. I sang in the Choir along with many Jewish friends. Our annual Christmas concert was a really big, sellout affair attended by both Christian and Jewish families. We sang both Christmas carols and songs for Hanukkah. In three years, I never heard a single word of concern, a remark about offensive or a complaint of any kind from anyone about anything to do with Christmas or Hanukkah. We were all good friends, Christians and Jews together. We respected and acknowledged each other's religious heritage and celebrations. At our fiftieth reunion, choir member sang several religious songs with complete joy and pleasure. The Feudals don't like that kind of harmony. They would have us at each other's throats, or at least divided into competing camps, each offended by the other's expressions of beliefs.

It is important to remember that the second amendment clearly says, "Freedom of religion" not what the anti religion crowd acts like it says, "freedom from religion." The difference of that one word is of major significance. It gives a lie to all of the removals and preventions the courts have caused.

Saturday, February 04, 2006

Attack Dogs and Political Bitches

I consider myself somewhat of a maverick politically in spite of what the very liberal members of my family have decided about me because of a few of my political stances they object to. I am equally disturbed by many if not most of the ridiculous, self-serving claims made by members of both parties in defense of their own and in condemnation of the members of their opposition. These ridiculous claims and statements, both in defense and in attack, are certainly neither honest nor objective. Trained as an engineer, I began searching for a pragmatic, rational answer to this vexing situation that would explain the very emotional, polarizing and paralyzing reason for this. When I looked into it in depth, I found what seemed to me to be at least partly responsible for this activity.

My first clue came from Jane Goodall in her long time study of the chimps at Gombe. Her report provided one telling insight, albeit somewhat remote. She noted that male chimps sometimes ran through the area where the troop was gathered, screaming, waving their arms, beating their chests and creating a major ruckus just to make themselves seem bigger and stronger than other male chimps. In so doing, they often raised their status and occasionally becoming the leader of a troop, some times even without a serious fight. Does sound a bit like some politicians, doesn't it? There was one particular lowly male who suddenly raised himself to very high status by doing this run through while batting old ten gallon cans along with his hands. The resulting clamor made so much noise the other chimps cowered in fear. This intimidation of other males gained him leadership without the use of the damaging biting fight that usually preceded a take over. Now that really does sound like a politician!

Fights for supremacy in primate societies often include recruitment of supporters willing to go to the mat with either the reigning monarch or his challenger. Alliances are formed, concessions are granted, deals are made–politics? It certainly sounds like it. Are our political battles merely upscaled primate king-maker battles? I really think so. Politics transcends all reason and feeds on pure emotion–the primal urge of all primate societies. We are, after all is said and done, just a large troop of naked apes who will argue, make loud noises to intimidate, fight and even kill to promote a leader or become one ourselves. Power is a strong driving force and a powerful aphrodisiac. The winner in most primate troop supremacy battles gets to father most of the next generation in the troop, or at least try to–just ask Bill. The sexual appeal of power is unmistakable. When I look at and hear all this political posturing I can't help but see the actions as those of monkey pretenders and the king they would depose.

There is another factor I see as possibly related in part at least to that of our simian cousins. That is the adversary principal so dear to the hearts of attorneys. This principal, applied so diligently in the courts, has come to be the guiding principal of the legal profession and has spilled over into politics along with the vast majority of politicians who are lawyers. Basically this principal forces the attorney to look at all things from the standpoint of that which favors his client or position. I call this the "attack dog" principal. Attack your opposition with everything you can conjure up while never accepting anything damaging to your client or position. "If it doesn't fit, you must acquit" and they did in spite of the evidence. Truth be damned conviction (or acquittal) is what we are after. Because, shouldn't we provide the best legal argument for our clients that money can buy?

The left has honed the adversary principal into a fine art. Their politicos have reached the point of literally screaming epithets– raw hatred in fact– at any who disagree with them. This is done at virtually every opportunity. Bipartisan has become a useless catch word if not a joke. Every utterance by one in power is followed by a stinging rebuttal from the opposition. Many now scream that this is their obligation, to oppose dramatically and vigorously anything proposed by the opposing candidate, legislator or office holder. No matter that the nation becomes severely damaged and polarization has become so pervasive as to dominate all reason and eliminate all cooperation. "If it's proposed by the opposition it must be bad!" (for us!) Is there any wonder that in a nation so evenly divided it is virtually impossible to change or reform anything? While I firmly believe the vast majority of Americans to be hard working, thoughtful, caring individuals who will cooperate in almost any endeavor for the good of the entire group, I see them cast aside reason and embrace pure emotion in any political venue. "I was born a Democrat and I will die a Democrat" comes from the lips of a whole lot of people as do comparable words from many Republicans. "Don't confuse me with the facts! My mind's made up!" could be considered the motto of many partisans, and they mean it!

You'll notice I have little respect for most politicians of any stripe with their duplicitous words and devious motives. They may spout meaningless pap to the public, posture mightily, make ridiculous laws, send our men to die in foreign lands, spend our money lavishly and often foolishly, feather their nests from the public treasury and a thousand other significant actions serving self rather than the nation, and promise many things while doing just the opposite, yet we are stupid enough to continue electing them time and again. I often wonder, how many public serving statesmen our nation has actually held in office the last two hundred and twenty some years. I'll wager there weren't many. I'll also wager there are more true and honorable public servants reporting to the board rooms of America than walking the halls of Congress and other public buildings in Washington. Politicians who win elections do so by appealing solely to our emotions. Hate wins elections so it is used increasingly. I believe this to be a creation of our modern world of instant communication. Politics has become a fist fight with no holds barred. Facts and reality be damned, he or she who hits the hardest and fights the dirtiest will probably win. Lie, cheat, steal, bear false witness, commit whatever dirty trick or crime will sufficiently tar your opponent is fair to be used to do so. Richard Nixon would be a saint in comparison to the politicians of today. Just smile sweetly into the cameras and praise America's "working families" and promote a "living wage" and you'll win. That's because the naked ape is not so far from the jungle and civilization is not really so civilized.

This brings me to my title, "Attach Dogs and Political Bitches." In the political world there are now both attack dogs and attack bitches. The emphasis is on the word "attack." Our political scene is peopled with these creatures. They have no concrete plans for progress–no ideas of how to solve problems–no records of creative work–often no record of any kind of productive work. What they do possess is the ability to attack and destroy. They are totally dedicated to attack mode. You find them on TV–at protest gatherings–at peace marches–at political rallies–on college campuses–on the streets in many cities. Their common denominator is hate, pure undiluted, primal hate. Like every insecure creature they hunger for attention–the TV camera–the radio interview–anyone to notice or pay attentions to them. They are demolishers, the opposite of builders–destroyers, the opposite of creators–breakers, not menders–dividers, not uniters–creators of chaos, not harmony–purveyors of hatred, not love.

There is a very old story about the differences between builders and wreckers. A man bought an old house and planned to tear it down and build a new one. The first bid he sought was for the demolition of the house. The bidders were all rough men in ragged, filthy clothes driving old, battered trucks. Each promised to do the job including hauling the rubbish to the dump. The next bid he asked for was for the design and construction of his new house. The bidders each arrived in shiny, expensive new SUVs and were dressed in fine clothes. Each spoke in glowing terms about his plans for a new modern house on the soon to be empty lot. A friend suggested he consider another alternative, a man who renovated old houses. When this man arrived it was in nice looking, but older sedan. Dressed tastefully but not extravagantly he offered to take the owner to visit a few of his nearby jobs, one of which was just underway. He pointed out that the finished job started out as a home much like his old one on the lot, sound, but a bit worn, out of style and in need of paint. It was now a charming home unique in the neighborhood and very comfortable feeling inside. The one just underway looked to be even shabbier than his. Several workmen were moving about skillfully removing sections of walls according to the plans shown by the builder. The man agreed to look at the builders plans and bid for renovating his old place.

Several weeks later the man and his wife were looking over the various bids and plans. Both were struck by several intriguing facts. Though the cost for the complete renovation was slightly more than construction costs alone for new, addition of the cost of demolition made the renovation considerably cheaper. Also, the renovated home would have all the latest advances in service, utilities and appliances as the new homes plus the charm of its uniqueness–it wouldn't look just like all the other new, cookie-cutter homes in the neighborhood. In addition, the two large trees that shaded the old house could be retained while both would have to be removed in the tear down and construction of the new. Of course they chose the complete renovation. There were three distinctly different groups of men involved in the bidding and selection process. Which of these groups would you chose to represent you politically? Men like the wreckers, rough, relatively untrained men who could easily tear down the old house, combined with those who would build completely new from the ground up requiring those standardized skills. Or would you select men who could take the existing basic structure and use those very special skills needed to select the best of the old and rework it into a comfortable new structure?

The liberal left (Feudals in my parlance) hate any form of personal freedom or individuality as they steal for themselves more and more decisions from the individual. At the same time, they mouth their mantras about the poor and downtrodden multitudes as they seek to enslave them. Ignorance is their ally, emotion is their tool and reason is their enemy. Mass hysteria is the tool they use to manipulate those who have lost the ability to reason. They have adopted this tool and the other tactics that Herman Goebbels used so effectively to enslave Nazi Germany for Hitler. This is nothing new. For all their pronouncements their only real goal is election and power for themselves. They will sacrifice anything, indeed, even bring our nation to its knees to gain or regain power for themselves. Power is their goal! Hate and destruction, even of our nation, are their tools

See quotes on Page 91

This explains the effectiveness of the Feudal's vote getting powers. Their "Tax and spend" philosophy is based in this reality and provides cheap vote buying. By pledging more and more money to more and more people, the Feudals are buying votes primarily from the poor, the weak, the helpless and anyone else looking for a handout. In spite of their "help for the downtrodden" rhetoric, they are not really interested in helping these people. They just want their vote, their blind obedience and political enslavement, promising anything to get it.

Feudals will do anything to control their people, even evil things they constantly accuse their opposition of doing. While eschewing racial bigotry, they practice political bigotry on a massive scale. For example, If you are pursuing a career in public service, academia or the entertainment world you had better speak like the Feudals or you will go nowhere. One conservative comment, or any statement in conflict with Feudal ideals and you will be black-balled. Many an aspiring social worker, actor or professor has had their career derailed after making a conservative political comment. Those in these fields are constantly being told by fellow aspirants never to speak their conservative political views or their hopes for advancement will be dashed

Remember, those attack dogs and bitches are the demolishers–political destroyers who haven't the skill or so much as a clue how to build. After demolition–complete destruction–others would come in, take over and build on the rubble and according to their completely new plans. Who knows what those plans might be? I certainly hear no concrete plans from the left. I hear lots of pap about peace, love, equality, human rights, fairness, feeding the poor, providing health care, and the favorite, "Surely the richest nation on earth can afford to support the poor." But where are the action plans to achieve these desirable ends? Hmmmmm?

The key is, as pointed out before: destruction is infinitely easier than construction, it takes little skill or mental effort to smash things to pieces compared to the massive skills and coordinated effort required to design and fabricate the simplest object or conceive of a new idea or concept. Example, 9-11. The comparison of the number and kind of men (not really men, but brain dead, inhuman pigs) who destroyed those buildings and the time required to carry out their destructive plan with the creative genius, skills, coordinated effort, and years of careful planning required to design and build those buildings is obvious. Is not this fact lost on those on the left.

Two year olds know the power of destruction and disruption all too well. They can hate and smash with little restraint until they become civilized and learn the value of cooperative humanitarian effort. The current crop of political hate mongers seem to have frozen their emotions at the age of two as they lack any creative thought and rely solely on hate and destruction to disrupt their opponents and derail any constructive efforts these opponents may mount. This is true no matter how important are these constructive efforts. Those out of power cannot afford for those in power to produce any programs or actions that will benefit the nation because it will erode even further their own standing. The better any program is for the nation as a whole, the more destructive and divisive will be the attacks of the out-of-power opposition. The more damage done to creative efforts regardless of how beneficial, the better their chances in the next election. They cannot let the majority achieve any goals the voters might see as beneficial. No matter the cost to our nation, the left will do everything in their power to prevent American success in Iraq because they know that success will spend defeat at the polls.

People have said to me, "Where are your plans? I hear your complaints too, but no plans." Well folks, I have several plans detailed in a new book I am currently writing titled simply, "Solutions." They are probably far from perfect, few single person plans are, but they are workable and useable and are certainly a start. Unfortunately, few legislators would even consider them because:

1) They don't require a huge government bureaucracy to implement.

2) They definitely keep the politician's hands out of the financial cookie jar.

3) They don't pander to any "special interests" other than the American public.

4) They are simple and direct and don't require a team of attorneys and accountants to explain them for us.

5) They provide for the poor and less fortunate, address affordable healthcare for all, help solve the illegal immigrants problem, add protection from terrorists.

6) They are written so real people can understand.

Since they don't promote liberalism the left will be against them and since they don't promote conservatism the right will be against them. Probably the only ones who would be for them are average, hard-working Americans without a political ax to grind or favor to ask. This is, of course, a shrinking portion of our populace in comparison to increasing numbers of miscreants, protesters, welfare freeloaders, government slackers, and other non-productive individuals demanding ever increasing amounts from public treasuries.

Below are listed links to several in my collection of workable plans to solve some of our most vexing problems–national and world-wide. To date I have addressed revision of our ridiculous tax structure, welfare, health care, global warming, atmospheric pollution, our dependence on foreign petroleum, the drug problem–and several others. I have also listed numerous other problems I plan to address in the future. Here are links to those plans I have posted to date.

Taxes & welfare - The Johnson Tax Code - **http://jtax.blogspot.com**

Drugs - A Real Answer to the Drug Problem - **http://hjdrugprb.blogspot.com**

Security - Solution to the ID security Problem - **http://hjidsecurity.blogspot.com**

What concrete plans do you have for our nation in the next fifty years? Remember, hopes, wishes and dreams, are not plans no matter how lofty, for they do not require any touch of reality. I'd certainly be eager to read of your plans. Or are you, like so many liberals, so caught up in anti-Bush, anti-war, anti-capitalism, anti-whatever effort you have no time for creative, productive, positive efforts at building? Maybe, like John Kerry, you have "secret" plans you will reveal once in office or ????? Or maybe, you are like the current administration, so bogged down in trying to compromise to suit everyone that you bring forth an unworkable program like the latest Medicare Rx Program that panders to everyone and satisfies almost no one. What do you think?

Thursday, January 26, 2006

The Reality of Liberalism

It is my very firm belief that power hungry, dictatorial, leaders of the liberals and of the liberal Democrats are doing everything they can to destroy the economy, integrity, freedom, military power, religion, and even the holy "civil rights" of our nation. The really sad thing is that good, decent, well intentioned Americans with liberal leanings are supporting these truly evil men who spout hatred for all who oppose them. These would be dictators are endorsed by a media that mostly says nothing good about America and current American policies, yet waxes eloquent in defense and support of all of our enemies. Unbelievably, they ally with all of our enemies in virtually every venue of communication and rhetoric. This has been going on for a long time.

The only possible conclusion that any reasonable, rational being could come to is that these self-serving individuals believe that they will be triumphant only if America were reduced to economic, political and physical rubble where they could rise from the ashes and "save" the country. The following is but one example of a great multitude that clearly illustrate the method and intent of these true enemies of America no matter how unknowingly they act.

It was 1987! At a lecture the other day they were playing an old news video of Lt.Col. Oliver North testifying at the Iran-Contra hearings during the Reagan Administration. There was Ollie in front of God and country getting the third degree, but what he said was stunning!

He was being drilled by a senator; "Did you not recently spend close to $60,000 for a home security system?"

Ollie replied, "Yes, I did, Sir."

The senator continued, trying to get a laugh out of the audience, "Isn't that just a little excessive?"

"No, sir," continued Ollie.

"No? And why not?" the senator asked.

"Because the lives of my family and I were threatened, sir."

"Threatened? By whom?" the senator questioned.

"By a terrorist, sir" Ollie answered.

"Terrorist? What terrorist could possibly scare you that much?"

"His name is Osama bin Laden, sir" Ollie replied.

At this point the senator tried to repeat the name, but couldn't pronounce it, which most people back then probably couldn't. A couple of people laughed at the attempt. Then the senator continued. "Why are you so afraid of this man?" the senator asked.

"Because, sir, he is the most evil person alive that I know of", Ollie answered.

"And what do you recommend we do about him?" asked the senator.

"Well, sir, if it was up to me, I would recommend that an assassin team be formed to eliminate him and his men from the face of the earth."

The senator disagreed with this approach, and that was all that was shown of the clip.

By the way, that senator was Al Gore!

This was censored in the US from all later reports. Why are valid and important news stories such as this almost always kept from the public? Who is it that wields such power over our "independent" news sources that they can squelch these stories selectively? Who is it that controls the news media so completely that only stories that harm America's image come out of Iraq, while positive and success stories that point out all the good we are doing, never see the light of day. Hmmmm?

Also:

Terrorist pilot Mohammad Atta blew up a bus in Israel in 1986. The Israelis captured, tried and imprisoned him. As part of the Oslo agreement with the Palestinians in 1993, Israel had to agree to release so-called "political prisoners."

However, the Israelis would not release any with blood on their hands, The American President at the time, Bill Clinton, and his Secretary of State, Warren Christopher, "insisted" that all prisoners be released.

Thus Mohammad Atta was freed and eventually thanked the US by flying an airplane into Tower One of the World Trade Center. This was reported by many of the American TV networks at the time that the terrorists were first identified.

Just who are those that would want to do this and why do they act as they do? To believe the mantra, "We must protect the civil rights of all. We must only act after the fact. We must provide all manner of legal (according to American law) protections to each individual terrorist or enemy combatant. If we do not, we have thwarted the intentions of our founding fathers." These men are either complete fools or very much in bed with our enemies. There is no other viable conclusion. Their only possible purpose is to so destroy America that they will be able to come to power over the devastated corpse of formerly free America and the American people.

Is this passion to destroy America and its successful capitalism and the unbelievable benefits of our free enterprise system a throwback to the battle with the robber barons of the late eighteen hundreds and early twentieth century? Wake up and look at reality, the capitalism of today is a very far cry from that of a hundred years ago. It has resulted in the highest standard of living for the most ordinary citizens in the entire world. Certainly, it is not perfect, just better by far than any other system. In the face of huge tax loads, terribly invasive and counterproductive government controls, constant streams of hatred, misinformation and outright lies from media who promote class and culture hatred against successful business people, business still survives. It also continues to pay virtually all the taxes to our government and is solely responsible for the vast majority of jobs for working Americans and continues to make profits. An evil word for liberals, profits would be abolished by liberals if they could. Should they succeed, where would the government satisfy its constantly growing appetite for cash? Hmmmmm!

With over-bloated and terribly inefficient governments taking in excess of forty percent of our GNP it amazes me that free enterprise capitalism has survived. That it has, is a testimonial to the marvelous and overpowering excellence of individual human enterprise for profit over any operations of governments. Knowledge and understanding of this fact is increasingly changing government policies and is bringing about a major economic revolution in a China long swamped with government bureaucracy. Will China soon replace the US as the nation most driven by individual freedom and free enterprise capitalism? Will liberals destroy the excellence that has been American free enterprise to third world status as they already have accomplished with American public education?

One of the characteristics of liberals that truly mystifies me is the complete absence of accepting or even listening to any words or thoughts that differ from the mantras handed to them from on high. Why is it that so many liberals didn't even know anyone who voted Republican. From the halls of academia to the offices of media writers to the meeting places of feminist supporters to their own clubs and homes, these people almost never interact with anyone who doesn't hate George bush, Republicans, business people, conservatives, corporate executives, talk radio, (especially Rush Limbaugh) etc. etc. They are so closed minded, so intellectually inbred, so completely controlled by the narrow, unyielding emotional confines of liberalism that there is no way they will permit even the exposure of their pure intellect to disturbing influences that question their veracity. Should anyone dare to communicate heretical (to liberals) thoughts or ideas they will be accused of being ignorant or stupid, but certainly far beneath the intellectual level of those lofty liberal concepts and holy beliefs. Their definition of truth seems to be anything liberal royalty says is truth and anything they disagree with is not true. Of course, by definition, anything a conservative or Republican says is a lie. The fact of this is so overpowering as to be laughable if it were not so very sad.

I pose a single example of the very different way liberals and conservatives react and believe, a real example.

The first amendment: Most Americans have no real knowledge and little understand of the first amendment. Because of so much media hype, most Americans believe the words, "separation of church and state" is part of the wording of this document. This is absolutely untrue. The ACLU and the out-of-control federal judges are dead wrong! Not only are they dead wrong, but they have grossly warped the meaning of the first amendment into precisely the opposite of what it clearly states and I can prove it. All anyone has to do is to read the exact words of the first amendment. That amendment states, "Congress shall make no law respecting an establishment of religion, or prohibiting the free exercise thereof; or abridging the freedom of speech, or of the press; or the right of the people peaceably to assemble, and to petition the government for a redress of grievances." That is the sum total of what it says - no more, no less. Between the ACLU, corrupt judges and wannabe Athiest dictators they have twisted those simple words to mean precisely the opposite of what they so clearly state. So, I ask you: Has the United States become an **Atheocracy?**

The removal and abolishment of anything remotely resembling religion or religious beliefs from all public places has become the current focus of the Atheist left. Plain and simply they are establishing "Atheism" or "Secular Humanism" as the state religion of the US in direct defiance of the First Amendment to our Constitution. "Congress shall make no law respecting an establishment of religion," Any removal or prohibition of religious symbols - Christmas - Hanukkah - God - Christ - Islam - Buddha - from public places is also in defiance of the first amendment, "or prohibiting the free exercise thereof...." Isn't it about time we fought back against these clearly illegal actions? Let's fight the ACLU and those corrupt judges and call them what they are. Without a higher power, they have no moral or even ethical basis for their words. They can say whatever they want with no consequence unless someone can legally prove they broke the law. They can lie, cheat, steal, even murder with complete confidence they will not be punished. Just ask Teddy Kennedy. I say, let's prove who and what the ACLU really is. Let's impeach every judge who ruled against religion and religious symbols and especially the ninth district court.

The First Amendment states clearly, "Congress shall make no law respecting an establishment of religion, or prohibiting the free exercise thereof..." These words are the sum total of those referring to religion, no more, no less. Clearly they are a statement embodied in the words, "Freedom **of** Religion" not "Freedom **from** Religion" that the left wants to impose and which the ACLU and the left leaning courts have so blatantly enforced..

The first part clearly states the Federal Congress shall make no law which establishes a religion. That includes only the United States Senate and House of Representatives. No mention is made of any state, county or municipality. In other words, the first amendment says any federal law which establishes a religion as the official, federal religion is constitutionally illegal. States are therefore able to determine whether any such clause appears in their state constitution. For this reason, all prohibitions against any religious expression or symbol of any kind in any state, county or city government property including schools is excluded as they are not federal property.

Clearly, conservatives and liberals differ substantially in this matter. Factually, legally and possibly, there is no question that the liberal position is in direct opposition to the true and actual meanings of the first amendment as described. Their gross and erroneous expansion and near reversal of the most basic meaning of this amendment is but a microcosm of their entire philosophy of politics and of government. The following is a gross generalization, but hits at the heart of the differences. Liberals seem to love government and hate corporations. Conservatives seem to love corporations and hate government. I would far rather have a fortune 500 with so many independent, self sustaining, groups of free individuals controlling 500 different entities who must make a profit to survive than a single government entity with no profit incentive whose only inducement for excellence is to expand by base line budgeting. Our government is indeed a hydra, producing little of value and totally dependent on the private sector including the fortune 500 companies for its financial support. I repeat: There is absolutely nothing government does or could do that could not be or is not done better, with less cost, safer, more efficiently, and with superior environmental and social effect by private, independent, profit making organizations and corporations. Besides this, they would be paying completely for whatever part of government remains. No socialist nation can match the excellence and benefit to so many of its citizens. Why is it that so many people risk life and property just to get to the US. How many take the same risks to get to Cuba, Spain or even Sweden?

Monday, January 23, 2006

Musings on the New Medicare Rx Benefit?

Forward from Nancy Grimm 1-23-2006

Just in case you all were wondering about the new Medicare Prescription Drug Plan, here it is from the horse's mouth.

You might want to share this with your folks. It will help to clear up the confusion around the new Medicare Prescription Drug Plan.

Subject: Bush Explains Medicare Drug Bill

Bush Explains Medicare Drug Bill -- Verbatim Quote

Submitted on 2005-12-13 16:35:14

WOMAN IN AUDIENCE: 'I don't really understand. How is it the new plan going to fix the problem?'

Verbatim response (PRESIDENT BUSH):

'Because the -- all which is on the table begins to address the big cost drivers. For example, how benefits are calculated, for example, is on the table. Whether or not benefits rise based upon wage increases or price increases. There's a series of parts of the formula that are being considered. And when you couple that, those different cost drivers, affecting those -- changing those with personal accounts, the idea is to get what has been promised more likely to be -- or closer delivered to that has been promised. Does that make any sense to you? It's kind of muddled. Look, there's a series of things that cause the -- like, for example, benefits are calculated based upon the increase of wages, as opposed to the increase of prices. Some have suggested that we calculate -- the benefits will rise based upon inflation, supposed to wage increases. There is a reform that would help solve the red if that were put into effect. In other words, how fast benefits grow, how fast the promised benefits grow, if those -- if that growth is affected, it will help on the red.'

Forward this to others -- so they, too, can understand.

Ho's reply:

Which end of the horse did you say this came from? This so called plan is no more than a blatant vote-buying instrument, completely idiotic, that probably creates more problems for more people than it solves and will cost infinitely more than the actual net amount of any real benefits. Like so much of the self-serving legislation that has come out of Washington for at least the past sixty years, its main beneficiaries are Washington bureaucrats, with Congress and the drug industry following behind in decreasing order of value. I'll give you an actual example from my own experience that could probably be echoed by millions of seniors all over the country.

Most of the major drug companies have had wonderful and very efficient programs to provide free drugs to seniors on low incomes like Social Security. During Barbara's last year we benefitted with an average of $1300.00 per month of her drugs provided absolutely free by drug company programs. (All but one of the drug companies announced they would discontinue their free drug plans once the new law took effect, and I can't really blame them.) The drugs and over-the-counters for her we had to pay for out-of-pocket amounted to nearly $1000.00 per month. My benefit was much less at about $120.00 per month. I calculated the lowest costs to us under the new plan. Because her costs were so high, she qualified for the maximum out-of-pocket expense so our total costs, including premiums for part D would have been over $4,000.00. annually, a savings of $8,000.00 on paper. The problem was that because many of her drugs as well as both of mine are not yet available in generic form, they are only partially covered by the plan and would add between $3,000.00 and $4,000.00 to our annual costs. It's very difficult to calculate accurately the actual difference.

Under the new law, the total cost for my drugs added to the premium cost for the insurance I must buy, will be in excess of $155.00 per month. If I buy the same drugs under the discount program of the privately insured supplement program I already have and pay for, my cost will be only $80.00 per month. (Provided I don't need additional new drugs) That is still $80.00 a month more than I was paying under the old system. Actually, since one of the drugs I take is from Pfizer my cost per month will only be $40.00. Amazingly, Pfizer alone among the major drug companies is continuing their free drug program for low income seniors, at least for the present.

This is terribly expensive legislation, even if measured by implementation, education, administration and policing costs alone. There is no question in my mind about who benefits the most from this program. Number one, the ravenous federal bureaucracy that must grow to administer and police the plan. Number two, Members of Congress.(supposedly pays for votes) Number three, the drug companies who are able to cancel their free drug programs. You'll notice I didn't mention seniors on medicare because they will gain the least if anything.

This is your government in action–Democrat, Republican, Independent–makes no difference. They're all made mostly of the same cloth. If I sound PO'd, I am! Oh yes, all you younger people please remember who is going to pay for this fiasco as well as all that other pork....you are!

Ho

- - - - - - - - - - - - - - -

Reply from Nancy:

Availability of reasonably priced prescription medication is a real issue, Uncle Mike, I know. Sorry that I touched a nerve. The attempt at levity was to point to our president's complete inability to get across a single point. Or maybe, more sinisterly, it's real obfuscation. I think the fundamental issue is that we should talk care of people when they are hurting or in need. That is consistent with our basic values and if we hold to those values, then we enact laws concerning health care and drug benefits that target those in need of health care, not those in need (supposed) of even greater profit.

Unfortunately, these are NOT the values of the people in power at the moment, which is why we continue to find ourselves in situations where we wonder, WHAT HAS HAPPENED? How is it that the republicans have succeeded in convincing us that we need tax "relief" as if paying for programs that help those in need is some sort of disease or afflication? How is it that ever greater numbers of our citizens cannot afford even basic health care? How can it be that we still have a significant poverty problem in this richest of all nations? I am afraid it is because all of us have bought into the notion that the cons have been selling for decades – that if everyone worked as hard as the conservatives purport to do (notwithstanding that much of their wealth is NOT earned), everyone would be able to take care of themselves; that if we reward the rich for their "hard work" somehow the poor will magically be pulled up....

OK I am rambling. Anyway, Uncle Mike I am sorry if what I thought was a sadly funny commentary on our leadership made you upset.

Love to all, nbg

Ho's reply:

Au contraire! Your words were but a trigger. I've been upset about the idiocy in Washington for many many years. I thought your commentary to be on the mark. I don't always agree with you, but I certainly do listen to what you say and value your opinion. You may even be surprised at how much of what ideas come from the liberal side of humanity I agree with. I see either side of the aisle as having a paucity of really creative ideas to deal with the multitudinous threats-- no--

menaces we now face with certainty. Mostly they deftly avoid even acknowledging these true menaces exist. In most things we may disagree on the method, and even on the reality of the situation, but are certainly close to congruent on the desired end results.

Ho goes on:

I reread your email and it triggered a more thoughtful response with some disagreement. I see little actual difference between the intentions or values of those now in power and their opposition. I have little respect for all but a very few members of our government including our elected representatives, aspiring or sitting executives, judges, et al regardless of their party affiliation. I have little real respect for many famous members of the entertainment industry including media, sports, TV, movie and music stars either. So many are active narcissists who are paid far too much money, get far too much attention, and have far too much influence over many Americans, particularly with respect to their true human value. I suppose, but don't specifically know, there are probably many in the world of business who would fall under the same category. Unfortunately, they don't usually get as much press as the others, Ken Lay and friends excepted.

Some months back I started writing a book, "Monkey Kings, Monkey People" to describe the interactions between those who control our society and those who are the subjects (or victims) of that control. (That book morphed into one titled, *The Feudals*.) Why, like pack animals, we have this social/political structural "worship" of heros, royalty, the famous, the beautiful, even the wealthy ("kings") never ceases to befuddle me. Is it so prevalent among we humans that it must be genetically controlled? Is the political struggle for power between the left and right a human aping (how about that little dual meaning) of the well know troop conflict structures of many primates including monkeys, baboons and apes? Once I got into it I became so infuriated with what I discovered that I shelved the project for later.

Republican versus Democrat, Liberal versus Conservative, black versus white, religious versus atheist, you name it, all dichotomies of this type are never about or for the vast majority of the people, but are about who of the elevated, the leaders, the "kings" have the most power over those ignorant peasants. Each caters to their own political power. Historically, Democrats and liberals cater to the powerful in labor, government, entertainment and education. Republicans and conservatives cater to the powerful in business, religion and the military. Democrats purportedly love the downtrodden, the disenfranchised, the failures in life while Republicans treat the successful, wealthy and powerful with equal ardor.

The truth is that with very few exceptions, neither party gives a whit about the little guy on either side of the political fence. Their only concern (of most, not all) is money and power. The money to get and stay in office and the power to control the government. Literally all the conflicts are between the very powerful to see who can tell enough lies well enough and promise enough pork to get elected.

The thing that disappointed me so much was that the stupid Republicans, once they got in power, seemingly decided to do to the nation what the Democrats had been doing for the previous forty years. That is, write increasingly complex and intrusive laws to extract money from the general populace for their own very special interests. To me, the Democrats became masters of deception and duplicity by vastly expanding their power base, the government bureaucracy, at the expense of the real people of the country. They were buying their way into power using taxpayer dollars.

When the Republicans came into power I thought things would change, but they didn't. These idiots seemed to think it was their turn to do the same thing the Democrats had been doing for so long. That damnable Rx Drug law is a classic example. The only difference between that and a Democrat version for the same purpose would be which group of power brokers got the money and the power.

Liberals, Republicans, conservatives, Democrats, by and large they're all the same hateful, power hungry, self-serving, pseudo criminals wearing different colors and speaking different languages. This is such an abomination as to bewilder the mind of any logical, reasonable, pragmatic individual. Most certainly realize that the vast majority of political speech in this country is completely void of the real truth and couched, like a lawyer's argument, strictly to make the desired point. I have found that there are real, practical, workable, creative systems out there, available from many intelligent, well-intentioned sources that could solve so many of our problems in ways so ingenious as to dazzle the mind. I have seen some and have written about others myself. Following is a small sample of what I am referring to.

EXAMPLES:

"The Johnson Tax Code" - a revolutionary proposal that most politicians would be against since it is simple, would cost much less to administer and would help keep their hands out of the till. See Page 200

"A New Solution to the Drug Problem" - an effective method for completely removing the financial incentive for illegal drug sales and the industry that flourishes in spite of "The War on Drugs." See Page 499

"A Solution to the Identity/Security Problem We can Live With" - one way to solve all kinds of identity problems that would satisfy Constitutional constraints and not force people to comply. See Page 206

"Job Growth Indiana" How Indiana (Or any other state) can attract many new businesses, greatly increase job growth, and vastly increase state revenue without new taxes. See Page 498

"The Antiquated Minimum Wage" - a proposal to correct the problems that costs jobs, drives industries out of the country, creates labor voids in some areas and doesn't do what it is supposed to do in most of the country. See Page 370

Case in point, taxes. It is a firmly established and proven fact that judiciously lowering taxes, far from reducing government revenue, actually increases revenue because of increased economic activity. Yet the left steadfastly curses Republicans for lowering taxes. On the other side and in spite of increasing damage to our environment, Republicans refuse to promote proven environmental issues even when the economics favor them. Both are merely playing the political music their bases want to hear. Neither seem to recognize or care about the facts or the nation for that matter, but only for their own political bank roll. Or, can it be they are too ignorant to understand the situation?

Instead of real concern, we now have a liberal Democrat party willing to do anything including the destruction of our nation to regain the power they have lost. There is no longer any doubt in my mind but that given the same situation, Republicans would be just as evilly stupid. This hunger for power totally destroys or prevents any use of real reform to make things better.

There is one thing I know that bears on this problem. It is a fact proven over and over again to reasonable people. That is: no matter what the project or problem, private, individual and group effort will provide a solution better, faster, cheaper, cleaner, and more effective overall than any government. If you doubt that, look at China today. After languishing in the throes of depression for decades because of endless and futile government collective farms, their farm economy took off when the government noted that the people were producing more needed agricultural output than the huge collective farms on tiny, individual plots worked and harvested by individuals and small groups for their own profit. By changing to farm ownership and encouraging individual entrepreneurship, China began an economic growth spurt that is just now reaching momentous proportions. To some extent the Chinese government realized that relaxing control and encouraging individual enterprise had exactly the opposite effect predicted by the Maoists.

China is moving toward less control on individuals while our people are facing staggering increases in controls, reporting requirements, and disincentives for success. Indeed, we now seem bent on challenging and even despising excellence and success in many areas of our social/political structure, especially in our education system. There is no such anti-excellence attitude in China. Is it any wonder we seem headed for third-world mediocrity?

Yes, China is still burdened with a huge, corrupt bureaucracy, but at least they are moving slowly away from it while we seem doomed to move rapidly into it. Has our huge, overgrown bureaucracy reached the point where neither political party can afford to rein it in? Is government of the people by the government and for the government our future fate? Or are we already there?

Saturday, January 21, 2006

What we need is more bureaucracy! Beaver dam

This is an actual letter sent to a man named Ryan DeVries by the Michigan Department of Environmental Quality, State of Michigan. This guy's response is hilarious, but read the State's letter first.

SUBJECT: DEQ File No.97-59-0023; T11N; R10W, Sec. 20; Montcalm County

Dear Mr. DeVries:

It has come to the attention of the Department of Environmental Quality that there has been recent unauthorized activity on the above referenced parcel of property. You have been certified as the legal landowner and/or contractor who did the following unauthorized activity:

Construction and maintenance of two wood debris dams across the outlet stream of Spring Pond.

A permit must be issued prior to the start of this type of activity. A review of the Department's files shows that no permits have been issued. Therefore, the Department has determined that this activity is in violation of Part 301, Inland Lakes and Streams, of the Natural Resource and Environmental Protection Act, Act 451 of the Public Acts of 1994, being sections 324.30101 to 324.30113 of the Michigan Compiled Laws, annotated.

The Department has been informed that one or both of the dams partially failed during a recent rain event, causing debris and flooding at downstream locations. We find that dams of this nature are inherently hazardous and cannot be permitted. The Department therefore orders you to cease and desist all activities at this location, and to restore the stream to a free-flow condition by removing all wood and brush forming the dams from the stream channel. All restoration work shall be completed no later than January 31, 2006.

Please notify this office when the restoration has been completed so that a follow-up site inspection may be scheduled by our staff. Failure to comply with this request or any further unauthorized activity on the site may result in this case being referred for elevated enforcement action.

We anticipate and would appreciate your full cooperation in this matter. Please feel free to contact me at this office if you have any questions.

Sincerely,

David L. Price – District Representative and Water Management Division.

= =

Response sent back by Mr. DeVries:

Re: DEQ File No. 97-59-0023; T11N; R10W, Sec. 20; Montcalm County.

Dear Mr. Price,

Your certified letter dated 07/19/2005 has been handed to me to respond to. I am the legal landowner but not the Contractor at 2088 Dagget, Pierson, Michigan. A couple of beavers are in the (State unauthorized) process of constructing and maintaining two Wood "debris" dams across the outlet stream of my Spring Pond. While I did not pay for, authorize, nor supervise their dam project, I think they would be highly offended that you call their skillful use of natures building materials "debris." I would like to challenge your department to attempt to emulate their dam project any time and/or any place you choose. I believe I can safely state there is no way you could ever match their dam skills, their dam resourcefulness, their dam ingenuity, their dam persistence, their dam determination and/or their dam work ethic.

As to your request, I do not think the beavers are aware that they must first fill out a dam permit prior to the start of this type of dam activity. My first dam question to you is:

(1) Are you trying to discriminate against my Spring Pond Beavers, or

(2) do you require all beavers throughout this State to conform to said dam request?

If you are not discriminating against these particular beavers, through the Freedom of Information Act, I request completed copies of all those other applicable beaver dam permits that have been issued. Perhaps we will see if there really is a dam violation of Part 301, Inland Lakes and Streams, of the Natural Resource and Environmental Protection Act, Act 451 of The Public Acts of 1994, being sections 324.30101 to 324.30113 of the Michigan Compiled Laws, annotated.

I have several concerns. My first concern is; aren't the beavers entitled to legal representation? The Spring Pond Beavers are financially destitute and are unable to pay for said representation -- so the State will have to provide them with a dam lawyer.

The Department's dam concern that either one or both of the dams failed during a recent rain event, causing flooding, is proof that this is a natural occurrence, which the Department is required to protect. In other words, we should leave the Spring Pond Beavers alone rather than harassing them and calling their dam names.

If you want the stream "restored" to a dam free-flow condition please contact the beavers -- but if you are going to arrest them, they obviously did not pay any attention to your dam letter, they being unable to read English. In my humble opinion, the Spring Pond Beavers have a right to build their unauthorized dams as long as the sky is blue, the grass is green and water flows downstream. They have more dam rights than I do to live and enjoy Spring Pond. If the Department of Natural Resources and Environmental Protection lives up to its name, it should protect the natural resources (Beavers) and the environment (Beavers' Dams).

So, as far as the beavers and I are concerned, this dam case can be referred for more elevated enforcement action right now. Why wait until 1/31/2006? The Spring Pond Beavers may be under the dam ice then and there will be no way for you or your dam staff to contact/harass them then.

In conclusion, I would like to bring to your attention to a real environmental quality (health) problem in the area. It is the bears! Bears are actually defecating in our woods.

I definitely believe you should be persecuting the defecating bears and leave the beavers alone. If you are going to investigate the beaver dam, watch your step! (The bears are not careful where they dump!!) Being unable to comply with your dam request, and being unable to contact you on your dam answering machine, I am sending this response to your dam office.

Thank you,

Ryan DeVries & the Dam Beavers

===

Here are a few observations prompted by the above which I received recently by email.

It has been said that truth is stranger than fiction, to which I might add (especially in this case), truth is funnier than fiction. I will also add a serious tone to this by noting it is an example of the kind of things we Americans face at the hands of a ponderously overgrown and still growing, monstrously inept, totally self absorbed government peopled with anal retentive, busy-body lawyers with no sense of reality and far too much time on their hands. This bloated bureaucracy serves mostly its own members, many of whom couldn't hold a productive job in the private sector because of their poor education, nonexistent work ethic, or combination of both. The only groups of sorrier, more questionable and more self-serving humans I can think of are our elected officials, and the Federal Congress in particular. This includes members of all political parties.

It is amazing to me that our republic has endured for so long at the hands of scoundrels and brigands. This is particularly true since these multitudinous, unproductive bureaucratic "Jabba the Huts" drain increasing amounts of hard-earned cash from the pockets of the ordinary, hard working, harder pressed populace who have no access to and little control over these monsters. Sadly, our supposedly watchdog media are more enthralled with ratings and promoting their own self protection, agenda, income and status than in exposing the real corruption and waste within these Frankenstein creations, the Hydras of government. I say this with due respect and apologies to the tiny percentage of government employees who actually do work, care and probably produce 99.9% of the effectiveness of government. I would wager that we could eliminate close to 99% of government jobs and the nation would move on forward with hardly a ripple noticeable by non-government individuals.

Thursday, January 19, 2006

Something You Won't Hear about on Main Stream TV

This is an email forward I want to share.

I sat in my seat of the Boeing 767 waiting for everyone to hurry and stow their carry-ons and grab a seat so we could start what I was sure to be a long, uneventful flight home.

With the huge capacity and slow moving people taking their time to stuff luggage far too big for the overhead and never paying much attention to holding up the growing line behind them, I simply shook my head knowing that this flight was not starting out very well. I was anxious to get home to see my loved ones so I was focused on my issues and just felt like standing up and yelling for some of these clowns to get their act together.

I knew I couldn't say a word so I just thumbed thru the "Sky Mall" magazine from the seat pocket in front of me. You know it's really getting rough when you resort to the over priced, useless sky mall crap to break the monotony. With everyone finally seated, we just sat there with the cabin door open and no one in any hurry to get us going although we were well past the scheduled take off time. No wonder the airline industry is in trouble I told myself.

Just then, the attendant came on the intercom to inform us all that we were being delayed. The entire plane let out a collective groan. She resumed speaking to say "We are holding the aircraft for some very special people who are on their way to the plane and the delay shouldn't be more than 5 minutes.

The word came after waiting six times as long as we were promised that I was finally going to be on my way home. Why the hoopla over "these" folks?

I was expecting some celebrity or sport figure to be the reason for the hold up. Just get their butts in a seat and let's hit the gas I thought.

The attendant came back on the speaker to announce in a loud and excited voice that we were being joined by several U.S. Marines returning home from Iraq !!!

Just as they walked on board, the entire plane erupted into applause. The men were a bit taken by surprise by the 340 people cheering for them as they searched for their seats. They were having their hands shook and touched by almost everyone who was within an arm's distance of them as they passed down the aisle. One elderly woman kissed the hand of one of the Marines as he passed by her. The applause, whistles and cheering didn't stop for a long time.

When we were finally airborne, I was not the only civilian checking his conscience as to the delays in "me" getting home, finding my easy chair, a cold beverage and the remote in my hand. These men had done for all of us and I had been complaining silently about "me" and "my" issues I took for granted the everyday freedoms I enjoy and the conveniences of the American way of life. I took for granted that others had paid the price for my ability to moan and complain about a few minutes delay to "me" while those Heroes were going home to their loved ones.

I attempted to get my selfish outlook back in order and minutes before we landed, I suggested to the attendant that she announce over the speaker a request for everyone to remain in their seats until our heroes were allowed to gather their things and be first off the plane. The cheers and applause continued until the last Marine stepped off and we all rose to go about our too often taken for granted everyday freedoms. I felt proud of them.

I felt it an honor and a privilege to be among the first to welcome them home and say "Thank You for a job well done." I vowed that I will never forget that flight nor the lesson learned. I can't say it enough, THANK YOU to those Veterans and active servicemen and women who may read this and a prayer for those who cannot because they are no longer with us.

GOD BLESS AMERICA! WELCOME HOME! AND THANKS FOR A JOB WELL DONE!!!!!

A HoJo comment:

I was reminded of the contrast to a scene I witnessed on TV some years back when a group of soldiers were marching through a crowd of jeering, cursing, screaming young people in shabby garb holding hate filled signs and raising fists and middle fingers at our soldiers. I wondered, was it the difference in the wars, the difference in the public opinion, the difference in the soldiers, the difference in the locale or the difference in the particular audience? My guess is that the difference was between an organized, politically motivated group of demonstrators playing to the main stream media who strongly favor the group's hate-filled agenda and a spontaneous, grateful, thankful group of successful Americans reacting to their deep, genuine appreciation and playing to no one but themselves.

There is no doubt in my mind that a great many of the casualties on both sides and in both wars would be alive and in good health and the world would be far closer to general peace if those who work so diligently and emotionally against both wars by providing comfort, encouragement, emotional support and thus direct aid to our enemies, would instead, spend the same energy helping in the physical and political rebuilding of Iraq and Afghanistan. The biggest beneficiaries of the efforts of these so-called, "anti-war" activists include terrorists who visit wholesale murder on their own people even more than on our troops. That their objective, far from solving the problems of despotism and the totalitarian oppression of people, is instead quite obviously the degradation and defeat of America strictly for political gain of their own, selfish, self-serving agenda.

These politically motivated groups care little for the lives or suffering of those we would rescue from tyranny or for our own people. No price in misery is too high for others to pay to aid them in their striving for political power. Power and control are their real goals. Government control over everyone with them in control of that government is their desired end.

Freedom–political, economic, religious, literary, you name it–individual freedom of virtually any kind is their sworn enemy. If you doubt this, just try to speak against any of their pet agendas at any place where they control a group of their "protesters." Example: conservative speakers at virtually any college campus in the country. Why is it so important for liberal cause groups to silence any opposing voices? Could it be their arguments are so weak as to be unable to withstand criticism. This happens so often as to be considered the normal course of things. Why is there never any comparable oppression of liberal voices by conservatives?

The answer is that conservatives generally encourage open well mannered discussions while liberals usually encourage only discussions that agree with their agenda and will often shout down any dissenting opinion. Relatively speaking, conservatives have open minds while liberals have minds closed to opinions that disagree with their mantras.

Liberal Democrats, lead by Howard Dean, who heads up the DNC, are almost apoplectic in their loud, angry expressions of hatred for Republicans. Hate has become the mantra of the Democrat party. Led by Dean and aped by Democrats, Kennedy, Byrd, Pelosi, McKinney and a host of others, liberal democrats mouth a constant stream of epithets of hate at Republicans, indeed, at any who do not agree with them. It seems to be a genetic condition of liberals. Totally bereft of even a hint of positive programs to solve any of the country's problems, all they can do is scream insults like frustrated schoolboys unable to get their way. They are so against practically everything, how can we expect them to spend any effort at practical solutions to anything? All we hear are epithets, slogans and mantras, all seemingly dutifully repeated after being disseminated from someone, somewhere–maybe Michael Moore, or moveon.org? What is the real motive of these people who scream with so much hatred for America?

Real Americans would like to know.

Tuesday, January 17, 2006

HJ response to the Message from The Fellowship of Reconciliation titled,

"Finding Dr. King's Moral Compass in an Age of Deceit."

I have the utmost respect for the memory of Dr. Martin Luther King, Jr. He was a great champion for his people and his efforts on their behalf was instrumental in the huge gains they have made in jobs, income, acceptance and respect. But I also know he contrived his words to convey meanings to fit his own agenda. In the mentioned quote from April 1967, "A nation that continues year after year to spend more money on military defense than on programs of social uplift is approaching spiritual death." The implication is in direct opposition to the actual facts. To make it accurate the word "nation" must be replaced by "government." In America these two terms mean very different things. Indeed the "government" did in 1967 and in 2004 and probably during all the years in between, spend more on defense than on social programs. If, however, you use the word, "nation" you must include all individual and corporate spending on social programs along with government. In this case, social spending of the "nation" far exceeds military spending. Fortunately, in America, the government is not the only socially active entity unlike most of the socialist nations of the world.

Regarding the "immoral" war, should Dr King's position on war been in effect during the period of WW II there is no doubt in my mind that Hitler would have won the war and Europe would now be under German domination. Japan would probably now control the western US and maybe the whole continent if Germany did not control the eastern half.

It is ridiculous to speak of the deaths in Iraq without mentioning the more than twenty times as many young Americans who are murder victims right here in the supposedly "at peace" US than die from enemy action in Iraq. Isn't it about time we addressed our own, home grown terrorists that murdered about 700 civilians in Chicago alone last year? Most of those, victims and perpetrators alike, were black. The so called disaster in Iraq pales in comparison to the disaster on our streets right here at home that vocal critics of the war completely ignore. I wonder what the real motive is for their anti-Iraq war stance? Hmmmmmm! I wonder why they were not active against the immoral war in Cosevo? Hmmmmmmm!

I seriously doubt the truth of the statement "a massive increase in hunger, with 36 million people, or 13% of the "U.S. population, experiencing food shortages in the past year," when all government statistics indicate the biggest health problem for America's poor is obesity.

The final paragraphs starting with, "But the journey to "spiritual death" encompasses..." merely reports the cultural moral degradation of our nation spearheaded by fifty years of efforts by the liberal left to secularize our nation, destroy religion and the American family in order to promote their own peculiar form of morality. Never have I seen more blatant and evil expressions of intense hatred and violence than from liberal Democrat politicians and in so called peace marches. Indeed the head of the Democrat National Committee, Dr. Howard Dean himself, screamed his hatred of all Republicans several times. Does that not mean he holds passionate hatred for at least half of all Americans: those who merely disagree with his politics?

Should the ACLU succeed in their massive efforts to make atheism or secular humanism the defacto state religion of our nation (in direct defiance of the first amendment,) will they destroy all of the government buildings like the supreme court building which have religious symbols? After all, these are definitely Judeo-Christian symbols at that.

As usual, these liberal, anti-everything individuals and organizations are completely bereft of any substantive positive programs of any kind. All they seem able to do is mouth meaningless slogan mantras and scream epithets and hatred at those in power. They angrily denounced the economic programs of this administration until it became so obvious the economy was growing exactly the opposite from their pronouncements that even the dullest individuals could see it. Then, they shut up about the economy and have shifted totally to the war in Iraq. Together with their puppets in the media they paint an extremely negative picture of Iraq in direct contrast to all truly factual reports. Their encouragement of the anti-American and anti-Iraqi terrorists is doubtless the reason for the continuing murder of Americans and Iraqis by foreign terrorists. With all the negative comments about Iraq, I wonder why the Democrat leader of the House, Nancy Pelosi, has come out in such a belligerent manner after Iran's atomic power announcements. Are the Democrats about to go to war with Iran? A curious American would like to know.

Ben Stein Comments, Especially About Christmas Trees

- Dec 12, 2005

If they know of him at all, many folks think Ben Stein is just a quirky actor/comedian who talks in a monotone. He's also a very intelligent attorney who knows how to put ideas and words together in such a way as to sway juries and make people think clearly.

~ ~

The following was written by Ben Stein and recited by him on CBS Sunday Morning Commentary, Sunday, 12/18/05:

~ ~

Herewith at this happy time of year, a few confessions from my beating heart: I have no freaking clue who Nick and Jessica are. I see them on the cover of People and Us constantly when I am buying my dog biscuits and kitty litter. I often ask the checkers at the grocery stores. They never know who Nick and Jessica are either. Who are they? Will it change my life if I know who they are and why they have broken up? Why are they so important? I don't know who Lindsay Lohan is either, and I do not care at all about Tom Cruise's wife. Am I going to be called before a Senate committee and asked if I am a subversive? Maybe, but I just have no clue who Nick and Jessica are. If this is what it means to be no longer young. It's not so bad.

Next confession:

I am a Jew, and every single one of my ancestors was Jewish. And it does not bother me even a little bit when péople call those beautiful lit up, bejeweled trees Christmas trees. I don't feel threatened. I don't feel discriminated against. That's what they are: Christmas trees. It doesn't bother me a bit when people say, "Merry Christmas" to me. I don't think they are slighting me or getting ready to put me in a ghetto. In fact, I kind of like it. It shows that we are all brothers and sisters celebrating this happy time of year. It doesn't bother me at all that there is a manger scene on display at a key intersection near my beach house in Malibu. If people want a creche, it's just as fine with me as is the Menorah a few hundred yards away.

I don't like getting pushed around for being a Jew, and I don't think Christians like getting pushed around for being Christians. I think people who believe in God are sick and tired of getting pushed around, period. I have no idea where the concept came from that America is an explicitly atheist country. I can't find it in the Constitution, and I don't like it being shoved down my throat. Or maybe I can put it another way: where did the idea come from that we should worship Nick and Jessica and we aren't allowed to worship God as we understand Him? I guess that's a sign that I'm getting old, too. But there are a lot of us who are wondering where Nick and Jessica came from and where the America we knew went to. In light of the many jokes we send to one another for a laugh, this is a little different: This is not intended to be a joke, it's not funny, it's intended to get you thinking.

Billy Graham's daughter was interviewed on the Early Show and Jane Clayson asked her "How could God let something like this Happen?" (regarding Katrina) Anne Graham gave an extremely profound and insightful response. She said, "I believe God is deeply saddened by this, just as we are, but for years we've been telling God to get out of our schools, to get out of our government and to get out of our lives. And being the gentleman He is, I believe He has calmly backed out. How can we expect God to give us His blessing and His protection if we demand He leave us alone?" In light of recent events...terrorists attack, school shootings, etc.

I think it started when Madeleine Murray O'Hare (she was murdered, her body found recently) complained she didn't want prayer in our schools, and we said OK. Then someone said you better not read the Bible in school . the Bible says thou shalt not kill, thou shalt not steal, and love your neighbor as yourself. And we said OK. Then Dr. Benjamin Spock said we shouldn't spank our children when they misbehave because their little personalities would be warped and we might damage their self-esteem (Dr. Spock's son committed suicide). We said an expert should know what he's talking about. And we said OK. Now we're asking ourselves why our children have no conscience, why they don't know right from wrong, and why it doesn't bother them to kill strangers, their classmates, and themselves. Probably, if we think about it long and hard enough, we can figure it out. I think it has a great deal to do with "WE REAP WHAT WE SOW."

- End of Quote -

~ ~

Funny how simple it is for people to trash God and then wonder why the world's going to hell. Funny how we believe what the newspapers say, but question what the Bible says. Funny how you can send 'jokes' through e-mail and they spread like wildfire but when you start sending messages regarding the Lord, people think twice about sharing. Funny how lewd, crude, vulgar and obscene articles pass freely through cyberspace, but public discussion of God is suppressed in the school and workplace. Are you laughing? Funny how when you forward this message, you will not send it to many on your address list because you're not sure what they believe, or what they will think of you for sending it.

Funny how we can be more worried about what other people think of us than what God thinks of us. (I realize that doesn't apply to atheists.) But, if you discard this thought process, don't sit back and complain about what bad shape the world is in.

Wednesday, October 12, 2005

A New Plan for Disaster Relief

Copyright © October 7, 2005 - Howard E. Johnson - Leesburg, Indiana - (hjdisrelief5B12 HTML)

Disaster Relief - A new way to disperse funds.

This is but an outline of a program that the author conceived of after the Katrina disaster and plans to fledge out into a full scale lecture.

Problem: The governments of Louisiana and of New Orleans are asking for the unprecedented amount of $268 billion to rebuild after hurricanes Katrina and Rita. This could set a very expensive precedent which, I'm sure, all other states will try to follow with all kinds and sizes of disasters. Can anyone imagine the efficacy of turning that much over to a corrupt state government with absolutely no strings, for that is what they ask.

Here's a better idea that could be used as a model for disaster relief throughout the country: Take the final estimate figure from the state and divide it in half. Take the total amount of insurance payments being made to property owners and subtract that amount from the first figure giving a net cost. Take the remaining net cost and divide it by four. That amount is what the state government must contribute. For every dollar the state contributes, the national government will contribute three up to the full amount of the net figure.

Here's how the money will be distributed: Half of the entire sum will be divided evenly between all of the registered voters in all areas designated as total disaster areas. In areas of less than total devastation the amounts will be lowered to reflect the actual percentage of damage. This will be done on an individual property owner basis. The money will be distributed in the form of debit cards to those deserving compensation. These debit cards may only be used to purchase food, clothing, utilities, and replacements for items, structures and building materials. Labor for any repairs and building will have to go to licensed builders and contractors and only for work not covered by insurance.

The other half of the funds will be designated for rebuilding and replacing infrastructure actually destroyed or damaged by the storms. No new construction is to be payed for out of these funds. FEMA will administer all federal funds and payments with the approval of the proper state, county and city government agencies. Accurate records of the dispersal of all funds will be kept and made available as public records.

Friday, October 07, 2005

Fantasy???

A Conservative Turns Liberal??

A WARNING: Closed minds, liberal, conservative or moderate, will not readily understand these words. If you think them a bit harsh, extreme and over the top I suggest you consider CAREFULLY the latest words of the liberals mentioned in the first paragraph, to the editorial pages of the New York Times and to the rants on moveon.org. These words are actually a very small extrapolation of their words and are definitely in the same vein. For those from Rio Linda, this is what's called a parody.

To sincere liberals: You may not like these words, but there are increasing numbers of Americans who see liberal Democrats as hate filled enemies of America in just this way. If you don't like these words, I suggest you step back from your own prejudices and take a look at the direction the liberal Democrat party is heading. How HATE! has become their watchword and deception their guide. Do you really see those individuals mentioned in the first paragraph as the leaders you would be proud to follow?

To all my liberal, conservative and moderate (mugwump) friends and family:

I have finally gotten the message. This formerly mostly conservative individual has decided to convert to the liberal side. I have listened thoughtfully to the carefully crafted words of those wonderful Americans, Ted Kennedy, Howard Dean, Louis Farakhan, Robert Byrd, Harry Reid, Al Sharpton, Barbara Boxer, Chuck Schumer, Charley Rangle, Nancy Pelosi, Jessie Jackson, the Clintons and most recently, Dick Durbin and Cynthia McKinney. I have finally caught the true wisdom, compassion and selflessness of their impassioned call for real Americans to stand up and join the noble liberal cause. Like any loyal liberal I promise to listen to, view and read only those with proven liberal agendas. I will refuse to hear, see or read anything that disagrees with our marvelous liberal philosophy. I will only have friendships with liberals and will cut off all those who don't share our liberal views. I will leave our little country church and join an atheist ethical society with liberal values. Then I won't know a single person who voted for that evil George Bush and his Republican cronies.

Thank you Katrina and Rita! These wonderful storms have provided us with many more opportunities to bash Bush and the Republicans. In the first place we can blame Bush for the storm because of his global warming strategy. Since so many of the New Orleans residents who couldn't get out of town in time were black we have made it a race issue to prove how Bush hates blacks. With Jessie Jackson, Louis Farakhan, Charley Rangle and Al Sharpton screaming their racial hatred rhetoric, our media can blast away at Bush, conservatives, Republicans and the current administration as being inept and maybe downright criminal in their poor response to the drowning of New Orleans blacks. Unfortunately the twenty-five thousand body bags sent to Louisiana turned out to be a bit of overkill as only a few hundred bodies have been found so far.

Whatever the count we can still blame Bush for the countless inhumane deaths of so many poor people. It's unfortunate that the predictions of thousands dead by our friends in the media didn't turn out to be true. Their reporting of untrue rumors about murder, rape and shootings as fact succeeded in making things worse for a while. Fortunately, people will remember the early sensational reports and mostly ignore the retractions. The fact that these false reports caused FEMA to hold off for the protection of their people will never be reported so we can still blame them for their slow response.

Never mind that Louisiana has received the most money of any state for Army Corps of Engineers projects. (I wonder where all that money went?) It was still Bush's fault that all that money was not used to raise and strengthen the dykes as has been recommended for more than thirty years. Never mind that the city didn't implement its own detailed evacuation plans and never used the many busses that were available before the storm hit. Bush must have scuttled all those busses, especially those that were used during the last election to carry voters from the black neighborhoods to poling places. The media will downplay that while concentrating on the slow response of the federal government. All in all Katrina and Rita have proven to be wonderful fodder for our propaganda mills. So what if it resulted in death and misery for some poor and helpless people, the most important thing is that it provided us with countless new opportunities to expand our hate rhetoric against Bush and the Republicans and will keep our voter base from learning the truth and deserting.

The problem about the New Orleans police having only about two thirds of the active duty police that were reported to the federal government seems to have been handled well by our media friends. What happened to all that federal money the city was supposed to be using to pay the non-existent police and how that information was kept secret will never see the light of day just like all that Corps of Engineers money. Our media friends will never mention it and will brand as liars those enemies of ours that do. Then when axed FEMA head Brown talked about the dysfunctional state and local governments - our good liberal Democrat friends in Louisiana - our media friends ignored the facts and branded him as having sour grapes and trying to shift the blame off of himself.

In spite of Katrina getting all the attention, I am pleased to see that Guantanamo Bay remains a focus of success in our attacks on the Bush Administration's illegal war. As long as we continue to pound away at the realities of this torture camp our purpose will be served. Even a few Republicans are joining our band wagon. This is really beginning to help those wonderful freedom fighters in Iraq and Afghanistan. With our aid in destroying confidence in the US military on the political side, these loyal freedom fighters have increased their attacks on both military and government workers of the US and the puppet regimes in Iraq and Afghanistan. They are encouraged by our constant condemnation of America's illegal occupation of their land. With our help, they may yet return the Taliban and even Saddam Hussein and his Baathists to power. With Al Queda freedom fighters so encouraged by the words of our liberal politicians I am sure they will succeed.

I'd like to thank the main stream media and especially the New York Times, the LA Times, NBC, ABC and CBS and all their affiliates for their unrelenting campaign against the illegal war in Iraq and the Bush administration. By concentrating on the killings by the freedom fighters and ignoring all the positive results in Iraq, our main stream media are beating down the spirit of Americans here at home. Fortunately, they are completely ignoring the growing amount of evidence being found about Al Queda connections with Saddam Hussein and WMDs being moved to Syria and Iran. By continuing to do so, they can continue to accuse Bush of lying to justify going to war in Iraq. We are encouraged that the constant diatribes of our liberal politicians and the never ending media barrage against the war is picked up by our friends at Al Jazeera to encourage the Al Queda freedom fighters. Another year of concentration on the evil American military and all the atrocities they are committing and we'll have those cursed conservatives and militarists on the run.

Our media campaign to drive the country into a recession is also having increasing success. In spite of the continuing real growth in jobs and unemployment lower than during most of the Clinton administration, our leaders keep pounding on the word, recession! recession! recession! With our lackeys in the media continuing to call the economy the worse since the great depression, the ignorant American peasants are becoming more and more depressed. One recent poll showed fear of job loss to be the number one concern of Americans. It made me chuckle as I realized this is a phenomenal result of our media campaign. Thanks to the lack of knowledge of our increasingly ignorant populace, it's becoming much easier for us to instill fear and hatred into their simple minds. Our efforts in the education system to dumb down the American people is showing increasing success. This coupled with the constant growth of illegal immigration is overloading our health care, education and welfare systems. The collapse of these systems will hasten the collapse of the hated capitalist system in America and encourage more hatred against the capitalists by the serfs, I mean common people.

Another tactic valuable to our cause is gaining momentum thanks to our friends in the media who follow and promote our actions. This tactic involves accusations of mischief or criminal activity by those on the right. No matter how questionable or baseless are our charges, our media friends will pick them up and act as if they are proven facts. Should we find the slightest hint of a possibility there could be bad activity we will call for a congressional investigation and a special prosecutor and then go ballistic and call for their heads. Since any activity that helps our cause is good and just we will do everything in our power to minimize it no matter how unethical or criminal it is. Those 700 or so FBI files that just appeared in the Whitehouse during the glorious Clinton administration is a good example of how our media friends can bury those things for us. Remember the liberal rule of definition: anything that favors our causes or agrees with our beliefs is true, good and intelligent. Naturally, anything that favors conservative, patriotic American or Republican causes or agrees with their beliefs is untrue, evil or stupid . After all, aren't those who agree with us and support us good people with fine minds while those who disagree with us are lying, evil, stupid dolts?

We must use all means possible to stop appointments of any federal judges who might disagree with our positions. Only those who agree completely with the ACLU have a right to be confirmed. We will make all manner of accusations against any possible appointee who does not share our perfect liberal philosophy. Remember, accusation is all we need, regardless of the true facts. Once we make those accusations, our friends in the media will trumpet them as if they are true no matter how baseless they may be. We don't care how much damage is done to our nation or the people. The only thing that matters is that we regain the positions of power we had when Johnson was president and both houses of Congress were under our control. We must continue to accuse the Republicans of voter fraud and of cheating in elections (even as our Democrat machines in the big cities succeed in stealing millions of votes without a single word from the media). Maybe we had better not brag about that as Mayor Daly did during the Kennedy election, at least not until we are back in power.

In closing I would like to remind all liberals that our mantra is, "No lie is too evil, ridiculous or vulgar if it promotes our agenda." I will reiterate our short term goals as:

1. Regain power by any possible means no matter how it damages our country.

2. No matter how good it is for our country, oppose and discredit any and all actions by Republicans or conservatives by any and all means possible.

3. Discredit anything Republicans accomplish no matter how good it is.

4. Promote hate for anything and anyone who disagrees with our agenda.

5. Continue to provide political aid to the freedom fighters in Iraq and help them defeat America and drive American troops from their soil. Remember, if America succeeds in Iraq it will be a huge success for the Bush administration and will set our agenda back for years.

6. Continue to repeat word for word the mantras coming from George Soros.

7. Use peace marches and protests to preach hate and violence like Georgia Congresswoman Cynthia McKinney did at the recent Washington protest.

And of course, remember our long range goals:

1. Complete destruction of the America capitalist system.

2. Complete destruction of the American military.

3. Complete removal of all Republicans, conservatives, Christians and their followers from any positions of power in all American organizations of any kind.

4. Complete destruction of the power of religion in America.

5. Complete destruction of the American family and replacement with government for all American serfs.

6. Adoption of atheist socialism as the power structure in the United States.

When our revolution is over and the power is in the hands of our glorious socialist people, things will be very different than under those capitalist dogs. We elite socialist government members will control everything without interference of self serving capitalist bosses. The grand homes we will live in, the expensive cars we drive, the dream vacation villas we use, will all rightfully belong to the people, not to wealthy individuals. We will own nothing, merely have their use as reward for our service to the people. The common folks will proudly serve us, their glorious leaders, knowing there are no longer any wealthy capitalists stealing money from the people.

I will close with a quote from one of our good European friends. A noted French government official, explains why he hates America and George W. Bush

"I hate George Bush's America because Bush Americans are so arrogant they think English is the only language. They use outdated religious principals to make judgements. Why don't they embrace atheist socialism as we have and enjoy the glories of freedom from religious restraints?

"When they invaded Iraq they cut off billions of dollars we were getting from Saddam Hussein and the UN 'oil for food' program. I actually had to stop construction on my vacation home on the French Riviera for lack of funds. For the same reason I'm unable to buy my wife the Ferrari I promised her and she may actually have to attend the next official soiree in a dress she has worn once before. It's positively horrid what those cowboy Americans have done."

We should follow the example of this good friend of ours. I realize I may not live long enough to view the coming changes, but at least I have the vision and foresight to see it coming and abandon old, worn out conservative, free enterprise capitalism.

With a newly enlightened mind and changed allegiance I say bravo to liberals and atheistic socialists everywhere.

Howard Johnson

A SPECIAL NOTE TO MY LIBERAL FRIENDS AND FAMILY:

If these words brought on an angry, or fearful response, I suggest you do a reality check on your own political thoughts and prejudices. You may spend so much of your time in such a cloistered group of other liberals that you have no idea what so many other Americans think and believe. I was recently told by one very liberal person that I was the only person they knew who planned to vote for George Bush in the recent election. That and some other remarks lead me to believe that this person has a totally closed mind and walks in political lock step with the group listed at the beginning of this little essay. I seriously doubt they ever listen to anyone outside the liberal camp. A mind that completely shuts out any expressions, opinions or beliefs that differ from their own or who accepts only those that agree will soon be crippled by mental inbreeding.

These individuals - indeed, all individuals of any persuasion - should sometimes listen to words that haven't come through the finely tuned filter of their own prejudices. There are increasing numbers of people who see the liberal Democrats as those who would destroy America and "bring her to her knees." They see "peace" marches and protests as vehicles used by bitter anti-Americans to denounce our nation with words of hatred and incitement to riot and violence. I fear these forces bent on the destruction of capitalism and free enterprise in America have taken control of the Democrat party.

The nearly forty years our nation was controlled by liberalism should be judged by the results of those forty years. The following has happened in America during that period:

1. Our education system has gone from the best in the world to so far down we are now among many third world nations. We have a very small percentage of our graduates in the fields of science or math - much less than many nations and especially China.

2. The poor, mostly minorities, have stayed relatively poor in spite of massive, liberal "give them a fish" programs.

3. The federal government has become far more intrusive into all of our lives.

4. The American family structure has been seriously and systematically destroyed. This is particularly apparent in many minorities.

5. Our college campuses have become a seething hotbed of hatred and contempt for religion, capitalism, conservative Republicans and even America.

About this parody: If it brought a laugh or smile of understanding to your face then you comprehend and are a true human being. You are also quite capable of chuckling at the antics of the bunch I mentioned in the first paragraph and their conservative contraparts; at Rush Limbaugh and Al Franken, at Sean Hannity and Alan Combes, and even at the talking heads and Bill O'Reilly and - - - well, you know what I mean.

The only difference I can see between the words of those mentioned and many more like them on right and left is the seething hatred coming from the left. I see no counterpart on the right to, for instance, the words of Democrat chairman Howard Dean who said, and I quote, "I hate Republicans, I hate conservatives and I hate Rush Limbaugh." He might well have added that he hates all Americans who don't agree with him.

Howard Johnson

How Indiana can grow jobs rapidly

Wednesday, September 28, 2005

How Indiana (or any other state) can attract new businesses, increase job growth, and substantially increase state revenues.

It is quite obvious that the current financial problems of California are caused by too many expenditures and too little income. Certainly, that is an oversimplification, but it is a basic truth. It is also true for many other states during the recent economic reversal, but that's not the only reason. Currently, California is experiencing substantial losses of revenue as business leave for overseas or for states where taxes on business are lower. What would happen if there were a state, say Indiana, where there were no taxes on businesses?

State lawmakers would have apoplexy over such a proposal. But look at a few facts:

All state revenue is ultimately paid by individuals in the prices paid for goods and services provided by business. This includes individual owners, stockholders, and all professionals. The state merely uses these businesses to collect tax money from customers or clients and turn it over to the state. This is true for any tax paid by business or corporations.

Many times, tax abatements and other tax incentives are offered to investors or businesses to get them to move to any given locale. If this is so successful for certain instances, why wouldn't it work for all instances. And who ultimately pays more to make up for the lost revenue? Individuals! Why is this done? To provide jobs and economic growth in the community which will ultimately result in a larger tax revenue for the community from increased individual income.

Since, in reality, individuals ultimately pay all taxes, why not move the tax burden directly to the individual and reduce the effort business now makes to collect those taxes and pass them on to the state? Granted, this would be very unpopular unless individuals understood the reality of transferring those taxes from hidden - in the costs of the goods and services purchased - to obvious - taxes paid directly by the individual.

Consider removing all taxes for business - what would be the results:

BENEFITS:

Businesses would have a substantial incentive to stay in Indiana or to move to Indiana from many other states. The changes could be phased in over several years. Start by offering immediate tax free status to any new business that moves to Indiana. The same could be done for a new investment by businesses already here. Follow this by removing all taxes from existing businesses over a two year period.

The added potential for job growth would be a shot in the arm for Hoosier workers. The actual potential would be difficult to assess until it actually happened, but there is no doubt it would be substantial. This is the argument always used for any tax abatement incentive for business. If it works on a small scale, why wouldn't it work as well on a state-wide scale.

Not only would the taxes on business be reduced but savings of the current costs of record keeping and reporting would enable Indiana businesses to pass these savings on to consumers in the form of lower prices. Think that wouldn't happen? Consider the business that now goes outside the state via mail order and the Internet because of competition by businesses with lower costs and taxes.

A Real Answer to the Drug Problem

It will work, but it's sure to upset most of the do-gooders, control freaks and drug sellers. Those with their hands in the illegal drug pot including some politicians will do everything in their power to prevent this from becoming a reality.

Wednesday, September 28, 2005

A Real Solution to the Drug Problem - 1999 - Rev, Jan 2008

In my opinion, our current "War on Drugs" should be renamed "War on Drug Symptoms." It comes to mind that the hard drug problem provides an example of how often we address the symptoms while ignoring the problem. I have a rather simple solution to the drug problem which would be easy to implement and would probably work! For some reason, simple, effective solutions to eliminate the root of a problem are frequently ignored in favor of complex, expensive, symptomatic ones. Sadly, the simple solution I propose would be opposed on moral grounds by the self-righteous, on political grounds by those politicians who benefit from the continuing drug problem and on financial grounds by all those people whose hands are in the drug pot. There are very many in each of these three groups all over the world who don't really want the drug problem to disappear.

The first thing to do is to really admit there is a root to the problem. We have admitted that there is a drug problem, but have been ignoring the root and treating the symptoms only. What is the root cause? Very simply, people who want drugs are the cause. Because drugs are illegal, there are powerful incentives for the young to use them. It's cool. Being illegal makes taking them exciting and very expensive! You'd think we would have learned that lesson from the results of prohibition. As with illegal booze, the high costs of illegal drugs make for high profits and provide wealth to many criminals involved along with the murders, turf wars and political payoffs that goes with it. All that money makes instant millionaires and many dead kids. It's a self feeding epidemic -- a demonic Hydra -- chop off one head and two more appear! Kid is given drugs! Kid wants more, but has no money. Kid steals to get money, then starts dealing to feed his habit and so the supply tree grows with the most vicious and deadly climbing the power ladder with many bodies dropped along the way to the top.

If you think that money doesn't add up to lots of power, look at my January 14, 2008 article about a Mexican drug house and the photos of literally hundreds of millions in cash at - http://hojo2rants.blogspot.com/

In precisely the same way prohibition made us a nation of drinkers and alcoholics, drug prohibitions made us a nation of users and addicts. While I do not propose removing the legal penalties for private drug possession and sales, I do propose a radical solution which will remove the monsterous profits from illegal drug sales and deprive organized crime of it's most lucrative money maker. Remove the profit from the illegal drug trade and the life blood of all associated criminal activity will drain away and the drug cartels will disappear, at least grow far weaker if deprived of American money. The rest of the world, or at least those nations not controlled by drug lords, might then adopt similar policies with similar benefits. All diligence must be taken to keep political hands out of the resulting system; difficult, but certainly not impossible. As long as the only source for these drugs is criminal enterprise the killings and degradation of addiction will continue. All that cash makes it so.

The heart of this very simple and effective solution, free drugs! Once drugs are free, all the associated criminal activity will cease. Without profit in it, there would be no kids out trying to get other kids to use drugs, no corner dealers, no crack houses, no drug lords and no one being killed for drugs. This is one thing our government could do if we could get over our massive ego driven self righteousness and all the anti drug rhetoric from those who don't really want the problem solved. Steps to the solution are as follows:

Part one. Create drug treatment centers as needed throughout the country.

Part two. Staff these centers with medical and support personnel whose financial incentive is based on getting patients off drugs.

Part three. Provide free any drug needed to any person who comes into the treatment center and registers as a user.

Part four. Leave all laws about dealing and possession in place, but remove all laws punishing use.

Part five. Negotiate for the cheapest source of all drugs to be purchased by our government for distribution to the centers.

The details:

Part one. Create drug treatment centers as needed throughout the country. There are already many drug treatment centers in existence. These would have to be expanded, redesigned and joined in a network with the many new centers required for the complete system. This would not happen overnight as the number of people coming to these centers after the required legal changes is a complete unknown. Many new centers should be planned as temporary since the number of addicts could decline quickly and drastically, particularly among the young.

Part two. Staff these centers with medical and support personnel whose financial incentive is based on getting patients off drugs. While there are already qualified people who could staff these centers, additional people would undoubtedly have to be hired and trained. A group and individual bonus program based on the number and quality of the individuals who left the program "drug free" could be an aid to effectiveness. Since the opportunity for mischief by staff members exists as it does in all situations, stringent rules would have to be in place. For instance, any staff member who took any drug for any reason or under any circumstance except the written prescription of a physician would lose their job immediately. Routine drug tests of all staff members would be conducted frequently. Keeping lowlife types off the payroll would require massive effort, but it would be worth the effort. Like many law-enforcement agencies, a previous felony conviction would disqualify any person from working at any drug center.

Part three. Provide needed drugs free to any person who comes into the treatment center and registers as a user. The operative word is "register" and this is how it works. A user must register and enter a treatment program to receive any drug. Drugs will only be provided for use at the center and under supervision. There would be no dirty needles and NO EXCEPTIONS! Hard cases could be housed in temporary housing at the center until they are ready and able to manage on their own. While the costs of this program would be quite high, I'm certain it could not be as high as the current cost of the drug "war" and associated evils. Unfortunately, by the time the politicians and bureaucrats finished creating the required legal and financial structure, costs would doubtless quadruple. Even with them filling their hands and pockets, the costs would still be a small fraction of the costs of the current system.

Part four. Leave all laws about dealing and possession in place, but remove all laws punishing use. Constant efforts would have to be in place to prevent theft and conversion of the drugs into the black market which is certain to evolve from the current drug economy. The drug economy would certainly be decimated by having to compete with a legal source of free drugs and would certainly vanish as a major problem for law enforcement. The "pusher" would become a creature of the past along with drug dealers and drug lords. Gangs fighting over drug "turf" would have nothing to fight over. The gang problem would stay, but their current major source of income would be gone. They would surely be far weaker and less dangerous than they are now.

Part five. Negotiate for the cheapest source of all drugs to be purchased by our government for the centers. Removal of criminals from the drug supply system would drop the costs dramatically. These costs would doubtless represent only a tiny portion of the costs of this Federal Drug Rehabilitation System. The required drug distribution system could be tightly monitored and controlled. Drug purity could be tested and monitored to prevent deaths from poisons or other impurities.

Drawbacks would include those who do not respond to treatment and continue to use drugs. Also, drug OD deaths would no longer remove people from the ranks of drug users. The numbers of those in these last two categories is completely unknown and would not be apparent until the program had been in operation for at least a year or two. There would always be those few who would refuse to come to the treatment centers and might support a small black market. Wealthy users, Hollywood druggy types, hardened criminals and a few other kooks with money would probably support a small criminal drug economy. Without the billions now flowing through the drug economy, the police would be far better equipped to handle them. It would be much like the difference between the problem with bootleggers during prohibition and the problem with bootleggers now.

Who would be against it? All those who profit from the multibillion dollar drug trade including not just those in the trade themselves, but those politicians and law officials who are bought and paid for by the drug traffickers. Also, the ultra moralists from both the right and left, who always turn to legislation to cure moral problems. Many of these people equate standards and requirements of their own culture with morality. They are relatively normal people with very strong feelings about right and wrong according to their own definitions. Lord deliver us from the legislation of the self-righteous!

This capsule description would have to be carefully expanded into an active program before it could be implemented. I'm certain many real and imaginary obstacles would have to be overcome for it to work. It would most certainly overcome drug crime and probably reduce substantially the number of drug dependents. Petty drug crime might persist for a while and marijuana is a special case, but removing the criminality of use and the billions of dollars of profit currently going into the criminal drug economy would go a long way toward complete elimination of the drug problem.

Tuesday, September 27, 2005

On Religion, Law and Education

I am quite pleased to report I have reestablished contact with Linda Williams, an email acquaintance and former SFN member from several years ago. We had an email exchange right after 9-11 which is included in my book, "Images of Pain." I have found our exchanges stimulating and very enjoyable. You can view her fiction blog -- Reality Skimming -- at **http://www.okalrel.org/blog/blogger.html**.

In her blog she states about me, "I find his advocacy of Biblical values as the only proper moral base for government and education to be plain blood-chilling scary." I really don't understand how she received that impression. If it was from some of my writing, I'd like to change it. In any event I shall respond with an attempt at clarification:

Biblical law was certainly the overwhelming contributor to our constitution and to our earliest laws, but certainly not the only one. I firmly believe in the first amendment and have two lectures I give on the subject. It is my belief and I so state in my lectures that the present actions by the courts regarding the "separation of church and state" are precisely the opposite of what that amendment states. I reread my lectures to see if that's where she formed her opinion and have now posted them in their entirety in my blogs. I can understand where she might get that idea and will soon redo both lectures to make my beliefs more clear. Links to current versions of my lectures are at: **http://hjbloglist.blogspot.com**

I firmly believe that for anyone to impose their belief system on others without their consent is evil. This includes atheism. I also believe that by far the most grievous wrongs going on in the world are because of fundamentalist religious beliefs of all types being forced on even those who do not agree. This includes what I call "fundamentalist atheism." How many wars can you think of where religion is not or was not a major factor? I have spoken to religious and non-religious groups and individuals with my lecture on science and religion for many years. Most listeners, including even fundamentalist Christians, whom I thought would be almost violently against my words entered into constructive discussions after the lecture. Several members of some science and engineering groups were not so open minded. Constructive discourse is always in danger from closed minds with firm beliefs.

I would certainly agree that the advocacy of Biblical values as the only proper moral base for government and education would be "plain blood-chilling scary." This if only because there seems to be an infinite variety of interpretation of Biblical values. I think it equally scary to contemplate removal of all Biblical values from government and education.

When I was in high school I sang in the choir. Our high school was about 50-50 Christians and Jews with a few other belief systems in the mix. The choir was about sixty percent Jewish and we were a fairly close knit group - good friends all. We sang in many different places including, schools, churches and synagogues where we performed both secular and religious music. One of our big events of the year was our "Christmas" concert. I never heard a single complaint from any Jewish member of the choir about singing Christmas music. During the concert we frequently sang Jewish and secular songs along with the carols. I remember two soloists, in particular, who sang "Ave Maria" and "I Wonder as I Wander." Both were Jewish. Our male soloist in several Christian pieces was an atheist. I truly cherished that atmosphere of understanding, acceptance of differences, and indeed, peace. To me, that is the epitome of comradeship, love and humanitarianism.

Most likely, that would never happen today. Instead, the ACLU would be stirring up animosity by suing the school to stop any such concert. I certainly don't call that progress. I see current political correctness activity inflaming anger and hatred for any possible differences of belief or purpose between people. I see current efforts at "diversity" promoting divisiveness and intolerance. Hate for anyone "different" has become the aleinating driving force in our country as exemplified by those who promote political, religious, racial, cultural and economical differences for their own purposes.

The modern media has become the stage from which hatred - noisy, quiet, clever, infuriating and even almost subliminal hatred - emanates under the name of news, entertainment and commentary. Indeed, so-called "peace marches" orchestrated by those who hate America have become an escalating vehicle for screaming nefarious hate mantras and subsequent incitement to angry actions. I fear serious mob violence lies ready to erupt just beneath the surface. The overpowering motive of those emissaries of hate are all too plain - power - and not for the people!

No, I certainly do not advocate Biblical values as the only proper moral base for government and education. Nor do I accept atheism, or the exclusion of Biblical values in the same role. I do accept that our Constitution was an extraordinary document with far reaching political effects. I just do not see it being corrupted in meaning to further the goals of a single group to the exclusion of all others. I see great harm in replacing human moral values with "political correctness" as seems to be happening.

Yes, the rights of minorities of any kind need to be protected, but to protect feelings and ask government to impose sanctions on any who might injure another's feelings is a recipe for hatred and violent mob actions. All reasonable concepts, religious or secular, have their place in law and education and should be so considered, but not necessarily adopted. Like language, morality is a constantly evolving, almost nebulous concept that is moved like a straw in the wind by our current beliefs. Even some very basic moral values have been changing, cut loose from religious and even ethical constraints. I get a bit nervous wondering about where all this is headed.

Sunday, September 18, 2005

I Have an Ugly Observation to Make and Share about Award Shows.

Never is there as much display of artificial breasts, lip puffs, male enhancements, vulgarly expensive clothes and jewelry as in the endless parade of award shows constantly being trotted out by the entertainment world. In addition to the five "big" award shows: Oscar, Grammy, Emmy, Tony and Golden Globe, the air waves are pummeled by numerous other "lesser" award shows. These include seven for music, five more for Hollywood, at least nine cable awards shows and countless other even smaller award shows. This is according to an article titled, "Utterly Meaningless Award Shows," by Coury Turczyn in Pop Cult Magazine. Coury goes on to say, "Some of these aforementioned programs are so spirit-crushingly awful that you would think there could not possibly be any worse ones. But leave it to corporate executives to devise award shows that are blatantly void of meaning, yet still believe they're legitimate enterprises that actually matter." And these people expect us to take their social and political activism seriously?

Ordinarily I don't agree much with Chris Rock, but in an Entertainment Weekly interview. Rock said he had rarely watched the Oscars, and called award shows "idiotic." "Come on, it's a fashion show," Rock told the magazine. "What straight black man sits there and watches the Oscars? Show me one. And they don't recognize comedy."

For your information, Chris, very few straight white guys watch either. Thank goodness I have not seen an award show in many years. I have long had my own opinion about these shows which I define as:

Group social masturbation by narcissists permanently frozen at the emotional and intellectual age of fourteen with far too much money and time on their hands and far too little respect for anyone or anything. I take great comfort in the news that these shows are drawing smaller audiences each year indicating that the number of entertainment world "groupies" similarly frozen at age fourteen is actually decreasing. I take even greater comfort when I happen to hear the names of the award winners and realize I don't recognize a single name and haven't the foggiest idea who they are. Of course, nearly all of the names from the entertainment world I do remember are dead!

Tuesday, September 13, 2005

Decimation of the Environment - The Real Culprit

An excerpt from the first part of the Discussion

I am going to talk to you about a very controversial subject. I hope to open your eyes and minds to a very real and present menace facing us all. While we direct increasing efforts to deal with the numerous symptoms of this menace, almost none is directed at the root cause. I may seem a bit crazy to some of you, but to those I address the following words by Angela Monet:

"Those who dance are thought insane by those who can't hear the music."

During 1953, while living in Long Beach California, I took my Professional Engineering qualifications training and examination. As part of our training, my group of six hopeful Professional Engineers were responsible for developing projections of population, food supply, fuel reserves, atmospheric conditions, raw material usage, technological advances and a few other conditions for the next fifty years of our planet's life. I ran across my copy of the resultant predictions while moving my personal belongings in 1981. I was startled at what I reviewed in those papers. Some of our predictions were uncannily accurate while some were far off the mark. The projections of fuel reserves and raw material usage were very accurate. Our population growth projections were a bit under the mark and those for our atmospheric conditions were over for some components and under for others. We grossly underestimated the speed of developments in rocketry, communications and computer technology based on silicon chips. We did not foresee the rapid decimation of the rain forests and the virtual extinction of so many wild animals, particularly the predators. Our projections of food crops were under-estimated while the collapse of the ocean fisheries was completely missed.

I have continued to read widely regarding these subjects from research papers, books and magazines written by scientists from universities all over the world. Most of these works direct answers to the many vital and controversial questions concerning the actions of the human population and their effects on our earth. This accumulation of facts points unerringly toward some disturbing conclusions about the very near future of our planet. These conclusions are extremely controversial and frightening and most people refuse to even listen to them let alone do anything about them. As part of the process of writing a book on this general subject I am accumulating those facts and ideas which cause my concerns. A small portion of these facts, concerns and conclusions are included in this essay. The opinions are my own, the facts I report are as accurate as possible.

THE DISTURBING FACTS:

POPULATION GROWTH: The human population continues to grow explosively. Despite the expressed concerns of a tiny group of people, there is no indication of any change in this growth. Currently, we are adding about 200 million people each year to our already crowded planet. That is about twice the population of Mexico. The only country doing anything about this problem is Communist China and they have been denounced by many for their efforts. In many nations with high birthrates, population pressures cause their excess population to emigrate or die of starvation. As they move to other nations, they bring their high birthrates with them and quickly overwhelm the resources of these other nations. The United States and Mexico are a classic example. Mexico's birthrate, among the highest in the world at 4.6 per woman, is being exported to the US at a dramatic rate with the tide of humanity crossing our southern border both legally and illegally. The Latino population of the US is rapidly surpassing the African population in numbers. At the present rate of immigration and high birth rate, Latinos will be a true majority in the US by the year 2030 when the US population exceeds a half billion! To survive we will become a net importer of food rather than the huge exporter we are today. Where will that food come from?

FOOD PRODUCTION: World human food production peaked during the nineties and is now declining. There are many contributing factors including the following ones:

1 All ocean fisheries, except the Indian Ocean, are declining. In fact, the North Atlantic area fisheries have collapsed and will take many decades, perhaps centuries, to restore. The use of new technologies has enabled commercial fishermen to decimate the most productive fish populations with uncontrolled harvesting. While there is a tentative world accord aimed at this problem, the worst offender nations have not signed the accord and continue to plunder the oceans with ever expanding fishing fleets harvesting far more than the fisheries ability to renew the resource. A byproduct of this gross harvesting of wild fish for food is the destruction of sea floor habitats by heavy bottom nets and the killing of millions of tons of non-food sea creatures. Add to this the destruction of many areas where ocean fish spawn and their young can grow, protected from predation.

2 Agricultural lands are now shrinking in area for the very first time. The clearing of forests while decimating wildlife habitats is now generating less agricultural land than that which goes out of production due to soil depletion and erosion.

3 Uses of chemical fertilizers, insecticides, weed killers and fungicides have reached a point of diminishing returns while polluting our watersheds. Harmful pest populations continue to develop immunities to these poisons much faster than do beneficial populations of insects, birds, plants and other natural pest controls which are higher up the food chain.

4 Slash and burn agriculture, used throughout the third world, is rapidly destroying not only habitats but the usefulness of much land for any purpose whatever! The soil is usually depleted after a few years use to where it will not produce crops. It then takes decades or even centuries for nature to return the soil to productivity again. A byproduct of this denuding of the land is air pollution and massive erosion with silting of the rivers and mud-slides of monstrous proportions. TV news programs increasingly show this happening all over the world. Many of these reports show bare ground, air so polluted by smoke it is dangerously unhealthy with low visibility over many square miles, and rivers so muddy all life is choked from them. Acid rain is but one more negative factor in a sea of bad news.

5 Fresh water supplies are shrinking all over the planet. Underground water reservoirs are being depleted drastically as water is mined much faster than it can be replenished. Rivers, damned for irrigation of marginal land, are frequently drying up before the water reaches their termination in lake or sea. Everywhere, lakes and wetlands are shrinking or drying up completely. Mexico City was once called the Venice of the Americas for its many lakes and canals. The city has so drained its aquifer that the lakes and canals are long gone and the land itself has sunk more than twenty feet. The shifting ground has broken so many of its water mains that leaks now waste up to a third of its water. Subsiding ground is a serious problem in many other parts of the world as well. Americans mining the water of the Ogallala reservoir underlying the great plains must go deeper and deeper as this huge reservoir shrinks. Already it is gone from parts of Texas. In China and India, some underground aquifers have shrunk so much water can no longer be reached and food production suffers. The Yellow River in China slows to a trickle before drying up because of upstream irrigation. This is also true of the once powerful Ganges, Nile and Colorado Rivers which barely reach the sea in dry seasons. Literally thousands of small rivers have completely disappeared. Tule Lake in California's San Joaquin Valley, once more than 100,000 acres is now less than one tenth that size and is little more than a knee-deep mud puddle. Diversion of water for agriculture has destroyed 90 percent of California's wetlands and caused the extinction of up to 39 of 67 native fish species. This trend is echoed world wide and is another way natural habitat is increasingly being destroyed.

These are all valid demonstrations of how finite resources are reacting to uncontrolled human population growth. How can anyone not see what is going on and be terrified.

THE EPIDEMIC THAT MOST MENACES THE EARTH

I received a copy of a commentary on sustainability on our planet by Jay Burney. His comments fit so well with my passion about population, I have included a few quotes in this piece. After the quotes, I will provide a number of responses. I do not disagree with Mr. Burney in the main. I strongly disagree with many of his comments about the causes and what needs to be done to change things. I see his efforts as reactions to symptoms and condemnations of those who see things differently. I see no one addressing the real problem with more than the most casual comments.

January 2002.- "In 1992 a report was issued by the Union of Concerned Scientists called 'World Scientists Warning to Humanity.' It stated bluntly that 'human beings and the natural world are on a collision course.' It says that our current practices and activities are altering the world in ways that make life unsustainable. The report was signed by over 1700 scientists representing 77 countries and by over half of the world's living Nobel laureates.

"A few years before that, in 1987, The World Commission on Environment and Development chaired by Norwegian Prime Minster Gro Haarlem Brundlandt issued a report called 'Our Common Future.' That report provided a definition of sustainability that stands today as a blueprint for thinking and action. It states that 'Sustainable development is development that meets the needs of the present without compromising the ability of future generations to meet their own needs.'

"That is a pretty good definition. It is not that complicated to understand. It is about learning to live within our means. And so we know that we have problems, and that we as humans, need to change how we live on this planet. Of course the devil, as they say, is in the details."

In his commentary there followed many statements including the following phrases: "globalization is defined by powerful economic interests" - "an approach to business and economic growth, that dictates that the bottom line is to make as much profit as possible at all costs." - "growth is promoted as good for business. And we are told, what is good for business is good for society." - "This approach fails to consider transcendent environmental and social costs including clean and renewable resource use, healthcare, hunger, and education." - "This myopic philosophy of business leads to environmental depredation, social unrest, and a widening of the gap between the rich and the poor." - "While it may serve the short-term needs of a few, it fails to even suggest sustainability" - "Businesses that put profit over social responsibility, and that do not recognize the true costs of environmental degradation are looting the natural wealth of the planet. Businesses that don't recognize this are stealing our future. We know that now it is the time to recognize that the real bottom line is the environment." - "Unchecked human population pressures are contributing to environmental, social, and economic problems. The world population in 1960 was 3 billion. Today it has doubled to a little over 6.2 billion. It will double again in less than 50 years.

We don't know how to feed the worlds population today. What will it be like in another generation? Two generations. We can only imagine what will it be like in a hundred years.

We do know that globalization has increased economic activity worldwide, soaring last year to an estimated $30 trillion. We also know that it has increased income inequality and environmental degradation."

I believe his opinions and blanket attacks on business reflect a type of bigotry that would not be tolerated if it were directed toward a racial or ethnic group. Not all businesses behave in such asn irresponsible manner. Business, like all other organized human efforts, including religions, political organizations, governments, social groups, occupations, professions and countless others, is a grouping of people with a common denominator. Many individuals belong to a number of these groups and can be identified as such. No one belongs to less than four including: sex, race or ethnicity, economic level, age and there may be more. As such, all groups of any kind have members ranging through many spectra: intelligent to stupid - belligerent to friendly - leaders to followers - educated to ignorant - power hungry to meek - rich to poor - humanitarian to sociopath, and countless others. This is true for groups as diverse as families, governments, businesses and churches. . . .

Tuesday, September 13, 2005

The Myth of the Separation of Church and State

This is the entire lecture in it's current form

Anytime religion is mentioned within the confines of government today people cry, "Separation of church and state". Many people think this statement appears in the First Amendment of the U.S. Constitution and therefore must be strictly enforced. However, the words: "separation," "church," and "state" do not even appear in the First Amendment. The First Amendment reads: "Congress shall make no law respecting an establishment of religion, or prohibiting the free exercise thereof...." The statement about a wall of separation between church and state was made in a letter on January 1, 1802, by Thomas Jefferson to the Danbury Baptist Association of Connecticut. The congregation heard a widespread rumor that the Congregationalists, another denomination, were to become the national religion. This was very alarming to people who knew about religious persecution in England by the state established church. Jefferson made it clear in his letter to the Danbury Congregation that the separation was to be that government would not establish a national religion or dictate to men how to worship God. Jefferson's letter from which the phrase "separation of church and state" was taken affirmed First Amendment rights. Jefferson wrote:

"I contemplate with solemn reverence that act of the whole American people which declared that their [federal] legislature should 'make no law respecting an establishment of religion, or prohibiting the free exercise thereof,' thus building a wall of separation between church and state." (1)

The reason Jefferson choose the expression "separation of church and state" was because he was addressing a Baptist congregation; a denomination of which he was not a member. Jefferson wanted to remove all fears that the state would make dictates to the church. He was establishing common ground with the Baptists by borrowing the words of Roger Williams, one of the Baptist's own prominent preachers. Williams had said:

"When they have opened a gap in the hedge or wall of separation between the garden of the church and the wilderness of the world, God hath ever broke down the wall itself, removed the candlestick, and made his garden a wilderness, as at this day. And that there fore if He will eer please to restore His garden and paradise again, it must of necessity be walled in peculiarly unto Himself from the world...."(2)

The "wall" was understood as one-directional; its purpose was to protect the church from the state. The world was not to corrupt the church, yet the church was free to teach the people Biblical values.

The American people knew what would happen if the state established a church as in England. Even though it was not recent history to them, they knew that England went so far as forbidding worship in private homes and sponsoring all church activities and keeping people under strict dictates. They were forced to go to the state established church and do things that were contrary to their conscience. No other churches were allowed, and mandatory attendance of the established church was compelled under the Conventicle Act of 1665. Failure to comply would result in imprisonment and torture. The people did not want freedom from religion, but freedom of religion. The only real reason to separate the church from the state would be to instill a new morality and establish a new system of beliefs. Our founding fathers were God-fearing men who understood that for a country to stand it must have a solid foundation; the Bible was the source of this foundation. They believed that God's ways were much higher than Man's ways and held firmly that the Bible was the absolute standard of truth and used the Bible as a source to form our government.

There is no such thing as a pluralistic society. There will always be one dominant view, otherwise it will be in transition from one belief system to another. Therefore, to say Biblical principles should not be allowed in government and school is to either be ignorant of the historic intent of the founding fathers, or blatantly bigoted against Christianity.

Each form of government has a guiding principle: monarchy in which the guiding principle is honor; aristocracy in which the guiding principle is moderation; republican democracy in which the guiding principle is virtue; despotism in which the guiding principle is fear. When people stop upholding good moral conduct, society soon degenerates into a corrupt system where people misuse the authority of government to obtain what they want at the expense of others. The U.S. Constitution is the form of our government, but the power is in the virtue of the people. The virtue desired of the people is shown in the Bible. This is why Biblical morality was taught in public schools until the early 1960's. Government officials were required to declare their belief in God even to be allowed to hold a public office until a case in the U.S. Supreme Court called Torcaso v. Watkins (Oct. 1960). God was seen as the author of natural law and morality. If one did not believe in God one could not operate from a proper moral base. And by not having a foundation from which to work, one would destroy the community. The two primary places where morality is taught are the family and the church. The church was allowed to influence the government in righteousness and justice so that virtue would be upheld. Not allowing the church to influence the state is detrimental to the country and destroys our foundation of righteousness and justice. It is absolutely necessary for the church to influence the state in virtue because without virtue our government will crumble -- the representatives will look after their own good instead of the country's.

Government was never meant to be our master as in a ruthless monarchy or dictatorship. Instead, it was to be our servant. The founding fathers believed that the people have full power to govern themselves and that people chose to give up some of their rights for the general good and the protection of rights. Each person should be self-governed and this is why virtue is so important. Government was meant to serve the people by protecting their liberty and rights, not serve by an enormous amount of social programs. The authors of the Constitution wanted the government to have as little power as possible so that if authority was misused it would not cause as much damage. Yet they wanted government to have enough authority to protect the rights of the people. The world view at the time of the founding of our government was a view held by the Bible: that Man's heart is corrupt and if the opportunity to advance oneself at the expense of another arose, more often than not, Man would choose to do so. They firmly believed this and that's why an enormous effort to set up checks and balances took place. Absolute power corrupts absolutely. They wanted to make certain that no man could take away rights given by God. They also did not set up the government as a true democracy, because they believed, as mentioned earlier, Man tends towards wickedness. Just because the majority wants something does not mean that it should be granted, because the majority could easily err. Government was not to be run by whatever the majority wanted but instead by principle, specifically the principles of the Bible.

The U.S. Constitution was founded on Biblical principles and it was the intention of the authors for this to be a Christian nation. The Constitution had 55 people work on it, of which 52 were evangelical Christians.(3) We can go back in history and look at what the founding fathers wrote to know where they were getting their ideas. This is exactly what two professors did. Donald Lutz and Charles Hyneman reviewed an estimated 15,000 items with explicit political content printed between 1760 and 1805 and from these items they identified 3,154 references to other sources. The source they most often quoted was the Bible, accounting for 34% of all citations. Sixty percent of all quotes came from men who used the Bible to form their conclusions. That means that 94% of all quotes by the founding fathers were based on the Bible. The founding fathers took ideas from the Bible and incorporated them into our government. If it was their intention to separate the state and church they would never have taken principles from the Bible and put them into our government. An example of an idea taken from the Bible and then incorporated into our government is found in Isaiah 33:22 which says, "For the Lord is our judge, the Lord is our lawgiver, the Lord is our king...." The founding fathers took this scripture and made three major branches in our government: judicial, legislative, and executive. As mentioned earlier, the founding fathers strongly believed that Man was by nature corrupt and, therefore, it was necessary to separate the powers of the government. For instance, the President has the power to execute laws but not make them, and Congress has the power to make laws but not to judge the people. The simple principle of checks and balances came from the Bible to protect people from tyranny. The President of the United States is free to influence Congress, although he can not exercise authority over it because they are separated. Since this is true, why should the church not be allowed to influence the state? People have read too much into the phrase "separation of church and state," which is to be a separation of civil authority from ecclesiastical authority, not moral values. Congress has passed laws that it is illegal to murder and steal, which is the legislation of morality. These standards of morality are found in the Bible. Should we remove them from law because the church should be separated from the state?

Our founding fathers who formed the government also formed the educational system of the day. John Witherspoon did not attend the Constitutional Convention although he was President of New Jersey College in 1768 (known as Princeton since 1896) and a signer of the Declaration of Independence. His influence on the Constitution was far ranging in that he taught nine of fifty-five original delegates. He fought firmly for religious freedom and said, "God grant that in America true religion and civil liberty may be inseparable and that unjust attempts to destroy the one may in the issue tend to the support and establishment of both."(4)

In October 1961, the Supreme Court of the United States removed prayer from schools in a case called Engel v. Vitale. The case said that because the U.S. Constitution prohibits any law respecting an establishment of religion, officials of public schools may not compose public prayer even if the prayer is denominationally neutral, and that pupils may choose to remain silent or be excused while the prayer is being recited. For 185 years prayer was allowed in public and the Constitutional Convention itself was opened with prayer. To this day, Congress is opened with a prayer that is written into the Congressional Record. If the founding fathers didn't want prayer in government why did they pray publicly in official meetings as they do to this day?

It is sometimes said that it is permissible to pray in school as long as it is silent. Although, "In Omaha, Nebraska, 10-year old James Gierke was prohibited from reading his Bible silently during free time... the boy was forbidden by his teacher to open his Bible at school and was told doing so was against the law."(4) The U.S. Supreme Court with no precedent in any court history said prayer will be removed from school. Yet the Supreme Court in January, 1844 in a case named

Vidal v. Girard's Executors, a school was to be built in which no ecclesiastic, missionary, or minister of any sect whatsoever was to be allowed to even step on the property of the school. They argued over whether a layman could teach or not, but they agreed that, "...there is an obligation to teach what the Bible alone can teach, viz. a pure system of morality." This has been the precedent throughout 185 years. Although this case is from 1844, it illustrates the point. The prayer in question was not even lengthy or denominationally geared. It was this: "Almighty God, we acknowledge our dependence upon Thee, and we beg Thy blessings upon us, our parents, our teachers and our Country." What price have we paid by removing this simple acknowledgment of God's protecting hand in our lives? Birth rates for unwed girls from 15-19; sexually transmitted diseases among 10-14 year olds; pre-marital sex increased; violent crime; adolescent homicide and suicide have all gone up considerably from 1961 to the 1990's -- even after taking into account population growth. The Bible, before 1961, was used extensively in curriculum. After the Bible was removed, scholastic aptitude test scores dropped considerably.

There is no such thing as a pluralistic society; there will always be one dominant view. Someone's morality is going to be taught -- but whose? Secular Humanism (Atheism) is a religion that teaches that through Man's ability we will reach universal peace and unity and make heaven on earth. They promote a way of life that systematically excludes God and all religion in the traditional sense. That Man is the highest point to which nature has evolved, and he can rely on only himself and that the universe was not created, but instead is self-existing. They believe that Man has the potential to be good in and of himself. All of this of course is in direct conflict with not only the teachings of the Bible but even the lessons of history. In June 1961 in a case called Torcaso v. Watkins, the U.S. Supreme Court stated: "Among religions in this country which do not teach what would generally be considered a belief in the existence of God are Buddhism, Taoism, Ethical Culture, Secular Humanism (Atheism) and others." The Supreme Court declared Secular Humanism to be a religion. The American Humanist Association certifies counselors who enjoy the same legal status as ordained ministers. Since the Supreme Court has said that Secular Humanism is a religion, why is it being allowed to be taught in schools? The removal of public prayer, indeed of any religious expression of those who wish to participate is, in effect, establishing atheism as the state religion of our nation while excluding all others and in particular, Christianity. This is exactly what our founding fathers tried to prevent with the First Amendment.

December, 2003, the ACLU threatened to sue a high school in Ohio if they performed Handel's Messiah in their annual Christmas concert. They sighted the ruling of the so-called separation of church and state in our Constitution. The choir cancelled the concert, an annual event for many years. This, like countless other similar actions by the ACLU and supported by ignorant or prejudiced judges and attorneys, is one more step in the promotion of Secular Humanism or Atheism by the state. This is the religion promoted by the ACLU and it has become the government sponsored religion of America in absolute defiance of the First Amendment. This has become a direct attack on Christians, Christianity and freedom of religous expression of any kind by our government. Unless something is done to stop and reverse this unconstitutional (and actually illegal) action, those who would destroy Christianity for their own purpose will succeed in perverting the First Amendment into doing precisely what it was written to prevent. The "Big Lie" is currently winning.

An interesting concept. Students in a school in Texas recently found a way to legally have prayer in their school. During an assembly, a student stepped to the lectern and said the following: "I will now read from the Congressional Record of the United States," whereupon, he proceeded to read the opening prayer from a recent session of Congress. There was no way he could be prevented from reading from the Congressional Record. The ACLU is steamed about it, but so far hasn't found a way to stop it.

1. Thomas Jefferson, Jefferson Writings, Merrill D. Peterson, ed. (NY: Literary Classics of the United States, Inc., 1984), p. 510, January 1, 1802.

2. John Eidsmoe, Christianity and the Constitution (MI: Baker Book House, 1987), p. 243.

3. M.E. Bradford, A Worthy Company: Brief Lives of the Framers of the United States Constitution (Marlborough, N.H.: Plymouth Rock Foundation, 1982), p. 4-5.

4. John Witherspoon, "Sermon on the Dominion of Providence over the Passions of Men" May 17, 1776; quoted and Cited by Collins, President Witherspoon, I:197-98.

A Hoax That Could Scare People

Redone with more accurate information it could be the basis for a new Sci-Fi novel or story.

PLANET-DISSOLVING DUST CLOUD IS HEADED TOWARD EARTH! is the title of an interesting but fictitious article.

By its obvious inaccuracies the article itself lets us know it's a hoax. The statement, "To avoid widespread panic, NASA has declined to make the alarming discovery public. But Dr. Sherwinski's contacts at the agency's Chandra X-ray Observatory leaked to him striking images of the newly discovered chaos cloud obliterating a large asteroid."

All "asteroids" are within our solar system. There are no "asteroids" as far as ten light years away from us. Besides, we have no instrument capable of resolving any object as small as an asteroid at that distance.

Following are several essays, emails, or commentary that don't seem to belong in either of the other book sections. They are added here and will be included in the table of contents.

Saturday, January 21, 2006

Greetings from Sunny (today) California!

It's Friday evening, January 20th and Deb should be getting home any minute now. I'm all settled in by now, know my way around town a bit and have started a few new adventures. Jake and Charlie have become good friends after a rather shaky start. They now chase each other around the yard in play, taking turns chasing each other. I take them on walks together with few problems other than an occasional twisted set of leashes.

I've spent today going through photos from many years. Many of them really took me back. I plan on retouching a number of them including several of my father when he was a boy and then a young man. I also ran across a number of Dolores as a baby, Barb as a young woman and many dear family photos. Naturally, there were a few tears shed. I hope to place several of these on this blog to share with you. I especially want to share one of our wedding photos because that's the Barbara I always remember. It's also the Barbara that my heart always saw when I looked at her those last months. She always was and always will be a beautiful little lady to me.

Well, Deb is home and I'll have to take a dinner break. As soon as I get the photos on the blog I will send out an announcement.

So much for HoJo's current chapter of, "Travels with Charlie" until the next chapter is written. I wish you all well.

Tuesday, January 24, 2006

We take a trip to Murphys, California

Sunday the 22nd, Deb and I went for a drive into the mountains about sixty miles east of Stockton to the little town of Murphys. It's a former gold mining town with a very checkered past and an interesting present. The main street is now an eclectic collection of shops, wine tasting cubby holes and unique little restaurants with much local flavor. We had a wonderful time walking down main street and stopping into one of the little wine tasting rooms sprinkled about in the town. On our way home we drove down from the mountains into one of the most spectacular bright orange and red sunset over the coastal range I have ever seen. Yes, his palette was definitely at work.

Deb and I ate lunch in one of the interesting little restaurant/delis in Murphys.

Sunday, February 12, 2006

Deb's Birthday

Today is February twelfth, my daughter Deb's birthday. It's a beautiful, sunny day and will probably be in the mid seventies by late afternoon. It's been like this all week making walking the dogs and working outside a really pleasant experience. I've become active in a little Methodist Church about ten minutes away where the atmosphere is just like home and the people are open and friendly. I'm singing in the choir, playing bells in the bell choir, playing Pinochle, helping with Wednesday night dinners and tomorrow, I attend my first rehearsal with their gospel/barbershop singers. I'm trying to give to the church as much as of myself as I can. I have received so very much from the church–the church community everywhere–that I wish I could do more.

This evening, Deb and I will go to see a modern dance group perform at the Bob Hope theater downtown Stockton. A play, and now a dance performance–whew! It's almost more culture than I can handle, but I'll manage it somehow.

Buford is all tucked away at a nearby storage facility 'til needed for whatever. On my out the fiberglass roof blew out about twelve feet along the left side. The manufacturer admitted they had problems with this particular roof and have a kit available to fix it. My unit is too old for them to provide any help with the replacement so I am going to do the work myself and save about a thousand bucks. I'm trying to get them to provide me with two kits free, one for each side as I was warned the other side would probably go too at any time. The kits cost nearly $200 each so I'm hoping Winnebago will help out at least. Of course, how can I apply any pressure for a unit that's eight years old? They did say the repair kits were very effective and relatively easy to install. It's just that they take quite a few hours labor and that's what runs up the cost of having the work done. Glad I have the tools to do the job with me–thanks to Bob Fee.

I must share the following letter I wrote for Deb's birthday. I call it, "Incredible Deb."

Yes indeed, Deb, you are incredible! I remember precisely where and where we met. It was on an elevator in West Suburban Hospital in Oak Park, Illinois in the early evening of February 12, 1951. You were the most beautiful newborn I had ever seen and your mother, holding you gently, was equally beautiful. Despite a bruised forehead from a difficult delivery, you were drop-dead gorgeous. Of course, I have never seen you as anything but beautiful from that first day to this. From that day the memories began to build.

Some were memories of pain: striking your head against the edge of a door when you were but a few months old. I was terrified I might have injured you seriously, but you recovered with no ill effects. In our house in Long Beach you kept hurting yourself by running your head into the edge of our kitchen table until I padded the entire edge of the table.

I remember a delightful little girl playing with her baby brother, then with a new sister, then with another new sister. I remember identical blue dresses for all my girls including your mother. I remember trips to Sequoia and Yosemite, a long trip home in our white Simca with a little brother. Stops at Tucson and in Monument valley during that trip. I remember a Christmas card picture with a little brother, taken in the old house on Eddy road, a little girl reciting "Madelaine" and "Krispins Krispian, the little dog who belonged to himself." on the couch in Lyndhurst, a first day at school in Mayfield Heights, and many other precious moments as the years passed so very quickly.

Suddenly I saw a beautiful young lady walk down the stairs in her first high heels in our house on Lynn Park. My little girl had metamorphosed over night into a woman, right before my eyes. Then there were summers at the lake, waterskiing, boat riding, even some fishing. Each day a wonderful joy seeing you, your brother and sisters, your cousins and friends so very joy filled and celebrating life and youth. Then it was studies and dances and snowball fights and learning to drive, laughter and a few tears. Far too soon it was off to college and my little girl, now a woman, had left the nest to make her own life. I was so very proud.

Then there was hygiene school, marriage and two wonderful sons. A proud father became also a proud grandfather. During this time my own life began to fall apart as I struggled with a failing marriage and violent internal turmoil. Had it not been for you, your brother, your sisters and the rest of our extended and quite wonderful family I would not have made it through. Even with all that support I made many mistakes costly and damaging to others and myself. Through all this personal hell, you stood strongly by my side, never wavering.

Then, I hurt for you as your own marriage fell apart. It is truly devastating to see one you love go through painful times and be unable to help. But love definitely makes such transitions easier and there was much love surrounding you. I was so happy for you when an old love came back into your life even as I myself was finding love once more. The happy days we shared culminated in our six-month visit in Visalia–a wonderful time of pain and joy where hidden rumblings of future disaster haunted both of us. These days were some of the happiest Barb and I shared and you were a big part of that happiness. Remember the laughing jag?

Now we are both recovering from terrible losses, different, but extremely hurtful. It is a treasure to me to be here with you at this time. I know it helps my healing process and I think yours as well. Your cheery "good morning" each day lifts my spirits no matter how low they have gone. We share laughter, memories, tears, dreams and sorrows in an almost magical way. You are a shining beacon of love and joy for me and I thank God for you, my incredible Deb!

Love and Happy Birthday! Dad.

Thursday, February 23, 2006

Washington's Birthday news!

It's a sunny day here in California–cool (60 degrees) and bright, but the sun warms your body when you are outside. I have to run up to Sacramento (about forty miles) today and will take Charlie with me. He so enjoys riding and is great company for me.

I had a rather "teary" Monday. While going through the boxes of papers and stuff I brought here to sort and organize, I ran across a little eight-page card Barbara gave me at least ten or twelve years ago. Reading those sentiments of love and seeing her ending comment, "No more... Barbara" I fell apart. I must have sobbed for thirty minutes or more immediately after reading the card and several more times before Deb came home. The card was bent and creased from being carried in my pocket for several years. When I shared it with Deb I once more broke down. Deb immediately put her arms around me and cried with me for several moments. We then ran through a litany of loved ones we had lost in recent years: Barb of course, Deb's mother (my first love), my mother, my sister, my father, her mother's parents who were also very dear to me. Then we talked about the wonderful memories—the words and snapshots of our lives with them. It was quite an emotional moment for us both. I thank God I have been so blessed with deeply caring children, other relatives and very dear friends. I'm sure you all will help me through other moments like these as they are bound to come.

Deb asked me about the seemingly strange signature line, "No more..." I explained it was a very special message, inexplicable without an interpretation from Barb or me. About the time we were married we started remarking to each other, "No more loneliness." or "No more longing." or "No more empty nights." We would vie with each other to come up with differing "No mores" to express our love. It was an almost secret language where finally, the words, "No more..." alone was sufficient to convey our message of love. Eventually, I took the booklet out of my pocket as I wanted to save it from being destroyed. I hadn't seen it for years until yesterday when I found it tucked away among some other cards we had exchanged and saved. That was just one of the memories of "magic" I will treasure as long as I live. No one or no event can erase or lessen those magic memory moments.

About the same time, a very dear friend emailed me the following quote saying it described my Barbara. I am sharing it with all of you because it says so much of who Barbara was. The quote was from Irma Bombeck:

"When I stand before God at the end of my life, I hope that I will not have a single bit of talent left, and can say, 'I used everything you gave me.'"

Sunday, Deb and I went to San Francisco to visit my niece, Marcia so I skipped church. It was a wonderful, sunny day even in Frisco–cool, but bright, clear and sunny. Marcia's sister, Leslie, had called Friday and told us she was leaving Sunday evening and wanted to get together before she left. We arrived at Marcia and Michael's about noon and had a nice visit with her. Marcia had surgery to remove a large, soft-tissue tumor from the inside of her right thigh on February ninth. She gets tired easily so we were careful not to over stay. She was her usual bright, cheery, upbeat self and doesn't look the worse for her ordeal.

After our visit, Deb, Leslie and I drove down to the Presidio and took a long walk with Charlie along the shore (a couple miles each way is my guess) from Crissy Field to Fort Point right under the Golden Gate bridge. Walking back, the lowering sun painted the city a bright almost white in front of us. When I get the photos from Deb's camera I'll enter them in this blog for all to see. After that we took the obligatory tourist trip down Lombard Street before heading back to Marcia's. There were so many people driving down Lombard Street it took us nearly an hour to get there.

We headed back for another short visit with Marcia before leaving for Stockton about seven. Leslie was heading for the airport and home and planned to meet with my sister and brither-in-law, Bobby and Bob Grimm whose flight was scheduled to arrive before her's took off. The senior Grimms were arriving from Buffalo, NY after Deb and I left. Whether here or in Frisco we will definitely be seeing them.

Well, it's about time for me to take Jake and Charlie for our daily walk so I'll leave you with this thought:

Youth is not a time of life, it is a state of mind, a product of the imagination, a vigor of the emotions, a predominance of courage over timidity, an appetite for adventure.

Nobody grows old by living a number of years. People grow old when they desert their ideas and ideals. Years wrinkle the skin and slow the steps, but to give up enthusiasm wrinkles and slows the soul.

Worry, self-doubt, fear, anxiety---these are the culprits that bow the head and break the spirit.

Whether seventeen or seventy, there exists in the heart of every person who loves life the thrill of a new challenge, the insatiable appetite for for what is coming next. You are as young as your faith and as old as your doubts.

So long as your heart receives from your head messages that reflect beauty, courage, joy, excitement and love, you are young. When your thinking becomes cloudy with pessimism and prevents you from taking risks, then you are old. For all her physical problems and challenges, my Barbara was always young. How can I do her memory any better than to stay always young even as she.

Thursday, March 30, 2006

A Shay Day - A True Story

Two Choices

What would you do? You make the choice! Don't look for a punch line; There isn't one! Read it anyway. My question to all of you is: Would you have made the same choice?

At a fund raising dinner for a school that serves learning disabled children, the father of one of the students delivered a speech that would never be forgotten by all who attended. After extolling the school and its dedicated staff, he offered a question:

"When not interfered with by outside influences, everything nature does is done with perfection. Yet my son, Shay, cannot learn things as other children do. He cannot understand things as other children do. Where is the natural order of things in my son?"

The audience was stilled by the query.

The father continued. "I believe, that when a child like Shay, physically and mentally handicapped comes into the world, an opportunity to realize true human nature presents itself, and it comes, in the way other people treat that child."Then he told the following story:

Shay and his father had walked past a park where some boys Shay knew were playing baseball. Shay asked, "Do you think they'll let me play?" Shay's father knew that most of the boys would not want someone like Shay on their team, but the father also understood that if his son were allowed to play, it would give him a much-needed sense of belonging and some confidence to be accepted by others in spite of his handicaps.

Shay's father approached one of the boys on the field and asked if Shay could play, not expecting much. The boy looked around for guidance and said, "We're losing by six runs and the game is in the eighth inning. I guess he can be on our team and we'll try to put him in to bat in the ninth inning."

Shay struggled over to the team's bench put on a team shirt with a broad smile and his Father had a small tear in his eye and warmth in his heart. The boys saw the father's joy at his son being accepted. In the bottom of the eighth inning, Shay's team scored a few runs but was still behind by three. In the top of the ninth inning, Shay put on a glove and played in the right field. Even though no hits came his way, he was obviously ecstatic just to be in the game and on the field, grinning from ear to ear as his father waved to him from the stands. In the bottom of the ninth inning, Shay's team scored again. Now, with two outs and the bases loaded, the potential winning run was on base and Shay was scheduled to be next at bat.

At this juncture, do they let Shay bat and give away their chance to win the game? Surprisingly, Shay was given the bat. Everyone knew that a hit was all but impossible 'cause Shay didn't even know how to hold the bat properly, much less connect with the ball.

However, as Shay stepped up to the plate, the pitcher, recognizing the other team putting winning aside for this moment in Shay's life, moved in a few steps to lob the ball in softly so Shay could at least be able to make contact. The first pitch came and Shay swung clumsily and missed. The pitcher again took a few steps forward to toss the ball softly towards Shay. As the pitch came in, Shay swung at the ball and hit a slow ground ball right back to the pitcher.

The game would now be over, but the pitcher picked up the soft grounder and could have easily thrown the ball to the first baseman. Shay would have been out and that would have been the end of the game.

Instead, the pitcher threw the ball right over the head of the first baseman, out of reach of all team mates. Everyone from the stands and both teams started yelling, "Shay, run to first! Run to first!" Never in his life had Shay ever ran that far but made it to first base. He scampered down the baseline, wide-eyed and startled.

Everyone yelled, "Run to second, run to second!"

Catching his breath, Shay awkwardly ran towards second, gleaming and struggling to make it to second base. By the time Shay rounded towards second base, the right fielder had the ball, the smallest guy on their team, who had a chance to be the hero for his team for the first time. He could have thrown the ball to the second-baseman for the tag, but he understood the pitcher's intentions and he too intentionally threw the ball high and far over the third-baseman's head. Shay ran toward third base deliriously as the runners ahead of him circled the bases toward home.

All were screaming, "Shay, Shay, Shay, all the Way Shay"

Shay reached third base, the opposing shortstop ran to help him and turned him in the direction of third base, and shouted, "Run to third! Shay, run to third" As Shay rounded third, the boys from both teams and those watching were on their feet were screaming, "Shay, run home! Shay ran to home, stepped on the plate, and was cheered as the hero who hit the "grand slam" and won the game for his team.

That day, said the father softly with tears now rolling down his face, the boys from both teams helped bring a piece of true love and humanity into this world.

Shay didn't make it to another summer and died that winter, having never forgotten being the hero and making his Father so happy and coming home and seeing his Mother tearfully embrace her little hero of the day!

AND, NOW A LITTLE FOOTNOTE TO THIS STORY: We all send thousands of jokes through the e-mail without a second thought, but when it comes to sending messages about life choices, people think twice about sharing. The crude, vulgar, and often obscene pass freely through cyberspace, but public discussion about decency is too often suppressed in our schools and workplaces.

If you're thinking about forwarding this message, chances are that you're probably sorting out the people on your address list that aren't the "appropriate" ones to receive this type of message. Well, the person who sent you this believes that we all can make a difference. We all have thousands of opportunities every single day to help realize the "natural order of things." So many seemingly trivial interactions between two people present us with a choice: Do we pass along a little spark of love and humanity or do we pass up that opportunity to brighten the day of those with us the least able, and leave the world a little bit colder in the process?

A wise man once said every society is judged by how it treats it's least fortunate amongst them.

You now have two choices:

1. Ignore the message

2. Forward this link to your email list - **http://www.ashayday.blogspot.com**

May your day, be a Shay Day, sunny today tomorrow & always!

Monday, April 10, 2006

April 10th report

Greetings all:

I may not be able to head back home as soon as I planned since I have to do some repairs to Buford's roof before I can leave. On my way out here I drove through some sixty mile per hour winds that blew out the left side of my roof. I didn't know it until almost two weeks after I arrived here when I discovered water leaking in over the driver's seat. When I got a ladder and took a look I discovered more than half of the curved section of the roof was missing–about eight inches wide by twenty feet long. I patched it up to keep the water out and ordered a repair kit ($600.00 worth) to fix it. When I finally found a Winnebago repair shop abut fifty miles north of us I took it in for an estimate. Would you believe $4,000.00 to repair the roof and clean up the water stains on the inside? My insurance will cover only a part of the damage repairs so I am doing the work myself. I have all the necessary tools with me. It's not a difficult job, just a long tedious process climbing around on Buford's roof. I figured about four full days and so far it has taken only two. I have been seriously delayed and will only be able to finish if it ever stops raining like it has been the last eight days in a row!

When I do head back, I'll run I-80 all the way to Elkhart, just thirty miles from home. I made it out here in three days so should be able to do the reverse in the same time period. That is if it ever stops snowing on the pass to Reno. I-80 has been blocked with snow for several hours numerous times in the last few weeks and they won't even let you drive it without chains most of the time. I might as well wait for an open day as it adds at least two days and more than 900 miles to go the southern route.

The repairs to Buford are almost finished. All I have yet to do is some caulking and cleanup on the inside. Of course, I can't finish the caulking until we have some dry hours and we are supposed to have showers today and the next five days in a row. My only hope of getting away soon is enough dry hours (I need at least three) between showers so Buford's roof can dry off and I can get the caulking complete. The caulking would have to set before the next rain. Then I will require at least a full day of packing, maybe more, before I can leave. The other problem is that mountain pass in the high Sierras on I-80. Even when it is open, chains are often required and chains for Buford are quite expensive and difficult to install. I was very lucky on my way here as all roads were clear and dry. It would be incredible luck if the same were true on my way home.

I had a really painful day yesterday–emotionally painful. In the church here I have been attending, we sang the cantata we have been practicing for many weeks and it went very well. As we started walking down the aisle with the opening section I suddenly remembered how much Barbara loved Palm Sunday. I thought of how she would have so enjoyed the cantata. I recalled so many special services she arranged for Palm Sunday. As a result, tears ran down my cheeks through most of the service. It wasn't easy for me to sing, but I managed. I also remembered an incident of about a week ago that should be of interest.

It was a very unusual happening. I went to sleep on the couch while watching TV. Of course I've never done that before. Any way, I awoke about 1:00am and turned off the TV. As I leaned back on the couch and prepared to head to the bedroom I was suddenly aware of a very faint fragrance. At first it was familiar, but I couldn't quite recognize it. Over the next few minutes it steadily grew stronger as I moved about sniffing many nearby items trying to find the source. All at once I recognized it, Windsong, the fragrance your mom always wore from when we first met. By this time I was making a serious effort to find the source; pillows, the couch, the floor, my clothes, nothing seemed to be the source. The fragrance was with me wherever I turned or moved. I checked the clock and realized I had been awake for at least fifteen minutes with that fragrance slowly intensifying until it was almost overpowering.

I sensed nothing but that fragrance, no tension, no person, no entity of any kind. I decided it had to be Barbara so I called out her name. Instantly the fragrance was gone. It didn't fade away it went from powerful and intense to absolutely and totally gone in an instant. It never returned. I am completely baffled and can't imagine where it came from and why it vanished so quickly. I refuse even to speculate. One thing I do know. I was not dreaming! That fragrance may have been completely in my head, but I was fully awake with it for at least fifteen minutes. That was an experience the likes of which I have never known. It was not frightening or worrisome, but it certainly did pique my curiosity. It also did make me think, but not speculate about a lot of things. Yesterday, I couldn't get it out of my mind.

I can hardly believe it! As I look out the window I see blue sky and sunshine! It's eight in the morning and if the weather holds I'll finish Buford's repairs today and be ready to pack.

Blessings to you all

Sunday, April 23, 2006

Travels with Charlie, California and back

letter of 1/23/07 continuation

I know, I write a lot and some of what I write (mostly re: politics) angers and upsets some of you. Well, some of what you express can anger and upset me, but mostly it's your gross misunderstanding of my meaning and intent. I find that anger is not nearly as strong as it used to be. No, I am not changing under pressure. In fact, if you know me at all, pressure applied will meet an equal or greater resistance to that pressure. (One of HoJo's laws) Maybe it's because my writing gives me an outlet for those energies as I tell the world what to do and how to go about it even if no one listens or reads. I am trying to be less strident in my words, but those know-it-all, self serving politicos (from all points of the political compass) are becoming more and more strident. Maybe I'm just becoming more mellow in my old age. Maybe my years with Barb toned me down a bit. She was an Irish liberal Democrat and we had great political discussions - emotional, but not angry. I don't know how we managed that.

Now, guess what? I'm involved with another Irish liberal Democrat, Daphne. How could I be so lucky? I wonder, could the Irish be genetically Democrats? So far no political sparks - a few little rubs here and there, but nothing remotely angry or confrontational. She has requested, "Be a bit less strident in your wording, just to lessen the possible anger of readers." She may be right so I am trying - not to change my positions - just to soften my rhetoric. I'm certain to ramble about quite a bit in this writing which is opinions, not news so feel free to buzz off at any time.

This letter ran amok so I decided to move the rest of it to my "HoJo's Rants" blog where it more properly belongs. In keeping with Daphne's wishes I have endeavored to keep it more friendly and less "strident." Click on www.hojo2rants.blogspot.com to continue.

Ho

Church doings and a special commitment:

Last week I was asked to take the place of our regular lay delegate at the annual meeting of the Northern Indiana Conference of the Methodist church. I went to this conference, held at Purdue, for six straight years with Barb when she was an active pastor. One of the reasons I elected to go was the memorial service they always held for pastors who have died since the last conference. I sat near the back of the music hall as I was quite sure I would have some teary moments during the service. I was devastated when I saw the list for the memorial and Barb wasn't on it. Somebody slipped up big time. I was so upset I walked out before communion service and walked back to my room. I was terribly upset and was still hardly over it by the end of the day. I didn't even attend the dinner that evening.

By the next day I was beginning to feel badly because of how I reacted. Maybe my little guardian angel was working on me. It would be just like her to be pointing out my resentment was not a very Christian thing to do. When a well thought out plan for renovation of Epworth forest facilities was proposed with a 16 million dollar price tag, I made a fateful decision and commitment. I have committed myself to raising one hundred thousand dollars within the three year period until the money is needed for and as a memorial to Barbara. All I want is an acknowledgment plaque with Barbara's name placed in a prominent place in the new facility. I'll furnish the plaque. It is something I can do in memory of my dear Barbara, and I will do it. I hope to walk onto the stage at annual conference in two or three years and present a check to the conference. Now I have a definite purpose. All I have to do is figure out just how to do it.

Changes here at home:

It's Saturday, June tenth and I am well into tackling this place and repairing and restoring four years of increasing neglect. I have made a check list (to which I add things daily) of things to do. I have done a great deal in the yard as that is one of the most neglected parts. I'm replacing Barb's flower beds with plants and shrubs that do not require the amount of work her flowers did. I will still have some beds of Impatiens, but they do not require much work. Many of her favorite perennials have died and I'm looking for easy-to-maintain replacements. For the first time her peonies bloomed profusely in beautiful maroon. Her french lilac and flowering almond were also so very spectacular this year. Oh how I wish she could have seen them. I've weeded part of the gardens, but much more attention is needed. Sadly, her flox, among her favorites, didn't make it through the winter for the first time since she planted them.

I've a whole bunch of RV trailers to get rid of on ebay and a garage full of yard sale items I plan to start moving this next week end. I also hope to rebuild the Viking deck-boat. Add to that all of Barbara's things I need to find homes for and I have a real challenge. I've photographed all of her jewelry and will do the same with the rest of her clothes, furnishings, furniture, knickknacks and memorabilia. It is definitely an awesome undertaking. Wish me luck!

Monday, June 12, 2006

Catching up and some future plans

Dear family:

A whole lot of water has gone under the bridge, and I mean a lot since I last added to this special family and friends blog.

First, I shall bring you up to date with my travels. It was late April when Charlie and I finally left Stockton for home in Buford. We drove uneventfully across the country on I-80 after pausing in Donner Pass to take pictures of Buford parked beside a wall of snow at least twenty feet high. After a stop, I drove on to the Detroit area for a visit with my girls. After our visit, I left Charlie with Mindy, Joe, Joseph and Chantel (thanks guys) for the next three weeks when I would be traveling.

May first I flew from Chicago to the Hawai'ian island of Maui where I spent a week doing many of the touristy things: boats, sights, beaches etc. Drove the road to Hana - spectacular! Then drove along the coast completely around West Maui - it's at least as spectacular as the road to Hana, maybe even more so, but not as famous. Drove to the top of Haleakala crater, but it was cold, cloudy and rainy. Could hardly see a thing. I even did a bit of promotion of "Blue Shift," dropping copies off to both Borders stores on Maui.

May eighth I flew to Kailua on the Kona Coast (west side) of the Big Island (Hawai'i). I had been invited to Hilo on the east side of the island to visit the Gemini telescope headquarters by Peter Michaud, their PR guy. The Gemini telescope was a featured part of "BlueShift" and I had shipped an entire box of books from California so they could be given to Gemini people. I was planning to sign them while there, but sadly, the US Postal Service screwed up and as far as I know, they have not yet arrived.

While on the Big Island, I visited many of the places I had been with Barbara almost fifteen years earlier. There were lots of memories and not a few tears. I also visited a macadamia nut grove and factory where they are harvested, packaged and shipped. (I have a great photo of Barb and I at the entrance to that building.) While there, I picked up about five pounds of nuts which I have shared with friends and am still enjoying. Boy are they ever great!

For the first time, I visited Greenwell Farms, a popular coffee plantation, and took a tour of the plantation. Our group saw several kinds of coffee trees (really just big bushes) and the plant where the fruits are washed and peeled down to the beans, the beans are dried out in the sun, and then are roasted and packaged. Their famous Kona coffee is shipped all over the world and especially to Europe. Starbucks in the US is one of their biggest customers. I bought twenty-one pounds and had it shipped home. That's a lot for a non-coffee drinker. Kona coffee is so good it made a coffee drinker out of me. At least of Kona coffee.

As it worked out, my visit to Gemini was put off 'til the very last day since Peter Michaud had been on vacation the week before and had a lot of catching up to do. It was quite a thrill for me to be given a VIP tour of the facility and watch computers display the work that had been done on the telescopes several nights before. I was amazed at how close the actual operations center was to my description of it in "Blue Shift." Especially so considering I had written that part of the story before they broke ground for the building. They gave me a very special T shirt and even invited me to come back and give a talk about how I chose Gemini to be the telescope in "Blue Shift." That was quite an honor so I hope to go back sometime next winter, maybe for a longer stay.

I also stopped to see my the last dental office I designed. It was for Dr. Brian Ito there in Hilo. Incredibly, it was just half a mile down the road from Gemini. Brian took me through the office and told me everything was very much as it had been for the sixteen years since it was built. He really like his facility and the Hickory cabinets I had designed and built for him. They still looked like new. I promised to contact him before my next trip out there as he wanted to take me to dinner and a visit.

May sixteenth I arrived back home faced with the monumental task of going through the house and clearing up so many problems left from four years of neglecting all but the most necessary maintenance and repairs. I started on the yard which needed the most work and the boats which hadn't been in the water for several years.

The week before Memorial Day I went to Florida to visit a friend who lives in St Augustine. I may end up wintering there if things work out. I enjoyed a big family gathering there on the weekend before heading for home on Sunday.

Monday our quartet, The Willows, sang at the Leesburg Memorial day services at the cemetery after the annual parade. It was something our quartet has done for many years. It was a very teary day for me for several reasons. Barbara sang with us the first few times we were in the service and May twenty-ninth is our anniversary, thirteenth this year. One more emotional milestone. We sang "I'm Proud to be an American," a very inspirational and patriotic song.

CAUTION! This paragraph is not politically correct! The parade, the memorial service and our song reminded me I am still very proud to be an American. This in spite of all the anti-American rhetoric from the main-stream media and the political left with their messages of hate created to attempt to divide us and degrade our image in the world. This effort is all because of their insatiable appetite for money and power. That small town parade and Memorial service is what America is to me. Fly over country is where the real Americans are who are willing to work for freedom for all people. The elitists of the left look down their noses at these Americans and their "misguided attitudes." With their "holy" dogma and corruption of our Constitution, they cannot understand the heart and soul of the increasing numbers of real Americans who are starting to take our nation back for real freedom and prosperity. They can't stand it that our economy is doing so well and that we are fighting for real freedom. They are doing everything in their power to scuttle and destroy our economy and our efforts for freedom no matter how damaging those efforts are to the nation. They've lost on the economy so their only hope to regain power is for us to fail in Afghanistan and Iraq. Should our efforts there result in successful democratic governments, they will lose a great deal of political capital and be out of power for a long time to come. For this reason they have become defacto supporters of our enemies, working and hoping for our defeat and humiliation in the middle east. I call that treason!

I've never figured it out - are those politicians from the liberal left pawns of the leftist main-stream media, or are the main stream media simply the voices of the liberal left? Maybe they are all merely the property of George Soros. Now, down from my soap box.

Future plans:

I plan to drive my Mercury with Barb's power wheel chair, mounted carrier and accessories to Dallas as a gift to my niece, Pam, who is partially paralyzed by a stroke. They have no means of doing what this rig will enable them to do and this will make life much easier for them. As it is, she can only go where Elbert takes her in her regular wheel chair and they would have no way to transport a power chair even if they could afford one. I've put more than $10,000 into that rig and probably couldn't get more than a couple of thousand if I sold it if that much. I hope to visit for a day or two with Pam and Elbert and also my son, Mike who lives nearby.

I've been invited to the wedding of a friend's granddaughter's in Orlando on July first and will fly there from Dallas after my visit in Texas. Then, on July third I will fly from Florida to Sacramento where Deb will pick me up. After a few days with Deb, I will head east in the neat little BMW sedan I'm buying from Deb. I plan to go through Jackson Hole Wyoming and view the Grand Tetons where, with a bit of good fortune, I may get in some trout fishing. I'll then head for the Black Hills and Badlands of South Dakota before driving home to the lake. This will trigger many memories for it is the exact route Dee and I took on our first vacation exactly fifty-six years earlier when she was pregnant with Deb. I've never been back to the Black Hills or Badlands since then. After I return, I will remain here until after Labor day.

Music has always been a big part of my life. Our quartet, The Willows, is working on some new numbers we plan to present at the lake service the Sunday before Labor Day. I cannot sing with the quartet without thinking of Barbara who was part of our group for several years before she went into the ministry. Recordings I have with her in the group are treasures that I will always be able to hear and will doubtless always bring tears. No music has more deeply touched my heart than hearing Barbara sing and especially Patsy Cline numbers. I cried every time she sang those songs and regrettably, I never recorded a single time she sang them. Fortunately, I have several really good recordings of her singing other music including when she sang, "Til There was You" to me during our wedding vows. That lady has made it very difficult for me to hope to find a new lady. She is certainly a tough act to follow. One of my friends said recently, "Howard, you know Barbara has ruined you for any other female." You know what my answer was? "No, she just taught me to seek and not settle for any but the best."

After Labor day I plan to take Buford east for a week or so. I plan to visit Bobby and Bob and other members of the family and some friends in the east. My precise route will not be set until I start and that will remain flexible depending on coming events, known and unknown.

Saturday, July 22, 2006

New Universe Theory

Recent discoveries indicate problems that could be explained by this theory. One is the perceptible slowing of the speed of light. The other is the possibility that red shifted light is not a doppler effect.

Friday, September 23, 2005

I quote from one reference: "It was 1576 when British astronomer Thomas Digges modified Copernicus' idea of the universe. What Copernicus thought was a clearly defined 'outer rim,' said Digges, was really unbounded space filled with stars stretching infinitely in every direction. Though Digges couldn't have known it at the time, a big-bang explosion started our universe in motion and, in doing so, produced cosmic microwaves. As Digges peered into the sky, these rays were traveling through that unbounded space; their detection confirmed the big-bang theory and earned Arno Penzias and Robert Wilson the 1978 Nobel Prize in Physics.

"The radiation led physicists to believe that space is expanding and that matter is spread more or less randomly through it. In the 1980s, Alan Guth at the Massachusetts Institute of Technology and Andrei Linde at Lebedev Physical Institute in Moscow came up with the idea that the universe ballooned in a rapid burst soon after the big bang, and that burst exponentially increased the size of the universe. This new theory of "inflation" set the stage for modern multiverse theory."

Another reference by Alan Montgomery, Mathematician, and Lambert Dolphin, Physicist, is as follows:

"The possibility that the velocity of light, c, is not a fixed constant is reconsidered by statistical analysis of the historical measurements collected from four sources. Our hypothesis testing of the selected data shows the measured value of the velocity of light has decreased over the past 250 years. Furthermore, the probability of some systematic or experimental problem was found to be low. Brief analysis of constants other than c suggests that those constants which involve atomic phenomena and units of time are also apparently changing. A third set of constants with no obvious dependence on c were analyzed and show no apparent variability with time. A variable velocity of light implies that atomic clocks and dynamical clocks do not run in step---that atomic time has been decreasing with respect to dynamical time."

Another about red shifted light from distant galaxies:

"Current cosmological models cannot explain this grouping of galaxy redshifts around discrete values across the breadth of the universe. As further data are amassed the discrepancies from the conventional picture will only worsen. If so, dramatic changes in our concepts of large-scale gravitation, the origin and "evolution" of galaxies, and the entire formulation of cosmology would be required.

"Several ways can be conceived to explain this quantization. As noted earlier, a galaxys' redshift may not be a Doppler shift, it is the currently commonly accepted interpretation of the red shift, but there can be and are other interpretations. A galaxys' redshift may be a fundamental property of the galaxy. Each may have a specific state governed by laws, analogues to those in quantum mechanics that specify which energy states atoms may occupy. Since there is relatively little blurring on the quantization between galaxies, any real motions would have to be small in this model. Galaxies would not move away from one another; the universe would be static instead of expanding.

"This model obviously has implications for our understanding of redshift patterns within and among galaxies. In particular it may solve the so-called "missing mass" problem. Conventional analysis of cluster dynamics suggest that there is not enough luminous matter to gravitationally bind moving galaxies to the system."

I have always wondered about that cosmic microwave background radiation. If it was produced by the big-bang fifteen billion years ago, how can that radiation still be around? If it traveled in a straight line, as most physicists and cosmologists believe it does, it would now be at the farthest reaches of the universe, long gone from our small inner corner of that universe. I have my own theory that can account for it being around and for numerous other strange conditions in a universe where radiation does not go in a straight line at all. In 1988 I wrote an essay about my theory. Since that time I have read nothing to refute it.

Relativity and a completely new concept of our universe - A very new and different way of thinking about our universe - by Howard Johnson - 1988

In 1905, Albert Einstein published his first dissertation on his new "Special Theory of Relativity." It defined special relativity which fits with and solves for elementary particles and their interactions. In 1916 he published his second dissertation defining general relativity which solves for cosmological and astrophysical interactions. The theory of relativity, or simply relativity, encompasses two theories of Albert Einstein: *special* relativity and *general* relativity. The special theory of relativity and the general theory are connected. The special theory applies to all inertial phenomena except gravity. It is based on spacetime that is flat, not curved. The general theory defines the law of gravitation, and its relation to other forces of nature. It says spacetime is curved, warped by gravitational fields.

The theory of relativity transformed theoretical physics and astronomy during the 20th century. When first published, relativity superseded a 200-year-old theory of mechanics stated by Isaac Newton. It changed perceptions.

The theory of relativity, was hardly noticed when it was first published. Among other new concepts, it proposed the path of light is bent or curved by gravity, in particular, the powerful gravitational force exerted by large objects like the sun, black holes, or groups of galaxies. On July 6, 1918 the following comment by Sir Arthur Eddington was published in Scientific American Supplement, "The position we have now reached is known as the principal of relativity. In so far as it is a physical theory, it seems to be amply confirmed by numerous experiments (except in regard to gravitation)."

The theory put forth in the 1916 paper lacked experimental proof. Several astronomers, including Arthur Stanley Eddington, in charge of Cambridge Observatory, used a solar eclipse of May 29, 1919 as an opportunity to test one prediction: light rays from a star would be bent as they passed close by the gravitational field of the sun. When the prediction appeared to be proved accurate, Einstein was hailed by the science community and achieved almost an apotheosis in the public mind. The following is an excerpt from the Scientific American Supplement of December 6, 1919:

"The results of the total solar eclipse of May 29 last were reported at a meeting of the Royal Astronomical Society, held on November 6. The results were most satisfactory. The star images are well defined and the resulting shift at the limb is 1.98", with a probable error of 0.12". This result agrees very closely with Einstein's prediction of 1.75". It was generally acknowledged at the meeting that this agreement went far to establish his theory as an objective reality."

I am an amateur cosmologist and claim no fame or special expertise to back up my own theory. It is merely a concept developed over many years of thought on the subject. For that reason I am presenting my theory as a thought provoking variation on the concept of how the universe operates. It is a combination and simplification of the many theories and ideas proposed over the years concerning the speed of light, the expansion of the universe (as conceived from information on red shifts of distant galaxies), the relation between gravity and the speed of light, and perceptions we seem to take for granted as true and factual. Is important to recognize that perception is reality to most people. The perception of the absolute linearity of light to the mammalian eye is the basis for our sense of space and time whether it is true or not. Humans and some primates are the only ones who can understand the spacial displacement of light passed through lenses and reflected by mirrors.

My reasoning is based on the following: It has been proven that the trajectory of light is bent (speed is changed) when light passes near a large object. (The sun, a star or a black hole.) Perhaps it never goes in a straight line, but is constantly wandering, bent by gravity as it passes by or through all kinds of collections of matter.

We, on our earth, are in a specific location in the universe and our movement relative to the universe is infinitesimal, even over very long (to us) periods of time.

The universe in its entirety has a huge mass and so a very large gravitational force. There is no question but that this force effects the path and the speed of light within the universe. This is true even though the dispersion of known mass (mostly in galaxies) in the universe is lumpy and irregular.

We perceive light as traveling in a straight line path no matter how circuitous is the actual path. Star photos taken during the May 29, 1919 eclipse proved this. The true position of the stars that appeared close to the sun was different from the apparent, observed position during the eclipse. Gravitational lenses in space sometimes cause multiple images of the same objects to appear in several positions, all different from the true position. No matter the true path light takes to a human observer, that observer perceives the light to be coming directly to him in a straight line from its source. That would be true, even if the actual path were a randomly distorted and irregular, spiral, helix, circle or arc. The red shifted galaxy we see so clearly could even be our own in the distant past should the light circle back and intersect our current path.

Would it not be true that at a position at or near the outermost reaches of the universe, the pull or force of gravity of the entire mass of the universe would be completely in one direction, that being toward the center of mass of the universe? Would it not be possible that this force of gravity would be strong enough to "bend" light back into the universe, keeping it from escaping? This would, in effect, provide an event horizon for the universe, much like that of a black hole, where light cannot escape, but would be turned back into the universe. Were this the case, the visual effect on an observer within the universe would be the same as that we presently see. Our universe could even be considered a type of "black hole" from which energy or matter can never escape.

If the above facts are true, all light we see is truly traveling in a path that is not straight but is affected or curved by the gravitational effect of the mass of the universe. The speed of light at the point in space time where we are is relative to the masses of all objects from planets to stars to galaxies to that of the entire universe in relation to our own position. If there is a way of calculating the relationship of the mass of the universe, our position relative to that mass and its dispersion, and our measurement of the observed speed of light, it is beyond my knowledge.

If this theory is true, our universe is a finite object with a specific mass, a specific size and a specific set of physical laws. It may or may not be expanding as the "red shift" of distant galaxies could be an effect of changes related to the position of ourselves as observers relative to the overall gravity of the universe. Such being the case, there could be many other universes of varying sizes distributed throughout space time in a similar fashion to galaxies within our universe.

Who knows?

Reflections on Male - female communications

Saturday, August 19, 2006

Battle of the sexes

I recently read a study that said women use an average of two and a half times as many words in a day (17,000 to 42,000) as a man. In M/F discussions I'll wager that ratio goes up to at least ten to one. This has probably been going on since words first replaced grunts for communication. Come to think of it, men probably used grunts for the first hundred centuries or so the women were using words. As a matter of common knowledge, a lot of men still use grunts in conversations with women.

---- The Female Dictionary for Men:

Understanding these closely guarded secrets of the female mystique is essential if you wish to live in peace with any woman. Your particular partner may place more or less importance to any of these, but rest assured, they are all in use.

"FINE" This is the word women use to end an argument when women feel they are right and you need to shut up. Never use "fine" to describe how a woman looks - this will cause you to have one of those arguments.

"WHATEVER" This is an invitation to argue. This means that the woman has much more to say on the matter and you must initiate more conversation or it will bite you in the butt so hard later you won't be able to sit for a week and half. Should you ever use this with her, "YOU ...." will start a war! - See last item.

"FIVE MINUTES" This is half an hour. It is equivalent to the five minutes that your football game is going to last before you take out the trash, so it's an even trade. Pacing around or hovering over the woman while waiting is unacceptable, just put on the TV but don't get too into a show because when she is ready you must be ready immediately.

"NOTHING" This means "something," and you should be on your toes. "Nothing" is usually used to describe the feeling a woman has of wanting to turn you inside out, upside down, and backwards.! "Nothing" usually signifies an argument that will last "Five Minutes" and end with "Fine"

"GO AHEAD" (With Raised Eyebrows) This is a dare. One that will result in a woman getting upset over whatever you had thought about doing like "Nothing" and will end with the word "Fine"

"GO AHEAD" (Normal Eyebrows) This means "I give up" or "do what you want because I don't care" You will get a "Whatever" in just a few minutes, followed by "Nothing" and then "Fine" and she will talk to you in about "Five Minutes" when she cools off.

"LOUD SIGH" This is not actually a word, but is a non-verbal statement often misunderstood by men. A "Loud Sigh" means she thinks you are an idiot at that moment, and wonders why she is wasting her time standing here and arguing with you over "Nothing"

"SOFT SIGH" Again, not a word, but a non-verbal statement. "Soft Sighs" mean that she is content. Your best bet is to not move or breathe, and she will stay content.

"THAT'S OKAY" This is one of the most dangerous statements that a woman can make to a man. "That's Okay" means that she wants to think long and hard before paying you back for whatever it is that you have done or that she imagines you have done. "That's Okay" is often used with the word "Fine" and in conjunction with a "Whatever."

"GO AHEAD..." At some point in the near future, you are going to be in some mighty big trouble.

"PLEASE DO" This is not a statement, it is an offer. A woman is giving you the chance to come up with whatever excuse or reason you have for doing whatever it is that you have done. You have a fair chance with the truth, so be careful and you shouldn't get a "That's Okay"

"THANKS" A woman is thanking you. Do not faint...! Just say you're welcome.

"THANKS A LOT" This is much different from "Thanks." A woman will say, "Thanks A Lot" when she is really ticked off at you. It signifies that you have offended her in some callous way, and will be followed by the "Loud Sigh." Be careful not to ask what is wrong after the "Loud Sigh," as she will only tell you "Nothing"

"YOU .....!" a simple declaration of war! All above harmful words will carry at least ten times the vehemence they carried before. Don't count on being able to get a single word in, even edgewise. You will now suffer for a very long time!

---- The Male Dictionary for Women - The Guys' Rules:

At last a guy has taken the time to write this all down. Finally, the guys' side of the story. (I must admit, it's pretty good.) We always hear "the rules"from the female side. Now here are the rules from the male side. These are our rules! Please note... these are all numbered "1" ON PURPOSE!

Guys: we know all of these don't apply to all of you, but for those that don't, you can surely find a similar one to substitute that will.

Ladies, take these comments to heart. Understanding them rationally will save many pointless conflicts which no one ever "wins" and make both of your lives more peaceful - if that's what you really want.

1. Learn to work the toilet seat. You're a big girl. If it's up, put it down. We need it up, you need it down. You don't hear us complaining about you leaving it down.

1. Sunday sports. It's like the full moon or the changing of the tides. Let it be.

1. Shopping is NOT a sport. And no, we are never going to think of it that way.

1. "Terminator" and "Indiana Jones" movies are what it's all about. "An Affair to Remember" and "Sleepless In Seattle" are chick flicks.

1. Crying is blackmail.

1. Ask for what you want. Let us be clear on this one: Subtle hints do not work! Strong hints do not work! Obvious hints do not work! Just say it!

1. Yes and No are perfectly acceptable answers to almost every question.

1. Come to us with a problem only if you want help solving it. That's what we do. Sympathy is what your girlfriends are for.

1. A headache that lasts for 17 months is a problem. See a doctor.

1. Anything we said 6 months ago is inadmissible in an argument. In fact, all comments become null and void after 7 days.

1. If you won't dress like the Victoria's Secret girls, don't expect us to act like soap opera guys.

1. If you think you're fat, you probably are. Don't ask us.

1. If something we said can be interpreted two ways and one of the ways makes you sad or angry, we meant the other one.

1. You can either ask us to do something or tell us how you want it done. Not both. If you already know best how to do it, just do it yourself.

1. Whenever possible, please say whatever you have to say during commercials.

1. Christopher Columbus did not need directions and neither do we.

1. ALL men see in only 16 colors, like Windows default settings. Peach, for example, is a fruit, not a color. Pumpkin is also a fruit. We have no idea what mauve is.

1. If we ask what is wrong and you say "nothing," we will act like nothing's wrong. We know you are lying, but it is just not worth the hassle.

1. If you ask a question you don't want an answer to, expect an answer you don't want to hear.

1. When we have to go somewhere, absolutely anything you wear is fine...Really.

1. Don't ask us what we're thinking about unless you are prepared to discuss such topics as baseball, the shotgun formation, or monster trucks.

1. You have enough clothes.

1. You have too many shoes.

1. I am in shape. Round is a shape.

1. Thank you for reading this. Yes, I know, I have to sleep on the couch tonight; but did you know men really don't mind that? It's like camping.

Pass this to as many men as you can - to give them a laugh.

Pass this to as many women as you can - to give them a bigger laugh!!

The Most Beautiful Will Ever Written

Wednesday, February 14, 2007

THE LAST WILL AND TESTAMENT OF CHARLES LOUNSBURY

I have searched for years to find a copy of the will purported to be that of a destitute Chicago attorney, found in his pocket when he died in a mental institution. Today I found it on the Internet and wish to share it with each of you. This will (the part in quotes) I heard read to the ADTA members at the annual meeting at the Palmer House Hotel in Chicago about 1970. The parts in bold arial were not read, but were discovered by me just today and are added for clarity and good knowledge. It touched me deeply at the time and does even more so now. To wit:

THE MOST BEAUTIFUL LAST WILL AND TESTAMENT EVER WRITTEN

A Last Will

He was stronger and cleverer, no doubt, than other men, and in many broad lines of business he had grown rich, until his wealth exceeded exaggeration. One morning, in his office, he directed a request to his confidential lawyer to come to him in the afternoon--he intended to have his will drawn. A will is a solemn matter, even with men whose life is given up to business and who are by habit mindful of the future. After giving this direction he took up no other matter, but sat at his desk alone and in silence.

It was a day when summer was first new. The pale leaves upon the trees were starting forth upon the yet unbending branches. The grass in the parks had a freshness in its green like the freshness of the blue in the sky and of the yellow of the sun--a freshness to make one wish that life might renew its youth. The clear breezes from the south wantoned about, and then were still, as if loath to go finally away. Half idly, half thoughtfully, the rich man wrote upon the white paper before him, beginning what he wrote with capital letters, such as he had not made since, as a boy in school, he had taken pride in his skill with the pen:

IN THE NAME OF GOD, AMEN

"I, Charles Lounsbury, being of sound and disposing mind and memory, do hereby make and publish this, my last will and testament in order, as justly as may be, to distribute my interests in the world among succeeding men.

"That part of my interest, which is known in law and recognized in the sheep-bound volumes as my property, being inconsiderable and none account, I make no disposition in this, my will. My right to live, being but a life estate, is not at my disposal, but these things excepted, all else in the world I now proceed to devise and bequeath.

"ITEM: I give to good fathers and mothers and trust to their children all good little words of praise and encouragement and all quaint pet names and endearments. And I charge said parents to use them judiciously or generously as the deeds of their children shall require.

"ITEM: I leave to children inclusively, but only for the duration of their childhood, all and every flower of the fields and the blossoms of the woods. And I devise to children the banks of the brooks and the golden sands beneath the water thereof and the odors of the willows that dip therein and the white clouds that float on high above the giant trees. And I leave the children the long, long days to be merry in a thousand ways, and the night, and the trail of the Milky Way to wonder at; but subject, nevertheless, to the rights hereinafter given to lovers.

"ITEM: I devise to boys jointly all the useful idle fields and commons where ball may be played, and all snow-clad hills where one may coast, and all streams and ponds where one may skate, to have and to hold the same for the period of their boyhood. And all meadows, with the clover blooms and butterflies thereof; and all woods, with their appurtenances of squirrels and whirring birds and echoes and strange noises; and all distant places which may be visited, together with the adventures there found, I do give to said boys to be theirs. And I give to said boys each his own place at the fireside at night, with all pictures that may be seen In the burning wood or coal, to enjoy without let or hindrance and without any incumbrance of cares.

"ITEM: To lovers I devise their imaginary world filled with the stars of the skies and the red roses by the walks, the bloom of the hawthorne and the sweet strains of music and ought else that they may desire to figure to each other the lastingness and the beauty of their love.

"ITEM: To young men jointly, being joined in a brave, mad crowd, I devise and bequeath all boisterous, inspiring sports of rivalry. I give to them the disdain of weakness and undaunted confidence in their own strength. Though they are rude and rough, I leave to them alone the power of making lasting friendships and of possessing companions and to them exclusively I shall give all merry songs and brave choruses to sing, with smooth voices to troll them forth.

"ITEM: And to those who are no longer children or youths or lovers I leave Memory, and I leave to them the volumes of the poems of Burns and Shakespeare, and of other poets, if there are others, to the end that they may live the old days over again freely and fully, without tithe or diminution; and to those who are no longer children or youths or lovers I leave, too, the knowledge of what a rare, rare world it is.

"ITEM: To our loved ones with snowy crowns, I leave the peace and happiness of old age, and the love and gratitude of their children before they fall asleep."

It was then reported and suggested, "This sublime request, my friends, was made by the late Charles Lounsbury, Chicago attorney at law, while confined in a mental institution. So you see, in this world filled with hate and greed and bigotry, this world filled with fear of total annihilation, which of us is to say who is the sanest?"

A little more Internet research on the subject brought up the following which I did not know until this moment:

About the most beautiful last will and testament in history written for Charles Lounsbury by Williston Fish.

— THE MOST BEAUTIFUL LAST WILL AND TESTAMENT EVER WRITTEN —-

When a person sits down with his or her attorney to prepare a last will and testament, one would expect the document produced by this meeting to be legalistic, dry, morbid. Certainly, one would not expect inspired prose verging on poetry.

Yet when Williston Fish, an attorney in Chicago, Ill., sat down in 1897 to draft a will for one Charles Lounsbury, what Fish produced as a testament proved to be sheer prose poetry. In its time, Lounsbury's will was printed and reprinted around the world. To generations of attorneys, it became a classic.

However, if a will is defined as "a written instrument legally executed by which a man makes disposition of his estate to take effect after his death," then the Lounsbury will was no legal will at all. It was, in fact, a literary article. There was only an attorney-businessman, and part-time author, in Chicago named Williston Fish who created the fictional will as a literary effort.

Williston Fish was born on January 15, 1858, in Berlin Heights, O., the eldest son in a family of 8 children. Self-taught in Greek and Latin, he briefly attended Oberlin College, then won appointment in 1877 to the U.S. Military Academy at West Point. In 1881, the year of his graduation, he married, and subsequently had 3 children. He remained in the Army for 6 years, studying law on the side. After resigning from the Army, he was admitted to the Illinois Bar in 1887, then chose to enter into a business career. But his heart was always in writing, and he published at least 3 books and 500 articles, stories, poems for periodicals.

In 1897, he hit upon the idea of a perfect will and upon a wealthy, nonexistent client named Charles Lounsbury.

As Fish recalled it later: "The name, Charles Lounsbury, of the divisor in the will, is a name in my family of 3 generations ago--back in York State where the real owner of it was a big, strong, all-around good kind of a man. I had an uncle, a lawyer, in Cleveland named after him, Charles Lounsbury Fish, who was a most burly and affectionate giant himself and who took delight in keeping the original Charles Lounsbury's memory green. He used to tell us of his feats of strength. . . . His brain, my uncle always added, was equal to his brawn, and he had a way of winning friends and admirers as easy and comprehensive as taking a census. So I took the name of Charles Lounsbury to add strength and goodwill to my story."

The will that Williston Fish had written found its way into print for the 1st time the year after it was created. It appeared in Harper's Weekly on September 3, 1898. It was picked up and reprinted widely. But in recent years, it has been forgotten.

Aftermath - Speaking of the numerous reprintings of "A Last Will," Fish wrote good-naturedly: "Whenever a newspaper did not have at hand what it really wanted . . . it would run in this piece of mine. In return for the free use of the piece, the paper, not to be outdone in liberality, would generally correct and change it. . . . Some writers can boast that their works have been translated into all foreign languages, but when I look pathetically about for some little boast, I can only say that this one of my pieces has been translated into all the idiot tongues of English."

Although a lawyer, Williston Fish devoted 35 years of his life working as a realtor and as an executive in many railroad companies. He retired in 1923, concentrated fully on his writing career, and died in Western Springs, Ill., on December 19, 1939, at the age of 81.

Blessings and love to you all, Ho

Writers and Women - a warning

Tuesday, December 15, 2009

A warning for women about writers, male writers.

Beware of starting a relationship with a writer. They are human and have some or all the foibles, the charms, the weaknesses, and inconsistencies exhibited by the male of the species. That being said, there are some things specific to artists, and a few peculiarities attributable to writers alone.

All of them have at least some of the following traits. Some of them have all of them. I repeat, All of them have at least some of the following traits. Some of them have all of them

Artists are unconventional people. They do not often follow the norms of polite society and this often puts them at odds with "normal" persons. If they follow rules they are often of their own making and do not necessarily follow society's rule book. The very few who gain fame and fortune are especially afflicted with these attributes.

Artists are frequently unkempt and unconcerned about their personal appearance, their place of residence or their workplace. Since they usually work alone they do not have to worry about interference of any kind from other people. As a result they often lack social skills and can be opinionated and even uncivil.

They treat money and finances in the same manner and rarely have enough to live on. Those who have money usually inherited it or have a sponsor, (or sugar momma) sometimes unwilling, who provides for their needs. When a windfall comes for any reason, even their own success, they give freely to friends and family, often to groupies or other leeches who disappear as quickly as the money. Much of their life is spent in poverty and they usually die penniless and alone.

Artists are emotional. They are usually driven by emotion more than by rational thought. Most people share this trait, but it is greatly amplified in artists. They are known for volatile, often unpredictable actions that can become very damaging. Their emotions frequently override their logic, particularly in situations where the powerful emotions like love, hate, revenge, remorse, and similar others are aroused. They frequently get themselves into situations where there are no possible favorable solutions. Those who do learn to leash in their emotions can do so up to a point. Once that point is passed, emotions can burst forth with tremendous force, drowning all rational responses.

They are subject to most acts of debauchery and are often found in a drunken stupor, sometimes in an alley or gutter. For this reason, most artists die quite young, often by their own devices. Quite a few die of drug overdoses. A few die at the hands of the husband of one of their conquests. They are not a good risk for life insurance or investment.

Though they often woo and marry women they love deeply, even beautiful, loyal women, they are prone to cheat, given the opportunity. For some women, artists have almost a magical charm. Why they start a romance with a known bounder and expect to change him is beyond understanding. Tragic stories of these foolish adventures abound in literature and folklore.

Writers have all of the above plus a few peculiar to the species. They are wordsmiths, trained and practiced in the art of using words to paint pictures and scenarios of imaginary people and things. They are completely unbounded by facts and some are not even bound by natural laws. Science fiction and fantasy writers in particular are limited only by their considerable imaginations. As a result, when their work turns out badly, what do they do? They either discard it or rewrite it. There is a common belief among writers touted in books and lectures, "rewriting is the key to success."

That would pose no problem if it were not carried over into the writer's life experiences. What sometimes happens in real life is that the writer jumps in and acts in a similar manner to his writing. It's, "If it doesn't work out right, rewrite it!" But life cannot be "rewritten." Things once said cannot be "unsaid. The vase once broken cannot be returned to its original condition. Real life happenings cannot be "rewritten." The entropy of the universe is always and only increasing.

The characters in their creations become as real people to the writer. In his mind he can hate them or love them. He can also use his talent as a wordsmith to manipulate their lives, even kill them, with no real consequences. He can even resurrect the ones he killed if he wants. Writers can come to view real live people the same way. They can become extremely disturbed when real people don't follow his "script" which, of course, they don't. There are many other problems associated with this imposition of creative writing into real life. One horrible true story is about a writer who became so enamored with one of his heroines that he committed suicide after writing of her sudden death. That's quite obviously carrying "method writing" a bit too far.

Just think about artists as normal people whose emotions are much stronger than most and can shift into overdrive in an instant. The emotional fish story of the artist would not turn the small fish into a bigger one, but into a virtual whale.

On the positive side, artists including writers can be quite wonderful friends or companions. They are usually quite sensitive and try not to be hurtful to those they care for. Emotions directed to positive action can be wonderful resulting in deep and abiding love, unbelievable acts of kindness, some quite altruistic. They are also quite sensitive and can be hurt deeply and quickly, even by unintentional acts. Those without the negative traits can make affectionate and loyal friends, lovers, and husbands. Ah, but finding those with all positive traits borders on the impossible. So if you take a writer into your life as a friend or lover, even a very good one, be prepared to accept a few warts . . . maybe lots of warts.

- Howard Johnson, December, 2009

Part III, A Collection of thoughts on many subjects

Personal concepts, Beliefs, Religion, Politics, and Love.

By

Howard Johnson

FROM THE AUTHOR

Much of the writing in this part describes concepts that make sense to me and are feelings I have personally experienced. I believe an individual's personal belief system will determine their social, religious, and political actions; their relationships with others; the kind of life they lead; and ultimately, the person they are at any given time. There are numerous pieces about my personal belief systems. They describe the most significant of my guiding principles. Many describe how I try to relate to my children, a most salient part of whom I am.

Howard Johnson quotes with the year they were written.

So think about writing. If there is a story, memory, or idea in you, give it the wings of the written word. Who knows how many others you may touch. —2011

There are times when admitting defeat is the greatest victory *—1973*

My measure of a man or woman is not how much they agree with me, but rather, how logical and persuasive are their arguments when they disagree. I also consider what kind of emotions play in these arguments. Do they lash out in anger with words of resentment and condemnation, or do they listen and make rational judgements? *—from a talk on communication given in 1969*

> When truth and belief come to conflict,
> it is better to change one's belief to fit the truth
> than to change the truth to fit one's belief.
> **Beliefs are the creations of men**
> while **Truths are the creations of God!** *—July 7, 1986*

For those offended by religion or use of the word, "God," in this, or any of my published work, simply substitute the phrase, "the order of things," or "natural laws."

Those who discount or will not read the Bible because it represents a religion, or because it is a religious work, deny themselves learning a great deal of ageless knowledge collected and preserved for thousands of years. This knowledge, mostly about human behavior and about interacting profitably and successfully with others, is real, practical, and valuable. A great many life rules and lessons explained and demonstrated, apply to almost any human situation *—1990*

A New Serenity Prayer

May God, the order of the universe,

Grant me the serenity to understand belief,

The courage to accept truth,

And the wisdom to know the difference.

—February 20, 2001

If you ignore the faith-based content of the Bible, it becomes a valuable history, a study of human nature, and an excellent guide to human behavior.

—1967

Religion and politics are closer to each other than either might prefer.

—2008

Perception, ah yes, perception, it is what drives our decisions, controls our emotions of love, anger, joy, disappointment, friendship, hatred, virtually everything we think or react to. Perception overrules facts, logic, and reality. Whether from love, avarice, or foolishness, and no matter how removed perception is from truth, it still rules us and determines our life decisions. We do not live in a real world, but live totally in a world created by and subject to our perceptions.

—1960

When one person suffers from a delusion it is called insanity; when many people suffer from a delusion it is called politics.
—1967

The liberal Democrat party in the US has a record of failure, corruption, lies, hatred, deceit, and greed so blatant that only an intellectual could ignore or evade it.
—2009

The really dangerous people are not those who believe in violence as a means to every end or they who believe in treachery as a means to most ends. Those can be overcome by resistance and by alertness. The truly deadly menace is the intelligent man or woman whose central vision, has been indoctrinated in the accuracy and supremacy of their belief system, their view of reality. They then impose their views as controls on others. This is particularly true of many elitist intellectuals, particularly when they gain political power and control. So often they become misdirected and confused until suspicion becomes their guiding principle and pure power their only end.

—1992

The United States will be a socialist dictatorship by 2030. At this time those leftist activists will happily extol the joys of socialism as they are being carted off to the salt mines.
—*2008*

To a liberal Democrat, socialist, or almost any intellectual, reality simply does not exist.
—*1998*

"We cannot continue to rely on our military in order to achieve the national security objectives that we've set. We've got to have a civilian national security force that's just as powerful, just as strong, just as well-funded."
—*Barack Hussein Obama - In a speech in Colorado on July 2, 2008*

It is interesting to note that among the numerous well-hidden provisions of the Obamacare law, there is one establishing and funding just such a force. Unlike the military, this force will be able to enforce federal law as police, and not forbidden to act as law enforcement as is the military. I wonder if they will be wearing brown shirts? I also wonder why the media has neglected to inform the public of this? Hmmmm?
—*in response to the preceding page quote from Obama's speech*

Patriotism has been called the last refuge of scoundrels, but anti-patriotism truly is much more so. Those who accuse opponents of any kind as using patriotism to hide their false intent are often the true scoundrels. False patriots are quite obvious to open minds.   — *July 4, 2011*

It seems the American Voter has come to admire failure, corruption, greed, and gross dishonesty in their politicians as long as they spew lies about and hate for the successful.
—*1993*

I have voted hundreds of times, but only five times have I voted **for** a major candidate. Every other time I had to choose the lesser of the evils presented on the ballot.   —*1992*

An untruth that conveys a true meaning from one person to another is, in fact, a truth—a truth that conveys a false meaning is in fact an untruth. Truth or untruth is not in the medium, only in the message!
—*1968*

Monkey Kings, Monkey People

In my book, *The Feudals*, I described our amazing passion for celebrity worship, adulation, and sometimes fanatical, group attachment to celebrities for many reasons, now mostly entertainers including TV news and sports celebrities, but also dictators, kings and political leaders. I believe this self subjugation to a charismatic leader or celebrity is a genetic trait we share with our primate cousins and maybe all primates who live in troops or packs. For this reason, the original title of, *The Feudals*, was *Monkey Kings, Monkey people*.

There is considerable evidence for this tendency being genetic from many university studies of primates. It is also obvious in many cohesive groups of other animals, mostly predators like wolves and even orcas. All of these animals live in packs, troops, tribes, pods, or other cohesive groups. Even some birds in flocks exhibit some of these tendencies. In many of these groups, the leader gets there by being, *the meanest SOB in the valley*, and fighting and killing his way to the top, or *her* way as is the case with spotted Hyenas.

Humans are unique among mammals in having many kinds of celebrities and/or leaders. The followers of these celebrities are called many different names. These include: fans, supporters, subjects, constituents, worshipers, groupies, etc. Many of these are quite irrational, even forming cult like organizations. *Trekies* who go bananas over both of the TV *Star Trek* series are but one example. They even have a national convention.

Americans fought a war to getaway from British royalty, but look at how we treat them now. For no rational reason, Americans so worship British Royalty that their every action is detailed in our media. We Ooh and Ah at the tiniest detail of their personal soap opera lives. How irrational is that? The same can be said about stars of sports, Hollywood or TV, including the so-called news. For all of them, their moral turpitude and scandalous behaviors seem only to enhance and encourage the adulation of adoring fans.

There must be a rational explanation of this irrational behavior. I have heard many, but the best one I have heard is that such behavior is instinctive and therefor not controlled by logic. It seems we are not so far intellectually from our simian cousins as we would like to believe.   *—2010*

I agree wholeheartedly with Ronald Reagan when he said, "the nine most terrifying words in the English language are, 'I'm from the government and I'm here to help.'"
                    a whimsical comment by Ronald Reagan in a speech in 1980

I have decided to rename our two dominant political parties according to their most distinguishing characteristics. The two are now the *Hate* party and the *Stupid* party. The *Hate* party uses accusations, condemnations, and fabrications in hate campaigns against their opposition. The *Stupid* party does the same, but only in primary campaigns against members of their own party. To a realist, it's obvious which is which.   *—2012*

True value in life lies not in finding that which we like, but in liking what we find. The secret of happiness is not in doing that which we like, but in liking that which we must do.
                    —December 1980

Deceit can destroy only deceivers. No liar can perceive the purpose of him whose heart is free from treason to himself. Guile is a form of wisdom that an honorable man may have and honorably use, persuading deceivers to employ their ill will ignorantly in the service of him whom they aim to destroy.   *—1968*

Find something nice to say to everyone, each time you meet. Then say something nice about someone else to that person. If you do these two things consistently, your life will be pleasant, you will have many friends, and no one will ever find fault with you. *—1980*

Deceit can destroy only deceivers. No liar can perceive the purpose of him whose heart is free from treason to himself. Guile is a form of wisdom that an honorable man may have and honorably use, persuading deceivers to employ their ill will ignorantly in the service of him whom they aim to destroy. *—1968*

Images of Pain

A Satanic burst of flame - Screaming, burning flesh - Bright tinkling shards of glass - Another monstrous flash of fire - Black smoke billowing - Heart-rending phone calls - Humanity in the stairwells - Electronic pictures burned into brains - A rumbling, crushing, obliterating collapse - Terrible showers of stone, steel, glass, dust, and flesh - Lives painfully obliterated as millions watch in horror and disbelief - Booming clouds of smoke and dust, then dooming silence.

Heroic thousands in vain efforts - Photos of lost loved ones - Withering hope - Veils of tears - Anguish a billionfold, but a few scream with joy - Faces of horrible pain of loss - Electronic images of child faces of evil - I cry, you cry, millions cry, God cries. Satan laughs! *—September 11, 2001*

The real, the sweetest taste of victory comes when you win in your adversary's battlefield, fought with his weapons and his set of rules at a time of his choosing, when losing would cost you no loss of stature. Even more so when you are your own adversary! *—1972*

Decide right, or decide wrong, but decide! It is sometimes better to make a wrong decision than to avoid making any decision. You must always decide among two or more options. Anyone can provide good reasons for selecting a particular course of action under consideration. If you wait for 100-percent proof, you'll wait forever; so make up your mind, make the decision, and carry it through. Errors can usually be corrected, but the indecisive person stays in a constant storm of confusion, seldom achieving anything. The only thing that truly needs weighing is the cost of the course and its probable rewards. But remember, not to decide is a decision which may have dire consequences. *—1985*

Beauty of face and body attracts only; it cannot hold, nor will it last for long. Beauty of heart, on the other hand, grows with time, holds people together, and brings joy to all who have the good fortune to share it. Ah! But beauty of soul, the greatest of all, makes life worth living for everyone touched by it, whether for a brief moment or a lifetime. *—1974*

Somehow, we always get back to the basics. Right and wrong, good and evil, like beauty, are in the eye of the beholder (or doer). Their rules are not immutable. They are lifestyle—cultural, social, or religious creations. They depend entirely on one's own situation—whose side you are in, to what group you belong, or who eats whom. I am sure Genghis Khan, Hitler, and Saddam Hussein had and have quite different views from their victims of right and wrong.

Good and evil, right and wrong have very different meanings for a lamb than for a lion.

—May 8, 2001

There only two possible results when the lion shall lie down with the lamb. The lamb will be eaten, or the lion will starve.   *—2004*

Many a great proverb is read, shared with friends, and then forgotten. What a pity all that wisdom goes to waste.   *—1998*

If you can't live your life the way you'd love to live it, then love your life the best way you can live it   *—1973*

Heroes and Oracles, Where Have They Gone?

Emerson remarked, "Each man is a *hero* and an *oracle* to somebody."

Noah Webster describes a *hero* as "a prominent or central personage taking an admirable part in any remarkable action or event; as the *hero* of a romance; hence, a person regarded as a model of noble qualities; as, Washington is more than a national *hero*."

He describes an *oracle* as "the medium by which God reveals hidden knowledge or makes known the Devine purpose; also, the place where the oracle is given."

Like it or not, we all have heroes and oracles who we use to shape our actions, character, and beliefs. They are the winds that bend the twig into the tree.

Pick carefully your heroes for as they are, so will you become! —1998

The past is that portion of time we carry in the storehouse of our memory and all before it. It includes memories, pleasant and unpleasant according to how our heart sees our experience.

The future is that portion of time we carry in the dreams and wishes of our hearts. It is colored bright or dark according to the intent of our spirit.

The now—today—that brief demarcation between past and future is where we act, live, dream, remember, plan, think, cry, laugh, and love. It is good or bad according to our motivating desire at that instant.   *—1965*

He who has no God is his own God and will live accordingly.   *—2007*

It is best to be careful what family you choose to be born into!   *—January 1999*

Ignorance can be cured with education and experience.
       Stupidity furiously resists all efforts at correction or cure.   *—1977*

A smile is a light in the window of a face that signifies the heart is at home.   *—1968*

A decision is necessary only when the facts at hand do not reveal the only course to take.
   —1960

Aye . . . like a snowflake in flight

       between sky and ocean are we.

              Beauty for an instant . . . Never to be again.   *—1973*

True beauty is not in the eye but in the **heart** of the beholder!   *—1968*

On Idealism

To be idealistic and naive is to lay oneself open to charlatans and con men of all types. To discard naivete only stops the most obvious of these, and at what price?

To discard idealism in order to keep oneself safe from frauds and connivers creates total constipation of the soul, a deplorable condition.

I believe it is best to be idealistic and naive, but secure wise counsel before making life-changing decisions. Ah, but securing wise counsel, there's the rub. A quote from Talbot Mundy: "When a number of men, for a number of different reasons, counsel me to turn aside from danger, I have usually found it wise to recognize the danger, but do the opposite of what they urge. Although they likely know it not, their counsel is directed either by their own necessity or by their love of comfort, good repute and profit."

Even in our pursuit of happiness, there is some sadness and even evil. This is because we are less than perfect beings, with less than perfect minds and hearts, communicating in less than perfect means, in a less than perfect universe. The best we can do in this less than perfect world is just that, the best we can do.   *—2010*

Here are a few suggestions for a pleasant and enjoyable life.

Recognize that life is never fair. Most of it is a random process.

Never look back. They may be gaining on you.

Once you've fallen in love, never stop loving that person.

Dream all the wild dreams you can dream, but plan and decide rationally.

Always show everyone you care about, even your pet, that you love them.

Use emotions for love. Use logic for decisions.

Savor and cultivate pleasant emotions. Minimize and weed out unpleasant ones.

Laugh every day, even if you don't feel like there is anything to laugh about.

Take frequent walks—through the woods if possible.

Get rid of everything you don't need or that doesn't hold treasured memories.

Use your last cent to buy a flower for someone.

Each and every day, share a treasured memory with someone you care about.

Tell everyone just how special your special someone is, and do it at every chance you get..

Consider that every statement you make to anyone is a commitment to make it true.

Never lose that child-like wonder at the world. Keep it alive and active.

Rid yourself of everything that is not useful, beautiful, joyful, or filled with wonder.

Forgive everyone of everything and especially discard grudges.

If you have a dog, give it all the love you can and as much freedom as possible.

Say something pleasant to everyone you meet every day.   *—2011*

To reach another mind and heart and touch with loving care that most tender, guarded, secret being hiding within impenetrable protective walls is my most passionate desire.

To let that being know that there are others like it—frightened, lonely creatures—in the midst of the hostilities of the surface world of sham people;

To form that tenuous thread of understanding between these secret beings;

To share life, this brief flash between two black eternities, with others of my ken . . . would seem to give it meaning.

I would be, or strive to be, a poet perhaps . . . a reacher . . . a dreamer . . . an artist painting thought pictures . . . a thought sculpturer using words as chisels . . . an architect of phrases.

But whatever, I must reach out and try to touch others.   *—1974*

One valuable thing I learned about children is they belong to themselves, not to their parents. As parents, we are charged with guiding the infant into childhood, the child into a young adult, and the young adult into a full person. It's an awesome responsibility for which so many are ill trained. Parents who try to *possess* their children make a serious mistake and frequently drive them away. God loans us children for a short while, charging us with guiding them to independent adulthood and completely equal status. They are for us to teach, enjoy, love, and set free.

—2010

As you think, you travel; as you love, you attract. You are today where your thoughts have brought you; you will be tomorrow where your thoughts take you. You cannot escape the result of your thoughts, but you can endure and learn, and accept and be glad. You will realize the vision (not the idle wish) of your heart—be it base or beautiful, or a mixture of both—for you will always gravitate toward that which you secretly must love. Into your thoughts you will receive that which you earn—no more, no less. Whatever your present environment must be, you will fall, remain, or rise with your thoughts, your vision, your ideal. You will become as small as your controlling desire, as great as your dominant aspiration. *—1971*

If you remain true to your idealism, you will surely be duped on occasion. But if losses are kept small while ideals and naivete are held, you will be able to smile at life and have numerous dear friends. Or perhaps, you search for something else? —May 25, 2001

The only truly stupid question is the one that is not asked. *—1960*

Ice-blue eyes - secret tears - pain hidden in the heart - bright laughter - running, running - broken child's world - stifled fears - steeled, hard-shell - soft love-warmth - sun and bright sky to black midnight - the now trapped - foiled understanding - tenuous dream-wish - listen, hear - being freedom - broken chains - fly to - reach - have - love - borrow - miss you. *—1965*

NOTE: For those of you who don't like the term "God given" please substitute "natural" or any other term that suits you. Everything except, of course, "government granted." *—2009*

To do what you know you must when the time comes;
To be who you truly are in the face of ridicule;
To stand true and tall against strong opposition;
To give without hope of reward or repayment;
To believe for the sake of truth only . . .
And to love for the sake of love only . . .
. . . is to live! *—1963*

True Hell is when you realize you've made a stupid mistake and that someone else has to pay for your error. *—1966*

Life, as inevitable as the universe itself, is defined as one thing only—that which can change its environment through the controlled use of energy. This seems a cold definition of life, but it could be that what we seek is a direction rather than a definition. There has only been one direction to life since its inception.

—1961

Absolutely anything repeated often enough will convince people to believe it no matter how blatantly false or ludicrous it is. In the same vein, there is nothing so destructive or misleading as a reality that is never mentioned and is deliberately withheld. Politicians and our main stream media talking heads are masters of both of these means of misinformation.   *—2010*

"Do Unto Others as You Would Have Others Do Unto You."

The golden rule (Matthew 7:12 and Luke 6:31) is a direction for a way of life. It is simple and direct yet difficult for most to comprehend. It is a way for a person to act toward others, not something to be expected of them. One who applies the golden rule is a giver in the finest sense of the word and takes pleasure in the *giving*, with no thought of receiving anything whatsoever in return. Acceptance of the gift alone is the greatest kindness that a giver can receive.

Too often, we forget that others do not see the world as we do and are troubled that they do not seem to reciprocate our own imagined goodness. The golden rule has no component that says we should expect *anything* from another person. That is truly a function of *their* world, not ours. To expect any act from another is to burden ourselves with a potential disappointment and create tension in our interpersonal relationship with that individual. It is, in fact, the single most unkind action one can take toward another person.

Courtesy, consideration, friendship, affection, love—these are all giving things as *it is only in giving that we receive.* What we do receive is the pleasure of knowing what we have done and lies entirely within our own psyche with no external component. To expect or ask anything in return is to debase oneself and bring negative, displeasing specters into one's being.

"Judge not, that ye be not judged" (Matthew 7:1).

Dr. Frank Crane reminds us, "The golden rule is of no use to you whatever unless you realize that it is your move!"   *—1978*

Most humans will take the path of least resistance. They eagerly will believe the truth of that which they want to be true or commit as true because that path requires little effort. Each time an unproven or untrue statement is made, commitment cements that belief stronger in the mind of the one making the statement. It takes diligent and often painful effort to search out real truth. Such effort is far more than most are willing to spend. This is especially so if it goes against one's previously stated positions or committed beliefs. Humans often follow leaders who espouse those beliefs, even to their own detriment. I think it's just human nature, or maybe overwhelming primate nature. Apes and monkeys do the exact same things on a quite different scale.   — 2014

For those who agree with the media portrayal of the Tea Party and Tea Party members, I ask a simple question. Are your expressed opinions based on actual experience? Have you been to a Tea Party rally? Or are you merely aping the words and images from the TV talking heads? I've attended several Tea Party rallies as well as several so called "peace" marches. The differences between the realities of both and the portrayals on TV are astounding and very revealing.

I ask another question: Did the original Boston Tea Partiers have any more valid objection to the rule of King George III than we currently have with the Washington ruling elite?   —*2010*

Find something nice to say to everyone, each time you meet. Then say something nice about someone else to that person. If you do these two things consistently, your life will be pleasant, you will have many friends, and no one will ever find fault with you.   —*1980*

There are three unforgettable moments, good ones, bad ones, and embarrassing ones.   —*1967*

The poet speaks - the mirror reflects - a few truly understand   —*1997*

✳   ✳   ✳

POLITICAL QUOTES FROM ALL OVER THE MAP INCLUDING A FEW OF MY OWN

Let us not seek the Republican answer or the Democratic answer, but the right answer. Let us not seek to fix the blame for the past. Let us accept our own responsibility for the future.

—*John F. Kennedy*

Suppose you were an idiot, and suppose you were a member of Congress; but I repeat myself.

—*Mark Twain*

One of the penalties for refusing to participate in politics is that you end up being governed by your inferiors.   —*Plato*

It is better to be violent, if there is violence in our hearts, than to put on the cloak of nonviolence to cover impotence.   —*Mahatma Gandhi*

If you put the federal government in charge of the Sahara Desert, in 5 years there would be a shortage of sand.   —*Milton Friedman*

The darkest places in hell are reserved for those who maintain their neutrality in times of moral crisis.

—*Dante Alighieri*

If you have too many regulations you destroy all respect for the law.   —*Winston Churchill*

Politics is not a game. It is an earnest business.   —*Winston Churchill*

Politics is not a game. It is an earnest business engaged in by all manner of despots who could not otherwise make a living.   —*Howard Johnson*

Most laws that prohibit, control, or tax what people desire, do not work, but make things worse. The laws about guns, liquor, gambling and sex accomplish three things. First, they only control the actions of honest citizens, not of any criminals. Second, they open the door for huge criminal organizations to step in and make scads of money supplying the forbidden. Third, they turn many otherwise honest citizens into criminals while promoting the very things that they prohibit, control, or tax.   —*Howard Johnson*

Healthy citizens are the greatest asset any country can have   —*Winston Churchill*

I am extraordinarily patient, provided I get my own way in the end.   —*Margaret Thatcher*

Democracy is when the indigent, and not the men of property, are the rulers.   —*Aristotle*

Whenever a man has cast a longing eye on offices, a rottenness begins in his conduct.

—*Thomas Jefferson*

It is enough that the people know there was an election. The people who cast the votes decide nothing. The people who count the votes decide everything.   —*Joseph Stalin*

Principles have no real force except when one is well-fed.   —*Mark Twain*

The modern conservative is engaged in one of man's oldest exercises in moral philosophy; that is, the search for a superior moral justification for selfishness.   —*John Kenneth Galbraith*

The whole aim of practical politics is to keep the populace alarmed (and hence clamorous to be led to safety) by menacing it with an endless series of hobgoblins, all of them imaginary.

—*H. L. Mencken*

I have no ambition to govern men; it is a painful and thankless office.   Thomas Jefferson

If the United States of America or Britain is having elections, they don't ask for observers from Africa or from Asia. But when we have elections, they want observers   —*Nelson Mandela*

A conservative is a man with two perfectly good legs who, however, has never learned how to walk forward.   —*Franklin D. Roosevelt*

A liberal is a person fully capable of working and paying his own way who, however, has never learned how to earn his keep and manages to get others to pay for all or most of his needs and wants.   —*Howard Johnson*

Perseverance is the hard work you do after you get tired of doing the hard work you already did.   —*Newt Gingrich*

Politics have no relation to morals..   —*Niccolo Machiavelli*

Yes they do! That relationship is one of total opposition.   —*Howard Johnson*

Life without liberty is like a body without spirit.   —*Khalil Gibran*

If voting changed anything, they'd make it illegal.   —*Emma Goldman*

Inflation is as violent as a mugger, as frightening as an armed robber and as deadly as a hit man.   —*Ronald Reagan*

If you have always believed that everyone should play by the same rules and be judged by the same standards, that would have gotten you labeled a radical 60 years ago, a liberal 30 years ago and a racist today.   —*Thomas Sowell*

Always vote for principle, though you may vote alone, and you may cherish the sweetest reflection that your vote is never lost.   —*John Quincy Adams*

In this world of sin and sorrow there is always something to be thankful for; as for me, I rejoice that I am not a Republican.   —*H. L. Mencken*

In this world of sin and sorrow there is always something to be thankful for; as for me, I rejoice that I am not a Democrat   —*Howard Johnson*

A fool and his money are soon elected.   —*Will Rogers*

The good news is that, according to the Obama administration, the rich will pay for everything. The bad news is that, according to the Obama administration, you're rich.   —*P. J. O'Rourke*

Those who stand for nothing fall for anything.   —*Alexander Hamilton*

Politicians also have no leisure, because they are always aiming at something beyond political life itself, power and glory, or happiness.   —*Aristotle*

I don't make jokes. I just watch the government and report the facts.   —Will Rogers

Hell, I never vote for anybody, I always vote against .   —W. C. Fields

If we don't believe in freedom of expression for people we despise, we don't believe in it at all.
                        —*Noam Chomsky*

    If the above is true, what does it mean when Democrats do everything in their power to muzzle any who speak against them including proposing legislation that will shut them up?
                        —*Howard Johnson*

If we don't believe in freedom of expression for people who disagree with us, we don't believe in it at all.   —*Howard Johnson*

The Democrats are the party that says government will make you smarter, taller, richer, and remove the crabgrass on your lawn. The Republicans are the party that says government doesn't work and then they get elected and prove it.   —*P. J. O'Rourke*

Politics has become so expensive that it takes a lot of money even to be defeated.
                        —*Will Rogers*

Politics is the art of controlling your environment.   —*Hunter S. Thompson*

Not true! Politics is actually the art of controlling the environment of others for your own benefit
                        —*Howard Johnson*

Politics: A strife of interests masquerading as a contest of principles. The conduct of public affairs for private advantage.   —*Ambrose Bierce*

Only government can take perfectly good paper, cover it with perfectly good ink and make the combination worthless.   —*Milton Friedman*

A healthy democracy requires a decent society; it requires that we are honorable, generous, tolerant and respectful. —*Charles W. Pickering*

We hang the petty thieves and appoint the great ones to public office. —*Aesop*

There ain't no answer. There ain't gonna be any answer. There never has been an answer. That's the answer. —*Gertrude Stein*

A free America... means just this: individual freedom for all, rich or poor, or else this system of government we call democracy is only an expedient to enslave man to the machine and make him like it. —*Frank Lloyd Wright*

When bad men combine, the good must associate; else they will fall one by one, an unpitied sacrifice in a contemptible struggle. —*Edmund Burke*

A leader in the Democratic Party is a boss, in the Republican Party he is a leader. —*Harry S. Truman*

You want a friend in Washington? Get a dog . —*Harry S. Truman*

Conservatives are not necessarily stupid, but most stupid people are conservatives. —*John Stuart Mill*

Liberals are not necessarily stupid, but most stupid people are liberals. —*Howard Johnson*

A liberal is a man or a woman or a child who looks forward to a better day, a more tranquil night, and a bright, infinite future. —*Leonard Bernstein*

A liberal is a man or a woman or a child who looks forward to a better day, a more tranquil night, and a bright, infinite future, all paid for by others. —*Howard Johnson*

The secret of getting things done is to act! —*Dante Alighieri*

In politics the middle way is none at all. —*John Adams*

We would all like to vote for the best man but he is never a candidate. —*Kin Hubbard*

Conservative, n: A statesman who is enamored of existing evils, as distinguished from the Liberal who wishes to replace them with others. —*Ambrose Bierce*

He who knows how to flatter also knows how to slander.   *—Napoleon Bonaparte*

I love power. But it is as an artist that I love it. I love it as a musician loves his violin, to draw out its sounds and chords and harmonies.   *—Napoleon Bonaparte*

The successful revolutionary is a statesman, the unsuccessful one a criminal.   *—Erich Fromm*

Bad politicians are sent to Washington by good people who don't vote.   *—William E. Simon*

Ninety percent of the politicians give the other ten percent a bad reputation.

—Henry A. Kissinger

I have been thinking that I would make a proposition to my Republican friends... that if they will stop telling lies about the Democrats, we will stop telling the truth about them.

—Adlai E. Stevenson

I have been thinking that I would make a proposition to my Democrat friends... that if they will stop telling lies about the Republicans, we will stop telling the truth about them.

—Howard Johnson

Any American who is prepared to run for president should automatically, by definition, be disqualified from ever doing so.   *—Gore Vidal*

Whenever men take the law into their own hands, the loser is the law. And when the law loses, freedom languishes.   *—Robert Kennedy*

When buying and selling are controlled by legislation, the first things to be bought and sold are legislators.   *—P. J. O'Rourke*

Fun is like life insurance; the older you get, the more it costs.   *—Kin Hubbard*

There are many men of principle in both parties in America, but there is no party of principle.

—Alexis de Tocqueville

A wise and frugal Government, which shall restrain men from injuring one another, which shall leave them otherwise free to regulate their own pursuits of industry and improvement, and shall not take from the mouth of labor the bread it has earned. This is the sum of good government, and this is necessary to close the circle of our felicities.   *—Thomas Jefferson*

One of the reasons people hate politics is that truth is rarely a politician's objective. Election and power are.   *—Cal Thomas*

It is not in the nature of politics that the best men should be elected. The best men do not want to govern their fellow men. —*George MacDonald*

Politics, it seems to me, for years, or all too long, has been concerned with right or left instead of right or wrong. —*Richard Armour*

In politics there is no right or wrong, only winning at all costs. —*Howard Johnson*

All the president is, is a glorified public relations man who spends his time flattering, kissing, and kicking people to get them to do what they are supposed to do anyway. —*Harry S. Truman*
'Tis the business of little minds to shrink; but he whose heart is firm, and whose conscience approves his conduct, will pursue his principles unto death. —*Thomas Paine*

Instead of giving a politician the keys to the city, it might be better to change the locks. —*Doug Larson*

A diplomat is a person who can tell you to go to hell in such a way that you actually look forward to the trip . —*Caskie Stinnett*

When I was a boy I was told that anybody could become President; I'm beginning to believe it. —*Clarence Darrow*

Hell hath no fury like a bureaucrat scorned . —*Milton Friedman*

The person who has nothing for which he is willing to fight, nothing which is more important than his own personal safety, is a miserable creature and has no chance of being free unless made and kept so by the exertions of better men than himself. —*John Stuart Mill*

Tradition means giving votes to the most obscure of all classes, our ancestors. It is the democracy of the dead. Tradition refuses to submit to that arrogant oligarchy who merely happen to be walking around. —*Gilbert K. Chesterton*

Radical changes in world politics leave America with a heightened responsibility to be, for the world, an example of a genuinely free, democratic, just and humane society. — *Pope John Paul II*

I hope we shall crush in its birth the aristocracy of our monied corporations which dare already to challenge our government to a trial by strength, and bid defiance to the laws of our country. —*Thomas Jefferson*

It only stands to reason that where there's sacrifice, there's someone collecting the sacrificial offerings. Where there's service, there is someone being served. The man who speaks to you of sacrifice is speaking of slaves and masters, and intends to be the master. *—Ayn Rand*

Writers love to write.

Writers live to write.

Writers love to live.

Writers live to love.

- - - - - Sometimes we cry.

—Howard Johnson 2008

Books written by Howard Johnson - Latest First

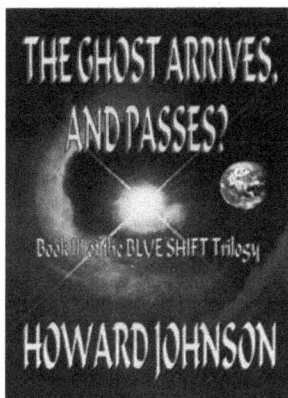

THE GHOST ARRIVES, AND PASSES? Book III of the BLUE SHIFT Trilogy — HOWARD JOHNSON	**Days of the High Morning Moon** — Howard Johnson	**HO'S RANTS** Ten Years of Ho's BLOGs & comments, 2005–2015 — Howard Johnson	**DOUBLE JEOPARDY** Book II of the Blue Shift Trilogy — HOWARD JOHNSON
SciFi novel - 2016 Blue Shift III	Action, Thriller With love interest	Non fiction, 10 years of Commentary	SciFi novel Blue Shift II
Sahm' Allah (The Arrow of Allah) **In St Augustine** — Howard Johnson	**Climate & Much Worse Dangers We [Face]** Is Another Ice Age Due? Is the population out of Control? Is Civilization Due to Collapse? — Howard Johnson	**The Crystal Feather** — Howard Johnson	**STARRING** — Howard Johnson Short Stories, Mostly SciFi
Action, Thriller with love interest	Climate Realities Latest facts and figures	SciFi novel FWA award winner	Short stories mostly SxiFi
Memoirs from The Lakeside Includes: Quotes, Letters, Essays, Poetry, and Commentary - Some from Other Authors — Howard Johnson	**Words from the Lakeside** — Howard Johnson	**ENERGY, CONVENIENT SOLUTIONS** How Americans can solve the energy crisis in ten years — HOWARD JOHNSON	**BLUE SHIFT** A Discovery Beyond Imagination, A Future Beyond Horror Book I of a trilogy — Howard Johnson
Memoirs II With many quotes	Memoirs II With many quotes	All about energy Past, present, future	SciFi novel, book I Of Blue Shift trilogy

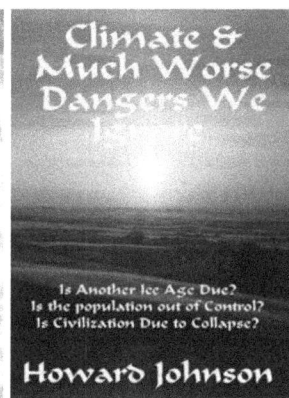

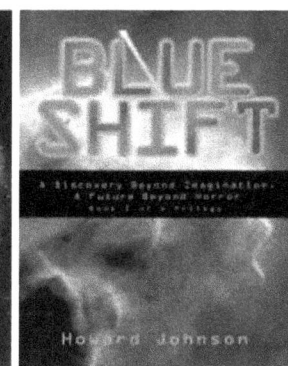

More Books by other authors, published by Senesis Word

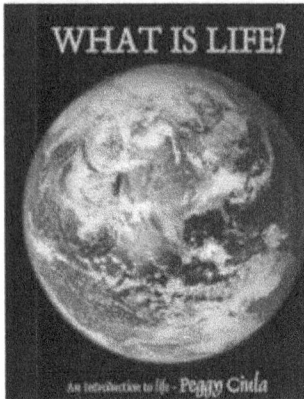

WHAT IS LIFE?

An introduction to life - Peggy Ciula

Biology for Grade school

Pass, Passed, Past

Jean Light Willis

Novella

Listen to Your Granny! You Know She's Never Wrong.

By Isabel Garner

This book of Granny Advice is for all our grandchildren as they leave home.

Sage teen advice

Christmas Poems for Everyone

Merry Christmas

By Isabel Garner

Christmas Poems

— Ho's Rants, comments, 2005 - 2015 —

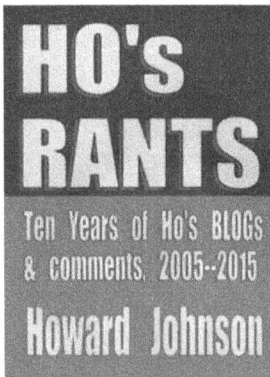

HO'S RANTS

Ten Years of Ho's BLOGs & comments, 2005--2015

Howard Johnson

The author says of this book, *Ho's Rants* - - "For the last ten years I have written a BLOG of mostly political with some other commentary in **http://hojo2rants.blogspot** as well as a number of individual BLOGs on many subjects. This book is a collection of these presented in roughly chronological order, oldest ones first. This is a large book of 596 pages.

I consider myself politically and socially as a **realist** as opposed to any other of the ISTs and ISMs so many people identify with. There is a long description of my beliefs and ideas early in the book. I see PC, Political Correctness, as an effort by elitists (another IST I am not and that I detest) to control the masses and coerce them into thinking and speaking as these elitists want them to.

I much prefer to make my own decisions about what I do and say with consideration for the balance between truth and hurtful comments for others. Should any of my words offend, ask yourself if this is because others have told you to be offended (PC) or if you merely disagree with my comments. Sometimes the truth is not pleasant and can even hurt. I try never to deliberately speak a truth that will offend a particular individual, but sometimes it happens."

Published 2015 - Released in October 2015.

To read an excerpt, goto **www.hosrants.blogspot.com**

— Days of the High Morning Moon —

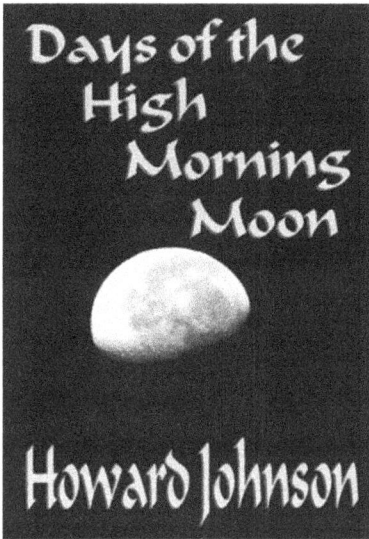

Days of the High Morning Moon is an adventure thriller that takes place in Northern Indiana in and around Lake Tippecanoe where the author lived for many years. A retired Chicago homicide detective, Ragan Yoder, moved to a home on the lake where he grew up and spent his formative years. Because of the influence of the son of one of his best friends from high school days, Ragan was soon involved in helping the local law enforcement agencies cope with a small but devastating crime spree. Murder, mayhem, theft and deception plague him as he becomes deeply involved in catching criminals of several different kinds.

Quite by accident, he meets and then falls for a lovely nurse who saves his life in an accident and changes his life dramatically. As soon as one pair of criminals pay for their crimes, another pops up and leads Ragan on a roller coaster pursuit that takes him and his lady into the Carribean and even up the Amazon to Manaus, Brazil. When his lady is in danger, he returns her favor and saves her life. There are many unforseen twists and turns in the story, incidents that challenge him, his lady, his associates, and even his friends from Chicago.

Published 2015 - Released in May, 2016.

To read an excerpt, goto **www.dayshmmm.blogspot.com**

— Double Jeopardy —

DOUBLE JEOPARDY is the second book of the BLUE SHIFT Trilogy. BLUE SHIFT, the first book, tells of the discovery of a star moving at 90 percent of the speed of light that could threaten life on Earth. See **Blue Shift**, Page 16.XXX

In this book, Dr. Charlie Botkin, from Cal Tech, one of the worlds top authorities on high energy physics is working to determine just what the effects of the star's passing so close to the Earth might be. Shortly after the mysterious disappearance of his uncle C he becomes deeply involved in the ongoing task of predicting how close the star will pass, and what damage it might do. Working with the original group from Gemini, Crazy Charlie helps in their effort to keep the public calm. Armed with increasingly accurate projections of the path and possible effects of the ghost star, Charlie predicts there is a good chance it will pass with little or no effect on the Earth.

In the midst of this, a new menace appears in the form of a large asteroid that is on a collision course with Earth. Angus Thomas's close friend, Pat Yamaguchi leads a team of astronomers from Arizona into the mountains of Tibet to observe and record the meteors where they will strike the earth. They make a perilous journey on horseback up to a high plateau where they set up their equipment. The trip down from the plateau is even more dangerous as they are forced to take an older trail when one of the meteor strikes obliterates the road they used for the trucks that brought them and their equipment up to the start of the horse trail to the plateau. International cooperation on an unprecedented scale is organized to try to solve this unexpected new cataclysmic danger.

The sudden discovery of a dust cloud and even possible planets around the Ghost disrupts their predictions and must now be dealt with.

Published 2015 - Released in May, 2016

To read an excerpt, goto **www.blushift2.blogspot.com**

— Sahm' Allah in St Augustine —

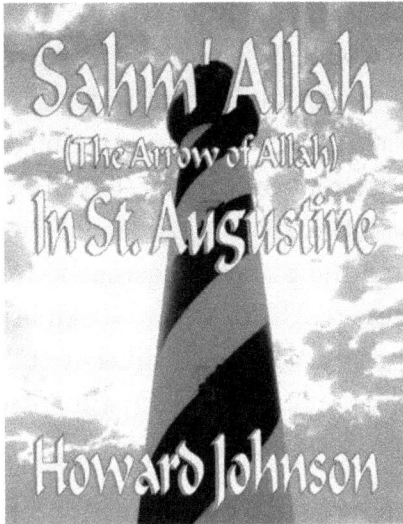

Sahm' Allah (the Arrow of Allah) in St Augustine, is an action adventure thriller that involves three protagonists in three very different and seemingly unconnected adventures that only come together in the last chapters. The lead characters include, Calder Voss, a geothermal engineer, Brooks McKibben, a child prodigy/computer genius, and Carol Mitchell, a Florida business woman who takes on an unusual role. Each of the three protagonists experience their own different adventures in their conflict with the same mysterious group of antagonists. There are some very unusual romances for several of the main characters, some great dangers and exciting adventures. Both the unconnected and finally the coordinated efforts of the three lead characters are needed to try to foil this planned and unusual cataclysmic event that is not fully understood until the climax at the end.

The action begins to take place in the high desert of Nevada. The scenes change to the Georgia hills north of Atlanta, Flamingo in the Everglades, Kansas City, and St Augustine. In three different and seemingly unconnected threads, they each face an unusual cadre of enemies of America who have infiltrated our federal government and are planning a major catastrophic event for America. Both the unconnected and finally the coordinated efforts of the three lead characters are needed to try to foil this planned unusual cataclysm. The dramatic climax takes place in St Augustine on Labor Day, 2015, at the culmination of the 450th anniversary celebration of the founding of the city.

Published 2015 - Released May, 2016

To read an excerpt, goto **www.SahmSA.blogspot.com**

—Climate and Much Worse Dangers We Ignore—

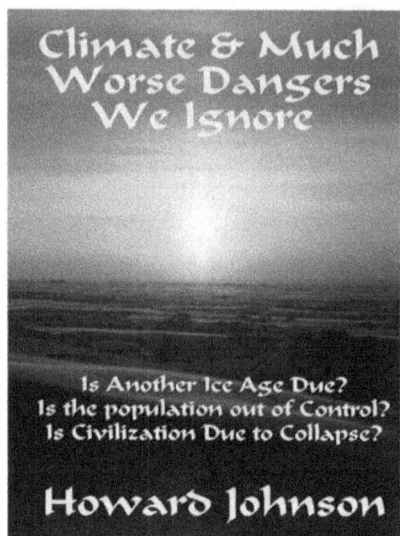

This non fiction book is a thought provoking and realistic look at what could be one of the biggest scams ever pulled off on the public worldwide. The physics and thermodynamics of the so called "greenhouse" gasses do not confirm the postulate that man's addition of carbon dioxide to the atmosphere is warming the planet dangerously. In fact, they soundly refute it. The planet may well be warming, but other factors are far more likely to be the actual cause than increased CO_2 in the atmosphere.

For example: one report used as confirmation of global warming by the supporters of AGW was the greatly diminished snows on Mt Kilimanjaro in recent years. The AGW supporters wrongly blamed that on CO_2 caused global warming. The truth is, man has caused this obvious change, but it had nothing to do with CO_2. Loggers have almost completely deforested the lower slopes of the mountain. Those forests once fed millions of tons of water into the air which flowed up the sides of the mountain and fell as snow near the top. With the forests gone the water no longer flows up the mountain so little or no snow falls. Deforestation of the slopes, a human activity, is the actual cause of the lack of snow on the summit. Deforestation worldwide is lowering the moisture in the atmosphere. This may cause a far greater increase in the Greenhouse effect than carbon dioxide at its worse.

Increasing numbers of scientists, particularly those well versed in the physical gas laws and how gas molecules absorb and radiate energy, are now speaking out about the grossly exaggerated claims of the IPCC and other promoters of anthropogenic global warming (AGW). It is becoming increasingly clear that not only is increasing carbon dioxide not detrimental to life on earth, but that it is highly beneficial. Learn of the fantastic agricultural benefits of increased CO_2 worldwide.

The book also outlines a recent theory linking global temperatures with the frequency of nearby super novas. Radiation from these explosions of giant stars links directly with global temperatures for the last 500 million years. There are a substantial number of detailed color graphics that demonstrate the correlation convincingly. The AGW people would kill to have such powerful confirmation of the physics they ignore. The theory is less than twenty years old, about where the theory of plate tectonics was when most scientists ridiculed that theory.

The book also describes other real and growing dangers man is perpetrating on our planet and its life. These dangers are very real, measurable, evidenced by many concrete happenings, and are increasing on a daily basis. These very real menaces are infinitely worse for humanity than the worst possible global warming scenarios, and there is no redeeming benefit like greatly increased crop growth.

Published 2014 - Edited and released in May, 2016.

To read an excerpt, goto **www.cmwdwi.blogspot.com**

— Memoirs from the Lakeside II —

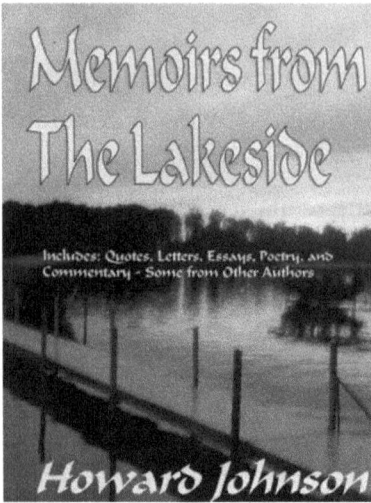

Memoirs from the Lakeside II

The new edition has a greatly expanded number of significant quotes that are now distributed throughout the books in what were white spaces at the ends of chapters or stories.

Memoirs from the Lakeside II is a combination anthology and collection of quotes, quips, poems, essays, letters, and memoirs. Many of my contributions were written as early as 1960. Some of the quotes of others writers and thinkers are from earlier times, dating as far back as before the Common Era.

Over many years I have collected a wide variety of sayings, letters, poems, essays and memoirs. All of the memoirs and essays are my own work along with many of the sayings and other writings. In any case, the sources and authors are acknowledged except for those marked, unknown or anonymous. Many of the memoirs are from my childhood and youth years around Lake Tippecanoe in Northern Indiana.

Because of the variety from one liners to complete memoirs, *Memoirs from the Lakeside II* an ideal read for a few minutes or for a relaxed hour. the memoirs recall memorable happenings from a very full life. I have had a blast for a life with many contacts with wonderful and fascinating people—friends, relatives, and those sharing but a single moment. Many of these haunting experiences are shared within the pages of this book.

Parts of the memoirs are very personal revelations. Most are fond memories of treasured experiences, often with loved ones. Some are memories that carry some unpleasantness, but that is just the way life happens.

Memoirs from the Lakeside II is actually a greatly expanded version of the original *Memoirs from the Lakeside,* containing quotes, essays, letters and memoirs. There are many additional memoirs and short quotes that were not included in the original *Memoirs from the Lakeside* book.

Excerpt, Dedication:

This book is a lot of who I am, what I think, what I believe, what I imagine, what I dream of, why and whom I love . . . in short, it is a collection of bits and pieces of my life—of me. It is a testimonial to all those beautiful human beings who, through love and some blunt trauma, helped me become the person I am. Therefore, I dedicate this book with great love and affection to all of my family, friends, and others, whose actions helped create, guide, inspire, stimulate, and mold my life into the person I am today. My passionate desire to please and never to displease them has guided me in positive directions throughout my lifetime. The family members, lovers, friends, mentors, and teachers who have left this earth are remembered fondly, appreciated greatly, and sorely missed. I am powerfully blessed to have known all of these incredible people, family, friends, colleagues, and acquaintances.

I have decided to list in this dedication as many of those people as I can without creating an entire new book. They are remembered in roughly chronological order. Many of these important people have roles in stories and essays in this book. I have been blessed with a close, loving relationship with members of my family, unique to each one. Those described as *special* were not loved any more than others. There was something different, maybe *magic*, about the two of us together. It defies definition. There were those, other than family, with which I felt a special connection as well. In this book, there is a description of a conversation with one of my grandparents that clearly illustrates my meaning. Those that are not listed are no less loved or appreciated. If I listed all of them, there would be no pages left for the burgeoning content already in place.

There is much more to the full dedication. See the book to read the rest.

Published in 2014, it has been extensively edited and released in May 2016.

To read a more extensive excerpt, goto **www.wlsmls.blogspot.com**

— STARRING —

STARRING has just been released and is now available in paperback through most book outlets, and as an ebook for the Kindle. It was originally titled, *Short Stories, Mostly SciFi*. A fellow writer and member of the Science Fiction Novelists group, D. Keith Howington suggested the title, *Starring* after seeing a copy of the cover of my book with the title, *Short Stories, Mostly SciFi*. Keith very graciously suggested this title and told me I could use it if I wanted to. Once I placed it on the cover, I immediately loved it and so I took him up on his offer. I will be sending him a copy from the very first printing of the final version.

From the text on the back of the book:

This collection of mostly SciFi stories is taken from the collection, *Words from the Lakeside*, recently released by the author. Howard Johnson says, "*Hard* science fiction is basically all fictional writing that uses extrapolation of real science—or actual science and technology expanded by the writer's vision—as far into the future, or past, as his or her creative imagination can take us. It is based on what we can imagine technology of the future to be. Jules Verne was a pioneer in this type of fiction. Look at all the things he imagined that have actually come to pass.

"Several of these stories deal with not only our own advanced technology, but with that of alien species from other worlds, other galaxies, even other universes. Yet all stories deal with mostly very human foibles, problems, interactions with others, sometimes even alien intelligent species. Many of the settings are on other planets where things like the atmosphere, gravity, the native flora and fauna, can be quite different from here on our small planet. While many of the writers of science fiction are scientists, enjoyable SciFi stories should be written so those not based in the sciences can understand and enjoy the action. Much of what we use every day would have been far out science fiction 50, 30, or even 20 years ago, the iphone for example.

When I was quite young, I was an avid reader of science fiction. The writing of Jules Verne and Robert Louis Stevenson whetted my appetite for later writers like Heinlein and Asimov. I was also fascinated by the sciences, primarily astronomy, and the possibility of space travel. I knew man would some day go to the moon, but I never dreamed then that it would be in my lifetime."

Published 2012 - edited and released in May, 2016

To read an excerpt, goto **www.StarringSciFi.blogspot.com**

— The Crystal Feather —

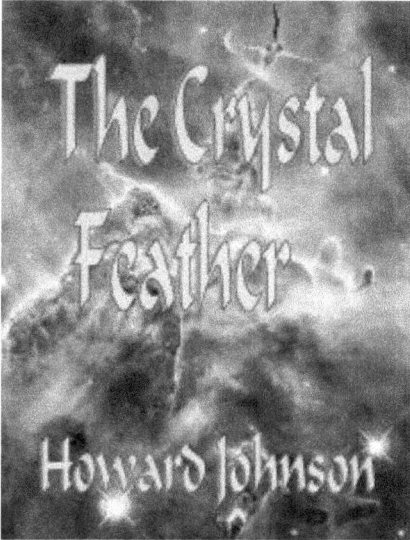

The Crystal Feather is my second hard science fiction novel and is very different from the first one, *Blue Shift*. In 2008 an early manuscript of *The Crystal Feather*, was submitted in the FWA Lighthouse novel contest. The first several chapters and a synopsis were the submission requirements. I was surprised when *The Crystal Feather*, entry came in first among a number of submissions. It took me three years to finish the novel which is now published and available in both print and ebook versions. The completed novel has been entered in the Florida Writers Association Royal Palm Awards contest. The awards will not be announced until October, 2014.

The story: Dr. Draxel Syl has a wild, off-Earth adventure with a drop-dead gorgeous lady named Leura Clauson. Reeling from this experience, he wanders about trying to learn what really happened, who Leura actually is, and what these strange happenings are about. This leads to his learning of and interacting with other humanoids from universes in other dimensions, actually other, parallel universes. In the process, he is abducted and transferred by "portal" to another part of our galaxy by a Segwah star ship captain. The Segwah are a humanoid species closely related to Humans, but from a different universe in a different dimension of space-time. The Scentar, another humanoid species, are from yet another universe in another dimension. The Scentar and Segwah have been at war with each other for millennia, invading each other's universes and killing each other.

Drax, a principal gravity scientist of the Eegis project in Pasadena has inadvertently created a slowly growing *rift* or *tear* in the space-time fabric between the Human and Scentar universes. This *tear*, caused by one of his research projects at Eegis, could cause the two universes to fold into each other, annihilating both. While the Segwah are virtually identical to Earth's Neanderthals, the Scentar are quite the opposite, slender and physically very beautiful by human standards. Both Scentar and Segwah have cultures very different from each other and from Humans as well. The Scentar are quite different in another way. There are twice as many females as males because each female birth is identical twins, while male births are always single. This makes their culture and morality based on two female twins bonding with a single male, a very unusual family structure and related sexual morality. Published 2012 - Edited and released in May, 2016   To read an excerpt, goto **www.CryFthr.blogspot.com**

The next two books were released some time ago.

— Blue Shift —

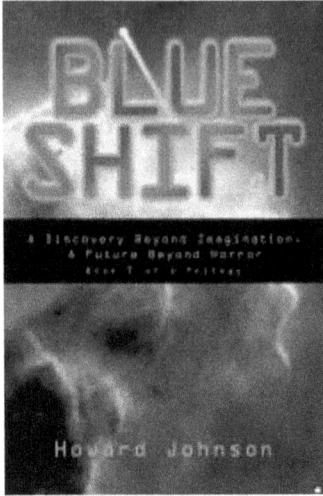

Blue Shift is my first book, a SciFi novel published in 2002. I received several rave reviews in newspapers, but sales were meager. That was mostly because of my inability to follow through on my publisher's marketing plan. My wife, Barbara's deteriorating health kept me from attending the speaking engagements and book publicity my publisher had arranged. The few book signings I did manage to have were quite successful. All told more than 400 books were sold, a very small number in the real world.

The story takes us from the big island of Hawaii to a Mohawk Indian reservation in upstate New York and back. The characters are mostly from the two very different groups of native Americans found there, Hawaiians and Mohawks. Using the new Gemini telescope on the island of Hawaii, astronomer Angus Thomas, a Mohawk Indian and popular pro football player, discovers a wayward star that threatens to destroy all life when it races past the Earth in about thirty years. Discovery of this inescapable menace unleashes snowballinig events that batter the former all-pro running back, his beautiful Hawaiian assistant, Lani Namahoe, their families and friends. This determined group of people battle ignorance, internal enemies and government agents as they deal with the discovery of this irresistible, unavoidable menace that man is absolutely powerless to change or escape. Then they face the awesome responsibility of publicly announcing the probable end of life on Earth while struggling against forces that want to prevent them from doing so. Love, adventure, and intrigue heighten the anticipation of the growing threat of annihilation.

The book is still available from most popular book sources and from my website. An ebook form for the Kindle is available, with other formats coming in the near future. Also coming in the future will be the second and third books in the *Blue Shift* trilogy. *Blue Shift II* deals with the significant people and events during the twenty eight years between the conclusion of first *Blue Shift* and the near approach of the *ghost star*. *Blue Shift III* deals with the last two years as the star approaches and what happens as it passes through the solar system, the final conclusion of the trilogy. I hope to finish and publish *Blue Shift II* in 2013, and *Blue Shift III* in 2014.

Here's a review from the Times Union Newspaper:

by Teresa Smith - Times-Union staff writer

"Blue Shift" appeals to the space lover

I've always been a science fiction fan. In the last few years, the genre has departed from scientifically supported scenarios to life on other planets, advanced space travel and strange aliens."Blue Shift: A Discovery Beyond Imagination, A Future Beyond Horror, Book I of a Trilogy" is a satisfying return to the basics.

The setting, characters and situation are exotic enough. The main setting is Hawaii - the Gemini Observatory on the island of Hilo. The main characters are of Mohawk or Hawaiian ancestry and their cultures are explored. The situation concerns the possible destruction of the Earth. That's the fiction.

The science is based on present-day astronomy - stuff a college student who took three semesters of astronomy 20 years ago, like me, can understand. Readers without the benefit of a couple of science classes will be able to grasp the situation, too, because author Howard Johnson describes the scientific concepts behind "blue shifts" so well. We are not talking about warp drives and interdimensional shifts here. We're talking modern-day observatories and methods.

In "Blue Shift" a former, extremely popular, NFL running back is the main hero in a novel packed with good guys and gals. Angus Thomas has returned to his first career choice - astronomy. He discovers a star traveling at 90 percent of the speed of light and calculates it will reach the Earth's solar system in 30 years by calculating the shift into the blue end of the spectrum. (A red shift means a star is moving away from Earth.) He figures the star hurtling through space threatens to destroy all life on the planet.

Astronomers, those late-night workers, tend to keep their discoveries to themselves until their work can be published. Thomas must confirm his conclusions, too, and does so with the help of his beautiful Hawaiian assistant, Mililani "Lani" Namahoe. Thomas and Lani, their family members and colleagues team up to prepare a series of press releases designed to ease the news to the public in a responsible way.

The enemies include a chauvinistic British astronomer who steals Thomas's rersearch and OSI agents who want to control the information about the star. It's full of people with character - intelligent, responsible individuals who hold their families precious.

At first, the dialogue is disconcerting because it's so, well, good. The characters' conversations are presented in perfect grammar. Their thoughts are complete; they compliment the contributions of others by acknowledging what they say. After a while we want everyone to speak and just plain get along like the "Blue Shift" characters. They follow through on their plans, think on their feet and strive over adversity.

Their circle includes a highly ethical journalist (imagine that!), loyal friends, efficient co-workers and supportive family members. It takes a while, after one gets used to the superb dialogue, to realize a couple of things are missing from the book - obscenities and the obligatory paragraphs retelling sexual encounters. We know how angry the characters are without any foul language. We know how much the characters are attracted to each other without one function described. The effect is powerful.

So if you'd like to try a little science fiction, not only is Johnson's book highly recommended, it will leave you hungry for the second installment.

— Energy, Convenient Solutions —

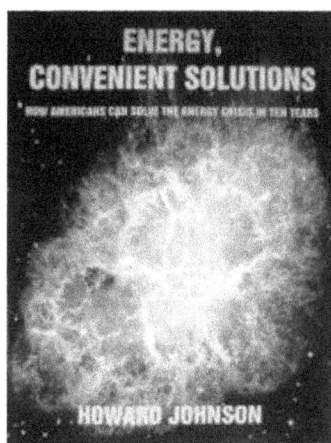

Energy, Convenient solutions, How Americans can Solve the Energy Crisis in Ten Years, is a non fiction book about energy. It is the culmination of ten years of my research into all manner of energy creation and use in a field where I have had considerable experience.

In the book I say, "We can replace all fossil fuels with renewable fuels and alternative energy sources within ten years and with relatively minor disruptions to present manufacturing and distribution systems. *Energy, Convenient solutions* describes most of the existing and proposed energy systems, all within current technology and capabilities. Some of these proposed systems are quite unusual and recently announced. It provides many unique and workable, long-term answers to growing concerns about energy, the economy, and dwindling supplies of petroleum. Adopting these new systems would improve our balance of trade, our economy, our job opportunities, and our technological presence while eliminating the CO_2 problem, regardless of its importance. We no longer have the luxury of time. The growing economic/political menace is here, now, real, and dangerous. If we don't act immediately, the consequences could be catastrophic."

Publication of the book was followed by publication of numerous articles in trade publications in many fields related to energy. Numerous book reviews, most quite positive have been written and published since publication early in the fall of 2010. Most of the negative reviews focused on the comments made about politics, Islam, and the lack of a single definitive answer. Obviously these reviewers failed to recognize the power that politics and politicians have over energy decisions, even though most are poorly informed on the subject. Anyone who doesn't see the danger oil-rich nations can pose, and the financial drain this causes the western world are wearing blinders. As long as petroleum remains our primary energy source, these factors must be considered. The answer is not a single system, or technology, but a combination of many, some effective in one field, others in different fields and industries. The one-size-fits-all solution so adored by politicians and the media, is completely impractical. The obvious difficulties and expensive collapse of many companies developing radical new technologies is just one of the lessons we must learn.

Since *Energy, Convenient Solutions* was released, I have given several well-attended lectures on energy to very diverse groups. One was to a group of mostly university professors on the MV Explorer, the semester-at-sea ship, during a voyage up the Amazon to Manaus. Numerous good questions were asked during the Q&A session that followed the lecture. This session was spirited, informative, and went well past the allotted time. Many of those who attended the lecture stopped me afterwards on the ship asking even more very good questions.

One editor describes it as,   **"The definitive book on energy for the 21st century."**

Here's a review from the Tucson Citizen Newspaper:

This book is written for anyone with any kind of interest in energy, power plants, vehicles---virtually any use of energy. While it covers some very technical subjects, it does so in ways that even laymen can understand. Author Howard Johnson has a knack of writing about very technical subjects in ways that most intelligent people can understand. The book covers all common and a number of rather uncommon energy systems. These systems include power generation, transportation, and use of all types of energy. It describes those from the past, a number of those from the present as well as some showing future promise.

The clear conclusion is that the future of energy might not look very much different from the present with most of the same systems and fuels and a few new ones, but with a very different mix. For example, we currently use coal-fired power plants for half of our electricity. That will probably drop to a much smaller percentage while several new technologies will move to the fore. We currently have a wide ranging mix of energy systems including more than a dozen power generation systems, a growing number of different vehicle power systems and fuels, and a well established investment in infrastructure. These massive systems will provide an inertial brake on rapid changes and will require a great deal of effort to modify.

The author describes what can realistically be done to bring about the evolutionary changes that will wean us from petroleum dependency. This alone could result in tremendous internal growth in energy and transportation industries. This would bring about an amazing growth in our economy and provide countless high amd medium level jobs for Americans. It would even satisfy the global warming crowd without any additional taxes.

The author describes a number of internal forces including established industries and politically active groups, that will oppose and interfere with these changes and will work against them. These activities do not bode well for these beneficial changes, changes that must be dealt with. Finally there are many reference to additional information about many of the new developments described in the book. The best answers to our energy problems could undoubtedly be found from combinations of technologies described in the book.

These are books published for other authors

—Speak, Memory—

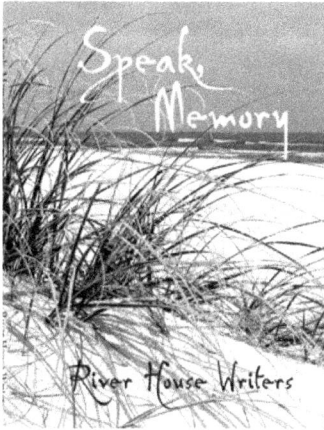

Speak, Memory is an anthology of memoirs written by a group called the **River House Writers**. It was released at the end of October, 2014. Within its pages are bits and pieces of the lives of this group of about two dozen writers, of which I am a member. They have met each Wednesday morning for the last four years at the River House of the St Augustine Council on Aging. Under the guidance of journalist, Peter Guinta they practice the art and craft of writing.

After members read their memoir, short story or other offering, the group offers comments and suggestions. The process can be exhilarating, funny, or emotional. Come read this intimate look into our lives as we share our realities.

—What is Life—

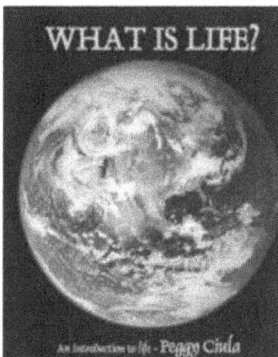

What is Life is an illustrated primer on biology for grade school students.

The author, Peggy Ciula, has taught high school and college biology for thirty years. She created this book to solve a problem she saw all to often. Many new students in her classes had little inkling of what biology and life actually are. She is trying to change that.

—Two New booklets by Isabel Garner—

—Listen to Your Granny—

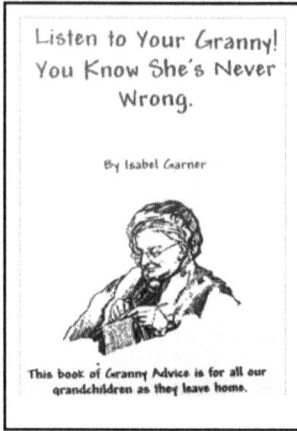

Listen to Your Granny!
You Know She's Never
Wrong.

By Isabel Garner

This book of Granny Advice is for all our
grandchildren as they leave home.

This one is a book of old-fashioned sage advice for young people. These are things about life that all children from six to sixteen would do well to read. Many adults could gain from reading them as well. Isabel's great sense of humor and reality makes these folksy instructions entertaining as well as valuable

—Christmas Poems—

Christmas Poems
for Everyone

Merry Christmas

By Isabel Garner

This other one is a collection of original Christmas poems that are witty and pleasing. Isabel has a clear, clever, and pleasing tone in all of her writing. Her down home language makes her writing appeal to a wide range of readers.

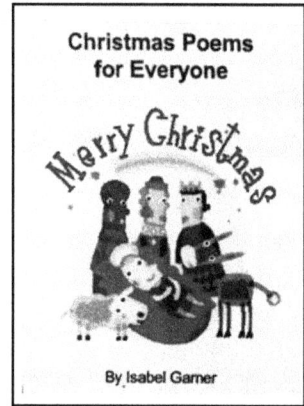

—Pass, Passed, Past—

Pass, Passed, Past is a novella, the first literary effort by artist, Jean Light Willis

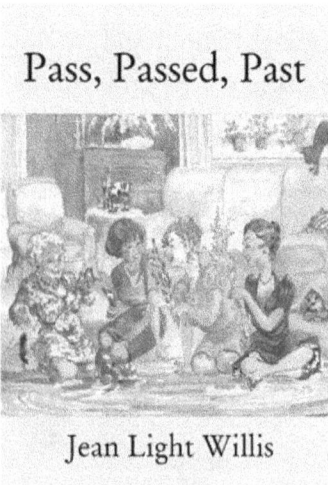

Pass, Passed, Past

Jean Light Willis

In a small town on the coast of North Carolina four ladies' bridge game is delayed as they cope with growing older. Will the hippie Stella find her long lost son? What is Penny hiding behind her socialite exterior? Can Lillian achieve fulfillment? How can Gert avoid being homeless? Is it too late for romance?

A native Virginian, Jean holds a BFA in Art Education from Richmond Professional Institute. After thirty years as a public school art teacher she opened an art gallery in St. Augustine featuring her plein air paintings and pen and ink illustrations as well as sculpture and weaving. With the love and support of her four extraordinary children she has turned to writing. An historical novel and a play are in the works.

Here are some small books Howard has published that are used in his lectures.

—Genesis 2012—

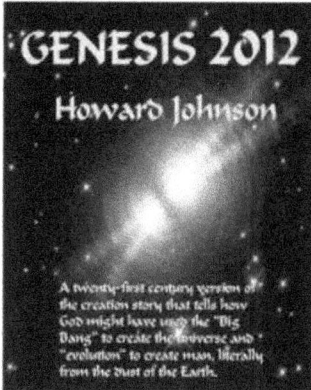

Genesis 2012 is one example of a number of booklets of 50 to 100 pages on a number of subjects. This one, *Genesis 2012*, is a rewrite of the book of Genisis to make it compatible with current scientific knowledge. It is the companion booklet to Howard Johnson's lecture,
Science and Religion, a Reconciliation.

The theory of relativity and a completely new concept of our universe. Some new, off-the-wall concepts of our universe. A new and different way of thinking about gravity , light, and the universe.

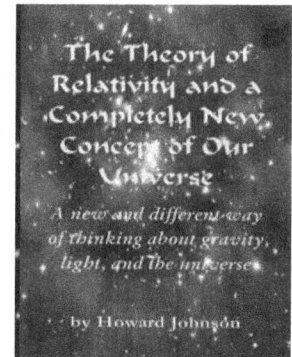

For those of you who don't know and might be interested, here's some information about my publishing company:

senesis word

Publishing Services for Unpublished Writers

104 Leeward Court - St. Augustine, FL 32084 - 904-687-1865
Cell phone: 574-265-3386 - *email:* senesisword@yahoo.com

A note from Howard Johnson, of Senesis Word

During any book event, I will talk about my books, describe them and provide excerpts. I will also describe my writing and how it has become my passion. I will describe the services of Senesis Word, the publishing company I started to help other fledgling writers. There are a number of personal commentaries that follow. The first one is a personal description of what has become my calling. This is followed by a description of my publishing company and then descriptions of my books including mini books of excerpts and links to excerpts on the Internet. These excerpts provide readers access to the *flavor* of my various writings.

Should you have interest in the services of Senesis Word, ask for, a copy of the flyer describing our services.

Many excerpts and small booklets are available on the Internet free or in print for a few bucks to be applied to any future purchase of the full book. Click **http://hojobooks.blogspot.com** to view excerpts of all of my books. Click **http://hjwrite.blogspot.com** where there are links to copies of all of these little books. If you would like a printed copy of any of these booklets, they are available for purchase.

In the next few pages, I will try to explain what has become my passion and my joy.

— My Last Hurrah —

I will try to explain what has become my passion and my last HURRAH so to speak. It has taken me about seventeen years to reach where I am with this passion and it is my hope that I will continue to grow from my experiences. I also hope you will take the time to read the pages that follow this short note.

Why I write

I am a story teller, both fiction and memoirs: fabricated and remembered. My writing dreams are bigger than I could possibly be. That alone should help keep me young at heart and always thirsting for another day, even at my age. Some time back I told everyone on my email list that I discovered I was a writer, but I didn't say why. Each story, thought, idea, or memory that I put into words brings forth from the depths of my mind and imagination, more stories, more thoughts, more ideas, and more memories. I am deliciously excited by writing these things. It has become my great passion, somewhat like this little phrase I wrote several years ago. *Those in their youth who can, dream. Those in their prime who can, do. Those in their old age who can, write.* For many years I was an avid reader, devouring all kinds of literature. Once I started writing, my reading time gave way to mostly writing time. Writing is so much more rewarding. Certainly I would like my words to be read, but my main pleasure lies in the writing. I would write even if I knew no one would ever read my words.

Why you should write:

Each of us has stories to tell, stories that should be told that others would love to read, especially family members. We all know how to write. We write letters, emails, we tell people jokes and little stories about our experiences. Not all of us can be writers. That's just a simple fact. However, many of you could write about things you would like to pass on to your children and grandchildren, things about you that you would like for them to know. My grandfather, George Dickinson told me many stories of his life growing up and as a young man. My father and mother did the same. I remember but a tiny portion of those stories. I would love to be able to read all of them, but they didn't write them down. Some of theses stories are imbedded in my memoirs. I do not want to deny my grandchildren access to the stories of happenings in my life so I have written and collected many memoirs. These are the little stories I would tell people about things that happened, significant things, things my progeny might like to know about before they were born or while they were very young. Not all of these are pleasant or happy stories for there are dark times in all of our lives. Still, time helps lessen the memories of trauma, physical and emotional. I therefore urge you to write. Write the stories of your life. Tell your as yet unborn descendants about your life so they will know you.

I remember just a few stories my parents told about my dad's parents and about my sisters before I was born. To me my paternal grandparents are virtually unknown other than those few stories and a few photos. How wonderful it would have been if they had written about their childhoods and lives. I would then at least have known something of my ancestry. As it is they are merely names and faces frozen at an advanced age. How did they meet? What about their parents? A hundred years from now, who will know anything about those ancestors just a few generations back? If you write about your life, your descendants will be able to learn at least some part of who you were, what you did, and how you lived your life. Think about it. What a gift that would be for your family.

I found that as I write one story or memoir, others come to mind, stories I would probably not have remembered had I not been writing the current one. I immediately make a note of their subject so I won't forget. Then, when writing that story, others too come to mind in a never-ending progression. I would wager that should you start writing stories of your experiences, you too will remember other stories and so grow a collection. This kind of writing is something you can do occasionally when you have the time or schedule regular times to write. Either system will work because these stories are in your memory. You can go back to them a day, a month, or a year later and they will still be there.

Should you make the decision to write, I would be pleased to offer help and instruction, mainly so you won't have to make the mistakes I have already made. Writing memoirs can be an exciting and rewarding experience and provide your family with valuable and permanent information.

So think about writing. If there is a story or memory in you, give it the wings of the written word. Who knows how many others you may touch.

—*Howard Johnson, 2011*

While at it, think on this well-said quote:

"There are many who find a good alibi far more attractive than an achievement. For an achievement does not settle anything permanently. We still have to prove our worth anew each day: we have to prove that we are as good today as we were yesterday. But when we have a valid alibi for not achieving anything we are fixed, so to speak, for life. Moreover, when we have an alibi for not writing a book, painting a picture, and so on, we have an alibi for not writing the greatest book and not painting the greatest picture. Small wonder that the effort expended and the punishment endured in obtaining a good alibi often exceed the effort and grief requisite for the attainment of a most marked achievement."

—*Eric Hoffer*

— My publishing company, *Senesis Word* —

Struggling with several kinds of publishing companies, agents and others for ten years taught me a great deal about this rapidly changing business. Actually, I have just scratched the surface. After two very expensive lessons, I dug in and learned a lot about what makes for a successful publishing of a book. Marketing a book is an entirely different subject. If you are not an established author or a celebrity or politician of some note, making a living writing is difficult, and for the inexperienced, virtually impossible. Having been engaged in this struggle, I decided to offer my services to others starting on the path I have already trod. As a result I started my publishing company, *Senesis Word*, to provide development assistance to the many unpublished and unheralded writers struggling to have their words published, if only for friends and family.

My website, **www.ho2jo.com**, can provide much information about the services offered. The costs for these services are surprisingly low and depend on just how much the writer asks me to do. An estimate of the costs associated with any project will be provided free of charge.

As an active member of the Florida Writers Association and several other groups of writers, I know many really good writers who have never made a penny from their work. I also know a very few who have at least made some money. Still, the all say, "Don't give up your day job until . . . ." There are, of course, those lucky, and usually hard working, writers who have cracked the best sellers lists after being noticed for any number of unfathomable reasons. Knowing someone already successful "in the business" can give you a leg up. Even then, there are a number of very necessary steps one must take to turn one's idea onto a finished book, and that's before a single copy is sold. Should you have any interest, I can and would love to provide you with invaluable information, books and reports on writing for both newbies and experienced writers.

I have become a prolific writer and work hard to make my writing clear, interesting and compelling. The seven books I have finished are available. Those in progress are described in this piece. I have numerous writing projects in stages from just started to half finished, and many more in the idea stage. Most, but not all of my fiction is *hard* science fiction. *Hard* science fiction is fiction in which the *science* behind the story is relatively accurate, possible—usually extrapolated from our current science—science pushed into the future—sometimes, far into the future. It is quite different from fantasy. There is no magic or suspension of the basic laws of physics, math, or chemistry. Sometimes fact catches up with fiction as new and real technologies replace previously fictional ones. From Jules Verne to Arthur C, Clark, Robert Heinlein, and Isaac Azimov, SciFi imaginings have become practical realities.

❖   ❖   ❖

Biographic sketch: My life has been a blast. I spent all of my growing up summers in and around Tippecanoe Lake in Indiana where I developed a love of water and the outdoor life. I spent part of at least 84 summers on the lake. I lived there full time most of the last 40 years.

I remain a part of a large, active, loving family which is my pride and joy. I am an avid fisherman, sailor, and water enthusiast. At 87, I have given up many competitive activities including: water skiing, sailing, and sports car racing. I love music and sang in many choruses and performed in musicals since I was eight. Now I write rather than do.

My pride and joy is my family. I am supremely blessed with five fantastic and beautiful daughters and a son who is equally fantastic, an even dozen terrific grandchildren, and several greats. I have spent the last nine years and as many more of the *golden years* as we can manage, with my marvelous and very dear lady, Daphne, who has an equally numerous and delightful family.

Professionally, I graduated from Purdue University as a chemical engineer in 1949. I spent a varied career including 20 years in the dental supply business with my father, Howard R. Johnson. After selling this business, I spent several years designing and building prestige dental offices all over the country. Starting in 1980, I worked as an independent consulting engineer for many major companies, NASA, the US Navy and Air Force. After retiring from engineering work in 1999 I started writing and was soon pursuing writing full-time.

I live in St. Augustine, FL with Daphne Fox and Charlie, our friendly, furry, four legged, Lhasa apso *child*. We travel frequently, often in our motor home. I am now active in the Florida Writers Association and the St Augustine Council on Aging programs where I meet each week with two Socrates discussion groups, a creative writers group, and a drama club. I am also available for lectures and discussions on a number of subjects I have written about in the books described earlier in this section.

Life has been unbelievably good to me.